# CHRISTIAN SPIRITUALITY
Origins to the Twelfth Century

# World Spirituality

*An Encyclopedic History of the Religious Quest*

# Board of Editors and Advisors

*Volume 16 of*
World Spirituality:
An Encyclopedic History
of the Religious Quest

# CHRISTIAN SPIRITUALITY

## ORIGINS TO THE TWELFTH CENTURY

*Edited by*
Bernard McGinn
*and*
John Meyendorff
*in collaboration with*
Jean Leclercq

CROSSROAD • NEW YORK

1989
The Crossroad Publishing Company
370 Lexington Avenue, New York, NY 10017

World Spirituality, Volume 16
Diane Apostolos-Cappadona, Art Editor

Printed in the United States of America

*Library of Congress Cataloging in Publication Data*

Main entry under title:
Christian spirituality.
(Vol. 16 of World spirituality)
Bibliography: p.
Includes index.
1. Spiritual life—History of doctrines—Addresses, essays, lectures.
I. McGinn, Bernard, 1937– . II. Meyendorff, John, 1926–
III. Series: World spirituality; v. 16.
BV4490.C464  1985    248'.09    85-7692
ISBN 0-8245-0681-2
ISBN 0-8245-0847-5 (pbk)

# Contents

# Preface to the Series

T HE PRESENT VOLUME is part of a series entitled World Spirituality: An Encyclopedic History of the Religious Quest, which seeks to present the spiritual wisdom of the human race in its historical unfolding. Although each of the volumes can be read on its own terms, taken together they provide a comprehensive picture of the spiritual strivings of the human community as a whole—from prehistoric times, through the great religions, to the meeting of traditions at the present.

The series was conceived in response to two trends that have emerged in the second half of the twentieth century: a growing interest in spirituality and an increasing encounter of the world's religions, especially between the East and the West. The plan for the series was initially prepared by Richard Payne and other editors of The Crossroad Publishing Company in consultation with such specialists as Jean Leclercq, Thomas Berry, Raimundo Panikkar, Seyyed Hossein Nasr, Arthur Green, and then with the full board of editors and advisers. It has been my privilege to work with the project from its earliest phase.

Drawing upon the highest level of scholarship around the world, the series gathers together and presents in a single collection the richness of the spiritual heritage of the human race. It is designed to reflect the autonomy of each tradition in its historical development, but at the same time to present the entire story of the human spiritual quest. The first five volumes deal with the spiritualities of archaic peoples in Asia, Europe, Africa, Oceania, and North and South America. Most of these have ceased to exist as living traditions, although some perdure among tribal peoples throughout the world. However, the archaic level of spirituality survives within the later traditions as a foundational stratum, preserved in ritual and myth. Individual volumes or combinations of volumes are devoted to the major traditions: Hindu, Buddhist, Taoist, Confucian, Jewish, Christian, and Islamic. Included within the series are the Jain, Sikh, and Zoroastrian traditions. In order to complete the story, the series includes traditions that have not survived but have exercised important influence on living traditions—such as Egyptian, Sumerian, classical Greek and Roman. A volume is devoted to modern esoteric movements and another to modern secular movements. It might seem problematic to include the secular in a series on spirituality, for to some the secular appears to be the very antithesis of spirituality and its greatest antagonist in the modern world. Yet precisely because it is problematic—perhaps the greatest problem for spirituality in our time—it is important to treat it within the series. Furthermore, the secular, especially in its humanistic forms, has affinities with certain classical traditions, such as Buddhism and Confucianism.

Having presented the history of the various traditions, the series devotes two volumes to the meeting of spiritualities. The first surveys the meeting of spiritualities from the past to the present, exploring common themes that can provide the basis for a positive encounter, for example, symbols, rituals, techniques. The second deals with the meeting of spiritualities in the present and future. It consists of a forum of the editors of the individual volumes, exploring the encounter of spiritualities in the midst of the challenges facing spirituality in our time. Finally, the series closes with a dictionary of world spirituality. Much more than a mere listing of technical terms, this is a creative enterprise that explores through the medium of language the diversity and unity of the human spiritual quest.

Each volume is edited by a specialist or a team of specialists who have gathered a number of contributors to write articles in their fields of specialization. As in this volume, the articles are not brief entries but substantial studies of an area of spirituality within a given tradition. An effort has been made to choose editors and contributors who have a cultural and religious grounding within the tradition studied and at the same time possess the scholarly objectivity to present the material to a larger forum of readers. For several years some four hundred and fifty scholars around the world have been working on the project.

In each volume the contents are organized according to a thematic or historical order, or a combination of both. Some traditions that have a highly developed sense of history have organized their material largely in chronological order. Others have followed chiefly a thematic order. Each tradition was urged to shape its material in the fashion most representative of its heritage. In every volume, care has been taken to cover adequately both central themes and pertinent historical material. Although the articles can be read as individual units, each volume as a whole is designed to provide the reader with an organic picture of the thematic content and the historical development.

In the planning of the project, no attempt was made to arrive at a common definition of spirituality that would be accepted by all in precisely the same way. The term "spirituality," or an equivalent, is not found in a number of the traditions. Yet from the outset, there was a consensus among the editors about what was in general intended by the term. It was left to each tradition to clarify its own understanding of this meaning and to the editors to express this in the introduction to their volumes. As a working hypothesis, the following description was used to launch the project:

> The series focuses on that inner dimension of the person called by certain traditions "the spirit." This spiritual core is the deepest center of the person. It is here that the person is open to the transcendent dimension; it is here that the person experiences ultimate reality. The series explores the discovery of this core, the dynamics of its development, and its journey to the ultimate goal. It deals with prayer, spiritual direction, the various maps of the spiritual journey, and the methods of advancement in the spiritual ascent.

Although focusing on spirituality, the series has a cross-disciplinary perspective, drawing from psychology, sociology, history, philosophy, theology, and other disciplines where these intersect spirituality. The essays contain necessary factual information on historical background, sources, personalities, works, and philosophical and theological concepts. The approach is historical in that the individual volumes present the development of each tradition and the series as a whole provides an overview of the spiritual quest of the human community. The treatment is encyclopedic, not through detailed alphabetical entries but through comprehensive coverage of each tradition and, thereby, of the spiritual quest as a whole.

In some sense the series is attempting to forge a new discipline in the field of religion, the discipline of spirituality. In the context of modern scholarship, this discipline has not been extricated from the history of religions, the philosophy of religion, and theology. Its central focus, its categories and concepts, and its distinct methodology have not been established to the point of being commonly accepted as conventions. Although this is true academically, in actual fact the realm of spirituality, as a body of wisdom, has been highly developed. The transmission of spiritual wisdom may be the oldest discipline in human history. Yet this ancient discipline needs to be accorded its own place in academic studies; at the same time it must integrate the findings of other disciplines such as psychology, sociology, and critical historical research. The challenge of this series, then, has been to develop the academic methods, skills, and tools appropriate for this corpus of wisdom.

The series has faced a second challenge: how deal with this discipline in a global context. We might say that there is emerging a new discipline: global spirituality. Such a discipline would study spirituality not merely in one tradition or one era but in a comprehensive geographic and historical context. And it would take into account this vast body of data not in isolation but in interrelationship. In this sense, the present series is attempting not merely to retrieve an ancient discipline in a modern academic mode but to lift it into a global context.

By presenting the ancient spiritual wisdom in an academic perspective, the series can fulfill a number of needs. It can provide readers with a spiritual inventory of the richness of their own traditions, informing them at the same time of the richness of other traditions. It can give structure and order, meaning and direction to the vast amount of information with which we are often overwhelmed in the computer age. By drawing the material into the focus of world spirituality, it can provide a perspective for understanding one's place in the larger process. For it may well be that the meeting of spiritual paths—the assimilation not only of one's own spiritual heritage but of that of the human community as a whole—is the distinctive spiritual journey of our time.

EWERT COUSINS

# Introduction

The written code kills, but the Spirit gives life.
2 Corinthians 3:6

I N THE COURSE OF CHRISTIAN HISTORY this quotation from Saint Paul has been most often applied to the understanding of Scripture, but its message is applicable also to what is presented in this volume. Throughout its long and complex history Christianity has always insisted upon the primacy of the inner meaning of Christian documents, rituals, and institutions—their spiritual depth. This volume and the two that will follow it in World Spirituality: An Encyclopedic History of the Religious Quest are an attempt to present the inner message of Christian belief and practice in a way that will be at once historically accurate and existentially pertinent.

Although "spirit" (*pneuma*) and "spiritual" (*pneumatikos*) are key terms in the New Testament and the words *spiritualis* and even *spiritualitas* were well known in Latin Christianity, "spirituality" does not necessarily have a self-evident meaning for all Christians today. Indeed, for many moderns, even modern believers, the term may have unfortunate connotations that suggest the kind of radically negative and pessimistically antimaterial understanding of Christianity that has dogged its history for many centuries. But spirituality correctly understood has rich dimensions and a field of meaning that no related term quite covers. For these reasons its use seems to be unavoidable for the kind of project presented here. The usefulness of the term "spirituality," like that of the term "religion" itself, is coupled with a singular resistance to easy definition or universal agreement.

The editors did not try to impose any single definition of spirituality upon the contributors to this or the subsequent Christian volumes. We did, however, circulate a brief working description of one understanding of the term for the contributors to use as a guideline if they found it helpful. This read, in part:

> Christian spirituality is the lived experience of Christian belief in both its general and more specialized forms. . . . It is possible to distinguish spirituality

from doctrine in that it concentrates not on faith itself, but on the reaction
that faith arouses in religious consciousness and practice. It can likewise be
distinguished from Christian ethics in that it treats not all human actions in
their relation to God, but those acts in which the relation to God is immediate and explicit.

What is contained in this and the subsequent volumes is obviously not
Christian spirituality in the first instance, the actual lived experience itself,
but reflection upon the historical manifestations of this experience, that is,
Christian spirituality as a discipline. The academic discipline of Christian
spirituality is a rather new one that does not, as yet, have a commonly
accepted niche or definition. Traditional Roman Catholic "ascetical and
mystical theology" covered much, but by no means all, of what is intended
by the term, especially because ascetical and mystical theology and even
what in more recent times has been called "spiritual theology" tend to
neglect the collective, social dimensions that have been so important to the
lived experience of Christian faith. Spirituality, both as lived experience and
as reflections on that experience, is a broader and more inclusive term than
either asceticism or mysticism. Although spirituality is intimately tied to
theology, particularly to what many today are calling practical theology, one
could argue that spirituality has an identity of its own.

It is our hope that a clearer and more adequate understanding of what the
various Christian communions have seen as the inner meaning of Christianity—and therefore "spirituality" in the root sense—will emerge from a
broad intra-Christian ecumenical enterprise of this nature. We see these
volumes also as an important part of the more general and more difficult
ecumenical project represented by the entire series, that is, a more fruitful
understanding of world spirituality or, perhaps better, world spiritualities.
The fruit of these hopes will appear in the final three volumes of this series.

Though many useful works on the history of Christian spirituality exist
(see the appended bibliography), these three volumes are unique in a number
of ways that require some comment and explanation. First, it should be
noted that the project has been totally ecumenical in planning and execution. This might seem a matter of course given the present situation in the
churches, but we need to remind ourselves of just how recent it is that the
ecumenical movement came to affect all the different communions and
groups that make up our still sadly fragmented Christian world. The editorial sessions that were responsible for the shape of these volumes were
exercises in the kind of forthright and profitable ecumenical dialogue that
in recent years has led, if not to the overcoming of all barriers, at least to
a better mutual understanding of how much we have in common. In choosing the contributors our desire has been to find the best possible scholars

and also, wherever possible, to choose those who could speak from a position within the respective traditions—Orthodox, Catholic, Protestant—on which they would write.

A second major editorial choice concerned the tone of the articles and the audience or audiences to which they are directed. Our intention has been to make these volumes accessible and useful to the general reader, especially to the many today so desirous of finding a solid and clear account of the history of Christian spirituality. We also hope that the articles will be profitable to those with more advanced knowledge who are anxious to reflect upon the issues presented in original contributions, even when these articles are not weighed down by all the trappings of the most detailed scholarship. To address such a dual audience is a task of delicacy and difficulty, one that makes great demands on the contributors, who as recognized scholars in their fields know all too well that it is frequently easier to write a long, technical piece than to synthesize large areas of material in a way that is both informative and original. The degree of success that we have achieved must be left to our readers to judge, but the editors would like to thank the contributors for their efforts in striving for this goal and for their generous responses to suggestions for modifications. No single, hard and fast model of the scholarly level of the articles was communicated to the authors aside from these broad guidelines. The variety of topics, both in terms of subject matter and chronological extent, would have made this difficult, and we felt that such a procedure would have placed undue constraints on our distinguished contributors, whom we hoped to give as free a hand as possible. Inevitably, considerable variation is found in the following articles, especially in the use of scholarly apparatus such as footnotes and bibliographies, but it seems to us that this variety is a positive feature as long as each of the articles fulfills its basic part in the plan of the whole.

The shape of the volume and the role of the individual articles in this overall plan require more detailed comment. Although these volumes are intended to serve as useful reference books (especially in relation to the *Dictionary of World Spirituality* that will appear as volume 25), their primary purpose is to give a synoptic presentation of the history of Christian spirituality. This meant that substantive articles of some length on the most essential stages and themes were needed rather than a series of brief entries that would cover every possible topic. This also indicated that the nature of the presentation needed to be primarily chronological rather than topical, though here a compromise was adopted that is evident in the division of the volume into two parts.

Part 1, "Periods and Movements," is designed to present the major stages in the evolution of Christian spirituality from roughly 100 to about 1200 of the Christian era. The choice of the twelfth century as the terminal date for this first volume can be argued on several grounds. First of all, from an ecumenical point of view, the gradually widening breach between East and West that had been building for centuries was still by no means definitive until the thirteenth century, when the tragedy (we might better say the great sin against ecumenism) that we call the Fourth Crusade occurred, which resulted in the Latin conquest and subjugation of the Greek East. Second, from the viewpoint of Western spirituality, the rich and original contributions of the twelfth century, though the source for much that followed in the later Middle Ages and beyond, could only serve in that function because they were the creative summation of the patristic past shared by both Greek and Latin Christianity. It was not for nothing that Bernard of Clairvaux, the foremost spokesman of twelfth-century spirituality and a writer revered in later ages by Protestants as well as Catholics, was called "the last of the fathers."

Part 2, "Themes and Values," studies the crucial topics that gave meaning to Christian spirituality during these same centuries. The decisions involved in selecting these themes out of so many possible ones were among the most difficult that the editorial board faced. Obviously, there are topics left out here that would have cried out for inclusion had more space been available. Given the constraints of the volume, our criteria for selection were two: first, that the theme was crucial for the understanding of the spiritual life of the first twelve centuries of the Christian faith; and, second, that it remains a significant part of the permanent spiritual treasury of Christian belief and practice. Full chronological accounts of each of these themes would have been impossible. Some of the articles in the second part have been able to adopt the format of a more or less complete chronological survey; others necessarily concentrate on the key moment or moments in the evolution of their subject, that is, the period, development, or persons that were formative for the entire tradition. In treating the themes it frequently proved necessary to respect the variety of Eastern and Western Christianity by dividing the treatment of such central topics as Trinity, anthropology, liturgy, and prayer into separate, but we hope interdependent, articles.

## The Individual Articles

The Scriptures of the Old and New Testaments form the basis for all Christian spirituality. No aspect of the life of the Christian religion can be understood apart from them. Given the physical constraints of this volume, it was impossible to think of giving a full analysis of the spiritual message of the whole New Testament and of the Hebrew Scriptures, or Old Testament, as read through Christian eyes. It was of vital importance, however, to begin the volume with a substantial article as a prologue that would highlight the place of Scripture as the foundation of Christian spirituality and explain how the tradition of "spiritual" exegesis that was the norm for so many centuries is to be understood. Sandra M. Schneiders has made an essential contribution to the volume in writing this prologue, especially in showing how contemporary hermeneutical theory allows for a new appreciation of the significance of the spiritual exegesis of Christian antiquity.

Part 1 begins with a paper by the Orthodox scholar John D. Zizioulas, "The Early Christian Community." It seemed especially important to have a Greek scholar responsible for this key article, which summarizes the formative era when Christianity was primarily a Greek-speaking movement whose identity centered in its liturgical celebration, a tradition that Orthodox Christianity has continued to maintain in uncompromising fashion. Robert M. Grant contributes next "Gnostic Spirituality," a study of the rich and varied movement that overlapped with several other religious traditions, whose history has been so much studied since the famous Nag Hammadi discoveries. Grant's paper argues against some of the more exaggerated evaluations of Gnosticism that have appeared in recent years by showing that, although the Gnostics played a considerable role in early Christianity and provide valuable confirmation of a number of the crucial values of the mainline Christian tradition, the exaggerations of the Gnostic position, especially with regard to the value of material reality, denied it a permanent role in the history of Christian piety.

Rightly among the longest articles in this volume is the magisterial summary "The Spiritual Message of the Great Fathers" by Charles Kannengiesser. The great fathers of East and West—Athanasius, the Cappadocians, John Chrysostom, Hilary, Ambrose, Jerome, and Augustine—remain the common patrimony of all Christians. This article situates these great teachers and men of the spirit in their proper historical context (a necessary procedure for evaluating their contributions as well as their human limitations) and provides succinct sketches of the bequest of each to the future of Christian spirituality.

Monasticism was the most characteristic and influential creation of Christianity in late antiquity; the monastic ideal and the ascetical and contemplative practices associated with it were of incalculable importance in the centuries to come. Two of the foremost historians of monasticism, both themselves Benedictine monks, have written the articles dealing with the rise, spread, and influence of monasticism. Jean Gribomont studies the complex issues involved in the rise of monasticism in Eastern Christianity from the late third through the seventh century, and Jean Leclercq contributes a characteristically wide-ranging and balanced account of monasticism in the West down to the end of the eleventh century.

The mysterious writer known as Pseudo-Dionysius, an anonymous, probably Syrian author of around 500 C.E., had a profound impact on theories of Christian spirituality for centuries to come. The difficulties of the Dionysian writings have led modern scholars to widely divergent views about their meaning and value. Rather than see the Dionysian writings as a Neoplatonic invasion or even perversion of Christianity, recent research has emphasized the fundamentally Christian and liturgical character of the Dionysian spiritual program, despite its Neoplatonic cast. Paul Rorem presents a balanced account of Pseudo-Dionysius and some aspects of his influence in a detailed article entitled "The Uplifting Spirituality of Pseudo-Dionysius."

The history of early Christian spiritual traditions has all too often concentrated upon Greek and Latin Christianity to the exclusion of the role of Christian belief and practice in other linguistic and cultural traditions. It seems especially important today—in the first century in which we can legitimately say that Christianity has become a truly global religion—to look back on early Christianity as it existed outside the Greco-Roman world. Here, too, hard choices had to be made (more space would have allowed the study of Christian spirituality in Coptic, Georgian, Armenian, and even Indian traditions), but it is clear that in the non-Greek East, Syriac Christianity, which was in many ways almost as ancient as the Greek-speaking variety, deserves special study. Roberta C. Bondi has contributed an engaging account of the spiritual significance of Syriac Christianity that illustrates the variety present in early Christian cultural implantations. Pierre Riché, a leading authority on the cultural history of the early medieval West, complements this piece with a clear and stimulating study of how the urban Christianity of the Roman Empire took on new forms as it adapted to the barbarian world of the Celts and Germans.

By the end of the seventh century the basic structure of Christian society was firmly established in the East. The same was not true in the West. In terms of impact on the history of spirituality, one must consider two closely connected stages in order to understand the development of Latin spirituality down through the twelfth century. The first is the Gregorian Reform, on which Karl F. Morrison has penned an insightful essay. Morrison shows that the two fundamental themes of the reform, those of sacerdotalism and papal monarchy, were as controversial in their time as they have remained down through the centuries. But it is clear that they enshrine values which were not invented in the eleventh century and which must be seriously considered in any current reappraisal of the meaning of Christian spirituality.

The final section of Part 1, "The Religious World of the Twelfth Century," deals with a topic of such scope and importance that it proved difficult to assign to a single author. Historians love to detect turning points, that is, periods when the course of history seems to take on a new shape that has a powerful influence for centuries to come. Scholars of medieval history have increasingly singled out the twelfth century (chronologically rather broadly defined, say ca. 1080 to ca. 1215) as a crucial turning point in the Middle Ages, at least in the West. There can be no doubt that the spiritual leaders of this era, especially Anselm of Canterbury and Bernard of Clairvaux, were figures of outstanding importance and that the twelfth century was a crucial watershed in the history of many of the spiritual practices that nourished Christian piety for centuries. The three articles that are devoted to twelfth-century spirituality here—"Anselm of Canterbury" by Benedicta Ward, "The Cistercians" by Basil Pennington, and "The Regular Canons" by Grover A. Zinn—stress the overriding importance of the great spiritual writers without denying the role of the changes in spiritual practices during this time. This concentration upon major writers rather than practices was a necessary, if difficult, choice: these writings continue to have a significant function in contemporary Christian spirituality, whereas the forms of piety of this era, important as they were, are frequently no longer integral to Christian consciousness.

To be a Christian by definition is to adhere to Jesus Christ as savior; hence, the first and in many ways the most important piece in Part 2 is John Meyendorff's article "Christ as Savior in the East," which in an original manner shows how the christology of Athanasius and Cyril of Alexandria forms the decisive core of the faith and practice common to East and West. Bernard McGinn has added to this article a brief appendix, which sketches the evolution of the distinctively Western view of Christ as redeemer that developed between the tenth and the twelfth centuries.

Faith in the three-personed God—Father, Son, and Holy Spirit—has marked Christianity from the start, however much this belief can be shown to have evolved in clarity and expression. For Christians in the ages covered by this volume, faith in the Trinity was not a piece of mere speculation but an intensely real part of Christian life, especially in prayer and liturgy. Thomas Hopko studies the trinitarian spirituality of the Greek fathers, concentrating on the role of the Cappadocians, and Mary T. Clark gives a perceptive survey of Latin thought and practice, especially as found in Marius Victorinus, Augustine, and Richard of St. Victor.

Belief in Christ as redeemer and in the triune God made a decisive mark on the Christian idea of humanity. Christian anthropology centers on the notion that human persons are made in the image and likeness of God (Gen 1:26) and that, although they have lost or damaged that image through sin, they have the possibility of having the image restored through the saving work of Christ, the perfect image of the Father. Lars Thunberg contributes a wide-ranging survey of the anthropology of the Greek fathers, and Bernard McGinn studies the Latin tradition from the fourth through the twelfth century. The way in which Christ restores humanity to its original goal is through the gracious gift (*gratia*) of divine life. In Eastern Christianity consideration of this communication of divine life did not evolve into a separate doctrinal or spiritual topic; it was presented through the teaching on Christ, the Trinity, and Christian anthropology. In Western Christianity, largely because of the challenge of Pelagius, Augustine of Hippo created a distinct theology of grace that has been central to Western theology and spirituality since the fifth century. J. Patout Burns contributes a clear and helpful article, "Grace: The Augustinian Foundation," to explore this theme.

The divine life communicated to the believer does not come in a private and hidden way, but communally and publicly through the sacraments and the liturgy of the church. Liturgical celebration is such an intimate part of Christian spirituality that it is eminently fitting that two extensive articles should be devoted to its role: that of Paul Meyendorff, "Eastern Liturgical Spirituality," and that of the eminent liturgical scholar Pierre-Marie Gy, "Sacraments and Liturgy in the West." The church's worship involves sacred art as well as ritual and ceremony. Though the role of art was equally vital in Latin Christianity, it was in the Greek East that consideration of the sacred image developed as a special theme of Christian spirituality. Leonid Ouspensky gives an account of this in his article, "Icon and Art." Liturgy is the privileged prayer of the whole church, but the development of other forms of prayer and contemplation, both communal and private, occurred in both East and West. These important aspects of Christian spirituality are studied in original fashion in the articles of Kallistos Ware for Eastern Christianity and Jean Leclercq for Latin Christianity.

The final three articles deal with themes that relate more directly to the practice rather than the theory of Christian spirituality. Once again it is important to note that these topics were chosen not only because they are distinctive expressions of the spirituality of the early centuries of Christianity but also because they enshrine elements of permanent validity for all Christians in our eyes. One of the most easily misunderstood aspects of Christian spirituality has been its adherence to the ideal of virginity, which was virtually unquestioned down to the Reformation and is still a vital part of many Christian communities. In a rich and subtle essay, Peter Brown explores the social and spiritual dimensions of virginity and notes its role in the evolution of Marian piety. Spiritual guidance has not played as large a role in Christianity as it has in some other religions, because in the Christian tradition the Holy Spirit is always the primary guide. But it cannot be denied that there is an important place for such guidance in Christianity, especially in the desert tradition, as (Sister) Donald Corcoran shows in a short piece devoted to this topic. Finally, although it is true that Christian spirituality in its earliest ages was frequently the creation of a spiritual elite of clerics and monks and nuns, we must not forget that the ideal of new life in Christ was intended for all believers, the whole body of those addressed in the First Epistle of Peter as "a chosen race, a royal priesthood a consecrated nation, a people set apart to sing the praises of God" (1 Pet 2:9). In a long and insightful article Jacques Fontaine looks at some of the implications of this in Latin Christianity in "The Practice of the Christian Life: The Birth of the Laity." An equally ample article might have been devoted to aspects of lay spirituality in the East, but Fontaine's article forms a fitting conclusion to this volume in its suggestion that the living out of the inner meaning of the gospel message has always been the ideal of all believers, those who have taken to heart the text in John's Gospel that says "the words that I have spoken to you are spirit and life" (John 6:63).

BERNARD McGINN

# General Bibliography
# and Abbreviations

## General Bibliography

### *Sources*

Migne, J. P., ed. *Patrologiae cursus completus. Series graeca.* Paris: J. P. Migne, 1857–66. 161 vols.

———. *Patrologiae cursus completus. Series latina.* Paris: J. P. Migne, 1844–64. 221 vols. and 4 index vols.

Sources chrétiennes. Paris: Cerf, 1940–. This rich collection, now more than 250 volumes, presents editions of texts with French translations and excellent introductions and critical apparatuses.

### *Studies*

Bouyer, Louis, Jean Leclercq, and François Vandenbroucke. *A History of Christian Spirituality.* 3 vols. New York: Seabury, 1982. Vol. 1, *The Spirituality of the New Testament and the Fathers.* Vol. 2, *The Spirituality of the Middle Ages.* Vol. 3, *Orthodox Spirituality and Protestant and Anglican Spirituality.* The original French edition of this series also included Louis Cognet, *La spiritualité moderne* as part 2 of vol. 3 (Paris: Aubier, 1966).

Cross, F. L., and E. A. Livingstone. *The Oxford Dictionary of the Christian Church.* 2nd ed. Oxford: Oxford University Press, 1974.

*Dictionnaire de spiritualité ascétique et mystique doctrine et histoire.* Edited by Marcel Viller, assisted by F. Cavallera, J. de Guibert. Paris: Beauchesne, 1937–. This is the most useful single work for the history of Christian spirituality. As of 1983 it had reached volume 12 (fascicles LXXVI–LXXVII) and the letter *P.* The richly detailed and lengthy articles, as well as the generally excellent bibliographies, make this an indispensable work.

*Dizionario degli Istituti di Perfezione.* Rome: Edizioni Paoline, 1974-. This work, devoted to the history of religious groups and orders, has thus far reached seven volumes, up to the letter *R*.

*The Westminster Dictionary of Christian Spirituality.* Edited by Gordon S. Wakefield. Philadelphia: Westminster, 1983.

## Abbreviations

ACW     Ancient Christian Writers. The Works of the Fathers in Translation. Edited by Johannes Quasten, Joseph C. Plumpe, Walter J. Burghardt and Thomas Comerford Lawler. Westminster, MD, and New York: Newman Press, 1946-. 44 volumes to date.

*ANF*     *The Ante-Nicene Fathers. Translations of the Writings of the Fathers down to* A.D. 325. Edited by Alexander Roberts and James Donaldson. Edinburgh, 1866-72. 10 vols. The most recent reprint is Grand Rapids, MI: Eerdmans, 1981.

*Dict. Sp.*     *Dictionnaire de spiritualité ascétique et mystique doctrine et histoire.*

Fathers     The Fathers of the Church. A New Translation. Edited by Hermengild Dressler et al. Washington, DC: The Catholic University of America Press, 1947-. 72 volumes to date.

LCC     The Library of Christian Classics. Edited by John Baillie, John T. McNeill and Henry P. Van Dusen. Philadelphia: Westminster Press, 1955-60. 26 volumes.

*MGH*     *Monumenta Germaniae Historica inde ab a. C. 500 usque ad a. 1500.* Begun under the editorship of Georg Heinrich Pertz; continued under many others. Hannover and Berlin, 1826-. There are many sections in this massive collection. Most frequently cited herein are the *SS,* or *Scriptores* of 52 parts in 54 vols. (1826-1934) and the *SRM,* or *Scriptores rerum merovingiarum.*

NPNF     The Nicene and Post-Nicene Fathers of the Christian Church. Edited by Philip Schaff and Henry Wace. Buffalo and New York, 1886-90. First Series of 14 volumes; Second Series of 14 volumes. The most recent reprint is Grand Rapids: Eerdmans, 1983.

*PG*     *Patrologiae cursus completus. Series graeca.*

*PL*     *Patrologiae cursus completus. Series latina.*

# 1

# Scripture and Spirituality

## Sandra M. Schneiders

### The Birth of Christian Spirituality

IT WAS HISTORICAL EVENTS, the exodus of the Hebrews from Egypt under the leadership of Moses and the covenant they made with Yahweh on Mount Sinai, that gave rise to and defined Jewish religious experience. Likewise, it was an event, the resurrection of Jesus of Nazareth, that inaugurated and shaped Christian spirituality. From the moment of that event, Christianity was distinct from Judaism even though it would be some sixty years (ca. 90 C.E.) before the break between the synagogue and the newly consolidated Christian community would be definitive.

Twenty centuries of exegesis and theology have not succeeded in fully elucidating that inaugural experience to which the disciples of the historical Jesus bore witness first by proclamation (e.g., Acts 2:22-24; 1 Cor 15:3-8) and then by narratives in which they described "seeing the Lord" (e.g., Luke 24:13-53; John 20:11-18, 19-23, 26-29). Some of the first disciples, utterly disillusioned by the Roman execution of the one they had believed to be the Messiah who would liberate Israel, testified to their experience that the same Jesus whom they had followed, who had been killed and buried, was alive with God and in and among themselves, alive with an indestructible new life which the disciples experienced in themselves as the guarantee of their own eventual and full triumph over sin and death.

They began to live as participants in the paschal mystery, that is, in the death and resurrection of Jesus, whom they now acknowledged as Lord and Messiah. They felt themselves to be free of the Mosaic law (see Gal 3:23-27), no longer bound to struggle to please God through the performance of good works, but, as graced children of God in Christ, empowered by his indwelling Spirit to live in love of God and one another (see Romans 8) according to the pattern that Jesus had given them during his life and described to them in the Beatitudes (Matt 5:1-12). Their joy and their mission were to

1

proclaim the good news (the gospel) of salvation in Christ available to every person who believed in him, was baptized, and lived faithfully within the community of believers who soon came to be called "Christians" after the one to whom they had given their lives. This salvation was offered equally to Jews and Gentiles, to men and women, to slaves and free people (see Gal 3:28). The salvation that Jesus had announced and made available was the universal salvation that the most deeply religious of the ancient Israelites had dimly foreseen as characteristic of messianic times (e.g., Isaiah 60).

Christian spirituality, that is, personal participation in the mystery of Christ begun in faith sealed by baptism into the death and resurrection of Jesus Christ, was nourished by sharing in the Lord's Supper, which the community celebrated regularly in memory of him who was truly present wherever his followers gathered (see Matt 18:26), and was expressed by a simple life of universal love that bore witness to life in the Spirit and attracted others to faith (see Acts 4:32–35; 1 John 1; and elsewhere). Within a very short time Jesus' followers experienced the same persecution that had cost Jesus his life (see Acts 3:1–4:31), and martyrdom, witness to the faith by the shedding of one's blood, became the most coveted crown of Christian life (see Acts 6–7).

## Christian Spirituality as Productive of Scripture

The resurrection experience, as well as the ignominious death of Jesus on the cross, required interpretation in religious categories that could be understood by the first disciples and those to whom they proclaimed salvation in Jesus' name. It was to Israel's sacred literature, the Hebrew Scriptures, that Peter and Paul and the other apostles turned for the religious language that enabled them to interpret the Jesus story as messianic salvation and Jesus himself as Lord and Savior. For the first Christians the Hebrew Scriptures were the word of God just as they had been for Jesus himself (John 10:34–36). However, the Christians began to interpret the Scriptures differently from the Jews, since the Christians regarded Jesus as the fulfillment of the messianic prophecies whereas Jews still awaited that fulfillment.

Furthermore, within two to three decades after Pentecost—when Peter and the others had experienced the outpouring of the Spirit upon themselves and had begun to preach the gospel—a body of original Christian writings began to develop. The letters of the apostle Paul to the communities he had founded began to be circulated and read in other communities. Sometime in the sixties the first narrative account of the life, preaching, work, death, and resurrection of Jesus, the document we call the Gospel of Mark, was composed and was followed by a number of other Gospels, three of which (Matthew, Luke, and John) have been included with that of Mark in the "canon," or official book of Christian Scripture. One of these Gospels, that of Luke, had a sequel, which came to be called the Acts of the Apostles and which described the life of the early church from Pentecost until the end of Paul's apostolic career. Finally, toward the end of the first Christian century, a piece of Christian apocalyptic literature was written, probably composed in the same community that produced the Gospel of John, and this book of Revelation, or Apocalypse, eventually became part of the Christian canon of sacred writings.

The most striking feature of the Christian writings that eventually came to be regarded as Scripture is that they not only transmitted the teaching of Jesus, namely, his announcement that the promised reign of God was imminent, but also identified that reign as having been inaugurated in and by the person and work of Jesus himself. Jesus, now believed to be the Son of God, Messiah, and Savior of the world, was the primary content of the Christian preaching. In confessing Jesus of Nazareth as the Christ, the Christian community expressed the centrality of his person to their monotheistic faith, a development that finally proved incompatible with the Jewish faith in one God as it was preserved and taught by the synagogue after the fall of Jerusalem in 70 C.E.

The first suggestion that these Christian writings were beginning to be considered "Scripture" appears in 2 Pet 3:16 (ca. 100–125), where the author refers to the writings of Paul as on a par with "the other Scriptures." In Justin's *Apology* 1.67, written about 150, we find an indication that some of the Christian writings, notably the Gospels, were being read along with the Hebrew Scriptures at Christian liturgies.

The most important development, in view of what will follow, was the attempt to situate the Christian writings in relation to the Hebrew Scriptures, which the Christians continued to regard as the inspired word of God even after the expulsion of the Christians from the synagogue (ca. 90). The struggle between Marcion, who rejected the Hebrew Scriptures, and the larger community, which accepted them, precipitated the formulation of the official position that Scripture is a single "book" composed of two Testaments. The earliest known reference to the Hebrew Scriptures as the Old Testament is that of Melito of Sardis, which is recorded in Eusebius's *Church History* (*Historia ecclesiastica*) 4.26 and dates from ca. 170. Tertullian, around 200, seems to have been the first to refer to the Christian writings as the New Testament.

The Christian designation of the Hebrew Scriptures as the Old Testament was an expression of an intuitive understanding of the process of revelation within history that has never been explained in a fully satisfactory way. The Christian community came to see itself as the "true" (and eventually as the "new") Israel, the inheritor of the promises made to Abraham and the covenant mediated by Moses. Thus, the Old Testament was regarded by the Christian community as its own literature, but only in the context of the new covenant established in and by Jesus Christ. What is the whole of Scripture for a Jew is only a part, and indeed a preparatory part, of the Sacred Scripture for a Christian. Consequently, the most fundamental law of hermeneutics, the mutually determining relationship of part and whole, entails a radically different approach to the Hebrew Scriptures by Christians. The problem of how the Christian is to interpret the Old Testament in light of the New and the New Testament against the background of the Old was the central hermeneutical problem of the Christian use of Scripture during the first half of the Christian era.

## The Role of Scripture
## in Early Christian Spirituality

The attitude of the first Christians toward Scripture differed in no significant way from that of believing Jews. Every word of the sacred text was pregnant with divine meaning and everything of religious significance was expressed in the context of biblical categories and by means of biblical language. Consequently, the entire religious experience of the early church was steeped in and articulated by biblical symbolism. At first this symbolism was drawn entirely from the Hebrew Scriptures. Later, as we have seen, the Christian community produced its own writings, which were themselves profoundly influenced by the Old Testament.

Proclamation, the preaching of the gospel to those who had not yet heard it, was the first task of the new community that was inaugurated by the resurrection of Jesus. As we see from the records of the earliest preaching by Peter, Paul, and the other apostles as recounted in the Acts of the Apostles, every effort was made to interpret the Christ-event in terms of the promises given to the ancestors in the Old Testament. Jesus was presented in the preaching of the early church as the New Adam, the New Moses, the prophet promised in Deuteronomy, the promised heir to the Davidic throne, the Isaian Suffering Servant, and the mysterious Son of Man in the book of Daniel. All of the titles that the early church employed in order to understand and proclaim Jesus as Son of God and Savior of the world were drawn from the Old Testament and transformed by the Christian experience of Jesus to become vehicles for the interpretation of his life, work, and destiny.

Catechesis, the further formation of new converts in the life of Christ, was likewise virtually entirely biblical as was the prayer life, both liturgical and individual, of the early Christians. The celebration of baptism in connection with the solemnity of the resurrection (Easter) was an initiation of the Christian into the mystery of Christ in his passion, death, and resurrection understood against the background of creation, the fall, the flood, the promise to the ancestors, the exodus, the covenant, the exile, and the return, all understood as types of the salvation finally effected in Christ and now communicated to the members of the believing community. Eucharist, the commemoration of the Lord's last supper with his disciples, was interpreted by the Christian community against the background of the paschal meal. Thus, the death of Jesus was understood as an exodus by which Jesus, the New Moses, leads the community to life and freedom in a new and eternal covenant that was sealed in his blood, shed for them on Calvary. The daily prayer of the early Christians consisted of the psalms of the Old Testament as well as the prayer that Jesus himself had taught them (the Our Father [see Luke 11:1-4]), which was itself profoundly scriptural.

Theology as it developed in the early church, beginning with the work of the apologists and that of the masters of the earliest catechetical schools of Alexandria and Antioch, consisted entirely in the exegesis of Scripture. In attempting to make the new teaching acceptable to the Jews, the Christians relied almost exclusively on the exposition of the Hebrew Scriptures as prophecy fulfilled in Jesus. For the Gentiles, especially those knowledgeable in philosophy, the exposition of the Scriptures aimed at showing the reasonableness of the biblical material and its compatibility with pagan learning. Indeed it was not until the high Middle Ages that theology began to take an independent dialectical form that relied primarily on philosophy rather than on Scripture.

In short, the Scriptures played the role in the religious experience of the early church that the Second Vatican Council claimed it should play in the life of Christians of our own day. Scripture was indeed the "pure and perennial source of the spiritual life" (Dogmatic Constitution on Divine Revelation [*Dei Verbum*], chap. 6, art. 21).

## The Problem of Interpreting Scripture in the Early Church

### *Underlying Assumptions*

The problem of how to interpret the Scriptures was crucial for the early church. Certain presuppositions about interpretation underlay all the exegetical efforts of these first centuries.

First, contrary to the assumptions of post-Renaissance exegesis, the early church assumed that the Bible, in some ways at least, was unlike any other type of literature. It was believed not only that every word of Scripture was inspired by God but also that every word was the bearer, in some way, of divine revelation. Consequently, the interpreter required divine assistance (usually understood as interior illumination) in order to understand the text aright. This led Origen, the early church's greatest biblical scholar, to insist that the students at his catechetical school in Alexandria lead a quasi-monastic life since the purity of their consciences and the intensity of their prayer were substantively determinative of the quality of their scholarship.

Because the Scriptures were the church's book, only the believer, working from within the believing community, could rightly interpret the biblical text. By the sixth century this position had developed into a theory of authoritative ecclesiastical interpretation that effectively brought an end to the creative period of patristic exegesis. But its original purpose was not to control the work of orthodox exegetes; rather it was to dispute the legitimacy and, therefore, the validity of the interpretation of the "heretics"—that is, those thinkers and teachers, such as the Gnostics, whose faith was no longer compatible with that of the great church. Justin, Origen, and the orthodox Tertullian among others invoked this principle against Jewish, Gnostic, and Marcionite interpretations, particularly in defense of the continued significance of the Old Testament for Christians, the christological interpretation of the Old Testament, and the defensibility of the Old Testament presentation of God, which some of the heretics regarded as too materialistic and anthropomorphic, if not blatantly immoral. Nevertheless, even if only the believer could achieve the proper interpretation of the Bible, the results of this interpretation were intended to be understood by and convincing to the well-disposed nonbeliever as well as triumphant in the struggle against the heretics.

A second presupposition underlying early Christian exegesis was that Jesus himself was the hermeneutical principle par excellence. Not only was he the fulfillment of the Old Testament (see Acts 2:22–36) and therefore the key to its true meaning, but also he was presented as supplying during his own lifetime the example of how the Scriptures were to be interpreted. Jesus made it clear that the Old Testament required an interpretation that was more than mere repetition or literalistic application of the Mosaic law (e.g., Jesus' response to the Pharisees on the question of divorce and remarriage [Matt 19:3–9]). He also showed repeatedly that all parts of Scripture were not of equal weight and that even the most sacred tenets of Torah, such as the observance of the Sabbath, must yield before the demands of the great law of love (see Mark 3:1–6). Furthermore, Jesus taught as one "having authority," that is, without appealing to either the law or the traditional interpretation of the law (see Mark 1:21-28), thus grounding the claim of the church that Jesus inaugurated a truly new covenant, which had become the norm for the interpretation of the old.

A third underlying assumption of early Christian exegesis was that biblical interpretation was simultaneously a work of scholarship demanding the best use of the most advanced methods and a work of faithful contemplation that would never be equal to the mystery of divine revelation. Related to this was the double obligation of the exegete to scholarly integrity and to the tradition of the church. Each of these two poles was accorded different importance at different times and in different places. Origen, for example, although deeply convinced that biblical interpretation was an essentially contemplative and ecclesial occupation, tended to place more confidence in the results of research than in the deliverances of tradition, whereas Irenaeus regarded tradition as the ultimate norm of scholarly work.

## The Problem of the Relationship between the Two Testaments

The primary focus of the early church's exegetical concerns was not the New Testament. Even though the New Testament itself (see 1 Pet 3:16) acknowledged that some of Paul's writings were "hard to understand" and that some people were trying to "twist [Paul's teaching] to their own destruction," the first Christian preachers and teachers were close enough in culture and language to the New Testament to assume an immediate access to its meaning, which could not be assumed with regard to the Old Testament. The primary problem for the early church was the relationship between the two Testaments, a problem that took two closely related forms.

First was the problem of trying to interpret the story of Jesus of Nazareth as the Christ-event for believing Jews, who would see the ignominious death of Jesus on the cross as God's repudiation of his teaching and of the claims of his disciples that he was the Messiah (see Deut 21:22-23). The first disciples had to interpret that death as part of God's plan, which was brought to its completion by the vindication of Jesus through resurrection and exaltation at God's right hand.

In telling the Jesus story, the first Christians attempted to show that the Old Testament itself was the basis for the messianic claim. This was done in various ways: by presenting Jesus' birth midrashically so as to show that he was the New Moses fleeing a contemporary pharaoh and returning from exile in Egypt as the mediator designated by God to save and form a new people (see Matthew 2); by showing that he was the fulfillment of Old

Testament prophecy (e.g., that he was the Suffering Servant of Deutero-Isaiah [see Luke 4:17–21 in relation to Isa 61:1–2]); or by showing how the events of Jesus' life and death, if properly understood, are seen as the global working out of a divine plan that can be discerned only now that it has been fulfilled in Jesus (see Acts 2:14–36).

The second task, even more difficult than showing that the New Testament was a fulfillment of the Old, was that of showing how the Old Testament could be interpreted in terms of the New. This was necessary if the Old Testament was to be "saved" from those who wished simply to abandon it as either totally irrelevant now that the new covenant had been established in Jesus or as unworthy of the God revealed by Jesus. The sound intuition of the early church was that the Scriptures that were so dear to Jesus, which had prepared a people for him even if not all recognized him when he came and which had been faithfully held to be the word of God from time immemorial, could not be rendered null and void—much less, evil—by the final revelation of God in the fullness of time. On the other hand, it was clear that priority had to be assigned to the New Testament and that the Old had to be brought into a relationship with it that honored the Old but subordinated it to the New. This is an example of the hermeneutical problem, the recognition that an ancient document is no longer assimilable purely on face value but that it is too significant to be abandoned as irrelevant or assigned merely historical interest. The actualizing of the perennial value of the classical text is the central task of interpretation.

In the New Testament itself the foundations are laid for the Christian interpretation of the Old Testament. Paul, for example, skilled as a rabbinical exegete, used the rabbinical techniques of verbal interpretation, so strange to the modern mind, to extract christological significance from Old Testament passages. An excellent example of this technique of interpreting words in isolation, without regard for the context, is Paul's building of a whole promise–fulfillment christology on the fact that the divine promise of salvation was made to Abraham's "offspring" in the singular, that is, to Christ, rather than to his "offsprings" in the plural (Gal 3:15–18). Therefore, Christ, by fulfilling the promise, validated the priority of promise over law. Paul also employed allegory, a term used rather inclusively of interpretation based on similarity. For example, in Gal 4:22–31 Paul develops the Old Testament story of Abraham's two wives and their respective sons as an allegory of the relationship between the two covenants, the old being a dispensation of slavery to the law, the new a dispensation of freedom according to grace. Paul's exegesis of the Old Testament, which he continued to hold in the highest esteem after his conversion, was thoroughly christological in content even though his methods remained largely rabbinic.

Another interpretive technique that appears in the New Testament itself is typological interpretation. A type is an Old Testament reality (person, place, thing, or event) that is understood, from a later perspective, to have been a foreshadowing of a New Testament reality. For example, Paul sees the rock that Moses struck to provide life-giving water for the Hebrews during the wanderings in the desert (Exod 17:6) as a type of Christ, the source of life for Christians (1 Cor 10:4). In John's Gospel Jesus himself is presented as interpreting the brazen serpent that Moses lifted up in the desert to save the rebellious Hebrews who had been bitten by fiery serpents (Num 21:6-9) as a type of the Son of man who would be lifted up so that all who believed in him would have eternal life (John 3:14-15). New Testament typological interpretation of the Old Testament is most strikingly evident in the Letter to the Hebrews, which is a prolonged explanation of how the Old Testament is fulfilled in the New, how the "law has but a shadow of the good things to come instead of the true form of these realities" (Heb 10:1).

Another New Testament basis for the christological interpretation of the Old Testament is found in the Fourth Gospel's presentation of the Paraclete. Jesus, according to John, had much to say to his disciples which his earthly companions were not able to bear (John 16:12-13); consequently, subsequent generations of Christians under the influence of the Holy Spirit would have to draw out the full meaning of the Christ-event. This interpretive activity, authorized by Jesus himself and guaranteed by the gift of the Holy Spirit, would consist partly in showing how Jesus and his messianic activity were already present in the Old Testament. The fourth evangelist himself is quite explicit in presenting Jesus as the one of whom Moses and the prophets spoke (see John 5:45-47; 12:12-16; 12:38-42).

## Differing Approaches to
## Biblical Interpretation in Antiquity

In the early church two basic approaches to the biblical text developed, which gave rise to two characteristic types of interpretation. As we will see later, traditionally these approaches have been called the "literal" approach and the "more than literal," or "allegorical," approach. These terms did not mean the same thing to the ancients that they meant in later times—and certainly not what they mean today. But they denote fundamental approaches, each of which gave rise to a tradition of interpretation that lasted until the high Middle Ages, when a philosophical approach to theology transformed the latter from biblical commentary and exposition into what finally became systematic and eventually scholastic theology.

The "more than literal" approach was developed in Alexandria in Egypt and can be traced back to the middle of the second century. It was related to the midrashic, typological, and allegorical interpretation that we find in the Old and New Testaments, but it was developed into a theoretically articulated exegetical method. The "literal" approach developed in Antioch in Asia Minor, partly in opposition to what was perceived as excessive allegorizing in Alexandria. As we shall see, the real differences between the two approaches had at least as much to do with intellectual heritage and temperament as with hermeneutical theory or exegetical method.

Another major tension at the heart of the development of early Christian biblical hermeneutics concerned the respective roles of scholarship and authority. The emphasis on thoroughgoing scholarly research as the basis for the interpretation of the sacred text was more characteristic of Alexandria, which was a center of the encounter between early Christianity and the Hellenistic culture of late antiquity. In Antioch, situated at the heart of the Jewish-Christian conflict and always beset with heterodox tendencies of the more exotic kind, the role of authority in the proper interpretation of the church's book was emphasized more, even though Antiochene exegesis relied on serious historical and linguistic scholarship. The emphasis on authority eventually prevailed, and by the sixth century exegesis had come to consist primarily in the compiling of *catenae* ("chains") of authoritative interpretations by the earlier commentators.

## The Two Schools of Exegesis in Antiquity

Before discussing spiritual exegesis as it developed in late antiquity and the early Middle Ages, especially in the Latin church, it is necessary to trace briefly the development in the East of the two types of exegesis that dominated the patristic period.

### Alexandrian Exegesis

Alexandria was a cosmopolitan city in Africa in which Hellenistic culture had reached a high level of development. It was the home of Philo the Jew (ca. 20 B.C.E.–50 C.E.), one of the most influential biblical exegetes of all time. Philo developed a method of allegorical exegesis, the purpose of which was to demonstrate the compatibility between the spiritual meaning of the Hebrew Scriptures and the loftiest insights of Platonic philosophy.

Philo's allegorical method is the background for the development of the exegetical school that arose in Alexandria. The school's first major scholar was Clement (ca. 150–215), a Christian intellectual who used Philo and found in allegorical exegesis a key to unlocking the scriptural symbolism

1. *Icon of Christ as Pantocrator,*
   Monastery of Saint Catherine,
   Mount Sinai, 6th century

within which were hidden the riches of Christian *gnōsis,* the secret wisdom reserved for the initiates in the faith. Clement was not primarily concerned with questions of exegesis but with humanistic Christian wisdom; his interpretations of the biblical text were often spiritual accommodations that appear fanciful to the modern reader.

Clement's greatest student, and certainly the greatest Christian exegete of antiquity, was Origen (ca. 185–ca. 254), who developed the theory of biblical interpretation that was predominant in the church until the high Middle Ages and who applied his theory in the production of a prodigious corpus of biblical commentary and scripturally based theological reflection. His *Hexapla Biblia* (ca. 240), a six-column presentation of Hebrew and Greek texts of the Bible, which enabled scholars to compare critically a variety of ancient versions, was an astounding scholarly accomplishment that adequately demonstrates Origen's profound concern with what moderns would call the literal sense of Scripture as the basis of exegesis.

Origen, in his *On First Principles* (*De principiis,* book 4), developed a theory of the threefold sense of Scripture which was the ancestor of the fourfold sense that became standard in the Middle Ages. This threefold division corresponded to the tripartite composition of the human person (body, soul, spirit) as this was understood by the Greek fathers. The literal sense (body) was the historical sense; the typological sense (soul) was the moral application to the individual; and the spiritual sense (spirit) was the foreshadowing of the new covenant in the old. Actually, Origen frequently proceeded according to a different method, distinguishing the literal sense from the spiritual sense, which he then often applied to the individual Christian soul. Origen's *Commentary on the Song of Songs* (*In Canticum Canticorum*, ca. 240) interprets the love of the spouses both as the relation between Christ and the church and as the relation between the Word and the Christian soul. (Both tradition and Origen thought of the Song of Songs as the wedding song of Solomon.) It is perhaps his most sustained and inspiring exercise of this method.

Origen had a number of significant successors in Alexandria, such as Dionysius (ca. 190–ca. 264), Athanasius (296–372), Didymus the Blind (313–398), and Cyril (376–444), but none was his equal in scholarship or creativity. The influence of the type of exegesis developed in Alexandria saturated the Christian West and retained its hegemony throughout the Middle Ages.

## Antiochene Exegesis

The catechetical school in Antioch in Syria developed its characteristic approach to exegesis largely in opposition to the allegorical approach of Alexandria. Its origins in the late third century are difficult to trace because the extant works of its scholars are few and fragmentary. It was founded by Lucian of Samosata (d. 312), who was followed by the school's major theoretician, Diodorus of Tarsus (d. ca. 392), who was himself overshadowed in the actual practice of exegesis by his famous pupil Theodore of Mopsuestia (350–428). John Chrysostom (347–407), more a theologian than an exegete, was a fellow student of Theodore and was basically Antiochene in his approach to the Scriptures. The last great figure of the school in Antioch was Theodoret of Cyrus (ca. 390– ca. 458). Antioch's influence reached the West through Julian, the Pelagian bishop of Eclanum (d. 454) and Junilius (ca. 540).

The opposition between Alexandrian (allegorical) and Antiochene (literal) exegesis has often been exaggerated. In fact, the scholars of Antioch were as adept at "more than literal" exegesis as were those of Alexandria, but their focus was different. Antiochene exegesis was heir to the type of verbal literalism that was characteristic of Jewish interpretation. But the Christian exegetes of Antioch were, of course, also concerned with interpreting the Old Testament in a Christian sense. Thus, on the one hand, they shared the Jewish conviction that history itself was the locus of divine revelation and that the literal (by which they meant the historical) sense, was of utmost importance, and, on the other hand, they needed a method for uncovering in the historical material a meaning that could have become apparent only with the coming of Christ. This twofold concern led to the development of a hermeneutical theory that embraced both typology and *theoria* and tended to center especially on the prophetic writings of the Old Testament.

The method of interpretation called *theoria*, the characteristic contribution of Antioch, attributed to the biblical writer a simultaneous perception of both the actual historical events that the prophet was describing and, in and through them, the future events that they foreshadowed. This theory presumed an ecstatic conception of biblical inspiration that grounded the attribution of revelation to every word of the sacred text, an approach characteristic also of Jewish exegesis of that period. This, in turn, led to a profound respect for the historical (or so-called literal) sense as the starting point of all interpretation and a greater interest on the part of the exegete in the perceptions of the human author in contrast to Alexandria's Platonic approach and its primary concern for the timeless revelation of the Holy Spirit hidden in the rather opaque wrappings of the historical material.

In summary, both the school of Alexandria and that of Antioch shared a double concern: for the starting point of all exegesis in the literal sense of the text and for the termination of exegesis in a spiritual sense consisting in the Christian (i.e., for them, the true) meaning of the Old Testament, which, by definition, had to exceed in some way the material content of that text. The primary locus of the spiritual sense for the Alexandrians was allegory (an inclusive term for all the literary vehicles of a more than literal meaning) and for the Antiochenes it was *theoria*, a less inclusive and flexible instrument even if one more closely tied to the historical sense.

Both schools of interpretation influenced the development of exegesis in the West. The Antiochene stream, far less influential than that of Alexandria, reached the West through the writings of John Chrysostom. The principles of Antiochene exegesis were espoused by Jerome (ca. 340–420), the most accomplished biblical scholar of antiquity in the West. But Jerome's work, in practice, was more Alexandrian than Antiochene. Jerome and Rufinus also translated many key works of Origen. Jerome's contribution to the understanding of the literal sense was his recognition that metaphors as such are part of the literal sense, something Origen never seemed to have realized. Jerome's greatest importance for the history of biblical interpretation in Latin Christianity was through his new translation, the Vulgate, begun in 382 at the request of Pope Damasus. Its style and language had incalculable effects upon the history of Western spirituality down to this century.

Alexandrian influence in the West was enormous. Although Ambrose of

Milan used Alexandrian exegesis, its most influential proponent was Augus-, tine of Hippo (354–430), whose approach to Scripture is set forth in his *On Christian Doctrine* (*De doctrina Christiana*). Augustine always commenced his exegetical work with the literal sense, that is, with Jewish history as presented in the sacred text, but he believed that all of Scripture had a spiritual sense, which was the true goal of interpretation. Augustine's book, designed to help the clergy in their central teaching task of interpreting and preaching the sacred text, was the Magna Carta of the biblical culture of the Middle Ages. The bishop's encouragement of the use of classical learning (e.g., *On Christian Doctrine* 2.4) was crucial in medieval education, and his exploration of the meaning of Scripture in terms of literal and figurative signs gave a new basis for the spiritual interpretation and enabled him to enunciate as the general principle of all exegesis the maxim "Scripture teaches nothing but charity, nor condemns anything except cupidity, and in this way shapes peoples' minds" (3.10). Only interpretations compatible with charity understood as correct belief and love ordered to the enjoyment of God were legitimate, though in the case of difficult passages such interpretations might well be multiple (e.g., *Confessions* 12.18–31).

The bishop of Hippo remained true to this program throughout his long career as an exegete. He did not neglect the interpretation of the literal signs of the Scripture, as his great *Literal Commentary on Genesis* (*De Genesi ad litteram*, 401–414 C.E.) shows, though the letter of the creation account for him revealed primarily the metaphysical structure of the universe. Other works, especially his lengthy *Discourses on the Psalms* (*Enarrationes in Psalmos*, ca. 390–420), which did so much to shape the prayer life of the Middle Ages, were explorations of the figurative meaning of the scriptural text.

The golden age of patristic exegesis came to a close with Cyril of Alexandria (376–444), in whom occurs a certain confluence of Alexandrian and Antiochene influences. There is no question that Alexandria exerted the greater influence on succeeding ages, but the primary concern and basic principle of both strands of the tradition can be summed up in Augustine's oft quoted line, "The New Testament lies hidden in the Old; the Old is enlightened through the New" (*Questions in the Heptateuch* [*Quaestiones in Heptateuchum*] 2.73).

## The Development of Exegesis
## in the Middle Ages

The early Middle Ages extends, for our purposes, from the fall of the Roman Empire in the fifth century to the rise of the cathedral schools at the beginning of the eleventh century. During this time of political and cultural upheaval the monasteries provided almost the only setting for the serious pursuit of the spiritual life, which was understood as a common life of prayer, study, and work. Study consisted primarily in the prayerful interpretation of Scripture under the guidance of the patristic writings collected in the *catenae*.

The prayerful study of the Scripture and the fathers, to which the monastics devoted several hours of each day, was known as *lectio divina*, and it was governed by the method of "fourfold interpretation" which John Cassian (ca. 360–435) introduced into Western monasticism in his *Conferences of the Fathers* (*Collationes*). This method, which consisted in drawing from the passage of Scripture its "four senses" was profoundly Origenist. The theory of the four senses, which corresponds better to Origen's actual exegetical practice than the three-senses theory he propounded, dominated exegesis until the high Middle Ages and is aptly summarized in a famous medieval couplet of uncertain authorship:

> Littera gesta docet, quid credas allegoria;
> Moralis quid agas, quo tendas anagogia.*

Thus, the literal sense refers to the events and realities of Jewish history. The other three are spiritual senses: the allegorical, which reveals the Christian or theological meaning of the text; the moral or tropological, which applies the text to the individual Christian's practice; and the anagogical, which points toward eschatological fulfillment. The classic example of fourfold interpretation is the understanding of Jerusalem as the Jewish city (literal), the church (allegorical), the soul (tropological), and the heavenly city (anagogical) (see Cassian *Conferences* 14.8). Gregory the Great (540–604), who became pope in 590, and the English monk Bede the Venerable (672–735), whose compilations heavily influenced later medieval scholarship, are classic proponents of this type of exegesis.

The interest in a more literal type of exegesis never completely disappeared during the early Middle Ages. It appears in the work of the Spaniard Isidore of Seville (ca. 560–636) and among the Irish monks. However, the dominance of the fourfold interpretation, that is, of spiritual exegesis, was never in question.

In the eleventh century the foundation of the cathedral schools in centers such as Paris, Laon, and Utrecht ushered in a new era of scholarship, during which systematic theology and biblical studies gradually became two quite distinct disciplines, until by the thirteenth century the separation of

---

*"The letter teaches what happened; the allegorical sense what to believe; the moral sense what to do; the anagogical sense whither we go."

functions was virtually complete. This development took place in many centers, not least the famous Abbey of Saint-Victor of Paris (founded 1110), in which monastic *lectio divina* and the dialectical methods of the universities met and mutually enriched each other. The spiritual sense of the Scriptures retained its importance, but intense interest in the Hebrew language and in Jewish exegesis revived a serious concern with the literal sense of the text. Scripture came to function quite differently in the lecture hall, where its literal sense was exploited in relation to doctrine and in the liturgical and contemplative contexts where its spiritual sense nurtured faith.

## Spiritual Exegesis: The Relation of Scripture to Spirituality

The approach to Scripture characteristic of the patristic and medieval periods is strikingly different from that of post-Renaissance or modern times. The contrast is often summarized somewhat simplistically, as the opposition between "spiritual" and "literal" interpretation, a distinction that is more confusing than enlightening. The confusion results, in large part, from the different meanings of the two labels in ancient and modern usage, as well as from the different contexts of interpretation characteristic of ancient and modern scholarship.

First, the term "literal sense" meant something quite different in the pre-Renaissance period from what it means today. For the ancient exegete the literal sense was the letter or "body" of the text as opposed to its religious meaning or "spirit," whether or not the latter was intended or even known by the biblical writer. Thus, for example, if this theory were applied to the New Testament, the literal meaning of the account of the crucifixion of Jesus would be restricted to the physical and political facts of the story. Its salvific significance (which is obviously the primary meaning the evangelists were trying to convey) would belong to the spiritual meaning. In contrast, for the modern exegete the literal sense is the meaning intended by the human author. Consequently, the meaning of the text would be identical to the historical facts only when the recounting of history is what the author intended. The literal meaning of a parable, prayer, poem, prophetic oracle, etc. would be determined by the literary genre in which it was written and the literary devices (symbol, metaphor, hyperbole, etc.) employed in it. These latter would belong to the literal sense because they belong to the meaning intended by the author even though they are not historical but literary, not literal but figurative.

Given these two very different understandings of literal meaning, it is not surprising that the ancient exegete saw it primarily as a door (albeit an important and usually indispensable one) to the true meaning of the text whereas the modern exegete, persuaded that the true meaning of the text is determined by the author, would consider the literal meaning to be identical with the true meaning.

Second, the term "spiritual sense" also had a very different meaning for the ancients from the meaning it holds for post-Renaissance exegetes. For the ancients the spiritual sense was the true meaning of the text, the message God wished to convey through Scripture to the believer. Consequently, although it might be obscure and never more than tentatively discerned, it was by no means arbitrary, fanciful, or subject to human manipulation. Indeed, for Origen, the same charism of inspiration was at work in the exegete as in the sacred writer, guiding the former to read truly under divine influence what the latter had written truly under divine influence. The theory of the necessity of divine illumination for the proper understanding of the Scriptures was a constant in the tradition of spiritual exegesis.

The problem for the modern reader in understanding and appreciating the ancient and medieval practice of spiritual exegesis arises from its underlying assumptions about Scripture, some of which appear valid to a modern reader and others of which seem quite doubtful.

1. Scripture was understood as inspired by God, something a modern believing interpreter might also hold. But inspiration was understood in premodern times according to a quasi-dictation model, which is hardly tenable today. According to this model, every word of Scripture is directly attributable to God and must, therefore, be suffused with meaning worthy of God. This led to the attempt to find serious religious significance in passages we today would easily relativize or even pass over. The attempt to find deep meaning where none probably exists led to the strained inventiveness of some patristic exegesis that moderns rightly find groundless or even fantastic.

2. The ancients were convinced that Scripture was concerned uniquely with God's revelation in Christ and that until the interpreter had uncovered the christological and salvific significance of the text he or she had not reached its true meaning. This true meaning could be conveyed straightforwardly by the literal meaning of the text, for example, in the Decalogue, but usually it was hidden in the dynamics of promise and fulfillment or the revelatory sacramentality of mundane realities and events. Typology and allegory, as literary vehicles, were not as sharply distinguished by the ancients as they later were by twentieth-century theorists. Typology referred to the foreshadowing of later realities by earlier ones, something which was intended by God, who inspired the whole of Scripture, but which could only be discerned by the later reader enlightened by Christian experience.

Allegory referred to all figurative meanings, a range that extended from genuine symbolism to pure accommodation of the most tenuous variety. Often typological and allegorical interpretation overlapped in actual practice, for both were founded on the same basic understanding of the unity of the two Testaments under the single revelatory intent of the divine author.

3. The patristic conception of Scripture not only allowed for but also created the expectation that the word of God had multiple meanings corresponding to the richness of the mystery of the Word made flesh (thus a spiritual and a corporeal meaning) and to the complexity of levels and phases in the realization of the Christian mystery (thus ecclesial and individual meanings; historical, contemporary, and eschatological meanings).

In contrast to this rich and theologically well-founded (although not always soberly used) understanding of the spiritual sense is that of post-Renaissance critical scholarship. For the latter, as it became progressively better equipped with philological, archaeological, and historical tools, the ideal of interpretation became the literal sense understood as the meaning intended by the human author, a meaning that seemed within realistic reach of the careful scholar. The spiritual sense became, in contrast, those meanings that had no real basis in the literal sense, whether such meanings be New Testament inspired christological interpretations of Old Testament prophecy (interpretations that could not be attributed to the Old Testament author) or edifying modern accommodations erected upon historical texts which had nothing to do with the later situation. Religiously committed Scripture scholars of the modern period have repeatedly tried to develop interpretive theories that could allow also for a contemporary—that is, relevant—meaning of the text that would be well grounded in the literal sense. However, these theories—such as modern approaches to typology, the theory of the *sensus plenior* or fuller sense, or various understandings of "salvation history"—have been characterized by a certain extrinsicism and arbitrariness. They invariably involve the building of an applied sense as a kind of superstructure on the literal sense, which remains imprisoned in the past, unable to transcend the world of the author.

Finally, a third difference between the patristic and the modern exegete concerns the relationship of each to tradition. For the ancient, the tradition of the faith provided the universally accepted context for all biblical interpretation. The instinct of faith, the sense of church, accepted theological development, and liturgical participation functioned normatively in the process of interpreting what was frankly acknowledged to be the "church's book." Caught up in the sense of the uninterrupted development of God's plan of salvation, the ancient interpreters responded aesthetically and religiously to the symbolic connections that guided their interpretation at a level unavailable to the modern exegete relying exclusively upon the tools of critical research.

With the Renaissance were born the quest for objectivity in the modern sense of the word and the profound suspicion of authority that would culminate in the scientific revolution and the Enlightenment. The immediacy of participation in an interpretive tradition was shattered. Scientific method became the sole guide of scholarly investigation, and mathematical exactitude and certitude the ideals of all knowledge worthy of the name. In such an intellectual climate the spiritual exegesis of the patristic and medieval scholars could only appear accidentally insightful at best and frivolously imaginative at worst.

In the late twentieth century, with the discovery of the serious limitations of scientific method in the humanistic sphere, the rediscovery of the power of symbolism and the ubiquity of metaphorical thinking and language, the development of a more adequate understanding of the constitutive function of imagination, and the raising of questions of language and interpretation in every field of investigation, a new appreciation of ancient biblical exegesis is also emerging. There can be no question of a simple return to the methods or conclusions of the patristic and medieval exegetes (although some of it looks much more credible than it did a century ago!). Historical criticism is an indispensable component of any responsible biblical interpretation and precludes the possibility of a scientifically responsible precritical approach to the texts. But postcritical interpretation, characterized by what Paul Ricoeur has called "the second naiveté," will no doubt involve an aesthetic appreciation and spiritual sensitivity that have long been almost absent from the world of biblical scholarship.

## Bibliography

### Sources

Augustine. *The Literal Meaning of Genesis.* Translated by John H. Taylor. ACW 41-42. 1982.

———. *On Christian Doctrine.* Translated by D. W. Robertson. New York: Bobbs-Merrill, 1958.

———. *On the Psalms.* Translated by Dame Scholastica Hebgin and Dame Felicitas Corrigan. ACW 29-30. 1960-61.

Gregory the Great. *Morals on the Book of Job.* 3 vols. in 4. Oxford: J. H. Parker, 1844-50.

John Chrysostom. *Homilies on the Epistle to the Romans.* Oxford: J. H. Parker, 1848.

————. *Homilies on the Gospel of St. John.* Translated by Sister Thomas Aquinas Goggin. Fathers 33, 41. 1957, 1960.

Origen. *Commentaries of Origen.* Edited by Allan Menzies. ANF 10. Includes his commentaries on Matthew and on John.

————. *On First Principles.* Translated by G. W. Butterworth. New York: Harper Torchbooks, 1966.

————. *The Song of Songs: Commentary and Homilies.* Translated by R. P. Lawson. ACW 26. 1957.


*Studies*

Barrett, C. K. "The Interpretation of the Old Testament in the New." In *The Cambridge History of the Bible,* 1:377–411. Cambridge: Cambridge University Press, 1970.

Brown, Raymond E. "Hermeneutics." In *The Jerome Biblical Commentary,* 2:605–23. Englewood Cliffs, NJ: Prentice-Hall, 1968. A good history of interpretation theory in relation to the Bible.

————. *The "Sensus Plenior" of Sacred Scripture.* Baltimore, MD: St. Mary's University Press, 1955. Contains a brief history of exegesis and an excellent bibliography from the period 1940–50.

Crouzel, Henri. "Spiritual Exegesis." In *Encyclopedia of Theology: The Concise Sacramentum Mundi,* 126–33. Edited by Karl Rahner. New York: Seabury, 1975. An excellent brief explanation of patristic and medieval exegesis and its relation to contemporary forms of exegesis.

de Lubac, Henri. *Exégèse médiévale: Les Quatre Sens de l'écriture.* 4 vols. Paris: Aubier, 1959–63. The classic work on the history of spiritual interpretation.

————. *Histoire et esprit.* Paris: Aubier, 1950.

Froehlich, Karlfried. *Biblical Interpretation in the Early Church.* Philadelphia: Fortress, 1984. A useful collection of texts.

Grant, Robert M. *The Letter and the Spirit.* New York: Macmillan, 1957. Good on the relation of early Christian exegesis to its classical background.

————, with David Tracy. *A Short History of the Interpretation of the Bible.* 2nd rev. ed. Philadelphia: Fortress, 1984. The best brief history of biblical interpretation.

Guillet, Jacques. "Les Exégèses d'Alexandrie et d'Antioche, conflit ou malentendue?" *Recherches de science religieuse* 34 (1947) 257–302. Treats the two schools of exegesis of the patristic period and the similarities between them.

Hanson, R. P. C. "Biblical Exegesis in the Early Church." In *The Cambridge History of the Bible,* 1:412–53. Cambridge: Cambridge University Press, 1970.

McNally, Robert E. *The Study of the Bible in the Early Middle Ages.* Woodstock Papers 4. Westminster, MD: Newman Press, 1959. A useful introduction.

Smalley, Beryl. *The Study of the Bible in the Middle Ages.* Notre Dame, IN: University of Notre Dame Press, 1964. An important study of exegesis in the twelfth and thirteenth centuries, concentrating on the return to the literal sense.

Steinmetz, David C. "The Superiority of Pre-Critical Exegesis." *Theology Today* 37 (1980) 27–38. Contrasts the multiple-sense theory of the ancients with the single-sense theory of modern historical criticism and concludes that the earlier theory was more adequate even if its practice left much to be desired.

Turro, James C., and Raymond E. Brown. "Canonicity." In *The Jerome Biblical Commentary,* 2:515–34. Englewood Cliffs, NJ: Prentice-Hall, 1968. Treats the topic both historically and theoretically.

# Part One
# PERIODS AND MOVEMENTS

# 2

# The Early Christian Community

## JOHN D. ZIZIOULAS

### Primitive Christianity

#### *The Eschatological Outlook*

T HE CHRISTIAN CHURCH was born out of the history and the expectations of late Judaism as the fulfillment of the destiny of the people of God announced by the Prophets, and Christian spirituality, therefore, emerged under the influence of the beliefs of contemporary Judaism. The eschatological outlook that marked the Hebrew mind, characterized by the expectation of the coming of the kingdom of God in the form of the "new aeon," the era of the Messiah, was inherited by Christianity and became the dominant factor in the shaping of its spirituality.

Unlike the pagan religions—and the Hellenistic mysteries in particular—which sought salvation in escape from time and history through myths leading to extratemporal experiences, Christian spirituality, under the influence of the scriptural mentality, was from the beginning focused on history. Unlike the Greek and pagan religions of that time, the church's outlook was not cosmological but historical; it was based not on the observation of nature (seasons, cyclical movement of stars, etc.) but on events. Creation, far from being eternal and "divine," was an event with a beginning. Its existence was contingent and constantly dependent on the will of God. Humanity's relation with God did not pass through nature but through obedience to the will of God, a fact that gave to Christian spirituality an ethical character ("doing the truth") and a strongly personalist dimension: it was through personal relationships that the human person's union with God was realized.

Related to these characteristics was the fact that in contrast to the ancient Greek mentality, which looked to the past for rational explanations of reality and therefore for the meaning of human existence (truth in the

23

Platonic sense was a "recollection" of the soul's original life), the biblical approach was eschatological; it involved an orientation of humanity toward the future. The Bible called human beings to look for the meaning of life in the final act of God in history, wherefrom all present and past events receive their explanation and significance. It was this final act of God, the *eschaton*, that became for the first Christians the source of their spirituality.

The expectation of the eschatological, messianic era was fulfilled in the person of Jesus Christ, who was for this reason regarded as identical with the expected figures of later Judaism, particularly with the Messiah (*christos*) and the Son of Man of the apocalyptic literature, mentioned for the first time in the book of Daniel (second century B.C.E.). Whether we accept the view that Jesus himself believed that he was the Son of Man or take the liberal position that it was the church that identified him with this apocalyptic figure, who was expected to bring the final judgment of God to the world and inaugurate the kingdom, the fact remains that this identification did take place already in the New Testament and constitutes a basic presupposition of faith and spirituality in all the New Testament writings. Christian spirituality was thus centered on the person of Jesus of Nazareth as the *christos* or the "Son of Man," the eschatological figure who brought into history the kingdom of God (other eschatological titles were also applied to him, such as servant of God [from Isaiah], king, prophet, etc.). Humanity's relationship with God became in this way dependent upon its relationship with the person of Jesus Christ, the historical figure who was at the same time the eschatological Messiah.

The entire historical life of the figure Jesus of Nazareth was important for the Christians of the first centuries, but it was mainly his passion and his resurrection that were of decisive significance. The eschatological Son of Man or Messiah was expected to be glorious and to be invested with full divine power and authority. The "suffering Son of Man" was a scandal, and yet Jesus, by accepting the cross, offered to be that scandal and thus to give to the eschatological reality a dimension of suffering, humility, and service as the way to glory. The cross and the death of Christ became cornerstones of Christian spirituality, in that they made clear from the start that the way to God passes through the "narrow gate" (Matt 7:13) of suffering, humiliation, and service, and not through domination and power. Only when Christians are "weak" can they be really "strong" ( 2 Cor 12:10); capacity is identical with incapacity, with loss of one's soul (Matt 6:39), of one's very life. Christian spirituality was based on accepting as one's own the very scandal of the crucified Son of Man, an acceptance that could lead to suffering and death, to martyrdom. It was not, therefore, an easy and uncostly spirituality.

But the decisive proof that the historical Jesus was the Christ of the last days came through the resurrection of Jesus. Without faith in the resurrection it would have been impossible for the early Christians to make the identification between Jesus and Christ. The risen Christ proved that God's final judgment on history had taken place in the person of Jesus and that the expected eschatological era was thus inaugurated. The end had already come in and through the resurrection of Christ. The decisive battle against the powers of evil had been won and the final destiny of the world, a destiny of unceasing and abundant life (John 10:10), of light (Matt 4:16), of justice (2 Pet 3:13), and of joy (Luke 2:10) had been granted to humanity and the entire creation in the person of the risen Christ. Humanity's relation with God is, therefore, marked by the celebration of this victory over the powers of evil and death. Christian spirituality was for the early church characterized by this celebration, which, as we shall see later, underlies the entire concept of the eucharistic community.

Faith in the risen Christ involved from the very beginning two apparently contradictory elements. On the one hand, it involved an encounter with the risen Lord especially in the form of sharing meals with him. On the other hand, it involved the expectation of his return, of his parousia, which would bring an end to suffering, injustice, death, and the persecution of his followers. This meant that Christian spirituality had to be experienced as a dialectic between history and eschatology, a firm conviction that the kingdom of God had come and at the same time a fervent prayer and expectation that it may come soon. The Lord's Prayer and the book of Revelation (Matt 6:9; Rev 22:17-20) give dramatic evidence of this dialectic, and other verses in the New Testament witness to it also. Christian existence was caught up between this "already and not yet" (O. Cullmann). Spirituality was experienced primarily as patience (*hypomonē*) and a vigilant expectation of the "hour" when the Lord would come back to ask for an account of his servants' deeds and to reward those who had remained faithful to him to the very end. This involved a demand of confession (*martyria*) of the name of Jesus before all persons, even unto death (*martyrion*), that is, taking upon oneself the very cross of Christ, while being absolutely convinced that the Lord would come soon to raise and glorify these martyrs for his sake, exactly as God did with Jesus in his resurrection.

It is evident from these remarks that the delay of the parousia, the return of Jesus Christ, acted as a force of decisive importance in the shaping of primitive Christian spirituality. The New Testament is full of evidence pointing to the problems, psychological as well as theological, which the delay of the parousia created for the members of the church. When will the Lord come? Where is he now? What is the state of Christian existence until the Lord comes? Such questions and the answers given to them by the early Christians determined the shape of Christian spirituality forever.

## Aspects of the Faith of the Early Christian Community

### The Worship of Jesus Christ and His Priestly Function

To the question "Where is Christ now?" the answer was given that through his ascension he was seated "at the right hand of the Father," where he intercedes for human beings as the eternal priest (*hiereus* or *archiereus*). By applying to Jesus Psalm 110 ("The Lord says to my lord, 'Sit at my right hand . . .'"), the early Christians attached to him the title Lord (*kyrios*) and recognized him as God—who together with the Father received prayer and worship and who, as head of the new redeemed humanity, the "first-born among many brethren" (Rom 8:29), presented the petitions and prayers of humanity to the Father. This was extremely important for the shaping of Christian spirituality in that it meant that Christian prayer was in essence nothing but Christ's prayer addressed to God *for* (*hyper*) us or *instead of* (*anti*) us. It meant also that only insofar as Christians are incorporated into Christ and are brought before the Father in the person of the only-begotten Son can they expect to be heard by the Father and receive the answer to their prayers. Christians, therefore, were taught to pray "in the name of Christ" and to do so corporately as "one," as the body of the one Lord Christ. The prayer par excellence was that which Jesus himself taught to his disciples, extending to them the unique privilege he had of calling God Abba (Father) and allowing them to address God as "Our Father who art in heaven" (Matt 6:9). It was in the spirit of the same privilege that the church experienced in the Eucharist, in which the "one" (Christ) was identified with the "many" (the church), the occasion par excellence of praying to God with the assurance that the prayer would be favorably received and answered by God, since the leader of the praying community was none other than the one and only Son of the Father, in whom God was "well pleased."

### The Holy Spirit

The place of the Holy Spirit in Christian faith was important from the very beginning. The very term "Christ" meant someone anointed by the Spirit (*kechrismenos, christos*) in the tradition of the Hebrew prophets and kings, with the difference that in the case of Jesus he was the Messiah—the last, the eschatological prophet or king, who would not only receive himself the fullness of the Spirit of God but also would give it to others as the gift of the last days (Joel 3:1–5). The resurrection of Jesus was the proof that he was this eschatological Messiah, and for this reason the resurrection was associated with the giving of the Spirit first to the disciples and then also to "all flesh" in the event of Pentecost (Acts 2:17). The delay of the parousia, therefore, did not result in leaving the Christians "orphans," but meant that another "comforter" (*paraklētos*) would undertake to guide and strengthen the Christians until the return of Christ (John 14:18). This made the role of the Spirit decisive for Christian existence between the resurrection and the second coming of Christ.

The fact that the Spirit was already given and at work after the resurrection and the ascension meant that the eschatological gifts of the Spirit were already present in the Christian community. The members of the church became "spiritual" (*pneumatikoi*). On the occasion of a certain controversy among the Christians of Corinth concerning "degrees" of spirituality, Paul taught that all members of the church were in one way or another bearers of the Spirit and the gifts of the Spirit and that true Christian spirituality does not allow for discriminations that place one gift above the rest, as if one member of the body could despise another or exist independently of the other members. The highest form of spirituality is love (1 Cor 13:13), because the Spirit is communion (*koinōnia*). Christian spirituality, therefore, could not be experienced outside the community, which involved a multiplicity and variety of spiritual charisms. The spiritual person is free from many things, including the law of the Old Testament, but is bound by one thing—the conscience of the other (1 Cor 8:7–13; 10:29; 2 Cor 5:11). Individualism is incompatible with Christian spirituality. None can possess the Spirit as an individual, but only as a member of the community. When the Spirit blows the result is never to create good individual Christians but members of a community. This became fundamental for Christian spirituality in the New Testament and was in direct line with the Old Testament mentality.

## The Church

Because the Spirit was regarded as "communion" and the gifts of the Spirit by nature corporate, the era of the Spirit, in which the Christians lived as they expected the parousia, was in a profound sense the era of the church, the community of those who were incorporated as one body into Christ and prayed to God in and through—or even *as*—the one risen Christ. Life in the Spirit was identified with belonging to the community of the last days, which was the community of the Messiah constituted in and through the gifts of the Spirit. The church was regarded as the eschatological community which the risen Lord would gather around him in his parousia and with which he would identify himself fully (Matt 25:30–31; Acts 9:5). In this sense the church as the body of the risen Christ and the church as the communion of the Spirit were one and the same thing. The Spirit did nothing but build up the body of Christ here and now. The Spirit did not act regardless of the person and the "body" of Christ, and Christ was not conceivable as an individual but always "in the Spirit," as a corporate person, as one who is at the same time many. Likewise, the many were never understood apart from the one, Christ. This paradox of the one who is many and of the many who are one was deeply rooted in the biblical mentality and formed the basis of Christian spirituality. Unlike other nonbiblical forms of spirituality, which could be understood individualistically, Christian spirituality was ecclesial in its nature. The church was not a means by which one would become spiritual in the sense that it provided the necessary instruction, worship, grace, etc. for such a purpose. The church was a set of relationships, which provided one with a new identity, different from the identity given by natural birth or society. For this reason being a spiritual person in early Christianity involved in the first place a "new birth," a birth in the Spirit (John 3:3).

## Baptism and the Eucharist

The idea of new birth or birth in the Spirit was associated in the early church with baptism. The deeper meaning of baptism for Christian existence involved on the one hand a death of the "old person," that is, of the way in which personal identity was acquired through biological birth; on the other hand it involved a birth, that is, the emergence of an identity through a new set of relationships, those provided by the church as the communion of the Spirit. Whereas biological identity is always bound by necessity, spiritual birth involves freedom: the spiritual person does not simply *act* differently from the natural person, the *psychikos* (1 Cor 2:14); the spiritual person *is* different in that personal identity is constituted in freedom from the necessity of nature. The new identity given "in the Spirit" was constituted through incorporation into the body of Christ, the church, through a new set of relationships. These relationships were identical to the relationship of Christ to the Father, and for this reason baptism amounted to sonship (Rom 8:15), to acquiring the privilege of calling God "Father" as Christ himself in a unique and eternal way does. In the same way this identity involved social relationships, which were acquired in and through the community of the church and not through the biological family or the state. One of the fundamental consequences of baptism was that the "new man" would not have his father on earth but in "heaven" (Matt 23:9) and that his "brethren" would be the members of the church. Similarly, he would have no citizenship on earth but in heaven (Phil 3:11), since his "city" would be the "future" (Heb 13:14) kingdom. Thus, he would be a stranger in this life. This was the existential meaning of baptism as "death" of "the old person" and birth of the "new" eschatological person. Its test was basically ecclesiological and not ethical or psychological as it is often thought. Spirituality had to do with acquiring new relationships and through them a new identity, since identities, whether biological, social, or "spiritual," always emerge from relationships.

It is against this background that we must see the importance of the Eucharist for Christian spirituality. The Eucharist was understood in the first centuries as the event that brought together the dispersed people of God "in the same place" (*epi to auto*) not only to celebrate but also to constitute the eschatological messianic community here and now. As such it was the spiritual event par excellence, because it was the eschatological reality manifested and foretasted in history. Baptized persons were led to this community in order to take their place in it, which involved the privilege of addressing God as Father—of acquiring the sonship that Christ has always had—and at the same time of addressing the other members of the church as "brethren" and sharing their eternal destiny. The Eucharist offered positively what baptism meant negatively: the death of the old, biological identity was replaced by the birth of the new identity, which was given in the eucharistic community. Since the old biological identity is based on natural necessity, it leads to death; whereas the new identity given in the Eucharist—based on free and undying relationships, above all on the eternal filial relationship between the Father and the Son, which was "lent" to the Christian in baptism—gives eternal life. The Eucharist is life eternal, primarily because it offers this set of relationships, which involves an eternal identity. Belonging to the community of the Eucharist is, therefore, tantamount to acquiring eternal life. Spirituality in this eucharistic context acquires an ontological and not simply a moral or a psychological context. It is not simply a matter of improving human nature and making it act and behave in a better way through moral achievement and virtue; it is not just a psychological experience of the fruits of the Spirit, such as peace, joy, patience, etc.; it is, above all, identical with overcoming death through the acquisition of a new identity based on new relationships which are identical with the Father–Son relationship of the Holy Trinity. The Christian becomes by grace what Christ is by nature—to put the matter in later patristic dogmatic terminology. In strictly biblical terms this very thing is expressed by Paul in his reference to baptism as giving the "spirit" of sonship in which we cry "Abba!

Father!" (Rom 8:15). Spirituality as the possession of the Spirit involves, above all, sharing in the same sonship of Jesus Christ, a relationship with God that gives an undying, eternal identity. Membership in the church as the body of those who through baptism and the Eucharist have acquired such an identity was the source of true spirituality. Spirituality is an ecclesial and not an individual experience.

The church, as the "image" or the "sign" of the eschatological community, offered through the Eucharist the foretaste of eternal life by providing believers with the set of relationships that would give them an undying, eternal identity as well as the experience of a life in which all natural and social divisions involving disintegration and death would be overcome in the unity of the body of Christ. This last point became extremely significant for the life of the church in the New Testament period. The way the eucharistic community was composed portrayed the "way of being" that will characterize the kingdom. Thus, the following characteristics eventually became permanent features of the eucharistic community in the early church. First, all the members of the church in a certain place should gather together in the same place (*epi to auto*) (1 Cor 11:20), exactly as all the dispersed people of God would be brought together from the ends of the earth in the kingdom (*Didache* 9 and 10). This meant in practice that there could be only one eucharistic community in each place (originally in a city, since Christianity started as an urban religion). Second, there is "neither Jew nor Greek, there is neither slave nor free, there is neither male nor female" (Gal 3:28) in the composition of the eucharistic community. All divisions, both natural (age, race, sex, etc.) and social (profession, social or economic status, etc.) are transcended in the Eucharist. This meant that the eucharistic community was a catholic community, and the members of this community were expected to show a catholic ethos in their spiritual life. Exclusiveness, based on natural or social discriminations of any kind ought to be foreign to Christian spirituality, because such exclusiveness contradicted the kingdom of God, of which the eucharistic community was understood to be a figure and an anticipation in history. Third, there should be ministries in the eucharistic community that would serve as types or images of the kingdom. A basic distinction between those who lead the eucharistic community by offering the Eucharist and those who confirm or seal this action with their "Amen" is already present in Paul's first letter to the Corinthians (14:16). This distinction became the basis of the church's order. The clergy-laity distinction (see *1 Clement* [ca. 96 C.E.]) marks the early church in a decisive way. Christian spirituality was conditioned by this order so strongly that it became necessary to introduce almost legalistic safeguards to spirituality so as to keep it ecclesial in its nature. The patristic era, as we shall see, is marked by this tendency, but the roots of this attitude are to be found in the New Testament view that Christian existence is in its nature eschatological and that it is in the way the eucharistic community is formed that we have the measure of our conformity to this eschatological model of life and spirituality.

## The Early Patristic Period

The factors that shaped Christian spirituality in the postapostolic age from the end of the first century until the beginning of the third century can be grouped under the following topics: (1) the gradual formation of the structure of the church on a eucharistic basis, (2) the challenge of Gnosticism and the patristic response to it, (3) the emergence of a Christian Gnosticism and its importance for spirituality, and (4) martyrdom as a form of spirituality and as an answer to Montanist spirituality.

### The Structure of the Church

The dominant influence in the formation of spirituality around the axis of the Eucharist and the structure of the church came from Ignatius, bishop of Antioch (d. 110 c.e.). In his seven letters, which are commonly accepted as authentic in their brief version (there is also a later longer version), Ignatius forcefully developed the view that salvation and spiritual or eternal life are realized and experienced through faithful communion in the eucharistic body of Christ. This body is "formed" in the community of the church, which brings together all the faithful under the leadership of the president of the eucharistic assembly, the bishop, surrounded by the college of the presbyters and assisted by the deacons. Ignatius insisted that no one can claim a relationship with God giving eternal life unless there is constant participation in this eucharistic community and, therefore, unless there is obedience to its head, the bishop.

At first sight these views of Ignatius seem to introduce into spirituality a sacramentalism almost of a pagan or magic kind, as well as a sort of legalism that attaches absolute authority to structures and ministries and demands obedience from the lay members of the church almost without any conditions. Ignatius called the Eucharist "medicine of immortality, an antidote against death" (*Letter to the Ephesians* 20.2), which has led scholars to the conclusion that we have here a pagan form of spirituality and a radical departure from the biblical mentality. Such a conclusion is hasty and unfair. Ignatius did not regard the Eucharist as an object that contains in its nature supernatural powers of immortality. For him the Eucharist is primarily and basically an event of communion, a *synaxis* (gathering together) in the same sense in which the Bible understood it in connection with the earliest eschatological expectations of the gathering of the dispersed people of God in the parousia. The meaning, therefore, of the expression "medicine of immortality" in the context of Ignatian theology is that eternal life stems not from the object of the Eucharist but from participation in the event of communion, the gathering of the community.

It is in this light that we must understand also Ignatius's emphasis on the bishop as a sine qua non for one's participation in eternal life. Whoever disobeys the bishop disobeys God or Christ himself, who is the true bishop of the church, because the bishop sits in the place of God or is the type of God. For Ignatius eternal and true life is an eschatological reality and is granted only through participation in the eschatological community, which is prefigured and manifested in the eucharistic community. In accordance with fundamental biblical ideas he maintained that salvation is not a matter of the individual but of belonging to the community of the people of God. Those who despise the eucharistic community and its head, the bishop, are arrogant and cut themselves off automatically from communion with God and from eternal life. The crucial importance of the bishop lies in his being the head of the eucharistic community and not in an office that he holds as an isolated individual. Like the Eucharist itself, the episcopacy is a relational ministry: both of these are crucial for spiritual life because they are crucial for the presence of the eschatological community here and now in history. The eucharistic and episcopocentric mysticism of Ignatius is therefore basically biblical in that it maintains the eschatological orientation and the community basis that mark the biblical approach to spiritual life.

Ignatius's views continued to dominate the church's life in the first centuries as is evident from other documents, such as the Syriac *Didascalia Apostolorum* from the beginning of the third century and the *Apostolic Tradition* (*Traditio apostolica*) of Hippolytus of Rome from about the same period. Both of these documents, which served as the basis for the development of church structure and life for many centuries, stress the principle that the eucharistic community and its head, the bishop, constitute the inevitable context of Christian spirituality. No one can participate in eternal life without passing through the Eucharist and the bishop. This idea led to the axiom "No salvation outside the church" (*extra ecclesiam nulla salus*), which we encounter in Origen and Cyprian and which seems to be presupposed throughout the early church. This axiom was misunderstood later on as implying institutionalism and legalism. In the first centuries, however, *ecclesia* (church) still meant the same thing as in Paul's letters to the Corinthians, namely, the actual eucharistic gathering. It should be paraphrased,

2. *Chalice of Antioch*, Early Christian Period

3. *The Trinity* by Andrei Rublev, Russian, 15th century

4. *Icon of the Descent of the Holy Spirit*, Russian

5. *The Riha Paten*, 6th century (central detail)

therefore, as follows: without participation in the eucharistic communion there is no salvation. This is another way of saying what the Fourth Gospel stresses—that unless we eat the flesh and drink the blood of the Son of Man we cannot have life; but according to the same Gospel it is the Spirit that gives life, and therefore it is the communion and the community of the Spirit, the church, that offers the context of spiritual life. The bishop is essential, since he is the head of this eucharistic community.

On the basis of such an interpretation it becomes evident that it was a fundamental assumption throughout the early church that only one Eucharist and only one bishop could exist in the same place. Since the bishop is important not as an individual but as the head of the eucharistic community and since the Eucharist is not a sacrament but the manifestation of the eschatological community in its totality, more than one bishop and more than one Eucharist would signify more than one church in a certain place. Ignatius and Cyprian were very strict on this matter, and so was the First Ecumenical Council, the Council of Nicaea, in 325 c.e., the eighth canon of which forbids the existence of more than one bishop in the same city.

The spiritual significance of this canonical provision is extremely profound. As we have already noted, the Eucharist is the place where all divisions, whether of a natural or a social kind, are transcended in the unity of Christ, in whose kingdom such divisions amounting to death will disappear. If the church celebrates a special Eucharist for the children or for the adults or for men or for women or for black or for white people, etc., this would lead to an eschatological affirmation of these natural divisions. The same would be true if there were special eucharistic celebrations for ethnic groups, professions, or social classes. In the Eucharist one must learn to accept all other human beings as belonging to the same body and sharing the same ultimate destiny. It is this profound "horizontal" dimension that the principle "one Eucharist, one bishop, one church" seeks to keep alive in spirituality. It is not enough to keep a so-called spiritual (in the sense of non-material) unity with other people. True Christian spirituality requires an actual bringing together—indeed, a material and historical experience of unity. Unless there is one concrete community and one head/bishop of this community, there is no spiritual experience that is, properly speaking, Christian.

This principle—one Eucharist, one bishop, one church—was maintained even when practical necessities, such as the rapid increase in the number of Christians from the late third century on, forced the church to create parishes and thus assign the role of eucharistic leadership to presbyters. It was a serious deviation from original ecclesiology to regard the bishops primarily as administrators of large dioceses and the presbyters as the celebrants of the

Eucharist. This took place in the Middle Ages, but in the fourth century the bishop was still *the* eucharistic president. The presbyters acted in the Eucharist always on the bishop's behalf and with his explicit permission. For a long time, especially in the West, the bishop would send a portion of his Eucharist to the parishes in order to mix it with the presbyter's Eucharist and thus make real the idea that there is only one Eucharist in each place, that of the bishop. This practice was known as *fermentum*. In the East what prevails even today is the practice of the antimension, a piece of cloth containing relics of saints (a sign of unity of the church in time) as well as the signature of the local bishop, which affirms that it is the bishop that makes the parish Eucharist valid, that there is only one Eucharist in each place.

Finally, the stress on the central and crucial importance of the actual and not simply the symbolic celebration of the Eucharist signifies that Christian spirituality is not based on contempt for or depreciation of matter. The Eucharist involves eating and drinking, that is, a meal. It also involves material elements, bread and wine, as well as human labor. All of these are sanctified in the Eucharist. Unlike ancient Greek, and especially Neoplatonic attitudes to spirituality, the patristic mentality, based on a eucharistic approach to life, stressed that being "spiritual" meant accepting and sanctifying the material world and not undermining its importance in any way. This point was particularly stressed by Irenaeus, bishop of Lyons (b. 140–160), and it was developed as an argument against the Gnostics. But on this we shall say more below.

## The Challenge of Gnosticism

Gnosticism was a movement both within and outside of the Christian church, which represented its own spirituality. (Gnosticism is the subject of another contribution to this volume, which deals with this movement in a more detailed manner.) Two aspects of Gnosticism, in particular, challenged the church in the patristic age. The first was its tendency to undermine the material world and to attribute creation not to God but to a demiurge, who is to be held responsible also for the evil that humanity experiences, and whose domain is principally in matter. Spirituality in this approach consists in an escape from matter and time, which would involve asceticism or its opposite, that is, a contempt for all ethical restrictions. The second major aspect of the Gnostic approach to salvation and spiritual life consisted in knowledge (Greek *gnōsis*, hence Gnosticism); those who have knowledge of the secret mysteries, which are revealed usually in the form of myths to a few privileged "Gnostics," can claim salvation and eternal life.

In rejecting Gnosticism during the second century, the church developed notions of spirituality that deny both of these two principles. This took place mainly under the influence of Irenaeus, whose writings against the Gnostics set down the fundamental principles of Christian spirituality for the church of the subsequent centuries.

Irenaeus faced the first of these two aspects of Gnostic spirituality (contempt for the material world) by referring emphatically to the tradition present in the writings of Ignatius of Antioch: the Eucharist is the "antidote against death" and therefore the source of immortality and eternal life. Irenaeus fought the Gnostics by stressing that the material world is a direct product of the one and only God, the Father, and that matter is good. In the same way he stressed that history and time are also good and constitute the ground and the context of the exercise of human freedom, which is an indispensable condition of spirituality. Adam was created by God and was placed in the material world, in the course of time and history, in order to reach full communion with God by acting freely and creating decisive events (*kairoi*), that is, history. The body was given to human beings as a link between the material world and the immaterial beings (angels and God). The spiritual person receives the Spirit of God in order to bring the material world through the body into communion with God and thus lead it to incorruptibility. This is what the Eucharist signifies and realizes until the final resurrection of the body.

This last point was of particular significance for Christian spirituality in the early centuries. One of the most difficult doctrines for the Greek philosophers of that time as well as for the Gnostics to accept was the faith of the Christians in the resurrection of the body. And yet this faith not only occupied a central place in the theology of the Christian writers of the second century (e.g., the apologist Athenagoras), but it was also introduced into the earliest creeds of the church. Christian spirituality was inconceivable without reference to the expectation of the resurrection of the flesh or of the body. Spirituality was so materially conceived that the human entity was regarded as lacking an essential part without the body. The immortality of the soul was not sufficient to console the Christian in the face of death. Irenaeus himself wrote that the souls after death await the resurrection of their bodies and only then do they enjoy full communion with God and eternal life. This resurrection will be the work of the Holy Spirit, who in the meantime sustains a form of communion with God through the communion of the church and especially through the Eucharist. But a spirituality that does not eagerly look forward to the resurrection of the body is not Christian spirituality.

The second aspect of Gnosticism that Irenaeus undertook to destroy was the principle that knowledge is the key to salvation and eternal life. On this point he was forced to correct, albeit implicitly, certain views that had entered the Christian tradition itself through important writers such as the apologist Justin (d. 165). The latter, in order to establish a bridge between Greek philosophy and Christianity, had developed the idea of the *logos* as the link between the world—especially human beings—and God, realized par excellence in Christ, the Logos of God incarnate. But by so doing Justin gave to the principle of knowledge a key role in salvation to the point of arguing that even before Christ and among the pagans true knowledge—and therefore salvation—was possible (for example, among the ancient Greek philosophers). Irenaeus modified this view by introducing another key idea in the place of intellectual knowledge. According to him, the apostles and those who live after Christ in the church have a superior knowledge of the Logos, in a sense the only true and valid knowledge, compared with the knowledge of those who lived before the incarnation. This is because the incarnation and the church offer a knowledge based on personal communion, not on truth as it is grasped by the mind. True knowledge of God, therefore, is a matter of personal relationships and communion, not of one's acceptance of certain rational propositions or even one's vision of the truth and of God.

Such an understanding of knowledge was extremely significant for spirituality in that it removed salvation from the realm of the intellect and placed it in the context of the community of the church. This served as a way of keeping alive the basic biblical approach to spirituality. The way to God has to pass through the relationship with the neighbor. Love is the only healthy basis of Christian spirituality. As it would be put later on by the ascetic fathers of the church, the instrument of knowledge is not the mind but the heart.

## The Emergence of a Christian Gnosticism

The tendency to approach spirituality through the intellect and to treat salvation primarily as a matter of revelation did not disappear altogether from the life of the early church. The line inaugurated by Justin was developed further in the catechetical school of Alexandria, where Greek philosophy was influential. Two great names stand out in this respect: Clement of Alexandria (d. 215) and Origen (d. 253). Their thought could be described as representing a kind of Christian Gnosticism with particular significance for spirituality.

Both Clement and Origen operated with the idea of the *logos* and used revelation as their starting point and primary motif in theology and spirituality. Clement stressed especially that faith (*pistis*) and knowledge (*gnōsis*) must coexist to produce the perfect Christian, who is at the same time the true Gnostic. Philosophy had at times an almost supernatural and saving role in Clement's mind, but he never became an intellectual in the strict sense. Faith, he said, is something superior to knowledge and is its criterion (*Stromateis* 2.4.15). This faith is primarily faith in the Logos of God, who is fully revealed in the incarnate Christ. It is he who alone reveals the otherwise unknowable God whose Reason he is. Salvation and eternal life derive from this Logos, who attaches himself to and illuminates the human *logos* or mind and thus grants salvation. The essence, therefore, of spirituality is the contemplation of the divine Logos or of God in and through the Logos. It is this that leads to love and not the other way around.

Unlike Clement, Origen wanted to be an *ecclesiasticus,* a man of the tradition of the church, and not a philosopher. Yet in fact he interpreted the Scriptures and the tradition of the church in such a way as to allow philosophy to dominate his theology. Like Clement he identified spiritual perfection with the true revelation and knowledge which the Logos of God grants to the human soul. But he was more mystical in his approach, and this made him a most influential force in the formation of Christian spirituality in the early church. His influence, however, accounts for many serious deviations from the early biblical mentality.

Origen's mysticism was Logos-centered. In his commentary on the Song of Songs of the Old Testament as well as in other works he speaks extensively of the union of the human soul with the Word in terms of love and marriage. But the fruit of this intercourse of the soul with the Word is described in terms of illumination of the mind. The Logos explains to the soul "all unknown and hidden things. This is the truer, closer, holier kiss which is said to be given by the lover, the Word of God, to his beloved, the pure and perfect soul" (*Commentary on the Song of Songs* 1). Spirituality is conceived very much in terms of Christian Gnosticism.

For the human soul to be deemed worthy of such a union with the Logos, it is necessary that the soul should purify itself from all passions (*pathē*) and reach freedom from passion (*apatheia*). Origen understood this very much in Platonic terms of an opposition between spirit and matter, the soul and the body. He insisted on asceticism, which would involve, among other things, virginity and chastity of the body (he emasculated himself in application of Matt 19:12, which he took in a literal sense). But he also insisted on studying the Scriptures and, above all, on prayer as ways of asceticism. The essence of all asceticism was for him the liberation of the soul, which he regarded in a true Greek fashion as immortal and even eternal—hence the highest and most precious thing—from the influences of matter and the body.

In all this, Origen, following the steps of Clement, made a clear distinction between the "simple" Christian and the "illumined" or "educated" or "Gnostic" one. He compared the first category with the multitude of the Gospel stories, which followed Jesus but did not have access to the mysteries of the kingdom. The spirituals or educated Christians are likened to the disciples of Jesus to whom the secrets of the kingdom were revealed. For him the Gospel itself consisted of a somatic, that is, bodily and material, part and a spiritual part. The outer, historical events—even the cross itself—had their significance hidden behind them (hence his famous allegorical method in exegesis). It is the knowledge and revelation of this significance that matter, and this is given to a few but not to all. The soul, by being purified from passions and being joined to the Word, sees the truth. This is the essence of spirituality.

Origen's enormous and lasting influence on the spirituality of the early church contributed distinctive ideas that proved to be both great possibilities and serious dangers for the church. First, Origen introduced as basic the notion of light, understood in terms of revelation, contemplation, and knowledge of the divine by the human soul, purified from passion and sin. Second, Origen attached the notion of holiness to perfection and, therefore, to a certain group of Christians, a spiritual elite. Thus, the idea of holiness was dissociated from the community of the church as a whole. This brought the danger of individualism or elitism and of conflict with the historical and canonical structure of the church. Finally, Origen shifted eschatology from the historical to the anthropological arena and made the expectation of the event of the parousia as well as the resurrection of the bodies of secondary importance to spirituality. All these characteristics can be observed in later monasticism, of which Origen can be regarded as the spiritual founder in many respects.

## Martyrdom as a Form of Spirituality

In spite of this Gnostic approach to spirituality, Origen himself shared the belief that had become predominant in the church since the New Testament, through Irenaeus in particular, that the highest form of spirituality is martyrdom. In his work *Exhortation to Martyrdom* (*Exhortatio ad martyrium*) he speaks of the true and perfect disciple of Christ as the one who is ready to go with him to the cross. True spirituality always involves some form of death. The ascetic and the martyr are for this reason the true spirituals of the church.

The view that the martyrs are the spiritual Christians par excellence was further developed in the church's struggle against a spirituality that was represented by a movement of the second and third centuries in Phrygia known as Montanism. Montanism was an enthusiastic movement characterized by the belief of its followers that they were under the immediate influence of the Holy Spirit and were thus experiencing the eschatological reality here and now. In this context they were claiming to have mysterious encounters with Christ and the Paraclete which led them to enthusiastic and at times hysterical manifestations.

Montanist spirituality was accompanied by austere asceticism and morality which impressed outsiders. A great Christian theologian of that time, Tertullian, joined the Montanists out of admiration for their strict morals, which included among other things forbidding second marriage and condemning escape at the time of persecution. In their spiritual zeal the Montanists showed disregard or even contempt for the ministry and the hierarchy of the church, apostolic succession, etc. What mattered for them was the Spirit, as opposed to organization, and the experience and virtue of the individual, as opposed to church structure and the eucharistic community.

As we have already noted, this view of spirituality was condemned by Paul when it first appeared in the Christian community of Corinth in the form of the belief that the Spirit was acting through charismatic individuals who possessed extraordinary gifts such as speaking in tongues, healing, and prophesying. Paul insisted that all these charisms are of no value whatsoever unless they are accompanied by love, which builds up the community of the church. He also taught the Corinthians that it is not only the extraordinary charisms that show the presence and activity of the Holy Spirit but also the most common and ordinary ministries of the church, including government, administration, etc. All ministries are charismatic, that is, gifts of the one Spirit, and all of them exist for the single purpose of the edification of the community.

The same Pauline attitude to spirituality was taken by people like Irenaeus at the time of Montanism. Two particular positions of Irenaeus expressed this attitude. The first was his stress on the historical and institutional aspect of the church. The office of bishop was regarded by him as carrying a "certain charism of truth," and the historical succession of bishops offered the guarantee of adherence to the truth. Spirituality was thus to be related to the bishop, who as head of the eucharistic community distributed the gifts of the Spirit to the members of the church (compare Ignatius). The second position taken by Irenaeus attacked the very root of the problem of Montanist spirituality and, in the final analysis, of Christian spirituality as a whole. In the Christian gospel, the Spirit always points to Christ, and spirituality is centered on the person of Christ. Irenaeus stressed this in opposition to Montanism by underlining the faith of the church that the spiritual

Christians, the "Spirit-bearers" par excellence, are the martyrs who die confessing the name of Jesus Christ as Lord. In an anti-Montanist letter written by Irenaeus to the martyrs of Lyons and Vienna and preserved by Eusebius in his *Church History*, it is stressed that those who possess the Spirit are not so much the Christians who prophesy and perform supernatural acts as the martyrs who give their lives for Christ. Thus, the Spirit is closely and inseparably joined to the historical Jesus. Spirituality becomes christocentric, though not christomonistic: the Spirit always acts in relation to Christ, but Christ himself is inconceivable without the Spirit. There is no genuine Christian spirituality unless there is at the same time some form of edification of the historical body of Christ, the church. Equally, however, the historical and institutional aspects of the church do not possess an intrinsic authority in themselves but exist only insofar as they are relational, that is, events of the communion of the Spirit in the context of the community.

## Toward Medieval Spirituality

The early patristic period bequeathed to the golden age of the fourth-century church and to the later patristic and Byzantine era certain fundamental principles of spirituality that were to become normative for the following centuries down to our own time. There were two basic mentalities or attitudes to spirituality that were involved in this historical bequest: on the one hand, the type of spirituality that was based on the eucharistic community and involved the community and its eschatological orientation as the decisive factors of spirituality; and, on the other hand, the type of spirituality that was based on the experience of the individual who struggles against passions and toward the achievement of moral perfection, a spirituality accompanied by a mystical union of the soul or the mind with the Logos of God. The first type was promoted under the influence of pastoral church fathers, such as Ignatius of Antioch and Irenaeus, whereas the second was influenced mainly by Origen and the theologians of Alexandria.

A study of the history of the church from the fourth century reveals that these two types of spirituality never ceased to coexist, but at the same time they were not easily compatible with each other. The Origenist type of spirituality was popular because Origen was widely read by the monks of Egypt in the fourth century. The purification of the mind from evil thoughts became the dominant theme of a certain strongly Origenist monastic tradition known as Evagrianism (from the name of Evagrius of Pontus, the founder of this spirituality). Evagrianism, together with Origenism as a whole, displayed very early its fundamental weakness and dangers and, in spite of its impressive expansion and influence, was finally rejected by the mainstream of the church. Origenism was officially condemned by the Fifth Ecumenical Council of 553 C.E.

Already in the course of the fourth century, alongside Evagrian spirituality, another spiritual type was flourishing, which was connected with writings attributed to Macarius of Egypt. This spiritual type represented a fundamental correction of Origenism in that it removed the center of spirituality from the mind (*nous*) to the heart (*kardia*), which it turned into the epistemological or gnoseological center of human existence. According to this spirituality, the heart as the bond of obedience and love was that which needed purification and spiritual ascetic exercise. Through Macarian monasticism, love, which did not allow for contempt of the sinner or for boasting of knowledge and spiritual perfection, became the spiritual theme par excellence and the source of inspiration for a whole series of spiritual fathers known as *gerontes* (literally "old men," possessing and guiding spiritual children). This was a most important development that saved Christian spirituality in the patristic period from the dangers of Origenism and somehow brought it back to its biblical and early patristic roots.

In spite of the influence of Macarian monasticism in the East, the problem of the survival of the Eucharist-based spirituality of the early days remained a serious one for many centuries. Macarian spirituality underlined the importance of the heart and of obedience and love, which made the dimension of communion decisive. But the question always remained open concerning the significance that the actual structure of the church, its ministries and sacraments, had for spirituality. Were the latter of the same importance for spiritual life as monasticism? Was a bishop as important a spiritual father as a *gerōn*, a spiritual father of a monastery? These questions underlie the history of spirituality of Byzantium and of many mystical currents in the West and make the contrast between this later period of history and the time of Ignatius or Irenaeus an obvious one.

The most important attempt to arrive at a healthy reconciliation of these two types of spirituality—the Eucharistic and the monastic (to describe them in general terms)—is to be found in the person and the writings of a Greek father of the late sixth and early seventh century, Maximus the Confessor. Maximus not only corrected Origenism and purified Evagrianism from the dangers they involved for spirituality, but, in a way that remained unique in the entire history of the church, he recovered and synthesized the old biblical and early patristic eucharistic approach to existence with monastic experience. For Maximus there is a deeply ecclesial structure and character in the world as a whole and in humanity in particular. Existence is eucharistic, and spirituality makes no sense if it is not an expression of this "cosmic liturgy," which gives meaning to everything. In his commentary on the Eucharist called *Mystogogia*, he sees the human being as the image of the whole church and places the meaning of human existence in a eucharistic context. Monastic experience is not an end in itself but receives itself meaning from the Eucharist, which fills with significance and purpose the entire creation. The great source of spirituality is once again the eucharist community.

In stressing this, Maximus brought back into spirituality another biblical element, namely, eschatology. Monasticism had started with a strong eschatological orientation as a sort of protest against the secularization of the church, but, unlike the biblical approach, it tended to dissociate eschatology from the eucharistic community. Maximus saw in the Eucharist itself a movement toward the end (*peras*) of the whole creation. Unlike the writings attributed to Dionysius the Areopagite (fifth century), which place the Eucharist in a primarily cosmic context (in the relation between heaven and earth), Maximus saw in the Eucharist a movement in time, an eschatological orientation in the old biblical sense that was previously preserved in fathers such as Irenaeus. Spirituality in this approach becomes a matter of participation in the eucharistic community as a way of overcoming individualism through the purification of the heart from all passions, but also through the actual gathering of the Eucharist, which places creation in the movement—in space and time—toward its proper eschatological end.

## Bibliography

### Sources

*The Apostolic Fathers*. Translated by Maxwell Staniforth. London: Penguin Classics, 1968.

### Studies

Bouyer, Louis. *The Spirituality of the New Testament and the Fathers*. Vol. 1 of *A History of Christian Spirituality*. New York: Seabury, 1982.
Pelikan, Jaroslav. *The Christian Tradition: A History of the Development of Doctrine*. Vol. 1, *The Emergence of the Catholic Tradition (100–600)*. Chicago and London: University of Chicago Press, 1971.
Zizioulas, J. D. *Being as Communion: Studies in Personhood and the Church*. Crestwood, NY: St. Vladimir's Seminary Press, 1985.

# 3

# Gnostic Spirituality

## ROBERT M. GRANT

GNOSTIC SPIRITUALITY is hard to define precisely, or even to describe, because the term "Gnostic" is so imprecise. Most of the ancient Gnostics (second to fourth century of our era) seem to have called themselves Christians or followers of their sects' founders. Few sectarians claimed to be "knowers"—which is what Gnostic means. At the end of the second century the Alexandrian Christian Clement used the term to denote his own circle of educated, Platonically minded, rather orthodox Christians. On the other hand, the Neoplatonist Plotinus denounced the Gnostics (*Enneads* 2.9) but did not use the term; it was appended by his pupil and editor, Porphyry. In spite of these difficulties, it is clear that to call something or someone Gnostic has some meaning, often invidious.

Gnosticism involves a negative attitude toward God or the gods and the world, an attitude of hostility or alienation, a feeling of being a stranger and afraid in a world created and governed by planetary angels and their allies. The spirit, different from soul and better than it, is, like soul for Plato, entombed in the body. It can be called a divine spark derived from the supreme Father above, unknown except by revelation. Its destiny is to come to awareness of itself and escape from its oppressors, passing through the planetary spheres to the truly heavenly realms above. Meanwhile it waits, perhaps anticipating its future life by taking part in various rites, and sometimes endeavoring to gain converts to self-awareness, especially among Christians in whose souls lie sparks of spirit.

In Gnosticism, as to some extent in Judaism and Christianity, there was an emphasis on contemporaneous divine revelation as the true source of knowledge about God, the gods or angels, the world, and humanity. Valentinus said that the Logos appeared to him as a little child. His deviant follower Marcus said that the whole first Tetrad appeared to him in female form. The author of the Hermetic *Poimandres* (1.1-4) saw "a being of an immense size," which turned into a "limitless vision, with everything become light, serene and joyful," followed by a whole series of transformations. The author of the *Apocryphon of John* saw a young man, then an old man, then a servant—one likeness with three forms. "I am the one who is with you forever. I am the Father, I am the Mother, I am the Son." Even a highly fragmentary Nag Hammadi document contains revelation: "The book of visions which were seen by Hypsiphrone" (XI, 4). More often than educated Christians, Gnostic authors tended to reject Greco-Roman education and learning. In a section not preserved at Nag Hammadi but found in Latin, the Hermetic *Asclepius* denounces scientific studies like arithmetic, music, geometry, and astronomy, for they turn one away from pure religious philosophy (§ 13). The Nag Hammadi *Tripartite Tractate* (I, 5) rejects all such studies. They are speculative and contradictory: "Nothing is in agreement with its fellows, nothing, not philosophy or varieties of medicine or varieties of rhetoric or varieties of music or varieties of logic (*organon*), but they are opinions and theories." Revelation is completely different from reason and transcends it. Indeed, this Gnostic view helps to explain why the church fathers insisted so strongly that Gnostics were inconsistent and had started out from misunderstood Greek philosophy. Irenaeus (late second century) discussed their disagreements and then turned to describe them at work: "When a text of scripture has been read, all of them frown and shake their heads, saying that here is a very profound word, and not all grasp the greatness of the meaning it contains; for this reason silence is the greatest thing in the opinion of the wise" (*Against Heresies* [*Adversus haereses*] 4.35.4). Irenaeus felt free to use irony, sarcasm, parody, etc. in dealing with such people. Indeed, at the end of the preface to his first book he seems to be parodying Ptolemaeus's *Letter to Flora*.

## Gnosticism and Morality

For many Gnostics, questions of conduct were of concern only to the world-creating legislator angels and to the human souls and bodies under their domination. Perhaps moral problems held less interest for many Gnostics than for the church writers attacking them, who naturally chose extreme cases. Church writers like Irenaeus cited Gnostic catchwords such as "gold in mud," a reference to Gnostics themselves as uncorrupted by life in the wicked world, and tended to portray the extremes as those of rigid asceticism and rampant license.

Asceticism was harder to attack than licentiousness, in view of the ascetic propensities of many orthodox Christians. Ascetic Gnostics were usually accused of denouncing marriage, wine, and meat. Their specifically theological errors must have been more important. On the other hand, the libertines were normally suspected of practicing promiscuous sexual intercourse in their rites, as well as infanticide and cannibalism. These charges were especially important because officials of the Roman state investigating Christian behavior suspected that Christians, like adherents of other foreign religions in earlier times, were guilty of such abuses. Christians in self-defense hastened to blame the Gnostics. By the fourth century even Gnostics blamed Gnostics. It is not clear that Gnostic behavior of this kind was always "mere" libertinism. Irenaeus tells how female disciples of a Gnostic named Marcus would say eucharistic prayers with him and also accept the gift of grace from him:

> Be ready like a bride awaiting your spouse, so that you may be what I am and I may be what you are. Place in your bridal chamber the seed of the light. Receive your spouse from me, make room for him in you and find room in him. Behold, Grace has come upon you: open your mouth and prophesy. (*Against Heresies* 1.13.3)

The gift of grace is the gift of prophecy. Irenaeus goes on to say that the union in question was physical. We cannot tell, any more than in regard to similar expressions in the Coptic Gnostic *Gospel of Philip*. Irenaeus also offers examples of what the "perfect" among the Gnostics would do in order to scandalize Christians. They would eat meats consecrated to pagan gods in the belief that they were not defiled by them (Paul had held this too). They took part in pagan festivities in honor of the gods. Some of them were present at the combats between gladiators and animals or with one another. And some "insatiably served the pleasures of the flesh," claiming that thus they rendered to the flesh what was fleshly, to the spirit what was spiritual (*Against Heresies* 1.6.3; compare the Gospel text about "rendering to Caesar," Matt 22:21).

The statement of Valentinus that "much that is written in the generally available books is found written also in the church of God" (Clement *Stromateis* 5.52.4) shows how much closer he was to Christianity than to any of the wilder forms of Gnosticism. Some Gnostics, however, resembled the Cynic philosophers who flourished in the Roman world, above all in their flouting of convention. The Cynics' hero Diogenes was famous for his lack of a sense of shame, even though Stoics concerned with ethics and religion portrayed him as one of themselves. Diogenes Laertius provided the more popular stories (*Lives of the Philosophers* 6.20–74). Almost any of them could have been told about the licentious Gnostics, whereas in fact there is only one original story, told from a rather hostile point of view. A Gnostic once asked a Christian virgin what she made of the text "Give to everyone who asks," and she hastened to reply, "On the subject of marriage, talk to my mother" (Clement *Stromateis* 3.27, trans. H. Chadwick). The licentious Gnostics also resembled the venturesome early Stoics, who wrote treatises, presumably theoretical, "on the state" or "on society," in which they shocked their readers as much as Diogenes did. When later moralists attacked them, their defenders would argue that these writings were the products of immature minds or perhaps were forgeries. It is not clear that, apart from Basilides and Valentinus, the Gnostics should be compared with teachers in philosophical schools. In fact, it is not clear how they spent their time, how they gained support (either financial or social), and what kind of "constituency" they had. The behavior of many left much to be desired, but we do not know whether this situation reflects the upper or the lower strata of society, or indeed whether any significant distinction (apart from the availability of leisure in some cases) can be drawn. Some of the church writers claim that they denied "Christ" when brought before Roman judges as Christians, but this need reflect little more than Roman police inefficiency. Obviously, if the Basilidians took as their model the Christ who stood laughing while someone else was crucified by mistake, their relations with Christians generally cannot have been good (though one must not exaggerate the prevalence of Christian martyrdoms). There also seems to be some relation between the usual Gnostic idea of a phantom Christ and the elusiveness of the Gnostic when pursued by the authorities.

## Gnostic Systems

Church writers generally treated the followers of Simon Magus (Acts 8) as the first of the Gnostics. This treatment was partly a matter of tactics, notably for Irenaeus (*Against Heresies* 1.23-31). By denouncing the rather simpleminded Simonians as the originators of heresy, one got some purchase on their successors, adherents of madly myth-minded sects, and finally on the more respectable followers of Basilides and Valentinus, not to mention Marcion (probably a Gnostic).

We shall deal first with the Simonians and their successors, then with the major schools. Simon is said to have claimed to have made the universe through an agent, his "first thought." The rebellious angels whom the agent made for the creation captured her, then exposed her to interminable insults, as she passed from body to body. She finally met Simon again when she was a prostitute in Tyre. She was Helen of Troy as well as Helen of Tyre. Simon himself came down from the highest heaven to rescue her, escaping the wiles of the planetary angels in disguise. What did this story do for his followers? Obviously they identified their own souls or spirits with the plight of the first thought; they too were prisoners of the angels. When freed by Simon's grace, they knew that the moral legislation of these angels was mere convention and that they were free to live as they chose. Some chose to practice magic, often love magic, or joined in the worship of Simon and Helen as identified with Zeus and Athena. Somehow combined with this notably Gnostic attitude were elements derived from Christianity. Simon, says Irenaeus, claimed to have appeared among the Jews as Son, in Samaria (his home according to Acts) as Father, and among the other nations as Holy Spirit. He was said to have identified Helen as the "lost sheep" of the Gospel parable (Luke 15:6), the one whom Jesus had come to save. By the third century the movement seems to have disappeared, though elements from the story of Helen flourished in other Gnostic settings, notably in the Coptic books from Nag Hammadi in Egypt.

Irenaeus calls another Samaritan—Menander—Simon's successor, but since Menander, like Simon, claimed to have been the savior it is hard to see the link between them. Menander's specialty was the donation of a "knowledge" that let his followers overcome the angels. By baptism in relation to him (in his name?) they "received resurrection" (see 2 Tim 2:18; perhaps 1 Cor 15:29). "They could no longer die, but went on living, ageless and immortal" (*Against Heresies* 1.23.5). Justin, writing about 150, had known some surviving disciples, but thirty years later Irenaeus found it pointless to look for them. Whether, of course, the disciples of Menander really took this language literally remains a question. Christian writers do not usually treat Ignatius's language about the Eucharist as the "medicine of immortality" as if it were literal, and perhaps equal consideration should be offered his Gnostic contemporary.

Saturninus, the third Gnostic in Irenaeus's canon, is perhaps the most interesting, for he definitely regarded Christ, not himself, as the Savior and provided a Gnostic reinterpretation of Genesis and the Christian gospel as his message of salvation. The usual Gnostic "unknown Father" made angels, who in turn made the world. They tried to make human beings "after the image and likeness" of a shining image from above, but they were too weak to have the beings stand erect, and only a "spark of life" (the spirit) could do so. Finally, the Father wanted to destroy the angels and sent Christ as the Savior. He was incorporeal though he seemed to be a man. He came to destroy evil persons and save the good. He therefore taught his good disciples to abstain from marriage and procreation (products of Satan). "Most of his disciples abstain from animal flesh and deceive many by this simulated asceticism" (*Against Heresies* 1.24.2). Presumably their asceticism was related to their doctrine of the weakness of the angels, the badness of the creation, and the ghostly nature of Christ.

Carpocrates deserves a brief mention simply because his interpretation of Jesus was quite different. Jesus was the son of Joseph. He was like other men, but better, because his strong, pure soul remembered its life before "incarnation" and could escape from the creator angels. Carpocrates' disciples were like Jesus, and some claimed to be better than the apostles. They had to experience "everything" for the sake of spiritual freedom and in order to avoid having their souls return to other bodies after death. They said that Jesus had secretly taught his disciples and apostles about these matters, for transmission to those who were worthy to know. An impressive statement presumably reveals how they set forth their own spiritual goals. "Salvation comes through faith and love. Everything else, since it is a matter of indifference, is called either good or evil in accordance with human opinion. Actually nothing is by nature evil" (*Against Heresies* 1.25.5). It is not clear whether or not Carpocrates' son Epiphanes was really a Gnostic or simply a radical communist who denounced private property, marriage, and the repressive nature of the Decalogue.

Here we must refer also to Marcion of Sinope in Pontus, a man quite different from the other Gnostics, but a Gnostic nonetheless. Marcion was obsessed with the uniqueness of the revelation in Christ, uniqueness especially in relation to the Old Testament and its God. Probably the date of his proclamation in Rome, rather soon after the unsuccessful and bloody Jewish religious revolt of 132–135, was related to the nature of his "gospel" of an incorporeal Christ-Savior, misunderstood by his earliest disciples though not by Paul. The Jewish-minded apostles interpolated the true Gospel and the genuine letters of the apostle, but Marcion himself, presumably by using philological methods like those employed for Homer in his time, was able to recover the original. His attitude was not that of a philologist, however, but of a religious reformer. His "antitheses," noting contrasts between true and false religion in the manner of Luther or, more exactly, Harnack, began with the hymnic affirmation "O wealth of riches! Folly, power, and ecstasy—seeing that there can be nothing to say about it, or imagine about it, or compare it to!" Philology thus served his mysteriously apprehended gospel. So too did Jewish or Jewish-Christian ideas. When Marcion differentiated the supreme God who was the good Father of Jesus from the ordinary Old Testament picture of God as just, his notion resembled Jewish distinctions drawn between the divine names Yahweh and Elohim.

When Irenaeus describes Cerdo, Marcion's predecessor at Rome around the year 140, we learn something also about Gnostic-Christian relations. Cerdo came into the Christian church there and publicly confessed his error. His views remained heretical, however, so that sometimes he taught them secretly and sometimes renewed his confession. Finally he was convicted of false teaching and was separated from the assembly of the brethren (*Against Heresies* 3.4.3).

Irenaeus also describes the missionary work of the Valentinians.

> They make public addresses for the sake of people from the Church, whom they call "common" and "ecclesiastical." By means of these speeches they capture the simpler Christians and attract them, imitating our sermons so that people will listen to them more often. They make complaints about us, claiming to think like us though we unreasonably refuse to be in communion with them. They say what we do and hold the same doctrine, but we call them heretics! When they have ruined the faith of some by their questions and have led their hearers not to contradict them, they take them aside and reveal to them the "ineffable mystery" of their "pleroma." [If someone actually joins their group] he thinks he is no longer in heaven or on earth but has entered into the "pleroma" and has embraced his angel. He walks about in self-esteem and arrogance, strutting like a cock. Some of them, indeed, say that a "man come from above" must have good morals—and this is why they affect a supercilious seriousness. Most, however, disdain such scruples as if being already "perfect." They live without shame and despise everything, calling themselves "spiritual." They say that they already know the place of their "rest" within the "pleroma." (*Against Heresies* 3.15.2)

These comments can hardly be taken literally.

The Valentinian system itself could be presented in various ways related to the circumstances. Thus, the *Letter to Flora* by Valentinus's pupil Ptolemaeus differentiates the supreme Father from the demiurge or creator while carefully claiming Valentinian teaching to be based on correct exegesis of the Old Testament and the Gospels. The Old Testament law was ordained neither by the perfect God nor by the devil. Echoes of this teaching recur in the more orthodox Christian writers Justin and Irenaeus. But Ptolemaeus speaks of a higher doctrine, which can be given Flora at a future date. It is this doctrine which is Irenaeus's principal target, though we also possess fragments from Valentinus himself (chiefly in Clement of Alexandria) and from other pupils such as Theodotus (excerpts in Clement) and Heracleon (notes on John cited by Origen in his commentary on the Gospel). Basically, the Valentinians tried to explain the movement from the one to the many, essence to existence, and the good to the evil by positing a primal principle, Depth, which existed in Silence. When the two united they brought forth another pair or syzygy; these were called Mind and Truth. Others made up a first Tetrad, then another for a total of eight, the Ogdoad. From the fifth and sixth proceed another ten, while from the seventh and eighth twelve more come forth—for a total of thirty, apparently related to the days of the lunar month. The thirtieth aeon, Sophia, wrongly wanted to know the

Father. Her purpose, called Achamoth (*ḥokmâ* is the Hebrew wisdom) took shape outside the pleroma or fullness of the aeons and was imperfect. Mind brought forth two more aeons, Christ and the Holy Spirit, to deal with the situation, and after a complex series of events in the spiritual world Achamoth produced the demiurge, and creation thus took place. The Savior Jesus came to save Achamoth and what she had produced. The point of all this for Valentinians was that they were, and knew themselves to be, essentially related to the pleroma. Psychic beings related to the demiurge were capable of being saved; these were ordinary Christians. Merely material beings were destined to perish. This whole system, as Tertullian intimated (*Against the Valentinians* [*Adversus Valentinianos* 4.2), is based on an older, even more highly mythological gnosis (*vetus opinio*).

The Basilidian systems occur in at least two forms, one of which is rather like the Valentinian notions of emanation; the other presents a "non-existent God" who makes a "non-existent world" out of nothing (Hippolytus *Refutation of All Heresies* 7.20.4). Christians could find some of their writings attractive, for Basilides himself wrote *Exegetica* on scriptural texts, and his son and disciple Isidore wrote *Ethics, On the Grown Soul,* and *Expositions of the Prophet Parchor,* apparently an oriental prophet revered by the Basilidians (see Eusebius *Church History* 4.7.7).

## Gnostic Practices

The Marcionites remained close to ordinary church practices in ministry and cult. They were led by bishops, presbyters, and deacons, and took part in baptisms, Eucharists, etc. Similarly, the Valentinians, as we know both from Clement and from Nag Hammadi, observed anointing, baptism, and Eucharist. Valentinus himself wrote a homily and at least one psalm, presumably for liturgical use. This is not to say that their goals were entirely Christian. Irenaeus gives us a baptismal formula which is almost a parody of ordinary Christianity. "Into the name of the unknown Father of All, into Truth the Mother of All, into the one who came down into Jesus, into unity and redemption and participation in the powers." Some of them said such formulas in Hebrew or Aramaic for greater effect (*Against Heresies* 1.21.3).

On the other hand, the Gnostic *Gospel of Thomas* represents Jesus' disciples as asking him, "Do you want us to fast? How should we pray? Should we give alms? What diet should we observe?" He replies, "If you fast you will generate sin for yourselves. If you pray you will be condemned. If you give alms you will do harm to your spirits. . . . Eat what is set before you" (logion 6, pl. 81.14). These Gnostics could have appealed to the New Testament precedent of Jesus and his disciples, who did not fast; on the other hand, such Valentinians as Ptolemaeus and Theodotus firmly accepted fasting, along with prayer. Some ancient philosophers rejected prayer, but like Christians most Gnostics advocated it, using it for their own purposes. "Judas said, 'When we pray, how should we pray?' The Lord said, 'Pray in the place where there is no woman'" (*Dialogue of the Savior* [Robinson, p. 237]; Origen too inclined toward this view). Almsgiving, absent from heterodox circles (according to Ignatius), was actually central in the late second-century *Sentences of Sextus* (in Coptic at Nag Hammadi) and in the ideas of the Gnostic Ptolemaeus. Finally, as among Christians generally, some Gnostics were more rigorous than others in regard to diet.

Irenaeus found the diversity in Gnostic rites especially displeasing. This was notably the case in regard to Gnostic rites of "redemption," regarded as superior to baptism or Eucharist and undertaken in relation to a "sacred marriage" (imitating the unions of the syzygies in the spiritual world) or unction with oil and water or balsam or a rite that has been called a "death-mass." As one would expect, other Gnostics rejected all these rites, claiming that "knowledge" was simply the opposite of ignorance and that, as spiritual, it was itself the redemption of the inner man (*Against Heresies* 1.21.4). So also a famous Gnostic formula quoted by Clement (*Excerpts from Theodotus* [*Excerpta ex Theodoto*] 78) states that "it is not the washing itself that liberates, but the knowledge of who we were, what we became; where we were, where we had been thrown; where we are hastening, whence we have been redeemed; what birth is, and what rebirth." Gnostics obviously spent much time in ritual acts and meditation on their meaning.

## Gnostic Literature

They also wrote books, and at considerable length. There were more than fifty-two books in the thirteen Nag Hammadi codices, even though some are duplicates and not all are Gnostic. In the second century Basilides composed at least twenty-three books of his *Exegetica*, which was mentioned above, and we have given the titles of some of his son's works. We have referred to some of Valentinus's writings; in addition, he composed letters that were preserved by his followers. Ptolemaeus made Valentinus's insights into a system and, more than that, explained how it was set forth in the prologue to the Gospel of John. Irenaeus cites many other examples of Ptolemaeus's New Testament exegesis. His assessment of the hidden knowledge in the Bible as a whole is reflected in his apologetic *Letter to Flora*. Another Valentinian, Heracleon, produced exegetical notes on at least the first eight chapters of John, and Origen had to take these into account when he produced his own enormous commentary. In these instances, at least, we find

6. Conclusion Page from *The Gospel of Truth*, Nag Hammadi Codex, I, 43

a spirituality not altogether different from what was flourishing within the churches. By the time we reach the "exegetical" treatises preserved at Nag Hammadi, however, we are in another world. The exegesis has overcome the Christian text. Sometimes the Bible is allegorized along with Homer; more often the subject of the "exegesis" is a Gnostic myth or group of myths. It seems no accident that at Nag Hammadi there were three copies of the *Apocryphon* (secret teaching) of John, one *Apocryphon of James,* and two works called *Apocalypse of James.* Gnostics were not content with allegorizing the Christian books but created their own. Indeed, in the *Letter to Flora* Ptolemaeus analyzed the various levels of inspired authorship in the Old Testament, relying on the teaching of Jesus as a guide. We may be tempted to think of this Valentinian as a fairly reliable exegete, but behind his expressions lies the Gnostic theory of the perfect God above the inferior demiurge. Ptolemaeus was a careful analyst. He classified Old Testament texts in relation to sayings of Jesus and thus reached the conclusion that some laws are derived from God (the demiurge, to be sure), some from Moses, and some merely from the elders of the Jewish people. In turn, the law of God can be further divided. It consists of pure legislation, not mingled with evil, which was completed by the Savior; a part that was typical and symbolic, transformed into the spiritual and invisible sphere; and a part mixed up with evil and injustice that the Savior abolished. As G. Quispel pointed out, the roots of this theory lie in the slightly earlier Christian apologist Justin, and the theory is worked out in Irenaeus and in the Pseudo-Clementine *Homilies.*[1] It represents one more point at which Valentinian Gnostics and orthodox Christians were largely in agreement, though of course the latter could not accept the Valentinian doctrine of God in its full ramifications.

## Sex and Asceticism

Almost all Gnostics, whether ascetic or libertine, were deeply concerned with human sexuality and its problems. Indeed, they often set the origin of sexuality not, as in Genesis, in the human situation but within the Godhead and throughout the spiritual realms above. We have seen something of how they spoke of the primal One or even of the primal Non-existent, from which twos were generated, or else they placed duality at the very beginning and described how pairs (syzygies) emanated from pairs in perfect harmony until the very last spiritual being became separated from *her* partner, spontaneously generated an inferior being—and thus the whole phenomenal universe began to come into existence. According to this kind of view, most often associated with the Valentinians, the goal of human spirituality is the recovery of the lost union with a spiritual partner and return to the realms above. According to Irenaeus (*Against Heresies* 1.6.4), the Valentinians considered themselves as being "in the world but not of it" (John 17:11, 14) as opposed to ordinary Christians who were "of it." They then differentiated their own morality from that of Christians. "Whoever is in the world and does not love a woman so as to possess her is not of the truth and will not come to the truth. He who is of the world and possesses a woman will not come to the truth because he possessed a woman with lust." It was important, the Valentinians condescendingly said (or so Irenaeus supposed), for "psychics" of the world, Christians, to practice continence and good behavior. Not so for them. Admittedly, this kind of teaching seems to contradict both Ptolemaeus and Heracleon, but it always remains possible that there were levels of moral teaching as there were levels of doctrine. In the Nag Hammadi books the morality is almost exclusively ascetic. This does not mean that libertinism was dead. Epiphanius (*Against Heresies* [*Haereses*] 26.17) tells us that in his youth he was approached by beautiful Gnostic women who tried to lead him astray, quoting Gnostic formulas to him. He resisted temptation and turned their names over to the local bishop. The date was not much earlier than much of the Nag Hammadi literature.

The goal and purpose of Gnostic spirituality are indicated in what Epiphanius said were the comments of the Gnostic missionaries. The most beautiful one said, "I am a vessel of election [a second-century phrase], able to save those led astray, but you [a less attractive Gnostic] were not strong enough." Again, they said to one another, "We were unable to save the young man, but left him in the hands of the Archon to perish." Epiphanius viewed them as completely deluded, but it is probably significant that the Hermetic treatise *Asclepius* (§ 21, in Coptic at Nag Hammadi) treats sex as a divine mystery, as does a Gnostic group described by Clement of Alexandria (*Stromateis* 3.27ff.). That group called it a "mystical communion" or a "sacred religious mystery," and Clement was horrified to hear that "it will bring them to the kingdom of God." Quite strikingly, he adds that "if these people spoke of acts of spiritual union as the Valentinians do, perhaps one could accept their view." In other words, in this regard there was little or no difference between Clement and Valentinus.

Indeed, on another crucial point one finds agreement: the nature of Jesus' asceticism. Clement quoted Valentinus for the point that Jesus was so ascetic that he did not evacuate any of his food; he was above corruption. Elsewhere he stated that in the "traditions" he had learned that when the beloved disciple touched Jesus he did not press any flesh. The "traditions" are, or are reflected in, the apocryphal *Acts of John*. These examples illustrate the eclectic or even syncretistic atmosphere of Alexandrian spirituality and the thin wall that separated some Gnostics from some Christians.

## The Goal of the Gnostic Way

It appears that all groups, perhaps because of their ties with Judaism and/or Christianity, spoke of both personal and communal eschatology. As was the case with Jews, early Christians generally did not look for the vision of God or any mystical experience during earthly life. As a Christian convert, the apologist Justin rather depreciated his goal as a Platonist: the vision of God. In regard to this matter, some Gnostics joined Neoplatonists like Plotinus by enjoying mystical experience here and now. The author of the Nag Hammadi *Gospel of Truth* is one who has already been in "the place of rest," the place from which he had (originally) come forth—indeed, the pleroma or spiritual world. It may seem that in the system of Justin the Gnostic the initiate entered into the spiritual world, but the oath of secrecy is the one which "our Father Elohim" swore when he "entered into the Good" and beheld the ineffable mystery and "was made perfect with the Good" (Hippolytus, *Refutation* 5.27.1–2). There is, of course, a call to those who are worthy to follow Elohim's example, but there is no assurance of a mystical vision.

For Gnostic spirituality, the ultimate goal was more important than any this-worldly experience. It was almost always escape, as we have said, that is, escape to the world beyond planets, beyond stars, the world at once infinitely remote and infinitely close because attainable within oneself. This is why Gnostics were likely to need not only semimagical formulas for dealing with the hostile powers they would surely encounter but also charts for locating their journey in the enormous desert of space. What supported them in this upward flight was not only self-knowledge but also awareness of what a warm welcome awaited them in or above the 365 heavens or in the pleroma. According to the *Gospel of Mary,* even the hostile powers would recognize the liberated soul as "conqueror of space," rising to "reach rest in the time of the moment of the Aeon in silence." Valentinians spoke of the ultimate salvation of both psychic and spiritual elements but laid emphasis on the spiritual, which would enjoy rest on the Lord's day with their mother in the celestial Ogdoad, bearing their souls like robes until the final end. Then the spiritual elements would put off their souls and when the Mother received her bridegroom they too would receive their angels as bridegrooms and would enter the bridal chamber and come toward the vision of the Father. They would have become intellectual aeons for intellectual and eternal (or aeonic) marriages of the cosmic syzygy (Clement *Excerpts from Theodotus* 63ff.).

Because of the Gnostic concern for travel through the heavenly spaces, it was not uncommon for them to have maps for their journeying. The anti-Christian writer Celsus managed to acquire one such chart and to describe it, claiming that it was Christian. Origen said that he himself found it, or one like it, only after "industrious researches." It came from the Ophites, "a most undistinguished sect in my opinion" (Origen *Against Celsus* [*Contra Celsum*] 6.24ff.). Apparently it owed something to astronomy or astrology, much to magic. At the top there were two concentric circles, the outer one outlining the Father, the inner one, the Son. The outer circle intersected a circle below it, which belonged to various angels; in turn, the lower circle intersected one still farther down with fixed stars outside the planets, and finally earth above, Gehenna-Tartarus below. The "game plan" was for the soul or spirit to escape upward through a first "diaphragm"—paradise leading upward via cross to life—into the middle circle, thence through the second diaphragm—Agape—into the circle of the Son surrounded by the Father. Presumably the Gnostic who carried such a diagram felt confident that he would reach his superheavenly destination. Origen was also acquainted with the magical formulas that the Gnostics were to use as they passed upward through the planetary spheres. (H. Chadwick notes that Plotinus too could speak of the upward way as accomplished with purifications for the approach to the vision of God. But of course Plotinus had neither charts nor formulas.[2]) At the highest gate the soul seems to address Michael thus: "Solitary king, bond of blindness, unconscious oblivion, I hail thee, the supreme power, preserved by the spirit of providence and wisdom; from thee I am sent in purity, being already part of the light of Son and Father. May grace be with me; yea, father, let it be with me" (Origen *Against Celsus* 6.31, trans. H. Chadwick). The resemblance of this kind of language to that quoted by Irenaeus is obvious. One may add that other Gnostics, like other Christians, descended to the level of crude magic and simply uttered vowels in sequence or incomprehensible groups of consonants.

## Attitude toward Creation

From this eschatological standpoint we can briefly consider the Gnostics' pictures of "creation." They were never willing to accept straightforwardly the accounts in the book of Genesis. Just as Philo had read them in the light of his own knowledge of Plato's *Timaeus* and Christians read them as allegorical narratives concerning the preexistent Christ, so the Gnostics, obsessed by the gulf between the unknown good Father and the alien hostile world, could never accept the notion of a God who actually made the world, took responsibility for it, and found it good. Compared with this difference, the disagreement between Christians who held that God created out of nothing and Greeks who held that God created out of something becomes trivial. Both rejected the pessimistic dualism of Gnostic thought.

Even Basilides, who verbally used Christian formulas (or parodied them?), was far away from Christian ideas. Before the creation "there was a time when there was nothing"; later "the non-existent God made a non-existent world." In this Gnostic system the process of "making" is explained away in considerable detail. We have seen how the Valentinians, presumably relying on more mythic antecedents, tell of a primeval pair and the subsequent emanations from them. The passion of the thirtieth, female aeon, not to mention her ultimate salvation, is quite complicated, but it serves to bridge the gap between the eternal and tranquil world of the primary aeons and the temporal, unruly created world. It does not quite bridge it, however, for Sophia has to produce a "psychic son," the demiurge, and the demiurge then creates the "world-ruler," the devil. Many other creation myths are to be found in the Nag Hammadi collection, but their basic pattern is one of distancing God from the world. The problem for the Gnostics' opponents was not so much the distancing as the ways in which they distanced. As Plotinus wrote, they "produce what they call the Demiurge and make him revolt from his mother and drag the universe which proceeds from him down to the ultimate limit of images" (*Enneads* 2.9.10). He concluded that "the man who wrote this just meant to be blasphemous." On the other hand, some Gnostics, perhaps followers of a certain Prodicus, had an apocryphal book with the following text:

> All things were one, but as it seemed good to its unity not to be alone [compare Gen 2:18], an idea came forth from it, and it had intercourse with it and made the Beloved. Because of this there came forth from Him an idea with which he had intercourse and made powers which cannot be seen or heard. (Clement *Stromateis* 3.29)

This is either a very physical or a very spiritual idea of emanation followed by creation. The relation of deity to the world is to be found in the Valentinian idea of the fall of Sophia, the last and youngest aeon. As we have noted, she felt a violent desire to see the supreme Father. According to some, she gave birth to a shapeless substance; when she looked at it, first she felt grief because of its imperfection, then fear that it might perish, then astonishment and doubt over its cause and the way she could hide it. From these passions she experienced conversion and tried to return to the Father, but without success. Her inferior daughter Achamoth experienced similar emotions, out of which the universe below arose. From the tears of Achamoth came what is humid; from her laughter (not mentioned for Sophia), what is luminous; from her grief and astonishment, the corporeal elements of the world.

As a Christian bishop, Irenaeus considered this ridiculous, but what the

Gnostics were trying to do was bridge the gap between God and the world and between the divine and the human. They were not content with traditional philosophical theology and its denial of emotion within the divine (compare the Gospel accounts of Jesus and also theological statements by Ignatius, Tatian, and Origen on the sufferings of Christ and even of God). One version of Valentinian theology has strong links with Christian orthodoxy, though also, as Hippolytus points out, with numerology in their scheme.

> The Father was alone ungenerated, without place or time, without counsellor or any other being that can be thought of in any way. He was isolated and at rest, himself alone in himself. But since he was productive (as the number one is productive of other numbers), it seemed good to him to generate and bring forth what he had in himself that was most beautiful and most perfect; for he was not devoted to isolation. For he was wholly Love, and love is not love unless there is something loved. (Hippolytus *Refutation* 6.29)

This early Christian emphasis, largely absent from the writings of the second-century apologists, was apparently being preserved among some of the Gnostics.

Gnostic spirituality, under a cloud in Christian and imperial circles for centuries, survived only in an attentuated, moderately theosophical guise among pagans and Christians who read, for example, the Hermetic literature—treatises and dialogues purporting to convey divine revelations but apparently derived from philosophical commonplaces. In the fourth century, Christian authors exploited the Hermetica for their own purposes and must have undermined Gnostic claims, although much of the Hermetic *Asclepius* is preserved in Coptic at Nag Hammadi. The fierce attacks by prominent Christians weakened Gnosticism, especially when combined with imperial pressure. Manichaeism, in some aspects a form of Gnosticism, tended to take its place. The emperor Julian, no friend of orthodox Christianity, denounced Arians for robbing a Valentinian community at Edessa in 362 and confiscated the church's property not for the Valentinians but for his soldiers and himself. Later Christian emperors sometimes included old Gnostic groups among those proscribed; thus, Marcionites and Valentinians are mentioned in 428 and Ophites in 438. It is hard to avoid the impression that this is mere antiquarianism. In the development of Christianity, whatever good the Gnostics may have stood for had been set in context and thus transcended. There was no place for libertinism in orthodox Christianity—at least not officially—but much room for the exercise of asceticism. Gnostic speculations about the unknown God and the world could be absorbed into meditations like those of Dionysius the Areopagite or, on another level, into the naming of the countless angels to be found, for example, in Coptic Christianity. In general, however, what happened to Gnosticism is that it simply came to an end. It may happen that those who reject the reality of the world and its historical actuality are rejected themselves.

## Notes

1. *Ptolémée: Lettre à Flora,* ed. G. Quispel (Sources chrétiennes 24; Paris: Cerf, 1949).
2. Origen, *Contra Celsum,* trans. H. Chadwick (Cambridge: Cambridge University Press, 1965) 346 n. 3.

## Bibliography

### Sources

Clement. *Stromateis.* Translated by H. Chadwick in *Alexandrian Christianity.* Edited by J. E. L. Oulton and H. Chadwick. LCC 2. 1954.
Foerster, W. *Gnosis: A Selection of Gnostic Texts.* 2 vols. Oxford: Oxford University Press, 1972.
Robinson, J. M. *The Nag Hammadi Library in English.* San Francisco: Harper & Row, 1983. The most accessible selection of texts.

### Studies

Grant, R. M. *Gnosticism and Early Christianity.* Rev. ed. New York: Harper & Row, 1966.
Jonas, H. *The Gnostic Religion.* 3rd ed. Boston: Beacon, 1970. A major thematic study.
Pagels, E. H. *The Gnostic Gospels.* New York: Random House, 1979.
Peel, M. L. *The Epistle to Rheginos.* Philadelphia: Westminster, 1969.
Rudolph, K. *Gnosis: The Nature and History of Gnosticism.* San Francisco: Harper & Row, 1983.
Scholer, D. M. *Nag Hammadi Bibliography 1948-1969.* Leiden: Brill, 1971. Continued in *Novum Testamentum.*
Wilson, R. McL. *The Gnostic Problem.* 2nd ed. London: Mowbray, 1964.

# 4

# The Spiritual Message of the Great Fathers

CHARLES KANNENGIESSER

THE MAIN CHRISTIAN THEOLOGIANS of the fourth and fifth centuries are called fathers of the church, because they conceived the dogmatic foundations of all Christianity down to our times. Their teaching helped to establish the dominant form of "true faith," recognized as the only orthodox dogma by the Roman emperors and their ecumenical councils. The Christian church identified itself as a faithful community on the basis of the creed canonized at these powerful synods, and no ecclesiastical "fatherhood" was ever to be attributed to those vanquished in the theological battles surrounding the synodal definitions. Men like Arius in the Alexandrian church of the early fourth century or Apollinarius (Apollinaris) in the area of Antioch during the second half of the same century or Pelagius in Rome at the beginning of the fifth century could exhibit personal sanctity and become influential as exegetes, theologians, and counselors. However, their spiritual message was obscured beneath misinterpretations and the severe distortions of their principles, imposed by their adversaries who became the "fathers" of the orthodox establishment in the churches of their times.

In recalling the spiritual message of the so-called fathers, one needs to be aware of the spirituality of the theologians they combated. For it was most probably through his biased rejection of the Arian view of salvation that Athanasius became the champion of a renewed doctrine of the divine incarnation. In Augustine's mature accomplishment as well, one may surmise that without his fierce refutation of the Pelagian ethics he would never have spelled out as forcefully as he did all that was presupposed by his African religiosity. In any case, the spiritual message of the fathers, valuable and inspiring as it remains for centuries in the churches of East and West, needs always to be located in its genuine setting, which was limited and conditioned by the polemics among Christians of their time.

Together with the polemic issues, there is another shaping force to be kept in mind. It is the mental pattern forged by the social origin and by the kind of education the fathers had undergone before they assumed leadership. If an awareness of their theological battles is vital to a more accurate understanding of the inner tensions proper to their spiritual message, it is equally important to consider the society and the culture that nurtured them. This is an indispensable key to their most vital and spontaneous convictions, the sort of unreflected certitudes that yielded the moral presuppositions behind their mystical enterprise.

Here a first observation, and a striking one indeed, is that of the family backgrounds of our heroes. Athanasius, bishop of Alexandria from 328 to 373, and Augustine, bishop of Hippo (born in modern Algeria) from 395 to 430, are the only ones among the outstanding spiritual leaders here considered who were *not* born into the ruling class—sons of the aristocracy or of very rich parents. The Christian spirituality of the fourth and fifth centuries, which was inherited by later traditions and universalized in Western civilization through more than a millennium, deserves to be relocated in its true birthplace, the domains of wealthy landowners and the refined circles of the upper class in the capitals of the Roman Empire around the Mediterranean sea. Except for Athanasius in the East and Augustine in the West, both linked by their middle-class origins and—should one say for that reason—the most creative founders of Christian spirituality in their centuries, all the other prominent figures we shall enumerate are of the same privileged origin: Basil of Caesarea, Gregory of Nyssa, Gregory of Nazianzus, John Chrysostom in the oriental provinces of the empire; and in its western part Hilary of Poitiers, Ambrose of Milan, Jerome, and, one may surmise, Leo the Great.

Rich among the richest but reduced to voluntary poverty in following the ascetical trend of their time, these church leaders enriched the whole Christian world by grafting onto the mystical vision of Christianity that they inaugurated the humanistic values of their old family traditions. Cultivated, even outstanding in their cultural achievements—in addressing the illiterate masses in the course of their pastoral duties or in facing the barbarians—these same converts and spiritual leaders introduced into the discourse of Christian spirituality very traditional attitudes of their pre-Christian roots and surroundings. Through their creativity in adopting the language of the contemporary elite, they formulated the Christian response to the spiritual needs of their generation.

Only one aspect of their founding initiatives, namely, that of their doctrinal and institutional contribution to the monastic movement, will be excluded—for redactional convenience—from our present analysis. Christian monasticism, in its first, very spectacular emergence, will nevertheless manifest almost all the spiritual traits we need to consider now in detail.

## Athanasius of Alexandria (ca. 300–373)

Athanasius was the founder of what may be called the fourth-century spirituality in the Christian church. His view of God seems to ignore the Gnostic pattern of theological inquiry refined and promoted by Origen until half a century before him in the Alexandrian church. He did not view the experience of faith in the Gospel revelation as a special case of the common aspiration for divine transcendency innate in human beings. His very idea of the revelation given by God to save the human race proceeded from a point of view that was no longer Origenian. Whereas the brilliant master of Christian catechesis in the third century started with the cosmic vision of God creating a hierarchized world of spirits and the universal process of saving the human spirits fallen into the lower spheres of a material world, Athanasius argued that Christian faith starts with the Gospel revelation itself. In contrast to the "psychological" view of salvation mingled with Gnostic metaphysics, as found in Origen, the Athanasian notion of faith seems "institutional," resting entirely on the historical revelation of God as communicated by the Gospel narratives. There is a decided shift from the Origenian focus on a supreme savior known through a scrutiny of the mysteries of the invisible cosmos and through the systematic assimilation of the general rules of human knowledge. For Origen, these rules were best applied in Christian terms in the ascetical and heroic behavior of the saints and best understood and taught to ordinary believers by elected individuals like himself. But, for Athanasius, the idea of God revealed along the classical lines of a religious cosmology—one of the main features of Hellenism—fades away, and the elitist and intellectualistic idea of a salvation assured to individuals according to their personal gifts and their abilities is replaced by a theory of the divine realities revealed by the Gospels. The founding intuition of Athanasius's spiritual message seems to lie here, in his seminal perception of the immediate access provided by God for everyone in the church to the realities of the divine presence in the Gospel revelation.

It comes as no surprise, then, that the first doctrinal treatise published by the young bishop of Alexandria, ten years after the Council of Nicaea in 325 and in the seventh year of his episcopacy, was entitled *On the Incarnation* (*De incarnatione*). This short treatise, still popular, was intended as a summary of the catechetical teaching recommended by the pontiff. It follows another, more traditional apology, *Against the Heathen* (*Contra gentes*), which opens with a Neoplatonic commentary on the creation of humankind according to Genesis 1-2. It is important to observe that from a strikingly Origenian opening, in which echoes of the Genesis narrative are sounded in Neoplatonic terms, the author draws his audience along a familiar sequence of Christian apologetics, still based on popularized Origenian arguments, to the christological synthesis of *On the Incarnation*, where the tune becomes eventually his own.

One recognizes in *On the Incarnation* the first appearance, at once firm and candid, of the incarnational spirituality proper to the Athanasian vision. The divine Logos, less defined in his own nature or in his being with God than Origen would have demanded, is insistently introduced as the incarnate Savior. Assuming the essential unity that keeps all human beings in the same bodily existence, Athanasius saw the human race as a single reality affected by the entry of the saving Logos into the physical structure. As a result, he emphasized the evangelical attractiveness of the Savior in realistic terms:

> He took to Himself a body, a human body even as our own. . . . For the solidarity of humankind is such that, by virtue of the Word's indwelling in a single human body, the corruption which goes with death has lost its power over all. . . . When, then, the minds of men had fallen finally to the level of sensible things, the Word submitted to appear in a body, in order that He, as Man, might center their senses on Himself. . . . (*On the Incarnation* 8, 9 and 16 [*PG* 25, cols. 109B, 112B, 124B])

Mediated by the magnetic radiance of the savior's body, divine grace streams into human souls through the senses, fascinated by the savior's miracles, by his death and his resurrection. Not only are the saving actions of the incarnate Logos open to the senses in the hearing and the subsequent memorizing of the Gospel narratives, but the savior's actions are actually experienced in the church because they are reproduced in the liturgy and in the virtuous imitation of Christ in the lives of the people.

Thus, the incarnational spirituality grounded by Athanasius on a genuine christological intuition developed into a vision of the church. From the treatise *On the Incarnation* to the numerous *Festal Letters* (*Epistolae Festales*) published by Athanasius each year to announce Lent, Easter, and Pentecost, the same theological focus is addressed again and again: in our contemporary experience of faith we are introduced into the paschal mystery of the Savior himself. Ecclesiology, in the sacramental sense of the fourth century, replaced the cosmological frame used by Origen for setting the journey of the Christian toward perfection.

Such a spiritual vision, saturated by a lifelong meditation on Scripture, detached from the rhetorical formalities of the learned school theology taught at that time in the university at Alexandria by commentators on Plato and Aristotle, located Athanasius in the orbit of Egyptian monasticism. Under the prestigious guidance of Anthony the Hermit and thanks to the organizational skills of founders like Pachomius, before the middle of the fourth century the "city in the desert" counted thousands of men and women striving for holiness. Focusing on the paschal mystery of Christ as revealed in the New Testament and made available in the church for any true Christian experience of faith, Athanasius's spiritual vision could easily integrate the values of the monastic movement. It is very probable that Athanasius was acquainted with the hermits and the monastic communities before he became a bishop. In his first years in office, he deepened his bonds of friendship with the monks and consolidated his hierarchical position. This partnership remained unshaken through the tumultuous decades of the Arian controversy (339–362), when the tough pro-Nicaean bishop of Alexandria opposed the religious policy of the emperor, Constantius II.

The Athanasian spirituality, based on the economy of God's salvific incarnation as actualized in the church, used dramatic circumstances for expressing its authentic message in two major writings. During the forced retirement of a six-year exile in the West, in 339–340, Athanasius completed a polemical work entitled *Against the Arians* (*Contra Arianos*) in two books (a third was added at a later date). Its pro-Nicaean stress showed that a systematic inquiry on God, Father and Son, needed to be focused by means of the mystery of the divine incarnation. The style and the composition of the work remained motivated by pastoral concerns. The message, even when sublime in content, never turned into pedantic or abstruse speculation. The more Athanasius elaborated a forceful dogmatic affirmation on the lines of his anti-Arian christology, the more he tried to communicate with the readers in the modest language of a homiletic catechesis. We still possess the letter by which he presented the work to the monks for whom it had been written:

> In compliance with your affectionate request, which you have frequently urged upon me, I have written a short account of the sufferings which we and the Church have undergone. . . . (*Against the Arians*, Preface [*PG* 25, col. 692A])

Referring to difficulty in communicating the doctrine of the Logos, he says:

> For the more I desired to write, and endeavoured to force myself to understand the Divinity of the Word, so much the more did the knowledge thereof withdraw itself from me; and in proportion as I thought that I apprehended it, in so much I perceived myself to fail in doing so. Moreover, I was also unable to express in writing even what I seemed to myself to understand; and what

I wrote was unequal to the imperfect shadow of the truth which existed in my conception. (*Against the Arians*, Preface [*PG* 25, col. 693B])

He concludes the letter with the following admonition:

Now when you have read this account, pray for me, and exhort one another to do so. And send it back to me immediately and suffer no one whatever to take a copy of it, nor transcribe it for yourselves. Like good money-changers be satisfied with the reading; but read it repeatedly if you desire to do so. It is not safe that the writings of us babblers and private persons should fall into the hands of them that shall come after. Salute one another in love, and also all that come unto you in piety and faith. (*Against the Arians*, Preface [*PG* 25, col. 693CD])

Behind the conventional literary commonplaces about the author's humility emerges the dogmatic awareness, linked with pastoral dedication, which characterizes Athanasian spirituality. The same attitude is clearly articulated later in substantial writings of the Alexandrian bishop, for instance in his *Circular Letter to the Bishops of Egypt and Libya* (356), or in the *Letters to Serapion on the Divinity of the Spirit* (357-359).

In 357, when hidden in the desert and protected by the monks during his third exile (356-361), Athanasius published his famous *Life of Anthony*, only one year after the latter's death at the age of 105. For a correct evaluation of this work—which soon became a worldwide "best seller" in the Greek-speaking Orient as well as in Latin translation circulated during Athanasius's lifetime—it is important to note the creative freedom with which the author treated his subject. Documentary data supplied to the exiled bishop were reworked by him in the form of a narrative biography, which radiates pure Athanasian spirituality: a strong dogmatic affirmation of the Nicaean view of Christ underpins the idyllic story of Anthony's life and fight in the desert. The hermit's struggles with the devils and with himself illustrate, not without some eccentricities, the victorious experience of faith promised actually to all Christians if only they trust in the reality of the divine incarnation, which is transmitted to them by the church.

In the pastoral strategy of his rule over the churches of Egypt and Libya for forty-five years, Athanasius appears as a prototype of the great bishops the Christian church would enjoy during the fourth and fifth centuries. In his last years he was praised by the young Basil of Caesarea for his responsible care of the whole church in the empire. Whether in the internal administration of his vast see or on the wider stage of the imperial politics in East and West, the secret power of the Athanasian spirituality emerged from the bishop's clear perception of the church as a whole in the actualizing process by which it forms the believing community into a liturgical, institutional, and theological celebration of the divine incarnation.

# The Cappadocians

Biographical data on the Cappadocians provides an entry into their spiritual universe, and their preaching and other documented pastoral activities provide a concrete encounter with their spirituality. Their strictly theoretical contributions to the development of Christian dogma also serve in the evaluation of their spiritual message. Under these three rubrics (biography, pastoral involvement, theory), let us examine the spirituality of the most famous Cappadocians among the bishops of the fourth century.

## Basil of Caesarea (330-379)

Basil, born in Caesarea in 330 and baptized at the age of twenty-seven, was chosen as a priest of Caesarea when he was thirty-two years old and was consecrated as bishop of Caesarea at the age of forty. He died there nine years later. This remarkable stability is paralleled by the unity and continuity of his mystical achievement. He was heir to a dual prominence, having been born into a family of saints and, through his father, having received immediate access to the culture of the wealthiest Cappadocians of his time. Thus, he institutionalized Christian sanctity as though it were a family affair under his direct responsibility, and at the same time he continued to address the rich and cultivated as his peers.

On his father's side, Basil's grandmother, Macrina the Elder, belonged to a very wealthy and politically influential family. She played a key role in Basil's Christian education. She had known Gregory Thaumaturgus, "the Wonderworker," a direct disciple of Origen. (Before he left the Origenian school in Caesarea of Palestine, Gregory had praised Origen enthusiastically in an address that still survives.) Macrina the Elder and her family became fervent Christians. Between 304 and 311, under the persecution of Maximus and Galerius her whole fortune was confiscated. On Basil's mother's side, several generations had been Christian, priests and bishops among them, and his mother had lost her father as a martyr. Basil's own father, called Basil the Elder, had recovered the wealth of his parents after the persecution. He added more real estate to it and became a renowned rhetorician, but he died when Basil was about twelve years old. The oldest of Basil the Elder's five daughters was Macrina the Younger, who exercised great influence over her brothers and formed a religious community of women around herself. After her death, Basil, the oldest of the boys, was recognized as the authority. His brother Naucratios died at the age of twenty-seven after five years of strict asceticism as a hermit. Another brother, Gregory, married and followed the profession of rhetorician, though later through Basil he became the bishop of Nyssa. Peter, the youngest, was consecrated as bishop of Sebaste. On Basil's father's side there was also an uncle, another Gregory, who was a bishop in Cappadocia.

Basil began his studies under his father and continued his education in Caesarea in Cappadocia, where he met Gregory, the future bishop of Nazianzus, with whom he completed his studies, during which time he spent five years in Athens. After his return to Cappadocia, impressed by Macrina's monastic foundation, he and Gregory founded a monastic community for men in Annesi, near his grandmother's domain and his sister's monastery. There Basil and Gregory were instrumental in the production of the *Philocalia,* a collection of carefully copied quotations from the works of Origen structured in three parts: Scriptural hermeneutics, apologetics from Origen's *Against Celsus,* and a treatment of the Christian doctrine of free will and divine justice. In this stage of his career, Basil's main couselor was Eustathius of Sebaste. It is to this period, before his priestly ordination, that several monastic rules are to be dated—rules edited by him at a later period but first sketched out and tested at Annesi.

The character of Basil's service to the church in Caesarea, first as assistant to the local bishop, Eusebius, and then as his successor, exemplified his spiritual achievement. He combined the Origenian mysticism, inherited through his family tradition, with the practical ecclesiology of his time. He joined typical Athanasian attitudes in defense of Nicaean orthodoxy and of the church community with Origen's scholarship and mystical fervor. He also manifested from the start an undoubted capacity for social leadership proper to his personal character and to his privileged extraction.

Basil inaugurated the tradition of bishops' assuming the role of rich patrons in helping the poor, the sick, and the refugees. This was instanced in a severe drought in 368–369 that brought with it famine and economic distress. After the earthquake that destroyed Nicaea on 11 October 368, Basil's "socialistic" sermons against the rich were accompanied by the building of a hospital and a hospice. Although the position of the young bishop was strong enough to resist the pro-Arian emperor Valens in 371–372 (Basil had opposed Arianism as early as 364), his principal contribution in the field of ecclesiastical doctrine was his teaching on the Holy Spirit.

His dogmatic teaching, like his biblical hermeneutics, remained inductive by nature. Basil's spiritual leadership in all his activities was rooted in the liturgy of the local church. It was from pastoral and liturgical practice that he claimed a more explicit formulation of trinitarian faith. We can tell the Spirit's divine nature by examining the Spirit's activity in the economy of salvation: the Spirit is holy like God and is truly divine, because a creature cannot sanctify others. The liturgy, through norms and rites, and the

Scripture, through the writings of both Testaments, are the immediate sources of Christian spirituality because they are inspired by the Spirit. In such a way, Basil reproduced and developed the Athanasian "incarnational" model of spirituality on the level of a much richer ecclesiology and of a stronger pneumatology.

Besides the three books entitled *Against Eunomius* (*Contra Eunomium*), written in 364, there is a collection of forty homilies, probably assembled by Basil himself as a guide for lay people similar to the rules that he provided for monks. Whether in his homilies *On Baptism* delivered between 372 and 375, or in his commentaries on various psalms or finally in the *Hexaëmeron*—his explanation of the six days of work of Genesis 1 preached during one week in Lent and published near the end of 378—Basil always used his rhetorical skills and theological notions with a pastoral purpose tuned to a mystical pedagogy. His sense of the hidden mysteries of divine revelation led him to insist on the stages of the spiritual progress in the Origenian mode; at the same time, his experience of popular piety inspired his celebration of the cult of the martyrs. Finally, in the many letters (over three hundred) that have come down to us are to be found the best witness to the richness of his character and the widespread influence of his pastoral initiatives.

## Gregory of Nazianzus (329/30-390)

Basil's lifelong friend was a son of the bishop of Nazianzus, Gregory the Elder, who was converted by his wife, Nonna, and baptized in 325 when he was about fifty years of age. As in Basil's case, the family belonged to the wealthy landowning upper class. Several priests and bishops, such as Amphilochius of Iconium, were Gregory's relatives, and he was himself consecrated to God before his birth. In 361 his father made him accept priesthood against his preference for solitude and contemplative asceticism; later, in 372, he was forced by his powerful friend Basil to become bishop of a place called Sasima, but he continued to stay in his hometown, where he assisted his father. Two years later, soon after the latter's death, Gregory retired into the wilderness of Isauria for four or five years of silence and contemplation. In early 379, the small Nicaean community of Arian-dominated Constantinople asked him to become its pastor. He preached in a chapel until November 380, when the new emperor, Theodosius, who favored the Nicaean creed, summoned him to preach, as bishop of Constantinople, in the basilica of the Holy Apostles. During the Council of Constantinople in 381, discouraged by the politics of some of his colleagues, Gregory resigned and went back to Nazianzus, where he administered the church until the election of his friend Eulalios in replacement of his father, about two years

later. He retired again to the family domain in Arianzum, where he dedicated himself until his death in 390 to asceticism and mystical writings—
chiefly poetic in form.

With Gregory of Nazianzus, the style of Christian spirituality of late
antiquity was no longer mediated by social leadership, as it was in Basil's
episcopal career. The same educated mysticism that drew Basil to the founding of monastic and pastoral institutions flowered in Gregory's gift as a
classical orator and as a poet. His genuine contribution to the history of
Christian spirituality in the ancient church is the invention of an appropriate metaphysics to support the triune notion of God. Gregory made the first
explicit use of the title "God" for the Spirit; he also distinguished three
"persons" or "hypostases" in the unique Godhead. With all the refined lyrics
of the Hellenistic tradition, Gregory introduced his own life into the realm
of theological inquiry as a source of autobiographical revelation (even before
Augustine). The poem On His Life (De vita sua) describes the inner life of
his soul with the accents of Augustine's Confessions. In his last decade he
wrote no fewer than four hundred poems, which reflected historical,
dogmatic, and autobiographical needs. He was the first Christian author to
publish a collection of his letters, and his epistolary legacy remains unchallenged in the Greek-speaking churches.

This brilliant and paradoxical figure with an innate talent for the creation
of literary forms was attracted by contemplative silence and ascetic macera-
tions more than by anything else. In his public speeches, he gave dramatic
utterance to his regret at the loss of privacy in being forced into clerical
office; his dedication to the church was as strong as his criticism of its
members, mainly priests and bishops, was severe. His denunciations of the
decay of clerical institutions were delivered with the pathos of an Old Testament prophet. Almost half of his addresses and sermons were delivered in
Constantinople between 373 and 381: among these twenty-two speeches,
seventeen were given in the small Anastasia, probably a private basilica.
Gregory denounced with learned disdain what he considered theological
propaganda in the streets and among the working class, and he showed no
interest in popular religion, which he viewed as linked with the cult of the
martyrs. His constant focus was the public, pro-Nicaean profession of trinitarian faith. In order to keep orthodoxy alive, he believed in the magisterium
of bishops and priests, but only if they were contemplatives, philosophically
trained. One of the most incisive critiques against the clergy of his time is
found in his panegyric for Athanasius (2 May 379), in which he insisted on
the need for biblical training for the clergy.

The most intimate encounter of the Christian and biblical traditions with
the Hellenistic mysticism in the Roman Empire is thus characterized by the

achievement of Gregory of Nazianzus. Classical images and allusions are threaded through his theological discourse, and his mystical sensitivity, marked by the metaphysics of late antiquity, communicates a new life to the Scriptural language of his sermons and poems.

## Gregory of Nyssa (ca. 331–after 394)

A younger brother of Basil, Gregory was reared at Annesi by his mother and his oldest sister Macrina before he went to school in Caesarea in 348. Between 360 and 364 he married Theosibia, who gave birth to a son, whom they named Cynegios. From 365 to 372 Gregory followed the profession of rhetorician. In 372, Basil who as bishop of Caesarea was already nearing the end of his brief career, asked Gregory to write a treatise on virginity, his first literary work, and appointed him bishop of Nyssa. After Basil's death, Gregory increased his doctrinal contributions far beyond the limits of his local church, and after the loss of his wife in 385 he intensified his dedication to monastic experience.

Most of Gregory's mystical writings were composed during the last ten years of his life, for example, *Life of Moses* (*De vita Moysis*), *Christian Way of Life* (*De instituto Christiano*), the fifteen *Homilies on the Song of Songs*, as well as the *Catechetical Oration* (*Oratio catechetica*). The *Creation of Man* (*De opificio hominis*) was probably written in an earlier period, after the death of Basil in January 373. The *Life of Macrina*, a masterpiece of Christian hagiography, followed quickly after the death of his sister in December 379. A few liturgical and dogmatic sermons and two or three panegyrics are also transmitted. In two homilies entitled *On the Love of the Poor*, both probably pronounced in Lent of 382, Gregory describes in a striking way the stark contrasts within the society of Nyssa and controls in a masterly fashion the sophisticated techniques of a professional *rhētōr* in his moving address. On Easter, Pentecost, and Christmas his sermons underscored the symbolic meaning of the liturgical feast; two other speeches were delivered at the councils of Constantinople in 381 and 383.

Gregory of Nyssa was the most systematic thinker among the Cappadocian fathers. After Origen, and in the pure style of a deepened Origenian vision, he elaborated the richest doctrine of Christian mysticism in the ancient Greek-speaking churches.

All the classical features of Christian Platonism are rejuvenated in Gregory's mystical theory. As a "microcosmos" created by God according to the harmony of the "macrocosmos," the individual human being experiences a divine image-likeness in the mind, the free will, and virtues, according to the revelation in Genesis 1:26. The primordial fall of Adam and Eve, which no longer postulates the Gnostic doctrine of a human preexistence as in Origen, signals the very nature of humanity, its metaphysical position on the border of two worlds—the spiritual or "noetic" one, and the material one. Being thus "positioned on the frontier" (*methorios*), fallen humanity keeps in principle the intuition of the "other," or invisible, world. Gregory insists on the present limitations of humanity in his repeated analyses of the moral, physical, or social miseries of the human condition and humanity's need of a divine savior; but he overcomes (at least in most instances) what would lead to dualistic pessimism by insisting on the incarnational foundation of Christian theology. Christ united us to himself and restored to us the divine friendship we had at the beginning. Within the framework of a restored Origenian soteriology, Gregory's eschatology propounds the doctrine of the incarnation of the Logos that was popularized by Athanasius. Christ's personal humanity redirects the dynamism of the universal human nature toward the divine in liberating it from the cycles of matter. We have been taught by Christ the necessary practice of the virtues. We have Christ himself as a source of our growth in the knowledge of God. The ongoing resemblance between God and us rests on the incarnate Christ, who will lead us to the perfection of such a resemblance, for in Christ alone God has become visible and therefore imitable.

On two distinct levels of mystical experience human beings are introduced into the contemplative life, which anticipates celestial beatitude. The first level is that of the "mirror of the soul": the divine illumination that occurs in the exercise of the "spiritual senses." Here humans recover a vision of the cosmos as created by God, which they had lost in their sinful passions:

> If a man's heart has been purified from every creature and unruly affections, he will see the Image of the Divine Nature in his own beauty. I think that in this short saying the Word expresses some such counsel as this: There is in you, human beings, a desire to contemplate the true good; but when you hear that the Divine Majesty is exalted above the heavens, that Its glory is inexpressible, Its beauty ineffable, and Its Nature inaccessible, do not despair of ever beholding what you desire. It is indeed within your reach; you have within yourselves the standard by which you apprehend the Divine. For He Who made you did at the same time endow your nature with this wonderful quality. For God imprinted on it the likeness of the glories of His own Nature, as if molding the form of a carving into wax. But the evil that has been poured all around the nature bearing the Divine Image has rendered useless to you this wonderful thing that lies hidden under vile coverings. If, therefore, you wash off by a good life the filth that has been stuck on your heart like plaster, the Divine beauty will again shine forth in you.
>
> For the Godhead is purity, freedom from passion, and separation from all evil. If therefore these things be in you, God is indeed in you. Hence, if your thought is without any alloy of evil, free from passion, and alien from stain,

7. *John Chrysostom*, Hagia Sophia,
Istanbul, 11th century

*Ambrose*, Cappella di Vittore,
Ciel d'Oro, Milan, 5th century

you are blessed because you are clear of sight. You are able to perceive what is invisible to those who are not purified, because you have been cleansed; the darkness caused by material entanglements has been removed from the eyes of your soul, and so you see the blessed vision radiant in the pure heaven of your heart. (Gregory of Nyssa *Homily 6 on the Beatitudes* [*PG* 44, cols. 1269D–1272B])

At the second and highest level of mystical experience reigns the darkness of the soul, in which the purified human being faces the infinite incomprehensibility of God. Here it finds itself engaged in a process of divinization through its perception of the presence of God in the soul. This process has no end; even in the celestial afterlife it continues to plunge humanity into the abyss of the mystery of God. The soul unites itself to the innermost presence of God as in a mystical marriage. Here again we find the assumption of a Neoplatonic trend in Gregory's mysticism, although he stresses that this spiritual achievement presupposes Christ's incarnation. The endless identification with Christ postulates the wound of divine love (Song of Songs 4:9), the crucified and pastoral unity between the church and Christ, the bridegroom. The mystical ascension means, first of all, that the soul is drawn toward the one who condescended to come down into it:

We can be lifted up toward the Most High only if the Lord who lifts up the humble has stooped down to what is below. That is why the soul that rises toward the things that are above asks the help of the Transcendent One and begs Him to descend from His majesty in order to become accessible to those who are below. (Gregory of Nyssa *Homily 10 on the Song of Songs* [*PG* 44, col. 988A])

Some of the dominant themes of Philo and of Origen are recapitulated in Gregory of Nyssa's mystical theory. The whole Alexandrian allegory of salvation as a partaking of divine transcendence revives in a unique metaphysical and literary celebration, but it is important to keep in mind that the Nyssean doctrine rests firmly on the Gospels and the Pauline message.

Further exploration of Gregory's dogmatic works, such as the books *Against Eunomius* or the *Refutation of Apollinaris* (*Antirrheticus adversus Apollinarem*), would reveal him as a fierce dialectician who often displayed quite candidly the intellectual and social prejudices of his class and time. Nevertheless, his doctrinal achievement represents the high point of the Cappadocians' contribution to the history of Christian theology. Basic spiritual convictions supported his fight against heresy, and they nourished as well his imaginative speculation about the afterlife. Their deep coherency is philosophically well articulated: God's absolute incomprehensibility is a logical principle for our created mind and finite nature. Through our own spiritual structure and through the universal mind establishing a harmony of the cosmos, the divine transcendence lies open to us as we ascend the path of virtue. The history of humankind, as witnessed by the Bible and discussed by philosophers, is a vast allegorical fresco of the drama of humanity's fall and of its salvation. It is the outstanding merit of Gregory to present a genuine synthesis of these basic convictions in authentic Christian terms.

## John Chrysostom (344/54–407)

Born in Antioch of noble and rich parents, John was trained by one of the most famous rhetoricians of his time, Libanios. The best Antiochene exegete of the fourth century, Diodorus of Tarsus, initiated him into theological matters. Chosen by the bishop Meletius, John was baptized and soon made lector in the main Christian church of Antioch in his early twenties. After two eremitic years that were damaging to his health, he became a deacon in 381 and was ordained a priest in 386, with a special mandate for preaching. From 386 to 397 in Antioch, and from 398 to 404 in Constantinople—after his unwilling promotion to the episcopacy—he excelled in the pulpit. His brilliant oratorical gifts never weakened the fiery spirituality of his ascetic ideal. John's many surviving sermons, preserved through private stenographers, still offer very rewarding reading. "Outspoken and direct, they remain today the most readable and edifying of all discourses among those of the Church Fathers, and are also a vivid source for the social history of the age."[1] A victim of his success, John died in bitter exile in Armenia.

About twenty years after the Cappadocians but still rooted in the same cultural setting, John was named "Golden Mouth" for his spectacular career in the pulpits of Antioch and Constantinople. More than Basil and the two Gregorys, John Chrysostom witnesses to the evangelical ground of their common spirituality. In his underscoring of the ethical issues faced by Christians—but too often ignored—he never tired of placing the Scriptures before them and inviting his audiences to contemplate Christ in vivid paraphrases of the Gospels or of the apostle Paul. He was enthusiastically dedicated to the latter.

During his decade as a priest in Antioch, John addressed the congregation thirty-two times in a series of commentaries on Romans, the longest and most comprehensive homiletic explanation of the epistle ever realized in the ancient church. In the same years, John preached forty-four sermons on 1 Corinthians, about thirty on 2 Corinthians, about twenty-five on Galatians, twenty-four on Ephesians, eighteen on 1 Timothy, ten on 2 Timothy, six on Titus, and three on Philemon. During the troublesome years in Constantinople, John completed his Pauline exegesis with at least fifteen sermons on Philippians, twelve on Colossians, and sixteen on 1 and 2 Thessalonians.

In the last months of his office he delivered thirty-four homilies on Hebrews. In other words, we possess about 280 of John's sermons, which communicate his knowledge of the letters of Paul. Hundreds of other sermons are transmitted—on Genesis, the prophets, Matthew, John, the Acts of the Apostles, and so on.

The dominant themes of John's powerful preaching are those of the traditional Antiochene catechesis. In a famous series of sermons entitled *On God's Incomprehensibility* (*De incomprehensibilitate Dei*), he pours forth a popular and oratorical adaptation of the Cappadocian anti-Arian theology. His dogmatic idea of Christ is as incarnational as possible, in the line of the Athanasian tradition; at the same time his christology is marked by the ethical and historical emphases proper to the exegetical teaching of Diodorus in Antioch. His "socialistic" speeches, filled with invectives against the ruling class, including the imperial family, denounce all sorts of abuses and injustices. The homilies for the main feasts of the liturgical year and paradoxically also a series of eight Antiochean homilies, *Against the Jews,* which were delivered in 386 and 387, reflect the needs and the spirit of the Christian community in its ritual gatherings. His notion of the Christian priesthood was the focus of a burning dedication to the church, which he considered the divine institution that actualized God's incarnate presence in society:

> For the office of the priesthood is executed upon earth, yet it ranks amongst things that are heavenly, and with good reason. For it was neither an angel nor an archangel nor any other created power, but the Paraclete Himself that established that ministry and commanded that men yet abiding in the flesh should imitate the functions of angels. Wherefore it behooves the priest to be as pure as if he stood in heaven itself amidst those Powers. . . . Picture to yourself Elias, and the immense multitude standing around, and the victim laid on the altar, and all in stillness and deep silence, while the prophet alone prays; and the fire forthwith descends from heaven upon the altar. Then pass from thence to the sacrifice which is now offered, and you will behold what is not only wonderful, but what exceeds all admiration. For the priest stands bringing down not fire, but the Holy Spirit, and he prays long not that fire may descend from heaven and consume the oblation, but that grace may descend upon the victim, and through it inflame the souls of all and render them brighter than silver fire-tried. . . .
>
> It is to priests that spiritual birth and regeneration by baptism are entrusted. By them we put on Christ, and are united to the Son of God and become members of that blessed head. Hence we should regard them as more august than princes and kings, and more venerable than parents. For the latter begot us of blood and the will of the flesh, but priests are the cause of our generation from God, of our spiritual regeneration, of our true freedom and sonship according to grace. (John Chrysostom *On the Priesthood* [*De sacerdotio*] 3.4–6 [*PG* 48, cols. 642B–644A])

No wonder John's warm and elegant speeches for the defense of religion in the light of the Gospel message became paradigmatic in his lifetime and have been imitated ever since. Countless pseudo-Chrysostomian homilies were added to his oratorial legacy, but the freshness and vigor of his own evangelical spirituality radiates, unmatched, through the centuries.

## Hilary of Poitiers (310/20–367)

Born in Poitiers, Hilary shows in his *Homilies on Psalms* (*Tractatus super psalmos*) a genuine acquaintance with the wealthy Gallo-Roman upper class of his time (see 118.14; 123.2; 140.14; 143,23; 146.13 [*PL* 9, cols. 540A, 675C–676A, 831CD, 853BD, 875A]). He describes his own conversion in philosophical terms that suggest a mature and adult decision. He was trained by excellent grammarians and rhetoricians, probably in Bordeaux. Hilary was married and was the father of a daughter called Abra. He was baptized by Maximinus, bishop of Trier, and it is possible that he sojourned for a while in this imperial capital of the West as an official or as a businessman. The Christian community of Poitiers elected him as its bishop around 350, and soon after this, in the aftermath of a pro-Arian synod held by Constantius II in Milan in 353, the Gallic bishops recognized him as their leader in their short-lived attempt to oppose the emperor's religious politics. Hilary was exiled by Constantius and sent to Phrygia, but he did not experience close confinement during the exile, which lasted from September 356 to the spring of 360.

On his return journey he went to Rome, where it is probable that he met the local bishop, Liberius, who had lately returned from his own banishment. In the fall of 360 or in spring 361, Hilary was again in Gaul. Almost immediately he became a key figure at the synod of Lutetia, the nucleus of modern Paris and then the headquarters of the new Caesar, Julian. There, and in a series of similar meetings, he succeeded in rallying the whole episcopacy of Gaul to pro-Nicaean orthodoxy. He also founded the monastery of Ligugé, near Poitiers, and the ascetic Martin of Tours was its first abbot (Hilary had admitted Martin to the ranks of the clergy in 355–356). The story of the inauguration of monasticism in Gaul is inextricably linked with the tales of the zeal and the wonders associated with Hilary's name. He died "in his home-town during the sixth year after his return," that is, in 367.[2]

During his short episcopal career Hilary emerged suddenly on the Gallo-Roman scene as a spiritual pioneer who acted on the scale of the whole imperial Christianity of his time. Before him the Latin-speaking churches of the West had produced Tertullian and Cyprian in North Africa and Novatian in Rome as creative leaders who oriented Christian spirituality in a way appropriate to the Western culture. Hilary learned much from the Africans in ethical matters and in basic Christian catechesis. He also knew the apologetical writings of Lactantius, another African, but Hilary's spiritual achievement is really his own.

At the very start of his ministry in Poitiers he wrote his *Commentary on Matthew* in the form of an *opus continuum*, the first biblical commentary of that sort ever conceived in Latin. The most remarkable feature of this carefully styled writing is its spiritual and symbolic richness, which can be attributed to Hilary's systematic use of what he called the *ratio typica* of the Matthean verses he discussed. This *ratio* allowed Hilary to discover divine mysteries related to Christian salvation behind the letter of the Gospel. Such a use of hermeneutical tools, which was taken over from his classical training, anticipated the creativity he showed in his encounter with the works of Origen while he was in the Orient.

In the first months of his exile in Phrygia, Hilary deepened his meditation on Scripture in a more polemical and dogmatic way by conceiving a presentation, in three books, of his faith in the divine Trinity. This treatise, *On Faith*, was later expanded by a refutation of current Arian exegesis and arguments and grew into no fewer than twelve books—Hilary's doctrinal masterpiece, *On the Trinity (De trinitate)*. In the introduction Hilary summarizes a report of his own conversion. This autobiographical sketch, contemporaneous with the long poem of the same type by Gregory of Nazianzus, anticipates Augustine's *Confessions*, which would be published one generation later. It keeps the attention focused on the intellectual itinerary of the religious conversion. The stages of this "quest for the Truth" begin with an experience of common sense (*opinio communis*, chap. 1) and then move on to a spiritual concern and dissatisfaction (*animus sollicitus*, chap. 4), a renovated religious awareness (*religiosa intelligentia*, chap. 6), a beautiful understanding (*pulchra intelligentia*) of God's infinity (chap. 7), and a theological training (*animus studiis imbutus*) that aims at the mind's peace in a faithful conversion (*fides*, chap. 8). The mind (*mens*) then undergoes a crisis in trying to transcend the common sense (chap. 10). It is perturbed (*trepida et anxia*) before being gifted by hope (*spes*, chap. 11). It becomes a happy mind (*mens laeta*) in being reborn by faith (chap. 12). This faith is total (*absolutissima fides*, chap. 13) and leads to a mind "secured in a self-confident rest" (*conscio securitatis suae otio*), in which "it relaxes, rejoicing in its fulfilled expectations" (*spebus suis laeta requieverat*, chap. 14).

The basic anti-Arian principles of trinitarian theology are taught in the remaining books of Hilary's *On the Trinity* with the same clear-minded firmness that distinguished the autobiographical prologue. The sole aim of the author is to capture the "complete meaning" (*absoluta significatio*) of

Scripture and to approach its "understanding beyond reasoning" (*inexplicabilis intelligentia*) through a more interiorized spiritual research. All through this splendid account of his trinitarian convictions Hilary multiplies in the form of prayers and comments the personal confession of his inability to speak correctly about the triune Godhead, yet in his logical capacity he surpasses Athanasius of Alexandria's writing on the same topic in his *Against the Arians.*

After his return from exile, Hilary published his vast *Homilies on Psalms.* In *On the Trinity* he had initiated his Latin fellow bishops into the dogmatic issues of the Arian controversy; in *Homilies on Psalms* he translated for them the exegetical teaching of Origen about the Psalter. Thus, Hilary represents the first mediator between the Old Latin versions of the Bible and the Septuagint. In a work of smaller size, the *Book of Mysteries* (*Liber mysteriorum*), he gives a complementary presentation of the hermeneutical rules of biblical exegesis. Finally, he composed a collection of hymns (*Liber hymnorum*). Some of these mystical and heavily theological poems were still sung in the liturgy of Toledo during the seventh century. They barely anticipated the more poetical and more famous hymns invented by Ambrose of Milan.

As a mediator between the Greek East and the Latin West in the Roman Empire, Hilary focused on christology and ethics in his pioneering contribution to Western spirituality. He delivered to the churches in Gaul, Italy, and Spain a spiritual message that combined solid doctrinal inquiry with a fervent reading of Scripture and a very responsible sense of the moral concerns of his society.

## Ambrose of Milan (334–397)

A contemporary of Hilary, Ambrose shared the Gallic bishop's position as a cultural mediator between Christian spiritualities in the eastern and western parts of the empire. He transmitted to the Latin churches the Alexandrian heritage by translating and paraphrasing Philo, Origen, and Athanasius; and he adapted the older Platonic tradition, as well as the more recent views of Neoplatonism, to Christian beliefs. In his busy twenty-two years as bishop of Milan, he sought transcendent truth with the fiery imagination and the rhetorical gifts typical of the scholarship of his times. His unique grandeur was to become a saint in the guise of a Roman aristocrat.

In the figure of Ambrose (a man only five feet four inches tall), the Roman ideal of Christianity, the *Romanitas Christiana*, reached its full stature. Close to his flock as a local pastor, Ambrose also exercised true statesmanship in dealing with different emperors, and his involvement in pastoral leadership and imperial politics never weakened his ties with a vast circle of friends and relatives. He was by nature dedicated to law and order. Although he faced unpredictable events in dramatic circumstances, his reactions were always measured and deliberate. Fearless in conflicting situations, he had a natural authority that led him to assume responsibilities with a clear view of the central issues. Ambrose created a social community with a fine sense of the necessary institutional initiatives. In defining the powers of church and state, he deliberately adhered to the newness of Christianity but also assumed the whole substance of his past. Thus, he transcended cultural boundaries in orchestrating foreign elements into his mellifluous celebration of the supreme moral values he identified in the Christian vision. A serene and powerful servant of the church in the episcopal office, Ambrose sanctified the national identity of his people and fused into a spiritual unity his faith in Rome and his adoration of Christ.

Ambrose was born in Trier about 334 in the immediate vicinity of the imperial court, and he spent twenty-five years, from 340 to 365, with his family in Rome. Only one childhood incident was recorded by his biographer, Paulinus. A swarm of bees swooped down and rested upon the eyes and lips of the sleeping child, which symbolized the future eloquence of the saint, sweet and nourishing as honey. Ambrose's education in Rome was that of the aristocratic upper class. When he was not yet twenty years old, his sister Marcellina received the veil of a consecrated virgin in a solemn ceremony held by the Roman bishop in the Vatican basilica. Throughout his twenties Ambrose witnessed the disruptions in the church that resulted from the Arian dispute. His own firmness in matters of faith when he assumed the role of a high-level defender of orthodoxy may reflect this earlier experience.

In about 370, having completed his formation in preparation for a career in public administration, Ambrose was named *consularis,* or governor, of the province of Aemilia-Liguria in northern Italy, whose capital was Milan. He exercised his office mainly as a judge in public affairs. In spring 374 he entered the Christian basilica on the day of the election of a new bishop, intending to restore enough calm among the opposed factions in order to avoid a riot. The opposing factions suddenly acclaimed him as bishop. He was not yet baptized, only a catechumen, and as such without complete Christian education. After a vain attempt to flee into a monastic solitude, Ambrose was baptized on 30 November of the same year and consecrated bishop a week later without having gone through the normal stage of the presbyterate.

Immediately after his consecration Ambrose handed over his immense wealth to the church. His brother Satyrus resigned his own position as provincial governor and came to Milan, where he acted as the financial manager of the episcopal palace. We can still read the letter of Basil of Caesarea congratulating Ambrose for his election. The new bishop's administration of the Catholic community of Milan was characterized by prudence, and he avoided any public reference to the Arian opposition. In his first writings he spoke of silence and discretion as the virtues most needed by militant Christians. He spent his nights and his rare free daylight hours in learning the doctrine of the church and in improving his scriptural training, with the Greek tradition as his school and the great Origen as his foremost instructor. From the beginning until his death, the many treatises he published arose out of sermons to his people or instructions to his clergy. As a rule, Ambrose edited his speeches in the quiet silence of the night, writing his works with his own hand.

In 377 he edited various sermons and exhortations, collected in three books entitled *Concerning Virgins* (*De virginibus*), complemented by *Concerning Widows* (*De viduis*), for a woman attracted by a second marriage. Against local criticism he justified his opinions in 378 in a treatise *On Virginity* (*De virginitate*). Ambrose did not reject marriage but stressed the evangelical excellency of virginity. The Son of God having chosen a virgin for his mother, "I am comparing good things with good things so that what is better may be seen more clearly" (*Concerning Virgins* 1.7 [*PL* 16, col. 209C). In the fall of 378, he gratified the nineteen-year-old emperor, Gratian, with two books, *On the Faith* (*De fide*), in which he began to struggle with Arianism. Two other books were added to the treatise near the end of 380, which collected recently delivered sermons. In March 381, the bishop sent to Gratian three books entitled *On the Holy Spirit* (*De spiritu sancto*), in which he imitated and partly copied Didymus the Blind and Basil. The clarity of Ambrose's style made his catechesis more convincing than its Greek models. Probably in 383 Ambrose incorporated two sermons for catechumens under the title *On Abraham* (*De Abraham*). A second book added a rather abstruse dissertation, but it contained too many etymologies, Greek quotations, and an almost fanatical denial of the values offered by pagan philosophers. In the midst of the battles that filled up the next ten years, Ambrose edited a tremendous number of homilies in the form of theological and ascetical treatises. Thus a vast compilation emerged: the *Hexameron*, based on Basil and Hippolytus of Rome; *On Sacraments* (*De sacramentis*); and commentaries on many books from Scripture, for example, *On Psalm 118* and *On the Gospel of Luke*. In *On the Duties of Ecclesiastics* (*De officiis ministrorum*), patterned after Cicero, he formulated the ethical rules imposed on Christians and showed clearly how the Christian's fidelity to the dominant form of the Nicaean orthodoxy meant, in his mind, true fidelity to Rome itself. Like Hilary, he crowned his literary career by composing hymns, though only a very few of them have survived.

Ambrose died on 4 April 397, in the same year that Augustine, whom he had baptized during his Easter vigil in Milan ten years before, published his *Confessions*. Therein the young bishop of Hippo tells the reader that he could not sleep during the night after the funeral of his mother. He tried a bath but found no relief. Then he slept a little, remembering as in a dream a hymn from Ambrose:

> For Thou art the
> Maker of all, the Lord,
> And Ruler of the height,
> Who, robing day in light, hast poured
> Soft slumbers o'er the night . . .
> (*Confessions* 9.12, citing Ambrose
> *Hymn* 2 [*PL* 16, col. 1473])

Later on, when accused by Julian of Eclanum in 429 of having invented original sin, Augustine replied, "My teacher in this matter was Ambrose." In his doctrine on sacraments and some general principles of ecclesiology, as well as in biblical hermeneutics, Ambrose exercised a decisive influence on his African convert.

The deepest continuity between Ambrose and Augustine, and perhaps the most significant feature of their fundamental contributions to Western spirituality, is linked with their role as preachers. Ambrose, the outstanding Roman moralist, and Augustine the religious genius from North Africa, incarnate the vital creativeness of Christianity in the spiritual crisis of their time, primarily because they preached to their ordinary congregations what they taught in their metaphysical and spiritual treatises. Driven by pastoral concerns, they effected a most unexpected and profound renewal of the classical heritage by submitting the written style of the contemporary intellectual elite to mediation through a spoken message addressed to the most popular audiences.

## Jerome (331–420)

Born in Stridon, Dalmatia, near the border of Pannonia (modern Yugoslavia), Jerome was the son of a wealthy landowner who had enough money to give Jerome a very expensive education. In the early 340s, he became a student of the grammarian Aelius Donatus in Rome, but he did not need to seek an occupation at the end of the year-long training by Roman rhetoricians. As a student Jerome had started collecting a library, which became in later years the most important private collection of the period. Another aspect of Jerome's student years is mentioned by J. N. D. Kelly, who said that "in youth and early manhood Jerome was strongly sexed."[3]

Jerome tells us that he was born into a Christian family, though he was only baptized in Rome around 366. After concluding his studies he went with a friend to Trier, where he copied two works of Hilary, *On the Synods* and the *Homilies on Psalms*. He met there for the first time Christian hermits, and he recognized the call to a much more dedicated form of Christian life. Soon after, in the circle of the bishop of Aquileia, Chromatius, he made the acquaintance of Evagrius of Antioch, famous for his elegant and widely read free translation of Athanasius's *Life of Anthony*. Jerome's departure for Antioch in 372 was marked by a painful rupture with his relatives.

In the Syrian desert for two or three years, then in Antioch itself from 376 to 382, Jerome began a more careful reading of Christian authors in the place of Cicero and the classics. Using young monks as copyists, he focused on biblical studies, for which he learned Syriac and Greek, while a Jewish convert started him in Hebrew. He was instructed in historical methods and in allegorical hermeneutics, and he became acquainted with the works of Apollinarius of Laodicea and Didymus the Blind. His first work was a *Life of Paul the First Hermit*, partly inspired by Athanasius's *Life of Anthony*. In Constantinople in 379 or 380, he was impressed by Gregory of Nazianzus, who introduced him to the works of Origen. He translated Origen's *Homilies on Jeremiah* and *On Ezechiel*. Back in Rome from 382 to 385, Jerome used his language skills, especially Hebrew, in working for Pope Damasus as a theological counselor and a very active translator. He put into Latin Didymus the Blind's *On the Holy Spirit* and Origen's commentary and two homilies on the Song of Songs. At the request of Damasus, he started the revision (or replacement) of the existing Latin translations of the Bible and the production of a single standard version. At the same time he gave session after session on Scripture to a group of upper-class women and girls who met on the Aventine with Marcella and Paula, two widows of illustrious descent and vast fortune who lived in personal seclusion and continuous austerity. Public opposition both to his new translations of the Gospels and the Psalms and to his excessive propaganda for virginity and asceticism drove him out of Rome in August 385 and back to Antioch. From there he undertook with Paula an unprecedentedly elaborate pilgrimage to Jerusalem, to many parts of the Holy Land, as well as to Alexandria and to the monastic areas in the Nitrian desert.

Residing in Bethlehem from autumn 386 to early 393, Jerome worked hard on his translations of Origen's biblical commentaries. After a few preparatory researches (*Hebrew Questions* and *Hebrew Names*), he started in 390 an entirely fresh translation of the Old Testament based directly on the

Hebrew, and he completed this astonishing task in 405, not without having dictated during that time numerous commentaries on the books of the Bible. These years were punctuated by violent quarrels with a former friend, Rufinus, and with the local bishop in Jerusalem and arguments against Jovinian and Pelagius, whose opinions he regarded as heretical. Unfortunately, he blindly supported the ambitious patriarch of Alexandria, Theophilus, in his shameful attacks against John Chrysostom. Warm-hearted, kind to the poor and the distressed, easily reduced to tears by their sufferings, Jerome was also inordinately vain and petty, jealous of rivals, morbidly sensitive and irascible, hagridden by imaginary fears.[4] His *Dialogues against the Pelagians* (*Dialogi contra Pelagianos*) and a few virulent letters were his last outbursts.

The problems of his personality, which indicated psychoneurotic imbalances, make it difficult to place Jerome in the front ranks of the saints of the ancient church. The extravagances of his campaign to exalt celibacy above marriage and his feverish studies, not to mention the restless controversies, show the same fateful limitations of his mind. But he still achieved a work of enduring importance for Christian spirituality. His version of the Old Testament raised the vulgar Latinity of fourth- and fifth-century Christians to the heights of great literature. His knowledge of Hebrew and his use of contemporary rabbinic exegesis contributed to a productive encounter with Judaism, like that of Origen in the third century, and for centuries provided an access for Western Christianity to the "Hebraic truth" of divine revelation. His biblical translations remained normative, as the so-called *Vulgata,* in all Latin-speaking churches until our time. In maintaining against his will his passionate love for classical authors, in absorbing—almost excessively—the Origenian and Christian Alexandrian literature, in reaching mastery over Syriac and Hebrew in an unusual way for his time, Jerome transmitted to the Western churches a priceless treasure of biblical information and spiritual edification. The appreciation of his legacy was apparent in the Medieval period, when his unquestioned popularity over the other church fathers was attested in a vast range of art works—whether he is regaled, quite anachronistically, in the purple robes of a cardinal or portrayed as the seminaked ascetic, rapt in biblical inspiration.

## Augustine of Hippo (354–430)

Augustine was born of poor parents in the small town of Thagaste in Roman Numidia (modern Souk Ahras, in Algeria). The determined ambition of Patricius, his father, and Monica, his Christian mother, together with the patronage of a rich fellow townsman, gave him a chance to develop innate gifts as a teacher. His years of studies in Madaura and Carthage until

375, though beneficial for his intellectual gifts, were also a time of unbridled sensuality. At the age of eighteen he entered into a common-law marriage, and a nameless woman would share his life for the next fifteen years. Their son, Adeodatus, died at the age of seventeen, in 390. Augustine's philosophical conversion to "wisdom," which resulted from his reading Cicero's *Hortensius,* was soon followed by his becoming a "hearer" among the Manichaeans for some nine years. He taught rhetoric in Carthage from 376 to 383 and from there he went to Rome. In the autumn of 384 he was sent to Milan, the seat of the imperial court, as the protégé of Symmachus, the prefect of Rome. His mother joined him a few months later. Her prayers (the efficacy of which was predicted by the local bishop, Ambrose), together with the support of a few close friends, guided Augustine out of the Milanese Platonic circle that had replaced the Manichaeans in his religious quest. Baptized with other catechumens by Ambrose in April 387, the young African forsook his career. After the death of Monica he went back to Rome, and before the end of 388 he was again in Thagaste. His monastic retreat was filled with writings against the Manichaeans and in defense of Christian faith. In 391, after his ordination in Hippo (modern Bône, in Algeria), he founded a monastery with a group of men, and they called themselves "servants of God," *servi Dei.* When he was consecrated as successor to the local bishop, Valerius, in 395, he was already a leading figure in African Christianity, thanks to his prolific writing and to his unquestioned ascendancy over his former friends, who were appointed bishops throughout Numidia. Augustine's passionate service to the church was characterized by brilliant sermons in Carthage and Hippo and countless letters to and decisive debates with schismatic Donatist bishops in a series of councils held in Carthage. From 412 on he was deeply involved in controversy concerning Pelagian views on divine grace and human freedom. A final battle with Arians—for example, Maximinus—marked the last years of his episcopacy until his death on 28 August 430.

As we stand on the threshold of the third millennium of Christianity, the literary legacy of Augustinian spirituality remains a vivid, unrivaled source of inspiration in the Western traditions, and no attempt at a brief summary can be adequate.[5] After an initial phase around the time of his baptism of imitating classical and Platonic literary models, Augustine focused on justifying God's spiritual nature and human free will against the Manichaeans in *On Genesis against the Manichaeans* (*De Genesi contra Manichaeos*) and in *On Free Choice* (*De libero arbitrio*). After he was ordained a priest, he collected his sermons in *Explanations of the Psalms* (*Enarrationes in Psalmos*), *On Faith and the Creed* (*De fide et symbolo*), and lectures on Romans, delivered in Carthage in July 394. His *Confessions,* written from 397 on, were addressed to his friends, mainly those who shared his monastic ideal, and served both as an apology and as an expression of the spiritual dimensions of his own journey through conversion to ecclesiastical ministry. In his main dogmatic works, such as On the Trinity (De trinitate), composed between 399 and 419, or On the City of God (De civitate Dei), composed from 413 to 427, a lifelong deepening of spiritual intensity illuminates the Augustinian thought. The "inner self" of the author had been analyzed in the Confessions with the acute philosophical interiority characteristic of the genius of late antiquity. Augustine considered this "inner self" to be the central issue in speaking of God and the Christian religion. He never changed his mind on this point. In his later teaching, such as On the Trinity or On Nature and Grace (De natura et gratia) (413–415) the theological analysis of the human self provided Augustine with new paradigms for his most sublime expositions of Christian dogmatics and apologetics. The same spiritual principle, nourished by the bishop's unremitting study of Scripture, also illuminated his ordinary preaching to his flock or to fellow bishops. With oratorical skills like those of John Chrysostom and with a wealth of systematic doctrinal insights—all the more striking in the poor pulpit of a Numidian bishop compared with those of the two Gregorys—in a variety of sermons Augustine introduced the immense spiritual treasures of antiquity into the church's basic language. He applied to the homiletic commentary on Scripture the gifts of a fine classical teacher, motivated by the pastoral care of a responsible bishop. After 400, Christian spirituality in the Latin West had to be "Augustinian"—a remarkable continuity unchallenged until the cultural ruptures that have marked the onset of modernity.

Early in his career, the African rhetorician, like Origen, had had a personal acquaintance with Gnosticism—for Augustine in its Manichaean variation. He shared also with the Alexandrian tradition a deep intellectual predilection toward Platonism, experienced by him in its Latin and Milanese revival. At the very moment of his conversion, he was linked with the spiritual legacy of Athanasius, whose Life of Anthony had such an impact on the first Christian monks in Trier. The story of their conversion fanned the ardor of his mystical passion in this crucial hour. With the wealth of Christian exegetical traditions at his back, Augustine interpreted Scripture, day after day, scrutinizing its letter, discussing its versions, and developing masterfully its allegories and its symbols. However much he received from the wider church, his affinity with African Christianity is manifest, especially in the intense demands and rigorous ethical concerns that inform the doctrines linking salvation and baptism, and in his whole ecclesiology.

Among the leading figures of the church in the fifth century Leo the Great in Rome (d. 461), Cyril of Alexandria (d. 444), Theodore of Mopsuestia, in the south of modern Turkey (d. 428), and Theodoret of Cyrus in Syria (d. 460) deserve more than the mere mention of their names. Like their colleagues, whose contributions were analyzed above (with the exception of Jerome), they ministered to their churches in the episcopal office. Leo excepted, they all also published extensive commentaries on the Bible. They applied themselves with creative vigor to scriptural hermeneutics and at the same time expressed their dogmatic visions as theologians invested with full pastoral authority. Their spiritual message is addressed in the first instance to the churches dependent on their leadership. Pastoral in its immediate motivation, rhetorical in its primary expression, and literary in its legacy for later generations, this message remained intimately bound to the intellectual process of the hellenizing of the apostolic tradition. It seems significant that such a message was proclaimed by bishops in the most important centers of Christianity during the fourth and fifth centuries—the very period in which the growing power of the monastic movement was already announcing deep structural changes in the established Christian spirituality.

### Notes

1. Henry Chadwick, *The Early Church*, 186.
2. Sulpicius Severus *Chronicle* 2.45 (*PL* 20, col. 157B).
3. J. N. D. Kelly, *Jerome*, 21.
4. Kelly, 336.
5. For other aspects of the spiritual message of Augustine, see the articles by J. Leclercq ("Monasticism and Asceticism II. Western Christianity"), M. Clark, B. McGinn, J. Patout Burns, P. Brown, and J. Fontaine in the present volume.

### Bibliography

#### Studies

Chadwick, Henry. *The Early Church*. The Pelikan History of the Church 1. Harmondsworth: Penguin Books, 1967.

*On Athanasius:*
Grillmeier, Aloys. *Christ in Christian Tradition: From the Apostolic Age to Chalcedon (451)*. Translated by J. S. Bowden. New York: Sheed & Ward, 1965.
Kannengiesser, Charles. *Athanase d'Alexandrie évêque et écrivain*. Paris: Beauchesne, 1983.
——, ed. *Politique et théologie chez Athanase d'Alexandrie*. Paris: Beauchesne, 1974.

*On the Cappadocians:*

Bernardi, Jean. *La Prédication des pères cappadociens.* Paris: Presses universitaires de France, 1968.

Daniélou, Jean. *Platonisme et théologie mystique: Essai sur la doctrine spirituelle de Saint Gregoire de Nysse.* Paris: Aubier, 1944.

Dörrie, Heinrich, et al., eds. *Gregor von Nyssa und die Philosophie.* Leiden: Brill, 1976.

Fedwick, Paul J., ed. *Basil of Caesarea: Christian, Humanist, Ascetic.* 2 vols. Toronto: Pontifical Institute of Medieval Studies, 1981.

*On John Chrysostom:*

Baur, C. *John Chrysostom and His Time.* 2 vols. Westminster, MD: Newman Press, 1959–60.

Kannengiesser, Charles, ed. *Jean Chrysostome et Augustin.* Paris: Beauchesne, 1975.

*On Hilary of Poitiers:*

Doignon, Jean. *Hilaire de Poitiers avant l'exil.* Paris: Études augustiniennes, 1971.

Kannengiesser, Charles. "Hilaire de Poitiers (saint)." In *Dict. Sp.* 7, cols. 466–99.

*On Ambrose of Milan:*

Duval, Yves-Marie, ed. *Ambroise de Milan.* Paris: Études augustiniennes, 1974.

Paredi, A. *St. Ambrose, His Life and Times.* Notre Dame, IN: University of Notre Dame Press, 1964.

Pépin, Jean. *Théologie cosmique et théologie chrétienne (Ambroise, Exaém. I, 1, 1–4).* Paris: Presses universitaires de France, 1964.

*On Jerome:*

Kelly, J. N. D. *Jerome: His Life, Writings and Controversies.* New York: Harper & Row, 1975.

*On Augustine:*

Brown, Peter. *Augustine of Hippo: A Biography.* Berkeley: University of California Press, 1969.

Burnaby, John. *Amor Dei: A Study of the Religion of St. Augustine.* London: Hodder & Stoughton, 1938.

Van der Meer, F. *Augustine the Bishop: Church and Society at the Dawn of the Middle Ages.* New York: Sheed & Ward, 1961.

# Monasticism and Asceticism

## I. *Eastern Christianity*

### JEAN GRIBOMONT

THE SPIRITUAL LIFE OF MONASTICISM is essentially hidden in the depth of human consciousness; however, its visible manifestations are found in institutions, in social and political conduct, in architecture and the arts, and, most of all, in literary works, which, for the period under scrutiny, are the most easily accessible source. It is self-evident that the very earliest period almost completely eludes us, though this is also the most significant one. Afterward, the manifestations show a degree of unity within provincial borders; consequently, a logical plan of study would be one imposed by geographical boundaries rather than chronological sequence. We may not always be able to find the most essential or most valuable information, but we do possess sufficient records of facts and personalities to justify an attempt to produce a historical sketch, factual and complex, before endeavoring to present a synthesis.

## The Beginnings:
## East of the Greek World

From 311 C.E. on, at the time when the peace of Constantine took effect and the Christian population started to adjust itself to the social and cultural structure of the empire, there arose a movement that in a variety of ways expressed a rejection of the conventional worldly values. It was not uncommon for such a movement to degenerate into an extreme form of heresy or rebellion, as, for example, the Circumcellians of Northern Africa; at the other extreme one finds sometimes a loyal and wise support of the authorities. The earliest beginnings of this movement are to be found in the distant past among Syrians and Copts. Their evangelization goes back to Judeo-Christian traditions, which were less formal but more exacting in their disciplines—such as celibacy, asceticism, fasting, periods of prayer, and poverty in general—than was the custom in the urban communities of the Mediterranean region.

In about 324 and then again in 334 and in the subsequent period there appeared in Christian papyri in Egypt the term *monachos* (monk) with its derivatives and synonyms: *apotaktikos* (he who denies himself), anchorite (recluse, hermit), or simply brother.[1] The papyri testify that such people had a religious reputation, that they could bestow blessings and make intercessions as well as intervene in church politics, generally against the powerful. The terms are purely Greek and were even adopted as they stood by the Coptic dialects. But there is reason to believe that *monachos* renders a Syrian technical term meaning "sole," "single," just as the word "abbot," which was used in the same milieu, is of Syrian origin. The main emphasis was on celibacy; however, at first its principal aim was to attain an inner unity, the opposite of sexual duality, even going as far as a union with "the only begotten Son" of God.[2] This line of thought was found mainly in the apocryphal *Gospel of Thomas* and seems to have been more or less forgotten by the fourth century. The Greek term *agapētos,* most used in the feminine for virgins, had approximately the same meaning around Antioch.[3]

It was the reputation of the Egyptian monks that finally spread their vocabulary and the concepts it established throughout the Christian world. The movement did not, in fact, spread exclusively from Egypt, because it originated in many provinces independently. However, it developed according to the Egyptian model; that is, it owes a great deal to (1) the saintly character of a few great personalities; (2) the geography of the Nile valley, which made it relatively easy to lead a marginal existence reduced to the strictest minimum; (3) the fact that Roman oppression of the Egyptian peasants had already created a movement known as "anchoritism," which referred to the flight into the desert of peasants who refused to assume the burden of agricultural labor; (4) the circumstance that at that time Athanasius, the charismatic leader of the local church in Egypt, spent many years in exile, defying official imperial policy (Arianism), so that rather than harass the rebels he sought refuge with them.

Shortly before the monks appeared in the Egyptian desert, there were in Syria fraternities of "sons (or daughters) of the covenant," who pledged themselves at baptism to a life of celibacy, prayer, and lay ministry in villages that had been in contact with itinerant prophetic teaching.[4] They formed the nucleus of Christian communities. The authorities lent them their support, while taking precautions to avoid abuses either by imposing controls on the relations between the sexes or by preventing individuals from profiting in a material way without rendering any services.

To the east of Asia Minor, near upper Mesopotamia, there also existed some active ascetics, who wandered as far as Constantinople, the capital, which was then still under construction. This agitation, stimulated by a certain Eustathius, bishop of Sebaste in 357, shocked Eusebius of Nicomedia, the bishop at the imperial court. He assembled a synod in Gangra (ca. 340), severely condemned the lack of discipline found in the ascetic communities, and tried in vain to persuade the Armenian bishops, his neighbors to the east, to join him in anathematizing Eustathius, who lived in their territory. The synod no doubt misrepresented the Eustathians when it accused them of frowning upon such institutions as marriage, family, social order, and the clergy. However, under their influence wives frequently freed themselves from their husbands, and children from their parents; slaves and soldiers refused obedience; ecclesiastic laws were disregarded; and the economic rights of the clergy were ignored. Still, by helping the poor and nursing the sick, they earned fervent love and devotion.[5]

Great biblical events that had happened in the desert (the exodus, the life of the prophet Elijah, John the Baptist, Christ's forty days of fasting), as well as eschatological promises which made life in the world seem irrelevant, were enough to attract the newly converted to Palestine. The numbers of Palestinian ascetics began to increase as early as 360. Etheria, on a pilgrimage in 384 to visit the holy places, found that liturgies and hospices were developed and maintained everywhere by ascetics.

From the very beginning of the fourth century Eusebius of Caesarea was struck by the structural similarities between monastic spiritual goals and those of the Essenes or the Jewish "therapeuts." The Christian monastic settlements in the deserts of Scetis and Judah developed in almost the same locations as had the Jewish ascetical communities earlier. The time lapse and the deeply evangelical nature of monasticism do not exclude a possible influence through Judeo-Christianity and its high moral ideals.[6] With regard to Buddhist ascetics or Manichaean "perfect ones," the sources are silent;[7] nevertheless, it is unlikely that the similarities that do appear are accidental, and we may assume that some latent cultural exchanges did occur but were subsequently ignored by monastic chroniclers, who considered them unimportant. In any case, it is possible to discern in the Christian documents a reinterpretation of the motifs and themes of asceticism in the light of the biblical doctrines of creation and redemption, the Christian concept of sanctification and of the expected advent of the kingdom of God. The same holds true for Stoic and Platonic influences, which are even more easily traced.[8] Here we deal with concepts that were widely accepted and respected by the elite as moral and metaphysical considerations, which the faithful believed were rediscovered in the Scriptures. Nevertheless, the elements inherited from Greek humanism always underwent changes. Hellenic borrowings were never more than of secondary importance and were modified fundamentally by strong Christian beliefs. The writings of intellectuals, who were experienced in understanding doctrinal nuances and were carried away by the words and the prestige of the philosophers, are seldom reliable guides, for the ascetic movement drew its following mainly from among the ordinary people.

## The Myth of Anthony

After the shock produced by the example of the life and death of Jesus of Nazareth, simple men who were little qualified to express themselves in writing were inspired to produce the various writings of the New Testament. Thanks to the communities of believers, these texts were circulated much more widely than the most famous classics. Something similar occurred at the beginning of monasticism. The uneducated picked up and preserved oral traditions, which monastics later recorded conscientiously, omitting that which no longer corresponded to the monastic institutions as they had developed. Writers would also take it upon themselves to interpret and add personal touches to the traditional accounts.

There is little doubt that the first text to be widely distributed was the *Life of Anthony* (d. 356).[9] This almost contemporary biography was the work of Athanasius, a man of extensive culture and learning but, more important, the indomitable head of the Egyptian church. Exiled by the emperor and hiding in the desert, Athanasius unconditionally approved of and endorsed Anthony's model of heroism. At the same time he outlined a set of orthodox rules that were deeply conscious of the true meaning of asceticism and could serve those following in Anthony's footsteps. Athanasius claims that Anthony died at the age of 106, which presupposes that the saint retired into the desert around 270. If his longevity was exaggerated by the biographer, the date of his embracing monastic life would have occurred shortly before 300. Anthony, the son of a well-to-do farmer, renounced his worldly possessions, in accordance with the teaching of the Gospels. At first Anthony imitated the humble ascetics who dwelled in the vicinity of his village, but he gradually retreated further and further into solitude and asceticism. Having conquered the temptations of evil spirits, he was greatly revered for the power of his prayer and for his miracles which set the tone for countless imitators. Athanasius certainly depicted a life as it was actually lived; however, some details in the biography recall the famous model first conceived

by the Neoplatonists Porphyry and Iamblichus in the legend of Pythagoras.
Thus, the biographer emphasized the self-imposed silence, freely chosen
poverty, superhuman wisdom, and psychological stability of his hero. Any
suspicion of bitterness or violent inner conflict about his break with the
world was eliminated. Anthony's knowledge of God, of Christ, and of the
human heart stands out the more brilliantly.

In this account, Athanasius alternates narrative with homily, the latter
being obviously the proper ideas of the biographer-theologian. Attention
has recently been focused on seven "letters" of the hermit, which have been
deemed authentic but were lost in the Greek version.[10] In a somewhat confused manner, they develop the "Gnostic" concept of rediscovering through
ascetic discipline and the Jesus prayer one's nature as pure intellect, as God
had originally created it before the fall. Restored by the incarnation, it will
recover its primitive state of perfection on the day when all will be redeemed.
This purely intellectual reality determines the spiritual progress made each
day. Anthony takes up this theme, eliminating the Origenist biases that
could raise objections. The principal facts concerning the life of the saint,
however, were treated very differently by his biographer, Athanasius, who
on the one hand presented him in a heroic light and on the other adopted
the traditional manner of the hermits as illustrated in the *Apophthegmata*,
which shall be dealt with later.[11] The monks recalled an Anthony who did
the impossible to escape temptation, who found himself frequently on the
verge of despair, who at times lost the strength to pray, who recognized his
total ignorance of the divine mysteries and of the Scriptures, and whose
supreme value was love toward his neighbor. To the distant reader, however,
Athanasius presents a brilliant, victorious hero, who goes forth into the
desert to brave the devil undaunted and whose fasting and silence reach
God. His prophetic wisdom penetrates the human heart and there performs
miracles. These two portraits are not as contradictory as they might appear:
the first reflects the perceptions of the saint himself and his disciples, and
the second is the impression he made on the episcopate and the general
public. If the devil had ever succeeded in converting the "divine man" to the
second point of view, Anthony would have failed in his saintly calling and
made a sham of the outward beauty.

## Nitria, Scetis, the Cells

Anthony had withdrawn farther and farther away from the Nile toward the
Red Sea. However, the three most famous centers of monastic life established
by his disciples were located in close proximity to one another to the west
of the Delta between Alexandria and Cairo. Ammun retreated into the

valley of Nitria (today El-Barnugi) about 325; later he withdrew to an even more isolated area, the Cells (*kellia*) about eleven miles farther south. Macarius of Egypt sought out an even more isolated wilderness when he went to Scetis about 330 (the present Wadi-Natrum, where four Coptic monasteries survive to this day). Mention may be made of yet another Ammun, who was the superior at Pispir, which had been founded by Anthony, and was later (360?) promoted to bishop by Athanasius. Ammun exercised a certain moral authority over the monks of the region and left remarkable letters that are simple and forceful.[12] Life in these places was semisecluded. The cells of the monks were fairly close to one other to permit visiting, and during the night from Saturday to Sunday a common liturgy was celebrated. Recent excavations by a French-Swiss team at the Cells have thrown more light on many facts alluded to in written documents.

Since the time of Athanasius, the patriarchs of Alexandria had considerably enhanced their authority. Monasticism could hardly continue to expand for long without provoking some clashes and raising problems of discipline. The first conflicts arose between the anchorites on the question of anthropomorphism—or how the simple, unsophisticated monks perceived the God whom they contemplated in their prayers. They accepted in all simplicity the Old Testament version of the face of God the Father and of his majestic and very concrete interventions. The more educated attempted, in the tradition of the philosophers and of Origen, to lift up their minds to a completely incorporeal God, explaining the Scriptures in an allegorical manner. This was the position followed by the bishops, and the obstinate character of their opponents provoked conflicts with the ecclesiastical hierarchy. True, there was a certain danger that traditional idioms would lose part of their meaning in the clever subtle formulations of allegory. From the sublime to the ridiculous there is but a small step. Archbishop Theophilus, who at first had opposed the anthropomorphites, reversed his position completely and in 400 started a bitter persecution of the Origenist elite. His actions had severe repercussions throughout the Roman world—in Palestine, in Rome, and in Constantinople, where John Chrysostom paid dearly for granting protection to the fugitives. Ultimately, this conflict brought about the decline of the great spiritual tradition of Egyptian monasticism.

A great many sources provide information about the golden age of monasticism, before its decline, thanks to pilgrims in particular who came from near and far to gather local traditions. Thus we have the *History of the Egyptian Monks,* an account of a pilgrimage by a monk from Jerusalem, made in winter of 394–395, translated later into Latin by Rufinus;[13] and the *Lausiac History*[14] of Palladius, memoirs of the twelve years the author lived in the desert (388–400). These works contain mainly ancient legends. Rufinus and Jerome, at the same time, had spent a few years in Egypt; John Cassian, however, had received his monastic education there, and his important doctrinal works, the *Institutions* and the *Conferences of the Fathers*, written in Marseilles between 425 and 429, reflect that training. But the most vivid portraits of the life, the wisdom, and humility of the anchorites are contained in the *Apophthegms of the Fathers*.[15] These are presented in the form of a few words of comfort or advice, inserted into a short anecdote that is not guaranteed to be as authentic as the apophthegm itself, as an answer from the elder to a person seeking spiritual guidance. Constantly attentive to their own consciousness and human consciousness in general, these monks saw into the depth of the human heart and discovered the most secret twists of self-righteous pride or presumptuous visions of false piety. Many of the apophthegmata are recorded in the first person, and some of the fathers emerge as distinctive, often warmhearted characters. Well over a thousand of these apophthegmata can be considered authentic, about forty of them dating back to Anthony himself. The questions raised deal chiefly with growth and perseverance in the silence of the cell. The example of Anthony had shown what abyss separated the monks from the clergy, the churches, the philosophers, and the writers with their speculations. The desert fathers offered answers to real questions after long hours of humble prayer. These were transmitted by word of mouth from one generation to the next, reduced to the essential without regard for logic or style. They were compiled by the disciples Poemen and Isaiah shortly before the Monophysite schisms and the barbarian invasions caused the breakup of the communities originally established in the desert. These compilations of apophthegmata were afterwards expanded with much cumbersome second-rate material, usually borrowed from edifying tracts, which further developed the original line of thought but destroyed its simple purity. Modern editions strive to retain as many anecdotes as possible, which is indeed as it should be; but the critical reader ought to detach the *verba* that go back to the desert fathers from the rest of the material.

The fathers had no mean sense of humor, which they not only practiced with great humility but passed on to their disciples as a fine instrument of education. "The Blessed Archbishop Theophilus went out one day with a magistrate to visit Abbot Arsenius and he questioned the elder to hear him say a word. After a short silence the elder said to him: 'If I say a word, will you do it?' Receiving the promise, he replied: 'When you hear that Abbot Arsenius is in a certain place, don't go near'" (*Apophthegmata*, Arsenius 7). Of course, identifying the patriarch here has an important purpose: it emphasizes the saint's renown, his humility, and his spirit of independence, which had grown out of his love for solitude. We must also acknowledge that the monks claimed complete autonomy vis-à-vis the authorities. If we were to generalize, we could say that the subject matter of the *Apophtheg-mata*, and thus the milieu that carried the oral traditions, reflects the spirit of Theophilus by scrupulously omitting anything faintly resembling Origenism. Yet this hierarchical censorship has not distorted the tone of the material that was transmitted and eventually written down. Since these collections of anecdotes do not furnish us with a clear set of doctrines which guided the monks, sources other than the *Apophthegmata* must be brought in to complete the picture.

## Pachomius and Cenobitism

Anthony was the typical hermit, whose solitude was all too often disturbed by small organized colonies of anchorites who settled around him. He was also joined by disciples who wished to be near the elder. But many felt the need for a communal life, which not only would serve to educate the young novices but also would offer the possibility of better practicing the virtues: charity, perfect poverty, disregard for material possessions, and freedom from self-deception. Although the hardships of ascetic life might be less obvious in a cenobitic life-style, every self-seeking, covetous thought in the very depth of the soul would be uprooted and severely chastised. Complete sub-mission to the guidance of a spiritual father—so judiciously practiced at Scetis—would become an integral part of the structure of communal life, closely tied to manual labor, prayer, and the struggle against all the vices. Thus, "families" of ascetics began to settle in various places. The most suc-cessful community was founded at Tabennisi on the Upper Nile, by Pacho-mius, a remarkable organizer and true pioneer-sociologist.[16]

Pachomius was born about 290 and he died in 346 or 347. About 313 he asked to be baptized after having been deeply impressed by the love Chris-tians had for one another. His biographer stresses that Abba Palamon had taught Pachomius all the virtues necessary for an eremitical life and that it was by no means out of weakness that he chose a cenobitic life. In 324 he began to gather "devotees," but when the initial attempt failed he concluded that nothing could be achieved without complete poverty and unquestioning obedience—two points that took him well beyond the anchoritic practice. Within a few years he had a following of nine thousand monks, and these numbers are probably not exaggerated. In some cases already established communities joined him in search of firmer control and discipline. The elder had received no secular education, but, knowing the Scriptures by heart, he understood perfectly the Gospel meaning of Christian self-denial. He knew the value of authority and had a deep compassion for human frailty. His perception of God and humanity was lucid and down-to-earth. His disciples loved him, even idolized him; and in spite of his austerity he was at times insanely jealous. His charismatic authority understandably led to conflicts with the authority of the local bishop, but Athanasius in far-off Alexandria appreciated his zeal and supported him with sympathy and good will. When Pachomius died his community was thrown into disarray by power struggles and differences of opinion. Finally, his successors Horsiesi and Theodore restored order by reviving and strengthening his disciplines. The *Rules* published under his name consist mostly of the cenobitic rules he had instituted, though part of the actual text may have been written by his successors. His personal writings, the *Letters,* written in code for his subordinates, have yet to be deciphered by historians. Some catechisms are attributed to him and to his successors. These texts, full of gaps, have been preserved in Coptic; the Latin versions, which together with the *Rules* were translated by Jerome in 404 from an incomplete Greek copy, make it difficult to appreciate the original version.

Though all this material is of considerable value, by far the most interesting are the *Lives* of the saint, told and retold hundreds of times by his successors in order to keep his spirit powerfully alive among the brothers. They are vivid tales of his inner conflicts and of his (prolific) creative dialogues with Theodore. Toward the end of Theodore's life (368) they were recorded in writing, when the oral tradition of the Copts was in danger of disappearing. The oldest *Life,* written in Greek, was composed by "brothers-interpreters" who had some training in the field. Since it was written with a distant public in mind, perhaps not too sympathetic, some of the more extraordinary traits of the elder, such as his charismatic powers, his visions, and his occasional ruthlessness in governing his flock, were readily attenuated. The Coptic *Lives* (and their Arabic versions), at first written for internal use, were much closer to the oral traditions and present a more authentic picture, marvelous in every sense of the word. The reader who approaches this charismatic personality with love and sympathetic understanding will return with interest to the *Rules* and catechisms; for here, in the commonplace routine of daily life, one encounters the real genius of this man, whose followers could in the intimacy of communal life discover, just like the hermits, their real motives hidden deep within the heart and overcome the sin of self-righteous pride. For the simple people who had remained closely attached to nature, a life of strict discipline completely devoted to the well-being of one's neighbor and to hard work for the community was the best possible path to becoming a true monk. The great attraction of this life can be measured by the innumerable eager candidates, often still catechumens, who flocked to Pachomius for *communion* (*koinōnia*) in the truest sense of the word.

## Basil of Caesarea
## and the Evangelical Fraternities

Whereas in Egypt monks by the thousands withdrew to the desert from cities and villages, those regions of the empire in which Hellenism was strong had greater difficulty making room for clergy and people who were adapting to the economic, civic, and family structures of the empire, as well as to more radical ideas from the East. Recent studies by G. Dagron have revealed that the apparent absence of information about monastic establishments in the city of Constantinople of the fourth century is no accident.[17] The monks feared that their forerunners would be linked to Bishop Macedonius, a candidate for the episcopacy from 337, elected around 344, deposed in 359, and strongly compromised in the Arian heresy. They also had no wish to bring into the open conflicts between the holy monasteries and the great John Chrysostom, who subsequently was canonized. In Pontus, in Cappadocia, and in Armenia—that is, in northeastern Asia Minor before 340—Eustathius set the example of complete detachment, self-denial, and a life of service to the poor. This found an echo in Constantinople in the popular party and influenced the future bishop, Macedonius. It was also in this city that the episcopate was most closely supervised by the state bureaucracy and where the population was the most difficult and disparaging. We know that later on as many as 345 monasteries for both men and women were counted, but this number is probably inflated since more than one name appeared for some communities. Only Rome surpassed this number. In the beginning, though, asceticism played a small role on the fringe of ecclesiastical society.

One forceful personality whose career and dynamic influence are well documented stands out in the region. In 358 Basil of Caesarea (330–379) asked to be baptized, with the intention of devoting his life entirely to the teaching of the Gospel. A son of the highest aristocracy, Basil was born with a strong sense of responsibility and never hesitated to take action where the common good was concerned. Having received a thorough education in Athens, he was the first to recognize the limitations of literary humanism and philosophy, but he knew how to make use of them. He went to live with his widowed mother, his sister, and several other family members who had joined Eustathius's friends and withdrawn from the world to a remote property in the forest. His younger brother Gregory, the future bishop of Nyssa, hesitatingly followed him from a distance. Another Gregory, of Nazianzus, also a Cappadocian, with whom he had formed a lasting friendship during their student years in Athens, encouraged Basil in his ascetic course and shared it in his fashion—in a more contemplative manner, surrounded by his own family.

The letters these young converts wrote radiate their joy. They blithely set out to persuade the educated elite to accept the paradoxical argument that salvation of the soul is a goal in every way equal to the highest form of philosophical wisdom attained by the Greeks. But in spite of the resounding rhetoric the ultimate cause of their success lay elsewhere. Basil fully appreciated the fact that Eustathius had unleashed religious and social passions that were highly ambiguous, but he was no less determined to embark upon religious reforms that would inspire confidence in the masses and provide an organization and support system. Following the example of Eustathius, he made a systematic tour of the great monastic centers of Syria and Egypt, gathering knowledge and experience. But the guiding principles for his movement were entirely based on a systematic study of the moral precepts laid down in the New Testament; no aristocratic wisdom or popular enthusiasm could be permitted to change them by an iota. He published these as a young man in a collection of about fifteen hundred short verses, under the title of *Morals (Moralia)*.[18] In a different vein, during those same years as a student spent with Gregory of Nazianzus, he worked on a compilation of extracts from the works of Origen, choosing passages designed to provide a theologically enlightened method for reading the Bible. Basil spent this period of learning in a retreat, in poverty, manual labor, and prayer, but the young convert did not for all that completely lose contact with the outside world. He participated actively in the theological and ecclesiastical controversies of the day—in particular those that preceded the councils of Constantinople (360) and of Lampsacus (364)—by publishing three scholarly volumes on the question of the Holy Trinity.

Basil did not share the Egyptians' predilection for solitude; consequently, he considered it completely natural, with his social and intellectual background, to become a priest. This step, far from changing his manner of living, led him to expand his field of action in Caesarea by founding a large hospice. When his activities gave rise to tensions between him and the episcopal administration, he pretended to withdraw, only to find himself recalled before long as altogether indispensable. When the bishop died (370), Basil succeeded him after a campaign in which a coalition between the popular party and his aristocratic or intellectual friends defeated an opposition of the bishops of the surrounding sees. This is almost the first instance in which a bishop was elected who took a very independent stand vis-à-vis the emperor, though his relations with the administration, which consisted mainly of men from his own social strata, were excellent. He was strongly supported by a devoted population, which had a keener insight than most into the essential problems of the universal church. Having been brought up in the traditions of the most privileged elite, Basil had transcended it through a sensitive love for the poor and his humble obedience to the divine commandments.

His works, entitled monastic *Rules,* are divided into two sections: the *Long Rules* and the *Short Rules.*[19] They consist of answers to questions put to him by monks and nuns whom he visited on his travels. It must be pointed out that these were not disciples trained by him but rather devoted laypeople influenced by Eustathius. The *Long Rules,* fewer in number, which constitute the first part of the book, are not a haphazard compilation but a systematic presentation of essential points. Basil did not consider these to be rules, a term suitable only for the commandments of the New Testament, but rather an *Askētikon,* a commentary. The book grew with the years: a first short edition, the Greek text of which is not extant, exists in a Latin version (Rufinus, 397) and a Syrian version. Here we can see an approximate chronological sequence and thus follow Basil's development through his ideas and institutions. It is highly unlikely that upon becoming bishop a man would not adopt more centralized and authoritarian views. It was characteristic of Basil to warn ascetics against overemphasizing the value of specific observances, such as ostentatious poverty, severe fasting, and excessive sentimentality in prayer, at the expense of true self-denial, meekness, and Christian love, which ought to be practiced by conscientious work, caring for the sick and the poor, submission of the individual members to the well-being of the entire body, and a prayerful, sober contemplation of God's revelation in the history of salvation through his sanctifying presence. The *Askētikon* tended to curb the zeal for prayer, poverty, and asceticism because the monks were likely to overdo it. In sermons, such as those on the Psalms or certain pages from his *Treatise on the Holy Spirit,* Basil showed less restraint, because he was addressing a public with different needs. Here, speaking of the soul as achieving union with God after having attained to a state of perfect purity, he clearly revealed himself as a disciple of Origen; however, he did not follow Origen in the speculations on the purely immaterial beginnings of the soul and its ultimate return to that state at the end of time. Basil had a very clear concept of *charismata.* He saw these as divine gifts bestowed upon everyone in virtue of the ministry each person is called upon to exercise in the church: for instance, guiding others, consoling or admonishing them, or expounding the apostolic teaching and deriving spiritual nourishment from it. Such a doctrine enabled him to avoid focusing on purely human or cultural qualities or even on the juridical power of a superior, whose authority derived solely from his position.

Next to Basil's extremely sensible, sober austerity, the two Gregorys, one of Nyssa, the other of Nazianzus, exhibit a more poetic style and a more lucid manner of developing their philosophic speculations. Beside Origen on their bookshelves we discover Philo, Plato, and the Stoics, all of whom Basil likewise had at his disposal but rarely manifested. Many a modern historian has been dazzled by the brilliant oratory of their intricate syntheses between the spirituality of the great thinkers of antiquity and the Christian way of purification of the heart. However, the two Gregorys wrote little until after Basil's death; one may wonder whether he offered them much encouragement to indulge in this sort of literary pursuit. The first, Gregory of Nazianzus, preached magnificent sermons, remarkable for psychological and doctrinal content, and his dreams and recollections can be found in his poetry. The other Gregory is known for his treatise on virginity, which, though somewhat utopian in outlook, reflected in a very concrete manner experiences his own brother, Basil, had encountered. After the latter's death (370), Gregory of Nyssa took great pains to maintain a loving, respectful relationship with the monastic communities, which met with an ever-increasing reticence on the part of the episcopate.

## The Encratites, the Sarabites, the Gyrovagues

Hermits and cenobites should by no means be considered the two opposing groups that dominated the entire world of monasticism. In a certain sense they were the same. The prologue to the *Life of Pachomius* claims Anthony as one of Pachomius's spiritual predecessors, after the patriarchs, the prophets, the New Testament, and the martyrs. The same *Life* notes in a eulogy after his death pronounced by Anthony that, if the "apostolic way" had existed in his lifetime, he would most certainly have embraced it.

On one point hermits and cenobites were in accord: those ascetics who had not evolved from the primitive form of monasticism, who scorned the two orientations sanctioned by Athanasius, who lived without rules, unstable, lazy, trying to sponge off benefactors wherever possible, deserved nothing but disapproval. The term "encratites," which means continent, became a derogatory term used to describe the sect that forbade marriage as well as certain foods. *Remnouth* or *sarabites*, Coptic words of doubtful etymology that have disappeared from the language, or *gyrovague* (always on the move, never settled) turn up in the works of some satirists to discredit the survivors of ancient monasticism by portraying them as the degeneration of asceticism run wild. Jerome, who satirizes his enemies in this manner, could even have been taken for one of them, except that he did agree to work.

A Syrian text, the *Book of Degrees,* is difficult to date (probably fourth century), but it gives a rather complimentary impression of the doctrines of the movement. A distinction is made between the "just," who are subject to all the commandments, and the "perfect ones," who, having renounced everything, need no longer own anything, perform any work, judge sinners, or shun them. Now and then the author accepts with resignation persecution at the hands of the "just," meaning the church. His doctrine is very similar to one that Basil tried to correct, yet it does have a certain moral dignity. It is rooted in a well-defined doctrine of creation and salvation that was undoubtedly Judeo-Christian.

Theodoret, a man with a fine Greek culture (d. 466) has left a whole series of vivid, picturesque studies of popular monks in his northern Syria.[20] The oldest ones date back to almost a century before his time. Whatever prejudices one may have about Symeon the Stylite, who elected to spend many years on the top of a column at the center of admiring crowds, those who had the good fortune to visit and pray at the site were forced to admit that this hermit showed a good taste in choosing a place of such extraordinary beauty. Furthermore, the enormous font at the side of the column, which was used in baptizing the newly converted Bedouin, proved his method effectual. Surely there is a place among God's saints for unorthodox souls unable to conform. Eternal wanderers, God's own pilgrims, even they will sometimes enter paradise.

## Messalians and Macarius/Simeon

As early as 370 at least some Syrian centers mention a sect that practiced rigorous asceticism, calling them Messalians, those who pray. They preached absolute detachment, including abstaining from any work and giving up all property, and they may have been antisocial, sentimental, romantic visionaries. The most unsettled vagabonds have left no trace; we can hardly expect them to have written or kept any sort of records. Those whom we do know were already on guard against extremists in their utterances; yet they are often all lumped together as representing one whole group. Besides, who has not had detractors, as the cases of Eustathius of Sebaste and the *Book of*

*Degrees* prove? Basil was maligned by Atarbios of Neocaesarea, and perhaps there was indeed some justification for criticism of the protection he granted the deacon Glycerios and the virgins who followed him into the desert.[21] Yet was it not he who had fought more than anybody else to establish hard work and sensible behavior as a vital part of monastic life?

After Basil's death, Gregory of Nyssa emphatically condemned all excesses but always deeply respected the venerable figures of ancient Syrian monasticism. The Antiocheans venerated cave dwellers of the mountains, although few had any illusions about their culture or usefulness to the church. John Chrysostom, who was educated in the ascetical school of Diodorus, ventured for four or five years into the desert and a life of solitude, until 380, when, physically exhausted, he abandoned this course. His understanding of charismatic powers differed essentially from that of Basil. For Chrysostom, charisms belonged to the New Testament times when the apostles raised the dead, and that is where they ought to remain. They should not be used as a pretext for slackening ascetic discipline. He supported his bishop, Flavian, in the persecution of Adelphius, Sabas, Simeon, and others, who under protest had been condemned as Messalians by the Council of Side in Pamphylia (390). These self-styled spiritual leaders were denounced for attributing too little importance to baptism and to the sacraments, because the sectarians believed that the sacraments merely remove the visible signs of sin without uprooting it entirely. The sectarians held that there were demonic powers confronting the Holy Spirit within the human heart even after baptism; in short, one had no choice but to rely entirely on the tangible experience of divine grace. Grace given through the church was never more than a beginning; it had to be rendered effective through a life spent in prayer and asceticism.

Some of their works, though condemned by the episcopate, are still in existence, which proves that the heretical texts have not all disappeared although their publication was hampered. In many instances these manuscripts have only been identified and examined in recent years. The *Fifty Spiritual Homilies*, ascribed to the name of Macarius, are selected writings published by Byzantine monks. These were received enthusiastically by the public and later had a significant influence on Lutheran pietism and Methodism. Modern research classifies this material as Collection II, along with Collections, I, III, and IV, as well as a few unclassified treatises. The author is called Macarius/Simeon because certain manuscripts bear Simeon's name, and a Simeon was among those persecuted for Messalianism.

Macarius/Simeon expressed his thoughts in a manner very similar to Basil. External discipline and institutions interested him very little; none equaled

him in his description of temptation, constancy in prayer, and purity of
heart. His vocabulary is forceful and picturesque without being artificial,
especially when he employs images borrowed from nature, from the wind
and the trees. His personal experiences seem to be those of an officer of
troops guarding the eastern frontier. Though his disciples had the right to
voice their objections, his answers frequently seemed illogical or not to the
point, and he preferred to turn back to his own favorite subjects. This
literary style, crowded with ideas and suggestions, little resembles that of the
Egyptians, but it too has its great charm. This author, often misunderstood
in his lifetime, was much appreciated by the Syrians, the Arabs, and subsequently by the Slavs, being very popular on Mount Athos. Macarius
expressed an inner spiritual freedom that found its complement in Basil's
rigorous discipline; neither could exist independently. If we attempt to oppose the two currents, disregarding Macarius's strong opposition to extreme
Messalianism, we would arrive at a spirituality that curiously resembles
those encountered in Persia and India.

Two important later writers whose dates are questionable, Diadochus of
Photice and Mark the Hermit, were generally labeled opponents of Macarius. More profound examinations show that they are his spiritual children,
who reacted vigorously, even more outspokenly than Macarius himself,
against the extremists.

## Evagrius the Intellectual

Evagrius of Pontus (d. 399), born at Ibora in Pontus about 345, was at first
a disciple of Basil but later turned to Gregory of Nazianzus, whose Gnostic
theology he preferred. Finally, he emigrated from Constantinople to join the
Origenists in the cells of the desert. Like Macarius/Simeon he too aroused
controversy as a theologian. No sooner had he died than he was condemned
by Theophilus of Alexandria and then again by Justinian in 553, because his
doctrine had caused great turmoil in the monasteries of St. Sabas in Palestine. Here again profound personal experiences clad in highly mystical
language lent themselves to questionable interpretations. His use of Neoplatonic philosophy is reflected in his writings in a certain monism, which
foresees that after all passions have subsided every soul shall enter into the
primorial unity following Christ.[22] All these speculations were linked to the
Gospel and to the mystery of the church and its sacraments. The spiritual
meaning, though highly refined, still appears closely tied to the literal sense,
all of which leads to a daring interpretation of a fundamentally Christian
faith. If we pursue the thought of either this master or his disciples to its

logical conclusion, it will appear preposterous nonsense. Therefore, the condemnations were not necessarily the result of stupidity or ill will. Macarius certainly never went this far. This does not mean that Evagrius did not provide stimulation for the well-educated monks: through Cassian for the Latin world; through Palladius for John Climacus; through Maximus the Confessor for the Byzantines; and through Philoxenus and others for Isaac of Nineveh and numerous Syrians.

Evagrius recognized that his doctrine was not, in its entirety, suitable for novices. In many of his works he took care to disclose only the very first elements of his doctrine, for example, in the *Praktikos* and the *Chapters on Prayer*.[23] His literary style, which consisted of enigmatic, obscure phrases, loosely connected, obliges the reader to meditate and study at length in order to arrive gradually at an understanding of the message. At the same time this style discourages quick prying eyes and the unfriendly curiosity of inquisitive minds. Less elementary are the *Kephalaia Gnostika* and the *Letter to Melania,* which have disappeared in Greek but have survived in Syrian or Armenian versions, well beyond reach of Justinian's soldiers. Even these versions contain a moderate, watered-down sort of Origenism, and the only manuscript that has preserved the compromising text of the *Kephalaia Gnostica* is a Syrian one, published in 1958 by A. Guillaumont.

Evagrius's basic training (the *ascetical* life) comprised Basil's moral teaching and the experiences of the desert fathers, who in their solitude attentively followed the movements of the heart. It demanded a detachment seemingly too perfect and a silencing of all passions, personified by as many demons, whose games Evagrius observed with incredible lucidity. Subsequently this analysis of thoughts and their hidden mainspring became an integral part of all great Christian spiritual traditions. The only exception was the degree of self-denial he expected, which appears unrealistic. He went well beyond all that the Stoics demanded concerning the self-image, respect for the humble, and the absolute humility of the creature before its creator. Evagrius's second stage (the *Gnostic* life) explained according to Plato, Origen, and Anthony that the soul is by nature pure spirit, condemned because of original sin to dwell in the flesh but redeemed through providence. This intellectual nature is able to achieve, through "essential *gnōsis*" and a religious science of nature, the revelation of the word and the contemplation of the One, which ultimately leads to a restoration where all duality is overcome and God is one in all. Love plays a part in the progression toward this goal, but Evagrius attached a highly refined and philosophical meaning to this word, far from what Basil understood by Christian love.

## Palestine: Gaza and the
## Desert of Judea, Sinai

In the fifth and sixth centuries the most active monastic centers moved to
Palestine where Cappadocians, Georgians, and Egyptians rather than Latins
gathered. The abbot Esaias, who had received his training in Scetis (ca. 431)
died in Gaza in 491. Despite certain objections, one can attribute to him or
to his disciple Peter, who published his works after his death, the corpus of
his writings in its various forms in the manuscripts and the oriental
versions. Esaias belonged to those who collected the *Apophthegmata;* he was
in contact with Evagrius and Macarius (certain texts of the two authors
appear in the corpus); and he created an intelligent balance in combining
various traditions. Gaza of the sixth century was dominated by the hermit-
monks Barsanuphius and John the Prophet (both died in 543); their disciple
Dorotheus added Basil's influence to that of the others. This milieu was close
to the Monophysites although without strong ties. The monks of the desert
near Gaza, on the other hand, in the end actively campaigned for Chalcedon, led by Euthymius (d. 473) and Sabas (d. 532). Thanks to the excellent
biographer Cyril of Scythopolis, we have the lives of a number of great personalities of this period, such as the story of a group of ascetics among
whom Evagrius's ideas caused considerable commotion, but we lack the
personal comments of the holy men. The monasteries they created still
exist, impressive testimonies to their creative genius. They instituted the
"lavras," a system grouping individual cells around a center, which offered
solitude to hermits as well as training for novices and common services on
Sundays. In this system Basil met Egypt. Anecdotes by John Moschus in his
*Spiritual Pasture* provide an insight into life in these lavras shortly after the
period of Cyril of Scythopolis.

Far to the south, in the Sinai peninsula, there were some scattered communities which sent a representative to Constantinople in 536. In the Sinai,
Justinian fortified the monastery of St. Catherine, famous to this day for its
library and for its icons, which escaped destruction by iconoclasts during
the later years of the Byzantine Empire. The holy mountain is the birthplace of an orthodox classic, *The Ladder of Divine Ascent,* by John Climacus
(d. after 650). This work is clearly inspired by Gaza, but it is more objective
and more laborious in its manner. Here we have the transition from the
"hesychastic" spirituality, inaugurated by unknown monks in the Sinai
desert, to a spirituality that subsequently flourished in Greek monasticism,
in particular on Mount Athos after the Arab conquest had cut off all contact
with the East. The ultimate goal was to overcome nature, and one of the
instruments to achieve this goal was a very simplified prayer, the constant

repetition of one sentence concentrating the mind on the name of Jesus and human sinfulness. The perfect monk could never be satisfied with his observance of the rules or his virtues; yet he never despaired in the face of his abysmal weakness.

Tales by the monk Anthony, as yet poorly edited, describe life in these deserts of the seventh century as rather more picturesque than profoundly spiritual in character. Here, with the Arab conquest, we have reached the final stages of the period under study. Relations with Byzantium and the West were giving way to new ties with Persia, Georgia, Armenia, Ethiopia, and Arabic Christian culture.

## The Influence of Ancient Eastern Monasticism

Monasticism gradually developed into a well-defined state with its territories, its departments, its laws, its characteristic garb, and its architecture. To the masses monasticism offered strength through its prayers, good example in practicing Christian virtues, and its theological and literary culture. Monastic culture naturally varied with time and place, while becoming more distinctive from secular culture and, at least in appearance, stereotyped and conventional. The Orthodox layperson attached great importance to this model of obedience to the Gospel teaching, an icon of love for God and one's neighbor, of inner peace and true bliss.

This same icon has illumined other Christian cultures despite their diversities. We know that in the West, for instance, the personality of Anthony, as portrayed by Athanasius, played a decisive role in the conversion of such personalities as Jerome and Augustine. Not only did it influence the biographer Sulpicius Severus, but before him Martin of Tours, his hero—even though the latter chose the life of community leader, bishop, and missionary. Jerome and Rufinus, on arrival in Aquileia some time before 374, adopted the Eastern practice. Thus, it was only logical that they proceed, one to the desert of Chalcis near Aleppo, the other to Egypt, before they met again in Bethlehem and Jerusalem. Assisted by a few women of the highest aristocracy, they translated Origen, Basil, and Pachomius or composed works more freely inspired by Eastern spirituality. John Cassian, another Latin who went to Egypt in search of spiritual masters, became an important influence in medieval monastic life. Basil's institutions, the lives of the fathers, and their *Apophthegmata* were all the surest guides in the centuries to come for the Latin monk on the path to perfection, as Benedict emphasized in the final chapter of his *Rule*.

From the very beginning, monasteries occupied a position of honor in the

Syrian and Coptic churches. In their most fruitful period the local culture grew vigorously in a climate of restrained rivalry with the sober intellectual approach of the Greeks. Neither were they intimidated by the secular authorities or by public opinion, nor did they forget a proper respect for the unity of the church. They displayed a constructive enthusiasm for the Gospel teachings, resisting the temptation of contesting social order for the pleasure of doing so. Disputes over christology and even Arab government did not prevent renewed periods of growth and spiritual leadership, but these occurred under much more difficult conditions.

Churches that developed in the Middle Ages, stimulated by struggles for national autonomy, reached back into early Christianity rather than build on the Byzantine evolution. Accordingly, medieval monasticism in Armenia or Ethiopia, just as in the Latin West, took on a distinctive character sometimes even in opposition to Byzantium. This did not diminish the important role played by religious texts translated from the Greek, together with ascetical practice and prayer inherited from their great precursors. That these tasks could be adapted to local social and family structures only underlines their vitality and sense of realism. Georgia experienced a similar development but remained more faithful to Byzantine orthodoxy. The Slavs, on the other hand, latecomers to the faith, plunged deep into the past in search of a particular form of humility, wisdom, and understanding, transmitted to them through Studite and Athonite monasticism. Here is not the place to examine the growth and flowering of this movement, to analyze its manner of adapting to diverse climates, or to scrutinize the fruit of supreme sacrifice.

## Invariables in a Variety of Forms

Those holy men and women who were truly monastics were always extremely reticent when speaking about the wonders of the spiritual life. Novices experienced a honeymoon in the deep joy following conversion and deliverance from sin. God has been manifested; angels, the church, and the brothers received with open arms the lost sheep returning to the fold. Evidence of such blessed moments appear in many a page of the texts discussed above. The more painful the trials, the more fierce the attacks of the evil one; the more heroic the struggle, the more frequent also become God's manifest interventions, God's consoling presence, and the direct experience that celestial joys surpass any pleasures that sinfulness and vanity might offer. There is Anthony, victorious in ferocious battles against foul creatures; there are the Letters of the young Basil (e.g., *Letters* 2 and 14) to Gregory of Nazianzus; and there is Cassian, in his rare moments of prayer in fire. However, the wise rarely dwell upon this kind of promise. Legends, for instance in the *History of the Monks in Egypt,* conjure up visions of fruits of paradise served by angels to the elect, who brave hunger and thirst beyond the limits of human endurance. Such descriptions do not attest to the authenticity of the documents.

More often the need arose to encourage the neophytes in moments of darkness and despair, when the demon of despondency attacks, the great tempter of the hesychast. The day seems endless, the imagination sets to work. The remedy: manual labor alternating with prayer—but, above all, remaining in the cell and an unshakable faith in God's promises and God's mysterious help. Generally speaking, Anthony and his followers had discovered the remedy against temptations of the flesh and spirit: complete confession of sins to a spiritual father and absolute trust in his advice and encouragement. This manner of spiritual analysis formed the basis for the treasure of the *Apophthegmata.* The best catechetical teaching and spiritual discourses also grew out of these analyses, though there is some danger in utilizing this literary genre, where true spiritual values often lie buried under much pious banality. Within the cenobitic communities personal crises were often less agonizing and mistakes less dangerous. Spiritual pride and hallucinations came to light more quickly, but overcoming the vice of despondency and penetrating into the innermost secrets of the heart were not as striking in this context.

A complete confession was sure to bring freedom from inner turmoil and phobias and to exorcize well-known demons. The hesychast was permitted to search for the most perspicacious and most congenial mentor, which avoided refusal of obedience to the first counselor in the hope of receiving different advice from the next one. How were the fathers able to live up to this trust? Primarily by distrusting their own perception and resorting to silence or generalities until such time as, in their simplicity of heart, the words of salvation would be revealed to them. The faith and trust of the disciple strengthened the master's vision and insight. Neither of them considered the response to be dictated by human wisdom; it was revealed by the Holy Spirit, who had been invoked, and through the Gospel, where that wisdom had already become manifest.

Hiding nothing does not invite yielding to vain chatter or self-satisfying introspection. Rather it demonstrates a willingness to learn complete humility. Even matters one would consider impossible to reveal except to God had to be laid without reserve before the elder. The foremost duty of the elder was to resist being tolerant or softhearted, because the rigorous defense would be useless against a truly divine manifestation. Zacharias had revealed one of his visions to his abbot, Carion. The elder, unable to discern the true nature of the vision, beat him in order to free him from evil delusions. But the vision persisted, and Zacharias, obediently visiting another elder, was told even before he opened his mouth that his vision indeed came from God. "But go," said the second elder, "and do as your father Carion tells you." When the same Zacharias was dying, Abbot Moses asked him, "What do you see?" "Is it not better to say nothing, Father?" and here the old man respected his untroubled peace. "Yes, my child, keep silent" (*Apophthegmata, Zacharias* 5). A silence more eloquent than words.

Those who had achieved a high degree of detachment seemed quite naturally able to speak with great purity of heart, either to a spiritual father, to a spiritual child, or, on a wider scale, to all those desirous of opening their conscience to a man of God, serene and wise, whose understanding went beyond anything psychology could ever hope for.

Two aspects, one a condition and the other a result, of the practice of confession may shock the modern psychologist: the extreme delight taken in confessing sins, and the recognition of one's inferiority and unworthiness. Whoever overlooks that this feeling is genuine could see in it a form of hypocrisy, a way of destroying one's basic self-esteem, a sort of masochism. Systematically creating a state of moral depression, debasing oneself in one's own eyes and in the eyes of one's peers—is this not in the nature of self-destruction? Fasting, dirty conditions, silence, and lack of culture betray the same state of mind, but they are less serious, because they do not have such a direct bearing on the mainsprings of life. There seems no doubt that this mortification of the body and the mind was perceived as running counter to the Greek "optimism." Nor can it be denied that the results will be destructive unless the disciplines are practiced with discretion, in the light of Christ's teaching. The wise knew this, be they cenobitic monks or hermits. However, experience has taught that a profound insight into one's own weakness has as a direct consequence serenity through trust in God, uninterrupted thanksgiving, and, to one's neighbor, unlimited forbearance and active kindness.

The hermit flees into the wilderness. A steadily growing procession of imitators—beggars and intellectuals anxious to share in his lights—pursues him. One word from his lips dispels sorrow and radiates peace. These are authentic facts, verifiable by anyone who opens a serious text and listens to the sound of the saint's words with that minimum of goodwill indispensable for sympathetic understanding. No one claims that success is easy; consequently, we find neither magic recipes nor formulas effective per se. All must submit to a true purification of the heart, total obedience, repentance, humility, and charity.

Progress occurs on two levels, complementary to each other. Asceticism engenders a growing inner peace and sense of fulfillment, so deep that no external upheavals can trouble it. On the mystical level, the image of God draws closer, becoming ever more tangible. Like the Son who knows the Father, it transcends words and ideas to appear as the pure light of the ineffable Trinity. Some possess the gift of expressing these experiences in theological terms and transmitting them to the church, since ascetics were often called to ministry in the world. Signs like this are unmistakable: compassion, joy, and angelic purity. Yet true fulfillment is found elsewhere, in self-denial and in mystical union.

*Translated by Marie Miklashevsky*

## Notes

1. E. A. Judge, "The Earliest Use of Monachos for 'Monk'," *Jahrbuch für Antike und Christentum* 20 (1977) 72–89.

2. A. Adam, "Der Monachosgedanke innerhalb der Spiritualität der alten Kirche," in *Glaube, Geist, Geschichte: Festschrift für E. Benz*, ed. G. Müller and Winfried Zeller (Leiden: Brill, 1967) 259–65.

3. A. Guillaumont, *Aux origines*, 38–45.

4. R. Murray, "The Exhortation to Candidates for Ascetical Vows at Baptism in the Ancient Syriac Churches," *New Testament Studies* 21 (1974) 59–80.

5. G. Dagron, *Naissance d'une capitale: Constantinople et ses institutions* (Paris: Presses universitaires de France, 1974); J. Gribomont, "S. Basile et le monachisme enthousiaste," *Irenikon* 53 (1980) 123–44.

6. A. Guillaumont, *Aux origines*, 14–66.

7. It is interesting, however, that Palladius wrote a book on Indian ascetics. See W. Berghoff, *Palladius: De Gentibus Indiae et de Bragmanibus* (Meisenheim: Anton, Meisenheim, 1967).

8. J. Leipoldt, *Griechische Philosophie und frühchristliche Askese* (Berlin: Akademie-Verlag, 1961).

9. Athanasius, *The Life of Antony and The Letter to Macellinus*, trans. Robert C. Gregg (New York: Paulist Press, 1980); A. Bouyer, *La vie de S. Antoine: Essai sur la spiritualité du monachisme primitif* (Begrolles-en-Mauges: Textes Monastiques, 1978).

10. *The Letters of St. Antony*, trans. D. J. Chitty (Kalamazoo, MI: Cistercian Publications, 1977).

11. H. Dörries, *Wort und Stunde I* (Göttingen: Vandenhoeck & Ruprecht, 1966) 145–225. The same volume contains fine analyses of the milieu of the Apophthegmites: work, study of the Bible, penitence, etc.

12. *The Letters of St Ammonas, Successor of St. Antony*, trans. D. J. Chitty (Kalamazoo, MI: Cistercian Publications, 1981).

13. *The Lives of the Desert Fathers*, trans. N. Russell (London: Mowbray, 1981).

14. Palladius, *Lausiac History*, ed. C. Butler (Cambridge: G. Olms, 1967).

15. *The Sayings of the Desert Fathers: The Alphabetical Collection*, trans. B. Ward (Kalamazoo, MI: Cistercian Publications, 1975). The most complete edition with the best index is *Les Sentences des pères du désert*, trans. L. Regnault (Sablé/Sarthe: Solesmes, 1981).

16. All the sources are translated into English with commentary by A. Veilleux, *Pachomian Koinonia*, 3 vols. (Kalamazoo, MI: Cistercian Publications, 1980–83).

17. G. Dagron, *Naissance d'une capitale*; J. Gribomont, "S. Basile et le monachisme enthousiaste."

18. Basil, *Ascetical Works*, trans. M. Wagner (Washington, DC: Catholic University Press, 1950).

19. Ibid.

20. D. Canivet, *Le Monachisme syrien selon Theodoret de Cyr* (Paris: Beauchesne, 1977).

21. J. Gribomont, *Commandements du Seigneur*, 100–101.

22. A. Guillaumont, *Les 'Kephalaia Gnostika' d'Evagre le Pontique* (Paris: Seuil, 1967).

23. Evagrius Ponticus. *The Praktikos. Chapters on Prayer*, trans. John Eudes Bamberger (Spencer, MA: Cistercian Publications, 1970).

# Bibliography

## Studies

Bouyer, L. *The Spirituality of the New Testament and the Fathers*. Vol. 1 of *A History of Christian Spirituality*. New York: Seabury, 1982.

Chitty, D. J. *The Desert a City: An Introduction to the Study of Egyptian and Palestinian Monasticism under the Christian Empire*. Oxford: Blackwell, 1966; repr. Crestwood, NY: St. Vladimir's Seminary Press, n.d.

Gribomont, J. *Commandements du Seigneur et libération evangelique*. Rome: Herder, 1977.

Guillaumont, A. *Aux origines du monachisme chretien*. Begrolles-en-Mauges: Textes Monastiques, 1979.

Hausherr, I. *Direction spirituelle en orient autrefois*. Rome: Herder, 1958.

———. *Hésychasme et prière*. Rome: Pontifical Institute of Oriental Studies, 1966.

Heussi, K. *Der Ursprung des Monchtums*. Aaten: Scientia, 1980.

Spidlik, T. *La spiritualité de l'orient chrétien*. Rome: Pontifical Institute of Oriental Studies, 1978.

*Théologie de la vie monastique*. Paris: Aubier, 1961.

Viller, M., and K. Rahner. *Askese und Mystik in der Vaterzeit*. Freiburg: Herder, 1938.

Vööbus, A. *History of Asceticism in the Syrian Orient*. 2 vols. Corpus scriptorum Christianorum Orientalium 184, 197. Louvain: Corpus scriptorum Christianorum Orientalium, 1958–60.

# II. *Western Christianity*

## JEAN LECLERCQ

IN ALL THE TERRITORIES where the church existed, both in the East and in the West, the fourth century witnessed the transition from a premonastic asceticism to an organized monasticism. This development was facilitated by the fact that in all parts of the Roman Empire, circulation of people and texts still encouraged an exchange of ideas. At the beginning of the latter half of the fourth century this process was disturbed by the invasion of the "barbarians," so called because they were not a part of the established civilization. They had in common the fact that they were new peoples, full of the vitality that characterized the young and vigorous. Yet the Huns, Goths, Vandals, Suebians, and later, in the sixth century, the Lombards, differed from one another. Wars and political rivalries arose among them, in addition to the division between Arian and orthodox among those who had come into contact with the Christian faith. In Gaul unification slowly arose with the appearance of a Frankish kingdom that would set the foundations for a Frankish church. This church, however, remained diversified because of the traditions that existed in each region. In a parallel fashion, under the influence of popes like Leo the Great (440–461) and Gregory the Great (590–604), the authority of the bishop of Rome was strengthened in the realm of doctrine and later in other domains, including the political.

In spite of all of these troubles in the West, the transformation of independent monasticism into an institution of the church gradually took place, following a course similar to that of the East. By pursuing holiness through asceticism, ordinary Christians—and they often were the simplest—won the esteem of the bishops, who helped and guided them. Some bishops would later rise from their ranks. Powerful inspiration came from examples offered by the East, particularly that of Anthony. The *Life of Anthony*, written by Athanasius, was widely influential, especially on Jerome and on Augustine in Milan. From the fourth to the seventh century, more and more texts gave witness to the existence and evolution of monastic institutions, particularly proceedings of councils, hagiographical narratives, and rules. More than a score of rules have come down to us.

Christian asceticism had ancient roots in the eastern half of the province of North Africa, which the Romans called the Proconsulate. Tertullian (d. ca. 220) and later Cyprian, the bishop of Carthage (d. 258), spoke of it; the term *monasterium* has been employed since their time. In spite of the

9. Monastery of Saint Catherine in the Sinai Desert, 6th century

10. Model of the third church at Cluny, 1892 reconstruction

persecutions of the third century and the Donatist schism of the fourth, monasticism expanded under the form of hermitages for solitaries and communities of virgins and "continents." Councils held in Carthage in 349 and in Carthage and Hippo at the end of the fourth century deliberated over some dangers that appeared in these settings. It was at that time that the African rhetorician Augustine, who had become a Christian in Milan under the tutelage of Ambrose, returned to his native country after having admired a form of monasticism in that city. Augustine had explored a variety of religious and philosophical schools and had experimented with a community life of "holy leisure" directed toward study at Cassiciacum in northern Italy. Some years after his return to Africa, in 388, he took up residence in Thagaste again in order to live with some companions in a kind of monastic seclusion; but it was only in 390, when he founded a community in Hippo near the cathedral of Bishop Valerius, that he began to speak of a "monastery." The instruction that he gave to the "servants of God" who lived there was marked by an insistence on the renunciation of all private property and on communal living which stressed charity and service to the local church. The transition to a recognizably cenobitic form of monastic life was thereby accomplished. After becoming bishop, Augustine continued to live in community with his clerics and thus was one of the originators of a kind of clerical monasticism that would have an influence in several regions of the West and that would evolve into what came to be called the "canonical life." The priests who were formed under Augustine soon became bishops and under their impulse monasticism, especially in this form, expanded throughout the Proconsulate and into the neighboring provinces of Byzacena, Numidia, and Mauritania. Monasteries of virgins and of nonclerics also existed. Writing against the monks of Hadrumetum, who aspired to do nothing but pray, Augustine composed a treatise, *On the Work of Monks* (*De opere monachorum*). He also left texts which, combined with others, were destined to enjoy a wide distribution under the title of *The Rule of St. Augustine* (*Regula Augustini*). These texts soon spread to Italy and Spain and, by way of these countries, to Gaul.

## The Iberian Peninsula

Beginning in the third century, Spain had its own Christian ascetics. One of them, Oriens of Cordova, took part in a council held in Elvira in 300. From that time on, consecrated virgins in the church would enter into a contract with God called the *pactum*. At the moment when Egyptian monasticism filtered into the West and tried to impose itself as the standard (around 375), a group of ascetics consisting of Priscillian and his disciples provoked a crisis. According to their opponents, these extremists, influenced by Manichaeism, declared marriage and certain foods to be evil and claimed that quasi equality between God and human beings was possible. Meanwhile, the behavior of some of them was causing scandal and their opponents also produced evidence of their insubordination toward the bishops.

In Visigothic Spain monasticism profited from the influences of other lands. A virgin named Egeria, who liked to travel, had an intense curiosity and was not lacking in personal resources. She gave an account of her recollections of traveling in Egypt, Mount Sinai, Palestine, and Asia Minor edited under the title of *Itinerary*. Iberian monsticism did have its own unique characteristics. First, a great emphasis was placed on the *pactum*, which for monks as for consecrated virgins and their spouses was irrevocable. Rules also appeared under the title *Book* (*Liber*) or *Book of Rules* (*Codex regularum*). Sometimes these rules were collections of Eastern or Western texts assembled for the use of abbots, and sometimes they contained the proceedings and decrees of regional synods of abbots. The collections passed down under the name "The Holy Fathers," and one entitled *Agreement of Monks* (*Consensoria monachorum*) contained Spanish elements. These kinds of works were sometimes authored by bishops who had been monks, like Fructuosus of Braga, Leander, and Isidore of Seville.

## Italy

As was the case everywhere, but perhaps especially in those places where Christianity had been established earlier, there were ascetics in Rome, Milan, and many other Italian cities during the second and third centuries. In Rome, Pope Damasus had promoted monasticism, which was not the case for his successor, Siricius. Jerome, from his monastic base in Palestine, provided the impetus for a whole group of monasteries toward the end of the fourth century. The influences that favored this development had come from all over. Hermitages and communities were scattered all about, and their abbots gave them rules inspired by those of other communities or by ancient Eastern texts. The *Rule of Paul and Stephen* appears to have been one of these. What was most original about this Italian monasticism was the fact that it developed largely in the cities, close to the basilicas, especially in the northern part of the country. Many bishops protected, and sometimes even founded, these clerical communities, which were closer to Augustine's than to Pachomius's groups. Monasticism was gradually integrated into the structures of the church and became assimilated into classical Roman culture.

Cassiodorus, a cultured layperson who had served four Gothic kings, founded a monstery at Vivarium in Calabria about 540, which he intended to make both a house of prayer and asceticism and a center for study. With this plan in mind he wrote *Introduction to Divine and Human Readings* (*Institutiones*), in which he proposed a complete intellectual program, almost too ambitious to be practicable. In fact, it *was* hardly practiced, since Vivarium soon disappeared; but it was not without influence on monastic pedagogy in later centuries. It is also known that there were four monasteries in Rome in the fifth century, and a dozen in the sixth.

It was at this time that three important historical documents appeared. The first two were rules: one is designated today as *RM*, the initials of its title, *Rule of the Master* (*Regula magistri*), and the other as *RB*, or the *Rule of St. Benedict*, because it was attributed to Benedict. These were followed by the *Life* of Benedict of Nursia in the second book of the *Dialogues* of Gregory the Great.

Historians are now nearly unanimous in recognizing that *RM* is an earlier document than *RB*, and that the latter is dependent upon the former. *RM* is the longest and the most detailed of the rules that we possess from this age. Drawn up in all probability during the first quarter of the sixth century in an area not far from Rome and depending on John Cassian, this document prescribed an observance marked by moderation—except on one point: suspicion of any exemption from community exercises. The exercises of prayer—the divine office, Eucharist, reading, silent prayers, blessings, rites, and ceremonies—gave witness to a concern that all the thoughts of the monk, all the activities of his day, be referred to the presence of God. Ascetical doctrine had as its point of departure a keen sense of the inclination to evil, which sin and the temptations of the devil placed in the human heart, and of the eternal punishment that awaited those who yielded to it. But the monk had recourse to Christ; he had confidence in the grace of redemption. He received the power to carry out, not without struggles or setbacks, a radical renunciation of all private property and of all self-will, a humble and absolute submission to his superiors, and a battle for spiritual control over the flesh and the attainment of purity of heart. This entire asceticism was rooted in a theology formulated on the belief that the monastic life, being nothing other than a fulfillment of the promises of baptism, was a way of approaching the Father through unity with Christ in the church, in which the abbot in relation to the monks played a role analogous to that of the bishop in relation to the faithful. The rule was as binding on him as it was on the rest of the monks. *RM* was too particular to be observed in places other than where it was written, but it remains valuable because of the concrete details it gives about the daily lives of the monks of central Italy during the sixth century. Without *RM*, it would be impossible to understand *RB* or to appreciate its value.

*RB* also appears to have been written not far from Rome, shortly after *RM*. An ancient tradition attributes it to an abbot named Benedict. What we know of him comes from what Gregory the Great said of him in the second book of his *Dialogues*, which belongs to the literary genre of monastic hagiography, though it integrates themes from ancient philosophical traditions and commonplaces inherited from classical Latin authors. These moralistic tales contained the entire spiritual itinerary of the "man of God," which Gregory wished to illustrate just as Athanasius had done in his *Life of Anthony*. The ascetic, the monk, and, above all, the abbot, was a Christian who renounced the world and overcame temptation, attained self-control in union with God, became capable of exercising spiritual fatherhood, and received—for the good of those around him—gifts similar to those of the saints of the Old and New Testaments. According to Gregory, Benedict was born in Nursia and founded monasteries at Subiaco in a valley situated east of Rome and later at Monte Cassino in Campania. The last specific event mentioned in the account was the death of the bishop of Capua, Germanus, which took place before February 541.

In comparison with all the other Western rules of the sixth and seventh centuries, the *Rule of St. Benedict* stands out as a masterpiece of practical wisdom and doctrine. It presents itself as a modest document, written for ordinary monks who were living in a difficult age when their institution lay open to dangers and gave rise to abuses. The *Rule* had no illusion about the adversities to which the monks were exposed, but this tranquil realism did not eradicate confidence in all the good that "God can accomplish" in those who serve him. If they are humble and submissive, and renounce all things, they will receive from God a joy that will "gladden the heart" and a peace that will bring happiness to the entire community. All the counsels given were of moderation, to build up the weak and to spur on the spirited. From beginning to end, one finds in this rule an admirable balance between prayer and work, submission and personal conscience, solitude with God and communal life, renunciation and the use of anything necessary to live cheerfully, generosity and prudence in austerity, silence and charity in interpersonal relations, the authority of the abbot and the right of the brothers to give their opinions. The divine office was only one of the prayerful observances in which God was encountered: reading, meditation, frequent and sometimes prolonged prayer were no less necessary. On all of these points, *RB*, like *RM*, was the result of experience accumulated over the course of many generations. Ancient manuscripts describing this evolution are extremely rare.

Gregory the Great had always shown great interest in the monasteries; he had founded six of them on his properties in Sicily. After becoming praetor of Rome in 572, he established one at his own home on the Caelian hill. He lived there after his return from Constantinople, where he had been sent as ambassador in 588. Gregory was elected pope two years later, and until his death in 604 he did not cease to concern himself, especially in his *Letters*, with the welfare of the monasteries. On the one hand, he stressed the contemplative nature of the life that the monks had to lead; on the other hand, he did not hesitate to entrust to them pastoral duties, even missionary work, when he needed them. And so, little by little, after a long crisis precipitated by wars and the vicissitudes of politics, a monastic renaissance became visible at the beginning of the second half of the seventh century.

## Gaul

The history of monasticism in Gaul is very complex. There, more than anywhere else, we see the intermingling of influences from the East, Africa, Spain, and the Celtic lands, to which must be added intellectual currents springing from different parts of Gaul itself. Up to the sixth century, one can speak of old Gallic (*altgallischer*) monasticism. Then, in the seventh century, monasticism can be designated, on the whole, as Iro-Frankish; in the eighth century, in one entire region, it was marked by a Benedictine influence of Anglo-Saxon origin.

Old Gallic monasticism emanated from three centers, Marmoutier, Lérins, and Agaune. The first one began with the arrival of Martin in the region of Poitiers, where he was welcomed by Hilary, the local bishop. For ten years, he led the monastic life at Ligugé. Beginning in 371, when he became bishop of Tours, he continued to live as a monk in a place located several miles from the city. It became for him and for posterity the "great monastery," Marmoutier (in Latin, *Maius monasterium*); monks and clerics prayed and worked there together. This Martinian monasticism, which was quite original, continued in the region after the death of Martin in 397 under Bricius and other successors. Above all, it expanded in proportion to the expansion of the cult of its founder, first along the river Loire, then beyond. Sulpicius Severus, a friend of Martin, wrote a *Life*, three *Letters*, and a *Dialogue* about him. The ideal of the bishop-monk which Severus presented aroused some opposition among bishops and clergy but admiration in many ascetic circles.

What Marmoutier had been in the west of Gaul, Lérins became in the southeast. On one of the islands that faced the city of Cannes a young man named Honoratus and his older companion, Caprasius, set out around 410 to live the monastic life, after they had visited the East. At that time,

Vandals, Suebians, and Visigoths were infiltrating all of Gaul. The prefecture had been moved from Trier to Arles, near which many nobles coming from the north took refuge. Such was the case for the two founders of Lérins.[1] Bishop Proclus of Marseille and his auxiliaries showed themselves favorable to monasticism. Being a true "spiritual father," according to the witness of his disciple and successor Hilary, Honoratus attracted "seekers of God," and Bishop Leontius of Fréjus ordained him a priest. The community grew.

John Cassian, a monk who had spent time in Egypt and absorbed the theology of Evagrius of Pontus, had been in Marseille since about 415. He published his *Cenobitic Institutions* between 420 and 424, and soon after, his *Conferences.* In the preface to *Conferences* 11-17, written about 426, he pointed to the example of Honoratus and his first companions as the "living rule" of community. After that time, two apparently contradictory tendencies emerged at Lérins. On one side there was an insistence upon the separation from the world that was implied by monasticism. Eucherius of Lyons, who was there for several years, in 427 wrote his *Praise of the Desert* and later, in 432, his tract *On Contempt for the World.* On the other side, a series of monks—and the fact that they were of noble descent and education is undoubtedly not irrelevant—became bishops in Provence, in the valley of the Rhône, and in the northeast section of Gaul. Perhaps to be identified with Lérins is the great monastic literary tradition of the *Rule of the Four Fathers,* the *Second Rule of the Fathers,* the *Rule of Macarius,* and the *Third Rule of the Fathers.* The influence of these rules on subsequent monastic legislation, including the *Rule of St. Benedict,* is quite significant.

The person who was able to synthesize successfully all the tendencies that emerged from Lérinian and Augustinian monasticism was Caesarius of Arles. Deeply touched by his reading of Julianus Pomerius's treatise *On the Contemplative Life,* which was filled with admiration for Augustine, he succeeded in being both an active pastor (to the extent of being primate of Gaul and president of several councils) and a promoter of the monastic life. He composed a rule for monks and a rule for virgins, and he often spoke of monks in his sermons. His written work was to have an influence on the spiritual literature of the Middle Ages.

Besides Marmoutier and Lérins, another center of monastic life began to exert an influence, the monastery which had been founded at the beginning of the fifth century over the relics of St. Maurice at Agaune, in the upper valley of the Rhône. The cult of this saint spread for more than two centuries, but it was a Lérinian, Eucherius of Lyons, who wrote the *Passion of the Martyrs of Agaune.* The founders of the "monasteries of Jura," Romanus and Lupicinus, had been formed near Lyons, where both St. Martin and

St. Honoratus were venerated and where spirits were nourished by the writings of Sulpicius Severus, Cassian, and Eucherius.

A new period began in the seventh century, determined by the interaction between two currents that caused it to acquire the name Iro-Frankish. One of the currents did, in fact, come from Ireland, mediated through Columban; the other originated in the monasteries founded by Merovingian descendants of Clovis and, after about 640, by the Carolingians descending from Pepin the Old. The first current, originating in Luxeuil, which was founded in 590, spread chiefly through the lands of Burgundy and to the east of the Seine; the second spread toward the west of Gaul under the Merovingians, then moved gradually toward the east under the Carolingians. Other traditions also intermingled—all of them offshoots of movements that came from Africa, Spain, Italy, Marmoutier, Lérins, and ultimately, through all these routes, from the East.

The strongest personality of the time was Columban. About 590, this energetic Irishman left his country with a group of disciples and became the founder of the monastery at Luxeuil in the Vosges. After quarrels with various bishops and princes, he traveled—less as a missionary than as a monk—through Gaul, Germania, Switzerland (where he left behind Gall and several companions), and came to settle at Bobbio in Lombardy, where he died in 615. His written legacy includes his *Rule for Monks* (*Regula monachorum*), *Rule for the Common Life* (*Regula coenobialis*), *Penitential*, and some letters, the fourth of which, written from Nantes to his "very dear sons" at Luxeuil, shows the delicacy of spirit of which he was capable. In his texts he reconciled prudence with severity.

Two features characterized this monasticism or, more exactly, these diverse forms of monasticism, which blended together or were superimposed on one another. The first was the variety of observances that were practiced— people have spoken of the system of the "mixed rule" (*regula mixta*). Most of the houses adopted the prescriptions of the rules of Caesarius, Columban, and others as well. More and more they adopted the *RB*, which everyone henceforth attributed to Benedict of Nursia, especially after the Greek pope Zachary (741-752) had the *Dialogues* of Gregory translated into his own language. Likewise, the traditions coming from the East, from Ireland, and from elsewhere joined together, and in this cross-fertilization process they opened up great spiritual and cultural possibilities. This richness, however, was threatened by a danger that arose from the second feature that marked this period. The monasteries were founded and endowed by the Merovingian and later the Carolingian princes or by the high nobility of the Parisian, Austrasian, Burgundian, or Bavarian courts. The nobility claimed power over the monasteries. Nevertheless, if the ideal was sometimes obscured, it did not entirely disappear. The two great convictions that had given birth to and continued to enliven monasticism since its beginnings were maintained: that of the necessity of a rigorous asceticism and that of the primary importance of prayer in the life of the monk as the source of all peace and spiritual freedom. Some had even practiced that form of monasticism which consisted in going into voluntary exile (*peregrinatio*), seeking holiness by exposing themselves to the dangers inherent in all travel during this turbulent age, and speaking to God's people, whether occasionally or on a more regular basis. Many saints of that time who have been described as missionaries had been (at least according to their original intention) nothing other than solitaries to whom had been given the additional possibility of sharing with others the faith, hope, and charity that they had received in their union with God.

## England

On this island, which was successively called Albion, Britain, and then England, there seems to have been a Martinian monasticism since the fourth century. In Scotland traces of the monastery of Candida Casa have been rediscovered; it was constructed during this period using white stones from the region of Tours, where Martin was bishop-monk. In the fifth century, Germanus of Auxerre came on a mission against Pelagianism (about 450), and the influence of Patrick was not unknown. In 563 Columba founded at Iona a monastery inspired by Irish monastic ideals, whose influence spread into Northumbria. Gregory the Great sent some Roman monks to Kent. Near Canterbury, which they founded, there had also existed a Martinian sanctuary. About 625, Bishop Paulinus, who had been sent by Gregory in 601, went as far north as York. At the Council of Whitby in 664 partisans of the Roman monastic traditions won a major victory, and monasticism in Britain no longer followed the Celtic tradition. The *RB* became known and increasingly followed, which assured a certain uniformity and prosperity. But that prosperity would be disturbed in the ninth century by the shock of the Viking invasion.

In the monasteries themselves, especially because of their schools, a spirituality developed which harmoniously united the heritage of classical Latin antiquity and that of the patristic era. The school of York, founded by Bishop Egbert, would give to the Carolingian renewal of the eighth and ninth centuries scholars such as Alcuin and other people of high Christian culture. The typical representative of this spirituality was the Venerable Bede (672/3-735), a simple monk from York who exerted a profound influence by his example and his writings. He spent all his life reading, teaching, and writing. He and his disciples lived out a spirituality that was wholly nourished by doctrine but simple in its expression, formulated in an admirable Latin. He was spoken of as the "miracle Bede" and contributed to the spirituality of the Anglo-Saxon church by writing works useful for the formation of youth and clergy, by creating a program for the pastoral life in his letter to Egbert, and by reacting against abuses that were introduced into the affairs of ecclesiastical and monastic institutions. It was with this reforming intention that he wrote his *Ecclesiastical History of the English People*, which was read both as a source of highly valuable historical information and as a deeply spiritual document.

## The Eighth and Ninth Centuries

In 768 Charlemagne inaugurated a reign that would be sixty-four years long, during which he would be crowned emperor in 800. By the time of his death in 814, he had made use of monasticism extensively and had set up a new structure for it. One of his sons, Louis the Pious (d. 840), attempted to continue the work he had begun, but all their effort resulted in only partial and ephemeral success. This did not lessen its impact on the institution. The soaring increase in the number of monastic foundations, which had not ceased to multiply under the first Carolingians, continued later on. Between 800 and 820, there were no fewer than six hundred monasteries throughout the empire, without counting those in Italy. They were of various kinds: there were basilical communities in the city and monasteries out in the country; in the border regions these were often simple houses owned by the local nobility. In Septimania in Aquitaine, on the Spanish March, the son of Count Witiza, who entered Saint-Seine in 780 under the name of Benedict, two years later became the founder or reformer of a whole series of important communities, beginning with the great Aquitainian Abbey of Aniane. In order to put an end to the reign of the "mixed rule," Benedict of Aniane, with Charlemagne's support, introduced or imposed the *RB* as sole norm in thirty abbeys.

To facilitate the implementation of this program of standardization and to extend it, if possible, to the entire empire, Benedict of Aniane compiled a collection of earlier rules, the *Book of Rules* (*Codex regularum*), which he used in his *Concordance of Rules* (*Concordia regularum*) in order to produce a kind of commentary on the *Rule of St. Benedict*. At the same time, he continued to preserve and develop the customs inherited from the earlier tradition. In this renewal of education, he was aided by Alcuin, the Englishman who had become abbot of St. Martin of Tours in 796.

All the work undertaken by Charlemagne and by Benedict of Aniane to reform the abuses that had crept into the monasteries resulted in the legislation passed by the councils held at Aachen under Louis the Pious in 816 and 817. To eliminate the cause of decadence, which was laxity of observance, the councils established a clear distinction between monks and canons with respect to habit, diet, and the observance of the rule. The *Rule of St. Augustine* was prescribed for the canons, and the *Rule of St. Benedict,* as interpreted by Benedict of Aniane, was imposed on the monks. The first two commentaries on this latter text soon appeared. The commentary of Smaragdus, abbot of Saint Mihiel, was written shortly after 817. The other circulated shortly after 845 in several versions and under several names, especially those of Paul the Deacon of Monte Cristo and Hildemar of Corbie, whose teaching it actually transmitted.

Nevertheless, the traditional ideal had survived. The quest for union with God through prayer and asceticism had preserved its priority, a quest that led the saints to successes which sometimes, from a human perspective, looked like failures, but which realized to a very high degree what was aspired to by all. The monks continued to be disposed toward difficult tasks that others would not undertake. Gregory of Utrecht molded Liutger (d. 809) into a bishop who was totally devoted to evangelization while living in voluntary poverty. Anschar, a disciple of Adalhart of Corbie in Picardy and later a monk of Corvey in Saxony, went into voluntary exile in order to "save souls" in Denmark and Sweden, before he became in 845 the archbishop of Bremen, where he died twenty years later. The ancient *peregrinatio,* which sometimes included some preaching, remained popular; even eremitism was maintained and reorganized. In the region of Metz, probably toward the end of the ninth century, an author whose name was perhaps Grimlaïc composed his *Rule for Solitaries.* He wrote for cenobites, but above all for hermits, including the recluses, who usually lived in association with a community. Their life was entirely contemplative, but this did not rule out a certain apostleship. Thus, the peculiar character of monasticism was safeguarded, even at this time, when everything had become subject to legislation. As an institution monasticism did not require that any one activity be its *raison d'être.* It had no end but the quest for God through prayer and asceticism; yet it allowed for the free expansion of personal vocations in the service of church and society.

## The Reforms of the Tenth Century

At the end of the ninth and the beginning of the tenth century, monasticism degenerated almost everywhere into a state of institutional decadence, and in certain countries, like England, it almost disappeared altogether. The secular powers—kings and feudal lords—continued to control the wealth of the abbeys, often favoring vassals who especially served their interests and whom they wished to reward. They often designated as abbots unworthy clerics and sometimes even lay people. Since the communities lacked resources, their members obtained them privately. They had personal savings, and they often lived outside of the monastery with a wife and children. To justify this, they apparently considered themselves no longer monks, but canons, and they lived without a rule.

It was at this time that a whole series of reforms appeared and were implemented throughout the tenth century. At certain points, the reforms received the support of popes such as Benedict VIII (1012-1024) and John XIX (1024- 1032). On the whole, their principal characteristic was that they were spontaneous and diverse. Rather than a reform there was a movement of reform or, even more precisely, a reformism, which manifested itself in independent and scattered reforms. Before the existence of institutional reforms there existed a need for spiritual conversion, which was inherent in monasticism. After all, monasticism was in itself an institution that reformed individuals and normally led them to reform the communities that they constituted, insofar as the circumstances and the institutions of each age permitted it. To this need for reform, which everywhere made itself felt, the *RB* offered a possibility: it anticipated the autonomy and, in this sense, the immunity of each monastery in temporal matters, that is, in the economic realm. One of the results of this was to restore to the monasteries their liberty (*libertas*). This was sometimes achieved in the older monasteries, which were closely bound to economic and political structures, but it was more often found in the newly founded monasteries, like Cluny, or in "refounded," "rejuvenated" monasteries, so to speak, like Gorze.

Although these reforms were independent of one another, there were similarities among them, because the saintly abbots who inspired them traveled about, met one another, came to know one another, and kept up friendly relations and exchanged ideas and texts (the collections of *consuetudines,* that is, the "customaries"). This convergence of an ideal, often symbolized and actualized by the saints, and this sharing of their experiences and aspirations insured the unity of the various reforms of the tenth century, which in turn prepared for those of the period that followed.

It remains for us to describe the most important of these reforms. The earliest was that of Cluny, founded in Burgundy in 909; it was a direct extension of the reform of Benedict of Aniane. Since the source of decadence was the seizure of property by seculars, the founder of Cluny, William the Pious, Duke of Aquitaine and Count of Macon, at the instigation of Bernon (who was already abbot of Baume and Gigny and became abbot of Cluny as well), gave this new monastery over to St. Peter and his successors, the popes. He commended it to the protection of the apostolic see and exempted it from the intervention of any other ecclesiastical or secular power. Thus, in effect, he assured its *libertas*. Cluny prospered in the tenth century, owing to the influence of great abbots who were saints: after Bernon (d. 927) came Odo (d. 942), Aymard (who resigned his position in 948), and Maïeul (d. 994). They contributed simultaneously to the consolidation of institutional liberty and internal organization and to the elaboration of doctrine. The long poem of Odo entitled *Occupatio* was a major accomplishment. The piece situated monasticism within the history of salvation insofar as it embodied a common life lived in charity, detachment, and purity of heart and insofar as it helped sinners (for whom it existed) to achieve for themselves and to give witness to the goal of all reform in individuals and in the church— namely, to return to the state of grace as symbolized by the Garden of Eden, to rekindle the fervor of the Jerusalem Christians after the resurrection of Christ, to actualize as fully as possible the mystery of Pentecost, and to anticipate, in a certain fashion, the celestial city.

In France there were other centers of reform, such as Fleury-sur-Loire, and, in Normandy, Mont Saint-Michel. In Lotharingia the chief centers of reform were Brogne in Belgium, which was associated with the abbeys of St. Blandin of Ghent and with Glastonbury in England, and Gorze in Lorraine, which was restored in 933 by John of Vendières and a group of laymen who became monks with him. In Italy the reformers exerted their influence in several areas. Romuald, a monk of St. Apollinaris of Ravenna, went first to San Miguel of Cuxa in Catalonia; then, until his untimely death in 1027, he founded or reformed numerous monasteries and hermitages in northern and central Italy, especially Fonte Avellana and Camaldoli. More than other reformers he insisted on the solitary life, though not exclusively. Even in Rome during the tenth century no fewer than sixty monasteries could be counted, some of which were of the Greek rite. The abbey of Sts. Boniface and Alexis on the Aventine was a meeting place for representatives of the various movements of reform that existed among the Roman houses. One of these representatives was Nilus, who founded a Greek monastery at Grottaferrata not far from the city. Nearly twenty-five Latin monasteries in Rome served the maintenance of basilicas.

Toward the end of the century, monks coming from Amalfi established a Latin monastery at Mount Athos. Although this long period, which has sometimes been designated as the "century of iron," had known so much violence everywhere and so much calamity in the papacy, it was also a time during which monasticism played a role that its origins destined it to play.

Under the internal impulse of an inherent need for spiritual renewal, it had been able to recapture, owing to this charismatic quality, the liberty that it needed to retain its identity. Despite the bankruptcy of institutions but with the support of Christian people of every sort—popes, bishops, laypeople— monasticism everywhere reformed itself and contributed to the reform of institutions. It remained distinct from the hierarchical structure of the church, but it became more and more associated with the work the church was given to accomplish in the world.

In England monasticism had almost entirely disappeared. The abbey of Canterbury itself was occupied by secular clerics, but Dunstan (ca. 909–988), who had been educated there, returned about 943. He replaced the secular clerics with monks following the *RB*. With the support of kings Edmund, Eadred, and Edgar, he promoted a genuine revival of monasticism. Exiled to Flanders from 955 to 957, he came into contact with the reform of Brogne. He was made archbishop of Canterbury in 959, and, in collaboration with Ethelwold, bishop of Winchester, and Oswald, bishop of Worcester, he reformed or founded thirty monasteries for men— several of which were cathedrals—and a dozen monasteries for women. Inspired by the practices of Fleury and Peter of Ghent, abbots and abbesses concurred in drawing up an agreement entitled *Regularis concordia*, which regularized observances. These monasteries became centers of spirituality and culture; they supplied England with many bishops and contributed to the evangelization of Scandinavia.

An outstanding representative of this renewal was Aelfric. Born about 955 and educated as a monk in Winchester under Ethelwold, he became abbot of Cerne and then of Eynsham in 987. He died between 1020 and 1025. Beginning in 991, Aelfric provided English editions of works that made the teachings of Bede accessible to the lower clergy and the people. Particularly influential were his two volumes *Sermones catholici* or *Homilies*. He also wrote lives of the saints and composed the first Latin grammar to be edited in English. He was the creator of a spiritual literature that was at the same time patristic and Anglo-Saxon.

## The Eleventh Century and the Gregorian Reform

The general characteristic of this reform, both in monasticism and in other areas, was to give an institutional and theoretical status to the reformist movement, which previously had been self-determined and had assumed a practical character. This goal was pursued through particular insistence upon the necessity of a certain amount of centralization and subordination to the papacy.

The means that were employed in the eleventh century at Cluny to sustain fervor were, on the one hand, an austerity tempered with discretion and, on the other, a striving for continuous prayer, which was manifest in the time devoted to spiritual reading, devotional exercises, and the celebration of the liturgy. To the "regular hours" were added supererogatory prayers, which were fulfilled by various groups of community members. Manual labor was mentioned as one of the practices, but there remained little time to attend to it. In turn, intellectual work was in favor and this resulted in a number of literary productions, which surpassed those of any other monastery of that period. The practices of Cluny spread far and wide—their diffusion was clearly evident throughout France, Spain, Portugal, Italy, England, and Germany. Throughout all of Christian Europe the number of houses that were more or less dependent upon Cluny increased from sixty in 1049 to about two thousand by the beginning of the twelfth century—if we are to believe some estimates. This monastery also exerted a reforming influence on the clergy and the laity. This was principally due to the bonds of "familiarity" it established with its benefactors and with those who worked within its domains and to the prayers of intercession promised for their deceased— hence the importance of necrologies for the history and geography of monasticism during this period.

In 1070, Lanfranc came from Bec to Christ Church of Canterbury, where he became archbishop. The influence of Cluny, which was already present in England, now increased. Malmesbury, St. Albans, and many other houses witnessed a flurry of intense literary activity, especially in the area of historical writing. Despite contrasts and sometimes conflicts, the similarities between the two currents represented by the ancient English tradition and the new Norman one coexisted and conferred upon English monasticism in the eleventh century a unique richness.

About 1030 in Tuscany John Gualbert founded the monastery of Vallombrosa, which would become the center of a vast community spread throughout central and northern Italy. Vallombrosa insisted on communal living and poverty; the observances seem to have been influenced by those of Cluny. In the subalpine region of Italy, the abbey of Fruttuaria, which was in contact with St. Romuald and with Ravenna, was the original house of William of Volpiano, who reformed St. Benignus of Dijon, and of John (who called himself "little John"), the abbot of St. Benignus and of "La Trinité" of Fécamp in Normandy. He was also in contact with England and Lotharingia. John of Fécamp left spiritual writings of a highly mystical and literary character, which circulated under different names, especially those of Augustine and Alcuin, and were widely read up to the end of the Middle Ages. Peter Damian continued the work of Romuald. In the *Life* that he wrote about Romuald (without having known him personally) and later in numerous other writings, he proposed a program of reform for monasticism and for the church. He was a hermit at Fonte Avellana and was named cardinal of Ostia in 1057. But after 1061 he was given permission to return to his hermitage, where he lived, for the most part, until his death (1072). In his works he presented to all monks—hermits and cenobites—a doctrine that was simultaneously austere and very human. He fought for all the causes of the Gregorian Reform, railing against simony, incontinence, the ignorance of the clergy, and the schisms that broke out in various cities, including Rome.

And so once more, owing to the independence rooted in its charismatic and not primarily institutional nature, monasticism, which led to the interior renewal of individuals, had prepared for and promoted reform in the church and peace in society. In northern and eastern Europe it took root in Sweden, Poland, and Hungary; and, because of its considerable vitality, Latin monasticism even expanded into the East. Christian Syria witnessed the settlement of Latin monks, who generally came from Italy, in Jerusalem, the valley of Josaphat, Mount Tabor, and elsewhere. There they practiced charity in all its forms: hospitality and care for the poor, the sick, and children. They quickly became prosperous and communicated among themselves and with monasteries in Sicily, Calabria, Rome, northern Italy, and other regions, as far as Lotharingia, France, and England. They also came into contact with the Eastern monks. In all of these contexts, texts and ideas continued to circulate. In 1054, a schism had officially separated the church of Rome from that of Constantinople, but, thanks to the interaction that continued to take place among some monks, there was a unity on the level of spirituality that was stronger than the division introduced on the level of religious politics.

*Translated by Dennis Tamburello*

## Note

1. Friedrich Prinz called the monastery a refuge (*Flüchtlingskloster*) for the aristocracy of northern Gaul (*Frühes Mönchtum im Frankenreich*).

## Bibliography

### Sources

*Aethelwold of Winchester: The Monastic Agreement of the Monks and Nuns of the English Nation*. Edited and translated by Thomas Symons. London: Nelson, 1953. Text and translation of *Regularis concordia*.

*RB 1980: The Rule of St. Benedict in Latin and English with Notes.* Edited by Timothy Fry et al. Collegeville, MN: Liturgical Press, 1981. Text, translation, and extensive commentary, along with a history of monasticism.

*The Rule of St. Augustine.* Translated by Thomas A. Hand. Westminster, MD: Newman Press, 1956.

*The Rule of the Master.* Translated by Luke Eberle with an introduction by Adalbert de Vogüé. Kalamazoo, MI: Cistercian Publications, 1977.

*St. Odo of Cluny.* Translated and edited by Gerard Sitwell. London: Sheed & Ward, 1958. *Life of Odo* by John of Salerno and Odo's *Life of St. Gerald of Aurillac.*

*Sulpicius Severus et al.: The Western Fathers.* Edited and translated by F. R. Hoare. New York: Harper & Row, 1965. The *Lives* of Martin of Tours, Ambrose, Augustine, Honoratus, and Germanus.

*Western Asceticism.* Edited by Owen Chadwick. LCC 12. 1958. Selections from Cassian and the text of the *RB.*

## Studies

Blair, Peter Hunter. *The World of Bede.* New York: St. Martin's Press, 1971.

Butler, Edward Cuthbert. *Benedictine Monachism.* 2nd ed. London: Longmans, 1924. Still a classic study.

Chadwick, Owen. *John Cassian: A Study in Primitive Monasticism.* Cambridge: Cambridge University Press, 1950.

Constable, Giles. *Medieval Monasticism: A Select Bibliography.* Toronto: University of Toronto Press, 1976. A useful tool.

Hallinger, Kassius. *Gorze-Kluny: Studien zu den monastischen Lebensformen und Gegensätzen im Hochmittelalter.* Studia Anselmiana 22-25. Rome: Herder, 1950-51. Fundamental work on the tenth- and eleventh-century reform movements.

Hunt, Noreen, ed. *Cluniac Monasticism in the Central Middle Ages.* Hamden, CT: Archon Books, 1971. A collection of essays; see especially those by R. Morghen, K. Hallinger, and J. Leclercq.

Knowles, David. *From Pachomius to Ignatius: A Study in the Constitutional History of Religious Orders.* Oxford: Clarendon Press, 1966. A brilliant study that includes a chapter on the development of obedience.

———. *The Monastic Order in England 940-1216.* 2nd ed. Cambridge: Cambridge University Press, 1963. A major work that includes a history of western monasticism to the twelfth century.

Leclercq, Jean. *Aux sources de la spiritualité occidentale: Etapes et constances.* Tradition et spiritualité 4. Paris: Cerf, 1964. Collects some of Leclercq's many articles.

———. *Études sur le vocabulaire monastique du moyen âge.* Studia Anselmiana 48. Rome: Herder, 1961.

———. *The Love of Learning and the Desire for God.* New York: Fordham University Press, 1961. A well-known study.

Lienhard, Joseph T. *Paulinus of Nola and Early Western Monasticism.* Cologne: Hanstein, 1977. Useful for the origins of monasticism in the West.

Lorenz, Rudolf. "Die Anfänge des abendländischen Mönchtums im 4. Jahrhundert." *Zeitschrift für Kirchengeschichte* 77 (1966) 1-61.

"Monachisme." In *Dict. Sp.* 10, cols. 1523-1617. A multi-author survey with excellent bibliographies.

Prinz, Friedrich. *Frühes Mönchtum im Frankenreich.* Munich and Vienna: Oldenbourg, 1965.

Rousseau, Philip. *Ascetics, Authority and the Church in the Age of Jerome and Cassian.* Oxford: Oxford University Press, 1978.

Schmitz, Philibert. *Histoire de l'ordre de Saint-Benoit.* 7 vols. Maredsous: Maredsous, 1948–56. A major history.

*Théologie de la vie monastique: Études sur la tradition patristique.* Paris: Aubier, 1961. Excellent collection of studies on figures from Origen to Aelred.

Vogüé, Adalbert de. *Community and Abbot in the Rule of Saint Benedict.* Kalamazoo, MI: Cistercian Publications, 1979.

Wollasch, Joachim. *Mönchtum des Mittelalters zwischen Kirche und West.* Munich: Fink, 1973.

# 6

# The Uplifting Spirituality of Pseudo-Dionysius

## PAUL ROREM

THE "SPIRITUALITY" OF DIONYSIUS the Pseudo-Areopagite remains veiled in the larger enigma of his true identity and specific historical context. We know not the man, but only his essays, few and relatively brief.[1] Near the start of the sixth century, the ongoing debate over the nature of Christ was suddenly compounded by the introduction of some difficult writings, ostensibly from the pen of Paul's convert in Athens, Dionysius the Areopagite (Acts 17:34). Initial skepticism regarding their authenticity was quickly dispelled. For centuries, patriarchs, popes, mystics, and other theologians ascribed the authority of the apostolic age to the ten "Dionysian" letters and the four treatises: *The Divine Names, The Mystical Theology, The Celestial Hierarchy,* and *The Ecclesiastical Hierarchy.*[2]

*The Divine Names* presents a philosophical, often convoluted exegesis of the many names of God found in the Bible, such as "Good," "Being," "Life," "Wisdom," and so forth. *The Mystical Theology* tersely summarizes the author's general method concerning spiritual knowledge; it begins with the famous example of Moses ascending into the "cloud of unknowing" on Mount Sinai and concludes with the principle of negating all presumed attributes of God, whether perceptible or conceptual. *The Celestial Hierarchy* first presents the concept of a hierarchy, whether angelic or human, and then concentrates on the three triads of celestial beings, as described in the Scriptures. *The Ecclesiastical Hierarchy* interprets the church's arrangement of rites and offices, specifically the three sacraments (baptism, Eucharist, and consecration of the myron-ointment), the three ordinations (of the hierarch or bishop, priests, and deacons), monastic tonsure, and funerals.

Although the author of these works was influenced by the Alexandrian-Cappadocian Christianity of Gregory of Nyssa, for example, and by the later Neoplatonism of Iamblichus and especially Proclus,[3] these debts were so artfully concealed that his pseudonym managed to survive even the penetrating criticisms of Renaissance humanists. It was conclusively exposed only in 1895.[4] Twentieth-century scholarship has identified the author's general context as a late-fifth-century mixture of Syrian Christianity and Athenian Neoplatonism. None of the various attempts at a more specific identification of the author has yet commanded a scholarly consensus.[5] The corpus may never be persuasively tied to a specific historical figure. There is, therefore, no historical basis for an investigation of the spirituality of this author except for his pseudonymous writings, which are so intentionally misleading about their original context and community.

The Areopagite's literary remains present a peculiar but coherent synthesis of Neoplatonic metaphysics, biblical exegesis, and liturgical interpretation.[6] The Neoplatonic framework of "procession and return," of descent and ascent, charts the Dionysian path of spiritual uplifting, an "anagogical" ascent to the divine summit itself. Guidance for this upward path comes through the interpretation of Christian symbols—both biblical and liturgical—according to a systematic program of negation. The Dionysian interpretation of scriptural and liturgical symbolism incorporates negation within the anagogical or uplifting journey, for such interpretation must negate and thus transcend the superficial appearances of the symbols in order to rise up to their higher, conceptual meanings. Then even the loftiest interpretations and purest conceptions must also be negated and abandoned in the final, silent approach to the ineffable and transcendent God beyond all speech and thought.

The intellectual climate that received this corpus so readily was dominated by late Neoplatonism, within and without the church, despite the increasing pressure of Christian emperors upon the official Platonic Academy, which Justinian closed or at least expelled in 529 c.e.[7] The Pseudo-Dionysian writings were first cited in 532 or 533. Although the extreme proximity of these dates may be coincidental, their relationship is suggestive. Forced underground, the Athenian Neoplatonism of Proclus and his school reappeared in the Pseudo-Areopagite's synthesis of Christian content and Proclean philosophy. Consciously or not, the first champions of these writings preserved much of the banished Neoplatonism within a Christian system which then influenced centuries of theology and philosophy.

## The Interpretation and Negation of the Perceptible

The motif of a spiritual uplifting or ascent is the second half of the metaphysical framework known as "procession and return." The Areopagite inherited and adapted this Neoplatonic construct, which is summarized so succinctly by Proclus: "every effect remains in its cause, proceeds from it, and returns to it."[8] As is apparent in the works of a predecessor like Iamblichus and a successor like Eriugena (John Scotus), the pattern can symbolize an ontological bestowal of being itself in a creating procession as well as a cosmic gathering of all reality back to the divine source in a saving return. Our author emphasizes the epistemology of this "downward and upward movement": the divine procession is God's accommodating self-revelation; the return occurs through knowing and "unknowing." The opening lines of *The Celestial Hierarchy* trace the trajectory of the divine light as a downward procession and an enlightening return:

> Inspired by the Father, each procession of the Light spreads itself generously toward us, and, in its power to unify, it stirs us by lifting us up. It returns us back to the oneness and deifying simplicity of the Father who gathers us in. . . . However, this divine ray can enlighten us only by being upliftingly concealed in a variety of sacred veils which the providence of the Father adapts to our nature as human beings. (*CH* 1, 120B.7–121A.1; 121BC.16–27)[9]

This "variety of sacred veils" is the scriptural and liturgical symbolism in which the divine is "upliftingly concealed." It is the concept of "uplifting" that links the Neoplatonic metaphysics of procession and return to the interpretation of Christian symbols. The return and the interpretive uplifting are one and the same ascent, "the uplifting and return toward God" (*CH* 9, 260B.16f.; *CH* 8, 240A.2–8; *CH* 15, 333B.24), although it is the author's discussions of anagogical interpretation that provide more detail. The process of interpreting biblical and liturgical symbols constitutes the first step in the ascent to God. For the Pseudo-Areopagite, symbols may serve to conceal spiritual truths from the uninitiated, but their primary purpose is to uplift the faithful from the realm of sense perception to the realm of the intellect (*EH* 1, 376D.36–377A.5; *CH* 2, 140AB.7–18, 145A.8–10; *Ep.* 9, 1105C.36–45, 1108A.7–20). Perceptible and material symbols for the conceptual and immaterial truths of the heavenly realm are not disparaged for their lowliness. They are valued for their uplifting role, since they provide the path upward, beyond themselves, to the higher realm. "Our hierarchy," writes Dionysius, "needs perceptible things to lift us up from them into the domain of the intellect" (*EH* 1, 377A.4f.).[10] The uplifting is not accomplished by the symbols in themselves, as if they possess any magical efficacy; it occurs in the process of interpreting them, in the contemplative movement from the perceptible "up" to the conceptual.

> For it is quite impossible that we humans should, in any material way, rise up to imitate and to contemplate the heavenly hierarchies without the aid of

those material means capable of guiding us as our nature requires. Hence, any thinking person realizes that the appearances of beauty are signs of an invisible loveliness. (*CH* 1, 121C.35–124A.5)

The type of interpretation sampled here—equally illustrative of biblical or liturgical symbolism—involves what is usually called "negative theology." Yet both words need clarification. In the Dionysian vocabulary, the word "theology" usually means the biblical "word of God."[11] The Dionysian statements of "affirmative and negative theology" must not be taken as abstract principles concerning religious language in general. They are the specific guidelines for his biblical exegesis and are also applied to liturgical interpretation. The term "negative" or "apophatic" is also elusive, for the Areopagite applies his program of negation to both the interpretation of perceptible symbols and the abandonment of all conceptual interpretations.

It is the Pseudo-Areopagite's method of exegeting the scriptural symbols for God and the angels that integrates negation into his overall synthesis, as seen in the second chapter of *The Celestial Hierarchy*. No one can read in the Bible that the celestial beings look like oxen or lions, he says, without formulating some method for interpreting such absurdities. He argues that scriptural language works in a double way. "It does so, firstly, by proceeding naturally through sacred images in which like represents like, while also using formations which are dissimilar and even entirely inadequate and ridiculous" (*CH* 2, 140C.25–28). For Dionysius, at stake here are not just certain incongruous descriptions of the angels, but all biblical language about God. Beyond the obviously inadequate depictions of God as a charging bear or a benign fire, even the designations "word" or "mind" or "being" fall short of describing the ineffable divine essence. So the Scriptures must also use negations, but they do so in a most complex way.

> Then there is the scriptural device of praising the deity by presenting it in utterly dissimilar revelations. He is described as invisible, infinite, ungraspable, and other things which show not what He is but what in fact He is not. This second way of talking about Him seems to me much more appropriate, for, as the secret and sacred tradition has instructed, God is in no way like the things that have being and we have no knowledge at all of His incomprehensible and ineffable transcendence and invisibility. (*CH* 2, 140D.41–141A.3)

As illustrative of "negative theology," this crucial text is best understood by distinguishing the two related functions of negation in the overall ascent. The first concerns the anagogical interpretation of perceptible symbols, most obviously the "dissimilar" ones that are applied to God or to the angels in the Scriptures. The second function of negation, discussed in the next section, entails the subsequent, "higher" abandonment of all mental interpretations and conceptions before the ineffable transcendence of God.

To understand how negation first functions within the interpretation of symbols, we must recognize that the scriptural statements to be affirmed and denied are arranged in a continuum of relative similarity and dissimilarity.[12] Even the most grotesque biblical symbol for God—a worm!—is in some way an appropriate depiction of some divine attribute. On the other hand, even the loftiest image ultimately falls short. A given symbol for God, such as "sun of righteousness" or a cornerstone or a lion, can be employed because of its relative similarity to some aspect of the divine nature, but it must at the same time be negated because of its ultimate dissimilarity. *The Divine Names* puts it succinctly:

> For the very same things are both similar and dissimilar to God. They are similar to Him to the extent that they share what cannot be shared. They are dissimilar to Him in that as effects they fall so very short of the Cause and are infinitely and incomparably subordinate to Him. (*DN* 9, 916A.8-12)

Symbolic statements about God or the angels are not automatically and indiscriminately negated. They are carefully interpreted in order to leave behind the apparent similarity which is affirmed in the symbol but is literally false and must be acknowledged as a dissimilarity to be negated, and in order to ascend toward what is really meant by the symbol and can thus be affirmed on a new, higher level. In this interpretation of the symbolic, affirmation and negation combine to move the interpreter beyond the perceptible up to the conceptual.

Far from compartmentalizing his method into "affirmative theology," "negative theology," and "symbolic theology," the Pseudo-Areopagite seeks to hold together affirmation and negation, similarity and dissimilarity as a dialectical way of understanding the many symbols of his tradition. A "dissimilar similarity,"[13] as he puts it, is *simultaneously* a similarity to be affirmed and a dissimilarity to be negated. This is part of the larger simultaneity of procession and return, which are not two successive moments but rather two ways of viewing the same continuum. Assertions, writes our cryptic author, are arranged from the most plausible "down" to the most incongruous. Thus, in the third chapter of *The Mystical Theology*, he says that his treatises begin with the lost or fictitious "Theological Representations," a work that concerns the scriptural doctrines of the divine unity and trinity, then proceeds "down" to the Bible's conceptual names for God in *The Divine Names*, and continues with the "lowest" assertions—those biblical depictions of God taken from sense perception—in "The Symbolical Theology," which is also lost or entirely fictional.[14] The downward procession is here identified with the assertions. The denials of these attributions or concepts, on the other hand, are arranged from the bottom "up." The uplifting return is thus associated with "negative theology," even though procession and return, and affirmation and negation can never be separated entirely.

> In the earlier books my argument travelled downward from the most exalted to the humblest categories, taking in on this downward path an ever-increasing number of ideas which multiplied with every stage of the descent. But my argument now rises from what is below up to the transcendent, and the more it climbs, the more language falters, and when it has passed up and beyond the ascent, it will turn silent completely, since it will finally be at one with Him who is indescribable. (*MT* 3, 1033CD.31–45)

These examples of life, goodness, air (the "still, small, breeze"), stone, drunkenness, and rage are all biblical examples exegeted elsewhere in the corpus.[15] The methodological point illustrated here is that the uplifting return begins by negating first the lowliest, most incongruous descriptions and then moves up the continuum to negate those that may seem more appropriate. For the purpose of spiritual uplifting, this method gives a crucial place to the most disgusting and startling descriptions of the celestial beings.

> Indeed the sheer crassness of the signs is a goad so that even the materially inclined cannot accept that it could be permitted or true that the celestial and divine sights could be conveyed by such shameful things. (*CH* 2, 141B.27–31)

Base images such as animals and inanimate objects start the novice on the right path upward, since these symbols cry out for an exegesis that will transcend such appearances. Once begun, the method of spiritual interpretation that negates and goes beyond the superficial meanings can rise up to the more attractive depictions and yet not be misled by their charms. The more advanced interpreter needs few reminders regarding the role of negation in the interpretation of all symbols. "The explanation of one incongruous image suffices for the like-mannered interpretation of comparable ones" (*CH* 15, 337C.31–34).

The concept of relative incongruity thus carries the principle of negation deep within itself and applies it to the spiritual interpretation of the liturgy as well. Liturgical symbols may not be so obviously base and shocking, and some are even called "precise."[16] Yet they are not exempt from the same method of interpretation. The methodological prolegomena of *The Celestial Hierarchy*, chapters 1 through 3, apply both to that treatise and to the subsequent companion piece, *The Ecclesiastical Hierarchy*. As previewed in *The Mystical Theology*, uplifting interpretation starts with the "lower" or more incongruous depictions, a process begun in *The Celestial Hierarchy*. By the end of that treatise, the role of "negative theology" in interpreting symbols is largely assumed. It is then taken entirely for granted in the next work, *The Ecclesiastical Hierarchy*. For the most part, Dionysian biblical exegesis and

liturgical interpretation employ exactly the same method. The single difference is that liturgical symbols are "higher" or less incongruous than those
mentioned in *The Celestial Hierarchy*. The relative congruity of liturgical
imagery is detectable in both form and content. Formally, the liturgical
tradition is said to be "more immaterial" than the biblical tablets since it is
"free from writing" (*EH* 1, 376C.27–34). In terms of their contents, the liturgical symbols emphasized by Dionysius depict God not in material objects
but in ritual movements. The medium is the "higher" dimension of time,
not the lowly realm of space, as in the material forms and objects associated
with God in the biblical exegesis of "The Symbolical Theology" or *The
Ninth Letter*, or with the angels in *The Celestial Hierarchy*, chapter 15. The
Areopagite's liturgical exposition slights all objects, whether the architecture
or vestments or the sacramental substances and their containers. He emphasizes instead the gestures and movements of the rites. These symbols are not
spatial materials but rather temporal movements, such as the "procession
and return" of the hierarch with the incense or the fraction and distribution
of the eucharistic bread and cup as symbolic of the incarnation.[17] Of course,
the celestial hierarchy in itself is far superior to the ecclesiastical hierarchy.
It is indeed through the angelic beings that all of this spiritual enlightenment
is mediated to the human hierarchy and lifts it up. But as stages on a spiritual
pilgrimage, the biblical exegesis of *The Celestial Hierarchy* as a treatise is
preparatory to the more advanced exercise of liturgical interpretation in *The
Ecclesiastical Hierarchy*. This sequence is reflected also in the liturgy itself,
where the biblical readings provide a general introduction, open even to the
catechumens and penitents, whereas the subsequent, sacramental portion of
the rite is shared with only the "higher" orders.[18]

It is within the framework of procession and a return through the interpretation of symbols that Dionysius employed the categories of "purification,
illumination, and perfection." This trio of "powers" is applied to the angels
and especially to the human interrelationships of the triad of clerics with
the three lay orders: those being purified (the catechumens, the possessed,
and the penitent), the laypeople, and the monks.

> The holy sacraments bring about purification, illumination, and perfection.
> The deacons form the order which purifies. The priests constitute the order
> which gives illumination. And the hierarchs, living in conformity with God,
> make up the order which perfects. As for those who are being purified, they
> are the ones who do not partake of the sacred vision or communion. The
> sacred people is the contemplative order. The order of those made perfect is
> that of the monks who live a single-minded life. (*EH* 6, 536D.38–44)

Although the Areopagite once tied baptism to the powers of purification
and illumination, and the Eucharist and the sacramental consecration of the

myron-ointment to the power of perfection, in the rest of the corpus all three powers are operative in all three sacraments, although with differing emphases (*EH* 5, 504BC.20–25). Similarly, the "three ways" themselves are not as distinct as it may seem. Dionysius does not use this triad to mean a moral purification and a unitive perfection, as distinguished from the middle power of cognitive illumination. The fundamental concern of all three is spiritual knowledge, in various degrees. The concept of purification can consider moral blemishes, but it also includes purification from relative ignorance (*EH* 6, 537ABC). Illumination, of course, concerns the enlightened contemplation of the sacred symbols (*EH* 6, 532BC). Perfection means not perfect union, but perfect knowledge, "to behold sacred things with a perfected understanding" or to be "enlightened in the perfect understanding of the sacred illumination" (*CH* 3, 165D.45–48; *EH* 5, 504B.12–20). Thus the entire trio of purification, illumination, and perfection concerns progress on the same path of spiritual understanding, especially regarding liturgical contemplation. Although featured prominently in the corpus, this triad is actually auxiliary to the larger framework of procession and return, particularly regarding the uplifting interpretation of scriptural and liturgical symbols.

The goal of this anagogical movement, the first step of the overall ascent, is spiritual knowledge, as often expressed by the metaphor of light.[19] The interpreter is uplifted to the domain of the intellect or "raised up to conceptual contemplations,"[20] as seen in the interpretations provided by each section of *The Ecclesiastical Hierarchy* entitled "Contemplation." Since all of this uplifting interpretation employs some negation of the perceptible, it is the interpretive enterprise detailed in *The Celestial Hierarchy* and *The Ecclesiastical Hierarchy* that provides the proper context for the fourth chapter of *The Mystical Theology:*

> Chapter Four. That the supreme cause of every perceptible thing is not itself
> perceptible.
> So this is what we say. The Cause of all is above all and is not inexistent, lifeless, speechless, mindless. It is not a material body, and hence has neither shape nor form, quality, quantity, or weight. (*MT* 4, 1040D)

In summary, one negates all things perceptible in order to be elevated through these symbols up to the realm of the conceptual.

## The Negation and Abandonment of the Conceptual

*The Mystical Theology's* fourth chapter, however, is not the end of that brief essay, just as the conceptual contemplation of God achieved through the uplifting process of interpreting biblical and ritual images is not the ultimate goal of the Dionysian odyssey. The Areopagite's ascent has two steps. The former, usually overlooked and thus emphasized above, is the interpretive movement from perceptible symbols up to the concepts symbolized. The latter and more familiar leg of this journey is the negation and abandonment of all such concepts. This bipartite ascent is summarized at the beginning of *The Divine Names:*

> In this life, we use whatever appropriate symbols we can for the things of God. With these analogies we are raised upwards toward the truth of the mind's vision, a truth which is simple and one. And then we leave behind us all our own conceptions of the divine. We call a halt to the activities of our minds and, to the extent that is proper, we approach the ray which transcends being. (*DN* 1, 592CD.40–47)

As introduced above, "negative theology" is involved in both steps of this ascent. In the first, the relative incongruity of all perceptible images meant that affirmation and negation were combined to yield the conceptual meanings of these symbols. In the second step, the principle of negation is systematically applied to this higher conceptual or intelligible realm of spiritual interpretations. As the supreme cause of all, God is proportionately revealed in all of the created order and in human knowledge. But as transcending all, God is not fully known in creation or in any human concept. "God is therefore known through knowledge and through unknowing" (*DN* 7, 872A.4f.; see also *MT* 1, 1000B). The Dionysian ontology of God's total transcendence entails an epistemology of "unknowing." "If all knowledge is of that which is, and is limited to the realm of the existent, then whatever transcends being must also transcend knowledge" (*DN* 593A.2–5).

All concepts are thus ultimately incapable of expressing the ineffable God and must therefore be negated in that they are all left behind as the journey nears its final goal. Even the most sublime conceptions, such as God's Unity or Trinity, and even the highest name, "Goodness," stand merely at the limited pinnacle of human language and thought. Ultimately, they too must be recognized as deficient and must be negated. The prefixed superlative "*hyper*," so common in the corpus, is an abbreviation for this entire enterprise of negating and transcending human language. One may say, biblically, that God is "good." Yet one should also say, again with the Scriptures, that God is not "good" in the human sense. Such a negation is true not because of a deprivation, as if God were less than good, but because of a transcendence, since God is "hyper-good" or "super-good" or "more-than-good." This negation does not issue in a new, higher form of affirmation as in the earlier negation of the perceptible realm, but brings one past all use of the mind.

11. *The Heavenly Ladder,* Johannes
Climacus Manuscript, 11th century
(Garrett Med. Ms. No. 16)

[The] preference is for the way up through negations, since this stands the soul outside everything which is correlative with its own finite nature. Such a way guides the soul through all the divine notions, notions which are themselves transcended by that which is far beyond every name, all reason and all knowledge. Beyond the outermost boundaries of the world, the soul is brought into union with God Himself to the extent that every one of us is capable of it. (*DN* 13, 981AB.4–22; see also *CH* 2, 140C)

As apparent in this text from the end of *The Divine Names,* the negation of all concepts is not merely a rational technique or an abstract theory of epistemology. It is an ascent, a "way up through negations," which stands the soul outside itself—renders it, literally, "ecstatic"—and guides it to union with God. Dionysius did not have a technical concept of religious "ecstasy" as in later mysticism. God's ecstasy, the deity's standing outside itself, is an excess of goodness that overflows in a loving and creative procession down to humanity. The human soul, on the other hand, is taken wholly outside of itself when it rightly understands and leaves behind all human language and conceptions about God and ascends through negations to be wholly of God. The divine "ecstasy" takes place in the procession, the human in the return.[21] Likewise, the negation and abandonment of all the knowledge previously attained through interpreting the Bible and the liturgy results in union with God:

The most divine knowledge of God, that which comes through unknowing, is achieved in a union far beyond the mind, when the mind turns away from all things, even from itself, and when it is made one with the dazzling rays. (*DN* 7, 872AB.14-19)

Thus, for Dionysius the final goal of this epistemological uplifting through all symbols and concepts is union with God, also expressed as deification or "theosis." Deification—"being as much as possible like and in union with God" (*EH* 1, 376A.1f.; see also *EH* 1, 376B.13-15)—is the result of the anagogical ascent:

We see our human hierarchy . . . pluralized in a great variety of perceptible symbols lifting us upward hierarchically until we are brought as far as we can be into the unity of deification. (*EH* 1, 373A.10-13)[22]

Beyond the fourth chapter of *The Mystical Theology* and its negation of the perceptible, as incorporated into the interpretation of biblical and liturgical symbols in *The Celestial Hierarchy* and *The Ecclesiastical Hierarchy*, the Dionysian ascent continues and nears its destination in the negation of all intelligible or conceptual truths, as summarized in the fifth and final chapter of *The Mystical Theology:*

Chapter Five.    That the supreme cause of every conceptual thing is not itself conceptual.
Again, as we climb higher we say this. It is not soul or mind, nor does it possess imagination, conviction, speech or understanding. Nor is it speech *per se,* understanding *per se.* . . . It is beyond assertion and denial. We make assertions and denials of what is next to it, but never of it, for it is both beyond every assertion, being the perfect and unique cause of all things, and, by virtue of its pre-eminently simple and absolute nature, free of every limitation, beyond every limitation, it is also beyond every denial. (*MT* 5, 1045D-1048B)

In the end, even denials must be left behind as incapable of expressing the divine goal of this ascent. Negation of the conceptual realm means negating and transcending even the concept of negation. Negations are themselves negated, not in order to yield a logical affirmation but in order to pass beyond all speech and thought.

Now we should not conclude that the negations are simply the opposites of the affirmations, but rather that the cause of all is considerably prior to this, beyond privations, beyond every denial, beyond every assertion. (*MT* 1, 1000B17-20)

Beyond the interpretive negation of the perceptible, and even beyond the subsequent negation or abandonment of the conceptual, the final Dionysian step goes past negation itself into complete silence. Affirmation and negation may combine to chart the approach, but the ultimate arena for meeting God is in neither, nor any combination, but in silence. "As we plunge into that darkness which is beyond intellect, we shall find ourselves not simply running short of words but actually speechless and unknowing" (*MT* 3, 1033B.28–30)

## Moses on Mount Sinai

The Areopagite himself summarized this two-tiered ascent in his advice to Timothy, the fictional recipient of *The Mystical Theology:*

> Timothy, my friend, my advice to you as you look for a sight of the mysterious things, is to leave behind you everything perceived and understood, everything perceptible and conceptual, all that is not and all that is, and, with your understanding laid aside, to strive upward as much as you can toward union with Him who is beyond all being and knowledge. (*MT* 1, 997B.16–22)

The advised ascent beyond "the perceptible and the conceptual" is, in fact, first the anagogical interpretation of perceptible symbols and then the abandonment of these interpretations and of all things conceptual. Another drastic abbreviation for this bipartite elevation substitutes the sense of sight for all sense perception, and also invokes the principle of negation:

> If only we lacked sight and knowledge so as to see, so as to know, unseeing and unknowing, that which lies beyond all vision and knowledge. (For this would be really to see and to know: to praise the transcendent One in a transcending way, namely through the denial of all beings.) (*MT* 2, 1025A.5–9; see also *Ep.* 5, 1073AB)

The paradigm for this entire discussion is Moses on Mount Sinai. Beneath the surface of the Areopagite's embellishment of that biblical ascent lie several subthemes. First, the "three ways" of purification, illumination, and perfection can be detected in the alternative terminology of purification, contemplation, and union: Moses is first purified, then rises up to contemplate the place where God dwells, then enters into union with God in the "cloud of unknowing" (*MT* 1, 1000C.34–1001A.11).[23] Second, the vocabulary used to describe this journey is reminiscent of the eucharistic actions of the bishop or hierarch, for whom Moses is in fact the prototype: Moses on Mount Sinai and the hierarch in the Eucharist are both "purified" and "separated" from the assembly, moving up to a restricted area with "chosen" clerics to "contemplate" the divine things.[24] These subthemes to the Mosaic narrative may be quite suggestive, but the more basic point is that Moses first ascends beyond the perceptible symbols of the trumpet sounds and the bright lights, and then beyond every conceptual contemplation of the mind into the cloud or darkness of unknowing (*MT* 1, 1000D44–1001A.11). The story of Moses is not just the example of a spiritual elevation in general; it is more specifically a paradigm for the two steps of the Pseudo-Dionysian ascent. First, the symbols of the Bible and the liturgy—the trumpets and the lights—are interpreted "anagogically," lifting the interpreter up through sense perception to the concepts symbolized. Then these resulting concepts are themselves negated and abandoned in a renunciation of the mind and in silent union with the transcendent Godhead.

The example of Moses as a summary of the Areopagite's uplifting spirituality highlights a controversial feature of the Dionysian system. In the entire framework of procession and return described above, no critical or even important function is given to Christ. The incarnation, death, resurrection, and ascension of Jesus Christ are not even the principal examples of this motif, much less its indispensable ground, source, or cause. If the essential structure of the Areopagite's thought and corpus is indeed the pattern of procession and return, as here argued, it must also be said that his occasional references to Christ are largely cosmetic.[25] His program of religious epistemology overshadows the historical particularity of orthodox christology. Thus, Pseudo-Dionysius converted the purpose of scriptural negations from a humble reluctance to identify God except as incarnate in space and time into a bold cognitive technique for ascending into the divine transcendence itself.

## Influence

From their first appearance and into the present day, the Pseudo-Dionysian writings have influenced many facets of Christian life and thought, in both East and West, yet not as profoundly as sometimes claimed. Although the Areopagite's influence was long, broad, and occasionally deep, it still awaits a comprehensive evaluation.[26] Some brief indications are here given regarding the afterlife of his "uplifting spirituality," as defined above. This selectivity, however, must exclude many medieval thinkers and entire areas of influence such as the hierarchical arrangement of the angels and of ecclesiastical authority, the specific names and attributes of God, the three ways (purification, illumination, and perfection), the emphasis upon physical light as a symbol for the divine, and even the traditional account of the assumption of the Virgin Mary.

Of course, there would have been little or no Dionysian influence at all had not the corpus been mistakenly received as apostolic soon after its "discovery" in the early sixth century. Although it seems to have been initially invoked to support the Monophysite view that Christ had one (divine) nature, it was also and immediately used *against* the Monophysites, in support of the orthodox, Chalcedonian view of Christ's two natures, human and divine. As in this debut debate, the corpus has always been considered complex, obscure, and even susceptible to heretical interpretations. Its earliest exegetes and defenders, John of Scythopolis and Maximus the Confessor (ca. 580–662), labored diligently to give orthodox Christian interpretations to the passages that sounded Monophysite, Neoplatonic, or otherwise suspect. Eventually mingled together under Maximus's name, these comments or *Scholia* were totally successful in claiming Dionysius as one of the early church fathers, sound in faith and doctrine.[27] Maximus in particular ensured the survival and impact of the Dionysian writings through his advocacy and reinterpretation in the *Scholia*, the *Ambigua* (discussions of ambiguous texts in Dionysius and Gregory of Nazianzus), and elsewhere. Yielding to the Aeropagite's own penchant for puns, a modern interpreter has remarked that it was a "Maximized" Dionysian corpus that made its influential way through the Middle Ages.[28]

Calling him "an all-holy man and truly a revealer of God," Maximus the Confessor honored Dionysius highly, not as a unique authority but as part of the consensus of the fathers.[29] Specifically, he put the Areopagite's writings in line with Chalcedonian orthodoxy and the prior theological traditions of Alexandria and Cappadocia. The concept of deification, to take an example central to Maximus and all of Byzantine theology, was claimed to be harmoniously shared by all the fathers, including Dionysius. Deification, synonymous with salvation, meant union with God, precisely the goal of the Dionysian ascent discussed above.[30] Maximus had to defend the largely cosmetic christology displayed by Dionysius at this point, but both of them held that the path to this union led necessarily through knowledge, indeed, through contemplation of the Scriptures and of the liturgy.[31] Commenting on the Dionysian connections between the three sacraments and the three powers, the Confessor wrote, "From the divine scriptures we are purified and enlightened in the divine birth [baptism], whereas in the synaxis and the sacrament of the myron-ointment we are perfected in our understanding" (*Scholia* on *EH* 5 [*PG* 4, col. 161D]). Maximus also called on Dionysius regarding negative knowledge or knowing the unknowable, in harmony with the tradition of Clement of Alexandria and Gregory of Nyssa. Since God transcends all being and all knowledge, agreed Maximus, only negations are true and only silence is ultimately appropriate. "The 'unknowing' of God by those who are wise in divine things is not an absence of education but rather a knowledge which knows, in silence, that God is unknown" (*Scholia* on *DN* 7 [*PG* 4, col. 341A]).

It is difficult to describe precisely how Maximus was influenced by the Dionysian writings themselves, apart from the overall tradition in which he placed them. But surely their subsequent influence, in East and West, depended largely upon Maximus and his alignment of the Areopagite with the fathers of the church. After Maximus, John of Damascus (ca. 670- ca. 750) harmonized the fathers, now including Dionysius, into an *Exposition of the Orthodox Faith* (*De fide orthodoxa*). In the iconoclastic controversy, supporters of icons made surprisingly little use of the crucial role for symbols in the Dionysian system, whereas their opponents, the iconoclasts, occasionally cited the Areopagite's work to argue that the only permitted icon of Christ is the Eucharist. Later Byzantine writers paid special honors to our author, since they supposed him to be at the head of the *consensus patrum*. With a "christological corrective," Gregory Palamas used Dionysius to expound negative theology, to oppose the Western "Filioque," and to counter Barlaam, who quoted the Areopagite extensively himself.[32]

The Areopagite's clearest influence in Byzantium, again through Maximus, was in the area of liturgical interpretation and the hardy genre of Byzantine literature called "liturgical commentaries." Certainly the Dionysian influence in the East was not limited to the Greek church and its missionary children. The very early translation of the entire corpus into Syriac led to an important Dionysian presence in that tradition, including a series of interpretations of the sacrament of the myron-ointment, for example, and especially of the "procession and return" of the incense from the altar and back to it.[33] But it is specifically the Greek tradition of commentaries on the liturgy that is often said to begin with Dionysius, after the necessary forerunners in the earlier patristic writings.[34] Here the traditional alignment of the Areopagite with exclusively Christian predecessors needs not to be reaffirmed but to be challenged. A line does seem to run from his *Ecclesiastical Hierarchy* through Maximus's *Mystagogia* and Germanus of Constantinople's *Ecclesiastical History and Mystical Contemplation* to Cabasilas's famous *Explication of the Divine Liturgy.* The historical "typology" of this tradition—that the actions of the liturgy symbolize events in the life and passion of Christ—came from Antiochene exegesis and sacramental interpretation, notably Theodore of Mopsuestia, long before Pseudo-Dionysius ever wrote. But its timeless allegory—that the liturgy symbolizes eternal truths about God, the soul, and the entire spiritual cosmos—began with Pseudo-Dionysius, at least among extant systematic expositions. The procession and return of the incense, to take the example mentioned above, symbolizes the ceaseless procession and return of the deity itself. This type of interpretation is often called "Alexandrian," meaning that Dionysius developed his procedure from the methods of biblical allegory used by Origen and followers, along with their few and fleeting references to the liturgy. But another precedent, perhaps even closer, should not be ignored simply because it concerns non-Christian rites.

Neoplatonic theurgy had its own "liturgy" of perceptible symbols and their allegorical interpretations, as discernible in *The Chaldean Oracles*, Iamblichus's *On Mysteries* and some works of Proclus. It seems unlikely that the Areopagite, so schooled in Athenian Neoplatonism, could have been unaware of their anagogical method for interpreting the religious ritual of theurgy.[35] Post-Dionysian liturgical exposition was no longer predominantly typological, but a mixture of historical typology and spiritualized, timeless allegory. In general, christocentric salvation history and eschatology, sacramental realism, and the corporate solidarity of Byzantine worship were all challenged by Platonism's timeless individualism and disparagement of the earthly and material as "merely" symbols of another realm.

While some studies tend to slight the Dionysian influence in Byzantine Christendom, even a balanced account should acknowledge the more specific results of the Pseudo-Areopagite's legacy in Latin Christianity. In the West, the influence of the Areopagite's "uplifting spirituality" can be best seen in three specific areas:[36] the motif of "procession and return," the uplifting from the perceptible to the conceptual, and the leap beyond all concepts into the silent darkness of unknowing.

First, the Areopagite's entry into the mainstream of Western thought featured an application of procession and return to all of cosmic history in the works of the ninth-century Carolingian scholar, John the Scot (John Scotus Eriugena, ca. 810–ca. 877).[37] John translated into Latin the entire Dionysian corpus (and some works of Maximus) and inherited many of its themes, including *exitus* and *reditus*. For Dionysius and the Neoplatonists before him, the cycle of procession and return was timeless and unrelated to any historical pattern. John the Scot, however, receiving the Dionysian system through Maximus, adapted it to the entire sweep of the history of God and the world. Methodologically, John started with the microcosm of the human mind's dialectical process: a problem is broken "down" or divided into its various parts so that it may be analyzed and then reassembled back "up" to its original unity. He then moved to the macrocosm of metaphysics and "meta-history": the procession downward is God's original creation; the return upward is humanity's future deification. In the Scot's major work, *Periphyseon*, God's initial creative procession down into plurality is counterbalanced by a final universal return back to God. In the history of Christian doctrine, John's influence (despite his official condemnation) was not least in merging the Greek language of "procession and return" with the Latin language of "nature and grace."[38] Along these lines was constructed the most famous document of medieval theology, the *Summa theologiae* of Thomas Aquinas (ca. 1225–1274). Thomas wrote a commentary on *The Divine Names*, quoted the Dionysian corpus often (in its Latin translation by

Saracenus), and knew it well, including the pattern of procession and return. Specifically, the three parts of the *Summa theologiae* present, respectively, God and the creative procession of all things from him, the movement of rational creatures back up to God, and Christ as the way for that return.[39]

Second, regarding the uplifting movement from the perceptible to the conceptual, the Dionysian understanding of Christian aesthetics and religious symbolism became incarnate in the stone and glass of Gothic architecture. Abbot Suger of St.-Denis (ca. 1081–1151) explained his ideas for the abbey's new church, the first structure in the style later called "Gothic," by invoking the authoritative writings of the abbey's patron saint and supposed founder, this same Denis or Dionysius. In planning, commissioning, and describing the building, Abbot Suger emphasized the glorious beauty of the doors, the precious gems, the soaring arches, and especially the uplifting light of the stained-glass windows, since these material things lifted the eye and the spirit up to the immaterial realm of celestial and divine beauty.[40] The rationale for this "uplifting"—still effective in the luminous and seemingly weightless atmosphere of Gothic structures—came from the Dionysian tradition through the works of John the Scot and Hugh of St. Victor, among others. It is one of the striking ironies in the history of the Western church that its most concrete and visible legacy should be linked to such an elusive, pseudonymous corpus.

Third, the Dionysian leap into the silent cloud of unknowing, beyond all names, interpretations, concepts, and words, has had an illustrious history of influence among medieval mystics and other spiritual writers in the West. Indeed, some of them were much more interested in how the Areopagite abandoned concepts than in how he arrived at them in the first place, through exegesis and liturgical interpretation. The fourteenth-century *Cloud of Unknowing* took its title from the Dionysian interpretation of the biblical account of Moses on Mount Sinai. This anonymous English author claimed the Areopagite's authority for his entire treatise, but misleadingly so, for the work considers preparatory humility and other non-Dionysian themes, invoking the Dionysian corpus only for the concept of unknowing: "That is why St. Dionysius said, 'the most godlike knowledge of God is that which is known by unknowing.'"[41] Similarly, the titles of Nicholas of Cusa's *On Learned Ignorance* or St. John of the Cross's *Dark Night of the Soul* might suggest, incorrectly, a direct and dominating influence of the Dionysian corpus. In reality, these works, and others by Jean Gerson and Jan van Ruysbroeck, for example, have long and complex pedigrees which the Dionysian corpus influenced only from a great distance and through many intermediaries, such as Thomas Gallus, to mention only one example. Meister Eckhart, however, cited Dionysius directly as a venerable authority, principally for the utter transcendence of God, beyond life and light and being itself. Eckhart used our author to confirm that God is beyond all concepts, that every description of God is ultimately incorrect, and that only negations and silence are finally appropriate.[42] Henry Suso, following Eckhart, took little interest in the Areopagite's exegesis or sacramental exposition, but carefully cited the final Dionysian leap beyond all things conceptual.[43]

Even restricting the inquiry to these three areas—procession and return, anagogical architecture, and the mystical ascent into unknowing—the Dionysian corpus had a more particular influence in the West than in the East. This legacy should not be overly exaggerated, however, for much more work is needed on the comparative influence of Dionysius, Boethius, Augustine, and others.

## Notes

1. Citations will refer to the Greek text in *PG* 3, with occasional adjustments based on the critical edition forthcoming from the Patristische Kommission der Westdeutschen Akademie der Wissenschaften (Göttingen), edited by A. M. Ritter, G. Heil, and B. Suchla. The following abbreviations will be employed: *CH* = *The Celestial Hierarchy; EH* = *The Ecclesiastical Hierarchy; DN* = *The Divine Names; MT* = *The Mystical Theology; Ep.* = *Epistles.* References to the text will follow this form: *CH* 1, 120B.7— 121A.1 = *The Celestial Hierarchy,* chapter 1, column 120B, line 7 to column 121A, line 1.

2. The English translations are taken, with permission, from the new version by Colm Luibheíd, forthcoming from Paulist Press.

3. See Stephen Gersch, *From Iamblichus to Eriugena;* and Walther Völker, *Kontemplation und Ekstase.*

4. See Hugo Koch, *Pseudo-Dionysius Areopagita.*

5. See Ronald F. Hathaway, *Hierarchy and the Definition of Order,* 31–35.

6. For more detail, see my monograph, *Biblical and Liturgical Symbols within the Pseudo-Dionysian Synthesis* (Toronto: Pontifical Institute of Mediaeval Studies, 1984).

7. H. Blumenthal, "529 and its Sequel: What Happened to the Academy?" *Byzantion* 48 (1978) 369–85.

8. Proclus, *The Elements of Theology,* trans. E. R. Dodds (Oxford: Clarendon Press, 1963) no. 35, p. 38. See also Gersh, especially pp. 46 and 286.

9. See also *CH* 121C.35–124A.15; *DN* 1, 592B.21f.

10. See also *EH* 2, 397C.29f.; *EH* 5, 501.44–46; *Ep.* 9, 1108C.34–37.

11. E.g., *DN* 5, 824D.49; *CH* 4, 180B.20; *CH* 9, 261C.38.

12. E.g., *CH* 2, 144C.34–145A.4.

13. *CH* 2, 137D.44f., 141C.37, 144A.5, 145A.14; *CH* 15, 337B.25.

14. *MT* 3, 1032D.1–1033B.30. On the sequence of treatises, see P. Rorem, "The Place of *The Mystical Theology* in the Pseudo-Dionysian Corpus," *Dionysius* 4 (1980) 87–98.

15. *DN* 1, 596ABC; *CH* 2, 144CD; *Ep.* 9, 1105B.

16. *EH* 2, 401C.35f.; cf. 404B.12f.

17. On the censing procession, see *EH* 3, 425B.21–25, 428D.21–429A.2; *EH* 4, 476D.38–45; on the distribution, see *EH* 3, 444A.6–14, 444C.28–30; especially 429A.8–15.

18. *EH* 1, 376C.32–34; see also *EH* 3, 428C.27–29; *EH* 4, 476D.45–477B.17; *EH* 6, 529D.7–532B.19.

19. E.g., *DN* 3, 680C.21–29; *CH* 12, 293B.19–22; *EH* 5, 504C.31–33; *MT* 1, 1000A.1–3.

20. *CH* 2, 140A.11; see also *CH* 2, 141C.35f.; *CH* 15, 328A.2; *EH* 1, 377A.4f.

21. *DN* 4, 712AB.1–19; *Ep.* 9, 1112C.28–36; *DN* 7, 865D.33–868A.2, 872D.45–873A.3. See Völker, 200–217.

22. See also *CH* 1, 124A.5–15; *EH* 1, 376A; *EH* 1, 376D.40f.; *EH* 3, 433C.30–36; *EH* 6, 536C.37.

23. Against J. Vanneste, "La doctrine des trois voies dans le *Théologie Mystique* du Pseudo-Denys l'Aréopagite," *Studia Patristica* 8 (1966) 462–67. Of course, see Gregory of Nyssa's *Life of Moses*, trans. A. J. Malherbe and E. Ferguson (New York: Paulist Press, 1978).

24. On Moses as the prototype, see *EH* 5, 501C.32–34. On the parallels, see *EH* 3, 440A.11–15; 436A.3–5; 425D.44–46. An extraordinary religious experience is also linked to the Eucharist in the examples of Hierotheus in *DN* 2, 648AB.10–20 and *DN* 3, 681C–684A.3, and Carpos in *Ep.* 8, 1097B.21–26. See my "Moses as the Paradigm for the Uplifting Spirituality of Pseudo-Dionysius," paper read at the Ninth International Conference on Patristic Studies, Oxford 1983 (forthcoming in *Studia Patristica*).

25. The Dionysian christology has always been controversial; see especially the defense by R. Roques, *L'Univers Dionysien*, 305–29.

26. Perhaps the best survey yet in print is by A. Rayez and collaborators, "Denys l'Aréopagite (le Pseudo-)," *Dict. Sp.* 3, cols. 286–318 (Orient) and 318–429 (Occident). Other pertinent literature is summarized by Barbara Faes de Mottoni in *Il "Corpus Dionysianum" nel Medioevo, Rassegna di studi: 1900-1972* (Rome: Società Editrice Il Mulino, 1977).

27. Beate Regina Suchla, "Die sogenannten Maximus-Scholien des Corpus Dionysiacum Areopagiticum," in *Nachrichten der Akademie der Wissenschaften in Göttingen. I. Philologische-historische Klasse* 3 (Göttingen: Vandenhoeck & Ruprecht, 1980) 31–66.

28. Jaroslav Pelikan, "The Domestication of Dionysius," paper read at the Eighth International Conference on Patristic Studies, Oxford, September 1979. See his treatments of Dionysius and Maximus in *The Christian Tradition*, vol. 1, *The Emergence of the Catholic Tradition (100–600)* (Chicago: University of Chicago Press, 1971) 344–48; and vol. 2, *The Spirit of Eastern Christendom (600–1700)* (1974) 8–36.

29. *Mystagogia* (*PG* 91, col. 660D).

30. *Scholia* on *Ep.* 2 (*PG* 4, col. 529BC).

31. See especially P. Sherwood's contribution to the article mentioned above in n. 26 (*Dict. Sp.* 3, cols. 295–300) and W. Völker, *Maximus Confessor als Meister des geistlichen Lebens* (Wiesbaden: F. Steiner, 1965).

32. See John Meyendorff, *A Study of Gregory Palamas* (London: Faith Press, 1964) 133, 185–92, 202–10.

33. See W. Strothmann, *Das Sakrament der Myron-Weihe* (Wiesbaden: Harrassowitz, 1977–78); and J. Thekeparampil, "Weihrauchsymbolik," in *Typus, Symbol, Allegorie*, ed. Margot Schmidt (Eichstätter Beiträge 4; Regensburg: Pustet, 1981) 131–45.

34. See R. Bornert, *Les Commentaires Byzantins de la Divine Liturgie* (Paris: Institut Français d'Études Byzantines, 1966) 66–72; and R. Taft, "The Liturgy of the Great Church," *Dumbarton Oaks Papers* 34/35 (1980–81) 45–75.

35. See my "Iamblichus and the Anagogical Method in Pseudo-Dionysian Liturgical Theology," *Studia Patristica* 18 (1982) 453–60.

36. This selectivity excludes several important authors such as Hugh of St. Victor, Honorius Augustodunensis, Alan of Lille, and various Cistercians of the twelfth century.

37. See Dom Maieul Cappuyns, O.S.B., *Jean Scot Érigène: Sa vie, son oeuvre, sa pensée* (reprint, Brussels: Culture et Civilisation, 1969) 302-80; and Donald F. Duclow, "Dialectic and Christology in Eriugena's Periphyseon," *Dionysius* 4 (1980) 99-118.

38. John the Scot, *Expositiones in Ierarchiam Coelestem*, chap. 1, ed. J. Barbet (Turnholt: Brepols, 1975) 1-6; I. P. Sheldon-Williams, "Eriugena's Interpretation of the ps. Dionysius," *Studia Patristica* 12 (1975) 151-54.

39. *Summa theologica* 1a, q. 2, prol. See M.-D. Chenu, O.P., "Le plan de la Somme théologique de S. Thomas," *Revue Thomiste* 45 (1939) 93-107.

40. Abbot Suger, *On the Abbey Church of St.-Denis and Its Art Treasures*, ed. E. Panofsky, 2nd ed. (Princeton, NJ: Princeton University Press, 1979) especially pp. 62-64. See also W. Beierwaltes, "Negati Affirmatio," *Dionysius* 1 (1977) 127-59.

41. *The Cloud of Unknowing*, ed. C. Wolters (New York: Penguin Books, 1978) 145, quoting *DN* 7, 872A.14f.

42. M. Eckhart, *Die deutschen Werke*, ed. J. Quint (Stuttgart: Kohlhammer, 1976) 3:223, 265.

43. H. Suso, *Deutsche Schriften*, ed. K. Bihlmeyer (Stuttgart: Kohlhammer, 1907) 190.5-14, 328.24-329.8, 342.15-18.

## Bibliography

### Studies

Brons, Bernard. *Gott und die Seienden: Untersuchungen zum Verhältnis von neuplatonischer Metaphysik und christlichen Tradition bei Dionysius Areopagita*. Göttingen: Vandenhoeck & Ruprecht, 1976.

Gersh, Stephen. *From Iamblichus to Eriugena: An Investigation of the Prehistory and Evolution of the Pseudo-Dionysian Tradition*. Leiden: Brill, 1978.

Hathaway, Ronald F. *Hierarchy and the Definition of Order in the Letters of Pseudo-Dionysius*. The Hague: Martinus Nijhoff, 1969.

Hornus, Jean-Michel. "Les recherches récentes sur le pseudo-Denys l'Aréopagite." *Revue d'Histoire et de Philosophie Religieuses* 35 (1955) 404-48.

———. "Les recherches dionysiennes de 1955 à 1960." *Revue d'Histoire et de Philosophie Religieuses* 41 (1961) 22-81.

Koch, Hugo. *Pseudo-Dionysius Areopagita in seinem Beziehungen zum Neoplatonismus und Mysterienwesen*. Mainz: Franz Kirchheim, 1900.

Roques, René. *L'Univers Dionysien: Structure hiérarchique du monde selon le pseudo-Denys*. Paris: Aubier, 1954.

———. *Structures théologiques de la Gnose chez Richard de Saint Victor: Essais et analyses critiques*. Paris: Presses universitaires de France, 1962.

Rorem, Paul. *Biblical and Liturgical Symbols within the Pseudo-Dionysian Synthesis*. (Toronto: Pontifical Institute of Mediaeval Studies, 1984).

Scazzoso, Piero. *Ricerche sulla struttura del linguaggio dello Pseudo-Dionigi Areopagita*. Milan: Società Editrice Vita e Pensiero, 1967.

Vanneste, Jan. *Le Mystère de Dieu: Essai sur la structure rationnelle de la doctrine mystique du pseudo-Denys l'Aréopagite*. Brussels: Desclée de Brouwer, 1959.

Völker, Walther. *Kontemplation und Ekstase bei Pseudo-Dionysius Areopagita*. Wiesbaden: F. Steiner, 1958.

# 7

# Christianity and Cultural Diversity

## I. *The Spirituality of Syriac-speaking Christians*

### ROBERTA C. BONDI

O NE IS ACCUSTOMED to regarding Greek and Latin as the two great languages and overlapping cultures of the patristic church. The Greek and Latin writers of the period have been studied extensively from the Renaissance to the present, and their influence on what we call Western culture has been enormous. But there is a third classical patristic language and culture which sometimes stands apart from Greco-Roman culture and sometimes is a part of it: It is Syriac, the form of Aramaic used in a geographical area that included the countryside around Antioch, all the way across the borders of the Roman Empire into the empire of Persia. But though the greatest Syriac-speaking writer of them all, Ephrem (ca. 306–373), was known and admired early in the West, it is only within the last century that the vast extant literature of Syriac-speaking Christianity has begun to be studied extensively and appreciated for what it is—a Christianity which, even though it shared a great deal with its Greek and Latin counterparts, nevertheless had a character that expressed itself in a spirituality all its own, from its earliest traceable beginnings.

What were these beginnings? Almost without a doubt, earliest Christianity in both Adiabene and Edessa, the two most likely places for its origin among Syriac-speakers, had very strong ties with Judaism. As for Edessa, we see the origin of Christianity in the legend of Addai recounted by Eusebius in his *Church History* as well as in a longer and later Syriac version. According to this legend, the king of Edessa, Abgar, invited Jesus to share his kingdom. Jesus declined, but he sent his disciple Addai, who brought Christianity to Edessa. In the later account, the detail is added that when Addai first arrived, he stayed with a Jewish merchant. Although the story itself is clearly legend, that Christianity in Edessa had real links in its beginnings with Judaism is almost certainly true.

Adiabene is the other likely place for the origins of Christianity among the Syraic-speakers. Whereas Edessa as a city was part of the Roman Empire and displayed many different influences, Adiabene belonged only briefly to the Roman Empire; for the most part, it belonged first to Parthia, then to Persia, and was, therefore, much more cut off from Greek culture than Edessa. Christianity there does not appear to have had the same early struggle with Gnosticism as it had in Edessa, and, indeed, the Christianity of Ephrem and Aphraat, the two most important Syriac-speaking writers of the fourth century, both of whom were from Adiabene, is, in the words of Robert Murray, "best accountable for as a breakaway movement among the Jewish community in Adiabene."[1] The Syriac version of the Old Testament, the Peshitta, is thought to be originally Jewish and from Adiabene, and this fact further supports the notion that earliest Christianity was connected to Judaism there.

Syriac spirituality had three characteristics that it retained throughout the period: individualism, asceticism, and a dependence on the symbolic as a mode of theological reflection.

## Individualism

Compared with Greek and Latin Christianity, Syriac spirituality tended strongly toward individualism. In the earliest information we have about the rise of Christianity in Edessa, we see a Christianity fragmented into many groups. This fragmentation apparently continued right into the fourth century, when Ephrem complained about it. Indeed, though we know very little about second- and third-century Syriac-speaking Christianity, we do know that it was extremely complex in its diversity—so much so that it is impossible to make assessments with regard to Christian orthodoxy from that period.

The rise of monasticism in this area also displayed a characteristic individualism. By Ephrem's time in the fourth century, the life of the anchorite had been the norm for a long time for those who wished to pursue a rigorous style of Christianity, and a monastic, communal life was more the exception than the rule. The picture painted by Theodoret (ca. 393–ca. 466) in his *History of the Monks of Syria* and supplemented by Ephrem depicts these anchorites as people who rejected civilization. Jacob of Nisibis, for example, lived out of doors, except in winter, when he lived in a cave. He did not eat food that he or others had worked for; what he ate, he ate raw, and he wore only primitive clothes. Ephrem's picture adds that the admired anchorites were covered with filth, had hair like eagle feathers, and lived on friendly terms with wild animals.

The first "monk" to represent a move toward communal living, Juliana Saba, a contemporary of Ephrem, still retained the old individualism. Having begun as an anchorite, at some point he accepted disciples, who lived in caves around his. They began and ended their day with common worship, but during the day itself they wandered in the old style in pairs. Juliana himself continued in the old style, which included constant traveling, refraining from meat, severe fasting, long vigils, poverty, and mortification of the body. Communal monasticism like that among the Greek speakers became common after the fourth century, but the tradition of the anchorite remained far beyond that time. Isaac of Nineveh (d. ca. 700), the great seventh-century Nestorian mystic, still modeled himself on it. He tells us that when he was living by himself for a number of years he received all his food from a bird, like Elijah in the wilderness.

Looking at the picture of the sixth-century holy men and women that is presented by the Monophysite John of Ephesus (ca. 507–586) in *Lives of the Eastern Saints,* we see this individualism expressing itself not so much in the desire to live a solitary life as in the need of each man and woman given over to the life of perfection to find a suitable expression of his or her individual style within the walls of the monastery itself.

This individualism within the Syrian tradition could sometimes express itself in what seemed at the time an overemphasis on personal religious experience and prayer at the expense of the sacraments and more institutional aspects of the Christian life. Called "Messalianism," after the Syriac for "those who pray," this tendency toward personal experience greatly enriched Syriac spirituality. Sebastian Brock finds it in the writings of Ephrem, and the *Macarian Homilies* (a Greek collection of homilies, almost certainly Syrian in origin and of great influence among Syriac writers from the fifth century on) and the *Book of Degrees* (fourth century?) share in this tendency.

Perhaps it is this individualism that accounts for the appearance of Stephen bar Sudaili (late fifth century) in Monophysite monasteries in Philoxenus of Mabbug's time (ca. 440–523). Stephen, influenced by the Origenist, Evagrius of Pontus (346–399), so interiorized and personalized the Christian faith that even Christ himself appears in Stephen's thought as a stage the mystic must surpass in the interior spiritual journey.

But this individualism did not always have to do with personal religious experience. As Peter Brown has so beautifully shown, to be a "stranger" in the world of late antiquity meant not to withdraw from society but to assume a special responsibility for it and power within it, drawn precisely from the status of "stranger."[2] This is a picture we see clearly drawn in John of Ephesus's *Lives*. Not only did the holy man act as missionary, teacher of children, healer, and arbitrator of disputes; he acted against the demonic itself in behalf of society. The expression of individualism, therefore, had as much to do with the maintenance of society as it had to do with the rejection of "the world."

## Asceticism

Syrian spirituality was, from its beginnings, fiercely ascetical. The Syriac New Testament supported an ascetical understanding of the teaching of Jesus. Until the fifth century, in the place of the "Divided Gospels," Syriac-speaking Christians used the Gospel harmony of Tatian (born ca. 120), called the *Diatessaron*. Tatian, a highly educated man, spent an important part of his career in Rome, perhaps as a student of Justin Martyr (ca. 100–165). Dissatisfied with what he considered to be the laxity of the Roman church, Tatian broke with it and returned to the East in 172, where he had great influence. His rigorism seems to have been in accord with the inclinations of Syrian Christianity. It is not known whether the original language of the *Diatessaron* was Greek or Syriac, but it is certain that this work contributed formatively to the character of Syriac-speaking spirituality. Tatian revised many passages in his conflation in the direction of stricter asceticism. For example, in Luke 20:27–40, where Jesus denies that there is giving or taking in marriage in heaven, Tatian corrected it to read, "The peoples of this world take a wife and make marriages; but they who shall be worthy of the life of that other world and of the resurrection of the blessed, will neither take wives nor make wedding feasts."[3] As well as rejecting marriage, Tatian was also against the owning of property, the eating of meat, and the drinking of wine. In Tatian's text, Jesus the True Vine of John 15:1 redescribes himself: "I am the tree of the fruit of the truth."[4]

Both the *Acts of Judas Thomas* and the beautiful early collection of hymns, the *Odes of Solomon* (first or second century), reflect the way in which baptism and sexual abstinence were originally linked together. For example, in the *Acts of Judas Thomas* the apostle on his missionary journey at one point preaches at a royal wedding and leaves behind him a bride and groom vowed to perpetual continence. In the *Odes*, which very likely were baptismal hymns, virginity and "holiness" (continence in marriage) figure prominently. It is not surprising that these remain important concepts within our period, though by the time of Ephrem the notion that one could not lead an ordinary married life if one were baptized was regarded as heretical. Nevertheless, in the Syriac-speaking regions, by the fourth century, it was thought that the sexual component of married life made it impossible for the lay Christian to approach perfection.

A life of virginity was certainly a prerequisite for membership in the "Sons and Daughters of the Covenant," a semiclerical group peculiar to the Syrian church. These people did not live isolated in monasteries but rather lived sometimes singly, with each other or with their parents within their own communities. Although they could not marry, they could own property, and they do not appear to have been under the same strictures with respect to other ascetical practices of the monks.

Like their fellows in Egypt, anchorites went off to dwell without worldly possessions. Most Egyptian and Palestinian monastics believed that they must do enough manual labor to support themselves—with a little left over to feed the poor—but many Syriac-speaking monks lived on alms, repudiating manual labor. This attitude may have had its origin in a deeper conviction among the Syriac-speakers concerning the evils of society than was prevalent among Greek-speaking monastics. Certainly there was a more pessimistic view of sin and human nature among the Syrians, and we must remember that in this area Marcionism and Manichaeism throve.

The more bizarre aspects of this asceticism we meet again in John of Ephesus. There we see within the walls of a monastery a man who lived in a hollow log, even in the snows of winter, and in the same monastery his brother, who lived on a previously occupied pillar. We hear in another place of a monk who had worn all the hair off his head from knocking it on the ground and who prayed every night by falling from a standing position first to his knees and then upon his face. Again, though there are stories that come out of Egyptian monasticism of great suffering caused by ascetical practices, most of them have to do with the deprivation of food, water, or sleep. A real creativity in what seems to the modern reader to be self-torture belongs to the monks whose native tongue was Syriac. Along with this trend, we find in Ephrem in the fourth century, Philoxenus in the fifth, and John of Ephesus in the sixth a strong desire to moderate this asceticism, to bring it more into line with the Christian affirmation of the goodness of creation.

Perhaps in the earliest period Syriac writers may have associated the body with sin. Certainly in the beginning the solitary life was understood to be a life of repentance and mourning. The gift of tears, mentioned first by Ephrem, was a highly prized spiritual condition in which tears of repentance ran down the face day and night without ceasing. Whatever was believed earlier, it would be wrong to say that, by the fourth century, these writers understood the body as the source of sin: they did not. Such a writer as Philoxenus, who was surely influenced by Evagrius of Pontus in many ways, nevertheless knew that the life of the monk entailed the firm control of the heavy body by the lighter mind, so that the mind, drawn upward, would not be hindered by the weight of the body, bloated and fattened by food. If the mind clearly established its dominance over the body, then the body would be its servant. But this does not happen by itself. This dominance only comes about through the ascetic discipline of the body.

## Symbolism

Syriac spirituality is characterized by a way of seeing and meditating upon the things of God that can loosely be called "symbolic."[5] It entails a kind of double vision that sees, simultaneously, the visible, physical world and the hidden realities of God concealed within it which are conveyed through Scripture, Christ, the church, and the sacraments, by means of faith and the Holy Spirit.

This way of seeing the Christian realities expressed itself best and most characteristically within the Syrian tradition in poetry. What is probably the oldest extant piece of Syriac literature, the *Odes of Solomon,* is a collection of beautiful and mysterious hymns that were possibly used in the baptismal liturgy. The Hymn of the Pearl, itself embedded in the *Acts of Thomas* and also very early, shares their elusive quality. But it was the great fourth-century teacher, Ephrem, who was the greatest master of Syriac Christian poetry; indeed, no Syriac literature outside of the Bible and the *Diatessaron* had such a profound effect on the Syriac writers who came after, whether they themselves wrote in poetry or not. Philoxenus in the sixth century states that many monasteries had no books apart from the Bible and Ephrem, and such Nestorian writers as Narsai (d. ca. 503) and Isaac of Nineveh and Monophysite writers like Philoxenus and Jacob of Sarug (ca. 451–521) equally bear his stamp on their theology, their style, and their imagery.

Ephrem's hymns are complex. They make free use of typology, wordplay, paradox, repetition, and metaphor to convey to the listener or reader the richness of the reality hidden in the visible *raze'* (symbols, sacraments) and *remze'* (signs). Always they are grounded in Scripture; yet at the same time, R. Murray has suggested, the roots of some of the language and images may go much farther back to prebiblical times. Ephrem's style and method can be seen in this verse from one of his hymns of virginity:

> O fairest ear [of wheat]
>     which grew among hateful tares
> and gave the Bread of Life
>     without labor to the hungry!

It undid the curse
   with which Adam was bound,
who had eaten with sweat
   the bread of pain and thorns,
Blessed is he who eats
   of that Bread of blessing
and makes the curse pass from him![5]

In the preceding stanza of this hymn addressed to Christ, Ephrem was meditating upon Christ the Grape, a theme found also in the other great fourth-century Syriac writer, Aphraat. He went quite naturally into this stanza, in which, using the bread of the Eucharist as the governing symbol, he moved from an interpretation of the parable of the wheat to John's reference to Christ as the bread of life, freely given to all who eat it. From here, he contrasted this bread typologically with the bread Adam ate, for which he had to labor outside of Paradise. Finally, the listener understands that Christ is the bread of the Eucharist, replacing Adam's bread, of which we all have eaten. Within this short verse, then, Ephrem moved the listener imaginatively through a parable, a saying of John, salvation history, the meaning of the Eucharist, and the listrner's own need. This verse is both intensely personal and experiential, and at the same time it reveals a perception of the individual's place in the whole of salvation history and the sacramental life of the church.

Ephrem's way of writing hymns had a profound two-pronged theological basis which was passed on to Syriac-speaking writers on the Christian life after him. On the one hand, like the Cappadocians, he opposed the Arians, against whom much of his writing was directed, with the insistence that God's nature, in all its mystery, cannot be understood through human "investigation" or rational argument. On the other hand, the deity has made itself available to us in the incarnation, so that through faith and love we are able to come to God, or, as Philoxenus states it, to "walk in the spiritual countries." Here, in the special place that faith and love have as a kind of second vision through which we approach God and the things of God in our own human sphere, is the real contribution of the Syriac tradition to the spirituality of the early church. It is painful to speculate, in fact, on how right the fifth-century Jacob of Sarug was, when, after the Council of Chalcedon, he was pushed to make a definitive statement that would indicate where he stood in the christological controversy. He complied, but he also declared that such an emphasis on pinning down and defining what is essentially a mystery in Christ could only be destructive to the church. Jacob's own extant writings, with the exception of a volume of letters, are all in the form of metrical homilies, full of imagery and metaphor drawn from Scripture, the tradition, and the Christian imagination that Ephrem had also loved. They lead the heart to the faith and love (sometimes for him interchangeable terms) by which it sees God.

By the second half of the sixth century, the writings of Evagrius of Pontus assumed a special place of influence in Syriac spirituality. Though his ideas were repeatedly condemned in the Greek-speaking church in the years following his death, in a modified form they were more than congenial to Syriac speakers. Philoxenus himself, touchy over the inability of Syriac to express Greek concepts, may well have been responsible for one of the two Syriac recensions of the strange *Kephalaia Gnostica*. In other writings, Philoxenus speaks of faith as so powerful that without it even God would be as though not. Nonetheless, he at places abandons the Ephrem-like language of faith and speaks in terms of Evagrius's *theoria* (contemplation), which is both the faculty by which one perceives the "knowledge of Christ" and the hidden reality in both natural and supernatural things that reveals itself to those who are prepared for it. Neither Ephrem nor Aphraat in the fourth century had used this term. In comparison with Philoxenus, Isaac of Nineveh, in the seventh century, had thoroughly assimilated even Evagrius's cosmic hierarchy and referred to him by name. Babai the Great, a seventh-century Nestorian bishop, went so far as to write a commentary on the *Kephalaia Gnostica*, in order to demonstrate, by what can only be called rich allegorical exegesis, its orthodoxy.

The Macarian writings also assumed a special place in Syriac spirituality. Although there was an austere strand in the Syriac style of spiritual life and a reluctance to seek or trust mystical visions of God, which had much in common with the *Sayings of the Fathers*, there was also an emphasis upon personal religious experience within this tradition. In the greatest of the Syriac masters of spirituality after Ephrem, Isaac of Nineveh, numerous Macarian themes appear, including an emphasis on the humility of God in the incarnation, the indwelling of Christ in the saint, the understanding of the human situation as war between soul and body, the linking of purity of heart, mercy, and humility, and the importance of the Holy Spirit.

## Feminine Imagery

In addition to its distinctive blend of individualism, asceticism, and symbolism, one final example marks the diversity of Syrian spirituality within the wider Christian world. Perhaps it stems from an underlying understanding of the comprehensive nature of truth, or perhaps it reflects a sense of the incompleteness of each name for God as it stands by itself, but Syriac writers gave a place to feminine imagery that was unique in the early church.

The *Odes of Solomon* speak freely about the milk of the breasts of the Father, and, although this language with respect to the Father was not retained, until the fourth century (including in the writings of Ephrem) the Holy Spirit was regarded as feminine. Further, Mary was always a central figure within this tradition. Murray hints that Mary's especially important place in the later period within the complex typology tying together sacred history, the incarnation, the church, and the sacraments may have arisen as a necessary response by Syrian Christians to the threatened loss of the feminine in Christian imagery after the Holy Spirit came to be regarded as masculine. Some of Ephrem's Hymns of the Nativity, as they meditate on Mary, reveal the depth and insight of one thoroughly attuned to the use of the feminine imagery in the spiritual life.

### Notes

1. Robert Murray, *Symbols of Church and Kingdom,* 8.
2. Peter Brown, "The Rise and Function of the Holy Man in Late Antiquity."
3. Cited in Arthur Vööbus, *History of Asceticism in the Syrian Orient,* 1:40.
4. Cited in Vööbus, 1:41.
5. Sebastian Brock, "The Poet as Theologian," 243.
6. Robert Murray, "A Hymn of St. Ephrem to Christ," 43.

### Bibliography

#### Studies

Beck, Edmund. "Ephrem le syrien (Saint)." In *Dict. Sp.* 4, cols. 788–800. Beck is the editor of the monumental critical edition of Ephrem's works, published over the years in Corpus Scriptorum Christianorum Orientalium.

Brock, Sebastian. "Mary and the Eucharist: An Oriental Perspective." *Sobornost,* incorp. *Eastern Churches Review* 1:2 (1980) 50–59.

———. "The Mysteries Hidden in the Side of Christ." *Sobornost* 7:6 (1978) 462–72.

———. "The Poet as Theologian." *Sobornost* 7:4 (1977) 243–50. Extremely helpful for the understanding of "symbolic theology" (Brock's term) in the Syriac tradition.

———. "St. Isaac of Nineveh and Syriac Spirituality." *Sobornost* 7:2 (1975) 79–88.

Brown, Peter. "The Rise and Function of the Holy Man in Late Antiquity." *Journal of Roman Studies* 61 (1971) 80–101. Reprinted in his *Society and the Holy in Late Antiquity.* London Faber & Faber, 1982.

Chesnut, Roberta Cowan. [Roberta C. Bondi] *Three Monophysite Christologies: Severus of Antioch, Philoxenus of Mabbug, and Jacob of Sarug.* London: Oxford University Press, 1976. Contains extensive discussion of anthropology and contemplation in Philoxenus and Jacob.

McCullough, W. Stewart, *A Short History of Syriac Christianity to the Rise of Islam.* Chico, CA: Scholars Press, 1982. A short history, much better on events than on thought, but easy to use.

Murray, Robert. "A Hymn of St. Ephrem to Christ." *Sobornost*, incorp. *Eastern Churches Review* 1:1 (1979) 39–50. I have quoted from verse 14 of Murray's translation included in this article.

————. "Mary, the Second Eve in the Early Syriac Fathers." *Eastern Churches Review* 3:3 (1971) 371–84.

————. "St. Ephrem's Dialogue of Reason and Love." *Sobornost* 2:2 (1980) 26–40.

————. *Symbols of Church and Kingdom: A Study of Early Syriac Tradition.* Cambridge: Cambridge University Press, 1975. An outstanding book on the thought patterns and theology of Ephrem and Aphraat as they fit into the earlier tradition. Includes a great deal on Aphraat, who is not discussed in this article. Contains exceptionally helpful bibliography.

Ortiz de Urbina, Ignatius. *Patrologia Syriaca.* 2nd ed. Rome: Pontifical Institute of Oriental Studies, 1965. A Syriac patrology.

Segal, J. B. *Edessa: 'The Blessed City.'* Oxford: Clarendon Press, 1970. Concentrates on Edessa from the Seleucids to 639 c.e.

Vööbus, Arthur. *History of Asceticism in the Syrian Orient.* 2 vols. Corpus scriptorum Christianorum Orientalium 184, 197. Louvain: Corpus scriptorum Christianorum Orientalium, 1958, 1960. Invaluable in many ways. It treats Mesopotamia and Syria in separate sections from Persia. His other works cover a broad spectrum of topics of importance to the Syriac church and its literature.

12. *Enthroned Virgin with Two Saints,*
Monastery of Saint Catherine,
Mount Sinai, 6th century

13. *Christ's Mission to the Apostles:*
*Ivory Relief from a Gospel Book Cover,*
Germany, 10th century

# II. *Spirituality in Celtic and Germanic Society*

PIERRE RICHÉ

THE CONVERSION OF THE CELTS and subsequently of the Germans between the fifth and the seventh centuries radically changed the conditions of Western religious life. Christianity, a religion of Mediterranean origin, was implanted little by little in the countries of northern Europe, which for centuries had had a unique civilization. For the history of spirituality this encounter marks a decisive turning point, on which the history of medieval Christianity depends. But in order to understand the novelty of this religious phenomenon, we must first recall briefly the characteristics of religious experience that preceded Christianity in the Celtic and Germanic countries.

The Celt—the religious person *par excellence*—lived amid gods common to the entire Celtic society, such as Lug, the luminous god, or Dagda, the chthonic god, or the gods of each tribe, fathers and protectors of their people, whose spouses assured the fertility of the cattle, fertilized the earth, and freed it from all hostile powers. Between the gods and the people were the heroes, from whom the princely families were descended, that is, Cuchulain, son of Lug, conqueror of the dark and gigantic gods, or Bran, whose valor was recounted in Irish or Welsh epics. The Celtic king's status approached that of the heroes: he was responsible for the material welfare of the people and for the balancing of cosmic forces. At the time of his enthronement rites he was invested with a magical power. His power was conditional upon his moral and physical integrity; if he lost this, he was deposed. His wife played an important role beside him. It must be added that in Celtic society, the women, whether they were virgins or mothers, had a privileged place, which they would maintain after the conversion to Christianity. At Kildare, in the temple of the goddess Brigit, nine vestal virgins kept watch over the fire, which burned continuously. The women practiced magic, took the form of fairies, and attracted men by their beauty and charm. The Celts came together regularly at the time of the four seasonal feasts: on Beltaine (May 1) fire and the sun, symbolized by disks such as "triceles" (triangular shapes) with spirals, were honored; Lugnasad (Aug. 1) was the feast of harvesting; Samain (Nov. 1) was that of the subterranean powers; and finally Oimelc or Imbolg (Feb. 1) was the feast of breeding. The druids (*drua* in Irish, *dryw* in Welsh) were more soothsayers and judges than priests. Having a rapport with the gods, they spoke in their name, declared lawful and ill-omened days and ritual prohibitions, explained dreams and visions, and were versed in the magical writing of *ogham.* They were also educators of youth. According to the practice known as *fosterage,* the children of the aristocracy were entrusted to foster parents, who gave them a manual, intellectual, and military education. Religious education, as far as we can tell from several traditions, dealt with the destinies of people, and in particular with their lot after death.

The Celts believed in the immortality of the soul. The Byzantine historian Procopius tells us that the inhabitants of Celtic Brittany carried the souls of the dead to Great Britian in seemingly empty boats and that at the end of the voyage a voice counted the passengers through calling them by name.[1] The souls could be reincarnated in other beings—even nonhuman—in insects or in birds. The souls could travel far from their native country through the fog toward mysterious islands whose marvels are described by later legends: land of the living, land of joy, island of women, etc. The journeys (*imrama*) of souls and of heroes were the object of many stories that remained after the Celts became Christians.

The religious experience of the pagan Germans is known to us indirectly through Latin texts, which denounce pagan practices, through archaeological material, and through the Scandinavian literature of the *Edda* and the *sagas.* Unlike the Celt, the German man was primarily a warrior. From the time of his birth, he was the trustee of a power and doggedly assured his destiny by putting all the odds in his favor. The warrior learned how to fight from the time of his youth, and with his companions, the *bersekir,* he put all his energy into achieving victory. To avenge himself, he killed in order to preserve his dignity: vengeance was a sacred right. The German avenged himself and his clan, for his destiny was tied to his extended family. If he was excluded from this family, he was desacralized, became an outlaw, and was destined for death.

The king was a warrior among others, the proprietor of the sacred (*heilig*). The king knew that he had to exercise his magical power for the good of the tribe. The German believed that the world was in a perpetual state of tension, subject to antagonistic, destructive, or creative forces. The *Ases,* superior gods, had overcome the *Vanes,* whose leader Odin (called Wodan in southern German lands) was the father of human beings and of the gods, the *Allvater.* As god of war and savage hunter, he transferred his powers to the king. Odin received the dead warriors in Valhalla, "the home of those who have fallen"—where the Valkyries lived, who welcomed the dead while pouring out mead for them. Odin was assisted by other gods such as Thor, or Donar, the god of thunder, protector of humans against monsters and giants, who also tried to destroy gods.

The Germans expressed their faith less by personal devotion than by collective celebrations. They were obliged to reconcile the natural powers during the year's great feasts of the solstice or new moon. These celebrations took place in areas that were presumed sacred, enclaves separated from the world by a palisade, forests, giant trees, fountains, etc. The Germans reconciled the divine powers through prayers that were magical incantations, of which several texts have been preserved for us. They wore phylacteries of animal (stags' horns, bears' teeth, sea shells) and vegetable origin (resins, hazel nuts) or objects covered with Runic characters, some of which archaeologists have recovered in tombs. Unlike the Celts, the Germans did not believe in immortality, but they nevertheless feared the action of people after their death. They therefore had either to cremate the corpse or to bury it with familiar objects and prevent revenge by offerings and animal sacrifice. They could not imagine the destiny of the person in the afterlife. The Venerable Bede tells us that a warrior, a companion to the Anglo-Saxon Edwin, compared human life to a bird that flew through the room where the king sat, coming from the world of tempests and going back into obscurity: "Such is human life of which we perceive a brief moment, yet we are ignorant of what precedes and follows it."[2]

However, the Germans believed that just as the world had been created, one also had to imagine its destruction. The gods lived in Asgard, the "enclave of the *Ases*," imagined to be a wooden palace held up by an enormous tree. The roots of the tree were gnawed by a dragon, who sought to destroy this abode. As long as humans collaborated with the gods for the preservation of cosmic order, the world would continue to exist; but one day it would have to disappear in a universal catastrophe. The "twilight of the gods," of which Wagner sang in his own fashion, was one of the most profoundly established beliefs of the German spirit.

## The Spirituality of the Celts

Christianity had penetrated the Celtic lands of Great Britian from the fourth century. Christian communities were organized and monasticism developed rather quickly. The ascetical and voluntary heroism of the monks rendered them susceptible to the ideas of one among them, Pelagius, who propagated his ideas in Britian before going to the Continent. In 429, Pope Celestine sent Germanus of Auxerre to fight Pelagianism at the same time that he sent Palladius to convert Ireland. But the real missionary of Ireland was the Welshman (?) Patrick, who in his *Confession* recounts the circumstances of his apostleship. Patrick, even though he describes himself as little educated, knew Scripture very well, as is attested by the more than seventy biblical citations found in his work. Ascetic by the call of God who spoke to him in visions, monk turned bishop against his will, Patrick succeeded in rapidly converting many leaders of the Irish tribes. He got them to abandon the cult of idols and, as he put it, he made them pass from the cult of the sun to that of the "true sun who is Christ" (*Confession* 60). His first disciples were women, whose importance in Celtic society we have noted. The tribal leaders, converted along with their subjects, organized monasteries in several regions of Ireland. The abbots, who often had the title of bishop, represented Christ, himself called the "Great Abbot," and played a role both spiritual and temporal. Women were called to direct monastic communities, such as Bridget, who was installed at Kildare, on the site of the old pagan sanctuary. There even followed the creation of double monasteries of men and women, directed by abbesses.

The Celtic monks devoted themselves to manual labor: tilling, rearing cattle, making jewelry (we still have magnificent examples), copying manuscripts. In the beginning these monks were not intellectuals, but since they had to read the Bible and celebrate the liturgy in Latin they applied themselves very soon to the study of this foreign language and were led to copy and learn the Latin grammarians and texts coming from the Continent. In order to nurture their spirituality, they meditated on the Bible, beginning with the Psalter, which was the fundamental book of readings in Celtic lands as it was in the Mediterranean world. Prayer included the daily recitation of the 150 psalms (the "three fifties") with arms crossed and kneeling. Recent studies have brought to light the Irish exegesis of the seventh and eighth centuries, which played a major role in the formation of the new medieval Christian culture. The Celts also applied themselves to the study of computation for the ordering of the liturgy, especially for fixing the date of Easter. Separated from the Mediterranean world, they adopted a system different from that of the Continent, and for a long time they remained faithful to this particular computation of Easter, which led to numerous conflicts with the Roman church.

The Celtic monks paid close attention to the education of children; in this they took the place of the druids. Hagiographical texts give us rather precise instructions regarding the practice of fosterage, which we mentioned above. The child was entrusted to a monk, who entered into a kind of spiritual parenthood with him. If sons of aristocrats were entrusted provisionally to a monk, they later returned to their families, or else, offered to God, they became novices in monastic life.

Celtic spirituality was characterized by a rigorous asceticism, which

recalled that of the Eastern monks. In order to combat the intensity of concupiscence, monks plunged into ice-cold pools and prayed for hours with
arms crossed. The *crosfigill* or "vigil of the Cross" gave birth to many legends,
such as that of Kevin of Glendalough, who for seven years remained leaning
against a board in such perfect immobility that birds built their nests in his
open hands. The diet was very strict: one meal a day without meat, fish, or
eggs, especially during the three fasts, "that of Elijah in winter, of Jesus in
spring, of Moses in summer." (It so happens that the practice of fasting was
already known in Celtic law before Christianity. In order to assure his
rights, a plaintiff could fast in front of the house of his adversary, but such
"hunger strikes" sometimes led to death.) These ascetical practices were
accompanied by unceasing prayers and by the recitation of long litanies
called *loricae* or "breastplates," which enabled the monks to triumph over
every snare and temptation. Let us cite some lines from the *lorica* attributed
to Patrick:

> I arise today
>> through God's strength to pilot me:
>> God's might to uphold me,
>> God's wisdom to guide me
>> God's eye to look before me,
>> God's ear to hear me,
>> God's word to speak for me,
>> God's hand to guard me,
>> God's way to lie before me,
>> God's shield to protect me,
>> God's host to secure me
>>> against snares of devils,
>>> against temptations of vices,
>>> against inclinations of nature,
>>> against everyone who shall wish me ill,
>>> afar and anear,
>>> alone and in a crowd.[3]

Thus, in lieu of bloody, red martyrdom, the monks wished to attain "white
martyrdom" in renouncing the world and "green martyrdom" in devoting
themselves to austerities.

Another characteristic of Celtic spirituality was the practice of private
penance. The abbot of a monastery had to be a spiritual doctor, an *amnchara*,
for, as an Irish saying goes, "a person without a confessor is like a body
without a head." The abbot was obliged to direct each monk in his religious
life and to impose an appropriate penance after the confession of his sins.
The little books called the "penitentials" have preserved for us the scale of

punishments. To each sin there corresponded a penance consisting of recitation of psalms, corporal punishments, fasting on bread and water, and excommunications. Following are some examples, which are taken from the oldest of the penitentials, that of Finnian, abbot of Clonard in the sixth century:

> If someone sins by abusive speech and forthwith repents, he will undertake a prolonged fast. If someone argues with a cleric and minister of God, he will fast for a week on bread and water. If a cleric has once or twice committed a theft by stealing a sheep, a pig, or another animal, he will fast for one year on bread and water and will pay back what he has stolen fourfold. If a religious has given birth to a child and if her sin is known to all, she will fast on bread and water for six years. If a cleric desires carnally a virgin or any other woman without having once confessed it, he will fast for seven days on bread and water. . . .[4]

Even transgressions that would appear to us as minor were penalized: one hundred blows with a stick for having soiled hands; forty days of penance for the cook who lets an impurity fall into a liquid; seven days of penance for vomiting from drunkenness; one hundred blows with a stick for false testimony in good faith and seven hundred blows plus one hundred fifty psalms for testimony in bad faith; etc. Very soon these penitentials were applied not only to monks but were addressed equally to laypersons, and they were particularly aimed at all sexual abuses.

The punishments provided in the penitentials could be substituted for each other, and tables of equivalence were arranged: one year of penance could be replaced by three days of retreat in the tomb of a saint. Those who could not sustain the fast could replace it with fifty psalms kneeling and sixty-six psalms without kneeling. The penitential of Cummean even provided that the penitent who did not know how to recite the psalms and was not able to fast could choose a monk who would perform the penance in his place.[5] The substitution could even be made monetarily: the compensation paid to the monastery recalls the legal arrangement known in Celtic legislation as the "price of honor," which was proportional to the gravity of the offense and to the social status of the victim.

The spiritual value of private penance has been much discussed. It is certain that the minutiae, the arbitrariness, the disproportion between the fault and the repayment, and the disagreement between the different penitentials can give rise to many criticisms. But it is equally certain that this penitential practice marked an advancement over public penance, which could not be repeated. Each time that a monk fell, he could obtain pardon. The confessor was an intermediary between the person and God, the bestower of grace. As Gabriel LeBras wrote:

Because they call for delicacy in the psychology of sin as in the choice of the penalty, the penitentials serve for the education of the cleric as of the faithful. They inspire them with a sense of material cleanliness as of moral purity. The justice of men draws as much from them as the justice of God. As initiators of the penitentials, respectful of principles, ingenious in application, the Irish have contributed more than any other people in the dark ages to the progress of the moral conscience in the West.[6]

These penitentials would be very successful when the Irish settled on the Continent.

Another form of Celtic asceticism to be noted is exile far from one's native country. Following the example of Abraham, who left his country on God's command, or the apostles, who abandoned all for Christ, the Celtic monks undertook *peregrinatio* by breaking all the bonds that attached them to their clan—and they were very strong—or to their monasteries. The Celts left Ireland, Wales, and Cornwall to settle either in England or on the Continent.

While the Celts of the sixth century had refused to convert their Anglo-Saxon enemies in order not to "meet them again in Paradise," to quote a famous saying, the Irish monks of the seventh century settled in Scotland and in northern England. The disciples of Columba or Columcille, coming from Derry to Iona, founded monasteries in Northumbria, a monastery for men at Lindisfarne and a double monastery at Whitby. They devoted themselves to a religious life consisting of asceticism and meditation on the Scripture, which, if the Venerable Bede is to be believed, assured them of great success.

Other monks, like the heroes in search of wonderful lands, embarked on boats that took them to the Continent. On the island of Armorica and along the coast they founded monasteries and hermitages, establishing a new type of religious life, which did not fail to disturb the Gallo-Roman bishops. In 590, the Irishman Columban of Bangor and his disciples crossed the English Channel and proceeded to settle at Luxeuil. Columbanian spirituality did much to restore a Merovingian church that was too entangled in the compromises of the century. Men and women of the aristocracy who desired a more demanding religious life offered the monks land, entrusted their children to them, and even entered the monasteries themselves. Private penance, unknown in Gaul at that time, was favorably received. In 644, when the bishops assembled at the Council of Châlon-sur-Saône, they recognized the value of this new penitential practice. The Columbanians restored vigor to the reading and study of Holy Scripture. Although many bishops continued to pride themselves on being versed in the liberal arts, the Irish monks restored the essential element of ascetical culture, namely, being trained in meditation on the Bible. The Columbanians recalled to mind that the human person, from the time of birth, was called to the contemplation of God. For them, the boundaries between the visible and the invisible world no longer existed. This new spirituality can be evaluated by examining the works of Columban and by reading the hagiographical texts written in Gaul in the seventh and eighth centuries. Let us cite an excerpt from the Life of St. Gertrude of Nivelles: "We see many people, even in this world, who live an angelic life, so that while corporally they live among humans, their spirit and their conscience are directed toward eternity and their heart is unceasingly taken up in divine contemplation" (*The Virtues of St. Gertrude* 1 [*MGH, SRM* 2:464]). The Columbanian monks set up their monasteries as an anticipation of paradise: they triumphed over satanic powers, they tamed wild animals, they regulated nature. The monks sought to reclaim the privileges that Adam had received from God and had lost by sin. Even in their lifetime, these monks were favored by visions that revealed to them the horrors of hell and the delights of heaven.

Another feature of Celtic spirituality, also related to the *peregrinatio*, was the desire to evangelize the pagans. The Celtic monk, even though he sought out "the desert," could not refrain from converting the peasants to Christianity, and he became a missionary in spite of himself. Gall and Eustace, disciples of Columban, converted the Alamannics and the Bavarians respectively. Omer, a disciple of Eustace, evangelized Flanders. Missionary fervor overtook monks on the Continent like Amand and Eloy. The monasteries they founded were "nurseries" for missionaries. Beginning in the eighth century, the Anglo-Saxon monks took their turn: they also were animated by the missionary spirit and undertook the conversion of Germany.

The Irish contribution to continental Christianity in the seventh and eighth centuries did not, however, mark the end of a distinctive Celtic spirituality. Although the Viking invasions limited Celtic contacts with the Continent after 800, important native developments took place. Foremost among these was the interaction between Irish monastic culture and the ancient pagan Celtic traditions that had been passed on orally for centuries. It is to Irish monks of the eighth through the twelfth century that we owe the preservation of the early Irish sagas—a task which these monks did not see as contradictory to their religious dedication. This monastic interest in vernacular literary culture was also at the root of one of the most appealing characteristics of early Irish spirituality, the fresh and charming nature poetry with which the monks hymned the splendor of God's creation. As one well-known hermit's song expresses it:

For I inhabit a wood
unknown but to my God

> my house of hazel and ash
>> as an old hut in a rath . . .
> For music I
> have pines, my tall
>> music-pines
> so who can I
> envy here, my
>> gentle Christ?[7]

Irish monasticism, intimately tied up with Irish tribal society, did not lack its own abuses and problems. An important native reform movement called the *Céili Dé* (servants of God), which began in the eighth century, did much to recall the monks to austerity of life and fervor of devotion.

## The Spirituality of Christian Germania

The first Germans converted to Christianity were those who made up the eastern group of Goths, Vandals, and Burgundians. By an accident of history, they passed from paganism to a form of Christianity which the orthodox catholics judged heretical. Under the influence of Ulfilas, they adopted Arianism, which had been condemned at the Council of Nicaea (325 c.e.). Although we know almost nothing about the spirituality of the Arian Germans, we can say that the strength of Arianism flowed from the national character of this religion. The Arian clergy was strictly submissive to the prince; a liturgy in the Gothic language brought together a faithful who, thanks to the translation provided by Ulfilas, had access directly to the Bible. The Burgundian and Vandal princes were concerned about theological controversies and tried by persuasion and force to convert the orthodox. The majority of their people remained faithful to their traditional beliefs and converted to orthodoxy only when their leaders agreed to receive catholic baptism in the sixth and seventh centuries.

The evangelization of the Germanic pagans—Anglo-Saxons, Franks, other peoples of Germania, then Scandinavians—was a work that required long labor. The conversion of the leaders led to that of the people, but the missionaries were unable to make ancient practices totally disappear. Thus was posed the problem of the "Germanization of Christianity," about which many historians, especially in Germany, have debated. Were the Germans converted to Roman Christianity, or did they rather retain the features of their old religious culture? Did the encounter of the two religions take place without one contaminating the other?

In order to evaluate the influence of the Germanic temper on Christian spirituality, it must be remembered that the evangelizers agreed to the preservation of ancient customs. They fought against idolatry but respected the localization of the cult and certain rites. Pope Gregory the Great himself urged the Roman missionaries who were sent to England not to destroy the temples but to empty them of idols and to institute other solemnities to take the place of pagan feasts, for "it is undoubtedly impossible to suppress everything at once in hearts so uncouth; whoever wishes to climb a mountain only succeeds by advancing step by step and not in leaps and bounds."[8] In a manner contrary to those who, like Charlemagne, wished to impose Christianity by force, the missionaries adopted a policy of persuasion. Already in the eighth century, Boniface applied the advice given to him by Bishop Daniel of Winchester. The preacher must show that he is not ignorant of pagan doctrines; he must get the Germans to speak of their gods and lead them to admit the improbability of their beliefs: "All that should be set forth with gentleness and moderation, not with an air of passionate or provocative controversy."[9] At the end of the century, Alcuin opposed the terrorist methods of Charlemagne by recalling that "the person who possesses a rational intelligence must be instructed and enticed by all manner of preaching so that he will perceive the veracious character of the sacred faith."[10] While fighting against the most grievous pagan superstitions, the missionaries accepted the preservation of social rites such as the libation of the coffin in Scandinavia. To replace the magical incantations employed by pagans, clerics introduced prayers which could be called "Christian incantations": the priest blessed the fields, the vineyard, the nuptial bed, the shaving of the first beard, the new well, the vase which had been contaminated by an animal, the soap which one used for the bath, etc. . . . Some prayers had the power to drive away thunder and tempests and also to protect against slugs and worms. In order to prevent a sick person from going to find some healer who was in effect a sorcerer, clerics recited formulas blending Latin, Greek, vernacular, and cabalistic words, all accompanied by many signs of the cross.

Leaving behind the rites, let us move to a deeper discussion of the religious psychology of the Christianized Germans. The social structure, and particularly the fact that the Germans belonged to groups of warriors, influenced their way of living Christianity. The prince to whom the Germans were bound by ties of fidelity was always considered a sacred personage. After 751, when the Carolingian kings were anointed by bishops, they reinforced their religious character. The Frankish king represented God on earth: his palace was described after the manner of paradise—he sat surrounded by his warriors and vassals, like God in the midst of the angels and saints. The king was master of the kingdom just as Christ was master of the heavens. Christ himself had his vassals, that is to say, the apostles. The poet of the *Heliand*

(*The Savior*) interpreted the Gospels in his own way in the Germanic language: he presented Christ surrounded by his disciples, among whom St. Peter played the most important role. The cult of the Prince of the Apostles spread from the beginning of the seventh century in the Germanic world, as witnessed by the numerous churches dedicated to him. He was considered to have always lived in Rome, where his relics became the object of numerous pilgrimages. It was to his successor, the pope, that the bishops who evangelized Germany appealed for help and advice. The feast of the Chair of St. Peter, February 22, which had lapsed into obscurity in Rome, was retained in the Germanic countries. Without going so far as to say that the cult of the leader in the Germanic lands had promoted the cult of St. Peter, one can think that the Germans saw the apostle as the doorkeeper of heaven, the one who could lead them to paradise.[11] Alongside Peter, other heroes were venerated: the saints, generally of aristocratic descent, whose relics were objects of both cult and "translation," that is, movement to more fitting locations. The saints also promised success and prosperity. A country newly converted to Christianity, such as Saxony, could only progress spiritually and even materially by possessing relics: relics of male saints but also of female saints, for, as in Celtic society, women played an important role in religious life. Many abbesses and cloistered nuns who lived in the monasteries in the eighth century were considered saints. More than in any other area, feminine sainthood occupied a great place in Germanic devotion.

Bound by the ties of kinship and of tribe, the Germans had a particularly strong sense of solidarity. They expressed it in the *Geldonia,* "mutual aid associations" of sorts, which brought people together periodically and were the occasion of much excessive drinking and frivolity, which the clerics tried to suppress. But this spirit of fellowship inspired the "confraternities for the dead" established in the monasteries. At the Synod of Attigny in 762, forty-four clerics devoted themselves to praying for the living and the dead. In Bavaria, a "confraternity of bishops and abbots of Bavaria for the benefit of deceased monks" was established. At the time of a Frankish monk's death, all the others were obliged to celebrate masses for him. Throughout the ninth century, these associations multiplied in numerous monasteries. Thus, the famous *Liber memorialis* of Remiremont set up an association of prayer among several monasteries of *Germania.* The monks could pray both for the dead and for the living.

Another feature of Germanic spirituality was related to its warlike tendencies: war was a judgment of God. It was God, the God of armies, who helped the warrior in battle as he helped the heroes of Bible: Joshua, David, and Judas Maccabeus. The military saints (Maurice, Sebastian) were models to be imitated. Carolingian soldiers prepared themselves for combat by days of fasting and prayer, and engaged in battle to the chant of *Kyrie Eleison.* Thus, the idea of the holy war conducted against the enemies of Christianity appeared as early as the Carolingian epoch. The Frankish soldier had already become the *miles Christi,* whose weapons were blessed by the clerics. As early as the ninth century, a pope promised eternal salvation to those who were going to die in combat for the sake of defending the church against the Saracens.[12]

For many Christians, war against the enemies of God was only an aspect of the battle between the opposing forces of Good and Evil. Satan and his dependents assaulted the celestial citadel and prepared to hurl sinners into hell. The visions recorded for us by the monks, undoubtedly influenced by the Celts, describe in realistic fashion the horrors of hell and the splendors of heaven. In the end, Satan is necessarily vanquished. In the *Muspilli,* written in a Bavarian dialect in the middle of the ninth century, the poet calls to mind the last judgment and the triumph of Elijah over the Antichrist. It can be compared with another poem of Scandinavian origin, the *Völuspa* or prediction of the prophetess. If the author was not a Christian, he or she was much influenced by Christianity, describing the cycle of universal history since the creation and ending with a vision of restored harmony:

> I see a palace rising with a golden roof more resplendent than the sun. There will the company of those who remained faithful have their abode, and they will enjoy happiness until the end of time. A powerful Lord is coming to judge in all sovereignty; he descends in his omnipotence to order all things. He pronounces judgments, he challenges discord, and he establishes a sacred harmony which will be eternal.

It was no longer a question of cosmic catastrophes, as in the time of paganism, but of the building of a heavenly Jerusalem.

*Translated by Dennis Tamburello*

## Notes

1. Procopius *History of the Gothic Wars* 8.20.42–58.
2. Venerable Bede *History of the English Church and People* 2.13
3. Patrick *Lorica,* lines 32–48, as translated by Ludwig Bieler in *The Works of St. Patrick* (ACW 17; 1953) 70–71.
4. An edition and translation of the Penitential of Finnian can be found in Ludwig Bieler, *The Irish Penitentials* (Dublin: The Dublin Institute for Advanced Studies, 1975) 74–95.
5. The Penitential of Cummean can be found in Bieler, *Irish Penitentials,* 108–35.
6. G. LeBras, "The Irish Penitentials," 126.

7. "Marban, A Hermit Speaks," as translated by Michael Harnett in *The Book of Irish Verse*, ed. John Montague (New York: Macmillan, 1974) 57–58.

8. Gregory's famous letter is preserved in Bede *History* 1.30.

9. For the letter of Bishop Daniel to Boniface, see *PL* 89, col. 708.

10. Letter of Alcuin to Arno, Bishop of Salzburg, in *MGH Epistulae* IV, p. 164.

11. See the famous statement of King Oswy at the Synod of Whitby (664) in Bede *History* 3.25.

12. Pope Leo IV's Letter to the Frankish Army, Ep. 28 in *MGH Epistulae* V, p. 601.

13. *Völupsa* 64–65, in *The Poetic Edda*, trans. Henry A. Bellows (Princeton, NJ: Princeton University Press, 1923) 26.

# Bibliography

## Studies

*Celtic Christianity*

Dillon, Myles, and Nora K. Chadwick. *The Celtic Realms*. New York: New American Library, 1967. A useful general survey.

Hanson, R. P. C. *The Life and Writings of the Historical Saint Patrick*. New York: Seabury, 1983.

Hughes, Kathleen. *The Church in Early Irish Society*. Ithaca, NY: Cornell University Press, 1966. An original social interpretation of major importance.

———, and Ann Hamlin. *Celtic Monasticism*. New York: Seabury, 1981. An Introduction.

LeBras, Gabriel. "The Irish Penitentials." In *The Miracle of Ireland*. Edited by Henry Daniel-Rops. Dublin: Clonmore & Reynolds, 1959.

McNeill, John T. *The Celtic Churches: A History, A.D. 200–1200*. Chicago: University of Chicago Press, 1974.

Maher, Michael, ed. *Irish Spirituality*. Dublin: Veritas Publications, 1981. Ten essays, the first five of which touch this period.

Rees, Alwyn, and Brinley Rees. *Celtic Heritage: Ancient Tradition in Ireland and Wales*. London: Thames & Hudson, 1961. A brilliant study of Celtic mythology.

Riché, Pierre. "Columbanus, his followers and the Merovingian Church." In *Columbanus and Merovingian Monasticism*. Edited by H. B. Clarke and Mary Brennan. British Archaeological Reports International Series 113. Oxford: British Archaeological Reports, 1981.

*Germanic Christianity*

Boyer, Regis. *La religion des anciens scandinaves*. Paris: Payot, 1981.

Dumézil, Georges. *Gods of the Ancient Northmen*. Berkeley: University of California Press, 1973. A major study by one of the great historians of religion.

Levison, Wilhelm. *England and the Continent in the Eighth Century*. Oxford: Clarendon Press, 1946. A classic study.

Löwe, Heinrich. "Pirmin, Willibrord und Bonifatius: Ihre Bedeutung für die Missionsgeschichte ihrer Zeit." In *La conversione al'cristianesimo nell'Europa dell'Alto Medioevo*. Settimane de Spoleto 1966. Spoleto: Centro di Studi sull'Alto Medioevo, 1967.

Manselli, Raoul. "La conversione dei popoli germanici al Cristianesimo: La discussione storiografia." In *La conversione al'cristianesimo nell'Europa dell'Alto Medioevo*.

Mayr-Harting, Henry. *The Coming of Christianity to England.* New York: Schocken Books, 1972. An important interpretation.

Musset, Lucien. "La pénétration chrétienne dans l'Europe du Nord et son influence sur la civilisation scandinave." In *La conversione al cristianesimo nell'Europa dell'Alto Medioevo.*

Riché, Pierre. *Education and Culture in the Barbarian West.* Columbia, SC: University of South Carolina Press, 1976.

Salin, Édouard. *La civilisation mérovingienne.* 4 vols. Paris: Picard, 1949-59.

Vogel, Cyrille. *Le pêcheur et la pénitence au moyen âge.* Paris: Cerf, 1969.

# 8

# The Gregorian Reform

## KARL F. MORRISON

The Gregorian Reform can be said to have begun under Pope Leo IX at the Council of Rheims (1049) and to have ended under Pope Calixtus II at the first Lateran Council (1123). It was one of many movements of Christian renewal in the eleventh and twelfth centuries. Among them it was the most prominent, and its results were the most lasting; for it was limited neither to a particular diocese, kingdom, or religious order nor to the lifetime of one inspired leader. A series of popes (notably Gregory VII [1073-1085], from whom it took its name) made its principles their program of government. As such, it reached into the political and spiritual life of all western Europe. For decades it served as a common point of reference from which other reforms were either nourished or repelled. The goals, achievements, and failures of the Gregorian Reform have to be understood in the context of the many programs that competed in the effort to renew Christian life by purifying the church.

All such programs sought to realize on earth patterns of life set forth in Scripture. All were guided by a vision of church unity. The distinguishing features of the Gregorian Reform were (1) that it derived from Scripture a pattern of life in which the priesthood was set aside from and over the laity in Christian society, and (2) that it taught a form of church unity that was indistinguishable from absolute papal headship. Sacerdotalism and the papal monarchy were guiding principles of the Gregorian movement. In time, they became self-justifying ends.

The two principles, sacerdotalism and papal monarchy, were ancient; by combining them the Gregorians revived a doctrine that had incited dispute in the early church. According to the Gospels, Christ confided the church to the apostle Peter, empowering him to confirm his brethren and promising, by prayer, to sustain Peter's own faith (Matt 16:18; Luke 22:31-32). By the late second century, the lines of conflict had been drawn. Some believed that Christ spoke to Peter as representing all the apostles and thus all their successors: namely, the whole episcopal order. For them, the unity of the church consisted in the charismatic harmony that united all bishops on matters of faith, a harmony derived by each bishop immediately from the Holy Spirit and expressed institutionally by the consensus of synods and councils. Others held that Peter's commission was a personal (not a representative) one and that it passed by inheritance to those who succeeded him as bishop of Rome. For them, the unity of the church consisted in the principate of Peter, an office that mediated between Christ and all believers, conveying to them their faith and, by command, whatever authority they had in the Church.

Lacking a centralized administrative apparatus, advocates of the papal principate (or monarchy) were unable to shape the world according to their ideal. They encountered obstacles during the patristic age. The political interests of the Eastern Empire, which opposed a dominant church in the West, favored the rise of autonomous patriarchates that claimed equivalence in power. Controversies among patriarchs encouraged the use of councils as ecumenical courts with jurisdiction even over the most eminent bishops. The barbarian invasions further divided hierarchic order in the West, for, in the emerging kingdoms, church administration centered on the nearest seats of power, the royal courts, rather than on the distant papacy. From the eighth century on, a new wave of barbarian invasions and the development of feudal institutions compounded regionalism. Between the late ninth century and the beginning of the Gregorian Reform (ca. 1050), conditions hostile to papal monarchy reached their zenith, for then the Roman aristocracy held the papacy itself captive in weakness and degradation.

Although prevailing conditions favored sacerdotalism and corroded papal monarchy, papal tradition nurtured the ideal that combined the two. It is ironic that one of the most ardent advocates of that ideal, Nicholas I (858-867), came to the throne of Peter just when the papacy entered the debasement from which the Gregorians delivered it. In the period between the age of the fathers and the beginning of the Gregorian epoch, doctrines and institutions took root that legitimated sacerdotalism without papal monarchy and held popes accountable to the consensus and judgment of the whole church. These doctrines and institutions were interwoven with the political order that took shape in Europe after the barbarian invasions.

The Gregorians launched a bold assault against them. In general, Gregorians agreed that the unity of the church was the sum of its holiness, catholicity, and apostolicity. Its holiness, they held, was epitomized in the pope, "who, if he is canonically ordained, is beyond doubt made holy through the merits of St. Peter."[1] From the sanctification of the pope came the inerrancy of the Roman church. Because the spiritual power was superior to the temporal, the pope, the chief repository of spiritual power on earth, epitomized the catholicity of the church. He was able to absolve subjects of their oaths to unjust rulers, to claim the service of Christian kings, and even to depose emperors. Having power from which there was no appeal to judge and depose bishops, to sanction decrees of councils, and to approve or reject texts as binding in canon law, the pope could be judged by no one. His decisions were not subject to review. He alone could be called "universal," and the catholicity of others was measured by their conformity with him. Finally, the apostolicity of the Roman church took precedence over that of any other church, for it was founded by Christ himself when he responded to Peter's confession of faith by committing the entire church to him and promising that he would forever sustain Peter's constancy in faith by his own prayers. What Christ committed and promised to Peter, he likewise committed and promised to those who followed him in apostolic succession, the bishops of Rome.

There is reason to think that, early in the Reform, sacerdotalism and the papal monarchy were considered institutional means to a greater spiritual end: the purification of the church from secular domination. The reformers identified three practices that intruded worldliness into the church: simony (the buying and selling of sacramental functions, notably ordination), Nicolaitism (marriage or concubinage of clergy), and the prerogatives that laypeople exercised in electing and installing priests in church offices. The reformers were particularly outraged when laypeople invested priests with symbols of spiritual powers (e.g., the bishop's ring and staff). The attack on this symbolic practice evidently undercut long-standing constitutional practices designed to secure the loyalty of clergy to their temporal overlords. It led to the series of disputes known collectively as the Investiture Conflict (ended in England in 1107 by the compromise of London; in France, at about the same time, by a series of agreements; and in Germany in 1122 by the Concordat of Worms). All three practices were sanctioned by long usage, but, arguing that they corrupted the formal order and polluted the inward purity enjoined by Scripture, the reformers attacked tradition in the name of what they considered to be truth.

The contribution of the Gregorian Reform to the spirituality of the Western church cannot be defined simply by the Gregorian program and that program's successes and failures in achieving its stated goals. Instead, the Gregorian contribution must be measured by the total dynamic of its attraction to and repulsion from other doctrines in the ideological repertory of reform.

All programs began from the same point: the doctrine of the church as the Body of Christ. All addressed the same subject: participation in that Body. The Gregorian program caused three major zones to form in which rival doctrines came into play. The first, located by the Gregorians' use of coercion, concerned participation in the Body of Christ by vocation, especially by a calling to government. The second, defined by the Gregorians' challenge to the validity of sacraments performed by their enemies, was participation by sacrament in the Body. The third, crystallized by the Gregorians' equation between the inward act of orthodox belief and outward discipline (hierarchic obedience), concerned participation by affective union between the individual soul and Christ: that is, by the most inward and incommunicable joy in which the soul passed over from its own finitude into God's infinite wisdom, power, and glory.

## Participation by Calling

The jurisdictional conflicts between the Gregorians and their enemies centered on the doctrine of vocation. It was assumed that kings, bishops, popes, and all others governing Christian society held office because God called them to rule the people. But were they accountable for their conduct of office to any human authority? Gregorian doctrines of accountability resemble the later idea of the absolute state. They portrayed the Body of Christ as a corporation over which the pope had been called by God to exercise arbitrary judgment, transcending all other rights. They identified the moral values of the corporation with the program of their regime and the commands of the pope with eternal law. They set forth a political order ruled by the inspired judgment of one man rather than by the inherited law of a whole community. Their doctrine that the pope was dominant over all and accountable to none by divine vocation required the use of coercion against dissidents.

The letters of Gregory VII provide an unusually clear survey of the reformers' idea of papal vocation and of the powers and obligations that they thought it bestowed. Gregory continually insisted that God, or St. Peter, had chosen him to be pope and that he had assumed the heavy burden of the church against his will and to his grief out of obedience to God and faithfulness to St. Peter. The apostle commanded Gregory, his representative, to rebuke criminals and sinners and to punish them by the power of the Roman see. He must not withhold his sword from blood: that is, Gregory added, withhold the word of preaching from its task of destroying carnal life.[2] However, the words could also be taken literally. Pope Leo IX had been captured while leading a military expedition in southern Italy. Early in his pontificate, Gregory VII proposed to lead a crusade in person to deliver Eastern Christians from Islam, a sanguinary task that his successor, Urban II, eventually confided to a papal legate. Gregory and his successors regularly promoted and engaged in military campaigns. Universal justice, truth, and the liberty of the church depended upon the judgments that Gregory believed he issued under divine inspiration and that the sword enforced at his command. Disobedience to the commands of the apostolic see was idolatry, the self-worship of the creature.

Cardinal Peter Damian (1007-1072), an early and constant supporter of the Reform, once wrote that the pope was "king of kings and prince of emperors" and that Christ had committed to him the powers of earthly and heavenly empire. Gregory VII also insisted that in Christian society the exercise of all power, spiritual and temporal, had been entrusted to the church and to the pope, its head. Christ committed to him the power to bind and loose on earth and in heaven, to judge both secular and spiritual matters, and to enforce his judgments. The priesthood had been instituted by God to guide people to heavenly life. Kingship, instituted by human lust for power, sought empty glory. Priesthood, Gregory argued, was therefore as much higher than kingship as gold was more valuable than lead.[3] It was in his charge to give and withdraw archbishoprics, bishoprics, and all other clerical offices. If those whom he condemned remained obdurately in office, he could, acting as the immediate spiritual head of every believer, forbid their subjects to obey them, to partake of, or even to witness sacraments performed by them. He could command their people to rebel against and to eject them. How could any doubt that he might strip offices of temporal government from those who proved unworthy and unprofitable and grant them to worthy men? He could even judge angels.

This vocation, Gregory argued, justified him in the most dramatic act of his pontificate, the excommunication and deposition of the Emperor Henry IV. Infected with the contagion of simony, Henry had rebelled against the church. Falling into the idolatry of disobedience by stubbornly ignoring Gregory's commands and admonitions and by breaking specific vows of obedience, Henry committed the paramount injustice, denying God due honor. Mindful of his vocation and of the account that as universal pastor he would have to give for Henry's soul at the Last Judgment, Gregory therefore declared Henry deposed, absolved his subjects of their vows of obedience to him, and sanctioned military rebellion against the excommunicated and deposed king. He begged God and St. Peter to annihilate Henry and thus, in the eyes of people, to authenticate Gregory's spiritual unity with the Prince of the Apostles.[4]

Conditions of association provided Gregory the opportunity and the apparatus for coercion, but such were the divergent theories of vocation that dissidents also possessed coercive opportunities and apparatus that could be used against the papacy. Except in theory, the papacy did not have a monopoly of power. The conditions of association included, for example, the Christian faith, sacraments (including priestly and episcopal ordination), the church hierarchy, common authorities (Scripture, the writings of the fathers, canons of orthodox synods and councils), property, and political loyalty to secular rulers. Weighing these conditions, dissidents could view Christian society not as a centralized empire but as a diverse federation. To them the Body of Christ had one head only, Christ himself. Within the Body of Christ, divine vocation created individual spheres of authority and an equilibrium of coercive powers that Christian society could bring to bear even against its most exalted earthly members.

Gregory asserted that his doctrine of vocation and the actions to which it led were sanctioned by Scripture, by the divinely inspired teachings of the fathers and by historical precedent. However, the identification that he drew between Christ's commission to Peter and his own accession to the papacy failed to convince his critics. They insisted that he had distorted the terms of Christ's commission and that, by failing to distinguish between the papal office and the man who held it, he wrongly understood Christ's promise of inerrancy to the church through Peter as a guarantee of the pope's personal orthodoxy. Therefore, they argued, he had violated the individual spheres of authority that divine vocation created in the church and he warranted the action taken by Christian society against him.

On balance, Gregory's opponents represented three spheres of authority that his policies threatened: (1) those cardinals who abandoned Gregory in 1084; (2) the higher clergy of Europe; and (3) the kings, represented most vociferously by partisans of Henry IV. The critics persistently argued that popes were fallible and that the unity of Christ's Body derived not from any personal sanctification of the pope through St. Peter's merits but from other patterns of vocation. The advocates of all three spheres were concerned with demonstrating that Gregory's accession to the papacy had been illicit, that his coercive and punitive actions against them had violated and divided the Body of Christ, and, consequently, that they were warranted in deposing him—or considering that he had deposed himself—and therefore in proceeding to the election of a new pope. They also resorted to juridical processes, military action, and incitement by rebellion as means to bring about Gregory's downfall.

It was evident to dissident Gregorians and to anti-Gregorians alike that, as Abbot Gregory of Vendôme (fl. 1112) wrote, a pope could by wrongful acts deprive himself of participation in the blessedness of Sts. Peter and Paul.

God had instituted other modes of participation in blessedness by diverse callings: for example, vocation to the cardinalate, to the episcopate, and to kingship. A pope who acceded by corrupt or bloody means or one who was heretical did not belong to the community of faith over which he purported to rule. In fact, he fought against it as Antichrist, confounding the divine order. Orthodox popes could be forced into issuing wrongful commands, as many thought was the case when Pope Paschal II, yielding to force, approved lay investiture in 1112. It was necessary for the church, as a community, to have institutional redress against such leaders, redress preserving the spiritual unity that God established in diversity of callings. Again and again dissidents from the Gregorian program and actions resorted to a constitutional device that the Gregorians themselves employed: the council. All sides agreed that the Holy Spirit could speak through the assent of the faithful in synodal judgment. There were many points of controversy over the relative powers of popes and councils, but conciliarism, like the imperialized papacy, was one addition that the Gregorian Reform made to Western spirituality.

Critics of the Gregorians correctly perceived that the Gregorian Reform also contributed to the growth of anticlericalism. Condemnations of both the Gregorians and their enemies divided many churches. The resulting confusion of administrative discipline and sacramental order was compounded by strategies of terror, desolation, and slaughter—notably in appeals to the laity to rise up against condemned clergy. Understandably, these aspects of the Gregorian Reform encouraged radical reformers—like Arnold of Brescia (d. 1155), who led a rebellion of the laity against corrupt clergy in Rome and against the Pope "because he was a man of blood who maintained his authority by fire and sword."[5] They also encouraged yet more radical reformers, who attempted to form a Church without property, power, or priesthood.

## Participation through Sacraments

Sacraments were both outward and physical signs and inward and spiritual causes of participation in the Body of Christ. The sanctifying grace that they conveyed stamped faithful souls with the character of Christ and "transformed" them into his divinity, so that he was in them and they in him. Plainly, the Gregorian Reform, seeking papal dominance over the priesthood, also required control over the administration of sacraments and consequently over the actions by which the visible church defined itself as the Body of Christ, admitting some to participation in his eternal life and excluding others from it.

Centralization of church order required sacramental uniformity. The Gregorians supplanted local rites with the Roman rite (most dramatically in Spain), and they consistently worked to uproot local deviations from the Roman norm. Sacramental theology was relatively undeveloped, but the Gregorians asserted the universality of Roman norms. For thirty years (1050–1080), Berengar, director of the cathedral school at Tours, raised objections to the doctrine of transubstantiation. His doctrines provoked relentless opposition from French prelates, but, early in the series of inquiries to which he was subjected, he convinced Hildebrand (later Pope Gregory VII) of his orthodoxy. Although Gregory eventually forbade him to dispute on the subject of transubstantiation or to teach (except to convert those who had been misled by his doctrines), the pope yet protected Berengar as a "son of the Roman church" and commanded his episcopal accusers and others to refrain from calling him a heretic and from punishing him for his doctrines. Gregory's imposition of theological uniformity in the case of Berengar enabled enemies to denounce the pope as "a disciple of the heretic Berengar" (Synod of Brixen, 1080). It also enabled Berengar to teach his dialectical methods over a long period of time and thus to play an important role in the formation of scholasticism.

The Gregorian Reform provoked wider controversy over sacramental participation in the Body of Christ on other counts, namely, by nullifying sacraments performed by simoniacs and Nicolaite clergy, by forbidding lay investiture, and by absolving subjects of their oaths of allegiance to Henry IV. Each of these actions addressed a perceived threat to spiritual freedom. The Gregorians annulled the sacraments of simoniacs and Nicolaites because they regarded such men as in bondage to fleshly concerns. The sacraments that they performed— particularly ordinations to the priesthood or episcopate—were impaired by the moral defects of the celebrants. Cardinal Humbert of Silva Candida (ca. 1000–1061), an extremist among the early Gregorians, contended that ordinations performed by simoniacs and Nicolaites were empty rituals, entirely void of sanctifying grace. More moderate Gregorian reformers held that the validity of sacraments received from the hands of simoniacs and Nicolaites depended upon the worthiness of the recipients. A man ordained by a simoniac or a Nicolaite might retain his orders if he could demonstrate his own innocence, though he had to be deposed if he were proved culpable.

The Gregorians' sacerdotalism demanded the prohibition of lay investiture, a ritual in which a layperson, using the symbols of spiritual office—for example, a bishop's ring and staff—invested a cleric with the temporal faculties of that office. The words of investiture appeared to confer spiritual

14. *Triumph of the Papal View of the Church*, Santa Maria in Trastevere, Rome, 12th century

faculties, and investiture with temporalities preceded the sacrament of ordination. Thus, the Gregorians logically argued that the laity preempted, counterfeited, and usurped the ritual by which priests, acting as representatives of the church, consecrated a man and delegated him to perform the spiritual functions of his office. Two acts only, they held, were essential to become bishop: (1) election by the clergy of the widowed church, seconded by the request of its laity; and (2) consecration by bishops. If action by laypersons superseded either act or rendered either nugatory, even if the bishop-elect were duly consecrated he was a pseudo-bishop.

Finally, the Gregorians held, the papal absolution of oaths of allegiance was warranted. Although not a sacrament—that is, an act instituted by Christ as a means of grace—an oath was sacramental because it was ratified by the church and because through ratification it had supernatural results for the salvation of souls. As a sacramental act, it gained validity through the action of the church; orthodox faith was a condition of fidelity to oaths. The question was whether one could keep political faith with religious unbelievers. Gregory VII forbade King Alfonso of Castile and Leon to continue permitting Jews to rule over Christians. Alfonso was accused of exalting the synagogue of Satan and pleasing the enemies of Christ, thus throwing contempt on Christ himself and showing to his Creator a disregard that he would not tolerate in his own subjects. True fidelity could not be vowed except in the Lord, nor could it be kept if adherence to the letter of an oath led one to depart from the Lord. Faithfulness to God, according to the laws of the church, was the essence of the fidelity promised in the oath.[6]

The Gregorians therefore argued that a ruler's disobedience to God, represented by the pope as vicar of St. Peter, automatically dissolved his subjects of their obligations toward him. Even in political questions no one was bound to obey a man if, by so doing, he would disobey his Creator. The choice for Henry IV's subjects was whether to commit perjury by breaking their oaths to him or to commit apostasy and perfidy by keeping them. Gregory VII resolved their perplexity by declaring that, through disobedience to God, Henry had already forfeited their loyalty, and Gregory formally absolved them of their oaths.

Opponents responded that the Gregorians had misrepresented the nature of sacraments. To question the validity of sacraments performed by simoniac and Nicolaite clergy was to ignore the fact that, as Augustine had argued, sanctification was conveyed by God, not by the ministrant of the sacrament. Those who held that the validity of a sacrament depended upon the moral or legal capacity of the ministrant revived the ancient heresy of Donatism.

According to its proponents, lay investiture was a practice of long standing that secured the political order established by God. It made no pretense of conferring spiritual faculties or of superseding the sacrament of ordination. Indeed, the canonist Ivo of Chartres (ca. 1040–1116) concluded that lay investiture involved no violation of the faith. Princes, he said, granted nothing spiritual in the ritual; they only assented to elections that had already taken place and granted temporal faculties to the men who had been elected. Conferring the ring and staff was not essential to the grant. Ivo claimed that the Gregorian prohibition of lay investiture had adminstrative force because it issued from the pope; but it was by no means an expression of eternal law.

Critics held that the Gregorians minimized the sacral character of kingship in their attack on lay investiture, a character that was ratified by the rite of coronation. In this world, anti-Gregorians argued, the church was governed by two authorities, the royal and the priestly. They were united in the church, the Body of Christ, because Christ had united and sanctified them in his person. By their coronation anointing, kings were set aside from the laity, and, as the anointed of the Lord, they had the power to rule over priests as had Moses and David. Bishops and popes did not confer the royal power when they administered the unction. They only blessed those whom God, through inheritance or election, had called to the kingship. No one could withdraw an office that he could not confer. Therefore, bishops had no power to judge kings or to raise their hands against the Lord's anointed, as Gregory had done by forbidding lay investiture and by releasing subjects from their oaths of fealty.

Gregory's critics also argued that he had erred in holding that the validity of oaths depended upon the action of the church. An oath created obligations between the giver and the recipient but also between the giver and God, by whom the oath was sworn. The case for excommunicating a king might be debatable, but there was no question that anyone who violated a duly executed oath was guilty both of perjury toward the recipient and of contempt toward God. Oaths formalized the overriding duty imposed upon Christians by Scripture to pray for their kings, even if they were not Christians, and to submit to them, even if, like Nero, they were wicked persecutors of the church.

The agitated debates over sacraments and sacramental actions did not reach a resolution in the period of the Gregorian Reform, but they did enrich the spirituality of the church by raising normative questions. They produced intense reflection on the role of sacraments in building up the Body of Christ. In theology, analytical definitions on the nature of sacraments and their effects began to be framed. Legal and moral capacities of ministrants and recipients were elucidated, and a juridical apparatus was articulated in the church to delegate and oversee the exercise of spiritual faculties. And yet as the debates advanced, with their practical effects of legal and military conflict, some Christians gradually discounted participation in the Body of Christ through the material signs of the sacraments. Especially in ascetic religious orders, sanctification was sought through affective union more than through sacramental union.

A similar but more radical tendency appeared among nonconformist sects. Those who denied the historical existence of Christ, denounced the visible church as a brothel, and rejected the use of material objects (including altars and church buildings) in worship also rejected the materialism of sacraments. For them, baptism, the Eucharist, marriage, and ordination were impious works of the flesh, and, as we shall see, it was remarkable how many nonconformists who ended in a spiritual inwardness without priests or sacraments began their spiritual careers as advocates of institutions favored by the Gregorian reformers.

## Affective Participation

In all their reforms, the Gregorians distinguished between the faithful, the minority, and the unbelievers, a hostile majority composed of pagans, Jews, heretics, and false Christians. Repeated in each believer, the individual and incommunicable act of faith, responding to grace, constituted the Body of Christ. By faith, all participated as spiritual members of that Body. The task of the visible church was to express, nurture, and enlarge the spiritual unity that already made the multitude of believers one in heart and soul in God. The individual believer's affective union of heart with God was prior to institutional and even to sacramental association.

The Gregorians derived these ideas from their monastic ethos and their extension of monastic discipline—for example, celibacy—to the clergy as a whole; their patronage of monasticism greatly encouraged devotional practices and ways of life that were thought to serve affective union. Because of close and continual interchanges between monasticism and the laity, this emphasis also transformed lay piety.

During the era of the Gregorian Reform, there were three chief forms of monastic life: the cenobitic (communities practicing collective discipline, represented by Benedictine monasteries), the eremitic (communities practicing the discipline of solitude), and the collegiate (communities living the common life in a semicenobitic fashion, represented by canons regular). The Gregorians drew strength from these forms of life and also contributed to their growth and transformations in the eleventh and twelfth centuries.

There were many personal and institutional points of exchange between Gregorian popes and monastic reformers. Pope Urban II (1088-1099) gave papal encouragement and protection to the foundation of the Carthusian order by his former teacher, Bruno of Rheims. The growth of the Cistercian order, destined to be the largest in Europe, was nourished by Popes Urban II and Paschal II (1099–1118), and their constitution was finally confirmed by Pope Calixtus II (1119–1124). Motivated by the ideals of the Gregorian Reform, Robert of Arbrissel (ca. 1047–1117) left the household of the bishop of Rennes to become an eremite, an evangelist for his mode of life, and the founder of eremitic communities. Beginning at a Lateran synod in 1059 where Hildebrand defended the establishment of a new, strict revision of collegiate life, the Gregorian popes fostered the spread of houses of canons regular. The Gregorian Reform itself is known to have won some recruits to this mode of life. Norbert of Xanten (ca. 1080–1134), a member of the chapel of Emperor Henry V, withdrew to the solitary life after the degradation of Pope Paschal II (1112), as Bruno of Rheims had earlier done, and, with papal sanctions, founded the Order of Prémontré, which eventually numbered about one thousand houses.

The Gregorian call to purity through discipline gained resonance by its interplay with modes of holy living taught by monasticism. Monastic discipline provided a practical way to achieve eternal life, love, and joy. Countless separate disciplines were combined in physical and mental austerities, denial of self-will under rules of obedience, daily and yearly cycles of liturgies, special devotions (e.g., to the Blessed Virgin), prayer and meditation on Scripture. As Bruno of Querfurt (970–1009) wrote, these disciplines aimed at salvation through the destruction of the self; Cardinal Peter Damian described how he combined the mortification of will and body in an exercise of self-flagellation performed while he recited penitential psalms and prayers. Such practices were designed to intensify devotion and fervor, particularly the sense of sharing in the poverty and suffering of Christ.

Practitioners of the monastic discipline witness to the feelings of guilt and pollution, the fears of vengeance and death, and the needs of dependency, vindication, and everlasting glory that motivated them. These motives were not limited to inhabitants of monastic enclosures. The vast spread of monastic houses witnesses to the spiritual needs of society as a whole, from which came the converts to monastic life and donations that established and sustained their houses. Like two other expressions of popular piety in the Gregorian epoch, the crusades and the pilgrimages, the spread of monastic orders provided ways for believers to satisfy their inmost needs, to endure suffering as proof of their faithfulness, and, if necessary, to unite the sacrifice of their own lives with the sacrificial and saving death of Christ and the passions of the martyrs.

There were many points of exchange between monastic and popular piety. For example, inspired by the description of the primitive church in the fourth chapter of Acts, a wide variety of movements sprang up that espoused "apostolic poverty": abandoning private property and having all things in common, followers of these movements sought to be of one heart and soul in God. Itinerant preachers spread the gospel of apostolic poverty to every level of society. Another illustration is that the Gregorians themselves acted as spiritual directors to lay men and women, counseling them on moral questions, preparing written texts to guide them in the discipline of prayer, and instructing them in ways to intensify their devotion.

Like their doctrines on vocation and sacraments, the Gregorians' teachings on affective union had some results that they did not seek. Not all itinerant evangelists, like Norbert of Xanten, who preached the extreme asceticism of apostolic poverty, could compromise with the visible hierarchy that at times seemed far from the literal prescripts of the Gospel. Radical noncon-formists, such as Henry of Le Mans (fl. 1116–1145), Arnold of Brescia, and probably Tanchelm of Antwerp (fl. 1112), began in the Gregorian fold and ended denouncing the hierarchic church for betraying the Gospel through worldly pomp and avarice. The preaching of the Gospel of poverty by Gregorian evangelists prepared the way for the spread of Catharism in the twelfth century. Nonconformists, like the Gregorians, drew strength from the laity, and their doctrines spread through the movement of tradespeople from place to place.

The great issue was how to harmonize the literal text of Scripture with the demands of conformity within the institutional church. Educated lay-persons were able to read the Scriptures in Latin, and this was probably true of the circle of nonconformists found in Liège and Arras about 1025, who practiced daily reading of the Scriptures and the "holy canons." Evidently itinerant evangelists did not appeal to peasants and artisans in Latin when they preached the Gospels. By the end of the twelfth century, German translations of the Scriptures were current, and Peter Valdes (fl. 1179), the founder of the Waldensian sect, had commissioned the translation of the Scriptures and of some patristic texts into the vernacular of Lyons. The institutional dangers of opening access to the Scriptures to the uneducated was apparent to Pope Gregory VII. Attempting to avert a chaos in which every person would be his or her own theologian, Gregory forbade the translation of liturgies (including Scriptural passages) into the vernacular. The proposal to do so, he said, was "vane effrontery:"

It is obvious to those who consider the matter thoroughly that God was rightly pleased for Holy Scripture to be veiled in some places, lest, if it were freely accessible to all, it would grow cheap and subject to contempt, and lest, perversely understood by the unskilled, it might lead them into error. Nor does it mitigate the case that some religious men patiently bore with this request, which the people made in their simplicity, or dismissed it without rebuke, for the early Church passed over in silence many things that the holy Fathers later corrected with keen scrutiny after Christianity had been established and religion was spreading.[7]

The Gregorians gave great importance to participating in the Body of Christ by affective union; they fostered doctrines and institutions to serve that union. Still, they wished affective devotion to stay within limits set by their principles of sacerdotalism and papal monarchy. The torrent of popular devotion that strengthened their program flowed over and around those restraints and, for many, undermined them.

It was ironic that in the election of Pope Gregory VI (1045) the Gregorians resorted to simony and lay intervention to gain control of the papacy. It was just as ironic that the political actions through which they sought to cleanse and unify the church produced disunity and evoked stubborn denials of their guiding principles, sacerdotalism and papal monarchy. Certainly the great centralization of church government, crowned in the pontificate of Innocent III (1198–1216) fulfilled their principles; yet the effects of their work did not move only in one line. In other respects their efforts to achieve unity were self-defeating. Attempts to impose papal supremacy over the Byzantine church provoked the schism of 1054, which has never completely healed. Dissent among the Gregorians themselves exacerbated factionalism in Rome and contributed to the destruction of the city in 1083, an event that earned Gregory VII and his partisans the hatred of the Roman people— a hostility that Gregory himself had long reciprocated.

The Gregorians declared that sacraments performed by unworthy priests should be avoided by all the faithful, and they stirred up popular resistance to unreformed or excommunicate clergy. But this tactic encouraged anticlericalism and gave unintended encouragement to a wide spectrum of movements, some of which entirely rejected the priesthood and the visible church. It put into the hands of the laity a weapon that could be used against the Gregorians themselves. One unintended result of the Gregorian reform was the proliferation of heresies in the twelfth century. The Gregorians employed synods as instruments of reform, but this tactic also encouraged counterdoctrines. The election of antipopes by synods of bishops who opposed the Gregorians, questions concerning the legitimacy of papal accessions and commands, and divided obedience in local churches allowed some to contest the inerrancy of the Roman church and eventually to see a supreme authority in a general council. Finally, the Gregorian Reform contributed to the splintering of Western Christendom into "national churches." The attack on lay investiture ended with compromise on the symbolic act of investiture, but secular rulers still controlled accession to church office. Indeed, the Gregorian attack gave a strong impulse from outside to the inner consolidation of territorial states that was under way in the eleventh and twelfth centuries, and it thereby contributed to the formation of the "national churches" that were recognized in the fifteenth century.

It must also be added that the Gregorian Reform had very partial success in its disciplinary measures. Toward the end of his life, Gregory VII lamented how few feared God and how few there were to perform priestly offices for good Christians. Even though the reform continued after his death, it failed to eradicate the practices of simony and Nicolaitism. Together with other abuses against which the Gregorians labored—such as the gross immorality and ignorance of clergy and their exploitation of the poor to support their own luxury—these persisted in an unbroken line to the sixteenth-century Reformation.

Thus, the Gregorian reformers succeeded in achieving control of the papacy and in developing its powers of administrative and juridical centralization, but their goal of spiritual unity in the church eluded them. That this was so was due partly to the circumstances of political life; however, it was due also to the fact that the Gregorian concept of church unity differed in many respects from concepts of church unity that guided other reformers. The latter did not define unity chiefly in the external terms of hierarchic obedience to which the Gregorians were committed. As they interpreted Scripture, holiness was imparted through immediate communion with God rather than mediated through canonical (or sacramental) act; catholicity, through inward conformity with the mind of Christ rather than through outward obedience to hierarchic superiors; and apostolicity, not through apostolic succession, the official succession of bishops to apostles as rulers of churches, but through the apostolic life, which was understood to be devout acceptance of the apostle's ascetic and self-denying way of life as described in the book of Acts. In themselves, such views were not incompatible with the Gregorian principles of sacerdotalism and papal monarchy. Even so, these models, derived from alternative understandings of Scripture, acted, at the least, as tests and correctives for the validity of papal actions. Pressed to extremes, they could be used to deny the legitimacy of the priesthood, hierarchy, and sacraments of the visible church. By making its ideal of government a test of orthodoxy, the Gregorian Reform stimulated this clash of doctrine and, through politics and war, embedded counterdoctrines like burning coals in the consciousness of Europe.

## Notes

1. *Dictatus Papae* (Gregory VII, *Registrum* II. 55a) 23. See also Gregory VII *Reg.* VIII. 21, where the Pope (quoting a Pseudo-Isidorian decretal) asserted that Peter either raised saints to his throne or, by his merit, glorified the successors who entered into his legacy. See *Das Register Gregors VII*, ed. Eric Caspar (Berlin: Wiedmann, 1920-1923; *MGH Epistulae selectae* 2) 207, 561. The *Dictatus Papae* is translated in Karl F. Morrison, *The Investiture Controversy: Issues, Ideas, and Results* (New York: Holt, Rinehart & Winston, 1971) 38-39. *Reg.* VIII. 21 is found in *The Correspondence of Pope Gregory VII: Selected Letters from the Registrum*, trans. Ephraim Emerton (New York: Columbia University Press, 1932) 174.

2. *Reg.* IV. 2 (Caspar ed., p. 296; Emerton trans., p. 104).

3. *Reg.* IV. 2; VIII. 21 (Caspar ed., pp. 295, 554; Emerton trans. pp. 104, 170).

4. Gregory took these actions in the Lenten Synod of 1076 (*Reg.* III. 10a [Caspar ed., p. 271; Emerton trans., p. 91]).

5. Malcolm D. Lambert, *Medieval Heresy*, 58, quoting John of Salisbury.

6. *Reg.* IX. 2 (Caspar ed., pp. 571-72; Emerton trans., pp. 177-78).

7. *Reg.* VII. 11 (Caspar ed., p. 474; my translation).

## Bibliography

The already voluminous bibliography on the Gregorian Reform continues to grow by leaps and bounds. For the latest studies, readers may refer to annual bibliographies, especially those published by the *Revue d'histoire ecclésiastique* and the *Archivum Historiae Pontificiae*.

Becker, Alfons. *Papst Urban II (1088-1099)*, I: *Herkunft und kirchliche Laufbahn: Der Papst und die lateinische Christenheit*. Stuttgart: Hiersemann, 1964.

Blumenthal, Uta-Renate. *Der Investiturstreit*. Stuttgart: Urban, 1982.

Cantor, Norman F. *Church, Kingship, and Lay Investiture in England: 1089-1135*. Princeton, NJ: Princeton University Press, 1958.

Carlyle, A. J., and R. W. Carlyle. *A History of Mediaeval Political Theory in the West*, vols. 3, 4. New York: Barnes & Noble, n.d.

Cowdrey, H. E. J. *The Cluniacs and the Gregorian Reform*. Oxford: Clarendon Press, 1970.

Fliche, Augustin. *La Réforme grégorienne*. 3 vols. Louvain: Spicilegium sacrum Lovaniense, 1924, 1925, 1937.

Lambert, Malcolm D. *Medieval Heresy: Popular Movements from Bogomil to Hus*. London: Edward Arnold, 1977.

Leclercq, Jean. *The Spirituality of the Middle Ages*. Vol. 2 of *A History of Christian Spirituality*. New York: Seabury, 1982.

Minninger, Monika. *Von Clermont zum Wormser Konkordat*. Cologne: Böhlau, 1978.

Morrison, Karl. *Tradition and Authority in the Western Church: 300-1100*. Princeton, NJ: Princeton University Press, 1969.

Schieffer, Rudolf. "Gregor VII.—Ein Versuch über die historische Grösse," *Historisches Jahrbuch* 97/98 (1978) 87-107.

Weinfurter, Stefan. "Reformkanoniker und Reichsepiskopat im Hochmittelalter," *Historisches Jahrbuch* 97/98 (1978) 158-93.

# 9

# The Religious World
# of the Twelfth Century

## I. *Introduction*

THE TWELFTH CENTURY in the Latin West was both a summation of the patristic past and a new departure that introduced themes, values, and practices that were to be influential in Latin Christianity for centuries. Janus-like, this era sits astride the course of Christian spirituality with an ambiguous glance in two directions. The fashion among historians has been to emphasize the innovative character of the age; and the evidence of demographic expansion, experiments in government, legal developments, changing art styles, the rise of the university and scholastic theology, and new literary genres and styles cannot be denied. But the twelfth century must not be viewed as a revolutionary break. Its intimate and varied connections with the past are evident at every turn and have prompted historians to make use of metaphors like renaissance, reform, renewal, and revival to try to capture the creative relation of this age to its heritage.

For all the new sense of nature and humanity found in the twelfth century and notwithstanding the note of "secularity" that hesitatingly broke through at times, the era remained a profoundly religious one in which the major motivating forces were inextricably bound up with spirituality. Some admirable books, most notably M.-D. Chenu's *La théologie au douzième siècle* (Paris: Vrin, 1957; see the partial English translation by Jerome Taylor and Lester K. Little, *Nature, Man and Society in the Twelfth Century* [Chicago: University of Chicago Press, 1968]) and R. W. Southern's *The Making of the Middle Ages* (New Haven, CT: Yale University Press, 1953), have done much to reveal the spiritual riches of the age; but given the complexity of the religious life of the period and the limited space available here, it would be difficult, if not impossible, to think of presenting a synthetic view of its total significance. The editors chose to ask three experts to describe the three basic religious movements that shaped twelfth-century spirituality and through it later Western Christianity—Anselm of Canterbury and the circle associated with him, the Cistercian monastic reform and its great spiritual writers, and the canonical movement, especially as it gave rise to the spiritual theology of the Victorines. These are not, to be sure, the only important things in twelfth-century spirituality.

In recent scholarship much attention has been paid to the twelfth century as a turning point in the history of many of the practices that shaped the daily lives of believers. For instance, the evolution of the crusading ideal and the formation of the military orders—ambiguous achievements though they were—can be described as a major form of lay piety that had considerable influence for many centuries. See the classic study, now available in English, of Carl Erdmann, *The Origin of the Idea of Crusade* (Princeton, NJ: Princeton University Press, 1977). Peter Dinzelbacher in an important recent book, *Vision und Visionsliteratur im Mittelalter* (Stuttgart: Hiersemann, 1981), has shown how the visionary literature that played such a large part in medieval piety underwent a substantial shift that began in the twelfth century. A turning point is evident also in medieval apocalypticism, especially in the thought of Joachim of Fiore (ca. 1135–1202), on which see Bernard McGinn, *Visions of the End: Apocalyptic Traditions in the Middle Ages* (New York: Columbia University Press, 1979). Benedicta Ward in her *Miracles and the Medieval Mind* (Philadelphia: University of Pennsylvania Press, 1982) has discussed the more universal and personal flavor that miracle accounts and collections began to take on in the twelfth century, and Jacques Le Goff in his *The Birth of Purgatory* (Chicago: University of Chicago Press, 1984) has tried to show that the birth of the idea of purgatory in the late twelfth century marked a decisive change in the history of Western Christianity. These few recent works are mentioned here as illustrations of the continued interest that historians have taken in the rich and changing world of twelfth-century spiritual beliefs and practices.

Further reflection on the contributions of the twelfth century can be found in other articles in this volume, notably "The Human Person as Image of God, II. Western Christianity," by Bernard McGinn; "The Trinity, II. The Trinity in Latin Christianity," by Mary T. Clark; and "Ways of Prayer and Contemplation, II. Western," by Jean Leclercq. The editors hope that what is presented here will be sufficient to introduce the student to the riches of one of the decisive ages in the history of Christian spiritual traditions.

# II. *Anselm of Canterbury and His Influence*

### BENEDICTA WARD

## "Faith Seeking Understanding"

ANSELM OF CANTERBURY was born around 1033 in Aosta, which was then in the kingdom of Burgundy. He left home after the death of his mother and three years later became a monk in the new abbey of Notre Dame at Bec in Normandy. Anselm became prior of Bec in 1063, when Lanfranc left Bec to become abbot in Caen; he became abbot on the death of Herluin in 1078 and was made archbishop of Canterbury in 1093. He remained archbishop during the reigns of William Rufus and Henry I and died at Canterbury on Wednesday, 21 April 1109. His friend and companion Eadmer wrote an account of his public life in his *History of Recent Events in England* and a more personal biography in his *Life of St. Anselm* (*Vita sancti Anselmi*). The span of Anselm's life covered one of the periods of fundamental change in the history of Europe, and, as one of the most vigorous thinkers of his day, Anselm stimulated many of the great changes that came about during and after his lifetime. This was particularly true in the realm of piety and devotion, where he was an innovator on a scene that had changed very little for centuries. His prayers and meditations were formed by the old world of patristic theology and monastic life according to the *Rule of St. Benedict,* and they offered the form of piety that shaped the whole of the later Middle Ages.

The underlying structure of the *Prayers and Meditations* of Anselm is a precise and solid apprehension of biblical and patristic tradition in theology. It is not too much to say that the approach to prayer that he himself experienced and communicated to others formed a bridge between the patristic and medieval ways of devotion in the West. Anselm was a philosopher and theologian of genuinely original thought, and his clear and incisive mind was able to explore and express the truths of the Christian faith with unrivaled clarity and precision. As a monk, he might be better called an ascetic theologian than a mystic,[1] but the key phrase for understanding Anselm as a spiritual writer is found in the second section of the *Proslogion:* "I believe so that I may understand, and what is more I believe that unless I do believe, I shall not understand" (chap. 2).[2]

The *Prayers and Meditations* of Anselm, his only writings concerned with prayer, form only a fraction of his work, but for his contemporaries they were of major importance. Eadmer mentions them as if they were well-known and available: "As for his prayers, which at the desire and request of his friends he wrote and published, anyone can see without my speaking about them, with what hope and love he addressed himself to God and his saints, and taught others to do the same" (*Life*, p. 14).[3] Anselm, therefore, was asked by his friends to teach them how to pray. He wrote down long meditations and worked over them with infinite care and finally sent them to those who had asked for them.[4] With these prayers, he gave some instructions about how they should be used, and it is in these directions that certain indications are to be found about his understanding of the approach to prayer. To his friend Bishop Gundolf of Rochester, to Princess Adelaide, and to Countess Mathilda of Tuscany, he propounded the same approach to prayer,[5] and this is expressed more fully in the preface usually attributed to him, which was copied as a part of the *Prayers and Meditations:*

> The purpose of the prayers and meditations that follow is to stir up the mind of the reader to the love or fear of God or to self-examination. They are not to be read through in a turmoil, but quietly, not skimmed or hurried through, but taken a little at a time, with deep and thoughtful meditation. The reader should not trouble about reading the whole of any of them, but only as much as, by God's help, he finds useful in stirring up his spirit to pray. (*Prayers*, p. 89)

In the context of a whole life geared toward God, Anselm recommended certain times of more precise concentration upon the "truths upon which religion rests" as a matter of personal understanding. The whole effort of the intellect is then to be brought to bear upon the text provided, in such a way that the emotions of fear and of love are released and brought into play to activate the will in relationship to God. The long tradition of compunction, of the piercing of the heart by sorrow for sin and desire for God, is here given a new vitality and a stimulus of mental excitement through reading with the purpose of praying that was rarely found in earlier Western medieval writings.

The method proposed by Anselm amounted to a revolution in devotional practice in the eleventh century, and the content of the prayers themselves bears out the pattern he proposed in the letters. What is necessary to prepare the soul to come before God? First of all, withdrawal, going apart, in a literal but also a mental sense.

> Come now, little man, turn aside for a while from your daily employment, escape for a moment from the tumult of your thoughts. . . . Enter into the inner chamber of your soul, shut out everything except God and that which

can help you in seeking him, and when you have the shut door, seek him. (*Proslogion,* chap. 1; *Prayers,* p. 239)

The second stage is to ask for the help of God in this work: "Teach me to seek you." Anselm is always aware that such a work is possible only by the power of God, that it cannot be simply a human effort and attainment. Each of the prayers follows the same process: there is the hard work of repentance, begun by sorrow for sin. Anselm mobilized everything at his disposal for this vital matter of self-knowledge, this true discernment of the reality of the situation of everyman as creature before the Creator, as sinner before the Savior.

> Alas, what have I made of myself? What was I, O God, as you had made me—and how have I made myself again. In sin I was conceived and born, but you washed me and sanctified me; and I have defiled myself still more. (*Prayers,* p. 128)

This is a precise theological reflection upon sin, which Anselm strove to bring home to himself as a matter of personal experience, rather than any sudden discovery of real or imaginary faults of behavior. There are no illusions here, either of unreal goodness or of wickedness that is merely emotional disturbance, but a perception of the reality of the human condition of damaged, broken, blinded humanity, incapable in itself of remedying its condition. The purpose of the prayer is to make this a reality to the person praying.

From this apprehension of reality Anselm proceeded in each of his prayers to the awesome and incredible fact that God, who knows human beings as they really are, is everlastingly faithful: "I fled from God and God came with me" (*Prayers,* p. 129). "But it is he himself, he himself is Jesus. The same is my Judge between whose hands I tremble" (*Prayers,* p. 224). The "second compunction" in which the heart is pierced by the love of God leads Anselm to consider the cross and passion of Christ in order to bring home to himself the cost of the faithfulness of God in his love for humanity. This assimilation of humanity to the cross of Christ is given a dramatic dimension, in order to involve the one who prays with the reconciliation of God in Christ at every level of understanding. The "Prayer to Christ" is the most realistic instance of this:

> Why, O my soul, were you not there to be pierced by a sword of bitter sorrow when you could not bear to see the nails violate the hands and feet of your Creator? Why did you not see with horror the blood that poured out of the side of your Redeemer? Why were you not drunk with bitter tears when they gave him bitter gall to drink? (*Prayers,* p. 95)

From this meditation upon the passion of Christ, Anselm moves into the final part of his act of prayer, which is, in each prayer, praise and thanksgiving. "O that I might see the joy that I desire"; "hope and rejoice, rejoice and love, O my soul." The second movement of compunction is the discovery of the glory of God and the reaction of the soul to this experience is praise. It is in this part of the *Prayers* that the specific question about Anselm and the experience of prayer can be most clearly posed. Anselm is moving in each prayer toward the vision of the glory of God: in what sense is this a "mystical" experience? In a letter to Princess Adelaide, Anselm described the effect that he wished the *Prayers and Meditations* to have on the person using them: "I hope and pray that Almighty God will so preserve and nourish that same devotion in you that on earth you may be filled with his dearest love and in heaven be fulfilled with the sight of his face" (*Prayers*, p. 172). There are two distinct stages: the reception of love while on earth and the full vision of love hereafter. This is a distinction borne out by the prayers themselves. In the longest and most subtle of Anselm's prayers, the *Proslogion*, the penultimate chapter describes in images the fullness of glory which will be enjoyed in heaven.[6] It is a picture of varied and transcendent glory, but it is "not such a good as we experience in created things, but as different as Creator is from creature" (*Proslogion*, chap. 24; *Prayers*, p. 262). The final section deals with the longing of the heart for God, which is presented as only reaching fulfillment in the vision of God after death:

> My God, I pray that I may so know you and love you that I may rejoice in you, and if I may not do so fully in this life, let me go steadily on to the day when I come to that fullness. Let your love grow in me here and there let it be fulfilled so that here my joy may be in a great hope and there in full reality. (*Proslogion*, chap. 26; *Prayers*, p. 266)

In his writings, Anselm stands primarily within the tradition of ascetic theology, but his experience of prayer, joined to the clarity of his expression of what he had understood, set in motion much of the mystical analysis of the soul that was to come. In the *Life of St. Anselm* by Eadmer there are also hints of a more mysterious area in Anselm's life. Eadmer knew Anselm and was constantly with him, listening to him and also hearing his reminiscences of his earlier life. The great phrase of Irenaeus, "The glory of God is a living man and the life of man is the vision of God" (*Against Heresies* 4.20.7), was in both parts true of Anselm, in his writings and also in his life. Because of Anselm's prayer and union with Christ in his passion, those who knew him could also see in his life the marks of the resurrection of Christ and the action through him of the powers of heaven. Eadmer shows us a living, human person, a rare thing in medieval biography, but he also shows

Anselm as one through whom God acts. The dreams, visions, interior and intuitive experiences that Eadmer recorded are presented as evidences of Anselm's deep union with God in Christ, and the miracles he performed are also signs of his restoration in the New Adam, in touch with the powers of heaven. As a boy Anselm dreamed that he went to heaven, for he "imagined that heaven rested on the mountains, that the court of God was there" (*Life* 1.2, p. 4), and that he received from God "the whitest of bread." As a monk at Bec he saw through the wall of the dormitory "the monks . . . going about the altar" (*Life* 1.8, p. 13); the monk Riculfus saw Anselm "standing in prayer in the midst of a great ball of blazing light" (*Life* 1.16, p. 25). Many regarded him as having power over disease and asked him to cure them, because of his contact with the kingdom of heaven. Eadmer says that he also had the gift of tears in prayer: "In his contemplation of the final blessedness and in his desire for the life everlasting, he shed profuse tears" (*Life* 1.8, p. 15). And yet Eadmer makes it clear that Anselm himself neither discussed nor analyzed these experiences, though he drew from them the communication of charity and instruction for others: "As for his prayers, which at the desire and request of his friends he wrote and published, anyone can see without my speaking about them with what hope and love he addressed himself to God and his saints and taught others to do the same" (*Life* 1.8, p. 14). Anselm's concern was for progress in others and not for dwelling on experiences of God. Even in the first childish dream of heaven, Eadmer says that the result was that he was "loved by all" (*Life* 1.2, p. 5), not that he remained absorbed in the experience; and the biography shows above all a man who was greatly loved because of the goodness that he communicated to others.

In his account of the composition of the argument for the existence of God, Eadmer presents Anselm as receiving the "proof" in an intuitive flash of understanding, which might be considered a mystical experience: "Suddenly one night during matins the grace of God illuminated his heart, the whole matter became clear to his mind, and a great joy and exultation filled his inmost being" (*Life* 1.19, p. 20). Whatever the previous exercise of thought—and Anselm himself describes it as very arduous indeed[7]—and whatever the literary sources behind the "proof,"[8] both Anselm and Eadmer saw the discovery as a flash of illumination, a gift of God, and not the result of human reasoning alone.

Yet neither Anselm nor Eadmer spent time or attention on the "experience" in itself; they were interested only in the results of the illumination. The subtitle Anselm gave to the *Proslogion* expresses his understanding of prayer accurately: "Faith seeking understanding."[9] This directive for the Christian in his relationship with God springs from Anselm's experience throughout his life, which was further illuminated by a flash of insight into the mysteries of God and was then directed not to repeating or analyzing the experience but to the sensible and sensitive care for others that is a mark of authenticity in those who pray: "It seemed to me that this thing which had given me such joy to discover would, if it were written down, give pleasure to any who might read it. So I have written . . . from the point of view of someone trying to raise his mind to the contemplation of God and seeking to understand what he believes" (*Prayers*, p. 238).

Anselm's prayers and meditations, as well as the *Proslogion*, were prepared with great care; they are serious reflections upon the central mysteries of faith and are concerned most of all with salvation. In this they belong to the central tradition of meditation as a way of doing theology, and most notably to the tradition of Augustine of Hippo. In another way also the meditations arose out of the earlier traditions of prayer: the earliest of the prayers were sent as additions to selections from the psalter to Princess Adelaide and were addressed, like so many earlier prayers, to the saints. The prayers of Anselm transform this tradition of praying with and through the saints, making the short collections of the Carolingians into extensive dialogues. The saints who are addressed are, with two exceptions, those saints mentioned in the Bible and given first place in the liturgical worship of the church: St. Mary, the apostles, St. Mary Magdalene, St. Stephen. Other prayers are to St. Benedict, an obvious choice for a monk, and to St. Nicholas, possibly because of the connection of Bec with the cult of Nicholas at Bari. Prayers for any abbot, for friends and enemies, prayers to God, to Christ, to the Cross, before the Eucharist, all contain reflections fundamental to traditional theology. The words and phrases are taken from the Bible, rising up from the text of Scripture, especially from the psalms, so that it is often hard to say where quotation ends and invention on the theme begins. So far, the prayers belong to the tradition of meditation on the Scriptures that Anselm inherited and was formed by. To this he added a new element—his own penetration of the text in terms of emotion, feeling, personal participation.

With those who imitated Anselm, it seems at times that the solidity of the archbishop is lost and that all that remains is the secondhand emotions aroused in others, which sound either sentimental or tedious or both. The additions to Anselm's prayers were very early, and they influenced the tradition of medieval devotion as greatly as the genuine prayers. It is therefore necessary to consider the diffusion of the Anselmian tradition of spirituality along with the direct influence of Anselm himself. Some of these additions were by near contemporaries of Anselm—John of Fécamp, Elmer of Canterbury, Ekbert of Schönau, Aelred of Rievaulx, Ralph of Battle. Of the twenty extensive meditations and seventy-five prayers printed in volume 158 of

*Patrologia Latina,* only three meditations and eighteen prayers are now known to be by Anselm. The work of distinguishing them was undertaken earlier this century by A. Wilmart, and the genuine prayers have now appeared in the critical edition of Anselm's works. They demonstrate the major influence of these imitators of Anselm (a few earlier prayers of a different type have been included) and also the continuing popularity of this genre in the later Middle Ages. For instance, Meditation 1 (*PL* 158, cols. 709-22) is the work of Anselm's friend and biographer, Eadmer; Meditation 15 (cols. 784-92) is by Aelred of Rievaulx; Meditation 18, by John of Fécamp; 20, by Elmer of Canterbury; and the long meditation on the Psalm *Miserere* (cols. 821-54) was unknown before the fourteenth century.

The method of exploring a text of the Scriptures or an incident in the lives of the saints and using this as a basis for personal prayer was not invented by Anselm, but he began the pattern of writing down such meditations, with all the exclamations and sighs of one praying, using the resources of language to enable another person to enter into prayer by using those words. Anselm also added the passion of repentance and the exhilaration of praise to the bare texts, involving the supplicant in an intensity of feeling and a deepening of understanding. In the intensity of sorrow for sin, he is the heir of Augustine of Hippo, and the language of the *Confessions* is very close to Anselm's self-revelation and repentance. The intense personal involvement of Augustine with the philosophical and theological expressions of the Christian faith is no abstraction. Starting from the Scriptures, his language colored by the words of the Bible at every stage, Augustine strains toward God in the monologue of the *Confessions,* aware of sin, pleading for mercy, cleansing, and above all for knowledge and love of God. This turning inward to discover God at the roots of experience of the self in thought and feeling is also the pattern of Anselm's prayers and meditations. They are in the same intensely personal literary form with the same awareness of the unity of thought and belief. Like Augustine, Anselm was concerned with *sapientia,* the knowledge which is love—but with a new emphasis. Where Augustine united knowledge and desire in each moment of prayer and thought, Anselm used the mind and the emotions alternately, aiming at certain effects. Words are used to trigger the emotions, to deepen feeling, and to stir the will toward further conversion in a series of leaps and recoveries. The influence of Augustine on Anselm can be discerned in the prayers as well as in Anselm's theology.

The great successor to Anselm in this kind of prayer was Bernard of Clair-vaux. Augustine presented a spirituality of knowledge which is love; Bernard, a spirituality of love which is knowledge. Bernard was the heir to Anselm's distinction between love and knowledge, and he gave a new and minor place to knowledge in prayer. It is no longer the *sapientia* of Augustine that is diminished, but the *scientia* of the schools. The emotional use of language reached new heights in Bernard. In many specific ways he popularized and expanded the piety presented by Anselm. For instance, the devotion to the name of Jesus so strongly associated with Bernard is expressed by Anselm in his First Meditation. Bernard's concern with friendship found one of its classic expressions in Anselm's *Prayer for Friends,* and the devotion of Bernard to Mary had its precursor in Anselm's three long and magnificent prayers to St. Mary. The idea of using the image of motherhood to express an aspect of the relationship of Christ to the soul, which occurs among the Cistercians, received vigorous expression in Anselm's *Prayer to St. Paul.* It is Anselm who is the catalyst between the spirituality of Augustine and Bernard. Whereas for Augustine true wisdom becomes a wise love and for Bernard the loving heart is given true knowledge, in Anselm the reasoning mind alternates to some extent with the emotions, held in tension, at times fragmenting, in his exploration of love and wisdom, feeling and knowledge.

The prayers and meditations of Anselm were for those to whom he sent them, as well as for himself, a path toward God. His imitators caught only a part of his thought and style. The style of devotion they helped to create is more dated than the genuine prayers. Since the genuine prayers and meditations have now been distinguished from the lesser imitations, it is possible to see them again not only as they appeared to the eleventh century and not only as a part of the Anselmian corpus but also as genuine prayers which, with the same "deep and thoughtful meditation" Anselm recommended, can still enable the reader to "ponder more deeply those things that make him want to pray."[10] There is here a unique combination of theological veracity and personal ardor which give the spirituality of Anselm a lasting value.

### Notes

1. Though Evelyn Underhill includes him among the mystics (*Mysticism: A Study in the Nature and Development of Man's Spiritual Consciousness* [New York: World, 1965] appendix, p. 458).

2. Anselm, *The Prayers and Meditations of Saint Anselm,* trans. Benedicta Ward, p. 244. Page references in subsequent citations of Anselm's prayers and the *Proslogion* are to this volume.

3. Eadmer, *Vita Sancti Anselmi,* 14 (hereafter referred to as *Life*). Page references in subsequent citations of *Life* are to the translation of R. W. Southern.

4. For a discussion of the composition of Anselm's prayers, see A. Wilmart, "Les propres corrections de S. Anselm dans sa grande prière à la Vierge Marie," *Recherches de théologie ancienne et médiévale* 2 (1930) 189-204.

5. To Bishop Gundolf, *Prayers,* p. 106; to Princess Adelaide, pp. 172-73; to Countess Mathilda, p. 90.

6. The *Proslogion* is best known for containing the famous "ontological argument," but it is in fact a meditation and not a philosophical treatise. See *Prayers,* 238-67.

7. *Prayers,* preface to the *Proslogion,* p. 238.

8. E.g., Augustine *On Christian Doctrine* 1.7.

9. *Prayers,* preface to the *Proslogion,* 239.

10. Preface to *Prayers,* 89.

# Bibliography

## Sources

### Editions

*Anselm. Memorials of St. Anselm.* Edited by R. W. Southern and F. S. Schmitt. London: Oxford University Press, 1969. Contains the less formal fragments of Anselm to complement the critical edition.

———. *Sancti Anselmi Cantuariensis Archiepiscopi Opera Omnia I-VI.* Edited by F. S. Schmitt. London and Edinburgh: Nelson, 1938-61. This is the critical edition of the genuine works of Anselm stripped of the additions of later centuries.

### Translations

Charlesworth, M. J. *St. Anselm's "Proslogion."* Oxford: Oxford University Press, 1965. A translation with text and introduction.

Henry, D. P. *Commentary on the "De Grammatico."* Dordrecht: Reidel, 1974. Includes a translation of the *De Grammatico.*

Honnor, Paschal. "Letters of St. Anselm of Canterbury to the Community at Bec." *American Benedictine Review* 14 (1963) 138-63, 319-40. A translation of some of the letters.

Hopkins, Jasper. *Anselm of Canterbury.* 4 vols. New York: Edwin Mellon, 1975-76. A translation of the major works excluding the prayers and the letters.

Pedrizetti, Anselm R. "Letters of Saint Anselm and Archbishop Lanfranc." *American Benedictine Review* 12 (1961) 430-60.

Southern, R. W. *Vita Sancti Anselmi by Eadmer.* Oxford: Clarendon Press, 1962. A contemporary account of the private life of Anselm.

Ward, Benedicta. *The Prayers and Meditations of St. Anselm with the "Proslogion."* New York: Penguin Books, 1984.

## Studies

Barth, Karl. *Anselm, fides quaerens intellectum.* Richmond, VA: John Knox, 1960.

Evans, Gillian R. *Anselm and Talking about God.* Oxford: Oxford University Press, 1978.

———. *Old Arts and New Theology.* Oxford: Oxford University Press, 1979.

———. *Anselm and a New Generation.* Oxford: Oxford University Press, 1980.

Hartshorne, Charles. *Anselm's Discovery.* LaSalle, IL: Open Court, 1965.

Henry, D. P. *The Logic of St. Anselm.* Oxford: Oxford University Press, 1967.

Hopkins, J. *A Companion to the Study of Anselm.* Minneapolis, MN: University of Minnesota Press, 1972. Includes a comprehensive bibliography.

Hick, John, and Arthur McGill, eds. *The Many-Faced Argument.* New York: Macmillan, 1967. Studies of the ontological argument for the existence of God.

McIntyre, J. *St. Anselm and His Critics: A Reinterpretation of the "Cur Deus Homo."* Edinburgh: Oliver & Boyd, 1954.

Pouchet, R. *La rectitudo chez saint Anselme.* Paris: Études augustiniennes, 1964.

*Spicilegium Beccense I* (Paris: Vrin, 1959). A useful collection of articles.

Southern, R. W. *Saint Anselm and His Biographer.* Cambridge: Cambridge University Press, 1963. An excellent introduction to the life and writings.

Wilmart, A. Sixteen articles of major importance for the establishment of the genuine prayers of St. Anselm published between 1923 and 1931 in the *Revue Benedictine, La vie spirituelle, Archives d'histoire et littéraire du moyen âge,* and *Recherches de théologie ancienne et médiévale.*

# III. *The Cistercians*

## BASIL PENNINGTON

## Historical Context

AROUND THE YEAR 500 Benedict of Nursia wrote a *Rule for Monks* which gradually grew in influence until Charlemagne decreed that it would be the rule for monks throughout his vast empire. A particular observance of it was fostered by the monk who influenced him in this, Benedict of Aniane, but such uniform observance became effective only with the rise of the great Cluniac family in the tenth century. Under the wise rule of a succession of holy abbots, Cluny came to hold sway over some two thousand monasteries. In this reform the monasteries not only lost their autonomy but also the balance of liturgy, sacred reading and personal prayer, and work which gave the Benedictine life its strength and characteristic simplicity. At the time of the Gregorian Reform, many new monastic ventures arose. They looked to the Gospels, to the ancient monastic traditions, and in some cases to the *Rule of Benedict.* They sought poverty, solitude, and simplicity of life.

Among the reformers of this period there was a monk who has come to be known in history as St. Robert of Molesme. He began his monastic life at Moutier-la-Celle, near Troyes. After seeking to reform a number of monasteries he finally succeeded in molding a group of hermits into a Benedictine community at Molesme. But success brought fame, money, recruits who were less dedicated, and a gradual falling away from Robert's high ideal. In 1098 he set out to try again, joined by his prior, subprior, and nineteen other monks. They established the New Monastery, later called Cîteaux, near Dijon. Although Robert had to return to his monks at Molesme, the New Monastery flourished, especially after the entrance of Bernard of Fontaines (better known by his abbey's name, Clairvaux) in 1112. As monks went forth from Cîteaux to establish new monasteries, Stephen Harding, the third abbot, formulated with the other abbots a *Charter of Charity* which united Cîteaux and the communities founded from Cîteaux either directly or indirectly to form a monastic order, the Cistercians, frequently called "White Monks" from their light-colored habits. This federation respected the autonomy of the individual monasteries, yet provided a visitation system and a general chapter (a form later adopted by almost every monastic and religious order) to support ongoing fervor in monastic observance.

In this favorable context there grew up not only a large family of observant monasteries—some 360 by the death of Bernard of Clairvaux in 1153—but also a school of spirituality which, even though it was monastic and mystical, nonetheless gained an immense popularity in its own time and has had a continuing influence on Christian spirituality down through the centuries. The order was slow to admit convents of nuns, but from the earliest days the Cistercian way of life and observance had been adopted by nuns. Their expression of Cisterican spirituality developed some special characteristics that flourished most notably in the next century in Flanders. Almost from the start the Cistercians welcomed unlettered men as full members in a class called *conversi,* and thus Cistercian spirituality was able to express itself in very simple ways among a working class as well as among the learned clerics of the cloister.

## Basic Monastic Spirituality

If someone asks what a nun or monk does, the spontaneous response will probably be, she prays, he prays. When the well-known courtier, Arsenius, turned to the Lord for direction he received a simple and clear response: "Flee, be silent, pray always."[1] Monastics go apart to find silence. In their solitude they embrace an ascetic life to silence the clamoring within. They seek silence so that they can pray, so that they can hear and respond to God. Men and women go apart, embracing the monastic life because they want to find the freedom and the support they need to enter into a complete union with God. They have somehow sensed that this is what they are made for. They may or may not immediately see that it is by such a union with God that they can make the greatest contribution to the well-being of all, that they can be most fully an instrument of God's creative and redeeming love, the source of all that is good. The whole of creation, all its being and activity, is the *opus* of God, God's masterpiece. Its meaning lies in God's glory. All is made to glorify God. The rest of creation can adequately glorify God only if it is lifted up to God through and by the mind and heart of the human person. For the human person alone is made in the full image of God, with a mind to know God and a heart to love God. The lover of God, the one who truly seeks God, is eager that the whole creation, in accord with the divine will, ascend to God in glory. Through obedience, monastics seek to be in constant harmony with this movement. Through their prayer services, which Benedict called the *opus Dei*, the work of God, they seek to give voice to this movement, taking care "that our minds are in harmony with our voices" (*Rule of Benedict* 19.7). When monastics stand in choir, using the divinely inspired texts and listening to the shared faith of the fathers, they best express and constantly increase their "zeal" for the *opus* of God, that longing that all that takes place in their lives and in the whole of creation is to the glory of the God they love.

## The First Cistercian Expression

One of the most basic elements in discerning the spirituality of the Cistercian founders is to understand their attitude toward the *Rule of St. Benedict*. The *Little Exordium*, the documentary account of the founding of Cîteaux, emphasized their great desire to live the *Rule* that they had professed, their sorrow at seeing it transgressed, and their attempt to abandon everything that was contrary to the *Rule* or superfluous to its observances. The *Rule* was to be obeyed in everything. They were preoccupied with precision and intensity in returning to the purity of the *Rule*. When confronted with this great emphasis on the careful observance of the *Rule*, historians sometimes attempt to devaluate it by pointing to differences such as the institution of the lay brothers (*conversi*), the omission of deans and oblates, and the confederation of the monsteries. These are realities and they show some real adaptation to the social and economic conditions of their times. But they are all ordered to a fuller living of the spirit of the *Rule* by the monks. This emphasis on authentically living the *Rule* is clearly brought out in the few remaining documents from the founders: the so-called *Psalter of Saint Robert*, Saint Stephen's *Letter on the Use of Hymns*, and in Thurstan of York's remarkable *Letter on the Founding of Fountains Abbey*.[2]

At the heart of the spirit of the founders of Cîteaux was the cultivation of charity in a life structured according to the order of St. Benedict's *Rule*. The founders set for themselves an ideal of poverty, to be "poor with the poor

Christ" with a remarkable simplicity. Solitude and effective separation from the world were important to them. Another aspect of Cistercian spirituality or asceticism was manual labor. This, if anything, seemed to be one of the distinguishing marks that set the Cistercian renewal apart from all the other monastic renewals that were taking place contemporaneously. Another note, which responds very much to our times, was the founders' authenticity. They had vowed to live according to the *Rule of St. Benedict* and this they determined to do. They did not want to promise one thing and do another. Another facet, one closely connected with the central emphasis on the primacy of love, was their concern about the experience of God—or what a later generation might speak of as mystical experience.

Amadeus Hallier, in his excellent work, *The Monastic Theology of Saint Aelred,* brings out clearly the fundamental and dominating role this element of experience played in the thought and spirituality of Aelred of Rievaulx.[3] Examples can readily be drawn from the other early Cistercians. Bernard of Clairvaux used many analogies for tracing the stages of the spiritual life; but whether the image was three kisses, or seven infusions, or eight beatitudes, or any other, it always led to "the quiet of contemplation" after the painful fatigue of action, to the fullness of love where God "is not so much perceived as vaguely felt and apprehended, and that in a passing way and by the light of a sudden momentary blaze of glory, so that a great flame of love is enkindled in the soul" (*Sermons on the Song of Songs* 18.6). When Bernard came to the central theme of Benedictine spirituality in his commentary on chapter 7 of the *Rule of St. Benedict,* this characteristic thrust of the Cistercian spirit was evident. For Bernard, Benedict's ladder leads directly to perfect love, to the banquet of King Solomon, to the delights and joy of contemplation. It leads to the chamber of the king, where the soul rests securely in the king's embrace. While in this chamber the soul "sees things invisible and hears things unspeakable which it is not given to the human person to utter" (*The Steps of Pride and Humility* 7). This mystical element of the Cistercian spirit is nothing more than an explanation of elements to be found in the *Rule for Monks,* the full flowering of the seeds sown by the legislator of Monte Cassino. Benedict would have his monks "run the way of God's commandments with unspeakable sweetness of love" and "come to that perfect love of God which casts out fear"; he would have them "attain to the loftier heights" (*Rule of St. Benedict,* Prologue 49, 7.67, 73.9).

If mystical experience is the key element in Cistercian spirituality, it must be remembered that for the Cistercian fathers such mysticism could not exist without an experience of ascetical living. One must be in touch with the depths of human misery in order to be properly disposed to ascend to the heights of union with God. The mystical writings will be intelligible

5. Abbey of Senanque in Provence

6. *Tree of Jesus,* Manuscript
   Illumination, 12th century
   (M. 724, single leaf verso)

only if we first understand the ascetical pages that go before them and prepare for them. Bernard often quoted, in substance if not always in exact words, Augustine's words *Deus, noverim te, noverim me* ("God, let me know you and know myself").

Finally, there is the absolute centrality of Christ. No one can come to the Father but through him. The whole of life is to be lived in him and patterned after his example. There is no contemplation for those who are, by their own fault, divided from Christ. Therefore contemplative life is first of all the realization of union with God in Christ. And this invisible union is impossible without a visible union, in the spirit of charity, with all those in him. We are speaking of the whole Christ, his Body, the church.

## The Four Evangelists of Cîteaux

Bernard of Clairvaux has been rightly called the "theologian of the Cistercian life" (Jean Leclercq). He was the master of this school of spirituality with many disciples gathered around him and following after him. Most prominent among his disciples, each one immediately and profoundly influenced by him, were William of St. Thierry, Guerric of Igny, and Aelred of Rievaulx. Together with Bernard they have been called the four evangelists of Cîteaux.

### *Bernard of Clairvaux (1090–1153)*

Bernard of Fontaines was a man of extraordinary caliber. When he decided to enter Cîteaux, which was still a small and rather obscure monastery, this twenty-three-year-old man brought with him some thirty relatives, including his older brothers, whose wives and sister Humbelina entered a Benedictine convent dependent on Molesme. Bernard had a good classical education and many gifts. Within three years he was sent at the head of a band of twelve monks to start a new monastery. Clairvaux would not only enjoy phenomenal growth but, through new beginnings or aggregations, it would incorporate hundreds of monasteries into the order of Cîteaux before Bernard's death forty years later. Bernard's first publications came within the first decade of his abbatial rule, and after that they never ceased to come forth from his busy and eloquent pen, assisted by a corps of secretaries. He was busily commenting on the Song of Songs, an eighteen-year project, when he died. Bernard's collection of eighty-six sermons on the Song of Songs is his greatest work, undoubtedly one of the richest and most profound mystical treatises ever written. Many of his works are the fruit of his chapter talks to his monks, sometimes greatly adapted for a wider audience. His most comprehensive work was the long series of *Sermons on the Liturgical Year,* which forms an extensive commentary on all the mysteries of the life of Christ and Christ's Body, the church. In addition, the saint left numerous other sermons (*Sermones de diversis*), as well as series of sermon notes (*Sententiae*) and allegorical stories (*Parabolae*) that he used in his preaching.

Bernard entered into serious theological questions at times, but with diffidence. His interests, both in his published works and in his letters, were primarily spiritual and especially mystical. His earliest work (ca. 1124) was his treatise *The Steps of Humility and Pride,* which summarized his teaching on the spirituality of Benedict's *Rule.* Almost contemporary is the *Apology,* which he wrote to his friend William of St. Thierry to defend the Cistercian reform and attack the Cluniacs. Among his other important treatises are his masterful summary of the mystical life, *On the Love of God;* his important dogmatic work, *On Grace and Free Choice;* and his work written to the Templars entitled *In Praise of the New Knighthood.* His final completed work, *On Consideration,* written for one of his spiritual sons who became pope in 1145 (Bernard Paganelli, Pope Eugene III), has been used by every pope in this century. Bernard's thought is generally quite developed and complex, his style very cultivated, and his writings carefully edited for publication. He was undoubtedly the center of the Cistercian school, the master and guide who profoundly influenced all the others. This is not to deny that there was some reciprocal influence on him, especially from William of St. Thierry.

## William of St. Thierry (ca. 1085–ca. 1148)

Moderns may feel more at home with William of St. Thierry than with some of the other Cistercian fathers. He speaks openly and personally, as a man of our times. The growth and development of his contemplative vocation can be followed step by step in his writings. William had been a good, scholarly Black Monk (Benedictine) for some years, probably the prior of his monastery, when with his abbot he visited Bernard of Clairvaux in 1119. The visit had a profound impact on him. Thirty years later he would still write of it in awed terms, using exalted liturgical analogy. It was an hour of conversion. He wanted to become what Bernard was. At almost that same hour he himself was chosen to be an abbot, and so he had a community with whom to share his new quest. Many of his treatises, I believe, are edited from conferences he gave his communities.

First William explored what contemplation is and how one can hope to acquire it, in his treatise *On Contemplating God.* The way is love, and so he turned his considerations to love in *On the Nature and Dignity of Love.* Then, in the true Cistercian way, he knew he had to get to know the lover and the power at work in him, that is, grace. Like so many of the other fathers, he then produced a treatise on the human person: *On the Nature of the Body and the Soul.* His treatise on grace, which followed, took the form of a commentary on the Epistle to the Romans, which is drawn largely from Augustine. William relied very heavily on the fathers and did not hesitate to use their very texts and words. When he was ready to turn his attention to the text that was at the heart of all Cistercian mystical doctrine, the Song of Songs, he did not immediately launch out on his own. He had begun an explanation with Bernard while they lay side by side in the infirmary at Clairvaux. He published this as the *Brevis Commentatio.* Next he searched through all the writings of Ambrose of Milan and Gregory the Great and drew out all they had to say, verse by verse, on the great love song. With all this behind him, he was ready to begin his own commentary, his *Exposition on the Song of Songs.*

Rich additional light is thrown upon William's development by his very personal *Meditations,* which were written through these same years and were published to help young men learn how to pray. We have from this same period a letter, or rather a treatise, on the Eucharist, a response to a request, which indicates how important a place the Eucharist held in the lives of the Cistercian fathers and their spiritual outlook.

As one grows in union with Christ, one comes to have Christ's mind and heart, to share all his loves and concerns. The Cistercian fathers were men of the Church. As much as they longed for Mary's part, for Rachel's embraces, they accepted Martha's role when such was demanded and became fruitful like Leah. When William thought that Abelard was imperiling the faith and true theology, he forsook his holy leisure and his love song and spoke out on the true nature of faith and its content in his treatise *The Mirror of Faith* for the sake of the young monks in his community and all who were being influenced and confused by the subtle dialectic. But William did not stop at a clear presentation of the theology of faith and of the central object of the faith, the most blessed Trinity. He went on to formulate a trinitarian mysticism in *The Enigma of Faith,* which stands as his greatest and most profound and lasting contribution to the development of Christian spirituality. After this battle was over, William sought deeper solitude for a time with the nearby Carthusians. To express his fraternal gratitude to them and again to help the young, he wrote his synthesis *The Golden Epistle.* Finally, as life drew to a close he began to paint an idealized icon of all this in the biography of his idol and lifelong inspiration, the incarnation of all he strove for, his beloved friend, the abbot of Clairvaux.

## Guerric of Igny (ca. 1090–1157)

Guerric of Igny was in some respects truly in the middle of things. He was the favored disciple of Bernard of Clairvaux. Later, as abbot, Guerric had Bernard as his Father Immediate (the abbot who came annually for a formal visitation) while at the same time he was the Father Immediate of William of St. Thierry, a monk of Signy since 1136. Guerric entered Clairvaux probably around 1123, before Bernard had been catapulted into his commanding ecclesial and social role, when he was still able to spend considerable time at home with his community. The choice of Guerric as abbot of Igny undoubtedly came through the influence of Bernard, which would indicate that the abbot of Clairvaux saw in him a man who had grasped well the spirituality he sought to impart and would be able to pass it on to others. For his part, Guerric, on his regular visits to Signy, because of his love for the man whom he called his master, would have sought out this master's closest friend and would have tried to learn from him all he could about their beloved Bernard. It was perhaps William's Father Immediate—just as later it would be Aelred's—who encouraged him to edit some of his past jottings and also to put on paper what was perhaps his finest work.

Guerric's corpus, at least what we have so far unearthed, is quite brief. There are fifty-three liturgical sermons and a sermon on the Song of Songs. His sermons are marked with simplicity, clarity, and practicality. They are, perhaps, among the least edited of the writings that have come down to us from the Cistercian fathers—the closest to what the monks might have actually heard as they sat in the chapter house. Guerric's sermons are full of good, down-to-earth practical teaching. There is a complete though concise theology of work, of poverty, of silence, of Mary, and a rich christology. His doctrine is not pedestrian—the ideal of contemplative union with God is always present. Guerric made no bones about it: all are called to this and many of his monks were having experience of it.

The beatitudes, which all the Cistercian fathers use at one time or another to sum up the way to holiness, are central for Guerric. The theme is first found in the Advent sermons and reaches its climax in the All Saints' Day sermon. He completed only the first sermon for this feast, explaining the general plan he had in mind. For his collection of sermons Guerric chose five sermons for each feast (during his eighteen years as abbot he probably preached on each of these feasts a dozen or more times). Each sermon begins with a verse or a line from the liturgy of the day, but often this is only a takeoff point. The development of ideas is not always logical (though some of the sermons can be outlined in scholastic form), but development takes place through the association of ideas, especially scriptural words and themes. It is a delight to follow this weave of thought that always ends up at the contemplative heart of things.

## Aelred of Rievaulx (ca. 1110–1167)

Aelred seems very different from Guerric, even though they sat together at the General Chapter during the last years of Bernard's life. This "Bernard of the North," as he was called, was born in Northumberland. He became a monk of Rievaulx in 1134 and novice master in 1142. The next year he was abbot of Revesby in Lincolnshire and four years later back at Rievaulx was abbot of that house. Aelred was a born writer, one of the few early Cistercians to write on purely secular affairs, but he did not make his debut on his own choice. Bernard, impressed by the thorough and clear grasp that Aelred had of the breadth and depth of basic Cistercian teaching, required this novice master to write a "manual" for novices, the *Mirror of Charity*. This foundational treatise gave rise over the course of many years, in fact most of the years of Aelred's abbacy, to a sort of appendix, which is probably the most popular of all the early Cistercian texts—Aelred's *Spiritual Friendship*. This later work can be properly understood only when it is seen in the context of the earlier, more basic piece. Besides these two major contributions, we have from Aelred many sermons and also his profane works and the treatise on the soul which may or may not be complete—it was still on his writing table when he died. Aelred's *Pastoral Prayer* sets forth in yet another form the early Cistercian ideal of the spiritual father and tells us much about the author and how he saw his role in life.

## Disciples and Followers

We can only introduce a very few of the other interesting and significant members of the Cistercian school here. Gilbert of Hoyland was a confrere of Aelred and was sent by him to bring the Cistercian way to Swinehead, a Savigniac monastery fifteen miles south of Revesby. Gilbert shared Aelred's reverence for Bernard and was privileged to continue the latter's commentary on the Song of Songs. However, Gilbert brought a decidedly different flavor to the work, speaking as he was—at least in part—to a community of nuns. While Etienne Gilson questioned the level of Gilbert's experience, more recent authors agree that "mystical experience would seem necessary to explain his writings."[4]

John of Ford was a spiritual son and disciple of Baldwin of Ford. The latter, who became archbishop of Canterbury in 1184, is best known for his writings on the sacrament of the altar. John completed Gilbert's commentary on the Song of Songs. While he was abbot of Ford and doing this work, two other monks of the abbey, Roger and Maurinus, were writing on the Blessed Mother. But the best known of the Marian writers among the early Cistercians is Amadeus of Lausanne. His eight homilies *In Praise of the Blessed Virgin Mary* were written after he became bishop of Lausanne in 1144, but they are the fruit of Cistercian spirituality in their Marian piety and biblical exegesis.

A scholastic vein among these early Cistercians found its most significant voice in Isaac, the controversial abbot of Stella, who seems to have ended his days in exile on the Isle of Ré off La Rochelle. Isaac was probably an Englishman. His writings show familiarity with the thought of the masters active in Paris and Chartres in the 1130s, such as Hugh of St. Victor, Peter Abelard, William of Conches (these last two both received the effective remonstrances of Bernard) and Thierry of Chartres. Thierry preceded Isaac into the Cistercian life. The end of the century found another of the foremost masters of that age spending his declining days at Cîteaux: Alan of Lille. For these men the wisdom of the schools and the wisdom of the cloister were not antagonistic but complementary. It was something less than the wisdom of the schools that would eviscerate monastic learning and life in the next century.

Much of the literary heritage of Cîteaux has come to us in the form of sermons, even in the case of these more scholastic fathers. Hugh of Pontigny, who entered with Bernard and became an abbot a year before him, has left a collection that, like Guerric's, is very close to the original Cistercian experience and forms probably the oldest collection we have. At the other end of the century we have the collection of Helinand of Froidmont, which shows a strong scholastic influence.

Another medium that was important for the Cistercian authors was that of the epistle or letter. The carefully edited collection of Bernard's letters is in itself a treatise that he reworked several times before he died. Again, at the end of the century we find a significant collection, the letters of Adam of Perseigne, and again the scholastic influence is present, yet without the loss of the monastic or biblical flavor.

## And Today

The importance of these Cistercian fathers and their influence has been renewed in our times by what Jean Leclercq speaks of as "the closing of the scholastic parenthesis." The rationalistic approach toward theology, which saw its first significant expression in the eleventh century, drove a wedge between theology and spirituality. When the queen of the sciences lost her solid grounding in the sacred page and the writings of the fathers (How well Thomas Aquinas knew his sources, but this was not so for many of his successors!), theology devolved into a sad sterility on the one hand and a less than stable vigor on the other.

With the development of the more rationalistic attitude toward the basic truths of life, a tendency later universalized by the proliferation of the printed word, a more and more conceptual stance has dominated the Western approach to life and spirituality. The power of thought—sometimes totally divorced from the heart—has prevailed. But today's world is less and less dependent on the written word. Multimedia communications, rich in imagery and touching all the senses, evoke a holistic response that gives prominence to the heart, to that which is beyond thought, to the transcendental. The heart, the whole person, has its reasons of which the mind knows nothing. The evolution of the global village, increased communications with the Far East, its religions and its cultures, have challenged the Christian West and are making it acutely aware of its need to get in touch with all the dimensions of its rich heritage. There is a great need to reach back to the other side of the "scholastic parenthesis" and pick up those currents of life which are more integrally and fully human, open to the divine and to the divinization of the human. Those who are experiencing with some liveliness the currents of global spirituality, an ecumenism beyond ecumenism, in these last years of the twentieth century, find themselves surprisingly at home with these existential, personalist, and transpersonal Cistercian fathers of the twelfth century.

## Notes

1. *The Sayings of the Desert Fathers: The Alphabetic Collection,* trans. Benedicta Ward (London: Mowbray, 1975) 8.

2. See "Three Early Documents" in M. B. Pennington, *The Last of the Fathers* (Still River, MA: St. Bede's Publications, 1983) 17–32.

3. A. Hallier, *The Monastic Theology of Aelred of Rievaulx: An Experiential Theology.* Translated by Columban Heaney, with a special introduction by Thomas Merton. Shannon: Irish University Press, 1969. Distributed by Cistercian Publications.

4. Lawrence Bracelond in *Gilbert of Hoyland: Sermons on the Song of Songs I* (Kalamazoo, MI: Cistercian Publications, 1978) 20.

# Bibliography

## Sources

The indefatigable labors of Jean Leclercq, assisted by Henri Rochais and Charles Talbot, have given us a splendid edition of the works of Bernard in eight volumes (*Sancti Bernardi opera* [Rome: Editiones Cistercienses, 1957-77). Some of the works of Adam of Perseigne, Aelred of Rievaulx, Amadeus of Lausanne, Baldwin of Ford, Guerric of Igny, Isaac of Stella, and William of St. Thierry have appeared in critical editions with French translations in Sources chrétiennes (Paris: Cerf, 1943-). More of Aelred is found in the first volume of *Corpus Christianorum, Continuatio Medievalis* (Turnhout: Brepols, 1965), with two more volumes promised. Some forty volumes of the Cistercian fathers have appeared in English translation with good introductions in the Cistercian Fathers Series (Spencer, MA; Kalamazoo, MI: Cistercian Publications, 1970-). Cistercian Publications has produced also some sixty companion volumes in the Cistercian Studies Series (Spencer, MA; Kalamazoo, MI, 1969—), including basic studies on Bernard by Leclercq (CS 16), William of St. Thierry by Jean-Marie Déchanet (CS 10), Guerric of Igny by John Morson (CS 25), Aelred by Aelred Squire (CS 50), and Isaac of Stella by Bernard McGinn (CS 15).

The flavor of the times can be found in such contemporary works as the *Exordium parvum* (ed. J.-B. Van Damme; Documenta pro Cisterciensis ordinis historiae ac juris studio; Westmalle: Typis Ordinis Cisterciensis, 1959), the *Exordium magnum* (ed. B. Griesser; Rome: Editiones Cistercienses, 1961), and the *Vita prima sancti Bernardi* (*PL* 185).

## Studies

Bouton, Jean de la Croix. *Bibliographie Bernardine 1891-1957*. Paris: Lethielleux, 1958.
———. *Histoire de l'ordre de Cîteaux*. Westmalle: Fiches "Cisterciennes," 1959-68. 3 vols. A historical study from the point of view of strict observance.
Gilson, Etienne. *The Mystical Theology of Saint Bernard*. Translated by A. H. C. Downes. London and New York: Sheed & Ward, 1958. Although rightly criticized for some of its assertions, this work retains its very real value.
Hoste, Anselm. *Bibliotheca Aelrediana*. Steenbrugge: Abbey of St. Peter, 1962.
Janauschek, L. *Bibliographia Bernardina . . . usque ad finem anni MDCCCXC*. 1891. Reprint, Hildesheim: Olms, 1959. Has been updated by Bouton and Manning.
Lekai, Louis. *The Cistercians, Ideals and Reality*. Kent State, OH: Kent State University Press, 1977. The best historical study.
Manning, E. *Bibliographie Bernardine 1957-1970*. Documentation cistercienne 6. Rochefort: Abbaye Notre Dame de S. Remy, 1972.
Pennington, B., and P. Verdeyen. "Bibliographie de Guillaume de Saint-Thierry depuis 1900." In *Saint-Thierry: Une Abbaye du VIe au XXe siècle*. Saint Thierry: Association des Amis de l'Abbaye de Saint-Thierry, 1979.

# IV. *The Regular Canons*

## GROVER A. ZINN

REGULAR CANONS ARE deacons and priests who live in a religious community governed by a rule that requires personal poverty of each canon. They were one of three major religious orders in the Middle Ages, the other two being monks and mendicant friars. Communities of regular canons first appeared in Italy and southern France in the mid-eleventh century and then spread rapidly throughout Europe. The high point of their development was in the twelfth century. Important foundations included Prémontré (near Laon), Arrouaise, St. Victor (at Paris) and St. Ruf (at Avignon) in France; San Frediano (at Lucca) in Italy; and at Reichersberg and Springiersbach in Germany and Austria. There had been earlier attempts in the Carolingian period to establish a common life under a rule for cathedral canons and other clerics. The regular canons added the crucial element of personal poverty. In insisting on this they were one among other movements that sought to recover the life of the primitive church (*ecclesia primitiva*) and to embrace the ideal of the apostolic life (*vita apostolica*) in the eleventh and twelfth centuries.

Regular canons found precedent for their communal life and renunciation of private property in two major sources, one apostolic, the other patristic: (1) the description of the early Christian community in Jerusalem, in which all were united in heart and mind and shared their possessions in common (Acts 4:32ff.); and (2) the customs of the episcopal household of Augustine of Hippo, who insisted on a full common life and total personal poverty for his clergy. Given the rapid changes in social and ecclesiastical institutions after Augustine's time, his practice had little practical impact beyond the future bishops who were formed in his household. But in Augustine's sermons, in the elements that went into the *Rule* that bears his name, and in the *Life* by Possidius, the ideal of a community of clergy pledged to personal poverty lay waiting to be put into practice.

As they founded new communities or reformed old ones, regular canons adopted practices in addition to poverty and a common life that were per-ceived as pertaining to the monastic way. These included asceticism, common hours of liturgical prayer, contemplation, an enclosed life, and the like. Some canonical houses, Prémontré for example, were founded in the wilderness like Cistercian houses. Regular canons provoked opposition from clerics and monks alike. Clerics criticized their strictness; monks were reluctant to accept this new order that in many ways resembled monastic life. A fairly extensive polemical literature developed between regular canons and monks in which each side sought to show its distinctive claims and/or superiority.

By the early twelfth century, regular canons in France had taken the so-called *Rule of St. Augustine* as their standard. Although the history of this rule remains somewhat obscure, by the twelfth century it consisted of two parts: (1) an opening section now called the *regula secunda* or the *ordo monasteriorum;* and (2) a much longer section, now called the *regula tertia.* The latter section was a masculine version of Augustine's *Letter 211,* which was written to a group of female ascetics. The *regula secunda* (of Italian origin, probably sixth century) contained specific regulations for liturgical hours, food, manual labor, poverty, and silence. These were sometimes judged ill-suited for northern Europe and were dropped, leaving the *regula tertia* as the body of the *Rule.* Although the *Rule* lacked detailed provisions for community life on the order of the monastic *Rule of St. Benedict,* it was full of sound advice. Joined with local customaries giving detailed regulations, the *Rule of St. Augustine* both guided the regular canons and pointed to their patristic source of authority.

In examining medieval religious orders, scholars have often sought to identify distinctive Benedictine, canonical, Franciscan, or other spiritualities. In comparing regular canons and monks it is difficult to isolate characteristics that are exclusive to either order. Historical origins go part way in explaining *perceived* differences in the twelfth century. Individual canons and monks were absolutely certain what they were *not;* the distinctive character of what they *were* might prove more elusive of definition. Neither ordination as a priest nor the care of parishes can be taken as a differentiating characteristic. More monks were being ordained and were claiming the right to preach and to have the care of souls, while not all regular canons (who were by definition priests) saw preaching and/or the traditional priestly ministry as part of their vocation. There seems not to have been an exclusively "canonical" spirituality, for many major themes and concerns of their spiritual life were shared with Benedictine contemporaries. This is not to say that there were not canonical (and monastic) groups with distinctive spiritualities. What is being examined here is the claim of a distinguishing characteristic across an entire religious order. The canonical saying that monks are meant to "weep and pray" while canons do something different is more of a polemical commonplace than an illuminating distinction. A recent suggestion that the difference between monks and canons needs to be sought in certain attitudes rather than origins, customs, life-style, or spirituality deserves recognition.

The attitude singled out is that of *teaching others by word and example* on the part of canons, in contrast to the Benedictine and Cistercian emphasis on being a learner set on a way of individual salvation.[1]

The types of canonical foundations were diverse, from new foundations outside of cities to the reform of existing canonical chapters. The mid-eleventh-century foundation of St. Ruf at Avignon was begun by four clerics who with their bishop's support established the regular life in a ruined church outside the city. Arrouaise began with three hermits in 1090 and obtained episcopal recognition in 1097. At Chartres the ardent canonical reformer Ivo of Chartres, the former head of the regular canons at St. Quentin in Beauvais, failed to get canons installed in the cathedral and had to settle for reforming St. Andrew. Perhaps the most striking new foundation was Prémontré, founded in 1120 by Norbert of Xanten. Having undergone a dramatic conversion while a canon in the imperial entourage, Norbert exchanged his elegant vestments for the rough garb of a wandering preacher. After attempting unsuccessfully to convert several groups of canons to his ideas of asceticism, common life, and poverty, Norbert was encouraged to start a totally new community. The result was Prémontré, located in an isolated area near Laon. The widely influential Abbey of St. Victor at Paris began less dramatically with William of Champeaux's decision to retire from his positions as archdeacon of the cathedral and master in the schools of Paris. William began a religious community outside Paris in 1108 at a small shrine dedicated to St. Victor. At the urging of others he resumed teaching and provided the impetus for the special Victorine combination of religious life and scholarly inquiry. St. Victor soon became a royal abbey and was a center for creative scholarship, liturgical development, and contemplative life. It also had a strong preaching tradition and was the penitential center for Parisian students. Canonical reform was not without strong papal support, especially from Gregorian reformers. Urban II expressed his support for the house of regular canons at Rottenbach by noting that they were recovering a lost discipline and were worthy, alongside the separate monastic movement, of support and encouragement.

Of all the houses of regular canons, the Abbey of St. Victor had perhaps the strongest impact on the development of medieval spirituality. For that reason we shall examine it more closely.

## Hugh of St. Victor

At the Abbey of St. Victor a distinctive spiritual tradition developed under the leadership of Hugh of St. Victor (d. 1141) and Richard of St. Victor (d. 1173). Others contributed variously and deserve brief mention before we continue with Hugh and Richard. Adam of St. Victor was a liturgical poet of unusual skill. He wrote a series of sequences that distill Victorine thought into poems of great power and theological complexity. Thomas Gallus (d. 1246) who became the abbot Vercelli, was attracted to the works of Pseudo-Dionysius the Areopagite and wrote commentaries on them, continuing Hugh's earlier interest. He also penned influential commentaries on that favorite mystical text, the Song of Songs. Achard of St. Victor (d. 1171) was an abbot whose sermons, recently edited and studied, have been for too long neglected. Andrew of St. Victor (d. 1175), who spent the latter part of his life at the Abbey of Wigmore in England, represents singleminded devotion to the Victorine emphasis on the literal meaning of Scripture. Godfrey of St. Victor (d. after 1194) continued the Victorine theological tradition in his *Fons philosophiae* (*The Fountain of Philosophy*) and *Microcosmus*. Finally, note should be taken of the strident voice of Walter of St. Victor (d. 1180) whose *Contra quatuor labyrinthos Franciae* (*Against the Four Masters of Confusion in France*) reflects a narrow, antidialectical spirit at odds with Hugh and Richard.

By the mid-1120s Hugh's teaching and writing were gaining him recognition as a leading master at Paris. His interests and accomplishments were remarkable, for they spanned philosophy, biblical exegesis, theology, and contemplation, with significant contributions to each. Hugh's creative genius appeared in many ways. His *Didascalicon* was a superb introduction to philosophical study and biblical interpretation. In it he proposed a sequence of studies that related the three senses of scripture (literal, allegorical, and tropological) to courses of study centered successively on history, theology, and the contemplative life. In exegesis Hugh placed a new emphasis on the literal, historical sense of scripture. In theology he wrote the first theological *summa* of the medieval period, *De sacramentis christianae fidei* (*On the Sacraments of the Christian Faith*), adopting the method of "questions" popularized in the schools of Laon and Paris by Anselm of Laon and Peter Abelard but insisting that history be an integral part of theology. Hugh wrote two treatises of special significance for the contemplative life, *De archa Noe morali* (*On the Moral Ark of Noah*) and *De archa Noe mystica* (*On the Mystical Ark of Noah*).

Hugh's two treatises on Noah's ark are based on a drawing that uses the ark as a structural symbol of the stages of the mystic's quest and the unfolding of sacred history. This symbolic ark is set in the center of a diagram of the cosmos that Christ holds in front of his body. By means of intricate iconographic devices, the drawing represents the origin of the world from its divine source, the return of humanity to the divine center through meditation/contemplation, and the final consummation of all in divine judgment. Hugh tells us that he placed the drawing (which is described in detail in *De arca Noe mystica*) before his fellow canons and invited them to gaze at it—not, he stressed, to enjoy the beautiful forms and colors but to form their lives upon the truth found manifest there. Thus, this symbolic drawing that linked cosmos, history, and the contemplative quest can be likened in form and function to classic mandalas found in Tibetan Buddhism.[2]

The ark is depicted as a truncated pyramid with three internal storeys. Drawn as if seen from above, it appears as three nested rectangles with a square (the summit) in the center. The pyramidal shape represents the ascent of the soul from the divided loves and chaos of the world to the peace and unity of recollection and contemplation. From each corner three ladders link the storeys and ascend to the summit, thus representing the three stages of each of the four divisions of the mystic quest. The first division represents awakening, with levels of fear, grief, and love. The second division is purgation or the flight from the vice of concupiscence, with stages of patience, mercy, and compunction. The third stage is illumination or the flight of ignorance, with levels of cognition, meditation, and contemplation. The fourth stage is union, which is not a flight from vice but a further advance in virtue; its levels are temperance, prudence, and fortitude. The threefold pattern of purgation, illumination, and union represents the influence of Pseudo-Dionysius. Hugh's addition of awakening is a note more Augustinian than Dionysian.

The contemplative experience represents humankind's original nondiscursive inner awareness of God's presence. As created, humans had three "eyes": the eye of the understanding to see divine things; the eye of reason to see the self within; the eye of sense to behold the world. In the fall the eye of the understanding was blinded, reason was weakened, and only sense remained intact. Christ represents a new second "external" approach of God to humans. Calling people outwardly and healing them through the sacraments, Christ shows the way and provides the goal for the contemplative's quest. Hugh, like Richard later, likens the image of God within to a mirror that is obscured by sin and cleansed by discipline with the result that the presence of God again shines within the individual through the image beheld by the eye of the understanding.

The ecstatic, unific, and transforming aspects of the contemplative experience can be seen in the iconography of the stages of illumination. Illumination overcomes ignorance, which Hugh depicts as a person breaking a vase, thus representing the fragmentation of knowledge in the fall. The first stage, cognition or thought, gazes at a book open to the words of Genesis 1:1, which indicates that the purified mind can now again read the "book" of the created world. Meditation, which Hugh understands as concentrated attention to a single matter and as a state of withdrawn interiorized reflection, begins to gather up the pieces of the shattered vase. Finally, contemplation, symbolized by a craftsman, melts the fragments with the flame of divine love and sends the liquid into the square (Christ) in the center of the ark, where the lost likeness to God is recovered. In this vivid symbolic presentation Hugh catches multiple aspects of contemplation: passage beyond one's ordinary state (ecstasy), reforming of the lost image/likeness, and unification with Christ, the center. The theme of unity is sounded even more strongly in the first homily on Ecclesiastes. Drawing on metaphors of burning wood, Hugh presents the thinking soul as being like a fire of green wood, much smoke and little flame. In meditation the smoke clears and tongues of flame begin to leap about. With contemplation the flame burns ever more brightly until, "in the pure fire of love, with the utmost peace and joy, the soul is gently beaten back. Then, the whole heart being turned into the fire of love, God is known truly to be all in all. For He is received with a love so deep that apart from Him nothing is left to the heart, even of itself" (*Homily on Ecclesiastes* 1 [*PL* 175, col. 117]).[3] This passage reminds us that the compelling power of love, the weight of love according to Gregory the Great, is the motive force behind the entire contemplative quest. In a moving short treatise Hugh describes love as the "road to God," and in *The Soul's Betrothal Gifts* (*De arrha animae*) he sees the world and the sacraments as betrothal gifts, given to the soul by the Bridegroom to lead her to the marriage chamber of mystical experience.

In conclusion, we may say that for Hugh the mystic seeks the stable center. The quest begins by asking, Why is the human heart restless? The answer, given in the complex construct of the ark treatises, is that a divisive love of the world leads to restlessness. One must recover a unified love of God and seek the stable historical, cosmic, and contemplative center represented by Christ, the creative, sustaining, contemplative, and judging Word.

## Richard of St. Victor

Hugh's successor at St. Victor was Richard of St. Victor (d. 1173). Richard probably came to the abbey in the early 1150s, well after Hugh's death. He became subprior, then prior. Through his teaching, preaching, and writing Richard continued to develop the Victorine contemplative tradition.

Richard represents a less global grasp of fields than Hugh and a more concentrated focus on one. Even though he summarized Hugh's *Chronicon*, commented on Scripture, preached sermons, and ventured creatively into theology (with *De trinitate* and its necessary reasons for a triune God), it was as a mystical writer that Richard was remembered by later generations, including Dante. His major mystical writings were two: *De duodecim patriarchiis* (*The Twelve Patriarchs*, also known as *Benjamin minor*) and *De mystica archa* (*The Mystical Ark*, also known as *Benjamin major*). In these works Richard, like Hugh, used a penetrating symbolic interpretation of biblical persons, themes, and events. He appears as the master of discretion, able to discern strengths and weaknesses, to guard against excesses, to offer sage advice on that most dangerous of all journeys, the journey within that strives to transcend the self in ecstatic contemplation.

Richard of St. Victor's ascetic and contemplative teaching assumes the cosmic and theological setting established by Hugh and pays special attention to noetic and psychological matters. Three concerns deserve special mention. First, Richard carefully presented a process of discipline for mind and body leading to the proximate goal of interior quiet and the ultimate goal of contemplative ecstasy. Second, he analyzed with great insight the levels of perception or awareness that are involved in ordinary and contemplative experience. Finally, he distinguished three modes of contemplation, ascribing quite different qualities to each.

The basic symbolic structure that Richard chose reveals his interest in a transformative *process*. In *The Twelve Patriarchs* Jacob's twelve sons and one daughter (Genesis 29ff.) furnish Richard with powerful personifications of stages of ascetic/contemplative development. Jacob stands for the rational soul; his four wives represent the will (Leah), sensation (Zilpah), imagination (Bilhah) and reason (Rachel). The birth order of the children provides the sequence of developmental stages. The symbolic value of each of the four mothers relates each stage (child) to the discipline of senses, imagination, will, or reason. Each biblical figure thus becomes a personification of a state and a set of experiences into which the contemplative-to-be must enter. One *becomes* Reuben (who represents "fear of God") at the point of awakening, Naphtali in using the symbolic role of the visible material universe to approach invisible spiritual realities, Joseph in achieving discretion, and Benjamin in entering ecstasy. With each stage Richard offers perceptive comments on proper and improper application of spiritual disciplines of body and mind, revealing again and again his skill as a spiritual guide.

With the birth of Benjamin, the last son, Richard introduces a new symbol, the transfiguration of Jesus. Climbing the mountain of the transfiguration is the discipline represented by Jacob's children; standing on the mountain represents the absolute interior stillness that is the goal of discipline; the pure white light of the transfiguration represents interior visions of light; the fainting of the disciples, like Rachel's death, represents contemplative ecstasy. These and other biblical images become powerful and moving symbols that evoke and communicate the depths of ascetic and mystical experience. Richard was a teacher, a spiritual guide, who entered into a world of biblical symbols and made of it a vehicle of spiritual instruction and transformation.

In *The Mystical Ark* the ark of the covenant and the accompanying two seraphim become symbolic representations of the six degrees of contemplation, ordered hierarchically according to the way in which the *object* of contemplation is known. For Richard things are known in three ways: through the imagination mediating sense experience; through reason abstracting from sense experience or reflecting on itself; or through the understanding (*intellectus*) that apprehends invisible spiritual realities that are otherwise inaccessible. Imagination and reason provide knowledge of the visible world and the self. The understanding offers access to a completely different level of experience, the realm of spiritual and divine realities. This use of "understanding" is totally unlike the present-day association of understanding and intellect with reason and rationality. For Richard, like Hugh, it is through the understanding that God is inwardly present to the soul.

The two lowest degrees of contemplation involve sense experience mediated through the imagination and are differentiated by whether or not reason analyzes the experience. The second two degrees refer to knowledge through reason, either depending on the images from the imagination (the use of the symbolic value of material things to approach invisible spiritual reality) or involving only the reflection of reason without any images. The fifth and sixth degrees involve the understanding that transcends reason and "knows" in a unique way. The ark symbolizes the first four degrees, the cherubim the last two.

Contemplation is a distinctive mode of awareness, a beholding defined by inherent qualities, not by the object contemplated. One may contemplate a rock, the causes of things, an interior visionary experience, or (in ecstasy) the Trinity. The degree of contemplation is defined by the way something becomes known (sense, reason, or a divine showing). Contemplation itself is defined as a beholding with wonder and amazement in an expansive, intuitive grasp of things. It is nondiscursive and nonanalytical; it is awareness in a state of complete inner quiet, rest, and reception.

There are three modes of contemplation: (1) enlargement of the mind, (2) raising up of the mind, and (3) alienation of the mind or ecstasy. Enlargement is the fruit of human effort, a kind of contemplation that can be learned and generally relates to the first four degrees of contemplation. Raising up of the mind involves human effort and divine grace together, the latter granting a visionary experience to the mystic. Richard, unlike some other mystics, gave a positive place to visionary experiences and made them part of the mystic path. Unlike ecstatic experiences, they remain completely accessible to rational reflection. Alienation of the mind, or ecstasy, is the third mode and has three causes: greatness of devotion, greatness of wonder, and greatness of exultation. In the first, the fire of divine love is kindled with such force that ecstasy results. In the second, a visionary experience impels the mind to an ecstatic state. In the third, the mind becomes inebriated with an interior sweetness that leads to ecstasy. In each of these cases there is something that can be called a "trigger" that initiates a breakthrough to a special level of awareness. Richard employs biblical figures such as Abraham, Elijah, Moses, and Aaron as symbolic representations of various states of ecstasy. He also makes effective use of "natural" symbols such as boiling water and light reflected upward from the surface of still water. Two particular biblical figures require special mention. When discussing ecstasy caused by greatness of wonder Richard presents the Queen of Sheba and the apostle Peter in chains as two archetypes. The queen questioning Solomon during her visit is the soul eagerly seeking divine truth. Solomon's answers are "divine showings" (visions). The queen fainting is the soul in ecstasy. Explaining the symbols Richard says:

> First she asks and hears; next she sees and understands; finally she is struck dumb with astonishment and faints. She asks questions in order that she may learn; she contemplates in order that she may marvel; she is astonished in order that she may silence the mind and experience ecstasy of mind. The first is by meditation; the second, by contemplation; the third, by ecstasy. (*The Mystical Ark* 5.12)[4]

Peter in prison (Acts 12:3-10) represents a very different point of departure. Peter in the dark dungeon is the downcast soul caught in concupiscence and ignorance. The angel visiting and freeing Peter is a divine showing that lifts the mind to ecstasy. The queen and the apostle reveal Richard's skill in using biblical figures to convey deep and complex psychological states that are real parts of the spiritual quest—intent meditation leading to ecstasy and spiritual depression lifted and transformed by a divine showing.

The process of transformation by divine love is powerfully presented in the treatise *On the Four Degrees of Violent Charity*. In the fourth degree the soul is not only reborn and reformed in the image and likeness of God but is also conformed to the humility and servanthood of Christ, becoming above all else a fearless guide who seeks to bring others to spiritual maturity, to a transformation that is also a rebirth.

It should be noted that Hugh and Richard were influential in bringing the ideas of Pseudo-Dionysius the Areopagite into the mainstream of Western

Christian theological and mystical thought. Hugh used the Dionysian scheme of purgation, illumination, and union in his mystical writings, and he also introduced in his theology the idea of the Eucharist as a "participation" in Jesus. The insistence of both Hugh and Richard that knowledge of invisible divine things is first mediated through the symbolic significance of material things is very Dionysian. The Dionysian theme of "divine darkness" is also found in Victorine writings, although it is tempered by the conviction that the mystical experience is one of light and that the darkness or unknowing applies as much to our ability to express what has been experienced as it does to the experience, which has a noetic quality.

Victorine influence on later mystics was substantial, especially through Richard. His influence can be seen in Bonaventure's *Itinerarium mentis in Deum* (*The Journey of the Mind into God*), the English *Cloud of Unknowing*, and such later works as Bernardino de Laredo's *Ascent of Mount Sion*. In the later Middle Ages there was a general revival of interest in the twelfth-century mystics, and the Victorines were in the forefront of that revival. Hugh's concern with discerning the point of stability within through the contemplative experience and Richard's eloquent presentation of the stages of the mystic's quest and the variety of contemplation stand as major milestones in the development of the Western contemplative tradition.

### Notes

1. On this see Caroline Walker Bynum, *Docere Verbo et Exemplo.*
2. See Grover Zinn, "Mandala Symbolism and Use."
3. Translated in Hugh of St. Victor, *Selected Spiritual Writings,* 185.
4. Translated in Richard of St. Victor, *The Twelve Patriarchs, The Mystical Ark, and Book Three of The Trinity,* 327.

### Bibliography

#### Sources

Hugh of Saint Victor. *Selected Spiritual Writings.* Translated by a Religious of C.S.M.V. London: Faber, 1962.
———. *Hugues de Saint-Victor: Six opuscules spirituels.* Edited and translated by Roger Baron. Sources chrétiennes 155. Paris: Cerf, 1969.
———. *Soliloquy on the Earnest Money of the Soul.* Translated by Kevin Herbert. Milwaukee, WI: Marquette University Press, 1956.
Richard of St. Victor. *Selected Writings on Contemplation.* Translated by Clare Kirchberger. New York: Harper, n.d.
———. *The Twelve Patriarchs, The Mystical Ark, Book Three of the Trinity.* Translated by Grover A. Zinn. New York: Paulist Press, 1979.

Thomas Gallus. *Commentaires du Cantique des Cantiques.* Edited by Jeanne Barbet. Paris: Vrin, 1967. No English translations of this important author exist.

## Studies

Baron, Roger. *Science et Sagesse chez Hugues de Saint-Victor.* Paris: Lethielleux, 1957.

———. *Études sur Hugues de saint-Victor.* Bruges: Desclée, 1963.

Bynum, Caroline Walker. *Docere Verbo et Exemplo: An Aspect of Twelfth-Century Spirituality.* Missoula, MT: Scholars Press, 1979.

———. "The Spirituality of the Regular Canons in the Twelfth Century." In *Jesus as Mother: Studies in the Spirituality of the High Middle Ages,* 22-58. Berkeley: University of California Press, 1982.

Chatillon, Jean. "De Guillaume de Champeaux à Thomas Gallus: Chronique d'histoire littéraire et doctrinale de l'école de saint-Victor." *Revue du moyen âge latin* 8 (1952) 139-62.

———. "Les trois modes de la contemplation selon Richard de Saint-Victor." *Bulletin de littérature écclesiastique* 41 (1940) 3-26.

Dereine, Charles. "Chanoines." In *Dictionnaire d'histoire et géographie écclesiastiques,* vol. 12, cols. 353-405. Paris: Letouzey et Ané, 1953.

Dickinson, John Compton. *The Origins of the Austin Canons and Their Introduction into England.* London: S.P.C.K., 1950.

Dumeige, Gervais. *Richard de Saint-Victor et l'idée chrétienne de l'amour.* Paris: Presses universitaires de France, 1952.

Smalley, Beryl. *The Study of the Bible in the Middle Ages.* Notre Dame, IN: University of Notre Dame Press, 1964.

Verheijen, Luc. *Le règle de saint-Augustin.* 2 vols. Paris: Études augustiniennes, 1967.

Weisweiler, Heinrich. "*Sacramentum fidei:* Augustinische und ps.-dionysische in der Glaubenauffassung Hugos von St. Viktor." In *Theologie in Geschichte und Gegenwart,* 2:143-69. Edited by J. Auer and H. Volk. Munich: Zink, 1957.

Zinn, Grover A. "Mandala Symbolism and Use in the Mysticism of Hugh of St. Victor." *History of Religions* 12 (1973) 317-41.

———. "Personification Allegory and Visions of Light in Richard of St. Victor's Teaching on Contemplation." *University of Toronto Quarterly* 46 (1977) 190-214.

# Part Two
# THEMES AND VALUES

# 10

## The Role of Christ

### I. *Christ as Savior in the East*

JOHN MEYENDORFF

ACCORDING TO ALL THREE Synoptic Gospels, Jesus, on the way to Caesarea Philippi, a few days before the end of his messianic ministry in Jerusalem, asked his disciples a question about their belief concerning his personal identity: "Who do you say that I am?" The answer came from Peter, declaring that Jesus was "the Messiah," *ho christos* (Mark 8:29; Luke 8:20), or "the Son of the living God" (Matt 16:16). Various theological schools have given different interpretations to Peter's answer, but all agree that the entire meaning of the Christian experience depended upon it. Indeed, whatever Jesus said, whatever he did, was in virtue of his messianic ministry; whatever he experienced on the cross, whatever was the concrete reality of his resurrection—depended for its ultimate significance on his personal identity. This significance would be radically different whether he were Elijah, Jeremiah, or one of the prophets (Matt 16:14), or an angel (Jewish eschatological thought), or a passionless theophany (the Gnostics), or a creature adopted by God (Paul of Samosata), or one of the many created "intellects" who did not submit to fallenness (Origen), or whether, by meeting him, one met Yahweh himself, so that Orthodox Jews would fall to the ground hearing his name pronounced (John 18:6).

In a sense, all the doctrinal debates of Christian history can be reduced to a debate on Christ's identity. In the period between apostolic times and the high Middle Ages, various christological positions were brilliantly expressed and passionately defended. However, if one envisages the fate of the historic catholic or orthodox Christian tradition, no christological stand was as decisive, in terms of the nature of spirituality, as that of two eminent bishops of Alexandria in Egypt: Athanasius and Cyril.

231

The achievement of Athanasius (d. 373) is relatively well known. He led the struggle for the faith of Nicaea (325), which firmly proclaimed the divinity of Christ. Almost singlehandedly, he secured a Nicaean triumph. But this victory was not only doctrinal, but also spiritual. The message of Athanasius was that only God himself could properly be seen and adored as Savior. Thus, the divine identity of Jesus, equal to (or "consubstantial" with) the Father, was not a matter of abstract or purely theological truth, but it indicated the misery of fallen, "mortal" humanity—which could neither save itself nor be saved by another "creature"—and the true nature of God, who being love, performed himself the salvation of the world rather than act indirectly through created intermediaries or through an all-powerful but mechanic *fiat*. For Athanasius, salvation is a restoration of direct fellow-ship and communion between God and humanity, because anything less than such a fellowship would imply a limitation of divine love. Hence his famous definition of salvation as "deification" (*theōsis*), which became a stan-dard of Greek patristic thought.

The affirmation of Christ's divinity in Nicaean and Athanasian categories inevitably raised the question concerning the historical Jesus as man. The issue involved long debates, schisms, and the search for appropriate defini-tions at councils—Ephesus (431), Chalcedon (451), Constantinople II (553), Constantinople III (680) and Nicaea II (787). The result was a commitment to a single christological dogma in the East and in the West, although differences remained in the spiritual vision of the reality of the "life in Christ." At the center of these debates stood the figure and the teaching of Cyril of Alexandria (d. 444).

## Cyril: Christ the Emmanuel

Before Cyril of Alexandria had engaged himself in bitter theological debates with Nestorius (428-31), the basic inspiration of his understanding of the Christian mystery appeared in his serene and noncontroversial exegetical writings, particularly his *Interpretation* of the Gospel of John and his com-mentaries on other New Testament writings. Here Cyril's main concern was not to provide his readers with a rational scheme of the incarnation but to express its kerygmatic meaning: God, who "alone has immortality" (1 Tim 6:16), is the only Savior from corruption and death. This was also the cen-tral inspiration of Athanasius in his early and famous treatise *On the Incar-nation of the Word*, which he maintained in his polemics against Arius: only God can save. Similarly, Cyril, engaged in controversy, once proclaimed quite naturally, paraphrasing Isa 63:9, that "it is not an elder, nor an angel, but the Lord Himself who saved us, not by an alien death or by the media-tion of an ordinary man, but by His very own blood."[1]

This recognition of God as the agent of salvation is shown also in the repeated use of the title "Emmanuel" (which in translation means "God with us," Matt 1:23) for Christ, particularly in Cyril's famous twelve anathemas contained in his third letter to Nestorius.[2] Like Athanasius before him, Cyril could not conceive of the divine love manifested in the incarnation to be really perfect unless it was an act of *self*-giving of God. "God so loved the world that he gave his only Son" (John 3:16). This implied the personal presence of God in the human reality of Jesus of Nazareth.

The christological trend that originated in Antioch with Theodore of Mopsuestia and was most openly preached by Nestorius was based on the fear that the humanity of Jesus would be totally ignored by the proponents of "deification." This is why the controversy against Nestorius, undertaken by Cyril with such energy and consistency, was centered on the two most human moments in the Gospel story of Jesus: his birth from Mary and his death on the cross. Although Cyril always recognized that both these moments belong to divine economy in the flesh—that is, that the eternal God by nature could neither be born in history nor die—he considered that the salvation of the world would not have occurred unless it was personally the Son of God who was born of the Virgin, and also personally suffered on the cross "according to the flesh."

The whole spiritual experience reflected in Cyril's christology implies two central intuitions: (1) God, in the search for fallen humanity (see the parable of the "lost sheep"), does not stop halfway, but goes where fallen humanity is—in death itself. (2) It is not an ideal, perfect humanity that the Son of God assumes, but that humanity which bears all the consequences of sin, particularly mortality and corruptibility. Except for sin itself—a personal act of rebellion against God to which Christ, being God, remained totally foreign—he assumed all the limitations of fallenness, including suffering and death.

During the bitter christological controversies of the fifth and sixth cen-turies, the christology of Cyril was challenged from two sides:[3] (1) First, the school of Theodore of Mopsuestia, eventually condemned in the person of Nestorius, archbishop of Constantinople, not only reflected a legitimate concern for the full and free humanity of Christ but also attempted to rationalize the mystery (How could the eternal Son "be born"? How could the passionless God "suffer and die"?). It accepted as absolute the Greek Platonic philosophical category of divine changelessness (*atrepsia*), which excluded such realistic affirmations as a divine birth in time or the death of the Son of God on Golgotha. (2) Second, the Cyrillian view of Jesus Christ was also challenged by those who interpreted it in an "Apollinarian" sense. Again on the basis of Platonism, Apollinaris, bishop of Laodicea, saw Jesus as God with a human body but without a human soul: why, indeed, was there a need in him for another spiritual center besides the divine Logos? But then was he truly a man, since he was lacking a distinctively human spiritual identity? Even more sophisticated than Apollinarianism, the teaching of Julian of Halicarnassus claimed that, since death came "through sin" (Rom 5:12), the sinless humanity of Jesus could not be affected by corruptibility (Greek *phthora*) and mortality. The consequence was that the humanity of Jesus was perfect, incorruptible humanity, in the sense of not being fully like our fallen nature, and that therefore his death was not like our death.[4]

There is no doubt that Cyril used ambiguous terminology (like his formula *one nature incarnated of God the Word,* which he unknowingly borrowed from Apollinaris), but his rejection of Nestorianism was motivated not by any "anthropological minimalism" (this expression used by Georges Florovsky is, therefore, probably incorrect) but, on the contrary, by the conviction that human destiny lies in communion with God—an ultimately maximalist view of humanity. Nestorianism consisted, on the contrary, in a rationalizing sense of incompatibility between the divine and the human: the person of Christ, in which divinity and humanity met, appeared as a juxtaposition of two mutually impermeable entities. According to Nestorius, the human nature of Christ kept not only its identity but also its autonomy. Christ's birth and death were human only. Mary was mother "of Jesus," not "of God." Jesus the "Son of man" died, not "the Son of God." It was this duality, which implied a different anthropology, that Cyril rejected. On the other hand, he simply could not remain logical with himself if he adopted a doctrine similar to that of Apollinaris or Julian. It is precisely because Christ accepted existentially complete humanity—in a fallen state, from which it needed to be saved—that the divine Logos had to assume suffering and death. In order to lead it to incorruptibility through the resurrection, he first came down where fallen humanity truly was—"in the depth of the pit" (Ps 88:6)—and then cried before dying, "My God, why hast thou forsaken me" (Matt 27:46). This moment was indeed "the death of God": the assumption by God himself, in an ultimate act of love, of humanity in its state of separation from its "natural" communion with God. Christ's humanity was, therefore, neither diminished nor limited: it was humanity in its very concrete fallenness.

It is obvious that some aspects of Cyril's christology needed to be more clearly defined. The Council of Chalcedon (451) affirmed the doctrine of Christ's two natures in their distinctiveness and the doctrine of a *hypostatic* (not a "natural") union of the two natures. But in no way did it disavow Cyril: it only attempted to answer the legitimate fears of the Antiochians that Cyril had fallen into Apollinarianism. Not only does the Chalcedonian definition itself specifically ascribe the title of *Theotokos* to the Virgin Mary, but—after some hesitation in the second half of the fifth century—the Orthodox church at the Fifth Council (553) reaffirmed that the criteria of christological truth resides in Cyril *and* Chalcedon.

As we mentioned earlier, Cyrillian christology implied that divinity and humanity were compatible, but also that Christ's own particular humanity, although it was assumed with all the consequences of the fall, was deified through the cross and resurrection and thus revealed the true purpose of creation in conformity with its divine model. Christ was the New Adam because, in him, humanity and divinity were reunited again.

The christological definitions of the councils of Ephesus (431), Chalcedon (451) and Constantinople II (553)—as well as the dogma of Constantinople III (680) on the two wills of Christ— entered the common tradition of Eastern and Western Christendom. However, the West remained somewhat reluctant in the face of the doctrine of "deification." Resistance against the council of 553—and the Roman popes who accepted it—lasted until the seventh century. Even later a more analytic and more rational concern for preserving the humanity of Jesus—in a way similar to the Antiochian tradition of Theodore of Mopsuestia—remained prevalent in Western christological thought. Redemption and salvation tended to be understood as a "reconciliation" with God rather than as a restored "communion" with God. Of this trend the Anselmian theory of redemption as "satisfaction" was the ultimate result.[5]

On the level of piety and spirituality, the image of suffering Jesus—"paying off" the price of our sins—began, in the West, to replace the Byzantine vision of the incarned Logos, triumphant over death and through whose victory resurrection has become accessible as an eschatological anticipation in the body of his church.

## "Perfect God and Perfect Man"

If Athanasius and Cyril, by defending the divinity of Christ and the unity of his being, provided Christian spirituality with its essential basis, their names and their messages remained somewhat controversial even after their deaths. One of the major reasons for the bitter theological debates that followed was that zealous followers of the two great masters tended to freeze their doctrines into verbal formulas. These were accepted literally and out of the context provided by the spiritual experience of the catholic tradition and the theology of the masters themselves. The struggle of Athanasius centered on the Nicaean creed and, in particular, the Greek term *homoousios* ("consubstantial"), used in that creed to affirm the common divine "essence" or "substance" of the Father and the Son. But the same term was used by Sabellians or modalists, who interpreted "consubstantiality" as incompatible with the trinitarian revelation of God. For Sabellians, to say that the Father and the Son are of "one essence" meant that God was not three persons, but a unique essence with only three aspects or "modes" of manifestation. Thus, the Nicaean and Athanasian formulation of the Christian experience—true as it was in its opposition to Arianism—needed further terminological and conceptual elaboration. This elaboration was provided by the Cappadocian fathers with their doctrine of the three divine *hypostases*, or really distinct persons. It did not imply any disavowal of Athanasius but a more sophisticated use of Greek philosophical terms. Paradoxically, the Cappadocians— better versed than Athanasius in ancient Greek thought—were more successful than he was in showing the incompatibility between biblical trinitarianism and Greek philosophical categories. But they did so by using Greek vocabulary as a tool, changing its meaning and making it into a manageable instrument of Christian witness.

The same—actually almost identical—process took place in the fifth century after the triumph of Cyril over Nestorius. This process is connected with the famous decree of the Council of Chalcedon (451). Cyril's christology has been both kerygmatic and polemical. Eutyches—a zealous, ultra-Cyrillian ascetic— interpreted the unity of divinity and humanity of Christ to mean that humanity was so totally "deified" that it ceased to be "our" humanity. Christ was certainly "consubstantial" with the Father, but not "with us." His humanity was absorbed by God. Eutyches was formally faithful to the christology of Cyril, but in fact he was depriving it of its meaning for human salvation: God, according to Eutyches, was not sharing human destiny—human birth, human suffering, human death itself—but, while remaining absolute, changeless, and transcendent, was absorbing that human identity which he had originally created. Was he then still the God of love?

The Council of Chalcedon came as a reaction against Eutychianism. But its definition of Christ was a rather elaborate formula which resulted from long debates and was intended to satisfy the different existing terminological traditions: the Alexandrian, the Antiochene, and the Latin. The latter expressed itself in the powerful intervention of Pope Leo the Great in his letter to Flavian of Constantinople. In this famous text, the pope, using a terminology inherited from Tertullian and Augustine, carefully established the integrity of the two natures (*naturae*) of Christ, and insisted that this integrity requires that each nature preserve fully its characteristics. The resulting Chalcedonian text is the following:

> Following the holy Fathers, we all with one voice confess our Lord Jesus Christ <u>one and the same Son, the same</u> perfect in Godhead, <u>the same</u> *perfect in humanity,* truly God and truly man, <u>the same</u> consisting of a reasonable soul and a body, of one substance with the Father as touching the Godhead, <u>the same</u> *of one substance with us as touching humanity, like us in all things apart from sin;* begotten of the Father before the ages as touching the Godhead, <u>the same</u> in the last days, for us and for our salvation, born from the Virgin Mary, <u>the Theotokos</u>, as touching humanity, <u>one and the same</u> Christ, Son, Lord Only-begotten, to be acknowledged *in two natures without confusion,* without change, <u>without division</u>, without separation; *the distinction of natures being in no way abolished because of the union, but rather the characteristic property of each nature being preserved,* and <u>concurring in one person, or hypostasis,</u> not as if Christ were parted or divided into two persons, but <u>one and the same Son</u> and Only-begotten God, Word, Lord, Jesus Christ; even as the prophets from the beginning spoke concerning him, and our Lord Jesus Christ instructed us, and the Creed of the Fathers [i.e., of Nicaea] was handed down to us.

In this famous text, for the convenience of the reader, the clearly Cyrillian passages are underlined, and the sentences inspired either by the Antiochenes or Pope Leo are in italics. On the Cyrillian side, particularly noteworthy is the repetition of the pronoun "the same" (*ho autos*) eight times (excluding the Nestorian "duality" between the Son of God and the son of Mary) and the use of the title *Theotokos*. On the Antiochene-Latin side is the insistence on the integrity of *each* nature, each keeping its respective properties within the union. The formula is clearly a "committee document," lacking the straightforward, kerygmatic and soteriological fire of earlier Cyrillian statements. But it reflects a "catholic," charitable—we would say today "ecumenical"—concern for possible objections from either side of the debate.

Can it be said that the Council of Chalcedon solved the christological problem? Certainly not. Like all balanced, conceptual formulas, it solved certain problems but created new ones. Actually, the fathers of Chalcedon were conscious of this limited character of all doctrinal definitions, including their own. Not only did they deny any novelty on their part and insist that their only intention was to follow the fathers and the prophets; they also formally declared their inability to exhaust the meaning of the mystery in a verbal form. This is the significance of the famous four negative adverbs included in the definition: "without confusion, without change, without division, without separation."

In spite of this declared humility of the Chalcedonian fathers, objections to their terminology were voiced immediately. Indeed, on the one hand, by declaring that Christ was to be seen "in two natures," they were using the word "nature" in a more abstract sense than Cyril did, for whom "nature" designated a concrete reality and was synonymous with hypostasis. On the other hand, by designating the union as "a concurrence" into one person, or hypostasis, they were not making it quite plain that this hypostasis was the preexisting hypostasis of the Son of God (although their Cyrillian expressions hinted in that direction). Finally, Chalcedonian theologians would always be at pains to try to explain how, according to the Cappadocian fathers, God was still one God, although in him there were three hypostases and one nature, whereas according to Chalcedon Christ was one hypostasis but in *two* natures.

These terminological problems clearly show that it is wrong to consider Chalcedon a kind of ultimate finale of the christological debates. Not only was it widely opposed by large Eastern Christian communities, which still exist today and are labeled (perhaps inaccurately) Monophysites (Copts, Armenians, Ethiopians, Syrian Jacobites); but the formal and conceptual terminology used in the definition could not pretend to fulfill any function other than that of a warning or a signpost. In the experience of a deified humanity, proclaimed by Athanasius and Cyril, the authentic, created, human nature and its properties do not disappear but, in a new communion with the divine, are fulfilling their real purpose, given to them at creation.

We have seen earlier that a certain tradition of interpreting Chalcedon as a factual disavowal of Cyril has existed in the West. In the East, on the contrary, Christian orthodoxy remained quite definitely Cyrillian. Furthermore, the implications of the Chalcedonian statement about "the preservation of the properties of each nature" were not always fully recognized in the East. For instance, many Byzantine spiritual authors explain such passages as Luke 2:52 ("Jesus progressed in wisdom and maturity") as some pedagogical tactic on the part of Christ rather than as a real change from ignorance to knowledge, from childhood to human adulthood. For them, Christ's divinity implied omniscience, and his humanity was modified accordingly. But was it then concretely identical with our humanity? This reluctance to admit human ignorance in Christ may have Hellenistic-Evagrian roots, which equated "ignorance" with "sinfulness," and may therefore be anthropologically, and not christologically, motivated. Other Byzantine theologians had no difficulty admitting human "ignorance" in Christ. Their opposition to "aphthartodocetism" also indicates a perception—both biblical and Chalcedonian—that Christ's humanity was, indeed, very similar to ours in every way except sin.[6]

The fullness of humanity in Christ will also be further defined in the theological synthesis of Maximus the Confessor and his doctrine of the "two wills," as well as in the affirmation during the period of iconoclasm of Christ's "depictability." The christological debates around Chalcedon—just like the trinitarian controversies of the fourth century—illustrate the limitations (actually recognized by the fathers of the church) inherent in doctrinal definitions and other conceptual formulas.

## Christ and Mary

In 431 the Council of Ephesus, which marked the first and decisive victory of Cyrillian christology over Nestorianism, expressed itself in a single doctrinal decision: the Mother of Jesus is to be properly designated in the prayers of the church, in preaching, and in theological dissertations as "Bearer of God" (*Theotokos*), or "Mother of God" (*mēter theou*). The decision was concerned with christology: it affirmed the personal identity of Christ as the preexisting and eternal Son of God assuming human nature (not simply a single human individual). Since a mother is necessarily the mother of somebody (not of a "nature") and since this "somebody" in Christ was God, her proper identity was indeed "Mother of God."

It was inevitable that the christological decision of Ephesus would also add a decisive new emphasis to Christian spirituality: a renewed veneration of Mary—the woman through whom the incarnation occurred; the one human person who, by free concurrence with the greatest act of God's love, made the union of divinity and humanity possible.

Actually, the attribution of the title of *Theotokos* was the only doctrinal decision taken by the church concerning Mary. However, the New Testament, particularly Luke, had already proclaimed her eminent position in the "economy" of salvation ("henceforth all generations will call me blessed," Luke 1:48), and, since Irenaeus and Justin, the theologians had discerned her role as the New Eve. Indeed, as Eve in paradise had freely accepted the offer of the serpent and led Adam to fall, so Mary freely accepted the archangel's announcement, making possible a new "recapitulation" of humanity in the New Adam, Christ. Preachers, poets, artists, and hymnographers, using not only direct theological language but also biblical symbols and analogies, glorified her as "the earth unsown," the "burning bush," a "bridge leading to heaven," "the ladder which Jacob saw," etc. Innumerable churches were dedicated to her and icons of her became the most prominent *palladia* of popular piety, especially in the East.

The very emotionalism and exuberance of Marian piety were undoubtedly expressing a spiritual discovery of the human side of the incarnation mystery. The role of that simple woman, who conceived in her womb the new life (her virginity was a sign of this "newness"), was a reminder of the humanity of Jesus himself, and it gave in a new form the message that free fellowship and communion with God were the true expressions of authentic human nature. One of the biblical analogies of this fellowship—that of the family—was fulfilled in the particular role of Mary, as the mother not only of Christ but of all the members of his Body, the church.

It is important to note, however, that the piety and theology of the early church never tended to separate the veneration of Mary from its christological context. There was no doctrinal definition of her position except that of her divine motherhood. Her exaltation, after Ephesus, did not mean that her belonging to fallen humanity was forgotten. Well-known passages by John Chrysostom, by far the most popular and authoritative father of the Greek church, continued to be read and copied. Commenting on such passages as Matt 12:46–49 ("Who is my mother, and who are my brothers?") or John 2:4, Chrysostom frankly recognized Mary's human failings and imperfections.[7] The mother of Jesus was therefore seen, within the mystery of salvation, as the representative of humanity in need of salvation. But, within humankind, she was the closest to the Savior and the worthiest receptacle of the new life.[8]

In the medieval West, the Augustinian understanding of original sin as inherited guilt made it inevitable that Mary be approached in terms of an "immaculate conception," as the object of a special grace of God that made her in advance worthy of divine motherhood. The East did not follow that trend, because the consequences of the sin of Adam were seen as inherited mortality rather than as guilt, so that there was no need to see Mary in isolation from the common lot of fallen humanity. However, there developed in the East the tradition of her eschatological glorification after death. Anticipating the general resurrection, her Son made her, as his mother, inseparable from his own risen body, above the angelic powers themselves.

## Christ and the Holy Spirit: The Synthesis of Maximus the Confessor

The place of Maximus the Confessor (ca. 580–662) in the history of Christian doctrine is primarily associated with his defense of Chalcedonian orthodoxy against Monotheletism (the belief that Christ had only one divine-human "will"). Indeed, for Maximus, real humanity is dynamic, creative, and endowed with a proper "energy": this was, indeed, the case with the humanity of Christ, who, being a man, possessed a human will distinct from the divine. This human will of Christ was restored in conformity with the original and eternal purpose of God, established before the fall. In monotheletism, the humanity of Christ, although accessible to "contempla-tion" (*en theōria*), did not possess any "movement" or energy proper to itself, and the Chalcedonian definition, which affirmed that "the characteristic property of each nature of Christ was preserved" in the hypostatic union, had lost its meaning. The merit of Maximus was, therefore, in having deci-sively counteracted a "monophysitic" trend which interpreted "deification" as an absorption of humanity into divinity. For Maximus, deification was to be seen not as a denial but as a reaffirmation and restoration of created humanity in its proper and God-established integrity.

However, Maximus at no point of his system was renouncing the essential message of Cyrillian christology. God became human, he always affirmed, so that

> whole people might participate in the whole God (*theos holos holois metecho-menos*), and that in the same way in which the soul and the body are united, God would become partakable of by the soul, and, through the soul's inter-mediary, by the body, in order that the soul might receive an unchanging character (*tēn atrepsian*) and the body, immortality; and finally, that the whole human being would become God, deified by the grace of God become man—whole man, soul and body, by nature—and becoming whole God, soul and body, by grace. (*Ambigua* (PG 91, col. 1088C]

As we have seen in the case of Cyril, the union between the "whole" God and the "whole" human being did not imply, for Maximus, any absorption of humanity or any lessening of the properly human, created energy and potential, but a fulfillment of the human being, because this union is a meeting of the living God and the creature in a communion of love—not a merger or confusion of impersonal essences.

This doctrine of deification, as understood by Athanasius, the Cappa-docian fathers, Cyril, or, finally, Maximus, is not based on a limited or narrow understanding of christology. It reflects the trinitarian "economy of salvation," and particularly the economy of the Spirit. What the role of the Holy Spirit in the mystery reveals is that deification "in Christ" is necessarily the result of a freely accepted new birth in the Spirit. According to Maxi-mus, Jesus himself has taken this choice in his humanity. Of course, the doctrine of hypostatic union implies that the subject of the choice was still the Logos, not a separate human individual named Jesus, but the choice was "human." Having reminded his readers that, according to the Genesis account, the man was first formed from clay in his physical reality and that afterwards God breathed the Spirit into him, Maximus recalls the birth of Christ in Bethlehem and then the descent of the Spirit at his baptism by John. Both of these two births were assumed by Christ. "The Incarnation," Maximus writes, "took first the form of a bodily birth because of my condemnation, but it was then accompanied by a birth, which had been neglected [by fallen humanity] in the Spirit at baptism, so that I may be saved by grace, so that I may be recalled, or, more clearly, so that I may be created again" (*Ambigua* [*PG* 91, col. 1348D]).

Free human decision and free conversion, sealed by the Spirit at baptism, are therefore the conditions of a synergy between human freedom and divine grace, which makes deification possible through the sharing of that humanity which, in Christ, was assumed by the Logos, deified, and made present in the church through the Eucharist. That encounter and that sharing are effected by the Spirit—the Spirit which came upon Mary (Luke 1:35), which descended upon Christ in the Jordan, which was sent by Christ upon his disciples after the resurrection, which is invoked by the church in the eucharistic mystery, and which effects the equally mysterious encounter between God and each human soul. Thus, "through His flesh," writes Maximus, "the Son has manifested the Father whom humanity ignored, and through the Spirit He led to the Father those whom He had reconciled with Himself."[9]

In Christ, the two natures—divine and human—were united into the single personal existence of the incarned Son of God. Both were dynamic realities, expressed in the two wills or energies of Christ. But theirs was not a simple juxtaposition or an alliance between concurring wills (as conceived in Nestorianism), but a communion, in which there was a "communication of properties" (*communicatio idiomatum, perichōrēsis tōn idiōmatōn*), a penetration of divine energy into humanity with the free acceptance of deification by Christ's human will, effected through the Spirit.[10] And it is the same Spirit that effects the union of those who freely choose to be "in Christ" with the deified humanity of the New Adam.

## Christ's Humanity:
## The Meaning of Icons

The central message of the Alexandrian theology of Athanasius and Cyril had been that the salvation of the world is not being accomplished by any created mediation, but by the Son of God, who makes himself accessible to human beings, sharing his own life with them by assuming humanity in his personal existence as a human being. In this perspective, however, theological consistency and spiritual experience require that Christ be fully human, for, indeed, to use the celebrated phrase of Gregory of Nazianzus, "what is not assumed is not healed, and what is united to God is saved."[11] Salvation understood as communion with God, or deification, implies that the fullness of humanity—not a part of it—be the object of God's love, and Maximus described that fullness as including specifically the "movement" or dynamism of created humanity: human will, human freedom and human creativity. All these were assumed by the person of the incarned Logos and became part, through his death and resurrection, of his eschatological new creation.

The last and, perhaps, the most decisive episode in the debates concerning the identity of Christ came with the so-called iconoclastic crisis in the Byzantine world (715-843). Quoting Old Testament prohibitions against graven images and idolatry, the iconoclasts objected to images of Christ: since he was God, his image was also, necessarily, an image of God and, therefore, an idol. Against this position orthodox theologians—John of Damascus, Theodore of Studios, Patriarch Nicephoros—affirmed the reality of Christ's humanity, which was historical and therefore "representable," "circumscribable," and seen with human eyes. However, since Christ's personal identity is that of the Son of God, an image of Christ is an image of God, who makes himself visible as man. "In former times," wrote John of Damascus, "God, who is without form or body, could never be depicted. But now [i.e., after the incarnation] when God is seen in the flesh conversing with men (Baruch 3:38 [English 3:37]), I make an image of the God whom I see. I do not worship matter; I worship the Creator of matter, who became matter for my sake, who willed to take His abode in matter; who, through matter, worked out my salvation."[12]

Thus, an icon of Christ became a complete christological confession of faith, presented visually—a mystery of salvation and communion that words can express only partially. In the Byzantine tradition, the intention of the artist was to represent the personal identity of the incarned God (hence the Greek letters in the nimbus, *ho ōn*, "the One-who-is," the Septuagint version of YHWH, the name of God),[13] but always under the historical traits of Jesus of Nazareth. So, to use the words of a sermon of John of Damascus on the Feast of Transfiguration, "the things human become those of God, and the divine those of man, by the mode of mutual communication, and the interpenetration without confusion of the one into the other, and of the extreme union according to the hypostasis [or "person"]. For He is one God—He who is eternally God, and who later became man."[14]

## Redemption: The Body of Christ, Head and Members

Central to the christology endorsed by the early councils was the vision of Christ as both the eternal Logos and the "New Adam," who restored the unity of the whole humanity with himself as the divine model according to whose image human beings were created in the beginning. However, as we have seen earlier, this restoration could not be automatic or magical: it required free human response to the Spirit and the cooperation (*synergia*) of each human person and a "gathering" of free believers within the assembly of the church. The "whole Christ" (*totus Christus,* according to Augustine) was manifested where two or three were gathered in his name (Matt 18:20) and where, therefore, the Pauline image of the Body could be concretely present. Indeed, that "Body" is the church realized most fully in the Eucharist.

Participation in the Eucharist was defined in christological terms: it was a participation in the resurrected and glorified humanity of Christ, assumed in the hypostasis (or "person") of the Son of God and—in virtue of the "communication of idioms" between the two natures—penetrated with divine life, or "energies," or "grace." Since, in Christ, there was no confusion of essences or natures, neither were "those in Christ" partaking of the "essence" of God, but of his human nature. John of Damascus wrote:

> Men do share in and become partakers of the divine nature, as many of them as receive the holy body of Christ and drink His blood; for the body and blood of Christ are hypostatically united to the divinity, and in the body of Christ with which we are in communion, there are two natures inseparably united in the hypostasis. We thus partake of both natures—of the body, corporally, and of the divinity, spiritually, or rather with both in both ways—without there being any identification between our hypostasis and that of Christ, for we first receive [our] hypostasis within the order of creation, then we enter into union by the mingling of the body and blood.[15]

Being "in Christ," therefore, does not involve personal or "hypostatic" identification with the Logos, because the person is that which is always unique. It involves a sharing, through the power of the Spirit, in Christ's glorified humanity—a humanity that remains fully human even after its glorification. In debates with iconoclasts, who claimed that Christ, deified in his resurrection, had become "indescribable" and therefore denounced the possibility of making images of him, Theodore of Studios objected: "If Christ were uncircumscribed after His resurrection, we also, who are one body with Him (cf. Eph 3:6), would have to be uncircumscribed."[16]

The iconoclastic controversy directly involved not only the doctrine of the incarnation and, in general, human relations with God but also and particularly the eucharistic doctrine. The iconoclasts—and more precisely, Emperor Constantine V—affirmed the Eucharist to be the only legitimate and biblically established *image* of God. For their orthodox adversaries, as we just have learned from Theodore of Studios, the Eucharist was, on the contrary, a true and real identification of the faithful with the risen Lord—not simply a vision of his image. In the theological and christological categories developed by the orthodox spokesmen of the iconoclastic period, the Eucharist was never the object of a vision: only the icons were to be seen. It is this general conception of the eucharistic assembly that justified the extraordinary development of the *iconostasis*—the system of icons covering the screen that separates the sanctuary from the nave of a Byzantine church. The eucharistic mystery performed behind it is not an object of visual contemplation but a meal, eventually distributed to the faithful, who otherwise communicate with God by contemplating and venerating icons.[17]

On this point Eastern eucharistic piety stands in vivid contrast to the late medieval Latin practice of the veneration of the Host, an expression, on the level of spirituality, of the doctrine of transubstantiation. In the East, no philosophical terminology was applied specifically to the eucharistic mystery, which was not considered in isolation from the christological facts: the transfiguration of the body of Christ, the "change" which occurred in it after the resurrection and which, through the power of the Spirit, is also at work in the entire body of the baptized faithful, that is, in the "total" Christ. Thus, to designate the Eucharist, the theologians used terms found in the ancient liturgical texts, such as *metabolē* ("change"), *metarrythmēsis* ("change of order"), *metastoicheiōsis* ("trans-elementation"), *metamorphōsis* ("transfiguration"). The language is always tentative, imprecise, and applicable not only to the eucharistic elements as such but also to paschal and eschatological notions, which reflect salvation in Christ of the entire people of God. "We confess," writes Patriarch Nicephorus (early ninth century) "that by the priest's invocation, by the coming of the Most Holy Spirit, the body and blood of Christ are mystically and invisibly made present . . . not because the body ceases to be a body, but because it remains so and is preserved as body."[18]

Perhaps more important than any speculative argument devised by theologians, the liturgical tradition has preserved the same christological and ecclesial dimension of the Body, manifested in the Eucharist. The eucharistic prayers or canons used in the various local traditions of the East or the West have several common features determined by that single vision. First, they are prayers of the community, formulated in the first person plural, so that communion with Christ is not a matter of individual piety but of joining together within his single Body. Second, they are addressed to the Father, by an assembly of baptized persons who, in virtue of their baptism are already "in Christ." The unbaptized catechumens, the excommunicated, and the penitents are not joining in the prayer. It is clear, therefore, that the prayer is being answered precisely because it is Christ himself, in the assembly and through the assembly, who offers it to his Father, whereas the members of the community are, through the power of the Spirit, his adopted children "in Christ" and, corporately, the "royal priesthood." In them and through them Christ offers the sacrifice. He is "the one who offers, and is offered, who receives and is received" (Byzantine liturgies of Basil and John Chrysostom), but they are inseparable from him: "For as many of you as were baptized into Christ have put on Christ," and "God has sent the Spirit of his Son into our hearts crying, 'Abba! Father!'" (Gal 3:27; 4:6). Third, in the Eastern eucharistic canons, the invocation of the Spirit (*epiklēsis*) is not an invocation on the bread and wine only—as if they were "elements" to be transformed somewhat independently of the gathered community—but on the assembly *and* the elements:

> We ask Thee, and pray Thee, and supplicate Thee: Send down Thy Holy Spirit upon us and upon these gifts here offered, and make this Bread the precious Body of Thy Christ, and that which is in this Cup, the precious Blood of Thy Christ, making the change by Thy Holy Spirit, so that they may be to those who partake for the purification of soul, for the communion of Thy Holy Spirit, for the fulfillment of the Kingdom of Heaven. (Liturgy of St. John Chrysostom)

In christological terms the eucharistic action implies that the Son of God, who assumed human nature hypostatically, brings that nature to his Father in a sacrifice, offered once for all, and that those who have received the same glorified nature by adoption (*thesei*) or by grace (*chariti*), are joining that one High Priest, through the power of the Spirit who anointed him as Christ. That same Spirit anoints all the faithful within the communion of the Body of Christ, which they have joined through personal acts of faith.

The approach to christology that was based on the notions of communion between divinity and humanity, of "deification," of "communication of idioms" between the two natures of Christ implied an interpretation of redemption within a context broader than the juridical images used by Paul in Romans. These Pauline images, conceived within the framework of a Christian reading of rabbinic law, were given a philosophical and metaphysical dimension in Western scholasticism, so that salvation began to be interpreted in terms of vicarious atonement: the sacrifice of Christ on the cross, because he was God, was sufficient before God's justice to atone for the sins of all humans. In this view, God and creation remain naturally external to one another and the work of Christ is seen as a satisfaction of an abstract notion of divine justice. In the East, symptomatically, during debates on the meaning of redemption, a series of councils meeting in Constantinople in 1156–1157, approved the approach of Nicholas of Methone (rejecting that of Soterichos Panteugenos) to the notion of sacrifice. According to Nicholas, redemption should not be conceived as an "exchange" (*antallagē* or *antallagma*), but as a "reconciliation" (*katallagē*) and an act of divine forgiveness. God, Nicholas wrote, "did not have to receive anything from us. . . . we did not go to Him [to make an offering] but He condescended toward us and assumed our nature, not as a condition of reconciliation, but in order to meet us openly in the flesh."[19]

This doctrine of salvation through deification could have been identified as a Neoplatonic conception of "merger" between God and creation, if there was not, at its very center, the strong "theopaschite" affirmation, defended by Cyril of Alexandria: "The Son of God suffered in the flesh." This implies that, far from being a metaphysical "merger," salvation was a tragedy of love, including the assumption of the cross by God himself. But, at the same time, it is clear that Golgotha is not simply *the* price, which by itself repays an offended divine justice, but only the ultimate point of God's identification with fallen humanity, which is followed by the resurrection and is a part of the entire economy or plan of salvation. Thus the Byzantine *Synodikon of Orthodoxy*—a solemn annual doctrinal proclamation—affirms (in connection with the same twelfth century christological debates) that Christ "reconciled us to Himself by means of *the whole mystery of the economy,* and by Himself and in Himself, reconciled us also to His God and Father and, of course, to the most holy and life-giving Spirit."[20] "Christ's sacrifice—and the redemption brought by Him—is truly unique because it is not an isolated action but the culminating point of an 'economy' that includes the Old Testament preparation, the incarnation, the death, the resurrection and presence of the Holy Spirit in the Church."[21]

Although offered freely to all, the new life brought into the world by the New Adam must be freely received through personal conversion and appropriated through personal ascetical effort. The insistence upon this personal dimension of the Christian experience, which is general in Eastern monastic literature, has provoked accusation of "Pelagianism" or "semi-Pelagianism" on the part of representatives of Western spirituality, dominated by the Augustinian doctrine of grace. Be that as it may, the idea of *synergy* between divine grace and human freedom explains the authority—moral and spiritual— attributed in the Christian East to ascetics and saints who personally experience the kingdom of God.[22] Thus, in the eleventh century, Symeon the New Theologian stood up as the real prophet of this christocentric and pneumatocentric experience of God by each true Christian, available now, as it was in the time of the apostles, in the mystery of the church. Criticizing the monks of his community who were refusing to follow him in seeking this direct experience, Symeon wrote:

There are those whom I call heretics: those who say that there is no one in our time in our midst who would observe the commandments of the Gospel and become like the Holy Fathers . . . [and] those who pretend that this is impossible. These people have not fallen into some particular heresy, but into all the heresies at once, since this one is worse than all in its impiety ... Whoever speaks in this way destroys all the divine scriptures. These anti-Christs affirm: This is impossible, impossible.[23]

The message of Symeon goes beyond the issue of charismatic "leadership" in the church, which—in his view and in the view of many other monastic personalities—performs a prophetic ministry side by side with the institutional hierarchy. It affirms that a direct experience of the Spirit is open to all Christians, as a sign of the authenticity of their faith. The extreme forms of that trend led to sectarian Messalianism, which denied altogether the necessity of baptism, of the sacraments, and of the hierarchy, and considered individual "pure prayer" as the only true means of communion with God. The Orthodox ascetic and spiritual tradition counteracted this individualistic charismatic movement by identifying the "pure prayer" of the monks as "Jesus prayer," based on the constant remembrance of that divine Name, which, in the Old Testament, was considered unpronounceable and which now has been revealed in the person of the historical Jesus.

This return to history, to the New Testament revelation on the level of spirituality, implied that the ascetical and "experiential" trend of Eastern Christendom was defining itself within the christological framework of the fathers and the councils.

The patristic and conciliar tradition of the identity of Jesus Christ was inherited by the church, both East and West, from the first nine centuries of Christian history. It was still an open tradition, which represented problems if one required more analytical understanding of exegetical issues concerned with the human psychology of the historical Jesus, or if one's mind was dominated by the Augustinian distinction between "nature" and "grace." These problems would have probably seemed unreal to theologians of the patristic period, for whom christological thought did not consist so much in analyzing the mystery of the hypostatic union (which, being unique, lends no grounds for analysis or comparisons) as simply in showing human beings a way to overcome death through communion with the risen one. Their existentially limited approach to christology was not necessarily a weakness: indeed, the kerygmatic and soteriological christology of the fathers was actually closer to open-ended accounts found in the New Testament than is some of the modern analytic exegesis, which claims to restore the meaning of scriptural "originals."

The "openness" of the patristic tradition of christology consisted not only in the fact that some problems remained unresolved but also in the availability of potential avenues for constructive thought. The conception, so characteristic of Maximus the Confessor, of a dynamic human nature, which, in order to be fully human, is called to perfect itself creatively and in conformity with a divine purpose, is expressed in the doctrine of a distinctly human will in Christ. This christology of Maximus provides created human life with a spiritual foundation and a meaning, which Christians are called to assume fully, since the divine Logos himself assumed it and died in the flesh for its salvation. Furthermore, during the period of iconoclasm, Orthodox theologians defended the human "describability" of Christ and, by the same token, succeeded in showing that divine presence not only is realized in words of teaching and preaching or in the sacramental mystery but also is manifested in works of art. The consequences of this witness for the validity of human culture are indeed invaluable.

Even if the traditions of theology and spirituality tended to bifurcate in the East and in the West during the second millennium of Christian history, they have preserved, consciously or not, the common Athanasian, Cyrillian, Chalcedonian, Maximian, and "iconodulic" past. This common spiritual foundation is the major hope for a future reintegration.

## Notes

1. Cyril of Alexandria, *Le Christ est un: Deux dialogues christologiques,* ed. G. M. de Durand (Sources chrétiennes 97; Paris: Cerf, 1964) 472. See the remark of A. Grillmeier: "Nestorius lets himself be guided by concepts and proceeds by way of meandering and repetitious *analyses.* Cyril is possessed by an *intuition* which rests on John 1:14 and the Nicene creed" (*Christ in Christian Tradition,* 365).

2. *Acta Conciliorum Oecumenicorum,* ed. E. Schwartz (Berlin and Leipzig: de Gruyter, 1914) I, 1, 1, p. 41.

3. On the christological controversies, see particularly Grillmeier, *Christ in Christian Tradition;* J. Pelikan, *The Emergence of the Catholic Tradition (100–600);* and J. Meyendorff, *Christ in Eastern Christian Thought.*

4. On Julian, see particularly R. Draguet, *Julien d'Halicarnasse et sa controverse avec Sévère d'Antioche sur l'incorruptibilité du corps du Christ;* see also Meyendorff, *Christ in Eastern Christian Thought,* 87–89. A certain resurgence in Julian's doctrine of ancient "docetic" views (which considered Christ's death an "appearance" or show [Greek *dokeō*]), explains the use of the term *aphthartodocetism* to designate his doctrine.

5. The trend persists among Western theologians of the modern period. Even if they are not particularly sympathetic to the Anselmian view, the christology of Antioch seems to them more respectful than Cyrillianism of the "autonomy of the secular"; see, for instance, the works of J. F. Bethune-Baker, *Nestorius and His Teaching* (Cambridge: Cambridge University Press, 1908); and C. Moeller, "Le Chalcédonisme et le Néo-Chalcédonisme," in *Das Konzil von Chalkedon,* ed. A. Grillmeier and H. Bacht, 637–720. Others, however, adopt a more understanding attitude toward the Alexandrian and Cyrillian view (see particularly the works of T. Torrance, L. Bouyer, and J. Pelikan).

6. For a discussion of this important issue, see Meyendorff, *Christ in Eastern Christian Thought,* 86–89.

7. See *Homily 44 on Matthew* (*PG* 57, cols. 464-65); *Homily 21 on John* (*PG* 59, col. 128).

8. A Byzantine Christmas hymn (which probably goes back to the eighth century) honors the Virgin Mary as "our offering" to Christ, paralleling the offering of the Magi and the shepherds. It is noteworthy, on the other hand, that the eucharistic canon known as that of St. John Chrysostom, which is used daily in the Byzantine tradition, lists Mary as the first *for whom* the eucharistic intercessions are offered.

9. *On the Lord's Prayer* (*PG* 90, col. 876B). On this point in Maximus, see particularly A. Riou, *Le monde et l'église selon Maxime le Confesseur* (Paris: Beauchesne, 1973); and F. Heinzer, "L'explication trinitaire de l'economie chez Maxime le Confesseur," in *Maximus Confessor: Actes du Symposium sur Maxime le Confesseur, Fribourg, 1-5 Septembre 1980,* ed. F. Heinzer and Christoph Schönborn (Fribourg: Editions Universitaires, 1982) 159-72. On the theology of deification in Maximus, the best general study is L. Thunberg, *Microcosm and Mediator.*

10. The essential but difficult issue of the relationship between "natural" will and "gnomic" will in Christ is not discussed here (see Meyendorff, *Christ in Eastern Christian Thought,* 147-51).

11. *Ep. 101 to Cledonius* (*PG* 37, cols. 181C-184A).

12. *On the Holy Images* 1 (*PG* 94, col. 1245A). English translation by D. Anderson (Crestwood, NY: St. Vladimir's Seminary Press, 1980) 23. On the debate around iconoclasm and its christological implications, see Meyendorff, *Christ in Eastern Christian Thought,* 173-92.

13. See the comments of Theodore of Studios on the meaning of the inscription (*Letter to Naucratius* 2.67 [*PG* 99, col. 1296AB]; *On the Holy Images* 3 [*PG* 100, col. 420D]).

14. *On the Transfiguration* 2 (*PG* 96, cols. 548C-549A).

15. *On the Holy Images* 3 (*PG* 94, col. 1348AB); trans. D. Anderson (modified), p. 81.

16. *On the Images* 2 (*PG* 99, col. 385B).

17. On this theology of the iconostasis, see L. Ouspensky, "The problem of the iconostasis," *St. Vladimir's Theological Quarterly* 8 (1964) 186-218.

18. *Contra Eusebium,* ed. J. B. Pitra. *Spicilegium Solesmense* (Paris, 1852-58; reprint, Berlin: Akademie-Verlag, 1963) 1:440, 447D.

19. *Treatise against Soterichos,* ed. A. Demetrakopoulos (*Ekklēsiastikē Bibliothēkē;* Leipzig, 1866; reprint, Hildesheim: Olms, 1965) 337-38.

20. The text of the *Synodikon* is printed in the liturgical book known as the *Triodion,* which contains the offices of the lenten period. For a critical and interpretative edition, see J. Gouillard, "Le Synodikon de l'Orthodoxie" in *Travaux et Mémoires* (Paris: Editions de Boccard, 1967) 2:74.

21. See Meyendorff, *Christ in Eastern Christian Thought,* 199.

22. On the importance of this trend, see the article in this volume by J. Gribomont, "Monasticism and Asceticism I. Eastern Christianity."

23. Syméon le Nouveau Théologien, *Catechesis,* ed. B. Krivocheine (Sources chrétiennes 96; Paris: Cerf, 1963) 421-24. Very popular throughout the Byzantine Middle Ages, the writings of Symeon have only recently become fully available in a critical edition and French translation in the Sources chrétiennes series. English translations gradually become available also; see particularly *Hymns of Divine Love,* trans. G. Maloney, S.J. (Denville, NJ: Dimension Books, 1975); and *The Discourses,* trans. C. J. de Cantazaro (New York: Paulist Press, 1980).

# Bibliography

## Studies

Bouyer, Louis. *The Spirituality of the New Testament and the Fathers.* Vol. 1 of *A History of Christian Spirituality.* New York: Seabury, 1982.

Burghardt, Walter J. *The Image of God in Man according to Cyril of Alexandria.* Woodstock, MD: Woodstock College Press; Washington, DC: Catholic University Press, 1957.

Draguet, René. *Julien d'Halicarnasse et sa controverse avec Sévère d'Antioche sur l'incorruptibilité du corps du Christ.* Louvain: Smeesters, 1924.

Grillmeier, Aloys. *Christ in Christian Tradition: From the Apostolic Age to Chalcedon (451).* Trans. J. S. Bowden. New York: Sheed & Ward, 1965.

———, and Heinrich Bacht, eds. *Das Konzil von Chalkedon: Geschichte und Gegenwart.* 3 vols. Würzburg: Echter-Verlag, 1951–54.

Kelly, J. N. D. *Early Christian Doctrines.* New York: Harper & Row, 1958.

Meyendorff, John. *Christ in Eastern Christian Thought.* Washington, DC: Corpus Books, 1969. Reprinted, Crestwood, NY: St. Vladimir's Seminary Press, 1975.

———. *Byzantine Theology: Historical Trends and Doctrinal Themes.* New York: Fordham University Press, 1974. Second printing with revisions, 1983.

Norris, Richard Alfred. *Manhood and Christ: A Study in the Christology of Theodore of Mopsuestia.* Oxford: Oxford University Press, 1963.

Pelikan, Jaroslav. *The Christian Tradition: A History of the Development of Doctrine.* Vol. 1, *The Emergence of the Catholic Tradition (100–600).* Vol. 2, *The Spirit of Eastern Christendom (600–1700).* Chicago: University of Chicago Press, 1971, 1974.

Thunberg, Lars. *Microcosm and Mediator: The Theological Anthropology of Maximus the Confessor.* Acta Seminarii Neotestamentici Upsaliensis 25. Lund: Gleerup; Copenhagen: Munksgaard, 1965.

17. *Baptism of Christ*, Monastery Church at Daphne, 11th century

18. *Descent from the Cross* by Benedetto Antelami, Parma Cathedral, 12th century (central detail)

# II. *Christ as Savior in the West*

### BERNARD MCGINN

MEDIEVAL LATIN CHRISTIANITY'S BELIEFS concerning the person and work of Christ the redeemer were fundamentally shaped by the patristic heritage sketched so well above by John Meyendorff. Although the great christological debates were primarily an Eastern affair, Latin participation in witnessing to the faith of the undivided church was of great importance in such cases as Pope Leo I's intervention at Chalcedon, Western support for Maximus the Confessor during the Monothelite controversy, or papal encouragement of the iconodule monks who fled the East in the eighth century. Nevertheless, the ways in which Latin Christianity appropriated and expressed the common faith gave special nuances to the place of Christ in Western spirituality. Although a number of the essays presented in this volume touch on some aspects of these Western attitudes to the person and saving work of Christ,[1] it seems appropriate to add this appendix as a brief summary of this crucial element in the Christian spirituality of the West.

The central issue of belief and practice in both Eastern and Western Christianity during this whole period was not the question of God but the question of salvation—not "Is there a God?" but "How are we to be saved?" Jesus the Christ, God's anointed one, brought humanity not only the message of salvation but its very reality in his person and in his life, death, and resurrection. Debate and definition about the constitution of Jesus as the incarnate God-man were never pursued for purely speculative reasons but always because of the connection with the essential issue of redemption. In looking at Latin Christian attitudes toward Jesus as redeemer we can best see the distinctive traits of Western christological spirituality.

We can use a famous text from Bernard of Clairvaux's *Letter against Abelard* as a way of setting the major issues:

> There are three things especially conspicuous in the work of our salvation, namely, the example of humility which God gave us by emptying himself of his glory; the measure of his charity which he extended even to death, yes, even to the death of the cross; and the mystery of redemption wherein he destroyed death by submitting voluntarily to its dominion. But it would be as impossible to save us by the first and second of these without the third as it is to paint a picture on the empty air.[2]

For the abbot of Clairvaux and for the Latin tradition in general, solid Christian spirituality—that is, the effort to appropriate Christ's saving work in our lives—always needs to be true to all three elements: the imitation of the humility and love displayed in the divine kenosis and death on the cross and the objective communication of the mystery of redemption, that is, the remission of sins and the communication of new life in Christ. It was because Bernard was convinced (rightly or wrongly) that Abelard had denied the necessity of the objective communication of divine justice in the work of salvation that he penned the splendid summary of the Latin understanding of redemption that one finds in this letter.

It will be most helpful to begin with an account of the developing understandings of the mystery of redemption and then to move on to a briefer account of the imitation of Christ's humility and love, especially in the crucial period of the tenth through the twelfth century. Jacques Rivière has shown that the patristic period contributed three essential themes to medieval understandings of the mystery of redemption: (1) divinization, conceived of as the restoration of immortality; (2) the notion of the "rights" of the devil, which stressed the redemption as overcoming Satan's dominance over humanity; and (3) the importance of the remission of sins, which emphasized Christ's death as primarily a sacrifice of reconciliation.[3] Latin theology of the redemption and the spirituality that accompanied it can be seen as a complex and evolving set of variations on these three themes.

Divinization (*deificatio*), whose central place in the thought of the Greek fathers has been demonstrated above, was by no means absent in the Latin tradition.[4] Augustine insisted: "God wishes to make you God [*Deus enim deum te vult facere*], not by nature as in the case of him who gives you birth, but through gift and adoption. In the same way that he came to participate in your mortality through humanity, he has made you participate in immortality through elevation . . ." (*Sermon* 166 [*PL* 38, col. 909]). In a famous passage describing the fourth and highest degree of *caritas*, Bernard had exclaimed, "O pure and sacred love! O sweet and pleasant affection! . . . It is deifying to go through such an experience."[5] Still, the interaction of the divinization theme with the other components of Western views of redemption gave it a more restricted role with a somewhat different flavor from that which characterized the Greek East. The distinctive qualities of Latin views of redemption are more readily seen through an analysis of the relations between the traditional rights-of-the-devil understanding of redemption and the conception of redemption as a remission for sin, which evolved into a full-blown theology of satisfaction. This evolution affected not only the understanding of how Christ's work changed humanity's relation to God and the devil but also how human persons were to appropriate this new relationship through the church's sacramental system and their own spiritual practices. The "characteristically Western understanding of Christ" that was produced during this period (the phrase is that of Jaroslav Pelikan)[6] and the new systems of piety that built upon and accompanied the understanding of redemption that centered on satisfaction were crucial developments in Western spirituality.

The rights-of-the-devil understanding of redemption made little sense theoretically, as Anselm of Canterbury was to show in 1098 in his epochal christological treatise *Why God Became Man* (1.1–10), but it had immense symbolic power that is evident in the christological piety of the early Middle Ages. The notion that the devil's successful temptation of Adam and Eve through the tree in the garden had given him the right to control humanity and that the God-man had to overcome this satanic thralldom through his victory on the tree of the cross called up images of a supreme battle between the forces of good and evil, which was more effectively presented by the poets than by the theologians. Devotion to the wood of the cross, Christianity's supreme relic, played a special role in this piety. In the sixth century, the mannered court poet Venantius Fortunatus surpassed himself and his age in the two great hymns "Vexilla regis" and "Pange lingua," he composed for the translation of a piece of the true cross to Queen Radegonda's new religious house in Poitiers:

> Faithful Cross! above all other,
> One and only noble Tree!
> None in foliage, none in blossom,
> None in fruit thy peer may be;
> Sweetest wood and sweetest iron!
> Sweetest weight is hung on thee.[7]

The late Roman poet blended many themes into one—the glory of the cross as *the* Christian emblem (*vexilla* = imperial standard), the theme of the deception of Satan the great deceiver through the lowly wood of the cross, and even an emotional sympathy for Christ's physical sufferings. The eighth-century Old English poem known as "The Dream of the Rood" is less complex in its incorporation of themes but at least as powerful in its concentration on the essential message, the victory of the young hero Christ over the forces of death through his supreme battle-weapon. The rood itself addresses us:

> Almighty God ungirded him,
>     eager to mount the gallows,
> unafraid in the sight of many:
>     he would set free mankind.

> I shook when his arms embraced me
>> but I durst not bow to ground,
> Stoop to earth's surface.
>> Stand fast I must.
> I was reared up, a rood.
>> I raised the great King,
> liege lord of the heavens
>> dared not lean from the true.[8]

The image of Christ as triumphant warrior king reigning from the tree of the cross is dominant in artistic presentations of the crucifixion from this era. The same symbolic understanding of the basic meaning of Christ's life is also found in the famous eleventh-century Easter sequence, the "Victimae paschali laudes":

> The Lamb has redeemed the sheep;
> The innocent Christ has restored sinners to the Father.
> Life and Death engaged in a wondrous battle;
> The Lord of Life, once dead, now reigns alive.[9]

The rich symbolism of early medieval piety toward Christ the victor over death and the devil was not forgotten, even when the theoretical bases of this spirituality were undermined through the genius of Anselm of Canterbury.

Anselm's influence upon Western christology was unique. While Bernard of Clairvaux was perhaps a more powerful spokesman of medieval devotion to Christ and Thomas Aquinas a more balanced exponent of satisfaction theology, the archbishop of Canterbury's combination of deep devotion and theological innovation made him the special catalyst of the distinctive Latin view of the role of the God-man. In his *Why God Became Man* the traditional Latin emphasis on redemption as the remission of sins is rethought on the basis of a clear and powerful concept of satisfaction. Sin is seen as an affront to God's "honor," that is, his transcendent being, and hence divine justice demands recompense either by satisfaction or by punishment (see 1.13, 19, 22). Since "you do not make satisfaction unless you repay something greater than that for the sake of which you were obliged not to commit the sin" (1.21), the infinite magnitude of the offense requires a like satisfaction, which can be achieved only by one who is both God (and therefore *can* make such satisfaction) and also a human being (who is *bound* to make it). Anselm's concern that a more adequate understanding of redemption should lead to a more profound personal appropriation of its reality in our lives is beautifully expressed in his "Meditation on Human Redemption":

> See, Christian soul, here is the strength of your salvation, here is the cause of your freedom, here is the price of your redemption. You were a bond-slave and by this man you are free. By him you are brought back from exile, lost, you

are restored, dead, you are raised. Chew this, bite it, suck it, let your heart swallow it, when your mouth receives the body and blood of your Redeemer.[10]

Traditional Latin devotion to the cross and the new theology of satisfaction tended to concentrate attention upon the crucifixion as the central event of redemption, but this did not lead to total neglect of the other mysteries of the *ordo salutis*, or plan of salvation. The growing sense of personal commiseration with the sufferings of the crucified Jesus, evident in changes in the manner of portraying the crucifixion and in the heightened language of some authors, also should not be exaggerated. Even the general sense of what R. W. Southern called "the new feeling about the humanity of the Savior," so movingly expressed by the great Cistercian authors, must always be seen in perspective.[11] A glance at the role of Christ in the writings of Bernard of Clairvaux will demonstrate this.

Bernard's understanding of the mystery of redemption is more traditional than that of Anselm, but it is still profound. Although he gives an important place to devotion to the humanity of the Savior, Bernard always viewed such devotion as a necessary but lower stage in the ascent to perfect spiritual love.[12] The abbot of Clairvaux saw Christ's work primarily in terms of the cosmic law of ascent and descent— through the false ascent of pride, humanity had fallen into the slough of sin and could be rescued only by the humble descent and death of the God-man (God alone was incapable of descending) and his victorious ascension from the grave and back into heaven. Bernard's theology of redemption could be described as ascension-centered rather than passion-centered.[13] He and his Cistercian contemporaries took up the Pauline theme of the solidarity of head and members in the one body of Christ—"It is indisputably fitting that just as the head has preceded, the members ought to follow."[14]

Being "conformed to the image of the Son" (Rom 8:29) is both an onto-logical reality and a summons to action: the new creation implies a call to following the example of Christ in all ways. For the Cistercians and for the other Latin authors of this period, personal appropriation of the mystery of redemption—perhaps most adequately expressed through the traditional theme of *imitatio Christi*[15]—is not something added on at the end, but is the goal and purpose of the whole. This imitation was more one of internal attitude than of external practices, though it did not exclude the latter. It centered on two fundamental virtues—the humility by which the divine Word humbled himself in taking on human nature and the love that was the motivating force of the whole *ordo salutis*. Although Bernard and his contemporaries added a new personal note in their expression, the strain they played was an ancient one:

Let us endeavor to be made like this Child. Let us learn from him because he is meek and humble of heart so that the great God may not have been made tiny man for no reason, nor have died for nothing, nor be crucified in vain. Let us learn his humility, let us imitate his meekness, let us embrace his love, let us share in his sufferings, let us be washed in his blood.[16]

The remission of sins and the communication of new life to the believer, of course, involved not only internal attitudes but also the objective mediation of the grace of redemption through the sacramental life of the church. In medieval Latin Christianity, where infant baptism was the norm, this mediation was increasingly tied to the sacraments of penance and the Eucharist. Jaroslav Pelikan has noted that the most obvious background for the concept of satisfaction is to be found in the developing penitential system of the church,[17] and there can be no doubt that there were many reciprocal influences between christological spirituality and the major systematization of the practice of penance that was taking place in the eleventh and twelfth centuries.[18] Similarly, the uncompromising insistence on the real physical presence of Christ in the eucharistic species in the struggle against Berengar and the conception of the Mass as an atoning sacrifice were also closely tied to the Western view of the work of Christ, which received its classic if by no means final formulation during the period from the tenth century through the twelfth century.

## Notes

1. E.g., M. T. Clark, "The Trinity in Latin Christianity"; B. Ward, "Anselm of Canterbury"; and B. Pennington, "The Cistercians."

2. Bernard of Clairaux *Letter* 190.9.25. I have used the translation of Ailbe Luddy, *The Case of Peter Abelard* (Dublin: Gill, 1947) 92.

3. J. Rivière, "Redemption," in *Dictionnaire de théologie catholique* (Paris: Vacant, 1902–50) vol. 13, cols. 1938–42.

4. See the article "Divinisation" in *Dict. Sp.* 4, cols. 1389–1413, for the period covered here.

5. *On Loving God* 10.28. See the translation in *The Works of Bernard of Clairvaux*, Vol. 5, *Treatises II* (Washington, DC: Cistercian Publications, 1974) 120.

6. Jaroslav Pelikan, *The Growth of Medieval Theology (600– 1300)* (Chicago: University of Chicago Press, 1978) 106. The third chapter of Pelikan's book ("The Plan of Salvation," pp. 106–57) is a good theological introduction to Latin christology in this period.

7. This, the well-known translation of J. M. Neale, may be found with the Latin text in Matthew Britt, *The Hymns of the Breviary and Missal* (New York: Benziger, 1955) 120; but anyone who has ever heard this hymn sung in Latin during the Good Friday liturgy will wince at any translation.

8. The translation of Michael Alexander, *The Earliest English Poems* (New York: Penguin Books, 1977) 107.

9. The text may be found in Britt, *Hymns of the Breviary*, 129.

10. The translation of Benedicta Ward, *The Prayers and Meditations of Saint Anselm with the "Proslogion"* (New York: Penguin Books, 1979) 234.

11. R. W. Southern, *The Making of the Middle Ages* (New Haven, CT: Yale University Press, 1963) 234. For a classic statement of this type of devotion, see Aelred of Rievaulx's sermon "Jesus at Twelve Years of Age," which is partially translated in M. F. Toal, *The Sunday Sermons of the Great Fathers* (London: Longmans, 1957) 1:248–53.

12. See his *Sermons on Different Subjects* 101 (*Sancti Bernardi opera*, vol. 6, p. 368).

13. See Bernard McGinn, "Resurrection and Ascension in the Christology of the Early Cistercians," *Cîteaux* 30 (1979) 5–22.

14. *On the Resurrection* 1.8 (*Sancti Bernardi opera*, vol. 5, p. 83).

15. For an introduction, see the article "Imitation du Christ," in *Dict. Sp.*, 7, cols. 1536–1601.

16. *In Praise of the Virgin Mary* 3.14 (*Sancti Bernardi opera*, vol. 4, p. 45).

17. Pelikan, *Growth of Medieval Theology*, 143.

18. Aspects of the evolution of penance are treated in the article by Pierre-Marie Gy below (see pp. 371, 376, and 380), but the full story of the reciprocal relations remains to be told.

## Bibliography

### Sources

*Anselme de Cantorbery: Pourquoi Dieu s'est fait homme.* Sources chrétiennes 91. Paris: Cerf, 1963. Critical edition of the *Cur Deus homo* with French translation and an excellent introduction by René Roques.

*Sancti Bernardi opera.* 8 vols. Rome: Éditiones Cistercienses, 1957–77. Translations of many of Bernard's works may be found in the Cistercian Fathers Series (Kalamazoo, MI: Cistercian Publications, 1969–).

### Studies

McIntyre, John. *St. Anselm and His Critics: A Re-Interpretation of the Cur Deus Homo.* Edinburgh: Oliver & Boyd, 1954.

*Saint Bernard Théologien* (Analecta Sacri Ordinis Cisterciensis 9.3–4 (Rome: Éditiones Cistercienses, 1953). An important collection of papers, including one by J.-M. Déchanet on Bernard's christology.

Southern, R. W. *Saint Anselm and His Biographer.* Cambridge: Cambridge University Press, 1963.

Weingart, Richard E. *The Logic of Divine Love.* Oxford: Clarendon Press, 1970. A study of Abelard's soteriology.

# 11

## The Trinity

### I. *The Trinity in the Cappadocians*

THOMAS HOPKO

ASIL THE GREAT, archbishop of Caesarea in Cappadocia (d. 379); Gregory the Theologian, bishop of Nazianzus and later archbishop of Constantinople (d. 390); and Basil's younger brother Gregory, bishop of Nyssa (d. 394) are known in Christian history as the Cappadocian fathers. They were the leaders of the orthodox party of the church of their day, which included such bishops as Basil and Gregory's brother Peter of Sebaste, and Gregory Nazianzen's cousin Amphilochius of Iconium, as well as a company of women whom these famous men gratefully acknowledged as their teachers and guides. Among these were Basil and Gregory's grandmother, mother, and sister, Macrina, Emmelia, and Macrina —as well as Gregory Nazianzen's mother and sister, Nonna and Gorgonia, all of whom are canonized saints of the church.[1]

Hymned in Eastern Christian liturgy as "two souls in one body, united by divine love," Basil and Gregory Nazianzen may certainly be joined by Basil's brother Gregory in their spiritual and theological unity.[2] Nevertheless, for all their oneness of mind and heart, the Cappadocians were very different people. Basil was a sound pastoral bishop, the incarnation of wisdom and practicality. He was an ecclesiastical activist, a liturgical reformer, a monastic organizer, a fearless defender of Nicene orthodoxy, a compassionate spiritual father and friend. His brother Gregory of Nyssa was a married man, yet wholly dedicated to the ascetic life.[3] More speculative and mystical in his thinking than Basil, though perhaps less gifted rhetorically, he was much more influenced by the Hellenistic culture of his day, and, because of this, he alone among the Cappadocians may properly be accused of defending ideas outside the bounds of classical Christian orthodoxy.[4]

Gregory of Nazianzus was Basil's best friend. They studied Hellenistic philosophy and letters together in Athens before going off to follow Christ in short-lived monastic solitude. Forced into the episcopate by Basil in order to defend the faith and protect the flock from Arianizing heresies, Gregory never fully succeeded in the pastoral ministry. A cranky person, thin-skinned and self-defensive, easily insulted and often offended, Gregory claimed to prefer the life of a contemplative poet to that of a warring bishop. Yet his greatest theological works, including the orations on the Trinity—which won for him the title "Theologian," after the author of the Fourth Gospel— were delivered in the heat of doctrinal battle. He never passed up an occasion to fight, especially when it allowed him to wax eloquent in defense of his theological vision and personal behavior. He was known even to force the prudent Basil into clearer and more forceful expressions of church doctrine, particularly regarding the Holy Spirit, than his careful friend may have wanted to make for reasons of pastoral "oikonomia."[5]

The greatest of the Cappadocians, however, was certainly Basil. The two Gregorys praise him as their father, teacher, and guide.[6] And the church honors him with the title "the Great." Without Basil's influence and inspiration the extraordinary gifts of his brother and friend, together with a whole company of like-minded men and women, would certainly have gone undeveloped and unexpressed, forever lost not only to the cause of Christian theology but also to the spiritual achievements of humankind as a whole.

Orthodox Christians praise the Cappadocians for their articulation of the vision and experience of God celebrated in the church's sacramental mysteries, confessed by the martyrs and saints, witnessed in the Bible and the writings of the fathers—particularly Athanasius of Alexandria—and doctrinally formulated at the Council of Nicaea. As should be expected, the Cappadocians accomplished this task by using the philosophical language and categories of their time, particularly those of "mystical Platonism."[7] They were the heirs of a Judeo-Christian intellectual tradition that came from Philo and Origen already steeped in Hellenistic doctrines and ways of thinking. But their glory, according to their disciples over the ages, lay in their ability to overcome those elements of this tradition that were incompatible with Christianity, particularly in regard to the vision of God, and to coin new terms and formulate new explanations to protect and preserve the authentic experience and proper understanding of Christians.[8] Although Cappadocian teachings exist—especially from Gregory of Nyssa—that have not found a lasting place in the classical orthodox Christian tradition, Cappadocian teachings have been accepted by Christians of East and West on the nature and action of God the Father, Son, and Holy Spirit, not only in their relationship to the world of their creation, particularly to human persons made in their image and likeness, but also in their eternal and divine communion.

## The Vision of God

Every reasoning creature, according to the Cappadocian fathers, must affirm the existence of God. That God exists is a matter of right thinking which only a fool can deny.[9] But what God is in the innermost being and life of the Godhead remains by nature forever hidden from creatures. It is not that God will not make known the essence of divinity; it is rather that God cannot. To do so would be a contradiction in terms, an ontological impossibility. A God who can be comprehended by creatures, contained by creaturely minds and circumscribed by creaturely concepts, would be no God at all. The essence of God, God's *ousia*, is absolutely inconceivable and incomprehensible.[10] "A Greek teacher of divinity," wrote Gregory Nazianzen referring to Plato, taught that "it is difficult to conceive God, but to define Him in words is an impossibility," but the Christian father added that "in my opinion it is impossible to express Him and yet more impossible to conceive Him." For, he continued, "what God is in nature and essence no man ever yet has discovered or can discover" (*Oration 28* 4.16).

Utterly transcendent in nature and fully beyond human (and angelic) comprehension in essence, the living God, according to the Cappadocians, nevertheless can, and indeed must, be known. He can be personally known in his self-manifesting actions in creating, redeeming, and sanctifying the world. Basil made this point emphatically in his letter to Amphilochius, where he opposed those who claimed that either the essence of God is fully known or that God is not known at all and that Christians are, therefore, wholly ignorant of whom they worship. Basil said that "we know the greatness of God, His power, His wisdom, His goodness, His providence over us and the justness of His judgments; but not His essence. . . . We know our God from His operations, but do not undertake to approach near His essence. His operations come down to us, but His essence remains beyond our reach" (*Letter 234* 1).

This expression, "His operations come down to us," is reminiscent of Gregory Nazianzen's interpretation of Moses' vision on the mountain when he sees the "back parts" of God (Exod 33:23). These "back parts" (LXX *ta opisō*) are identified by Gregory as God's "majesty" or "glory which is manifested among creatures," through which "that Nature" of the Holy Trinity "at last reaches to us" (*Oration 28* 3). This too is Gregory of Nyssa's doctrine when he interprets Moses' vision of God in the burning bush as the uncreated light of the divine nature which has "reached down even to human nature" (*Life of Moses* 2.19-21). And he develops this same theme in his famous commentary on Christ's beatitude "Blessed are the pure in heart, for they shall see God" (Matt 5:8), when he says that God "whose essence is above every nature; invisible, incomprehensible. . ." becomes "visible in his operations (*energeiai*)," appearing to people whose hearts are purified by God's grace "in those things which surround Him (*en tisi tois peri auton kathorōmenois)*" (*On the Beatitudes*, Sermon 6). Basil summed up this common Cappadocian teaching in the letter referred to above in this way:

> Recognize that the voice is the voice of mockers when they say, if you are ignorant of the essence of God, you worship what you do not know. I do know that He exists; what His essence is I look at as beyond intelligence. How then am I saved? Through faith. It is faith sufficient to know that God exists, without knowing what He is; and "He is a rewarder of them that seek Him." So knowledge of the divine essence involves perception of His incomprehensibility, and the object of our worship is not that of which we comprehend the essence, but Him of whom we comprehend that the essence exists. (*Letter 234* 2)

## One God and Father

The knowledge of "Him of whom we comprehend that the essence exists" is the God of Israel, the Father of Jesus Christ, the "one God, the Father Almighty" of the Nicene Creed. Believers come to know him through his self-manifesting actions in the world in a personal relationship based on faith. Gregory of Nyssa affirmed this in his allegorical reflections on the journey of Abraham.

> Abraham passed through all the reasoning that is possible to human nature about the divine attributes, and after he had purified his mind of all such concepts, he took hold of a faith that was unmixed and pure of any concept, and he fashioned for himself this token of knowledge of God that is completely free of error, namely the belief that God completely transcends any knowable symbol. . . . For in his life we are taught that for those who are advancing in the divine paths there is no other way of drawing near to God than by the intermediary of faith; it is only through faith that the questing soul can unite itself with the incomprehensible Godhead. (*Answer to Eunomius' Second Book*)

Only by following in faith does the believer come to see the Lord. Gregory drew this conclusion in his interpretation of the "back parts" of God, which Moses saw on the mountain: "So Moses, who eagerly seeks to behold God, is now taught how he can behold Him: to follow God wherever He might lead is to behold God" (*Life of Moses* 252).

When people follow God in faith, according to the Cappadocians, they come to see that God is not alone in his divinity. This, for the Christian fathers, is the mystery of all mysteries, the truth of all truths. God has a Son. God is a Father by nature. And his Son, because he is God's Son, is divine with the Father's very own divinity. This was the faith declared at the Council of Nicaea, the doctrine of Athanasius, whom to praise, according to Gregory Nazianzen, is to praise God himself (*On the Great Athanasius* 1).

> We believe in one God, the Father Almighty . . . and in one Lord Jesus Christ, the Son of God, the only-begotten, begotten of the Father before all ages. Light from Light, true God from true God, begotten not created, of one essence with the Father (*homoousion tō patri*); through whom all things were made.[11]

God is not Father because human beings have projected this title onto him from their human experiences. God is Father because he has a Son by nature as a necessary element, so to speak, of his divine being and life. This, according to the Cappadocians, following Athanasius and Nicaea, is the teaching of the Bible. They saw in the Scriptures of Israel that the true and living God is never without his Word and Spirit. He is never devoid of his Wisdom, or empty of his Power and Glory. Together with the author of the Fourth Gospel, considered by Eastern Christians the first theologian and "author of theology," they see the Word of God (*logos tou theou*) as "God" with the God whose Word he is, the divine agent of creation without whom "was not anything made that was made."[12] They identify this divine Word of God not only with God's Image (*eikōn*), Wisdom (*sophia*), Power (*dynamis*), Seal (*charaktēr*), Radiance (*apaugasma*), and so on, but also with God's only-begotten Son (*ho monogenēs huios*), incarnate in human flesh as the real man Jesus of Nazareth, the Messiah of Israel and the Savior of the world.[13] And through the Son they come to know the Spirit of God, who proceeds from the Father and abides in the Son, who spoke through the prophets and dwells within the believers, guiding them into all truth.[14] By following God in faith, therefore, they discover their beloved Trinity, which, as Gregory Nazianzen testified, delighted their hearts and captivated their minds from the first encounter.

> From the day whereon I renounced the things of the world to consecrate my soul to luminous and heavenly contemplation, when the Supreme Intelligence carried me hence to set me down far from all that pertains to the flesh, to hide me in the secret places of the heavenly tabernacle; from that day my eyes have been blinded by the light of the Trinity, whose brightness surpasses all that the mind can conceive; for from a throne high exalted the Trinity pours upon all the ineffable radiance common to the Three. This is the source of all that is here below. (*Poem on Himself* 1)

For the Cappadocian fathers, as for Athanasius and Greek theology generally, the one God of faith is first of all the Father almighty. There is one

God—indeed, one might dare to say that there is the Trinity—because there is one Father. In this too they considered themselves faithful to the Bible, where the term "God" as a proper name belongs exclusively to him whose Son, Word, and Image Jesus Christ is, the One whose Spirit is the Spirit of God. And in this they also claimed to be one with the church, where those who are baptized "in the name of the Father and of the Son and of the Holy Spirit" offer eucharistic sacrifice of praise to the Father through the Son in the Spirit and have as their ultimate prayer the Our Father, which the Son gives and the Spirit inspires in all who worship the Father "in spirit and in truth."[15]

> For us there is one God, for the Godhead is One, and all that proceeds from Him (i.e., the Father) is referred to the One, though we believe in Three Persons. . . . When, then, we look at the Godhead, or the First Cause, or the Monarchia (i.e., the Father), that which we conceive is One; but when we look at the Persons in whom the Godhead dwells, and at Those Who time-lessly and with equal glory have their Being from the First Cause (i.e., the Son and the Spirit from the Father), there are Three whom we worship. (Gregory Nazianzen *Oration 31* [*On the Holy Spirit*] 14)

Basil virtually copied these words of his friend when he said that the "God who is over all alone has one special mark of His own person (hypostasis), His being Father and His deriving His person from no cause; and through this mark He is peculiarly known" (*Letter 38* 4).

For the Cappadocians, therefore, the one God of faith is the Father, who is "greater" than his Son and Spirit as the "sole cause of the Godhead" and the "cause of the cause of all things," that is, the Son, who yet shares with them the absolute unity and perfection of his incomprehensible divinity in an essential identity of nature.[16]

> This I commit to you today; with this I will baptize you and make you grow. This I give you to share and to defend all your life, the one Godhead and Power, found in the Three in Unity, and comprising the Three distinctly . . . the infinite conjunction of Three Infinite Ones, Each God when considered in Himself . . . the Three One God when contemplated together; Each God because of the one essence (*to homoousion*); One God because of the Monarchia (of the Father). No sooner do I conceive of the One than I am illumined by the splendor of the Three; no sooner do I distinguish Them than I am carried back to the One. (Gregory Nazianzen *Oration 40* [*On Holy Baptism*] 41)

> For us there is but One God, the Father of whom are all things; and One Lord Jesus Christ by whom are all things; and One Holy Spirit in whom are all things; yet these words do not denote a difference of nature . . . but they characterize the personalities of a nature which is one and unconfused. (Gregory Nazianzen *Oration 39* [*On the Holy Lights*] 12)

## The Tri-Personal Godhead

The one God who is love is not alone in his divinity. This, we have seen, is the Cappadocian conclusion drawn from the experience of faith, a conclusion not in contradiction to the Hellenistic insight that the Good must be in some sense self-sharing.[17]

A uni-personal monad God (not to speak of a nonpersonal or suprapersonal divinity) is not only contrary to the facts of divine revelation, according to the Cappadocians, but is abhorrent to "reason" as well—certainly "reason according to the apostles," which Gregory Nazianzen claimed for Christians contrary to those who think "in the manner of Aristotle" (*Oration 23* 12). God must express himself to be God. And he must do so divinely, according to nature, and not merely by his goodwill. He must do so in a manner befitting his majesty and glory, an ineffable and incomprehensible manner appropriate to his Godhead. The creation of the world cannot possibly satisfy the essential need of God for perfect self-expression.[18]

> But Monarchia is that which we hold in honor. It is, however, a Monarchia that is not limited to one Person, for it is impossible for Unity if at variance with itself to come into a condition of plurality; but one which is made of an equality of nature and a union of mind, and an identity of motion, and a convergence of its elements to unity—a thing which is impossible to the created nature—so that though numerically distinct there is no severance of essence. Therefore Unity having from all eternity arrived by motion at Duality, found its rest in Trinity. This is what we mean by Father and Son and Holy Spirit. (Gregory Nazianzen *Oration 29* [*On the Son*] 2)

God's eternal and uncreated self-expression is the divine Word, his only-begotten Son. This fact is affirmed for the Cappadocians not only by reference to the Christian Scriptures, particularly the writings of John and Paul, but also by reflection on the law, prophets, psalms, and wisdom literature of Israel in the light of Christ, as well as by consideration of the metaphysical and mystical insights of the Hellenistic philosophers who approached this sublime truth but failed to comprehend it clearly and fully because of the limitations inherent in the fallen state of human minds and hearts. It was Hellenistic errors on this issue, which had made their way into Christian thinking, that led to the various heresies of the fourth century against which the Cappadocians felt themselves called to do battle.

The Cappadocians identified Jesus the incarnate Son of God with God's Word and Wisdom witnessed to in the Hebrew Scriptures, as they identified the Spirit of Christ with God's Spirit who inspired the law and the prophets. They also identified Jesus with the word and wisdom of the Greek philosophers.[19] But against both Jews and Greeks the Christian fathers were compelled to defend the absolute unity of the Godhead by showing how God's Word and Wisdom, as well as his Spirit, were necessary and essential to his very being, yet personally, or hypostatically, distinct from him and in no way inferior. They argued that God's Word and Wisdom, and his Holy Spirit, could not be created since God never was, and indeed never could be, without them.[20] They argued that if God has a Son, Word, and Image (and, if he is love, he must), then this Son must be exactly what the Father is, for to consider him, and his Spirit, as inferior would not only denigrate the begotten but would also denigrate him from whom he is born, "for the lowering of those who are from Him is no glory to the Source" (Gregory Nazianzen *Oration 40 [On Holy Baptism]* 43). They argued that in any case, and indeed in every case, what is begotten is necessarily of the *same* essence (*homoousios*) as the one who begets, so that, when a being gives birth to another, the one born necessarily possesses an identical nature with the begetter and not one that is merely *similar (homoiousios)*—not to speak of one that is utterly *different (heteroousios)*.[21] They argued also that an image must be identical to its archetype in every way—certainly the divinely perfect image of the divinely perfect archetype who is divine perfection itself. Thus, they insisted, the Image of God, who is God's Son and Word, his Wisdom and Radiance, must be distinct from the Fatherly archetype only insofar as he is an image. He cannot be different in substance and certainly cannot be inferior or defective. And a personal God must have a personal Image and Word. He must be a personal Father with a personal Son whose very existence as person is to be exactly what the Father is—not the Father himself but the personal expression of his divinely personal being and life. Indeed the Son of God must be God's being and life itself in a personal, or hypostatic, form.[22]

The contribution of the Cappadocians to Christian theology was the formulation of the distinction between hypostasis or person (*prosōpon*) for the concretely existing subject (*hypokeimenon*) of God the Father, and so of the Son and of the Holy Spirit, and essence (*ousia*) or substance or nature for their identical divine being. This distinction, with the specific definition of terms it produced, entered the Christian tradition and quickly became part of the technical language of the church in dogmatic statements and liturgical prayers. It was taken up in the theological controversies of later ages concerning the person and nature of Christ, for example, and the relationship between God's unknowable essence (or supraessence, *hyperousios*) and God's actions and operations (*energeiai*) in the world.[23] It remains even today a live issue of debate among Christian thinkers on contemporary issues.[24]

In the Cappadocian corpus the key writings on this theme are the letter of Gregory of Nyssa *To Ablabius: On "Not Three Gods"* and the famous letter to Gregory by his brother Basil, *Letter 38*, which scholars think may have been Gregory's own work. One also finds the teaching clearly presented in the orations of Gregory Nazianzen. The idea presented is a rather simple one. *Hypostasis*, a stronger and much more appropriate word than *prosōpon/* person, designates the concrete existent which is noted in divine and human beings by their proper names.[25] It answers the question, Which one? Or, for personal beings, Who? Essence (also, in English, substance or nature) designates the general or common. It answers the question, What? Every being that exists, created or uncreated, exists hypostatically, that is, as a particular, specific, concrete existent. Yet every being that exists has its being in common with others that are essentially, substantially, naturally the same. Thus, for example, in the created order all animals called horses are essentially the same in their being horses. Yet each one is unique in its concrete, specific existence. There is no such thing as horse-in-general. There are only existing horses, any one of which will produce the same definition when asked about its being. The description becomes different, however, when the question is about a particular horse. In that case its specific hypostatic characteristics must be presented.

The example used by the Cappadocians has to do not with horses, but with people. In the above-mentioned letters and in Gregory Nazianzen's oration *On the Holy Spirit*, the fathers ask their hearers to imagine three men—Peter, James, and John; or Paul, Sylvanus, and Timothy. As human beings, they tell us, the three are identical. Their humanity is one and the same. But as unique human beings concretely existing, they are distinguished one from another as persons, distinct hypostases, each with his own name and personal characteristics (*idiotētes, idiomata*).

> That which is spoken of in a special and peculiar manner is indicated by the name of the hypostasis. Suppose we say "a man." The indefinite meaning of the word strikes a certain vague sense upon the ears. The nature is indicated, but what subsists and is specially and peculiarly indicated by the name is not made plain. Suppose we say "Paul." We set forth, by what is indicated by the name, the *nature subsisting*. This then is the hypostasis or *"under-standing"*; not the indefinite conception of the essence or substance, which, because what is signified is general, finds no *"standing,"* but the conception which by means of the expressed peculiarities gives *standing* and circumscription to the general and uncircumscribed. It is customary in scriptures to make a distinction of this kind. . . . (Basil *Letter 38* 3)

"Transfer, then, to the divine dogmas," the author continues, "the same standard of difference which you recognize in the case both of essence and of hypostasis in human affairs, and you will not go wrong" (*Letter 38* 3). The specific "mode of existence" (*tropos hyparxeōs*) of the Father is to be the source and cause of the Godhead, the begetter of the only-begotten Son, the one from whom the Holy Spirit proceeds. The Son's "mode of existence" is to be the begotten one, the hypostatic Image and Word of the unbegotten God. And the Holy Spirit's "mode of existence" is to be not another Son (thus the distinction between "generation" and "procession") but "the Spirit of God, the Spirit of Christ, the Spirit of the Lord and himself the Lord. . . ."[26] Thus, the essence of the three hypostases being one and the same, the peculiar characteristics of each person are preserved.

The weakness of this argument when applied to the Godhead was obvious to the Cappadocians, and they dealt with it directly. This was the specific purpose of Gregory of Nyssa's letter to Ablabius. Although we admit a commonness to human beings, and even a complete identity of nature, we still speak of "three men" when confronted with Peter, James, and John. And we still count three separate beings. Why, then, do we not speak of "three gods" when we meet the Father, Son, and Holy Spirit and count them as three divine beings? The Cappadocian answer—and that of the tradition born from their spiritual vision and intellectual conceptualization—has to do with the characteristics of God's essence or, as we might put it today, the nature of God's nature.

Whereas all created natures are limited and finite, and (with the exception of angels) in some sense material and bodily, located in space and time and therefore growing and changing, the nature of God transcends these categories in every way. God is holy. God's being is incomparable to created beings. God is completely different from everything which he has made. As such, the essence of God is beyond every creaturely word, symbol, image, and concept. Nevertheless, the Cappadocians taught that there are concepts that are "proper to God" (*logoi theoprepeis*), at least formally and schematically.[27] And so, in regard to God's being and life they defended the vision that the divine nature which is beyond creaturely categories of definition in its innermost content is in fact the nature of three divine persons: the one God and Father; his only-begotten Son, Word and Image; and his most-holy Spirit. And they insist that the three hypostases are not "three gods" or three distinct divine individuals or beings, because of the absolute unity and perfection of the identical nature which they share—indeed, which they *are*—which is, first and foremost, that of God the Father himself.

But God, Who is over all, alone has the special mark of His own hypostasis, His being Father and His deriving His hypostasis from no cause; and through this mark He is peculiarly known. Wherefore in the communion of the essence we maintain that there is no mutual approach or intercommunion of those notes of indication perceived in the Trinity, whereby is set forth the proper peculiarity of the Persons delivered in the faith, each of these being distinctively apprehended by His own characteristics. Hence, in accordance with the stated signs of indication, discovery is made of the distinction of the hypostases; while so far as relates to the infinite, the incomprehensible, the uncreated, the uncircumscribed and similar attributes, there is no variableness in the life-giving Nature, in that I mean, of the Father, Son and Holy Spirit, but in Them is seen a certain communion indissoluble and continuous. (Basil *Letter 38* 4)

These words of *Letter 38* are forcefully repeated by the Cappadocians again and again to deny the charge against them of "tritheism." "Against those who cast it in our teeth that we are tritheists," says Basil, "let it be answered that we confess one God not in number but in nature" (*Letter 8* 2). And Gregory Nazianzen, insisting that it is "better to take a meagre view of the Unity than to venture on a complete impiety," added that "each of these Persons possesses Unity; not less with that which is United to it (i.e., the other divine Persons) than with itself, by reason of the identity of Essence and Power. And this is the account of the Unity, so far as we have apprehended it. If then this account is the true one, let us thank God for the glimpse He has granted us; if it is not let us seek for a better" (*Oration 31* [*On the Holy Spirit*] 12,16).

And when I say God, I mean Father, Son and Holy Spirit; for Godhead is neither diffused beyond these, so as to introduce a mob of gods, nor yet bounded by a smaller compass than These, so as to condemn us for a poverty-stricken conception of Deity; either Judaizing to save the Monarchia, or falling into heathenism by the multitude of our gods. For the evil on either side is the same, though found in contrary directions. Thus then does the Holy of Holies Which is hidden even from the Seraphim, and is glorified by a thrice-repeated Holy, meet in one ascription of the title Lord and God. . . . (Gregory Nazianzen *Oration 45* [*On Easter*] 4)

Gregory of Nyssa grounded the unity of the three persons in the unity of their actions and operations in the world. "We," he wrote to Ablabius, "following the suggestions of Scripture, have learned that that Nature is unnameable and unspeakable. . . . Hence it is clear that by any of the terms we use, the Divine Nature Itself is not signified, but some one of its surroundings is made known" (*To Ablabius, On "Not Three Gods"*). We have already seen that, for Gregory, the "surroundings" of God refer to his actions (*energeiai*).[28] These actions are always those of the three persons, yet they are always perfectly one.

But in the case of the Divine Nature we do not . . . learn that the Father does anything by Himself in which the Son does not work conjointly, or again that the Son has any special operation apart from the Holy Spirit; but every operation which extends from God to creation . . . has its origin from the Father, and proceeds through the Son, and is perfected in the Holy Spirit. For this reason the name derived from the operation is not divided with regard to the number of those who fulfill it, because the action of each concerning anything is not separate and peculiar, but whatever comes to pass, in reference either to the acts of His providence for us, or to the government and constitution of the universe, comes to pass by the action of the Three, yet what does come to pass is not three things. (Gregory of Nyssa *To Ablabius, On "Not Three Gods"*)

Because every action of the Trinity—and the effect of every action of the three persons—is one action and one effect, it is strictly impossible, Gregory said, to speak in any sense of "three gods."

## Communion in the Trinity

A foundational teaching of the Cappadocians was that human beings, male and female, are made in the image and likeness of God, the Holy Trinity. Human nature mirrors divine nature. And human being is made to reflect not only the unity of the Trinity but also the "union" (*henōsis*) of the three persons.[29] "He did not make the heavens in His images," wrote Gregory of Nyssa, "nor the moon, the sun, the beauty of the stars, nor anything else which surpasses all understanding; you alone (O Man) are a similitude of Eternal Beauty . . . whose Glory is reflected in your purity. Nothing in all creation can equal your grandeur" (*Commentary on the Canticle,* Sermon 2).

Following the Scriptures, the Cappadocians also taught that human beings have failed in their calling. They have soiled their original purity and disfigured their primal beauty. They have, to refer again to Gregory of Nyssa, "looked toward the serpent and held his image" rather than the image of God (*Commentary on the Canticle,* Sermon 5). But God has acted to restore the image, to purify the nature, to replace human beings on the proper way, to return them to their original dignity, and even much more. God has acted to make his creatures divine, to deify them through the action of Christ, the incarnate Son of God, and the working of the Holy Spirit, by whom they were originally made. This is the doctrine of deification (*theōsis*), for which the Cappadocians, and Greek theology generally, are so very well known.[30] Gregory Nazianzen proclaimed this in a sermon for the feast of Theophany, when, after reminding how humans are created in God's image, bearing "in themselves the magnificence of the Creator-Word" since God has placed within them a "Breath taken from Himself," he went on to say how "the Word of God . . . the Light from Light, the Source of Life and Immortality, the Image of the Archetypal Beauty . . . came to His own image and took on flesh for the sake of our flesh, and mingled with Himself an intelligent soul for the sake of my soul, purifying like by like, and in all points except sin was made man" (*Oration 38* [*On the Theophany*] 13).

> And He who gives riches becomes poor, for He assumes the poverty of my flesh, that I may assume the richness of His Godhead. He that is full empties Himself, for He empties Himself of His glory for a short while, that I may have a share of His Fulness. What is the riches of His Goodness? What is the mystery that is around me? I had a share in the image; I did not keep it. He partakes of my flesh that He may both save the image and make the flesh immortal. He communicates a second Communion far more marvelous than the first, inasmuch as then He imparted the better Nature, whereas now He Himself partakes of the worse. This is a more godlike action than the former, this is loftier in the eyes of all men of understanding. (Gregory Nazianzen *Oration 38* [*On the Theophany*] 13)

Gregory continued this teaching in a sermon for Easter, which he called "the Passover to the honor of the Trinity." He said that "created to be made happy," and "cast out because we transgressed," we "needed an Incarnate God, a God put to death, that we might live" (*Oration 45* [*On Easter*] 2, 28).

> We were put to death together with Him, that we might be cleansed. We rose again with Him because we were put to death with Him. We were glorified with Him, because we rose again with Him. Many indeed are the miracles of that time: God crucified, the sun darkened . . . blood and water from His side . . . the rocks rent . . . the dead raised . . . the signs at the sepulchre which none can worthily celebrate; and yet none of these is equal to the miracle of my salvation. A few drops of Blood recreate the whole world, and becomes for all people what rennet is to milk, drawing us together and compressing us into unity. (Gregory Nazianzen *Oration 45* [*On Easter*] 28–29)

The Theologian completed his preaching about the deification of human persons within the unity of the Trinity in a sermon for Pentecost, in which he emphasized the work of the Holy Spirit, whose deity he clearly proclaimed, and whom he honored plainly with the title "God" (*Oration 31* [*On the Holy Spirit*] 10).

> The Holy Spirit, then, always existed, and exists, and always will exist. . . . He was ever being partaken, but not partaking; perfecting, not being perfected; sanctifying, not being sanctified; deifying, not being deified; Himself ever the same with Himself and with Those with whom He is ranged. . . the Spirit of adoption, of truth, of wisdom, of understanding, of knowledge, of godliness, of courage, of fear . . . by Whom the Father is known and the Son is glorified; and by Whom alone He Himself is known. . . . (Gregory Nazianzen *Oration 61* [*On Pentecost*] 9)

Basil was reluctant to state clearly that the Spirit is God. But he responded to Gregory's chiding and carefully demonstrated the divinity of the Holy

Spirit in his treatise dedicated to that end, in which he also clearly proclaimed the Spirit's deifying power:

> Through the Holy Spirit comes our restoration to paradise, our ascension to the kingdom of heaven, our adoption as God's sons, our freedom to call God our Father, our becoming partakers of the grace of Christ, being called children of the light, sharing in eternal glory, and, in a word, our inheritance of the fulness of blessing, both in this world and in the world to come. (Basil *On the Holy Spirit* 36)

Gregory of Nyssa identified the Holy Spirit with the kingdom (or kingship) of God. In his *Commentary on the Lord's Prayer* he said simply that "the Holy Spirit is the kingdom" (Sermon 3). Elsewhere he states that "the Anointing One is the Father; the Anointed is the Son; and the Unction itself, the 'Oil of Gladness,' is the Holy Spirit" (*On the Holy Spirit*). Those who belong to Christ are anointed together with him by the Spirit of God and become God's children, "gods" by grace.[31] This is the Cappadocian teaching about communion of human beings with God and, indeed, *within* the Godhead—the union with the Father, through the Son, in the Holy Spirit.

Like the God in whose image they are made, human beings are not intended to be separate individuals in relationship with one another in an external manner. Neither are they called to exist as a "collective" without personal "standing" or integrity. They are rather, like their Creator, made to be persons in community, distinct hypostases in an identity of nature, called to a perfect—and, according to Gregory of Nyssa, ever more perfect—union of being and action in fulfillment of all virutes, the greatest of which is love.[32] Such perfection, the Cappadocians taught, is possible only by the power of the Holy Spirit. And the Cappadocians themselves, many would claim, were the surest proof that such perfection for human persons is real.

> Only when a person has been cleansed from the shame of his evil, and has returned to his natural beauty, and the original form of the Royal Image has been restored in him (through Christ), is it possible for him to approach the Paraclete. Then, like the sun, He will show you in Himself the image of the invisible, and with purified eyes you will see in this blessed image the unspeakable beauty of its Prototype. Through Him hearts are lifted up, the infirm are held by the hand, and those who progress are brought to perfection. He shines upon those who are cleansed from every spot, and makes them spiritual people through communion with Himself. When a sunbeam falls on a transparent substance, the substance itself becomes brilliant, and radiates light from itself. So too Spirit-bearing souls, illumined by Him, finally become spiritual themselves, and their grace is sent forth to others. From this comes knowledge of the future, understanding of mysteries, apprehension of

hidden things, distribution of wonderful gifts, heavenly citizenship, a place in the choir of angels, endless joy in the presence of God, becoming like God, and, the highest of all desires, becoming God (*theon genesthai*). (*On the Holy Spirit* 23)

## Notes

1. See Gregory of Nyssa *Life of Macrina;* Gregory Nazianzen *Oration 43* (*Panegyric on St. Basil*); *Oration 7* (*On His Brother Caesarius*); *Oration 8* (*On His Sister Gorgonia*); *Oration 18* (*On the Death of His Father*).

2. Feast of St. Basil (January 1): Matins, Canon 2, Ode 7, Troparion 3. The line is taken from Gregory Nazianzen *Oration 43* (*Panegyric on St. Basil*) 20.

3. Gregory of Nyssa's wife, "Theosebeia," may have been the sister of Gregory Nazianzen, who praises her in his *Letter 95* to Gregory as "the fairest, the most illustrious even amidst such beauty . . . the true priestess, the yokefellow, the equal of a priest" (see *NPNF,* series 2, vol. 5, p. 3).

4. Such ideas of Gregory of Nyssa are, for example, his teaching about double creation and the provisional character of human sexuality made in prevision of humanity's fall (see *On the Making of Man* 16–22) and his doctrine of universal salvation "even including the introducer of evil himself," that is, the devil (see *The Great Catechism* 26; and *On the Soul and Resurrection*).

5. See *Oration 43* (*Panegyric on St. Basil*) 68; and Gregory's *Letter 58 to Basil.*

6. *Oration 43* (*Panegyric on St. Basil*); Gregory of Nyssa *On Virginity* 24; *Letter 10 to Libanius.*

7. See J. Daniélou, *Origen,* trans. Walter Mitchell (New York: Sheed & Ward, 1955) 85–86; see also idem, *Platonisme et théologie mystique: Essai sur la doctrine spirituelle de Saint Gregoire de Nysse* (Paris: Aubier, 1944).

8. See Daniélou, *Platonisme et théologie mystique;* V. Lossky, *The Vision of God,* trans. A. Moorhouse (London: Faith Press, 1963; reprint, Crestwood, NY: St. Vladimir's Seminary Press, 1983).

9. Gregory Nazianzen *Oration 28* 5–6; Gregory of Nyssa *The Great Catechism,* prologue; idem, *On the Soul and Resurrection.*

10. Gregory of Nyssa: "Now the divine nature as it is in itself, according to its essence, transcends every act of comprehensive knowledge and it cannot be approached or attained by our speculation" (*On the Beatitudes,* Sermon 6).

11. The Symbol of Faith of the Council of Nicaea, known as the First Ecumenical Council.

12. Vesper hymns of the Byzantine liturgy, Feast of St. John the Theologian, September 26 and May 8. See also John 1:1–18.

13. See Col 1:15; 1 Cor 1:24; Heb 1:3 (translated as verbs, rather than literally as nouns, in the Revised Standard Version) and John 1:1–18, where some ancient sources read "only-begotten *God*" (*theos*) in place of "only-begotten Son" (*huios*).

14. See John 15:26; 16:13.

15. See Matt 28:19; Rom 8:15–16; Gal 4:6; John 4:23–24; see also Basil *On the Holy Spirit* 58–64.

16. Basil *Letter 38* 44. For the Cappadocian interpretation of Jesus' words, "the Father is greater than I (John 14:28)," which they consider to refer to *origin* rather than *nature,*

see Basil *Letter 8* 5; Gregory Nazianzen *Oration 29* (*On the Son*) 15; *Oration 30* (*On the Son*) 7; *Oration 40* (*On Holy Baptism*) 43.

17. On the relationship between the Trinity and the Platonic idea of the self-sharing Good, see Gregory Nazianzen *Oration 29* (*On the Son*) 2; *Oration 38* (*On the Theophany*) 9; *Oration 45* (*On Easter*) 5.

18. See Gregory Nazianzen *Oration 29* (*On the Son*) 6-10.

19. Gregory of Nyssa *The Great Catechism* 5.

20. See Gregory of Nyssa *The Great Catechism* 1.

21. See Basil and Gregory of Nyssa's writings *Against Eunomius;* see also Gregory Nazianzen *Oration 29* (*On the Son*) 10-14.

22. See Gregory Nazianzen *Oration 30* (*On the Son*) 20; *Oration 38* (*On the Theophany*) 13; Basil *Letter 38* 8.

23. For the application of Cappadocian trinitarian language to issues of christology, see J. Meyendorff, *Christ in Eastern Christian Thought* (Washington, DC: Corpus Books, 1969; reprint, Crestwood, NY: St. Vladimir's Seminary Press, 1975). For the application of these terms in later controversies about the essence and energies of God, see, for example, V. Lossky, *The Mystical Theology of the Eastern Church;* idem, *The Vision of God.*

24. For a contemporary application of Cappadocian trinitarian theology, see *Women and the Priesthood,* ed. T. Hopko (Crestwood, NY: St. Vladimir's Seminary Press, 1983). See also its use for the development of a social philosophy in N. Fydorov, *Filosofiya Obshogo Dela* (*Philosophy of the Common Task*), an extract of which may be found in English in A. Schmemann, *Ultimate Questions: An Anthology of Modern Russian Religious Thought* (New York: Holt, Rinehart & Winston, 1965; reprint, Crestwood, NY: St. Vladimir's Seminary Press, 1982) 173-223. For an encounter between the Cappadocian tradition and contemporary process theology, see T. Hopko, *God and the World: An Eastern Orthodox Response to Process Theology* (Ph.D. diss., Fordham University; Ann Arbor, MI: Xerox University Microfilms, 1982).

25. See Gregory Nazianzen *Oration 39* (*On the Holy Lights*) 11; Basil *Letter 210* 5.

26. See Basil *Letter 38* 3-4; Gregory Nazianzen *Oration 31* (*On the Holy Spirit*) 29; Gregory of Nyssa To Ablabius, On "Not Three Gods."

27. See Gregory Nazianzen *Panegyric on St. Basil* 68; *Oration 21* (*On the Great Athanasius*) 35; Basil *On the Holy Spirit;* Gregory of Nyssa *Answer to Eunomius' Second Book; Life of Moses* 2.176-78.

28. See above, pp. 262-63; Gregory of Nyssa *On the Beatitudes,* Sermon 6.

29. See Gregory Nazianzen *Oration 30* (*On the Son*) 8; *Oration 31* (*On the Holy Spirit*) 17; *Oration 42* (*The Last Farewell*) 15.

30. E.g., Gregory Nazianzen *Oration 21* (*On the Great Athanasius*) 2.

31. Gregory of Nyssa *Commentary on the Canticle,* Sermon 15; *Commentary on the Beatitudes,* Sermons 1, 5, 6; see also Gregory Nazianzen *Oration 38* (*On the Theophany*) 7; *Oration 40* (*On Holy Baptism*) 45.

32. Gregory of Nyssa *Commentary on the Canticle,* Sermons 13-15; see also idem, *On Perfection.*

## Bibliography

*Studies*

Kelly, J. N. D. *Early Christian Doctrines.* New York: Harper & Row, 1958.
Lossky, Vladimir. *In the Image and Likeness of God.* Edited by John H. Erickson and Thomas E. Bird. Crestwood, NY: St. Vladimir's Seminary Press, 1974.
———. *The Mystical Theology of the Eastern Church.* Translated by the Fellowship of St. Alban and St. Sergius. Cambridge: James Clark, 1957; reprint, Crestwood, NY: St. Vladimir's Seminary Press, 1976.
Payne, Robert. *The Holy Fire: The Story of the Fathers of the Eastern Church.* New York: Harper & Row, 1957; reprint, Crestwood, NY: St. Vladimir's Seminary Press, 1980.
Pelikan, Jaroslav. *The Christian Tradition: A History of the Development of Doctrine.* Vol. 1, *The Emergence of the Catholic Tradition (100–600).* Chicago and London: University of Chicago Press, 1971.
Prestige, G. L. *Fathers and Heretics.* London: S.P.C.K., 1949.
———. *God in Patristic Thought.* London: S.P.C.K., 1959.

# II. *The Trinity in Latin Christianity*

## MARY T. CLARK

EARLY CHRISTIAN PRAYER indicates a primitive, undeveloped faith-awareness of the trinitarian God by Christians who experienced a threefoldness in God's revealed dealings with them. They recognized the creative, redemptive, and sanctifying work of God, Christ, and Spirit, naming them liturgically and privately in prayer. This devotion to Father, Son, and Holy Spirit was visible in the eucharistic liturgy, which was trinitarian, in the baptismal and other sacramental rites, which invoked the trinity in the setting of Christian community; and in the various doxologies of the New Testament and the liturgies. Yet the triadic formulas used in confessing God were not originated as statements that God is a Trinity. Early Christians were unaware of concepts like nature, person, or hypostasis. Not until the third century did Christians concentrate theologically on the equal divinity of the three. The theological speculation was the inevitable attempt to understand the faith, an understanding that was evolving slowly and not always accurately.

Such speculation was grounded in Christ's revelation of his divine Father and the promising and sending of the divine Spirit. In Christianity the term "spirituality" is most apt for indicating not the philosophic life but the life in the Spirit who makes it possible to pray "Abba! Father!" (Rom 8:14–17). Union with Christ in the Holy Spirit, in whom one becomes a child of the Father, is the foundation of Christian prayer and life.

This fact provides some insight into the significance of the Trinity for Christian spirituality. The diversity in God revealed by Christ is deeply related to the basic aspirations of the human person for openness to the transcendent; for interpersonal dialogue with God, and for living always and everywhere in God. No one goes to the Father except through the Son, and neither can anyone recognize the Son except in the Spirit (John 14:7; 15:27). Here we see how necessary are the divine three for the authenticity of Christian religious experience.

The Trinity is the theoretical cornerstone of Christianity. Within the Trinity is synthesized the economy or order of God's actions in behalf of the human race: creation, salvation, glorification. Although these functions help to distinguish Father from Son and both from Holy Spirit, the revelation of the Son's generation from the unoriginate Father, and the Holy Spirit's procession make known the constitution of the divine persons to be by relationship. The Trinity is then seen as the paradigm for the inter-relationship of all things and for the basic unity of reality.

The Trinity therefore has practical significance. Trinitarian spirituality denotes certain basic attitudes that are evoked by God's reality as Father, Son, and Spirit, namely, silence before the Ineffable, love-obedience with the Son toward the Father, experiencing God the Spirit in all things. Some religious traditions stress one of these attitudes more than the others. In the ancient Christian world the attitude that prevailed was that of union with Christ in love and in obedience to the Father. Paul spoke of Christ as the image of the Father (Col 1:15). In the Genesis account of creation we read: "God said, 'Let us make man in our image, after our likeness'" (Gen 1:26). Following Irenaeus, the Eastern fathers used "image" to denote natural powers and "likeness" to denote supernatural gifts. Within the Augustinian concept of image there was not only derivation from the trinitarian God but also an implied likeness and a dynamic note of tendency toward the Exemplar-Principle. The return to God by likeness was the goal of trinitarian spirituality. Some theologians, notably Marius Victorinus, following Paul (Rom 8:29) taught that, since Christ is the Father's image, human beings created in the image of God were created in the image of Christ. Others, like Augustine, following Genesis 1:26 interpreted creation by the Trinity to be creation in the image of the Trinity.

This image-theme emphasizes the practical connotations of the doctrine of the Trinity. Here is the human vocation to deification, an affinity by

19. *Philoxeny of Abraham*, San Vitale, Ravenna, 6th century

nature and grace to union with God. The Augustinian notion of image, as we said, refers not only to the natural image of the Trinity in the soul but also to its dynamic tendency toward the trinitarian God, a call to community with Father, Son, and Holy Spirit and with all others invited into that same community by creation. Although this is based upon the natural capacity to remember, understand, and love God, it is God's grace or gift of faith, hope, and love that actualizes this capacity. The graced soul is the true likeness of the Trinity. Perfect likeness will only be achieved at the resurrection, according to Victorinus (*Against Arius* 1.19). The interconnection of this image-theme and the theme of the Trinity is emphasized in Augustine's teaching that a human being is *capax Trinitatis*, because one bears within oneself always an image of the Trinity (*The Trinity* 14.8.11).

Instead of giving the history of the theological development of the doctrine of the Trinity, which can be found elsewhere, I shall consider the major representatives of the link between the doctrine of the Trinity and the doctrine of the image, because of the significance of this link for Western spirituality. These representatives are Marius Victorinus, Augustine of Hippo, and Richard of St. Victor—a layman, a bishop, and a canon.

## Marius Victorinus

Marius Victorinus Afer (281–ca. 365) had the benefit not only of the thought of the Greek fathers but also of the reflections of Tertullian (160–ca. 220) and of Hilary of Poitiers (315–ca. 358).

Tertullian, an African influenced by the Greek apologists and by Irenaeus's teaching on the divine "economy," taught that God is Trinity and unity. The key to his theology is the Stoic notion of nature. In his work on *Prayer*, the first formal trinitarian treatise we have, he recommended that one pray three times daily in honor of the Trinity. He viewed the incarnation as the way of salvation because it opens a participation into the reciprocal relations of the divine persons. The projection of the Word into the world did not separate it from God, nor was God divided by the various missions. In the Trinity the unity is not destroyed but distributed. Tertullian introduced legal terms into theology, but he also used ordinary words and metaphors. He had a vivid understanding of the Father as the source of life, of the Son as the agent of life, and of the Holy Spirit as the giver of life. To denote this order he used these images: rooted in the Father, the Holy Spirit is the fruit plucked from the branch (the Son); or, the Father is the spring, the Son the river, and the Holy Spirit the stream; or, the Father is the sun, the Son is its sunbeam whose point (*apex*) is the Holy Spirit, bearer of warmth and life. Such symbols were common in the tradition, but inadequately portray the equality of the three (Tertullian *Against Praxeas* 8). Tertullian deeply appreciated the role of the Spirit. He believed that the Spirit came from the Father through the Son to give friendship with God. Only if Son and Spirit are truly God do Christians really receive divine life to make friendship a reality. In his theology of unity and Trinity, Tertullian ascended from the actions of God to the immanent life of the Trinity and then to the dignity of human life as capacity for God's life through the Spirit.

Hilary of Poitiers refused to repudiate Athanasius as demanded by Emperor Constantius, who favored Arianism. Hilary was therefore banished to Phrygia, where he learned of the controversies in the Eastern church concerning the *homoousion* or the consubstantiality of Father, Son, and Holy Spirit. There he wrote *The Trinity* out of a desire for himself and for others to have an authentic prayer life, honoring God as he is, not alone but threefold. He wrote with apostolic ardor, convinced that faith in the Trinity was the source of salvation. Therefore he argued against three prevailing heresies: (1) subordinationism or Arius's doctrine that the Son was a creature of God; (2) modalism or Sabellius's doctrine that the Father, Son, and Holy Spirit were merely three different names for one and the same divine person; (3) Photinianism or Photinus's denial of the preexistence of the divine Christ. Arius had reasoned that, since the Father alone is unbegotten, he alone is therefore eternal and true God; Arius conceived of God as *essentially* unbegotten. Although Arius had died in 335, the new representatives of his subordinationist heresy were Ursacius of Singidunum and Valens of Mursa. In his treatise Hilary held together the Nicene stress on the consubstantiality of Father, Son, and Spirit with the emphasis on the special status of the Father found in Origen, Tertullian, and the Cappadocians. Hilary learned from the Greek fathers to speak of one God in three, each of the three containing one another (*circuminsessio* or *perichōrēsis*). Although the heresies he was opposing made him argue for the divinity of the Son, Hilary taught that Father and Son testified to the divinity of the Holy Spirit, and he also pointed to indications of the Trinity in the Old Testament, which did not become evident, however, until after the New Testament revelation of the Trinity. He believed that people should easily be convinced of the reality of the Trinity from Matthew's testimony of the Lord: "Go therefore and make disciples of all nations, baptizing them in the name of the Father and of the Son and of the Holy Spirit, teaching them to observe all that I have commanded you; and lo, I am with you always, to the close of the age" (Matt 28:19; Hilary *The Trinity* 2.1).

Hilary called the Father the source of all things; the Son, the only-begotten through whom are all things; and their Spirit, the gift in all believers. He distinguished between God, who in nature is Spirit and therefore omnipresent, and the Holy Spirit as gift to believers that enables them to know God and to worship him in spirit and in truth. The Spirit as gift to believers is fully God and omnipresent (*The Trinity* 2.31-32). The Spirit guides persons into truth. This gift is offered to all but has to be freely accepted and then retained by fidelity to God's commandments. With this gift comes hope and the overcoming of the fear of death.

Marius Victorinus was a Roman orator who was born in Africa, had a classical and philosophical education, and wrote both Greek and Latin. The story of his conversion to Christianity is told in the eighth book of Augustine's *Confessions*. He had early responded to the Neoplatonic call to the interior life of knowledge, a call to live intellectually rather than materially. He found in the Neoplatonic triad of *esse, vivere, intelligere* a trinitarian image in the soul. As a Christian theologian, he used this triad to demonstrate against Arius and the semi-Arians the reciprocal presence and equality of being, life, and understanding, where the Father as being is the source of the outgoing of life (the Son) and of the return by understanding (the Holy Spirit). Christ is universal life, bringing into the sensible world a higher life and knowledge of God to lead people to God. After Christ's death, the hidden Christ continues to act in the Holy Spirit, principle of the return to God by knowledge. The contemplative return comes from the Holy Spirit's presence in the human person who is opened to the trinitarian life of love. This love cascading within the Trinity is the great kerygma of the incarnation, the revelation of "how God so loved the world." Victorinus read of this divine condescension in John and Paul and synthesized it with what he had learned of the human vocation from the Neoplatonists. In his first book *Against Arius* he wrote:

> For this is a great mystery: that God "emptied Himself when he was in the form of God," then that he suffered, first by being in the flesh and sharing the lot of human birth and being raised upon the Cross. These things, however, would not be marvelous if he had come only from man or from nothing, or from God by creation. For what would "he emptied himself" mean if he did not exist before he was in the flesh? And what was he? He said: "equal to God." But if he were created from nothing, how is he equal? That is why it is "a great mystery" which was manifested in the flesh. (1.26)

The mystery is that of the trinitarian missions. It includes not only the descent of divine life through the Son into the world, into souls at baptism, but also the soul's ascent by contemplation through the Spirit to the Father:

> For the darkness and ignorance of the soul, violated by material powers had need of the help of eternal light so that the logos of the soul and the logos

of the flesh after destroying corruption by the mystery of that death leading
to resurrection, could thus raise up souls and bodies under the guidance of
the Holy Spirit to divine and lifegiving intelligences, uplifted by knowledge,
faith, and love. (Victorinus *Against Arius* 1.48)

The role of the Holy Spirit in the Trinity and in the baptized soul was
discussed more by Victorinus than by his predecessors. Calling the Holy
Spirit the feminine principle in the Trinity, he spoke of the Spirit as the
principle of the identity of the three divine subsistences. For Christians the
Spirit also is the principle of union with God. The ascetical life detaches one
from sensible knowledge to unite one with the divine Spirit of wisdom and
revelation. Faith is the knowledge of God given by the Spirit, a first resurrection to divine life, preparing for wisdom. The soul as predominantly life is
an image of the Son, who is the Father's image. In Christian action the soul
becomes like God. To become like the trinitarian God the soul needs a social
quality, charity leading to contemplation or conversion to the Father.

Like his predecessors, Victorinus taught that all divine activities *ad extra*
were accomplished by the Trinity as unity and yet reflected the threefold
essence:

> In the Three
> A threefold action
> But only one,
> O Blessed Trinity.
> (*Hymn* 3)

## Augustine

Augustine (354–430) learned of Neoplatonism through some Latin translations made by Victorinus, yet the latter's trinitarian theology does not
seem to have influenced Augustine's. In their spirituality, however, both
Victorinus and Augustine saw the human person's being made in the image
of God as the key to a divine vocation. Although Victorinus spoke of this
as a vocation to Christlikeness because of Paul's statement that Christ is the
image of the Father, Augustine took care to say that the human being is
made in the image of the Trinity and is called to the re-formation of that
image, which was deformed by original sin. Faith teaches that if we think
of that image of which it is written, "Let us make man in our image, after
our likeness," not in my image or your image, we must believe that human
beings were made in the image of the Trinity (Augustine *The Trinity*
14.19.25). Moreover, the trinity of the human mind is God's image and
likeness not because the mind remembers, understands, and loves itself, but

because it remembers, understands, and loves its maker. And in doing so it attains wisdom (Augustine *The Trinity* 14.12.15). Because Adam was created in this image and likeness, every child of Adam is *capax Dei*. Faith, hope, and charity will restore the likeness, gradually bringing purity of heart and peace. Only the pure of heart will see God and only the peacemakers will participate in his wisdom. One proceeds from faith to love, from seeing the image of God the Trinity in the mind to seeing God in his image, the human being. Likeness to God enables one to see him, but in a glass darkly, not face to face.

This creation in the image of the Trinity is a call to divine intimacy and community. Augustine used the language of *"reditus"* or return sometimes to indicate introversion in contrast to preoccupation with the sensible world, more often to indicate Godlikeness or that primary state of graced perfection to which the soul yearns to return, the image's clear manifestation of its Exemplar, to that God-given reality of intimacy with the Trinity intended by God and expressed as wisdom, the knowledge and love of God, the happy life of rejoicing "in You and to You and because of You," a joy in truth, that is, in God (Augustine *The Happy Life* 1.4.35).

Augustine's own conversion was his re-formation to the image of the Trinity through the gifts of faith and charity. The capacity for likeness to God is actualized through the Son but refers to the Trinity. If the soul is made in the image of the Son of God, as Paul taught, then in fact it is made in the image of the Trinity, since Christ said: "I and the Father are one." The image can be reformed only by the Trinity who originally made Adam in the image of God in holiness and justice. The Trinity reforms persons not only to intimacy with the three divine persons but to Christian community as well, a community only to be achieved by faith and charity.

The movement of return to God is initiated by the Word of God, who in receiving all in love from the Father returns all in love. Love is the special name of the Spirit, but since God is love and God is Trinity, the Father is love as is the Son. As love, the Father is the principle of creation and providence; as love, the Word is the principle of conversion and illumination; and the Spirit as the principle of love is the principle of return to the Father. Loving intimacy with the Trinity is true contemplative wisdom, and wisdom is the true and only image of God, a dynamic process of involvement in God, society, and the world through love. In intimacy with the divine persons the soul attains likeness to wisdom and shares in divine creative and providential action, illuminating and loving action.

The image, according to Paul (1 Cor 13:12) is a mirror that more or less perfectly reflects God. But, because the image is located in the intellectual acts of remembering, understanding, and willing, there is no suggestion here of a material image like a picture but rather of an activity directed to God the Trinity by the Trinity. There will come the day of transformation when one is "changed into his likeness from one degree of glory to another; for this comes from the Lord who is the Spirit" (2 Cor 3:18). This is interpreted by Augustine to signify spiritual progress, when he says: "This is what takes place in those who are making progress steadily day by day" (*Confessions* 7.10). And so he prayed: "May I remember You, understand You, and love You. Increase these gifts in me until You have re-formed me completely" (*The Trinity* 14.17.23).

Augustine constantly dwelled upon the mystery of the incarnation, but this never meant that he considered the mystery of the Trinity unimportant for spiritual life. The two mysteries are intimately connected. Christ as incarnate lived his trinitarian life. The Holy Spirit led him to the desert to speak with his Father. And Christ made known to his followers the existence of the Trinity, as does the church at every baptism, consecrating each one to these three as related to one another. Like Victorinus, Augustine was humbled by God's love for creatures and saw this as a reflection of the life of love within the Trinity.

Influenced by the Latin and Greek fathers, especially Gregory Nazianzus, Augustine developed a distinctive trinitarian theology. The Son is the perfect substantial expression of the Father, the generation of his self-knowledge; the Holy Spirit proceeds from Father and Son by spiration, a shared kiss. Therefore the Spirit proceeds from Father and Son as from one principle. From the Father as source the Son holds the power to send the Spirit forth at Pentecost. Father and Son meet in a love common to both, the Holy Spirit. Although he emphasized how the visible missions (the incarnation and the Spirit taking bodily form at the baptism of Jesus and at Pentecost) make us aware of the divine relationships, Augustine was more concerned with how the spiritual life of Christians is transformed by the invisible missions, the indwelling of the triune persons in the souls of the justified. He learned of this presence of the Son from John and Paul (John 14:23; 17:23; Gal 2:20; Rom 8:10; Eph 3:17) and of the presence of the Holy Spirit from Paul (1 Cor 6:19; 12:11; Gal 4:6).

The Trinity is present to actualize by their own communion the friendship of persons with God and with one another. The mystery of the Fatherhood is the mystery of self-giving, the ecstasy, the kenosis. He surrenders himself completely as Father of the Son and breathes forth the Spirit, love substantialized. All things are known in his Word and created in his love, the Holy Spirit. To creatures the Son reveals the Father, and in the hearts of the faithful the Spirit plants a spirit of adopted children so that they may know and cry out to their Father in heaven. The Son glorifies the Father, the Spirit glorifies the Son (John 16:14) and pours love into the hearts of believers. The willingness to be continually created by God in his image and likeness is the beginning of Christian perfection. Like the Son we are to receive all from the Father, and like the Father we are to make a gift of self, releasing self-will to become available to God in prayer and to neighbor in service like Christ, who washed the feet of his apostles (John 13:14–17), and like the Spirit, ever glorifying Father and Son.

The value of Augustine's trinitarian theology for Christian spirituality resides in his reflection upon the creation of Adam in the image of the Trinity and upon love as the ground of trinitarian relating in community. He made relationship not merely a theological tool for explaining the Trinity but the central issue of Christian life. Under the influence of Paul, Augustine cited charity as the fundamental end of the contemplative life. Although Victorinus was the earliest theologian to work out the Holy Spirit's consubstantiality with Father and Son, he identified the Holy Spirit with knowledge, whereas Augustine concentrated on the unifying function of the Spirit in the Trinity as expressive of love's centrality in Christian life. He was the first to identify the Holy Spirit explicitly with love (*The Trinity* 9.12.17).

> Wherefore the Holy Spirit also subsists in this same unity and equality of substance. For whether he is the unity between both of them, or their holiness, or their love, or whether the unity because he is the holiness, it is obvious that he is not one of the two. Through him both are joined together; through him the begotten is loved by the begetter, and in turn loves him who begot him; in Him they preserve the unity of spirit through the bond of peace (Eph 4:3) not by participation but by their own essence, not by the gift of anyone superior to themselves but by their own gift. And we are commanded by grace to imitate this unity, both in our relations with God as well as among ourselves. On these two commandments depend the whole Law and the Prophets (Matt 22:37–40). (Augustine *The Trinity* 6.5.7)

The imaging of the Trinity does not confine itself to the activities of mind. It required a synthesizing of knowledge, love, and action. The real relations within the Trinity are the paradigm for Christian life, which is the community life of real human beings. All material things, all actions, and all natural knowledge are to be used in the service of love. Commenting on the epistles of John and of Paul, Augustine said: "Charity is the soul of the Scriptures, the virtue of prophecies, the salvation given by the Sacraments, the foundation of knowledge, the fruit of faith, the riches of the poor, the life of the dying" (*Commentary on the First Epistle of John* 5.7; *Commentary on the Epistle to the Galatians* 4.5).

Openness to the Spirit for the strengthening of love will form the communion of saints. The Christian community is universal rather than exclusive; it has one mind and one heart. The community described in the Acts of the Apostles inspired Augustine's *Rule* for monastic life. He looked upon monasteries as centers for the education of love in order to realize a more perfect imaging of the Trinity in response to the prayer of Christ: "That they may be one even as we are one, I in them and thou in me, that they may become perfectly one" (John 17:23).

## Richard of St. Victor

Trinitarian spirituality permeates the teaching of Richard of St. Victor (d. 1173), who belonged to the community at Paris founded by William of Champeaux. Hugh of St. Victor was the moving spirit of the speculative and affective mysticism of the Abbey of St. Victor. Richard systematized the mystical doctrines of Hugh and became a spiritual master of the Middle Ages. The inspiration for a mystical ascent to the Trinity primarily through love responsive to God's presence in the human soul was Augustinian, an influence that reached Alexander of Hales and Bonaventure through the Victorines.

In Richard of St. Victor's *The Trinity* we see religious devotion closely linked with the understanding of faith. His theology manifested his faith and expressed his personal assimilation of the *credo* into his life. This way to a closer union with God was recommended by Richard to the young religious in the Abbey of St. Victor. Authority was used as a beginning rather than as an ending to thought, and thought itself was for the sake of love. Influenced by Augustine, Dionysius, Boethius, Anselm, and Cassian, his trinitarian theology was nevertheless original. The fundamental metaphysical intuition guiding his thinking, an Anselmian one, was that God is perfect existence. But Richard, inspired by John and Augustine, went beyond Anselm and called charity the most perfect property of the most perfect Being.

Perfect charity requires a trinity of persons: love of friendship requires another person, but perfect love of friendship implies a third to share the regard in which the lover holds the beloved and is regarded by the beloved as the beloved is regarded by him. Thus to the "mutual love" of Father and Son cited by Augustine, Richard added "shared love," the lover wishing to share with a third person his own joy in the beloved. The lover also wishes that the beloved share in the kind of love that is complete giving and not only a return of love; in this way the Son gives his all to the Holy Spirit as the Father gave his all to the Son (Richard of St. Victor *The Trinity* 3.19).

The love of two persons is not merely mutual but unites into one love, a common love for another that establishes them in the deepest possible union.

Shared love, the characteristic of perfect love, is not present in the Trinity unless there is a third person. Thus, the Holy Spirit proceeds from Father and Son as from one principle. The personal properties are limited to the three kinds of love: gratuitous, responsive-gratuitous, responsive. To give is the personal property of the unbegotten Father, to receive is the property that distinguishes the person of the Son, who also gives to the Holy Spirit, who is totally receptive from the Father and the Son from both of whom he simultaneously proceeds. The Father is giver, the Son is receiver and giver, the Holy Spirit is gift, as Hilary of Poitiers had perceived. Distinguished by their relations of love, the divine persons are constituted by their origins.

Richard's faith-understanding of God as Trinity illuminates the experience of interpersonal love as self-transcending. The spiritual life begins in carnal love which is gradually liberated into perfect charity, a love of the other as other and yet one with oneself. But in order that natural love be deified, there needs to be participation in the Holy Spirit. The Holy Spirit is not only gift within the Trinity but also gift to human souls, urging them to turn toward God in what can only be "responsive love." The action of the Spirit on the human spirit transforms it to the likeness of Spirit (Love) as fire transforms iron (Richard of St. Victor *The Trinity* 6.14). This transforming union with the Holy Spirit leads to spiritual marriage and makes human souls fruitful in the works of love.

The interpersonal love in the Trinity illuminates what is expected of human love, which is an image of God. Rather than merely being the source of individual satisfaction, love is intended to be the source of community expressed by communication and reciprocity.

Richard expressed that spirituality which had been lived by the many who recognized in the Trinity the exemplar of the communal love of authentic Christians. Christians are baptized not only in the name of the Trinity but are baptized into the believing community which by charity reflects the Trinity. They are called to strengthen that reflection. This is assisted through the Eucharist, which is not only a community celebration but also a trinitarian liturgy promoting community as openness to the Spirit of love, excluding none.

The spiritual life of the early and medieval Christians was an absorbing effort to return to the Father with the risen Christ. Spirituality did not mean immateriality, a repudiation of half of human nature, the body. It was a communion with the Father through the Son in the Holy Spirit and with one another by a shared love for God. Martyrdom and monasticism were positive rather than negative forces. They enabled Christians to identify with Christ in his passion and death and to enter into trinitarian life by contemplation and love. Proceeding from the union of Father and Son the Spirit of love is creative of community, binding all to Father and Son and to one another. This is the great mission. Spiritual life is no flight from the "alone to the Alone," but a relating to all in the threefold way of Father, Son, and Spirit. It includes the interiority of openness to the Father's generosity, to the Son's wisdom, to the Spirit's love expressing itself in community. This was early noted by Tertullian, when he said, "See these Christians, how they love one another" (*Apology* 39).

Trinitarian spirituality manifested in the prayer and attitudes of Christians preceded and followed the development of the dogma of the Trinity. The divinity of Christ was firmly rooted in Christian belief when the epistles and Gospels were being written (Heb 1:8–9; John 1:1; 1:18; 20:28; 1 John 5:20; Titus 2:13; Rom 9:4; 2 Pet 1:1). The New Testament echoes the oral tradition of faith in Jesus Christ the redeemer who declares himself to be only Son to the Father, one with the Father, and with the Father sending the Spirit. The oral and scriptural tradition was expressed in the Roman creed of the second century transmitted as the Apostles' Creed, reproduced in early form in the first-century *Didache* and in the second century in Justin Martyr's *Apology* and *Dialogue with Trypho the Jew*. The move from this symbolic expression to conceptual expression took place at Nicaea in 325, where, in opposition to Arius, the Son was declared to be consubstantial with the Father because everything true of the Father is true of the Son except that the Son is not the Father. Paul taught that the Spirit is no less than God (Rom 8:14–18) and John intimated the personhood and divinity of the Holy Spirit, the other Paraclete (John 14:16; 5:26; 16:7). This divinity of the Spirit realized in devotion and symbolized in Scripture was conceptualized by Athanasius and Victorinus and was formulated as a dogma in the Council of Constantinople (381), which completed the definition of the Trinity begun at Nicaea. The faith of Christians in the Father, Word, and Spirit expressed itself first in prayer, attitude, and action; only later was it articulated in the dogma of the Trinity: *lex orandi, lex docendi.*

Just as conciliar and dogmatic formulations do not claim to encompass the totality of the divine reality, to say all that can be said, so the spirituality to which they give rise should not succumb to complacency. The effort to live out what has been understood of God's revelation in any age does not remove the mystery of the Trinity, which will always ground an apophatic experience of the Father as well as a ceaseless development in affirmative theology, giving rise to always more integral spiritual attitudes. The spirituality of the medieval world grew out of patristic spirituality with its theological character and its view of the universe as the vestige of God, of the human being as the image of God. There was no opposition between progress in the spiritual life and the love of learning. The origin of the Son and the Spirit was articulated as proceeding from knowledge and love. When knowledge and love promoted each other in human life, a strong and authentic spirituality nourished great mystics. There was no return to God without knowledge and love. The return to divine unity was begun by the transformation of these two in faith and charity. It was a religious experience that led to ineffable union with God.

Thus, the early and medieval Christians did not consider the Trinity to be irrelevant to Christian life. It made them conscious of interiority and of eschatology. But in focusing upon the riches of the interior life and of future life, did trinitarian spirituality show sufficient respect for the human, for the bodily? Augustine, it is true, found the image of God in the soul, as did Victorinus and Richard of St. Victor. Yet Victorinus who taught that the human being was made according to the image of Christ said that because Christ was incarnate, then the whole human person, body and soul, was made in his image. Although he did not accept this position, Augustine realized that Christ is the way to our knowledge of the Trinity and to our life in the Trinity. He is the exemplar of how to live a trinitarian life open to the mystery of the Father, acting in love-obedience in a world where God as immanent is to be respected and cherished in all things. The incarnate Son, the Word, makes possible the process of entering deeply into the human and the cosmic to sacralize them. Just as the Son's life in the Trinity enabled him to unify the divine and the human, so the Trinity's image in the human soul enables a human person to unite the divine and the human, including the body, in the movement toward the absolute, a movement that restores all things in Christ. The re-forming of the soul's trinitarian image is effected through the Father's image, Jesus, our exemplar and mediator, who lived in time and history.

The doctrine of the Trinity, when linked with the image doctrine of Genesis, provides a sense of the dignity of being human. A person differs from animals not merely by rationality but by being made in the image of God. All have divine vocation to the unity of the Trinity: a community of friendship with God and with others. Through grace and free choice one's obedience to the new law of love, which Christ vividly manifested, reforms the defaced image of God in the human being and reveals God in his reality as Trinity, that is, as community.

# Bibliography

## Studies

Bouyer, Louis. *The Spirituality of the New Testament and the Fathers.* Vol. 1 of *A History of Christian Spirituality.* New York: Seabury, 1982. A chronological development of Christian spirituality that shows the concern of the fathers to preserve by dogmatic exactitude the integrity and authenticity of spirituality.

Daniélou, Jean. *The Origins of Latin Christianity.* Philadelphia: Westminster, 1977. A rich, detailed exposition of Latin theology, preceded by a study of Latin Judeo-Christianity.

Hill, William J. *The Three Personed God.* Washington, DC: Catholic University Press, 1982. A historical and systematic study of the doctrine of the Trinity that differentiates the patristic-medieval understanding of the Trinity from that of the nineteenth- and twentieth-century thinkers and offers a reinterpretation of the Trinity according to new insights on personhood.

Panikkar, Raimundo. *The Trinity and the Religious Experience of Man.* New York: Orbis Books, 1973. A brilliant exposition of the interrelatedness of the ultimate mysteries of the world and an ecumenical approach to diversity in spirituality.

Prestige, G. L. *God in Patristic Thought.* London: S.P.C.K., 1959. A careful presentation of patristic theology developed with philosophical precision.

Sullivan, John E. *The Image of God.* Dubuque, IA: Priory Press, 1963. A fine synthesis of the main images of God set forth by Augustine, followed by a discussion of his originality and influence.

# 12

# The Human Person as Image of God

## I. *Eastern Christianity*

### Lars Thunberg

IN CHRISTIAN SPIRITUALITY the human being as a person is of decisive importance.[1] This does not mean that Christian spirituality is individualistic. The human person is always seen in a social context. It is the person together with neighbors who is the subject of Christian spirituality. This means, too, that anthropology and ecclesiology (the understanding of the human person and the understanding of the church respectively) are interrelated.

The human being as a person is also always understood as being created in the image of God. The image character of a person's being and the image purpose of a person's existence constitute the characteristics of Christian spirituality. Therefore, the human being as person and God as the co-personal counterpart are seen as the decisive factors in this spirituality. What Martin Buber, from a Jewish point of view, called "the I-Thou relationship" is thus relevant also for Christian thought. The human being as image of the divine reality is never understood merely as a reflecting mirror, but as an individual subject, challenged in freedom by God and responding in action and worshipful recognition—or sinful revolt—to that challenge.[2]

The basis of this Christian spirituality was laid in the early church. Its authoritative writers and spiritual fathers developed its anthropology into a concise foundation for their reflections on spiritual development. In this context the two concepts of "image" and "person" are crucial. The human person is basically understood as a being who is the bearer of an "iconological" purpose in relation to God within the created order, and who is, at the same time, a person, that is, a being who is able to develop a self, which is neither just an individual within a species nor a disloyal resistance center within a given order. The concepts of image and person, as a matter of fact, belong together. Divine life is understood as personal. God is divinity in three persons—and thus the human being, as bearing the image of God, is necessarily a person.

It belongs to the genius of the early church that it was able to concentrate its attention on theological themes that were decisive for human spirituality. Three such themes are predominant, and at each point a peculiar Christian perspective is worked out: (1) the understanding of God, in which the divine reality is conceived of as trinitarian; (2) the understanding of salvation, in which Christ, the Savior, is conceived of as a *theandric* (i.e., a divine/human) *mystery;* and (3) the understanding of human beings, conceived of as *persons carrying the image of God in themselves.* In relation to all these three themes the concept of person is relevant.

In the development of its trinitarian theology the early church saw God as one substance actively manifesting itself, outwardly and inwardly, as three persons—the Father, the Son, and the Holy Spirit. This led to the insight that person is an individualization within the same nature or species, but more than that, since *God is the persons.* Especially in the Eastern tradition of the ancient church it is evident that the divine nature is not something that exists in itself, so that the persons of the Trinity could be understood just as three subordinate manifestations of their common nature, but that it exists only in so far as it manifests itself in Father, Son, and Spirit.[3]

This has repercussions for Christian anthropology. In the development of its christology (which is its doctrine of salvation) the ancient church saw Christ as a divine/human *person* (Greek *hypostasis,* Latin *persona*), which means that *the category of person transcends the limits of what is naturally given.* Christ consists of two natures but is nevertheless one person, as the Council of Chalcedon in 451 stated.[4]

Finally, in the development of its anthropology, the ancient church concentrated its attention on humans as composite beings—body and soul—and yet a unity, charged by God with a purpose in the world that is linked to their being "in the image of God." This unity is relevant to one's being a person, and yet one's personal being is intimately and exclusively related to one's "image" character.[5]

Thus, in the ancient church, no evaluation of human beings is possible without consideration of their relationship to God—one in three persons—or to Christ, the divine/human Savior, who is one person in two natures.

# Humans and Christ
## in their Image Character

What we have now stated is, of course, the fruit of a development that took place over centuries. No spiritual insight of this kind is mature at the outset. The roots of this anthropology are obvious. One of them is ancient biblical tradition. In Gen 1:26 God is said to have created man in his image and likeness. The Hebrew words here are *ṣelem* and *dĕmût*, both of which express the same idea: that the human being, in virtue of God's intention, is given a special position within the created universe—to name, to rule, to summarize, and to keep together under God. That is, the human being is God's viceroy on earth. Yet this is only one of the biblical stories of the creation of humankind. In Gen 2:17 we learn that God created the human out of dust and breathed his own spirit into the human's nostrils in order to make the human alive. The early church was bound to take both these accounts of creation seriously, and it did so in struggling with the possible meaning of the two stories in relation to each other.

At the same time, the early church was the steward of an apostolic tradition where humanity was seen both as fallen in Adam and restored again in Christ, the New Adam (Paul's contention in 1 Cor 15). Paul, too, saw the human being as the image of God, but especially in Christ, and as a being endued with God's Spirit at the end of times thanks to Christ's redemption. Likewise, the early church emerged within a Hellenistic cultural context. It was thus bound both to deal with Greek philosophy and to handle the Old Testament in its Greek version, the Septuagint. And there the rendering of Gen 1:26 seems more explicitly distinctive: the human is created not only "in the image of God" (*kat' eikona*) but also "into his likeness" (*kat' homoiōsin*), and this seems to imply a distance between what is given at the outset and what could be realized within the category of time. And if this is combined with the concept of humanity's fall and sinfulness, it might lead to an understanding of humans as in tension between their "ontological" image character and their "moral" similitude.[6]

In Christian tradition *Christ is always the true image of God* (both as identical with the creative Word, the Logos, and as incarnate in humanity), and actual human beings are only *according to* this image, that is, an image of the image.[7] The Logos is seen as the prototype, which God used in creating humans in his image, and Christ is seen as the archetype of what it is to be human. But Christ is, in his duality, also a person. And thus human beings, in reflecting the archetype successively, may develop their likeness to God as *personal* fulfillment. Let us now see more in detail how this general perspective was developed in the early church.

## Humans as Composite Beings

Early Christian tradition saw human beings as dual. They consist of both body and soul/spirit. This fact represents a problem but also a possibility. As a problem it is reflected, for example, in Origen (d. ca. 254), who, basing himself on Genesis 1 and 2, constructed a theory of a double creation: the first being one of pure spirits gathered around God, but finally falling into corruption; the second being effectuated by God in the act of rescuing fallen creation, giving humans bodies to gather up their falling and frozen souls (*psychai*).[8] This theory was later condemned as heresy, since it was in conflict with the biblical understanding of creation as basically good (see Gen 1:31), but it remained influential in later times. As a possibility, human duality was first elaborated by Irenaeus of Lyons (d. ca. 200), who regarded Adam as not yet mature but endowed with a divine task to develop his capacities to their fullness. This development was interrupted by the fall, but, since humans are restored in Christ (recapitulating their history in himself), they are in their freedom free to become what they were intended to be.[9]

Gregory Nazianzen, the Cappadocian father (d. 389), wrestled considerably with the problem of the composite makeup of human beings. They are a "mixture" or a "mingling" of body and soul. They are "at the same time spirit and flesh," and yet it is precisely as this mixture that they are rulers on earth, "a kind of second world," "fully initiated into the visible creation but only partially into the intellectual."[10] And this fact is not only an expression of the fallenness of human beings (as in Origen) but also, and foremost, a sign of their being preserved—by God in creating them both body and soul—from the most disastrous destiny (exemplified by the fallen angel Lucifer) of a creation that revolts against its Creator.[11] In the development of Christian thought, it thus becomes more and more clear that humans' composite being is to be regarded as their special prerogative, putting them into a unique position within the created order without letting them either usurp the exclusive position of God or be absorbed by material creation. They are in a position *in between,* which implies struggle, and it is precisely this position that renders humans both weak and pretentious. In the Eastern tradition of Christian thought the first aspect predominated; in the Western, the latter.

To Origen there was no initial coexistence of body and soul, although God in his providence used their secondary coexistence in his pedagogical scheme.[12] Later Christian writers, however, having rejected this theory, were able to see in the coexistence of body and soul in humans a divine instrument from the beginning. Gregory of Nyssa, another of the Cappadocian fathers (d. ca. 395), in his *De hominis opificio* (*On the Creation of Man*) claimed that the Origenist position was intimately connected with an idea of *metempsychōsis,* and he argued that a fall into the material world would not imply a purification but rather successive falls—or a superiority of sensual life over against spiritual life.[13] And this would again be in opposition to humanity's bearing the image of God.

For a later father, Maximus the Confessor (d. 662), who similarly started from a rejection of the Origenist theory, it was evident that body and soul cannot exist separately. They are by necessity linked to each other. But this is the very secret of human beings; they are a composite nature. God willed it in this way.[14] Leontius of Byzantium (the sixth-century monk and theologian) was of the same conviction. It is part of God's plan that human beings should consist of body and soul.[15] For Maximus, however, this plan was expressed in the very constitution of the human being. Body and soul not only form a composite nature, with its own principle of being, but also a complete species.[16] Thus, the human as a composite being is unique, and it is this uniqueness that is "according to the image."

Now, this again is of a special soteriological relevance, since there exists an *analogy between humanity's composite nature and the unity between divine and human nature in Christ.* Cyril of Alexandria (d. 444) used this analogy extensively and made it popular among contemporary and later church teachers.[17] Since Christ is the true image of God, this analogy seems to convey to the whole of humanity a secondary image character, which is fundamental and basic, even if it remains a fact that the early church located the image of God in humans in the soul, particularly in the higher part of the soul, the mind (*nous*).

## The Human as Microcosm

The dual composition of humanity was, thus, in early Christian tradition not only a problem but also a possibility. This possibility was often elaborated in terms of the human being's character as *microcosm.* The view of the human as microcosm goes further back than Christian thought. Its presence in Greek antiquity was probably due to Oriental influences. Already Democritus stated that the human being is a microcosm, and, although Plato never used the term, the whole dialogue of *Timaeus* is marked by the fact that the world is described as one great human being. In Aristotle we find the explicit terminology, but the concept does not play a very important role. Stoic philosophy, however, caused the idea to flourish, for there it was intimately connected with a corresponding idea of God's immanence in the world. On this basis the following formula could be devised: "What God is to the world, the soul is to the human being," the analogy between the two being taken for granted. Generally, however, the idea was conceived in such a way that humans simply reflect the world around them, even though Plato rather described the world in human terms.[18]

In the Christian tradition, therefore, a new element had to be added to the idea. It remained true that the world was seen as macrocosm, and the human as microcosm, but the microcosm character of humans is related also to their relationship to God. The human being is microcosm—in a wider sense—precisely because it is created in the image of God. Ancient Christian use of the concept probably developed under the influence of Philo, the Jewish philosopher and theologian. For him, however, the matter was more complicated than in the pagan philosophers, since he related himself to the biblical concept of humanity. Philosophically he relied more on the Platonic than on the Stoic tradition. Philo made a strict distinction between human beings created in the image of God and human beings formed from the earth. The analogy between humanity and the world has, thus, to include a dual perspective. In the end, the real analogy is that which exists between the Logos and the human mind (*nous*), on the one hand, and the material world and the human body, on the other.[19] Some Christian writers used precisely this duality in order to make a positive evaluation of humanity's status and task.

This is obvious already in the Cappadocian fathers, who seem to have used the concept of the human being as microcosm rather frequently. Basil of Caesarea (d. 379) thus stated that human beings are, by attending to themselves, able to see the wisdom of the Creator as in a microcosm, thereby referring to the interplay between the different elements within the human being, as an analogy to the cosmic order, in both of which God's creative wisdom is reflected.[20]

In Gregory Nazianzen, a microcosm motif is present in many places, although he generally did not use this term for the human as a mixed being.[21] On one occasion, however, he explicitly used the expression "the little world" about human beings and there in reference to the receptive powers of humans in their relation to the outside world, on account of which the human soul may be said to contain this world within itself.[22] But in doing so the soul is also performing a task open to humans precisely because they are microcosms: the soul is called to bring the body into living relationship to God. The human being, as a unity of distinctive elements, one intellectual and spiritual and the other limited and material—precisely in this capacity—is "a king on earth and a praiser of God."

Gregory of Nyssa, finally, used the concept of the human being as a microcosm in several places, although he is eager to point out that humanity's
likeness to the created universe is not the reason for its greatness. Created
multiplicity is an element in the analogy between microcosm and macrocosm, but in order to bring this fact into its right proportion, reference must
be made to the doctrine of the image of God in humanity. Human beings
are, in fact, *called to mediate between the intelligible and the sensible world.*[23]
This again, of course, actualizes humanity's fall and sinfulness and the consequent disorder in creation.

Thus, to early Christian thought, humanity's immature state in the beginning (in the way in which this idea was first developed by Irenaeus) as well
as its composite nature invite human beings to function in relation to creation as fulfillers of a higher purpose, and this means that the character of
microcosm is linked to a task of mediation. This becomes particularly
explicit in Maximus the Confessor and, before him, in a Syrian writer,
Nemesius of Emesa. To the latter, human beings are not primarily passive
reflectors of the created universe; they are called to perform a function
precisely as microcosm. They are called to *act* as microcosm in uniting in
themselves the opposite elements of the world. This task of human beings
means that they have to join together things that are opposites: mortal
creatures with immortal; rational beings with irrational. In Nemesius the
tension between the idea of the human being as a microcosm, reflecting the
outside world, and the idea of the human being as created in the image of
God is more definitely reconciled through the insistence on the *function* of
the human being in the world. This particular combination we find again
in Maximus the Confessor, who developed it into a theology of humanity's
fivefold mediation, as we shall see later. For the time being, it may be
enough to state that it is thus the human being as created in the image of
God who is at the same time a composite being, whose unity makes it
possible for him to work out his character of image both as personal fulfillment (liberated in Christ from sinfulness) and as a task of mediation within
the created world, linking that world to the Creator in worshipful
perfection.[25]

## Image and Likeness:
## an Important Distinction

In order to conceptualize humanity's constitution as a task, the early church
frequently made a distinction between image and likeness in the biblical
story about creation. We have stressed that the Hebrew terms *ṣelem* and
*dĕmût* do not convey any such distinction but are simply synonyms. But

in the Greek Old Testament, the terms *eikōn* (image) and *homoiōsis* (like-ness) seem to be more open to a distinction between two meanings. Origen linked this to his observations about the two creations. In Gen 1:26 it is God's final intention that is sketched out, and, therefore, both image and likeness are mentioned. But in 1:27 only the image is mentioned (God explicitly leaving out the likeness), and this indicated to Origen that the human being received in the first creation the dignity of image but that the perfection of the likeness was reserved for the end of history (on account of God's pedagogical efforts as well as humanity's positive imitation of God). Thus, for Origen likeness was acquired by human beings through imitation of God.[26]

Later Christian writers partly followed Origen in this line. The distinction as such, though, is older than Origen. To Clement of Alexandria (d. ca. 215) likeness meant something more than what is naturally given. And Irenaeus might have been the first church father to use the distinction, since the human character of image is to him no sign of human perfection, but indi-cates a task, the culmination of which is supposed to be likeness to God. Yet not all ancient Christian writers used the explicit distinction, partly because of a reaction against excesses of scriptural interpretation,[28] but first of all because too sharp a distinction (completed in the spirit of Origen) might bring with it the idea that something is lacking in created humanity as such and that the mind, which alone carries the divine image, is bound down through its relationship to the body and has to free itself through ascetic efforts in order to gain the divine likeness.[28] Thoughts on this line were a temptation to the Cappadocians, particularly the two Gregorys, and perhaps for that reason they hesitated to use the distinction.[29]

Later, however, it again became popular. Maximus the Confessor, for example, might at this point have been influenced by Diadochus of Photice (present at the Council of Chalcedon in 451), for whom likeness was above image.[30] But this is certainly not the only explanation. His use of it must be seen in contrast to a rather massive refusal to use it (e.g., in most of the Latin fathers and in an influential Greek father such as Cyril of Alexan-dria).[31] For Maximus, however, the use of the distinction did not seem to cause any difficulties, possibly because he had access to what was the real sense of the distinction when it was used. And this sense was shared by the majority of his predecessors.

The sense behind the distinction is not necessarily linked to Origen's particular theory of creation. For the point is that *the very concept of image contains a dynamism.* Image represents not only a status but also a potentiality, and this potentiality blossoms only when human beings are set free by Christ from enslavement to sin and are able to develop the potential capacities given at creation to their full maturity. If the distinction is used, it thus primarily serves the purpose of underlining this dynamic aspect of the concept of image. Human beings are created in the image of God, in order that they may become like God. And this likeness is both their own maturity as human beings and their fulfillment of a microcosmic and mediating task within the created universe.[32]

All through Christian thought humanity's particular position within the created order was underlined. The concept of the image of God was instrumental in bringing this out, and the concept of likeness helped to underline the active consequences of humanity's status. However, the status and task of human beings, who are created in the image and likeness of God, were also viewed from different points of view. In order to make the idea more concrete at this point, it seems wise to concentrate on some particular illustrations and also to bear in mind how humanity's status is regarded as both a personal and a collective one. When the Christian tradition talks about human beings, it sees them as representative in all respects:[33] microcosmically representative in relation to the rest of creation, individually representative of humanity, and representative of the created order in its relationship to God, Christ being both the primary image and the primarily representative man in full likeness.

Thus, let us in turn consider three aspects of the question: (a) the position of human beings under the aspect of their dominion; (b) the task of human beings under the aspect of their contemplative capacity; and (c) the unity of human beings as the unity of humanity, created and restored in Christ the Logos. With the first of these aspects we shall deal at greater length, since it summarizes in many respects what is characteristic of early Christian anthropology.

## Human Beings as God's
## Rational Viceroys on Earth

Today the Christian tradition is often accused of having evaluated humanity's place in creation so highly that it involved an open invitation to use nature's resources to extremes and to destroy nature at will. This is, however, a false accusation both in regard to medieval theology and, not least, in regard to the theology of the early church. And precisely at this point what we stated at the very outset of this article is relevant: Christian anthropology as it was developed in the early church was primarily concerned with the spirituality of human persons. Their dominion over the earth, part of their image character, is understood in terms of a spiritual enterprise, and, when human beings become absorbed by the material side of this enterprise, this is regarded as an expression of their sinfulness rather than of their rightful sovereignty.

The attitude of the early church at this point, of course, was not entirely uniform. Characteristic, however, for its thinking in general, was the fact that the interplay between what is biological and what is spiritual was understood differently at that time from the way it is now. For the early church human beings were primarily souls, having also bodies, through which they were related to what we might call biological/material creation. As such they were regarded as microcosms that reflected the universe. To us today, on the contrary, human beings are biological beings with such a degree of psychic and spiritual capacity as to allow them to survey and transcend their own biological conditions. To the early church it was important to underline that human beings, in spite of their materiality and corporeality, were capable of maintaining themselves as spiritual beings, whereas we in our time rather take the biological constitution of human beings for granted and find it important to underline that to this biological capacity there belongs also an ability to give consciousness to biological life and make it subservient to a mindful purpose—an ability, though, that can be used for good or bad.[34]

Gen 1:26 and 1:28 form, of course, the biblical basis for the ideas of the early church also about human dominion. Dominion is part of humanity's image character. But this also means that God's dominion becomes a model for humanity's, and human beings can rule on earth only as God's viceroys. Generally speaking, thus, all early Christian reflections about God's relationship to the created world are at stake. It is not surprising that the biblical stories about creation were frequently commented upon in the early church. In an inventory, once made by Yves Congar, we find the following remarkable names from that period: Theophilus of Antioch, Hippolytus, Clement of Alexandria, Origen, Victorinus of Pettau, Ephrem the Syrian, Basil of Caesarea, Eusebius of Nemesa, Prudentius, Gregory of Nyssa, Ambrose, Augustine, Theodore of Mopsuestia, Theodoret, Procopius of Gaza, Jacob of Sarug, Isidore of Seville, etc.[35] Yet this list refers only to works that deal explicitly with the subject. Shorter references are, of course, even more numerous.

Here we shall concentrate on a few important viewpoints in the early church that are related to the concept of human dominion as part of humanity's being created in the image of God.

A primary point is the fact that the biblical narrative about creation was regarded as answering fundamental questions raised in regard to the function of humanity. Thus, *the narrative primarily states a fact* rather than implies a moral appeal. The story about God's creation is more an explanation than a command. The recognizable fact is the actual carrying out of God's command and intention. A basic power to change the conditions of created order fundamentally was not presupposed in the time of the early church. A number of writers testified indirectly to this fact.

Origen could be mentioned as an example. In a homily on Gen 1:26 he simply registered that humanity holds a position in creation that corresponds to what is said in the text. Origen's main interest, however, was allegorical interpretation, to which we shall return.[36] Another example is Basil's tenth homily on the days of creation (a text which, although perhaps not by Basil himself, is nevertheless representative of the ideas of the early church), where the basic attitude is a similar one: simple observations about humanity's role in relation to the animals show the situation that Gen 1:26 refers to. When a human's shadow falls upon a pond, the fishes do not dare to come to the surface. The dolphin gets scared, when a human approaches, and, although the lion is feared by all other animals, a human is capable of putting it into a cage, etc.[37] The attitude of the author may seem a bit cruel, but the point is that it is a matter of pure observation, not of morality.

Thus, we can conclude that to the early church humanity's dominion to a great extent consists in its very status and not in activities that interfere with the created order. But it is as rational beings that humans exert their dominion. The concept of dominion thus acquires an ontological or even formalistic character, although in Western tradition there emerged a somewhat different attitude: humanity's dominion (as well as other expressions of its sovereignty) is also due to an explicit divine commandment, for which an additional gift of God is provided. However, to be able to rule is one thing, and actually to do so is another. Here it is a logical conclusion that humanity lost a considerable part of its factual dominion through its fall and sinfulness. The writers of the early church partly oscillate between these two positions, an optimistic one and a more pessimistic one, but neither position invites arbitrariness.

In the tenth homily on the days of creation, attributed to Basil the Great, we noticed a reference to observable facts. But these facts also have an explanation. *Human beings exert dominion thanks to their rationality.* Since human beings received the power to command on account of the superiority of reason, they are able to exert dominion over the animals. They cannot fly like the birds, but the human mind moves everywhere, and thanks to human intelligence, everything is under humanity's dominion.[38]

However, this is only one side of the matter. To the early church it is clear that human beings exert a factual dominion on earth but also that they misuse their position to satisfy their own egoistic needs. What Adam possessed in the beginning, he partly lost through his fall. Only thanks to Christ's restoration of humanity's rightful position are human beings capable of dominion in the proper sense of the word. But this means that the dominion aspects of humanity's image character are qualified through christology. On the one hand, it remains a fact that human beings exert their dominion on account of their created rational nature. John Chrysostom stated that nothing on earth is superior to humanity and that everything is thus submitted to it.[39] And Theodoret of Cyrus noticed that human beings exert dominion already in building houses, walls, cities, ports, ships, etc.[40] On the other hand, Cyril of Alexandria underlined that the actual exertion of dominion is also owing to an additional gift of God, since everything that we possess is a gift of God. What Adam possessed in the beginning was lost through the fall and was regained in Christ. And this means, consequently, that humanity's rightful exertion of dominion is, in the last instance, a fruit of redemption.[41]

This view may be expressed dialectically. On the one hand, dominion is given through the rational nature of human beings; on the other hand, its exertion depends on the relationship of human beings to God. Isidore of Pelusium even went so far as to state that the image character of human beings is due rather to their factual dominion than to their nature. When Adam actually exerted his likeness to God, he had the power to give names to the animals, but when he became disobedient this power was taken from him. Noah and Daniel were unique among humanity, since they were righteous: Noah was able to gather the animals in the ark, and Daniel frightened the lions. But such powers were refused to ordinary sinful human beings.[42] Even though Isidore's attitude is more characteristic of Western tradition, the fact remains that for the ancient church as a whole human beings partly abdicate their dominion over the earth through the fall and regain this dominion through Christ.

There is more to say about the understanding of human dominion in the early church. Especially within the Alexandrian tradition a considerable spiritualization of the whole concept took place. This is important, since this tendency, too, relativizes the idea of human dominion. For the Alexandrian, spiritualization implied that the dominion of human beings is dependent on their mastering their own passions, and that, in turn, depends on a proper development of their spirituality.

With some support in Philo, Origen introduced this spiritualizing interpretation of the creation narrative. Philo understood the dominion referred to in Gen 1:26 as a dominion over the passions, since the passions are a manifestation of what humanity shares with the animals. Thus, only human beings who master their own passions show their image character to the full. Origen fulfilled this line of interpretation within Christian tradition, and after him it was considered to be one of several possible interpretations.[43] The implication of it is that what human beings *are* becomes more important than what they do. And what human beings *are* in this respect is due to their rational souls, and not primarily to their bodies, even though they are a unity of both.

We might summarize with two parallel consequences of this kind of thinking, which are relevant for the early church as a whole. First of all, human dominion within creation has to be exerted through reason and has to have God's dominion as its model. And second, human dominion over the earth has to be exerted in parallel to the development of mastery over bodily passions. Thus, again, human dominion in its rightful sense cannot be arbitrary.

In this context—and this is our final observation at this point—we must not forget that the speculations in the early church about the so-called *logoi* of creation establish an important relationship between human dominion and the fixed natures and aims of created beings. Again Origen was the first Christian writer to develop the theology of the *logoi* fully. Inherent in the created order are *logoi* or principles, and these principles are related to the divine Word, the Logos. These *logoi* are, as it were, present within the Logos. Athanasius, however, said that God, realizing that a world created according to its own independent *logoi* would be a world falling to pieces, created the world according to his own Logos. A similar idea is found also in Augustine, who talks about the *rationes* as eternal and unchangeable principles. Other expositors of the idea of the *logoi* are Evagrius of Pontus (d. 399) and Pseudo-Dionysius the Areopagite (of the sixth century). For the latter—and for his commentator John of Scythopolis (also of the sixth century)[44]—the *logoi* were not only regarded as ideas that constituted substances but also as *divine intentions* (an understanding that anticipates the later Palamite doctrine of the uncreated divine energies).[45] Maximus the Confessor followed this line. To him the *logoi* were identical neither with God's own essence nor with the factual existence of things in the world. To Maximus every created being has its own nature, but this nature may be more or less manifest in each individual case.[46]

What is important in the present context is that human beings, on account of their rational, "logical" constitution, are able, *through contemplation of things* in their *logoi*, to keep the created universe together and to refer it to its primary cause, that is, in Christ and under God. This capacity is the prerogative of human beings as viceroys on earth, but it is only through their contemplative power that they exert it. Thus, human dominion is no threat to created beings. They find their higher unity in their relationship to God, mediated to them by human beings in the image of God and as beings capable of contemplating the very principles of their coming into existence. Human dominion, thus, does not imply a subjugation of the created order to human will in opposition to other purposes, but a creative communication with the universe in its differentiation, the purposes of which rest immobile in God's own intention.

These conclusions, however, lead us immediately to our second example: the task of human beings under the aspect of their contemplative capacity.

## Human Beings, Created in the Image of God, as Contemplating Beings

Contemplation, according to the early church, particularly in the East, starts in the ontological and ends in the mystical. Accordingly, contemplation is a threefold activity. It consists, according to Maximus the Confessor, in "natural contemplation" (i.e., contemplation of natures), in spiritual contemplation of what is revealed through Scripture, and in mystical contemplation of the triune God himself.[47] Contemplation in this sense is, now, only possible because humanity is created according to the image of God.

In Greek thinking there was a general rule that stated that "equal knows equal," and thus it is precisely human beings as carrying the image of God who are able to know God—but also, as a matter of fact, to know created things according to the divine intention for them. As rational beings humans themselves possess *logoi*, which are able to communicate with the *logoi* of the created order. Thus, humans as rational beings also keep the created things together under God, and they do so by using their contemplative faculty.

This faculty, though, is also effective in relation to God's self-revelation in the Scriptures. Scripture also has a "logical" content, and this is because the words (*logoi*) of Scripture are regarded not only as words but also as divine intentions, inherent in Scripture. And, therefore, human communication with Scripture implies a contemplation of these intentions themselves.[48] Thus, in reading Scripture, human beings as restored to their image character are able to read God's basic intentions in it. This form of contemplation, however, is only an intermediary state before mystical contemplation, the culmination of human intellectual activity.

In a part of the early Christian tradition mystical contemplation is called *theologia*. That is to say that the highest form of contemplation was also regarded as theology proper. Theology proper now establishes knowledge of God himself.[49] In the last instance humanity's image character leads to mystical communion with God. Such communion, however, is realizable only in what the fathers called "pure prayer,"[50] or in a kind of ecstasy on the part of one outside of oneself, and in the cultivation of the "heart." Pseudo-Macarius (an unknown writer of the early fifth century) said that the heart is the master and king of the entire bodily organism.[51] Therefore, when the human heart is filled with the presence of the incarnate Word, it is also open— organically, as it were—toward the living God. Baptismal grace lives in the heart, an understanding that is, in its turn, related to the ancient Christian idea that the Logos-child is born in the heart of the believer and grows in the believer as long as it is nurtured by the gifts of the Spirit.[52] Thus, John Climacus (d. ca. 649) said that the "hesychast," that is, the contemplative monk, tries to contain the incorporeal in a bodily habitation, his own physical/spiritual being.[53]

Therefore, all practical activity, all thinking, and all energy are potentially present in this human center, having its peace in Jesus Christ. Gregory of Sinai (from the end of the thirteenth century and the beginning of the fourteenth) said that this implies a return to the original simplicity of the morning of creation.[54] Simplicity, as a matter of fact, is both in biblical thinking and in that of the early church a restoration of God's primary intention for humanity, and it implies a liberation from the powers of evil (which try to split up humanity and the world in unlimited multiplicity) and also a liberation for personal development in multiple spirituality. The desert fathers were especially eager to underline this aspect. To them human simplicity implied both goodness and fulfillment of the call extended to humanity in creation to become like God himself.

However, this simplicity of humanity—restored in Christ—is not an individual capacity and prerogative only; it belongs to humankind as a whole. Therefore, our next example is that of the ancient Christian understanding of humankind as being made in the image of God.

## The Collectivity of Humanity and Its Image Character

In the early church human beings were regarded in their "adamic" unity. It is the biblical conviction not only that Adam was the first human being but also that he contained in himself all the human race. This conviction was also that of the early church. The doctrine of God's incarnation in Christ— reestablishing humanity's unity in itself—thus implies not primarily that

God became one person among others but that he adapted human nature to himself and became all that humanity is and could be. All human beings are, therefore, affected by the incarnation, and for some of the ancient Christian writers it thus became a problem how to distinguish this from the question of the personal salvation of the individual. A doctrine of *apokatastasis* (general restoration) was thus close not only to Origen but also to Gregory of Nyssa. Only through a distinction between an ontological level and a personal/soteriological level, where human freedom may be exerted, did it become possible for the early church to deal with this tension. It remains, however, a fact that humanity and its restoration in Christ are seen in a collective perspective and that humanity's image character is related to all human beings in their universal fellowship.

That fellowship is realized in the church, understood in a Pauline sense as the Body of Christ. Thus, there existed in the early church an ecclesiological aspect of humanity's likeness to God. According to Gal 3:28 there is in Christ—that is, also in the church—neither Jew nor Greek, neither bond nor free, neither man nor woman, but all are one in him.[56] Transferred to the sphere of spirituality this now means that human beings in Christ, keeping their whole species together, are obliged to abstain from war, to neglect the difference between free people and slaves, and even to disregard the splitting up of religion into factions and sects. At least this was the conclusion drawn by Maximus the Confessor. To him the church, too, was a "great man" gathering together in itself all that is human and related to the whole cosmos in this respect.

But the collectivity of humanity in this sense is not self-evident. To fallen human beings it is a matter of their restoration from sinfulness, and their working out of their task of mediation. This aspect of ancient Christian anthropology will thus terminate this article.

## Human Beings
## as Fallen and Restored and as
## Mediators in the Universe

A considerable amount of ancient Christian thinking was, of necessity, devoted to the fall of humanity and human sinfulness. Again, pure observation was sufficient to convince the Christian writers of the accuracy of the narrative of Genesis 3. Humanity's part in and guilt for the process that led to its sinful self-destruction and the consequences of the fall were some of the main questions to be dealt with.

Generally speaking, humanity's fall was seen in the early church as a revolt, but West and East were not completely in agreement on where to put the main stress. In the East the revolt was linked more to the composite nature of human beings and the temptations that emerge from the senses. The sovereignty that human beings experience over against the rest of the world invites them to neglect the dangers inherent in dependence upon the senses and the satisfactions offered by the sensible world. In monastic tradition this line of reflection led to the establishment of a list of eight capital vices, in which the first two were gluttony and fornication. (The temptation narrative of Genesis 3 was taken quite literally and at its face value.) In the West more emphasis was put on the revolt properly speaking—and humanity's fall was also often judged more radically—in that the initial impetus was one of pride. In its superiority humanity denied God his rightful reverence, and from that sin of pride all the other vices emerged as a consequence. As Augustine put it, humanity's basic drive was converted into its opposite, into *cupiditas*, sinful concupiscence, which turned humanity's attention to the created world instead of toward the Creator. In Christ this *cupiditas* again was converted into *caritas*, charity, so that humanity might be orientated in the direction meant for it from the beginning, that is, toward God, who is both the source of life and the goal of fulfilment.[57]

In both cases—and the difference between the two basic concepts is not all that important—considerable stress was put on *human freedom*. Freedom belongs to human nature. In conveying freedom to humanity, God calculated with the possibility of the fall and revolt. The role of Christ as Savior, therefore, was also planned before the beginning of time, although that role was not exclusively understood as one of restoration. Humanity's freedom is also restored in Christ, and thus the ancient church, after much discussion, came to the conclusion that there must be two wills in Christ, one divine and one human (codified as doctrine at the Council of Constantinople in 680-81), although in him the human will always follows the divine. But with the freedom of will is also connected the possibility of development.

Within the line of thought that emanated from Irenaeus, which was described above, humanity's restoration necessarily meant a new starting point. What was given at the beginning as a possibility (humanity's image character as a potentiality) is now free to be used in developing humanity's likeness. Christ recapitulates, according to Irenaeus, humanity's past history but also brings it to a new start, from which a history of fulfillment, in the life of individuals and of the human race, can emerge. Here freedom again plays an important role. The destiny of human beings is the result of their own choice. Gregory of Nyssa and Gregory Nazianzen insisted on this.[58] And what human beings might choose lies beyond their merely natural capacity.

In order to see more clearly what are the implications of this statement for the ancient church, we must consider the parallel concepts of incarnation and deification. The ancient church wrestled for centuries with what the prologue of John's Gospel really implied. In that process it rejected any idea of Christ as a half-God or a half-man. Christ's full divinity and full humanity were affirmed by the councils of the church, and at the Council of Chalcedon in 451 this conviction was also expressed, even though paradoxically, in a way that decided the perspective from which the incarnation would be seen in the future.

From Chalcedon on incarnation was to be understood as the hypostatic (i.e., personal) union of what is divine and what is human, both in their full capacity, without any false mixture between them or any destruction of either part. Incarnation, thus, *is* this "theandric" paradox or mystery, together with the implications it may have for the understanding of humanity's status and destiny. It is precisely this doctrine that also confirms human beings in their image character and opens up the road to its realization in full development of their likeness to God. And it is the same doctrine that seems to bind God in a perpetual salvific intercourse with human beings, a personal "I-Thou relationship" that can have no other worthy end and fulfillment than in mystical union.

And precisely here the concept of deification becomes relevant. Irenaeus already indicated and Athanasius explicitly stated that God became human in order that human beings might become God.[59] This was a paradox from the beginning, since the early church was never in doubt about the fact that human beings belong to the created order. And the created order and all that belongs to it always remain finite, whereas God is infinite, unlimited, eternal. But the paradox contains the conviction that human beings, in spite of their limitation, may enter into such a relationship with God that they, without losing their proper nature, may be in full communion with the divine reality. In doing so their likeness to God is fully realized, and at the same time the full implications of their being persons are manifested. Human beings are drawn into the dynamism of the divine Trinity, and that dynamism becomes manifest also in the life of the church as the fulfilled life of humanity.

Thus, human beings as microcosms may also function as mediators. Of all the fathers of the church, Maximus the Confessor was perhaps the most explicit on this point. For him, as for his predecessors, sin meant disintegration of humanity itself and of the created order. But restored in Christ humanity may reintegrate the whole universe and finally bring it into permanent salvific relationship with its Creator. At this point Maximus spoke of *five mediations*. These are: between the sexes (since disastrous antagonism is overcome), between paradise and the inhabited earth, between heaven and earth, between sensible and intelligible creation (so that all is held together by the universal principle, *logos*, intended by God at the creation), and, finally, between God and the whole of creation through ecstasy and mystical union, so that God becomes all in all, without destroying any created differentiations or anything of humanity's instituted free will, yet bringing all to its fulfillment, gathered around humanity in perfect likeness to God.[60]

This vision is a kind of culmination of all that the early church envisaged in its painful struggle to find a true anthropology, worthy of beings created in the image and likeness of God, beings who, in their relationship to God and in developing their spiritual capacities, are also able to transcend their own limits.

## Notes

1. The concept of person does not, therefore, have to be identical with a modern one or with that which is characteristic of modern personalist philosophers, but it is a fact that the modern concept of person has some of its roots in early Christian speculation on the triune God, on Christ as one person in two natures, and on human beings as composite beings.

2. See V. Lossky, "The Theological Notion of the Human Person," in Lossky, *In the Image and Likeness of God*, 111–23.

3. On the history of the development of this trinitarian understanding of God in the early church, see J. Pelikan, *The Emergence of the Catholic Tradition (100– 600)*, 211–25.

4. On the history of the ancient Christian idea of Christ as the God-man, see Pelikan, *The Emergence of the Catholic Tradition*, 226–77.

5. See Lossky, "The Theology of the Image," in Lossky, *In the Image and Likeness of God*, 125–39.

6. For a summary of the presuppositions of ancient Christian thought on this point, see H. Crouzel, *Théologie de l'image de Dieu chez Origène*, 31–70.

7. See Crouzel, 57, referring to the Pauline foundation of this idea.

8. The idea of a double creation (based on the two different creation narratives in Genesis 1 and 2) is found already in Philo, the Jewish theologian (see *On the Creation of the World* 134; *Allegory of the Jewish Law* 1.31) but was modified and changed by Origen (see *Commentary on John* 20.22 and a number of other places). On this see Crouzel, 148–53.

9. See *Against Heresies* 4.38. On Irenaeus, see in general G. Joppich, *Salus carnis: Eine Untersuchung in der Theologie des hl. Irenäus von Lyon* (Münsterschwarzach: Vier-Türme Verlag, 1965).

10. See *Oration 38* 11.

11. On Gregory's anthropology in general, see A.-S. Ellverson, *The Dual Nature of Man;* and for this particular idea of the providential preservation of humanity from an even more disastrous fall, see especially pp. 48, 55f., 58f., 62f., 67f., 72f.

12. See Crouzel, 149; and M. Harl, "Recherches sur l'origénisme d'Origène . . . ," *Studia Patristica* 8 (1966) 373–405.

13. *Doctrine of Man* 28; cf. *De anima et resurrectione* (PG 46, col. 108B).

14. See L. Thunberg, *Microcosm and Mediator.*

15. See Thunberg, 104–5.

16. Thunberg, 105–6.

17. See Thunberg, 108.

18. See Thunberg, 140ff.

19. Thunberg, 142.

20. Thunberg, 143.

21. See Ellverson, 16, 19, 38f., 51, 73.

22. *Oration 28* 22.

23. Thunberg, 143f.

24. Thunberg, 144f.

25. Thunberg, 145–52.

26. See Crouzel, 217–23.

27. See W. J. Burghardt, *The Image of God in Man according to Cyril of Alexandria,* 5.

28. See Thunberg, 131f.

29. On Gregory Nazianzen, see Ellverson, 43; on Gregory of Nyssa, see J. Gaïth, *La conception de la liberté chez Grégoire de Nysse,* 71f.

30. See Thunberg, 132f.

31. On this, see Burghardt, 6.

32. See Thunberg, 132–37.

33. Lossky struggles with what this might imply ("The Theological Notion of the Human Person," 120).

34. On this last point reference may be given to the thinking of Pierre Teilhard de Chardin.

35. Y. Congar, "Le thème du Dieu Créateur et les explications de l'Hexaéméron dans la tradition chrétienne," in *L'Homme devant Dieu: Melanges offerts au Père Henri de Lubac, I: Exégèse et patristique* (Paris: Aubier, 1963) 190–222.

36. *Homily on Genesis* 1.16.

37. Basile de Césarée, *Sur l'origine de l'homme,* ed. A. Smets and M. Van Esbroeck (Sources chrétiennes 160; Paris: Cerf, 1970) 186–95.

38. Ibid.

39. *Homilies on Genesis,* chapter 1 (*PG* 53, col. 72).

40. See *PG* 80, col. 105.

41. See Burghardt, 53ff.

42. Burghardt, 61f.

43. Origen *Homily on Genesis* 1.16. On the ancient Christian interpretation of Genesis in general, see G. T. Armstrong, *Die Genesis in der alten Kirche.*

44. On John of Scythopolis as a commentator on Pseudo-Dionysius, see H. Urs von Balthasar, *Kosmische Liturgie,* 644–72.

45. See Thunberg, 77f. n. 4.

46. See further Thunberg, 77–84.

47. As a matter of fact, Maximus referred to a threefold embodiment of the Logos: in the things of creation, in the letters of Scripture, and in Christ incarnate; see A. Riou, *Le monde et l'église selon Maxime le Confesseur,* 62f. On the different forms of contemplation, see Thunberg, 363–74.

48. On this understanding of Scripture in Maximus in relation to the *logoi* of creation, see *Ambigua* 10 (*PG* 91, col. 1128).

49. On the concept of *theologia* in the Eastern Christian tradition, see J. Meyendorff, *Byzantine Theology,* 8f.

50. On "pure prayer" in ancient Christian tradition, see Thunberg, 384–91.

51. On Pseudo-Macarius and the "prayer of the heart," see Meyendorff, *Byzantine Theology,* 68f.

52. On this theme, see H. Rahner, "Die Gottesgeburt: Die Lehre der Kirchenväter von der Geburt Christi im Herzen des Gläubigen," *Zeitschrift für Katholische Theologie* 59 (1935) 333–418.

53. On John of the Ladder, see Meyendorff, *Byzantine Theology,* 70f.; and for a wider treatment, see W. Völker, *Scala Paradisi.*

54. On Gregory of Sinai, see J. Meyendorff, *St. Gregory Palamas and Orthodox Spirituality,* 63ff.

55. On the ideology of the monastic movement and of the desert fathers in particular, see D. Chitty, *The Desert a City.*

56. On the interpretation of Gal 3:28 in Maximus the Confessor, see Thunberg, 325.

57. On Augustine's understanding of the fall of humanity in general, see Pelikan, *Emergence of the Catholic Tradition,* 299ff.

58. On the importance of freedom in Gregory of Nyssa, see Gaïth; and on freedom in Gregory Nazianzen, see Ellverson, 43.

59. For a summary of the idea of deification in the ancient church, see Thunberg, 454–59; see also Lossky, "Redemption and Deification," in Lossky, *In the Image and Likeness of God,* 97–110.

60. On the five mediations according to Maximus, see Thunberg 352–454.

## Bibliography

### Studies

Armstrong, Gregory T. *Die Genesis in der alten Kirche.* Tübingen: Mohr-Siebeck, 1962.

Balthasar, Hans Urs von. *Kosmische Liturgie: Das Weltbild Maximus des Bekenners.* Einsiedeln: Johannesverlag, 1961.

Burghardt, Walter J. *The Image of God in Man according to Cyril of Alexandria.* Woodstock, MD: Woodstock College Press; Washington, DC: Catholic University Press, 1957.

Chitty, D. J. *The Desert a City: An Introduction to the Study of Egyptian and Palestinian Monasticism under the Christian Empire.* Oxford: Blackwell, 1966.

Crouzel, Henri. *Théologie de l'image de Dieu chez Origène.* Paris: Aubier, 1956.

Ellverson, Anna-Stina. *The Dual Nature of Man: A Study in the Theological Anthropology of Gregory of Nazianzus.* Uppsala: Almqvist & Wiksell, 1981.

Gaïth, Jérome. *La conception de la liberté chez Grégoire de Nysse.* Paris: Vrin, 1953.

Garrigues, Juan Miguel. *Maxime le Confesseur: La charité avenir de l'homme.* Paris: Beauchesne, 1976.

Lossky, Vladimir. *In the Image and Likeness of God.* Edited by John H. Erickson and Thomas E. Bird. Crestwood, NY: St. Vladimir's Seminary Press, 1974.

———. *The Mystical Theology of the Eastern Church.* Translated by the Fellowship of St. Alban and St. Sergius. Cambridge: James Clarke, 1957; reprint, Crestwood, NY: St. Vladimir's Seminary Press, 1976.

Meyendorff, John. *Byzantine Theology: Historical Trends and Doctrinal Themes.* New York: Fordham University Press, 1974. Second printing with revisions, 1983.

———. *St. Gregory Palamas and Orthodox Spirituality.* Crestwood, NY: St. Vladimir's Seminary Press, 1974.

Pelikan, Jaroslav. *The Christian Tradition: A History of the Development of Doctrine.* Vol. 1, *The Emergence of the Catholic Tradition (100-600).* Vol. 2, *The Spirit of Eastern Christendom (600-1700)* Chicago: University of Chicago Press, 1971, 1974.

Quasten, Johannes. *Patrology.* 3 vols. Westminster, MD: Newman Press, 1949-60.

Riou, Alain. *Le monde et l'église selon Maxime le Confesseur.* Paris: Beauchesne, 1973.

Roques, René. *L'Univers Dionysien: Structure hiérarchique du monde selon le pseudo-Denys.* Paris: Aubier, 1954.

*Théologie de la vie monastique.* Paris: Aubier, 1961.

Thunberg, Lars. *Microcosm and Mediator: The Theological Anthropology of Maximus the Confessor.* Acta Seminarii Neotestamentici Upsaliensis 25. Lund: Gleerup; Copenhagen: Munksgaard, 1965.

Völker, Walther. *Kontemplation und Ekstase bei Pseudo-Dionysius Areopagita.* Wiesbaden: F. Steiner, 1958.

———. *Maximus Confessor als Meister des geistlichen Lebens.* Wiesbaden: F. Steiner, 1965.

———. *Scala Paradisi: Eine Studie zu Johannes Climacus und zugleich eine Vorstudie zu Symeon dem Neuen Theologen.* Wiesbaden: F. Steiner, 1968.

Wolfson, H. A. *The Philosophy of the Church Fathers.* Cambridge, MA: Harvard University Press, 1956.

# II. *Western Christianity*

### Bernard McGinn

"KNOW YOURSELF"—this maxim sent down from heaven and inscribed on the temple of the Delphic Apollo stands at the center of several Western spiritual traditions. Christian authors loved to cite this Greek counsel, though they felt that the Greeks had never grasped the full answer to the mystery of the human person. The triune God alone had revealed it, first in the Old Testament by teaching that humanity, though fallen, had been created "in the image and likeness of God" (Gen 1:26), and then by sending the only-begotten Son of the Father to take on flesh so that we might become true images of his Son (Rom 8:29; cf. 1 Cor 15:49, 2 Cor 3:18, Col 1:15-20). Anthropology forms a complex and pervasive topic that touches upon almost every area of Christian belief and practice.

Despite this scope and variety, it is possible to gain an understanding of some of the principal spiritual dimensions of traditional Latin anthropology by studying its central theme, the human person as made in the image of God (*imago Dei*), though an image now in need of reformation through the saving action of the Son, the perfect image of the Father. As one medieval author succinctly phrased it: "Since the Almighty himself has expressed his image in the mid-point of creatures, namely in humanity . . . , the same Creator sent the person of the Son of his deity into the world to take to himself this already-formed image to reform it to a better state" (Ralph Glaber *Histories* [*PL* 142, col. 663A]).

## Prolegomena

The ways in which Latin authors understood how humanity was made in and reformed to God's image were much influenced by their inheritance from both Jewish and Greek sources. The Hebrew view of the human person as called by God to acts of loving obedience was a resource always present to Christian authors in the sacred books they called the Old Testament. The anthropology of the Greek philosophers, especially of Plato and his followers, with its notion of the soul as bearing an image (*eikōn*) of divinity,[1] was almost equally influential. There were, of course, important differences between Jewish and Greek anthropologies, especially in the Greek split between the body and soul which led to an emphasis on the latter as the true person and an insistence that the soul's immortality was the true human destiny. Traditional Jewish anthropology knew nothing of the distinction between body and soul, and in its apocalyptic phase had created the notion of the resurrection of the body in order to vindicate divine justice in a time of persecution. Still, the emphasis that both traditions placed on the human person as a conscious agent with a unique relation to God and a special position in the universe was a crucial shared value that facilitated attempts to combine the two.

Given this dependence on two other religious traditions, what was new about Christian anthropology, especially that of Latin authors from the fourth through the twelfth centuries? One way to approach this question is to ask about the relationship of humanity to the universe, to the self, and finally to God. Traditional Christian anthropology would rightly insist that these relations are correlative; but they can be examined independently for the sake of clarity.

In terms of humanity's relation to the world, we can distinguish between the temporal and the exemplary dimensions of the human mystery. Christian understanding of the temporal nature of human existence built upon the theology of the "mighty acts" of God found in the Old Testament and also on the vision of divine predetermination of universal history that was present in intertestamental apocalyptic literature. This understanding was decisively altered by Christian confession of the ultimacy of the Christ-event. The Savior's resurrection, originally understood in apocalyptic fashion as

20. *Koimesis of Mary*, Kariye Caime, Istanbul, 13th century

21. *Creation of Adam*, Cathedral of Chartres, 13th century

the beginning of the new divine aeon, was also envisaged as early as Luke-Acts as the decisive middle point of history, upon which the new community was to model itself as it spread throughout the world. Augustine of Hippo worked out the full dimensions of this theology of history; his contributions to anthropology are inseparable from his theology of history.

Greek philosophical thought viewed the soul as the center of the cosmos, the median reality that joined together the extremes of the material and spiritual realms. For the Greeks the soul participated in divinity whereas the body to which it was joined exemplified the structure of the cosmos. In its material component humanity was thus dignified as the *microcosm,* or world in miniature. Christian thinkers down through the Renaissance were to make the theme of microcosm central to their anthropological speculations,[2] but Christian understanding of the microcosm frequently took on a character of its own through consideration of the way in which the union of the Logos with human nature achieved the completion of the physical universe.

Anthropology involves not only the way in which persons view their relation to the world but also how they conceive themselves. Here too the classical component in Christian anthropology is important, but not determinative. The Greek notion of contemplation (*theōria*) has had a long and important history within Christian thought and practice that cannot be pursued here.[3] In most Christian thinkers, both East and West, the ascent to vision or contemplation of God usually involves starting in a true contemplation of the self by some introspective technique. Christian authors were much influenced in this regard by Neoplatonists such as Plotinus, who advised: "We must close our eyes and invoke a new manner of seeing, a wakefulness that is the birthright of us all, though few put it to use" (*Enneads* 1.6.8); but whereas pagan philosophers withdrew from the external world to contemplate the divine spark buried within, Latin Christian authors after Augustine used introspection as much to highlight the tragic gap between human aspirations and accomplishments as to signal the presence of a divine element in the soul.

Pauline Christianity implied a concept of human freedom and its relation to history that marked a radical break with the traditions of classical philosophy. Its revival in the fifth century in Augustine's victory over Pelagius and his followers was a decisive, but perhaps not unexpected, event. The introspective knowledge to which medieval Latin Christians were invited was always more than a knowledge of the nature and powers of the soul. Rooted in an existential recognition of our sinful condition, it was a knowledge of both the grandeur and the misery of humanity—one of the major rhetorical themes of the medieval Latin tradition.

"Like is known by like," as an ancient Greek maxim had insisted.[4] In knowing him- or herself as made in the image of God, each human person is
called to a new and more adequate knowledge of God. The young convert
Augustine prayed that he might know God and the soul, nothing more—
and nothing less! (*Soliloquies* 1.7). The way within, that is, self-knowledge
by way of introspection, is also the way above: the ascent to God. Here too
we can see similarities to traditions inherited from the classical world and
important innovations, for, however much Christian authors made use of
Greek philosophical language in explaining their anthropology, the trinitarian and christological character of medieval understanding of the *imago
Dei*, the source of our likeness to God, was radically new. Divinization, a
concept taken over from the Greeks, was given a new content in Christian
belief and practice, not only through the new religion's insistence on the
necessity of grace to restore the image but also because Christian understanding of the image itself was based not upon a fluid Greek notion of
divinity but rather on the mystery of the one God who had revealed himself
as Father, Son, and Holy Spirit.

## Three Traditions of
## Western *Imago Dei* Spirituality

It is possible to isolate three traditions of *imago Dei* spirituality in Latin
Christianity between the fourth and the twelfth century: that which finds
the image of God primarily in the person considered as an intellectual subject; that which concentrates on the freedom of the subject as the true location of the image; and that which emphasizes the interpersonal character of
the image. Obviously, these are not to be thought of as discrete traditions.
Elements of each will be found in all the major spiritual teachers, but the
emphasis given will vary considerably from author to author and a study
of these variations will help to bring out the riches of medieval Latin
anthropology.

### Augustine and the Intellectual Subject

Marius Victorinus and Augustine both made use of important elements of
Neoplatonic thought in their efforts to understand what it meant to be
made in God's image and likeness.[5] In his first and second treatises *Against
Arius* (359), Victorinus distinguished between the Logos, who is the true
*imago Dei*, and the human soul, which is created *ad imaginem*—that is, after
the pattern of the Logos (*Against Arius* IA.20). The African teacher held that
the original human person whose creation is described in Gen 1:26 bears the

divine image—the soul possesses "to be," "to live," and "to understand" in conformity with the three divine persons, whereas the body's division into two sexes as recounted in the story of the creation of terrestrial humanity in Gen 2:7 mirrors the double nature of the Logos as both male and female (*Against Arius* IB. 61-64).

Like Victorinus, Augustine placed the *imago* character of the human subject primarily in its intellectual nature, but his rich thought involves elements of all three traditions and thus forms the crucial watershed for subsequent Western anthropology. We shall concentrate here upon the bishop's explicit statements regarding the *imago Dei*, but it is important to point out that almost all his writings are in one way or another involved with the mystery of the relation of the human person to God.

Augustine's most read work, the *Confessions* (397-400), is a two-part study of human destiny: books 1-9 tell the story of one man as everyman, and books 10-13 present two theological meditations on the human mystery— an analysis of *memoria* (book 10) and an interpretation of the creation account as the story of the soul's fall (books 11-13). In this subtle work Augustine decisively broke with Neoplatonic anthropology by using his own life story to convey a universal message: human destiny is no longer seen as the absorption of the individual back into the All, but as the recovery of the true self through divine reordering of the will. The true human person comes to expression through the act of *confessio*, a direct interpersonal address to God which is simultaneously confession of our own sinfulness (e.g., 2.1, 2.3, 10.1, 10.4) and praise of God's loving-kindness toward us (e.g., 1.1, 1.6, 1.15, 7.6). Augustine showed how his intellectual conversion, in which Neoplatonism played such a large part (7.9 and 20), did not enable him to overcome the conflict of the carnal and spiritual wills within him, which ". . . wasted my soul by their discord," as he put it (8.5). The stalemate between the two directions of the will could be broken only by the intervention of the grace of Christ, so graphically portrayed in the famous conversion scene in the garden (8.8-12).

Although Augustine was telling the story of his own life, the message he presented in the *Confessions* was no individualistic one. No soul either falls from God or returns to him by itself. The incidents that illustrate the sinful journey away from God, like the theft of the pears in 2.4-10, are always expressions of that solidarity in sinning which began in the Garden of Eden. The famous Ostia vision of book 9 that presents the paradigm of restored humanity has Augustine in company with Monica enjoying a brief experience of the "touching of Divine Wisdom" (9.10), the goal of the human pilgrimage. The fact that it is the unlearned woman Monica who shares in this mystical experience not only underlines that human destiny is the work of grace and not of our own efforts; it shows also that the goal is open to all. Finally, as book 10 makes abundantly clear, the reformation and restoration of the human person that divine love was working out in Augustine's life were never permanent accomplishments, but always a tenuous and ongoing process. Continuous conversion is the essence of the Christian life.

The *Confessions* lay down the fundamental lines of Augustine's anthropology, which broke not only with pagan Neoplatonism but at least in part with earlier Christian understandings of humanity that placed less emphasis on the effects of original sin and gave more weight to the inherent value of ascetic striving toward God. After 400, theological controversies, especially that with Pelagius, led Augustine to deepen and often to harden his positions. He abandoned some of the more Platonic elements found in the *Confessions,* such as the notion of the fall of the soul and the role of the natural desire for God, as he moved toward a more and more uncompromising stand on the operative efficacy of grace in the process of salvation.[6] During this period the trinitarian analogy in the soul, which he briefly noted in *Confessions* 13.11, was developed into a full-blown theology of the *imago Dei* in his great work *The Trinity* written between 400 and 417.

Augustine developed a sophisticated notion of an *imago* as a particular kind of likeness (*similitudo*) by which something both relates to and expresses its source. "Certainly, not everything in creatures, which is in some way or other similar to God, is also to be called his image, but that alone to which he himself alone is superior; for the image is only then an expression of God in the full sense when no other nature lies between it and God" (*The Trinity* 11.5.8). Such an image is expressive of its source not only because of proximity but also because its nature is formed through conversion, that is, a dynamic turning back toward the source in the very moment of its creation.[7] Like Victorinus, Augustine admitted that some images can have a relation of equality with their source, because the perfect *imago Dei* whose formative activity gives being to rational creatures and, in a somewhat different way, to all things is the Word, the consubstantial second person of the Trinity. Unlike Victorinus, Augustine insisted with Paul (1 Cor 11:7) that the human person can be said not only to be made *ad imaginem* (i.e., according to the Word) but also to be in itself a true *imago Dei* (e.g., *The Trinity* 7.6.12).

Unlike some Greek fathers, Augustine refused to see the sexual division of humanity as a result of the fall (e.g., *City of God* 14.21). This, coupled with his insistence that the image resides in the interior person (*homo interior*), makes it clear that Augustine did not conceive of the image in a sex-specific sense as if the male alone bore the true image of God (on this see especially the *Literal Commentary on Genesis* 3.22.34). However, in several of his works he did make use of an allegorical interpretation of the account of the fall that goes back to Philo, in which the serpent stands for the sense faculty, the woman for the inferior reason that is directed to the things of this world, and the man for the superior reason directed to God.[8] This became a popular theme in later Western anthropology. Thus, we may say that, although in his essential teaching Augustine insisted on the equality of men and women as partakers in the *imago Dei*, the symbolic value he gave to the genders shared the limitations of his culture. Still, Latin Christian authors in general made it clear that both biological males and females possessed all levels of the human spiritual powers. The goal of reformed humanity was not the suppression of any of these, but their harmonious integration, so that the highest power symbolized by the *vir*, or "man," in the soul regained its original role as the link between humanity and divinity. Such an integration was as open to women as to men, as the desert abbess Sara indicated when she exclaimed, in a language we moderns may find difficult to appreciate, "I am a woman in sex, but not in spirit."[9]

In his early works Augustine had explored how the whole of created reality mirrored the triune God and how the inner person had been created as a special image of the one God. This pattern was expanded after 412 in the later books of *The Trinity*, where the bishop insisted that the external world and even the outer person (*homo exterior*) bear only the vestiges of the Trinity (*vestigia Trinitatis*) and that only the inner person can be seen as a real *imago Trinitatis*. For God said: "Let us make man in our image and after our likeness," and a little later it was said: "So God created man in the image of God." It would certainly be incorrect to say "our," because it is a plural number, if man were made in the image of one person, whether of the Father, or the Son, or the Holy Spirit; but because he was made in the image of the Trinity, it was therefore said: "to our image" (*The Trinity* 12.6.6).[10]

Augustine was clear that this image resides only in the *mens*, or the higher dimension of the soul. "From this we are to understand that man was made to the image of God in that part of his nature wherein he surpasses the brute beasts; this is, of course, his reason (*ratio*), or mind (*mens*), or intelligence (*intelligentia*), or whatever we wish to call it" (*Literal Commentary on Genesis* 3.20.30). Since the *mens* includes both the intellectual and volitional aspects of the human subject (*The Trinity* 9.12.18), Augustine developed understandings of the human person as trinitarian image based both upon love and knowledge. A line of thought exploring the relation between the Trinity and our experience of interpersonal love was developed in *The Trinity* 8.5–8, before the bishop turned his attention to more extended analyses of the mind's knowledge and love of itself as the primary image.

The major effort of the last books of *The Trinity* is devoted to exploration of the intellectual soul as a trinitarian image. Augustine's complex variations on this theme might prompt the view that books 9–15 are primarily an exercise in philosophical speculation; but, though they contain much philosophical insight, they must be understood within the broad spiritual program of meditation on the image as the best way to cooperate with God's reformation of the damaged *imago* to its trinitarian exemplar—as is made clear in the magnificent prayer that closes the work.

Augustine explored how the mind's presence to itself (the *principale mentis* of 14.8.9 or *abstrusior profunditas memoriae* of 15.21.40) gives rise to acts of love and knowledge of self through the production of the inner word (e.g., 14.7.10, 15.12.22). The bishop's fascination with *memoria*, begun in the *Confessions*, reached a culmination in the last part of *The Trinity*, where *memoria* as the basis for all human intellectual activity mirrors the Father's role as the ground for the procession of both the Son, understood as an act of consubstantial knowledge, and the Holy Spirit, conceived of as one of equally consubstantial love (e.g., *The Trinity* 15.23.43). Augustine explored these triune structures of the inner, noblest part of each human person, especially in his masterful analyses of the triads *mens–notitia sui–amor sui* (e.g., 9.3.3) and *memoria–intelligentia sui–voluntas sui* (e.g., 10.11.17). Nevertheless, the exercise of understanding the mind as the *imago Trinitatis* is not the goal.

> Hence this trinity of the mind is not on that account the image of God because the mind remembers itself, understands itself, and loves itself, but because it can also remember, understand and love him by whom it was made. And when it does so, it becomes wise; but if it does not, even though it remembers itself, knows itself, and loves itself, it is foolish. (*The Trinity* 14.12.15)

It is only because the human person retains the image of the Trinity even after sin that it is possible for God's grace to restore that image through acts of knowing, remembering, and loving him. Augustine insisted that by ourselves we can do nothing: "We can deform God's image in us; we cannot reform it" (*Sermon* 43.4.4 [*PL* 38, col. 255]). According to this creationist model, in which the intellectual being receives its nature by conversion to the Word, "recreation" can take place only through a new conversion to the Word incarnate—the two halves of Augustine's view of human history fit together in seamless fashion.

Finally, we must remember that Augustine's view of the human subject as the *imago Trinitatis* always needs to be considered in the light of his thoughts on the mystery of grace and freedom. Some interpreters have seen in the late Augustine a diminution of the concept of freedom in humanity to the point of extinction, but such a view depends upon a concept of freedom that the bishop did not share. Augustine was resolutely opposed to any conception of freedom as the unhindered autonomy or self-determination of the individual subject. For him freedom was always in need of a modifier—it was freedom "to" or freedom "from." Adam's freedom had a degree of versatility (*posse peccare et non peccare*) not open to his descendants. After the fall humanity was freely bound *to* sin and enjoyed a perverse freedom *from* justice; Christ restored true freedom (*libertas*) to our power of free choice (*liberum arbitrium*) by granting freedom from bondage to sin and the freedom to cooperate with grace in living according to *caritas*. Augustine's ideas on freedom, though central in Western Christianity down to the Enlightenment, were not accepted without some modification. The more rigorist predestinarian implications of his theology were modified in the century after his death,[11] and Augustinian anthropology intermingled in rich fashion with other elements in the history of medieval Latin spirituality.

## *The Early Middle Ages*

In the midst of a dying civilization in which day-to-day survival was the most pressing concern, exalted insights into the meaning of human destiny could survive only by finding cultural and intellectual institutions to embody them and transmit them to future generations. Benedictine monasticism served as the primary vehicle for the preservation of Augustinian anthropology in the Middle Ages. The monks, to be sure, tended toward a position that found it hard to conceive of achieving full human destiny outside the monastery, just as the Platonic elements in the anthropology they inherited made it easy for them to conceive of the soul alone as the true image of God to the detriment of a full appreciation of the bodily reality of the human person. Monastic elitism and classical soul–body dualism were real difficulties in traditional medieval Latin spirituality, but their effect has at times been exaggerated. Various other elements in the tradition, especially the stress upon the microcosmic understanding of the human body and the grand vision of the restoration of perfect harmony to the cosmic hierarchy, served to outflank the dualism implied in some of the inherited philosophical categories. In a similar way, although the monks did tend to see the monastery as the only arena in which true restoration of the *imago Dei* was possible in this life, they never dared to claim that only monks and nuns could be saved. The mysterious workings of divine grace could not be limited to one institution or locale, though the disciplined monastic environment of obedience, humility, and prayer exemplified what Christian teaching regarded as essential foundations for trying to live the life of perfection.

Two rather different authors can serve to mark out some of the major contributions of Western anthropology between the fifth and the twelfth
century. Pope Gregory the Great (590–604) had little interest in philosophical questions, but no one did more to form monastic culture and its
mentality, especially in areas dealing with the situation of the human
person. The bases for Gregory's anthropology are largely Augustinian, but
his development displays a genius of his own. Gregory's acute sense of
human misery as a result of sin—strongly enforced by the lugubrious times
in which he lived—was joined to an intense realization of how compunction
for our sinful state gives rise to the desire for the experience of God as a foretaste of the perfect life to be enjoyed in heaven. If he insisted, on the one
hand, that "in contemplation of God a person recognizes his own worthless-
ness," he was equally convinced that "in that contemplation the taste of
interior quiet is already exerienced" (*Homilies on Ezechiel* 1.8.11; 2.12.14).
Jean Leclercq has observed: "The search for God and union with God are
explained in Gregory in the form of a generalized doctrine of the relationship of man to God."[12]

In the ninth century John the Scot, an Irish thinker resident at the Carolingian court, attempted to fuse the insights of some of the Greek fathers
with the Western tradition based upon Augustine. John's *Periphyseon* contains a profound theological anthropology of a pronounced Neoplatonic
character. Although it never became the basis for a spiritual program in the
way that Augustine's anthropology did through its assimilation into Benedictine monasticism, John's thought was not without influence in the
twelfth century. His understanding of humanity as created *ad imaginem* (the
Word is the true *imago*) stands primarily in the intellectualist tradition. The
image resides in the human person's higher intellectual nature and bears a
trinitarian structure. All this is traditional, but John went further by insisting that the idea of humanity (*homo*) is the first of the primordial causes in
which God created all things: ". . . man was made among the primordial
causes in the image of God; [so] that in him every creature, both intelligible
and sensible, of which he is composed, as of various extremes, should
become an inseparable unity, and that he should be the mediating term and
unification of all creatures."[13] The first creation was a spiritual one in which
all things were united in the primordial idea of the First Man, Adam. His
fall through pride produced the differentiated material universe in which we
now live, but this world of division is being led back to its pristine unity
through the saving work of the New Man, Christ the incarnate Word.

This grand architectonic scheme explains the peculiarities of the Irishman's anthropology. For John the proper definition of humanity is the ideal

one—"humanity is a particular intellectual idea eternally created in the mind
of God" (*Periphyseon* 4.7)—and the real similarity between the image and its
divine Exemplar paradoxically resides more in ignorance than in knowledge.
God knows all things under him, but he cannot know what he is because
he is not a "what," that is, a particular reality capable of being defined. God's
knowledge of himself is a transcendental awareness of his limitless mystery.
We are most truly image of God in our inability to grasp or define our true
nature, which precisely as *imago Dei* remains forever mysterious.

> What is more wonderful and beautiful to those thinking upon themselves and
> their God is that the human mind is more to be praised in its ignorance than
> in its knowledge. For it is more praiseworthy in it not to know what it is than
> to know that it is, just as negation is greater and more consistent than affirma-
> tion in the praise of the divine nature. . . . (*Periphyseon* 4.7)[14]

The spiritual wisdom of John the Scot can be described as an apophatic
form of the intellectualist understanding of humanity as the image of God.

## The Twelfth Century

The twelfth century has long been seen as a turning point in the history of
Latin spirituality. From the viewpoint of the understanding of the human
person as the image of God, the period is both a culmination of the development of traditions rooted in the patristic past and a time when new religious
experiences and innovative institutions and practices began to transform old
symbols and values. Some have gone further in claiming that the twelfth
century witnessed "the discovery of the individual" in its heightened pursuit
of self-examination, its new stress on intention and motivation, and its concern for interpersonal relations. However, exaggerated claims for a new
individualism neglect both the complexity of the ties of twelfth-century
thinkers to the past, especially to Augustine, and the differences between
twelfth-century notions of the self formed by interaction with a community
or group and by way of conformity to an archetype or model and those of
more modern notions of individualism.[15]

Whatever weight we wish to assign to the new aspects of anthropology
of this time, there can be no argument that the twelfth century was fascinated with the mystery of the human person as *imago Dei* and brought to
the study of this mystery a systematic ordering mentality not seen before.
The age was also remarkably creative in finding new institutional forms and
spiritual practices to foster the restoration of the image and the ascent to
God. The great mystical theologies of the Cistercians, Victorines, traditional
Benedictines, and Carthusians were rooted in anthropology.

The space available precludes a complete survey of all the spiritual masters who wrote on anthropology, as well as the various changes in prayer and practice reflected in and influenced by their views.[16] Following our general theme of the three traditions of image spirituality, we will concentrate on two representative figures: Bernard of Clairvaux, who saw human freedom as the site of the image, and Richard of St. Victor, whose thought contains profound reflections on how the interpersonal human subject is an image of the three-personed God.

Many twelfth-century monastic authors wrote treatises on the soul (*De anima*) and the related topic of conscience (*De conscientia*). Although Bernard did not, there can be no denying that anthropology was at the center of his thought. Despite the theological depth of other Cistercians who wrote in this area, notably William of St. Thierry and Isaac of Stella, Bernard was the master of the Cistercian school. In his ability to use Latin prose as a tool to penetrate self-consciousness and to portray emotion, he was Augustine's only rival among medieval Latin authors.

Bernard's insistence on self-knowledge is well-known: the primary path and first step along the way is self-knowledge. "Heaven was the source of the maxim: 'Know yourself!' Does not the spouse say the same to the beloved in the canticle of love: 'O most beautiful of women, if you do not know yourself, go forth . . .' (Song 1:7). Self-knowledge consists of three things, that a person know what he has done, what he deserves, what he has lost."[17] As the final sentence indicates, Bernard was always more interested in the practical consequences of self-knowledge than in its theoretical components. Self-knowledge that did not directly serve to increase the individual's sense of sinfulness and profession of humility—but that became diverted into *curiositas,* that is, pure intellectual exercise divorced from moral reformation—was anathema to Bernard. This attitude was the basis of the harsh attacks on Abelard and others who he rightly or wrongly thought had been guilty of this perversion. Still, the abbot recognized that spiritual reform rightly conceived could not be divorced from hard thought and analysis. In terms of insight into human motivation his *Steps of Humility and Pride* is a masterpiece of observation and introspection; his *Grace and Free Choice* is the most profound doctrinal treatment of this theme in the era; and his treatise *On Loving God* and the *Sermons on the Song of Songs* are unrivaled presentations of the path from self-knowledge and self-love to the heights of loving union with God.

As Etienne Gilson recognized in his classic essay "Christian Socratism," Bernard ". . . finds the image of God *par excellence* in human free will."[18] The abbot, of course, was no proponent of freedom conceived of as individual autonomy. Like Augustine's view of freedom, Bernard's was fundamentally

theocentric in the sense that God's unfailing goodness as the free and spontaneous expression of the divine being is the basic source of all liberty. In
the divine will spontaneity and rectitude can never be in conflict; in human
beings, at least as long as they are in this life, such conflict is always either
potential (as in Adam before the fall, or in the justified in the present) or
actual (as in those still under the domination of sin). The freedom to commit sin for Bernard, as for Augustine, was never more than the dim and
damnable vestige of the true freedom of voluntary and unfailing adherence
to the good found in God.

Bernard did not lack for predecessors who had stressed human freedom as
the true location of the *imago Dei,* but his own understanding of this was
conditioned by the role that love played in the life and thought of this most
passionate of monks. In an age filled with famous lovers and speculation on
love, Bernard was second to none in the power and singlemindedness of his
affections. Existentially what seemed to impress him the most about the
power of love was that it could be both voluntary and yet also totally
absorbing in a way that allowed no hint of an alternative. The paradox of
a totally free yet fully "obsessive" love is at the heart of Bernard's anthropology and the mysticism that is its flower. The activity of loving is the fundamental point of contact between God and humanity, as a famous text
from the *Sermons on the Song of Songs* says: "Of all the motions, the senses,
the affections of the soul, it is love alone in which the creature is able, even
if not on an equal basis, to repay its Creator for what it has received, to
weigh back something from the same measure."[19]

Voluntary consent or free choice (*liberum arbitrium*) Bernard defines as
"a self-determining habit of soul"; it involves both the spontaneous expression of the will and an accompanying judgment of the intellect.[20] Freedom,
understood in its most general form as the absence of external coercion, is
the inalienable characteristic of the human person as human. But how can
we say that human persons trapped in the endless cycle of sinning since the
fall are free? Here Bernard introduces his famous distinction of the three
states of freedom based upon Paul. What human beings always possess, both
before and after the fall, is *liberum arbitrium,* or the *freedom from necessity*
(i.e., external coercion) that assures that the sins they commit are voluntary
expressions of their own perverted wills. What humanity lost in the fall was
the *freedom from sin,* or free counsel. Christ restores this freedom to his
followers and thus puts them on the road that leads to the possession of the
third and crowning freedom, *freedom from sorrow* (free pleasure), that is, the
unfailing enjoyment of the goodness of God in heaven. The abbot
summarizes:

Here below, we must learn from our freedom of counsel not to abuse free choice, in order that one day we may be able fully to enjoy freedom of pleasure. Thus we are repairing the image of God in us, and the way is being paved, by grace, for the retrieving of that former honor which we forfeited by sin.[21]

Like most of his contemporaries, Bernard found the distinction between image (*imago*) and likeness (*similitudo*) of Gen 1:26 useful for describing how humanity retained its basic relation with God even after the fall, but lost its higher conformity. Different authors conceived of this distinction in different ways,[22] and even Bernard gave us a number of variations. In *Grace and Free Choice* the image is identified with free choice, and the progressively restored likeness is free counsel and free pleasure; whereas in the *Sermons on the Song of Songs* the image consists in the greatness (*magnitudo*) and uprightness (*rectitudo*) of the soul (and hence in what is lost through sin), and the likeness is found in the permanent simplicity, immortality, and free choice of the soul.[23] Despite these variations in Bernard and his contemporaries, there is a common basis to the *imago Dei* anthropology of the twelfth century evident in the conviction that even though humanity is fallen in sin, it remains open to God (*capax Dei*), especially to the action of the triune God reforming humanity's powers of knowing and loving toward the ultimate experience of *unitas Spiritus,* loving union with God in this life (see 1 Cor 6:17).

This dynamic process of restoration and ascent to union was not an individual effort for the twelfth-century writers, any more than it had been for Augustine. They insisted upon the ecclesial, communal, and above all interpersonal aspects of realizing human destiny. For Bernard and the other Cistercians, the monastery was the "school of charity" in which the abbot acted the part as much of a nurturing mother as of a decision-making father.[24] The cult of friendship that the Cistercians and many others pursued with such passion and subtlety was an integral part of the return to God. "Here we are, you and I, and may Christ be the third among us," as Aelred of Rievaulx so beautifully put it (*Spiritual Friendship* 1.1).

There are many ways to approach the complex topic of how twelfth-century authors understood and utilized interpersonal relations in their spiritual programs. In choosing to take a brief look at Richard of St. Victor's understanding of the human person and how this affected his understanding of the Trinity, we shall have space to examine only a small part of the extensive program of only one of the important authors who might be considered. Nevertheless, even this brief look can be indicative of the contributions of this age.[25]

Bernard of Clairvaux (though not some other Cistercians) showed little interest in developing a detailed faculty psychology; Richard's intense concern for analysis of the affective and intellectual powers of the soul and the ways in which they take part in the ascent to God is more typical of the twelfth-century passion for the ordering of experience and knowledge.[26] For Richard, as for all his contemporaries, the soul has two fundamental powers, love and knowledge, the two feet by which we journey to God, as the Cistercian Isaac of Stella put it (*Letter on the Soul* [*PL* 194, col. 1880B]). If love is the higher power in which the actual transformation or divinization of the person takes place, it is not an anti-intellectual love that reaches this goal, but a love that is itself a form of knowing—*amor ipse notitia est*, as a famous phrase from Gregory the Great had it (*Homilies on the Gospels* 27 [*PL* 76, col. 1207]). True *caritas*, as opposed to the false self-love of *cupiditas*, by definition implies another person to which it is directed. It was in exploring the implications of this that Richard of St. Victor made some of his most important contributions.

Richard followed Augustine's lead and developed an understanding of how the three persons can be one God through an analysis of the nature of *caritas*. God, who is by definition perfect charity or outpouring generous love, requires someone equal to himself toward whom to direct this love. "And in those who are mutually loved . . . the perfection of each, in order to be completed, requires with equal reason a sharer of the love (*condilectus*) that has been shown to them" (*The Trinity* 3.11).[27] This understanding of the Trinity as the supreme shared love of three equal persons is based upon a sensitive analysis of the experience of human love found in Richard's *The Trinity* 3.14–20, and it leads to a new definition of the divine person as "an incommunicable existence of the divine nature" (*The Trinity* 4.18, 22). It is important to stress that in this definition "incommunicable" (*incommunicabilis*) means "individual," that is, a self-identity capable of being shared. To put it in another way, a person (divine or human) is an individual self because only a "self" can choose self-transcendence. Richard works out his new notion of the person primarily in terms of the Trinity, but since the divine mystery and the human mystery are always correlative, the definition can be used analogously to apply to the human person as an incommunicable, or individual, existence of a rational nature (4.23–24). The human person, then, like the divine person, is called to share love: this is what makes it what it is truly meant to be. Being made in the image and likeness of God means being made to share in the shared love of the Trinity, and like the Trinity to communicate that love to others. This becomes especially clear in the fourth degree of Richard's treatise *The Four Degrees of Violent Charity*, where, after the liquefaction or transformation or death of the soul into God in the third degree, there is a higher stage in which the "new creature" rises with Christ to live a life of loving service to others. For Richard of St. Victor the true meaning of being an *imago Dei* is to become an *imago Christi* in this life.

The limitations of traditional *imago Dei* anthropology and the ascetical and mystical programs to which it gave rise have become obvious with the passage of time. The concentration on the soul, or inner person, as the true image and the difficulties that thinkers in this tradition had in expressing the substantial union of body and soul led to systematic ambiguities that encouraged depreciation of the body and sometimes skewed the sanity of ascetical observances. Although the Latin traditions in general insisted on the equality of both men and women in their possession of the image, actual practice frequently regarded women as somehow inferior in conformity with the symbolic values assigned to the female. Still, an unprejudiced look at the spirituality of traditional Latin anthropology shows that it brought to light values of permanent worth that have not always been remembered or fully appreciated in succeeding centuries. Foremost among these is what we might call the "anthropological turn," that is, the conviction that the mystery of God and the mystery of the human person are strictly correlative. Self-knowledge is the recognition of both the grandeur and the wretchedness of the human person—grandeur as the image of God, wretchedness as caught in the toils of sin. Introspection and humility then form the starting point of the journey toward God, a pilgrimage that is also a discovery of the true self; but this dynamic creation of the new person is possible only because the divine Word made the experiment first by becoming fully human for our sakes.

## Notes

1. Alcibiades 1.133c (whether by Plato or his immediate followers).

2. On the microcosm theme, see Rudolph Allers, "Microcosmos from Anaximandros to Paracelsus," *Traditio* 2 (1944) 319–409.

3. The most detailed study is the article "Contemplation," in *Dict. Sp.* 2, cols. 1643–2193.

4. For the implications of this principle on Plato's notion of divinization, see *Timaeus* 90cd.

5. See P. Hadot, "L'image de la Trinité dans l'âme chez Victorinus et chez saint Augustin," *Studia Patristica* 6 (1962) 409–42. See also the article by Mary T. Clark, "The Trinity in Latin Christianity," in this volume.

6. For further details, see the article by J. Patout Burns, "Grace: the Augustinian Foundation," in this volume.

7. This appears in *Confessions* 13.2 and is developed in the *Literal Commentary on Genesis* 1.4–5 and 15.

8. E.g., *The Trinity* 12.13.20. The root in Philo (somewhat differently interpreted) may be found in *The Creation of the World* 56–60.

9. As found in "The Sayings of the Fathers," in *Western Asceticism*, ed. Owen Chadwick (LCC 12, 1958) 121.

10. Cf. *Literal Commentary on Genesis* 3.19.29.

11. Especially at the Second Council of Orange, held in 529.

12. Jean Leclercq, *The Love of Learning and the Desire for God* (New York: Fordham University Press, 1961) 42–43.

13. *Periphyseon* 2 (ed. I. P. Sheldon-Williams, 2:29).

14. The two central texts for John's anthropology are *Periphyseon* 2.28–29 (ed. Sheldon-Williams, 134–64) and 4.7 (*PL* 122, cols. 762–72). The text cited is from col. 771BC.

15. For exaggerated claims, see Colin Morris, *The Discovery of the Individual 1050–1200* (New York: Harper & Row, 1972). For criticism, see Caroline Bynum, "Did the Twelfth Century Discover the Individual?" in *Jesus as Mother: Studies in the Spirituality of the High Middle Ages* (Berkeley: University of California Press, 1982) 82–109; and John Benton, "Consciousness of Self and Perceptions of Individuality," in *Renaissance and Renewal in the Twelfth Century*, ed. Robert Benson and Giles Constable (Cambridge, MA: Harvard University Press, 1982) 263–95. Cf. M.-D. Chenu, *L'éveil de la conscience dans la civilisation médiévale*.

16. See the article of Benedicta Ward, "Anselm of Canterbury," and that of Jean Leclercq, "Ways of Prayer and Contemplation: Western," in this volume for further particulars.

17. *Sermons on Different Questions* 40.3 (*Sancti Bernardi opera*, 6:236). See also *Sermons on the Song of Songs* 34–38.

18. E. Gilson, "Self-Knowledge and Christian Socratism," in Gilson, *The Spirit of Mediaeval Philosophy*, 211–12.

19. *Sermons on the Song of Songs* 83.2 (*Sancti Bernardi opera*, 2:300–301).

20. *Grace and Free Choice* 1.2–2.4.

21. *Grace and Free Choice* 8.27 (*Sancti Bernardi opera*, 3:185).

22. Robert Javelet lists six different groups of variations (*Image et ressemblance au douzième siècle*, 1:214–24).

23. Cf. *Grace and Free Choice* 9.28–10.35; and *Sermons on the Song of Songs* 80–82.

24. See Caroline Bynum, "Jesus as Mother and Abbot as Mother: Some Themes in Twelfth-Century Cistercian Writing," in *Jesus as Mother*, 110–69.

25. See Ewert Cousins, "A Theology of Interpersonal Relations," *Thought* 45 (1970) 56–82.

26. See the article by Grover Zinn, "The Religious World of the Twelfth Century: The Regular Canons," in this volume.

27. For more on Richard's view of the Trinity, see the article of Mary T. Clark, "The Trinity in Latin Christianity," in this volume.

## Bibliography

### Sources

Augustine. *Confessions.* Translated by Rex Warner. New York: Mentor-Omega, 1963.
———. *The Literal Meaning of Genesis.* Translated by John H. Taylor. ACW 41–42. 1982.
———. *The Trinity.* Translated by Stephen McKenna. Fathers 45. 1963.
Bernard of Clairvaux. *Sancti Bernardi opera.* 8 vols. Edited by Jean Leclercq et al. Rome: Editiones Cistercienses, 1957–77.

———. *On Grace and Free Choice*. In *Bernard of Clairvaux: Treatises III*. Cistercian Fathers Series 19. Kalamazoo, MI: Cistercian Publications, 1977.

———. *On the Song of Songs I, II, III, IV.* Cistercian Fathers Series 4, 7, 31, 40. Kalamazoo, MI: Cistercian Publications, 1971, 1976, 1979, 1980.

John the Scot. *Johannes Scottus Periphyseon: Libri I, II, III*. Edited by I. P. Sheldon-Williams with the collaboration of Ludwig Bieler. Dublin: Dublin Institute for Advanced Studies, 1968, 1972, 1981. Books IV and V are to follow.

Richard of St. Victor. *The Twelve Patriarchs, The Mystical Ark, Book Three of The Trinity*. Translated by Grover A. Zinn. Classics of Western Spirituality. New York: Paulist Press, 1979. No full translation of *The Trinity* exists.

*Theological Anthropology*. Translated and edited by J. Patout Burns. Sources of Early Christian Thought. Philadelphia: Fortress, 1981. A selection of patristic texts.

*Three Treatises on Man: A Cistercian Anthropology*. Edited by Bernard McGinn. Cistercian Fathers Series 24. Kalamazoo, MI: Cistercian Publications, 1977.

## Studies

Chenu, Marie-Dominique. *L'éveil de la conscience dans la civilisation médiévale*. Conference Albert-le-Grand 1968. Paris: Vrin, 1969.

———. *Nature, Man and Society in the Twelfth Century*. Chicago: University of Chicago Press, 1968. See especially the first essay.

Courcelle, Pierre. *Connais-toi toi même de Socrate à saint Bernard*. Paris: Études augustiniennes, 1974–75. A massive study of the history of the Delphic maxim.

Gilson, Etienne. *The Spirit of Mediaeval Philosophy*. New York: Scribner, 1940. Chapters 9–11 form a still unrivaled introduction to medieval anthropology.

Javelet, Robert. *Image et ressemblance au douzième siècle*. 2 vols. Paris: Letouzey et Ané, 1967. A wealth of material, though poorly organized.

Ladner, Gerhart B. *The Idea of Reform: Its Impact on Christian Thought and Action in the Age of the Fathers*. Cambridge, MA: Harvard University Press, 1959. An important study of the notion of reform in the patristic period.

*L'Homme et son destin d'après les penseurs du moyen âge*. Actes du premier congrès international de philosophie médiévale. Louvain and Paris: Nauwelaerts, 1960. An important collection of papers.

McGinn, Bernard. *The Golden Chain: A Study in the Theological Anthropology of Isaac of Stella*. Washington, DC: Cistercian Publications, 1972.

Otto, Stephan. *Die Funktion des Bildbegriffes in der Theologie des 12. Jahrhunderts*. Beiträge zur Geschichte der Philosophie und Theologie des Mittelalters 40/1. Münster: Aschendorff, 1963.

Pegis, Anton C. *At the Origins of the Thomistic Notion of Man*. The St. Augustine Lecture 1962. New York: Macmillan, 1963. A brilliant essay on the Augustinian roots of Thomas Aquinas's anthropology.

Sullivan, J. E. *The Image of God: The Doctrine of St. Augustine and Its Influence*. Dubuque, IA: Priory Press, 1963. A useful survey.

# 13

# Grace:
# The Augustinian Foundation

### J. PATOUT BURNS

IN THE WESTERN CHURCH, the understanding of the role of God's grace
was shaped by the interaction of three traditions. Each contributed a
particular element to the doctrine that was forged in the writings of
Aurelius Augustine (354–430), the bishop of Hippo in Roman Africa
at the end of the fourth and beginning of the fifth century. Augustine's
teaching served as the foundation for the subsequent Latin theology of grace.

From the traditions of Platonic spiritualism and Gnostic antimaterialism
came the conviction that the human spirit is derived from and drawn to a
natural union with the divine principle, which transcends not only the
limitations of the world of bodies but even the person's status as a creature.
As the initial step toward this union, asceticism frees the mind from attachment to the illusions and pleasures of the senses. Contemplation introduces
the person to the unchanging Truth and Unity which are the source of true
joy. This type of thinking was mediated by Origen (185–254) and was
reflected in the writings of Augustine's older contemporaries, Gregory of
Nyssa (330–395) and Ambrose of Milan (339–397).

A second tradition asserted that all creatures, even the spiritual, are by
nature unlike the divine and can be united to God only by an exercise of
free choice in which the creature conforms to the divine will. The person
who freely and fully obeys God's commandments will be rewarded through
a creative intervention in which God raises the body to immortal life,
confirms the will in the good that has been chosen, and transforms the spirit
so that all the person's desires are fulfilled. This tradition stressed the body
and refused to limit the hope for beatitude to the mind or spirit. The roots
of this viewpoint may have been in the Stoic insistence on free submission
to the divine will ruling the universe. Its Christian form is evident in the
writings of Tertullian (160–220) and Cyprian (d. 258).

Finally, a third element was introduced from the Pauline meditation on God's sovereignty over the initiative and freedom of creatures. The human exercise of free choice between good and evil is neither unrestricted nor autonomous. Customs established by repeated sin restrict freedom and God's providential control directs even evil decisions and actions to God's own good purposes. Christian commentators on Paul recognized the dependence of human faith on God's call and of good willing on the liberating grace of Christ. Thus, God was to be praised for the success of human efforts. Augustine's meditation on the Pauline writings carried beyond this traditional interpretation to a more radical understanding of the necessity and efficacy of grace.

These three traditions contributed differently to early Christian interpretations of the interrelation of divine grace and human freedom. Some regarded the human spirit's natural longing for God as a sign of divine promise that every person would eventually be converted and brought to salvation; others understood the frustration of this desire as the source of terrible suffering in the condemned, who are eternally deprived of the union with God for which they were created. Some viewed the exercise of free choice as a process of appropriation and development of the good with which God had endowed the person in creation; others saw it as a performance of prescribed tasks to win God's favor and so to qualify for the reward of re-creation, which would transform the original capacity of human nature. Most acknowledged that God assists and cooperates with a self-determining creature; a few asserted that God may direct a decision or even effect a new orientation in a person who had opposed him.

These three sources had been combined in the understanding of grace that prevailed in Western Christianity during the second, third, and fourth centuries. Theologians as diverse in outlook as Tertullian and Ambrose assumed a common doctrine of grace and freedom. God had endowed human nature with an inalienable capacity to choose good and reject evil. The exercise of the power of self-determination can be enhanced or restricted only by prior personal choice. Whatever the effects of the fall of humanity in Adam, the divine commands in the Scripture clearly indicate the capacity of human nature for good. Because God does not require the impossible, each person must be able to do the enjoined good and avoid the forbidden evil. Substantial obedience will be rewarded and significant failure punished. This common doctrine generally limited the role of divine grace to clarifying true good and evil, facilitating what can be done by natural power and forgiving the failures of those who repent. The Christian is encouraged by the revelation of God's love and forgiveness, by the example of Christ and the saints, by the promise of reward and threat of punishment. In bestowing grace, God acts by the highest justice. Some assistance is provided impartially to all; special graces are given to particular individuals because of their prior efforts or foreknown response.

In the fifth century, this common doctrine of grace and freedom was represented by John Cassian (360–435) and by Pelagius, who led the opposition to Augustine's attempt to overturn many of its foundational assumptions. Although much of this earlier viewpoint endured in the religious practice of the Western church, it did not prevail in its theology. Augustine introduced a new interpretation of the Pauline epistles and utilized the Platonic tradition to challenge the assumptions of human autonomy and capacity for good will and action. His innovative understanding of the Holy Spirit's operation in the Christian became the foundation of Latin theology.

The exposition of Augustine's doctrine of grace proceeds by a series of increasingly specialized considerations, beginning with the relation of nature and grace and terminating with its gratuity and efficacy.

## Nature and Grace

Augustine sharply contrasted the spiritual and material realms. The world of bodies has a certain completeness and a definite limit. In creation, God endowed matter with various potentialities which were subsequently actualized through forces and agents within the created universe. God establishes and maintains the material world in its goodness by a providential governance exercised through angels and human beings.

Spiritual creatures also enjoy certain natural endowments. Their natures include life, immortality, and the capacity for knowledge and free choice. The resources for their proper functioning and their development are not, however, inherent in their natures or even in the created realm. Spiritual creatures are established in goodness only by being turned back toward the origin of their existence, by being constantly and immediately nourished through union with divine truth and beauty. The divine Word illumines the creative mind and communicates an understanding of universal principles, such as unity and mathematical proportion, according to which the world is created and governed. The human spirit is guided by these principles in maintaining its own body, in performing bodily actions, and in judging and working on the material world. The human mind that turns away from the divine light loses both moral wisdom and the power to integrate the bodily functions so that corruption and death are prevented. Such understanding of universal truth as remains in sinful humans comes not from the natural capacity of the mind but from an obscured divine illumination.[1]

Augustine also asserted that the creature loves the divine beauty and desires created goods according to their true value only through the indwelling of the Holy Spirit, the grace of charity. This divine love acts as a gravitational force that moves the creature to delight in God and thereby both to love self and other persons and to desire bodily goods in their relationship to God. Angels and humans sin by pride when they prefer their own goodness to God's and glory in their power over the material world. When love is so distorted, all the person's willing is sinful. Only the intervention of the Holy Spirit can convert the creature and restore the true hierarchy of love.[2]

Unlike the material world, created spirits cannot be established in goodness and truth by any created principle. Spirits function properly only when they are informed and guided by divine Wisdom and Love. God himself works the perfecting conversion to himself both in the original creation and in the restoration of the sinner. Thus Augustine explained that all the person's good willing and working derived from God's grace, God's prior self-communication as truth and beauty.

In this understanding of the spiritual creature's relation to God, Augustine laid the foundation of his particular doctrine of divine grace and human freedom. This religious metaphysic excludes the autonomy or independence of a created spirit; it finds the Creator's activity at the heart of all the creature's functions. It guided Augustine's interpretation of Scripture and the elaboration of religious experience into doctrinal theology. From it flowed the peculiar theses of divine operation and human cooperation, of the primacy of the Spirit's gift of charity, and of the liberation of the will by grace, which came to characterize Western Christianity.

## Spirit and Flesh

Many Christian authors use the ontological categories of mind and matter to interpret Paul's description of a conflict between spirit and flesh. The material body was characterized as the seat of insatiable and insistent appetites, of passion and emotion, of the lust for domination. All these passions seem to arise from the necessity of securing and consuming limited resources in order to sustain bodily life. The needs of the body and energies directed to satisfying its appetites were recognized as the source of social conflict and the principal means of exercising dominion over other humans. In contrast to the body, the mind was characterized as stable in life and intrinsically free of passion, nourished by inexhaustible and indivisible truth, and the seat of the love that moderates lower instincts, harmonizes creatures with one another, and unites them to God. Unlike bodily appetites, the desires of the spirit admit a progressive and even permanent fulfillment. Because of these differences, many Christian authors regularly described the path to human fulfillment and beatitude as the limitation of the demands of the body and the cultivation of the resources of the spirit. Happiness for the whole person would finally be attained in the transformation of the flesh and its assimilation to the life of the spirit.

This ontological interpretation of the opposition of spirit to flesh required some clarification of God's intention and purpose in the constitution of the human person. The actual condition of the human body and its resistance to the spirit were generally explained as the consequences of a deliberate deviation, usually a sin of sensuality, introduced by Adam and Eve. This first sin shattered the original unity in which God had created human nature; it brought mortality to the flesh and burdened the spirit with the demands of a weakened body. Among the principal functions of redemptive grace were strengthening the spirit in its struggle to dominate the body by asceticism and restoring the flesh to a spiritualized condition in its resurrection from the dead.[3]

Augustine acknowledged the conflict that humans experienced among various bodily and mental operations. This tension, however, was understood as the manifestation of a more fundamental division within the created spirit itself between love of God and love of self. The human spirit was originally created and established in union with divine truth and beauty. Guided by wisdom, the soul harmonized all its operations by directing them to the highest good, God. The original sin of humanity, like that of the angels, was a disordered love of one's own individual goodness and of dominion over the material world. The creature rejected the guidance of divine wisdom and proudly exercised autonomous choice. Thus, Augustine explained the Pauline notion of spirit and flesh as two opposing orientations of a single soul: charity or submission to God and pride or creaturely autonomy. By opposing its natural orientation to God, by preferring its derived goodness and power, the created soul divides against itself and becomes "flesh."[4]

Turned from divine wisdom, the mind loses its clear understanding of unity, proportion, and harmony; it then fails to integrate all its bodily and mental operations. The spirit no longer governs the body perfectly and does not maintain its original health, which precludes corruption and death. The appetites and energies of bodily operation are poorly governed. The resulting conflict experienced within the body manifests a more fundamental disharmony in the human spirit itself. In order to regain control and co-ordination of its complex activities, the human mind must establish patterns of evaluation, affective response and operation. These customs or habits make most activities routine and thus enable the person to concentrate attention and energy on more important, spiritual objectives. Once established, however, these customs give particular sensible objects the power to attract or repel; they limit the person's capacity to modify a response and initiate a new type of behavior. Virtuous customs maintain the person in good choice and performance. Habits rooted in self-love, however, resist subsequent good intentions and may prevent them from issuing in action. Customs can bind the will to evil.[5]

Thus, Augustine offered a double explanation of the division and conflict designated by the Pauline terms spirit and flesh. This conflict occurs within the human mind, which the grace of the Holy Spirit is converting back to God. The love of self and pride, which seek domination over the material world and other human beings, oppose the Spirit's gift of love of neighbor and submission to God. Second, the inattention to divine wisdom and loss of divine love weaken the human spirit and give rise to concupiscence: the mind's inability to control and direct bodily appetites and functions for its own purposes. The mind and will are enslaved to evil by the loss of divine guidance and the customs by which it has been replaced. When a person is converted to charity, the love of God overcomes pride and begins to restore harmony in desire and action. Concupiscence will be extinguished and full integrity restored only when charity reaches its perfection in resurrection from death and the vision of God.[6]

Spirit and flesh, therefore, are opposed not as mind and body, but as grace and sin. Life according to the spirit means love of God and personal integration by this love. Life according to the flesh is ruled by pride and characterized by conflict within the spirit, the body, and human society as well.

## Free Will

Augustine's notion of the freedom of the will was a part of his general understanding of nature and its relation to grace; it differed significantly from the common understanding of freedom as autonomous choice between good and evil. The early Christian notion of freedom assumed that the person was endowed at creation with an inalienable capacity for self-determination by which each individual becomes responsible for both good and evil actions. Such freedom and responsibility were considered the necessary basis for reward or punishment. This type of personal responsibility restricted the role of grace to facilitating the creature's performance of good and rejection or repentance of evil. Divine operation would never supplant or displace the creature's autonomous decision.

Augustine's understanding of the necessity of divine grace for the proper functioning of the spiritual creature undermined the prevailing assumptions on the nature of freedom. In his view, the creature can recognize the good only by divine wisdom and can accomplish it only through divine love. Instead of focusing on autonomy, Augustine explained created freedom as a participation in God's unfailing love of goodness and thus of each creature according to its degree of sharing in that goodness and being. He identified the freedom that deliberates and chooses between good and evil, the power to sin or not to sin, as a deficient form of true liberty.

Spiritual creatures are naturally endowed with the power of choice, of recognizing and selecting among options. This capacity is exercised properly when a person responds to the hierarchy of goods: higher or fuller goods are to be loved more than lower or lesser ones; the particular must be subordinated to the universal, and the individual's good to the common good. Since evil is nothing real or positive in itself but only the corruption of an existing good, a creature distorts the power to love not by choosing an evil but by deviating from the true order of good. Thus, a person sins by pride in preferring self to God or to the common good of society, by sensuality in loving bodily more than spiritual good, and by curiosity in attending to sensual experience of individual objects while neglecting intellectual understanding of principles. In this theory, the goodness of the willing derives not from the creature's autonomy or self-determination but from its correspondence to the order of the goodness of its objects.

In order to love God as the highest good and to love creatures in their relation to God, the created person must participate in God's own love for God and for the world as God governs it. This love is not an activity of the creature alone; it is the effect of the grace of charity and the fruit of the indwelling of the Holy Spirit. Augustine explained that because only God is indefectibly good, charity is not a part of the natural constitution of any creature. Nor can creatures initiate such love by their own natural powers since they would thereby make themselves better than God made them. The person is perfected not by the addition of some created quality or property but by the indwelling and operation of the Holy Spirit, by participating in God's own love. Augustine based this doctrine on Rom 5:5, "God's love has been poured into our hearts through the Holy Spirit which has been given to us." In the absence of this uncreated grace, creatures may choose and select among the lower goods but they cannot love God above all nor will they follow the true order among lower goods. Any willing which is independent of the Holy Spirit's influence and belongs to the creature alone is disordered and sinful. Thus, for Augustine, true freedom is the fruit of grace rather than the property or achievement of nature. When deprived of the Spirit, the creature is unfree, in bondage to sin.

Augustine's notion of freedom, therefore, does not value autonomous choice. The divine will is by nature identical with unfailing love of goodness. Although God enjoys the supreme freedom, the divine will cannot even deliberate on a choice between good and evil. The highest level of created freedom belongs to the angels and saints in glory, who enjoy a full union with God and cannot fail in their proper love of good. At the opposite extreme stand the fallen angels and condemned humans: they are fixed in self-love and have no freedom to love a higher good. Only humans on earth who have received the Holy Spirit's gift of charity have a freedom that can be exercised in good or evil willing. The Holy Spirit's charity draws them to love and accomplish the good while concupiscence and residual habits of pride, sensuality, and curiosity oppose this tendency. The saints on earth may advance in the divine love and approach a full love of God. Until they receive the fullness of charity in the vision of God, their love can fail by their turning from God to self or to lower goods. Sinners on earth are in bondage to disordered love but are not fixed in it. The Spirit might still liberate them, turn them back, and join them once again to God.

The indwelling of the Spirit, therefore, the gift of charity, neither gives a creature the bare power to choose properly nor does it force an unwilling person to perform what God commands. Charity draws and attracts a person to good so that the will is moved by desire and delight. Love functions as a gravitational mass bearing or carrying the will to good.[7] Concupiscence and sinful customs, which draw their power from the sinful willing of the creature, attract the person to self and lower goods. Even when the Holy Spirit turns a person back to God, the habit of sinning continues to exert its contrary influence and restricts the freedom born of grace. In the eighth book of his *Confessions,* Augustine described the conflict of opposing forces that divided his will and prevented a full commitment to God. He traced the process by which the Spirit gradually liberated him from the dominance of these evil dispositions and opened him to the influence of divine beauty. In the tenth book of the same work, he detailed the continuing influence of sinful orientations even in a Christian bishop who was ruled by charity.

## Human Solidarity

Augustine, and after him most Western theologians, considered human persons not simply as individuals but as joined together in two peoples or cities. The human city is a solidarity in the sin of pride, which originated in Adam and continues in his offspring. The divine city was established in the humility and obedience of Christ and extends to all who are joined into him in faith and charity. During their earthly lives, the citizens of the heavenly city are not completely freed of the self-love that opposes their love of God. They are also mingled with the adherents of the earthly city to form the visible human community that is unified by a love of temporal peace. The two peoples have been mixed together from the earliest times and will be segregated only in the final judgment.

God originally endowed humanity with a participation in divine wisdom and love. The first human beings, Adam and Eve, understood the principles by which God created and governs the universe; they were moved by love to act in accord with his intention. Following divine guidance, their minds integrated the vegetative and sensitive operations to maintain their bodies in harmony and perfect health. No conflicting desires or corruption were experienced in mind or body. Had Adam and Eve continued in submission to God's governance, they would have been confirmed in goodness. Instead, they sinned by pride and lost the divine gifts of understanding and love. Then they fell prey to the devil's temptation and sinned by sensuality, as is recorded in the third chapter of Genesis.[8]

Once the mind had turned its attention from the principles of unity and proportion, it could not perfectly coordinate its own vital functions: the body began to corrupt. Similarly, selflove turned the human spirit against its fundamental orientation to God; conflict erupted among its appetites and affections. The three characteristics of fallen human existence followed from the loss of these graces: ignorance, concupiscence, and mortality. The offspring of Adam and Eve are born deprived of grace and subject to these effects of the deprivation.

Although its citizens are counted from Abel and include the patriarchs and prophets as well as the holy angels, the city of God was established in the death and resurrection of Jesus Christ. Jesus won the forgiveness of sins and restored the gifts of the Holy Spirit, by which humans love God for God's own sake, love created persons for God's sake, and desire lower goods in their relation to God. To be incorporated into Christ, a person must believe in Christ's saving work and seek the sacrament of that faith. Before the coming of Christ, God's people believed the promises of salvation and bound themselves to Christ by circumcision and the other rituals appropriate to the time. After his coming, they believe the preaching of the gospel and receive baptism in the church.

Every human being belongs to one of these two cities or peoples. Each is born of Adam through carnal generation into the earthly city and may enter the heavenly city by rebirth into Christ through faith and baptism. The condemnation of those who are not joined into Christ is justified not only by the universality of personal sin among adults but also by the participation of all, even infants, in the original sin of Adam. Although he never succeeded in explaining the mechanism of transmission, Augustine asserted that all Adam's offspring are subject to the guilt and condemnation of that original sin of pride.

This doctrine of inherited guilt was based upon two dogmas. Christians confessed that Jesus Christ is the sole savior, the only one who reconciles humans to God. Western Christians, and particularly North Africans, believed that a person could share the Spirit of Christ only in union with the church. Infants can be incorporated into Christ by baptism alone and converts to whom baptism is unavailable before death may be joined to Christ by faith and love. The infant who dies without baptism and the pagan who never hears the gospel both remain in Adam and are condemned for their shared sin.[9] Although Augustine was the first to articulate this doctrine of inherited guilt, it won general acceptance in Western Christianity. It was affirmed by the African Synod of Carthage in 418, reasserted at the Council of Orange in 529, and confirmed by Pope Boniface II (d. 532).

In developing this doctrine of the two cities, Augustine explained that individuals are constituted a people by shared love. The city of God is established by charity and includes not only the saints on earth but also the angels and the blessed in glory. As an earthly reality in the period between the resurrection of Christ and his return to judge, this city is not fully identified with the church, the visible Christian community. It is that group of holy people within the church which Augustine named the society of saints. The Holy Spirit unites these people by shared charity, although they may not be able to identify one another. This mutual love not only unites the saints; through their patience and forgiveness, it forms the visible communion of the church. Sinners, who do not share this love, are held in the unity of the church by the active love of the saints. Schismatics reject the unity of the church and refuse to tolerate sinners; they sin against charity and lose the Holy Spirit. Catholics who are unjustly excommunicated and who continue to exercise love remain members of the heavenly city outside the visible church. Finally, God knows those who are still to be converted and joined into his people. Thus, the heavenly and earthly cities are intermingled both in the church and in civil society.

Augustine defined two other social functions of charity. Following Cyprian, the martyr-bishop of Carthage, he linked sanctifying power and unity as twin gifts of the Holy Spirit in the church. He refused, however, to follow Cyprian in identifying the bishop as the guardian of unity and agent of sanctification. Since many bishops were clearly unworthy of their office, they were judged unable to possess and communicate the Holy Spirit. Augustine explained that the power to forgive sins is given by Christ to the society of saints, the holy people within the catholic communion. Ordained leaders administer the sacraments as agents of this group whose prayers win

22. *Creation and Fall of Adam and Eve*, Manuscript Illumination,
13th century (M. 638, folio 1 verso)

God's sanctifying grace. A Christian who originally received the sacrament of baptism without an inner conversion may subsequently receive the grace of faith through the prayers of the saints and then receive charity in their union. Since charity is the principle of both unity and sanctity, it can be received and exercised only in a social context, the society of saints, within the catholic communion.

Finally, Augustine explained that the exercise of love within the unity of the church provides the basis and test of one's confession of faith. Most events of the life of Jesus may be identified through similar human experiences of birth, preaching, healing, and death. The concept of God, however, seems to have no common experiential basis that provides its meaning and gives content to the words of the creed. Augustine observed that, according to 1 John 4:7-8, God is love and can be known only in the sharing of love within the community. Thus, he identified participation in the charity that constitutes the Christian community as a privileged experience of the God who is confessed in faith. Further, a Christian cannot profess belief in the saving work of Christ while refusing to share the love that motivated Christ. The social experience of charity in the community belongs to the essence of Christian faith.[10]

Augustine's doctrine of the role of the Holy Spirit in the constitution of the city of God and of the dependence of faith on charity grew out of controversies on the nature of the church which divided North African Christianity from the end of the second century. His debates with the Donatists forced him to develop his understanding of the divine presence and operation within the Christian community. This teaching provided a theological foundation for the communitarian spirituality that characterized Western Christianity. His reflection on the social dimension of grace challenged the assumption that access to God could best be attained through solitary contemplation and withdrawal from human society. He found the Father of Jesus Christ revealed in the operation of the Holy Spirit's gift of charity in the monastery, the church congregation, the family, and even in civil or military service. This influence may be detected in the confident statements of the *Rule of St. Benedict* that monks living in a monastery are the best, surpassing the hermits who provided the ideal for Augustine's contemporary, John Cassian.

## The Historical Process of Salvation

Paul's division of the personal history of the Christian into existence prior to the law, under the law, and in Christ provided the framework for Augustine's analysis of the process through which a person moves from sin in

Adam, through grace in Christ, and thence to the glory of the heavenly city. These stages will be examined in this section and the two major transitions, from the law to grace and from grace to glory, will be studied in the next section.

In the first stage, humans live as fallen children of Adam, deprived of both understanding and love of the true order of goods. They follow and seek to satisfy self-love; they experience conflict only among their own disordered desires, not between sin and grace. While living in this condition, they establish the habits that complete their bondage to sin.

In the second stage, the initial movement of grace brings a restoration of the knowledge of the true order of goods and of specific actions that ought to be accomplished or avoided. God provides this kind of grace through both the interior illumination of the mind and the exterior teaching of his messengers, particularly Moses. Those under the law recognize the good they ought to do and acknowledge the justice of the punishment threatened for refusal or failure. Attempts to conform to God's law, however, prove unsuccessful. The person is motivated by self-love and does not fulfill the first and greatest of the commandments: to love God with one's whole being. The person's self-love and desire for temporal gratifications oppose and overcome the purpose of avoiding some future punishment. Under the law, the will is divided against itself and the person faces an apparently inevitable condemnation.

Many theologians did not accept this interpretation of Paul's assertions on the function of the divine law in the economy of salvation. They believed that a just God commands only what the subjects can accomplish; they used the law as a measure of human nature's unaided capacity for good. They assumed that the grace of Christ became operative only after his death and resurrection; thence they inferred that human nature functioned alone in the patriarchs and the saints of Israel. Augustine responded that this viewpoint implied that the sacrifice of the cross was not absolutely necessary and that Christ was not the New Adam, the savior of all who enter God's kingdom. He concluded that the uniqueness of Christ required that his grace was operative even before his incarnation, that the city of God was indistinguishable from the kingdom of Christ. Augustine's perspective prevailed.

The person whose self-reliance has been shattered by the failure to fulfill God's commandments and escape the condemnation God threatens has been prepared to hear the preaching of Christ's gospel. Augustine argued that in order to make the transition to the third stage, a person must believe in the saving power of Christ and pray for the gift of his Spirit. Through the grace of charity, the believer is moved to love God and is incorporated into Christ as a member of his Body. By the sanctifying power inherent in the church, the convert is forgiven the guilt of Adam's sin and of all personal sins.

The grace of charity is the presence and operation of divine love, the Holy Spirit, in the creature. Charity restores the proper order of love so that fuller goods are preferred to more limited and the universal good to the particular. Charity overcomes the established power of pride, sensuality, and curiosity. Augustine changed his interpretation of the seventh chapter of Romans, applying Paul's description of the ineffective desire for good to the situation of the Christian who seeks to fulfill God's law perfectly but fails because of the continuing resistance of habit and concupiscence. As charity increases in a person, these contrary desires are more regularly overcome and the divisions within the person are gradually healed. The Holy Spirit grants only a partial sharing in charity to the saints on earth. They must pray daily for strength and forgiveness and are thereby preserved from falling once again into pride. Since charity is the sanctifying force in the church which covers a multitude of sins, a person who holds to the love of God and neighbor in the church is forgiven all other transgressions and failings.

The Christians who persevere in love, good works, and the unity of the church until the end of their lives on earth are brought by God into the fullness of grace. In this fourth stage, glory, they are illumined by the vision of God and participate fully in God's own love for himself and for the world he creates. This full sharing in divine truth and love establishes them in true freedom and perfect goodness. Liberated from every contrary orientation and tendency, they are confirmed in grace and are incapable of sin. In the resurrection of the flesh, the body is restored to immortality and the whole person attains a unity and integrity that cannot be lost.

Augustine's description of the four stages by which humans pass from sin to glory was widely used to explain the structure of the Christian life. His explanation of the way in which charity strengthens a person to follow the commandments by inspiring delight in good moved Western Christian theology beyond a narrow moralism. His characterization of charity as a love that unites creatures to God opened the West to the riches that Eastern Christianity had assimilated from Neoplatonic spirituality. This Platonic Christianity tended, however, to separate the soul's purification through obedience and asceticism from the higher spirituality of contemplative union with God. Augustine countered this by his focus on union by love that is not restricted by imperfect knowledge and by his assertion that good works are an expression of love, not a preparation for it.

## Free and Effective Grace

Augustine understood the grace of charity as the indwelling of the Holy Spirit who inspires love of God and of the good he commands. This doctrine won general acceptance in Western Christianity. His explanation of the Spirit's operation in a Christian's transition from sin to grace and from grace to glory contradicted firmly held convictions and was approved only in part.

In a series of attempts to explain the ninth chapter of Romans, which culminated in *To Simplician on Different Questions,* Augustine pondered Paul's twin assertions that God had preferred Jacob to Esau without reference to any meritorious works of either and that God alone must be praised for the success of the efforts through which a person reaches salvation. After considering several explanations, Augustine concluded that God himself had caused the good merits for which he then preferred Jacob as heir of the promise to Abraham. Applying this understanding of election to the process of conversion of adult Christians, Augustine asserted that God chooses particular individuals to receive the grace of faith in Christ without regard for their prior or subsequent good works. Since all human beings deserve condemnation for the common fall of humanity in Adam and for sins that they had added individually, no one has a right to this grace. God justly condemns all whom he does not choose to convert. Augustine refused to believe that those who do become Christian are more deserving of God's grace than those who never hear the gospel and never have the opportunity to convert. He made infants who die before any personal choice a paradigm of divine election: those baptized are saved and those unbaptized are condemned; neither have personally done good or evil for which they might be rewarded or condemned. On the basis of scriptural texts such as John 6:45, 65; Phil 2:13; and 1 Cor 4:7, Augustine argued that the grace of conversion and the charity that follows it are absolutely gratuitous, bestowed without regard for personal merit, even in adults. According to Rom 9:18, God has mercy on whom he wills and withholds mercy from whom he wills.

Moreover, Augustine rejected the standard interpretation of Rom 9:16, "So it depends not upon man's will or exertion, but upon God's mercy." By his reading, this text excludes independent human cooperation with divine initiative; it asserts that divine operation actually causes human cooperation in good willing and working. He applied this interpretation to the two important transitions in the process of salvation: conversion from sin to grace and perseverance in grace unto glory. He argued for the gratuity and efficacy of the Spirit's action in each case.

The process of conversion involved the preaching of the gospel and the response of the believer. Augustine argued that the Holy Spirit works within the person God has chosen and causes the decision to repent, to believe, and to pray for charity. No one converts without choosing it, but the Holy Spirit makes the sinner willing. The sudden conversion of Paul through the interior and exterior working of the Holy Spirit became Augustine's paradigm for the efficacy of this divine operation. He described the working of the same grace in his own life and in the lives of those to whom he preached.

This doctrine of divine election, of the gratuity of charity, and of the efficacy of the grace of faith met significant opposition. Through the efforts of energetic proponents and the cooperation of the Roman bishops, however, it received basic approval at the Council of Orange in 529 and eventually won general acceptance.

In the final five years of his life, Augustine applied the principles of election, gratuity, and efficacy to that perseverance in good willing and working which is necessary for the Christian to come to glory. The grace of charity does not eliminate temptations to pride and sensuality, nor does it eliminate the difficulties that arise from evil habits and inherited concupiscence. Thus, charity gives the Christian a limited freedom in good: the power to sin or not to sin. The person who does sin is responsible for an avoidable failure. The person who consistently exercises the power to do good, however, has been assisted by a further grace, has been moved by God to will and perform the necessary good.[11]

Augustine explained that God causes the actual willing by which those he has elected persevere in charity and its works. By providential control of the environment, God prevents certain temptations and arranges an opportune moment of death. By an operation similar to that which preserved Christ from all sin, the Holy Spirit moves chosen Christians to will good or repent of a fall into evil. The Holy Spirit does not force a person to remain faithful; the grace of perseverance supports the person's own desire for good and makes it prevail over temptation. Those Christians whose goodwill the Spirit does not sustain in this way themselves fail to maintain the commitment charity inspires in them; they abandon good and are justly condemned. God chooses the elect and causes their persevering; God only foreknows and does not cause the sin of those whom he calls but does not choose.

Augustine also maintained that God gives the grace of perseverance in charity without regard for a person's prior or subsequent merits. He had earlier made the same assertion about the gratuity of the grace of conversion. Prior to conversion, of course, all a person's actions are sinful and merit only condemnation. The good works that follow conversion are the effects of the divine gifts of faith and charity. Thus, a person has no good merits that are independent of the grace of conversion and might thereby serve as a basis for claiming that grace. Christians living under the grace of charity, however, are responsible for their cooperation in good willing and working. Still, Augustine argued that without the further grace of perseverance they will not sustain this cooperation. Thus, he concluded that the merits of charity do not provide an independent basis for the reception of perseverance. Without regard for any prior merits, God gratuitously sustains the elect in charity and then gives eternal life as a reward to the perseverance he has himself effected. God does not prevent the free choice by which the nonelect fall from grace; he punishes their sin, which could have been avoided by their exercise of the power given in the grace of charity.

Augustine's doctrine of the gratuity and efficacy of divine operation was guided by his interpretation of the ninth chapter of Romans: glory and praise for salvation belong to God alone; the creature cannot claim a reward from God for achievements that are produced by his grace. The focus of the theory is, of course, the saints who are brought to glory, not the sinners who are condemned. Many theologians judged, however, that the gratuitous election of some implies an ungrounded rejection of others who are no less deserving, either of heaven or of hell. Augustine's doctrine seemed to involve a double predestination by which God achieves his intention to save and condemn by granting an effective grace and withholding a necessary assistance. The divine purpose in withholding the grace of perseverance from Christians who had already been given the graces of faith and charity proved particularly difficult to comprehend. Finally, the distinction between actuality and necessity proved too subtle: without the grace of perseverance, Christians who can remain faithful invariably fail to do so; by this grace, those who can fail actually stand firm. The gratuity, efficacy, and necessity of the grace of perseverance seemed, at least to minds less subtle than Augustine's, to make God alone fully responsible for both salvation *and* condemnation.

In the controversy that greeted Augustine's articulation of this doctrine, most theologians opposed it. At the Council of Orange in 529, the thesis of divine predestination to both glory and punishment was explicitly condemned, and the doctrine of divine operation in the perseverance of the elect was ignored. In the ninth century, the church condemned the double predestination propounded by Gottschalk. The doctrine was revived by John Calvin in the sixteenth century and was condemned in the Decree of Justification of the Council of Trent in 1547. In yet another form, it was propounded by the Jansenists in the following centuries.

Augustine modifed the prior tradition and laid a new foundation for the doctrine of divine grace in Western Christianity. This understanding may be summarized in a series of propositions. The principal form of grace is charity, which moves a person to love God, to seek the good of the neighbor, and to delight in created goods according to their relation to God. This grace is absolutely necessary for religious and moral actions; without it all willing and working are sinful. Charity is the indwelling and influence of the Holy Spirit, not a created quality that might be possessed by the creature. This doctrine laid the foundation for the thirteenth-century distinction of the natural from the supernatural order, as well as the assertion of the incompleteness of the nature of the created spirit. The initial grace of conversion, faith, and forgiveness is both gratuitous and efficacious. It is neither earned by prior good action nor accepted by autonomous, independent consent. The subsequent grace of charity, however, does require a free human cooperation, which it facilitates but does not produce. This cooperation with grace in good willing and working is necessary for eternal salvation.

Augustine also transformed the earlier doctrine of sin. The guilt of Adam's original sin is imputed to every human being born in his line. This guilt brings eternal condemnation to those for whom it is not forgiven through the saving grace of Christ. Pride or love of one's own goodness and power is the foundational sin or basic deviation of every spiritual creature from God. Augustine explained concupiscence and lust as consequences of a prior sin of pride.

Although the religious metaphysic and understanding of the activity of created spirits, which were integral to these doctrines in Augustine's own thought, did not attain general acceptance, the interpretation of Paul upon which the theses were grounded did prevail. The Augustinian presentation of divine grace was to shape the religious experience of Western Christians for more than a thousand years.

### Notes

1. *On Music* 6.5.8-13; *On Genesis against the Manichaeans* 2.7.9; 2.11.15.

2. *On Genesis against the Manichaeans* 2.15.22-2.17.26; *Confessions* 13.9.10; 13.21.31.

3. See, for example, Gregory of Nyssa *On the Creation of Man* 16-18; and Ambrose of Milan *On Paradise* and *Letter* 21 3-10.

4. *On Genesis against the Manichaeans* 2.15.22-2.17.26; *Literal Commentary on Genesis* 11.5; 11.27-32.

5. *On Music* 6.5.9-14; *On the Lord's Sermon on the Mount* 1.12.34-36.

6. *Letter* 140 22.54; *Against Two Letters of the Pelagians* 1.10.17-1.11.24.

7. *Confessions* 13.9.10; *City of God* 11.28.

8. *Literal Commentary on Genesis* 11.5; 11.27-32; *City of God* 13.20-21; 14.10-13.

9. *On Nature and Grace* 4.4.
10. *Treatises on the First Epistle of John* 5.7; 6.13; *On the Trinity* 8.4.6–8.9.13.
11. *On Condemnation and Grace* 10.26–12.38.

## Bibliography

### Sources

Though there are many more recent critical texts of individual works of Augustine, the most complete edition remains that of the Benedictine Maurists (1679–1700), reprinted in *PL* 32–47.

### Studies

Brown, Peter. *Augustine of Hippo: A Biography.* Berkeley: University of California Press, 1969.

Burnaby, John. *Amor Dei: A Study of the Religion of St. Augustine.* London: Hodder & Stoughton, 1938.

Burns, J. Patout. *The Development of Augustine's Doctrine of Operative Grace.* Paris: Études augustiniennes, 1980.

Cochrane, Charles Norris. *Christianity and Classical Culture: A Study in Thought and Action from Augustus to Augustine.* New York: Oxford University Press, 1957.

Evans, Robert F. *Pelagius: Inquiries and Reappraisals.* New York: Seabury, 1968.

Gilson, Étienne. *The Christian Philosophy of Saint Augustine.* New York: Random House, 1967.

Holte, Ragnar. *Béatitude et sagesse: Saint Augustin et le problème de la fin de l'homme dans la philosophie ancienne.* Paris: Études augustiniennes, 1962.

O'Donovan, Oliver. *The Problem of Self-Love in St. Augustine.* New Haven, CT: Yale University Press, 1980.

Portalié, Eugène. *A Guide to the Thought of St. Augustine.* Chicago: Regnery, 1960.

Teselle, Eugene. *Augustine the Theologian.* New York: Herder, 1970.

# 14

# Liturgy and Spirituality

## I. *Eastern Liturgical Theology*

### PAUL MEYENDORFF

IN 988, ambassadors sent by Prince Vladimir from Kiev visited Constantinople and attended the liturgy at Hagia Sophia, the famous church erected by Emperor Justinian to be the cathedral church of the "New Rome." The emissaries reported that they did not know whether they were "still on earth, or in heaven." The writer of the *Russian Primary Chronicle* claimed that this experience was the cause of the adoption of Byzantine Christianity by the Russians.[1] This is an apt illustration of the influence of the liturgy of the "Great Church," which was felt not only by barbarian nations who received Christianity from the Greeks but also by other Christian peoples who had their own traditions, including the Syrian Jacobites, the Armenians, and even the Romans. Of course, the Byzantine liturgy itself was not autonomous, for it evolved from Syrian sources and was itself influenced by external sources, by the Jerusalem liturgy in particular. It can thus be argued convincingly that the Byzantine liturgy, because the majority of Eastern Christians became its adherents and because of its eclectic nature, is representative of the Eastern liturgical ethos. For this reason and because of limitations of space, our study will focus chiefly on the Byzantine approach to the liturgy, particularly with respect to developments in the Eucharist.

The scope of this article will be further limited to an examination of only two sacraments, or "mysteries," as they are traditionally called: baptism and Eucharist. The choice is not accidental, for these two were considered the source and summit of the Christian life and remained so in the East throughout the period in question. Baptism was the means by which one was made a member of the church, and the Eucharist was the means by which one affirmed this membership and experienced it. For the experience of the liturgy was precisely the experience of Christianity, and thus it became the very possibility and source for the knowledge of God and for participation in divine life itself. This is the meaning of the Eastern concept of *theōsis*, or divinization, and the liturgy was perceived as its most perfect expression and realization. This is also why theology and liturgy remain so closely linked in the East, for one is not considered possible without the other.

## Baptism

Characteristic of the Eastern understanding and practice of baptism throughout history is the unitive aspect of the sacrament. The rites of initiation, comprising baptism, chrismation (or confirmation, as it was later called in the West), and Eucharist are seen as one continuous action. Much has been made of the fact that chrismation either followed (in the West) or preceded (in the East) water baptism, but this has frequently been in the context of explaining or justifying the much later split of the rite of initiation into separate and distinct sacraments. Initiation, which comprises all these elements, marks the entrance of the neophyte into the church, the Body of Christ, and its culmination is the sharing of the eucharistic banquet, which is open to all the baptized faithful, including infants. In the East, these actions remain inseparable.

During the first centuries, East and West followed divergent practices in the rite itself. The early Western practice, which is seen, for example, in Tertullian and Hippolytus, consisted of water baptism, anointing with oil, and the laying on of hands. The anointing was connected with the anointing of Aaron by Moses, and the laying on of hands was seen as the imparting by the bishop of the gift of the Holy Spirit. In the East, the order was reversed, and anointing often preceded baptism. This is seen in such sources as the *Acts of Judas Thomas* (early third century), the *Didascalia* (mid-third century), and the Syriac *Acts of John* (early fourth century). The prebaptismal anointing was seen in some places as fully imparting the gift of the Holy Spirit. This practice was probably derived from baptismal practices described in Acts (e.g., 10:44–48; 9:17–18), where the Holy Spirit is imparted before baptism. In some cases, the anointing was not seen as having anything to do with the gift of the Spirit. John Chrysostom associated the granting of the Spirit with the immersion itself (*Second Baptismal Catechesis* 25–26). These divergences in practice, however, did not create any difficulties, for as long as the unity of the rite was maintained, it mattered little how the various elements were distributed through the actual rites. Indeed, it is remarkable how much uniformity exists, for, despite differences in how these elements are distributed or explained, the same chief elements are present throughout the Christian world.

In this early period in the East, before the fourth century, baptism was seen primarily as a reenactment of Christ's baptism in the Jordan. The font is called the womb, out of which a new, reborn person emerges, the "son of God." This is what we find in the *Didascalia Apostolorum*, which is of Syrian origin:

> [It is] the bishop, through whom the Lord gave you the Holy Spirit, and through whom you have learned the word and have known God, and through whom you have been known of God, and through whom you were sealed, and through whom you became sons of the light, and through whom the Lord in baptism, by the imposition of the hand of the bishop, bore witness to each one of you and uttered his holy voice, saying: "Thou art my son: I this day have begotten you." (*Didascalia* 9)

Similarly, the *Acts of Judas Thomas*, which originated in Ephesus, speak of baptism as "the bringer forth of the new man" and the "establisher of the new man in the Trinity." Later, Theodore of Mopsuestia (d. 428) always spoke of the baptismal font as the "womb," which introduces the Christian into a new life. Characteristic of this literature is the absence of a theology of baptism strongly connected to Rom 6:3-5—baptism as the reenactment and sharing in the death and burial of Christ.

This latter interpretation became dominant only in the fourth century, a pivotal period in the development of the church. The years that followed the recognition of the church and its transformation into the official state religion saw a massive influx of new members into the church, people of varied backgrounds and motives. Constantine launched a massive building campaign throughout the empire and particularly in Jerusalem, which had been until then an insignificant town. The church had to adapt to these new conditions, to provide its new members with proper teaching, and to develop adequate rites and explanations. At the same time, theological disputes were raging, and these too exercised significant influence both on the rites and especially on the theology behind them.

The process of historicization of the liturgy was felt most strongly in Jerusalem. The construction program begun under Constantine was responsible for a whole complex of buildings, the Holy Sepulchre, Sion, Golgotha, and others. These churches soon became centers of pilgrimage. The liturgy of the church at Jerusalem, which took place at the very sites where the major events of Christ's earthly life were believed to have occurred, could not but be influenced by the milieu. The liturgies of Holy Week in particular, reaching their climax at the Easter vigil, became largely a reenactment of the gospel events, complete with colorful processions to the appropriate sites, as we can see from the description provided by the pilgrim Egeria.[2] This type of stational liturgy had a powerful effect on eyewitnesses, and the liturgies of the major centers of the empire, Rome and Constantinople in particular, were soon patterned after it. The calendar, particularly the cycle of fixed feasts, owes much of its development to this phenomenon of historicization. This also marks a shift from a primarily eschatological emphasis in the feasts of the church to a more historical one, although this should not be exaggerated.

This historicizing trend strongly influenced the understanding of baptism, first in Jerusalem and then elsewhere. In particular, the baptismal rite, with its procession to the font, triple immersion, and emersion, began to be interpreted as the reenactment not of Jesus' baptism in the Jordan but of his death and resurrection. This interpretation, based on Romans 6, had of course always been present, but now it came to the foreground. Cyril of Jerusalem applied this theology to the liturgical ceremony in Jerusalem. The movement to the font was explained as the procession bearing the body of Christ to the tomb. The triple immersion he explained as the three-day sojourn in the grave. The emerging from the pool was a sign of the resurrection. Thus, our baptism is an imitation (*mimēsis*) of Christ's suffering in figure (*en eikoni*), but we are saved in truth (*en alētheia*) and have a share (*koinōnia*) in the true sufferings of Christ (*Mystagogical Catechesis* 2.5). The other leading catechists of the period—Ambrose, Chrysostom, and Theodore of Mopsuestia—also commented on this rite and used the same methodology but ascribed various meanings to each part of the rite. The historicizing trend, however, is evident in all of them.

Yet it is not sufficient to point only to the influence of Jerusalem and its rites to explain this trend. It was also part of the response by the church to the massive influx of new members, to whom the mystery of Christ had to be explained in an attractive and dramatic fashion. Moreover, it was a way to stress the historical basis for Christianity, which was in sharp contrast to the antihistorical bias of the Hellenistic culture. This was not a systematic approach, but a pastoral one. The church no longer consisted of a small, dedicated elite, but of a crowd that needed and demanded a clearer and more immediate structure.

All these factors led, in the fourth century, to the development of a new type of literature—catechetical literature, particularly the mystagogical catechesis. This was made necessary by the large number of converts, who had to go through the now structured catechumenate, or period of preparation for baptism. The final stage of this catechumenate took place during Lent, the period of preparation for Easter. This consisted of fasting, exorcisms, reading of Scripture, and instruction, which usually comprised explanations of the articles of faith contained in the creed. The description provided by Egeria gives a detailed outline of this program, and Cyril's *Procatechesis* and eighteen *Catechetical Orations* are an example of the sort of instruction that took place. The fourth-century Jerusalem creed, a baptismal profession of faith like all other early creeds, formed the basis for the so-called Nicene Creed, which remains in use today throughout the Christian world. At the Easter vigil, baptism took place: the neophytes then processed to the Martyrium, the Constantinian basilica, for the Eucharist. Then, during the octave of Easter, the newly baptized assembled each day at the Anastasis to listen to the mystagogical orations. These were explanations of the mysteries of baptism and Eucharist, which they had just experienced. For it was not until after they were initiated, after they had experienced them, that the mysteries of the Christian faith were explained to them.

Several important conclusions are to be drawn from this. First, the message of Christianity, its content, was revealed in a liturgical context. This is characteristic of the Eastern churches also today. Creeds were primarily baptismal confessions of faith at first. Second, Scripture was read and explained in a liturgical context. Third, the experience of the liturgy, of baptism, of Eucharist, preceded any explanation of them. The liturgical rites existed before their explanations: the explanations were secondary to the rites themselves and were often changed to accommodate the pastoral and polemical needs of each age. The explanations can in turn influence the form of the rites, though their basic structure, fixed very early, remains essentially unchanged.

The method with which the great catechists approached the rites is also significant, for they applied the method of scriptural exegesis to the liturgy, particularly to the visible actions of the rite. Already in the New Testament, Scripture was seen as having both a literal and a spiritual meaning. Moreover, the spiritual meaning was not secondary. From the time of Origen, the two senses of scripture were referred to as (1) literal or historical and (2) spiritual, mystical, or allegorical. Later, the spiritual sense was further subdivided into three aspects: (1) allegorical—the dogmatic aspect, which interprets the Old Testament as referring to Christ and the church; (2) tropological—the moral and spiritual aspect, which relates the allegorical to the mystery of Christian life, what we believe to what we do; (3) anagogical—the eschatological aspect, which refers to the final accomplishment we await in the kingdom.[3] From the fourth century, this became the traditional method in the East, though the various commentators stressed one or another aspect in their mystagogies. This will be examined later as it relates to the Eucharist. In Cyril's description of the stripping of the candidate before baptism we can see how this method is applied to the baptismal rite:

> You were stripped of your clothing, and this was an image of the putting off the old man with his deeds. Having stripped yourselves, you were naked; in this also imitating Christ, who hung naked on the cross, and in his nakedness spoiled principalities and powers and openly trampled over them on the tree.... Oh marvel, you were naked before all, and you are not ashamed. For, in truth, you were in the image of the first man, Adam, who was naked in paradise and was not ashamed. (*Mystagogical Catechesis* 2.2)

This exegesis, here applied to a ritual action that was at first only a practical act, provides a multifaceted meaning to the simple act of stripping. The "putting off the old man with his deeds" provides the tropological, or moral, level. The nakedness of Christ on the cross and his triumph over the powers —a brief summary of the theological meaning of the cross—represent the allegorical, or dogmatic, sense. And the reference to Adam in paradise is a sign of our insertion into salvation history, our passage into a new dimension of existence, into eschatology: this is the anagogical plane. It is easy to see how attractive and useful a preaching tool this exegetical method offers, but it also has its dangers, particularly when the individual elements of a rite begin to be seen in isolation from the rite as a whole, which does happen later.

After the fourth century, we find little literature on baptism. This is attributable largely to the generalization of child baptism. Although child baptism had existed for centuries, the majority of new members had been adult converts. In addition, many had postponed their baptism until late in life, including such figures as Constantine, Chrysostom, and Basil. With the generalization of child baptism, the need for baptismal catechesis declined and the catechumenate began to disappear. The result, in both East and West, was that baptism began to be taken for granted and thus began to lose its prominent position in the theology of the church, particularly in ecclesiology. In this period, too, was the beginning of a significant difference in approach to the rites of initiation between East and West.

Under the influence of Augustine's anti-Pelagian theology, with its strong emphasis on original sin as the *guilt* brought upon humanity by Adam, the West began to understand baptism chiefly as the remission of sin. Thus, the theology of baptism became primarily negative. Children were considered to be born guilty and thus to be in need of the palliative of baptism. Further, the Western requirement that confirmation, done by the laying on of hands, be performed only by a bishop eventually led to a split in the rite of initiation into two distant elements, since the bishop could not possibly be present at all the local churches on the traditional baptismal days of Easter and Pentecost. This, in turn, led to the withholding of the Eucharist from children until after they completed the process of initiation.

The East did not accept Augustine's notion of original sin and saw its consequence not as guilt but as mortality. Guilt is only acquired through the personal exercise of the free will, through personal sin.[4] Thus, baptism is perceived not primarily as remission from guilt but as liberation from mortality and incorporation into the life of the church. This is an eminently positive theology:

> Blessed is God . . . who makes all things and renews them. Those who were captive yesterday are today free persons and citizens of the church. Those who were formerly in the shame of sin now have boldness and righteousness. They are not only free, but saints; not only saints, but just; not only just, but sons; not only sons, but heirs; not only heirs, but brothers of Christ; not only brothers of Christ, but his co-heirs; not only his co-heirs, but his members; not only his members, but temples; not only temples, but instruments of the Spirit. . . . Have you seen how many are the benefits of baptism? Whereas many think that its only benefit is the remission of sins, we have enumerated as many as ten honors conferred by it. This is why we baptize even small children, even though they have no sins, so that they may also receive righteousness, adoption, inheritance, the grace of being brothers and members of Christ, and that they might become the dwelling of the Holy Spirit. (Chrysostom *Baptismal Catechesis* 3.5-6)

The baptized person is called to *theōsis*, deification, whose goal is understood as participation in divine life itself. The gifts received in baptism are then to be actualized in the life of the Christian. The *Apostolic Constitutions* (ca. 380) presumes the baptism of children, makes no mention of original sin, and places strong emphasis on a good Christian education and formation (6.15). Baptism is a free gift, not dependent on human choice, a promise of new life. The baptismal formula in the East is consequently always in a deprecatory form: "The servant of God . . . *is baptized* in the name of the Father, the Son, and the Holy Spirit." This indicates that baptism comes from divine, rather than human, initiative—to which the Christian is in turn called to respond.

The East sees baptism, as it does all the sacraments, as a trinitarian act: it is the gift of the Son, by the Father, made effective by the Holy Spirit. This is shown first of all by the trinitarian baptismal formula. Further, the prayers for the consecration of water and chrism are strongly epicletic, asking the Father to send down the Holy Spirit. Cyril of Jerusalem drew a direct parallel between the epiclesis over the bread at the Eucharist and the epiclesis over the chrism (*Mystagogical Catechesis* 3.3). Thus, the baptized, like Christ in the Jordan, are anointed by and with the Holy Spirit (*Mystagogical Catechesis* 3.1). Joined to Christ and filled with the Spirit, the Christian begins the process of human divinization. This understanding of baptism remains standard in the Byzantine church.

## Eucharist

This process of divinization fulfills itself in the Eucharist, which is a real participation in the glorified body of Christ. The eucharistic elements are seen in very realistic terms by all the great figures of the fourth century, including Basil, Gregory of Nyssa, Chrysostom, and Cyril of Jerusalem. Communion, the source of both immortality and unity, is essential for the Christian life:

> It is good and beneficial to communicate every day and to partake of the holy body and blood of Christ. For He distinctly says, "He that eats my flesh and drinks my blood has eternal life" (John 6:55). And who doubts that to share frequently in life is to have manifold life? I indeed communicate four times a week, on the Lord's Day, on Wednesday, on Friday, and on the Sabbath, and on other days if there is a commemoration of any saint. (Basil *Letter* 93)

The dramatic events of the fourth century also strongly influenced eucharistic theology and practice. The rites themselves, which were already firmly set in their basic structure and content, changed very little—only in external and peripheral aspects. But the understanding of the Eucharist underwent strong changes. The churches were now crowded with many new or potential members, but the catechumens and penitents could not communicate. Postponing baptism was common. Then, very important, the preachers began stressing the elements of fear and awe with regard to the Eucharist— in response to a perceived need to protect the mysteries from the "masses." The faithful responded by abandoning communion, and thus the community was split into a communicating elite and the majority of others. No longer an act of "communion" (*koinōnia*), the reception of communion became an act of personal devotion. Thus the traditional notion of the Eucharist as a meal, as fellowship, began to break down, to be replaced by a different understanding, where this active participation was not so essential.[5]

In addition to the important social changes in the period, theological debates determined the paths these new approaches to the Eucharist were to take. The Arian crisis led to a renewed emphasis by the orthodox on the preexistent divinity of Christ, in reaction to subordinationism and adoptionism. The orthodox leveled the doxological formula (". . . to the Father, *and* the Son, *and* the Holy Spirit") and stressed the two-natures formula. The Alexandrians laid stress on the divinity of Christ and saw his mediatorship as primarily a divine function; they paid little attention to the historical economy of Christ's saving work. The Antiochenes, on the other hand, stressed the humanity and the historical activity of Christ and his human mediatorship. These divergent approaches to the fundamental Christian mystery also reflected the different exegetical methods of the two schools. The Alexandrians, students of Origen, stressed the anagogical, or spiritual, sense of Scripture, whereas the Antiochenes emphasized the literal and historical sense.

Thus, the Antiochene liturgical writers, applying their exegetical methods to the rites and texts of the liturgy, saw it as an imitation (*mimēsis*) or memorial (*anamnēsis*) of the saving acts of Christ's life and the anticipation of the heavenly liturgy. This approach was synthesized by Theodore of Mopsuestia, who wrote his catechetical homilies between 392 and 428.

> Every time, then, there is performed the liturgy of this awesome sacrifice, which is the clear image of the heavenly realities, we should imagine that we are in heaven. . . . Faith enables us to picture in our minds the heavenly realities, as we remind ourselves that the same Christ who is in heaven . . . is now being immolated under these symbols. So when faith enables our eyes to contemplate the commemoration that now takes place, we are brought again to see his death, resurrection, and ascension, which have already taken place for our sake. (*Catechetical Homily* 15.20)

He went on to describe just how the rites represent Christ's ministry. In describing the procession of the transfer of gifts, he says that "we must see Christ now being led away to his passion and again later when he is stretched out on the altar to be immolated for us" (*Catechetical Homily* 15.25). The resurrection is effected through the consecration, and the sharing of the gifts is like the appearance of the risen Lord. Theodore also adopted the topographical system of church symbolism, which developed in Jerusalem. The altar was seen as the tomb, the apse as the cave of the sepulchre. This type of interpretation was to enter the Byzantine tradition through Germanus in the eighth century.

The Alexandrian approach, heir to the spiritualizing tendencies of Origen, is quite different. Writing late in the fifth century, Pseudo-Dionysius saw the liturgy as an allegory of the ascent of the soul to the invisible reality:

> Let us leave to the imperfect these signs which, as I said, are magnificently painted in the vestibules of the sanctuaries; they will be sufficient to feed their contemplation. As far as we are concerned, let us turn back, in considering the holy synaxis from the effects to their causes, and, thanks to the lights which Jesus will give us, we shall be able to contemplate harmoniously the intelligible realities in which are clearly reflected the blessed goodness of the models. (*Ecclesiastical Hierarchies* 3.3)

There is no room here for biblical typology and no reference to the earthly activity of Christ, except for the incarnation. Salvation is union with the prototype, and deification is achieved through moral perfection. Dionysius never spoke of the Eucharist as the body and blood of Christ.

In the seventh century, Maximus the Confessor was the great spokesman for this tradition. He adopted the Dionysian spiritualizing approach but added his own interpretation, which saw the liturgy as the memorial of the divine economy in Christ and the anticipation of the parousia and the eschaton. Thus, the liturgy represents all salvation history: the church building is the type and image of the whole universe; the Gospel reading is the consummation of the world; the bishop's descent from the throne, the expulsion of the catechumens, and the closing of the doors represent the descent of Christ in parousia, the expulsion of the wicked, and the entrance into the mystical chamber of the bridegroom (*Mystagogy* 14–16). Though slightly more realistic than Pseudo-Dionysius, Maximus too had a primarily symbolic view of the Eucharist. The strength of the Alexandrian approach was its strong eschatological emphasis, so characteristic of pre-fourth-century liturgy: its weakness became apparent in the iconoclastic controversies that shook the East in the eighth century.

The Byzantine tradition prior to iconoclasm generally followed the Alexandrian approach of Pseudo-Dionysius and Maximus to the liturgy. In the eighth century this led to a debate over the nature of the Eucharist. At the iconoclastic council of 754 the iconoclasts, appealing to long-standing tradition, declared that no images of Christ are acceptable, and that the Eucharist is the only valid symbol of Christ.[6] The defenders of images, particularly Theodore of Studios and Patriarch Nicephorus, rejected this position and affirmed that the Eucharist is not "type" but "truth," which is the very "flesh of God," even after his glorification. In reaction to the iconoclastic, spiritualizing position, the orthodox began to take a much more realistic, more representational approach, along christological and soteriological lines. Thus, in iconography, Christ could no longer be represented symbolically as a lamb but could be depicted only as a man.[7] And the anagogical approach to the liturgy was supplemented by the more historical, representational interpretation of the Antiochene school. Patriarch Germanus, a defender of orthodoxy against the iconoclasts, who was deposed by them in 730, composed a mystagogy on the divine liturgy, entitled *Historia*, which was his attempt to combine the two traditions. The following is a typical passage:

> The cherubic hymn, by the procession of the deacons and the representation of the fans, which are in the likeness of the seraphim, signifies the entrance of all the saints and righteous ahead of the cherubic powers and the invisible, angelic hosts, who run in advance of the great king, Christ, who is proceeding to the mystical sacrifice. . . . It is also in imitation of the burial of Christ, when Joseph took the body down from the cross, wrapped it in clean linen,

anointed it with spices, carried it with Nicodemus, and placed it in a new tomb hewn out of a rock. (chap. 37)

Thus, to the more primitive imagery of the heavenly liturgy, clear in the very text of the *Cherubicon* (introduced in 573–574 under Justin II), was added the later symbolism, of Antiochene origin, which saw the gifts at the transfer as representing the body of the already crucified Christ. The various liturgical items, the eiliton, the paten, cover, and aer are all interpreted in this second sense. This latter tradition was very influential in the development of the secondary rites, the prothesis, or preparation of gifts, in particular. But Germanus's approach to the anaphora, or eucharistic prayer, is completely biblical and devoid of allegory. It must be remembered that throughout the period in question, although the interpretation of the rite varied, the rite itself remained essentially unchanged, both in structure and in its two focuses—the liturgy of the word and the anaphora. In addition, the attention of the commentators was drawn chiefly to the visual aspects of the liturgy, the processions, the liturgical space.

The post-iconoclastic period saw the development of that peculiarly Eastern phenomenon, the iconostasis. A development of the primitive chancel barrier, it now became a real wall, covered with icons. This emphasized, in the Byzantine mind, the "mystery" element of the Eucharist. Moreover, the Eucharist was not something to be seen through physical eyes, but to be received as food. The mystery was *seen* through the program of icons on the walls, and particularly on the iconostasis, with their images of Christ and the saints. Thus, a cult of the eucharistic elements, such as that which developed in the medieval West, was not possible. Moreover, the Byzantines never used the term transubstantiation (*metousiōsis*) in connection with the Eucharist, for they always saw the elements themselves as bread and wine, which, like the human body of Christ, are divinized. Thus, the epiclesis in the anaphora ascribed to Chrysostom calls for the Holy Spirit to be sent "upon us and upon these gifts." The focus is not so much on the bread as on the people gathered together as the church. The fruits of the Eucharist are "purification of soul, remission of sins, communion of the Holy Spirit, the fulness of the Kingdom of Heaven." But the development of the iconostasis and the heightening of the mystery dimension led to a deepening of the split between clergy and laity, for the now-concealed sanctuary was the exclusive preserve of the clergy. This also manifested itself, in the ninth century, in the removal of the cup from the laity. From that time, though communion continued to be distributed under both species, it was given by means of a spoon.

It is significant that it was an argument over liturgical interpretation that served as the occasion for the so-called schism of 1054. The issue in dispute between East and West was the use of azymes. The West used unleavened bread for the Eucharist, whereas the East used leavened bread. The Greeks maintained that the leavened bread symbolized the *animated* body of Christ: the fact that the Latins used azymes showed that they were Apollinarians, for they denied that Jesus had a human soul. The Greeks further maintained that the eucharistic bread must be normal, everyday leavened bread so as to be consubstantial with humanity—"our daily bread." They understood bread to be the "type" of humanity, of our humanity, which changes into the transfigured humanity of Christ. Latin medieval piety, on the other hand, emphasized the "supersubstantiality," or otherness of the bread. The Latins, not attaching much significance to this apparently minor rubrical detail, only wanted the Greeks to stop condemning the Latin custom and were perfectly willing to allow them to continue using leavened bread. This was the chief dispute and the primary reason for the dramatic events of 1054: at that time, the Byzantines did not even bring up the other points of conflict.

This Byzantine intransigence about such an apparently trivial point reveals much about their liturgical piety. First, they see liturgical texts and rites as sources of theology. This is why the traditional methods of biblical exegesis can be applied to the liturgy. For the liturgy, together with the Bible, is the primary source and manifestation of the life of the church and the revelation of the eternal truth. A rite or liturgical text, like a passage from Scripture, must have not only a literal but also a spiritual meaning—and the spiritual meaning is just as important and just as true as the literal. The dangers in such an approach are obvious, particularly when the flights of allegorism are unchecked by a coherent and consistent vision, and when the attempt is made to parcel out meanings without regard to the rite as a whole. Nevertheless, the notion that the liturgy is a primary source for the theology of the church, as well as its primary expression, remains characteristic of the Eastern church.

Closely linked with this was the proliferation of hymnography in the Byzantine world, hymnography that was quite unlike the few surviving early Christian hymns. The *kontakia* of Romanos the Melode, and then of many imitators, were in fact poetical homilies. These found their way into the office. The monks, always a presence in Byzantine Christianity, at first opposed such poetry as unbiblical and rejected the music to which it was set as too secular, but later they developed their own hymnography. This monastic hymnography, largely composed during the great theological debates of the sixth through the eighth centuries, is a compendium of Eastern patristic theology. These hymns found their place chiefly in the monastic office, which was gradually to displace the cathedral office totally after the eleventh century. This hymnography remains a primary source for the study of Eastern piety, asceticism, and theology, though it is difficult to use because of its great volume and diversity.

The liturgy was expressed in the context of the church year—a liturgical calendar composed of periods of feast and preparatory fasts. The year was seen as a reenactment of the salvific acts of God, as well as of the chief events of Christ's life: by participating in these, the Eastern Christian assimilated himself into salvation history, into Christ's life. The Eucharist was the culmination of each day or period of celebration: it was removed during periods of fasting, particularly during "Great" Lent, which lost its primitive meaning as a time of preparation for baptism and became a period of preparation for Easter, the central mystery of salvation—a period during which each Christian was called to rediscover his sinful nature and thus his alienation from God.

If any conclusion can be drawn from all these developments, it is that, together with scripture and tradition, the liturgy is an essential ingredient of Eastern spirituality. It is also the means by which the faithful, assembled as the church, become what they are meant to be, members of the Body of Christ and sharers in divine life. Thus, the liturgy cannot be separated from any aspect of Christian faith and experience. It is integral to christology or soteriology, because it is through the liturgy that we come to know Jesus as the incarnate one, to share in his incarnate body, and to become divinized by assimilating ourselves to him. It is integral to anthropology, because it is through the liturgy that the theocentric nature of humanity is revealed. It is integral to ecclesiology, because it is at the liturgy that the church becomes what it truly is, the living Body of Christ. It is integral to trinitarian theology, because in the liturgy the acting Trinity is revealed and experienced. The liturgy is a bearer of tradition, for through it the message and experience of God are passed on. Thus, for the Eastern believer, no Christianity is possible without the liturgy.

### Notes

1. S. H. Cross, trans., "The Russian Primary Chronicle," *Harvard Studies in Philology and Literature* 12 (1930) 199.

2. John Wilkinson, ed., *Egeria's Travels* (2nd ed.; London: S.P.C.K., 1980).

3. R. Taft, "The Liturgy of the Great Church," 59-60.

4. For an outline of this Eastern theology and its contrast to the Western approach, see J. Meyendorff, *Byzantine Theology*, 143–46.

5. Taft, 68–69.

6. G. D. Mansi, ed., *Sacrorum conciliorum nova et amplissima collectio* (Florence: Zatta, 1759–98) xiii, 261D–264C.

7. Quinisext Council in Trullo, canon 82 (Mansi ii, 977–80).

## Bibliography

### Studies

Bornert, R. *Les Commentaires byzantins de la divine liturgie du VIIe au XVe siècle.* Archives de l'Orient Chrétien 9. Paris: Institut français d'Études Byzantines, 1966.

Erickson, J. H. "Leavened and Unleavened: Some Theological Implications of the Schism of 1054." *St. Vladimir's Theological Quarterly* 14 (1970) 155–76.

Mother Mary and K. Ware, trans. *The Festal Menaion.* London: Faber & Faber, 1969.

Meyendorff, J. *Byzantine Theology: Historical Trends and Doctrinal Themes.* New York: Fordham University Press, 1974. Second printing with revisions, 1983.

Riley, H. *Christian Initiation.* Catholic University of America Studies in Christian Antiquity 17. Washington, DC: Catholic University Press, 1974.

Schmemann, A. *Introduction to Liturgical Theology.* London: Faith Press, 1966.

Schulz, H.-J. *Die byzantinische Liturgie: Glaubenszeugnis und Symbolgestalt.* Sophia 5. 2nd ed. Trier: Paulinus-Verlag, 1980.

Taft, R. "The Liturgy of the Great Church: An Initial Synthesis of Structure and Interpretation on the Eve of Iconoclasm." *Dumbarton Oaks Papers* 34–35 (1980–81) 45–75.

Whitaker, E. C. *Documents of Baptismal Liturgy.* 2nd ed. London: S.P.C.K., 1970.

Yarnold, E. J. *The Awe-Inspiring Rites of Initiation: Baptismal Homilies of the Fourth Century.* Slough, England: St. Paul Publications, 1972.

23. *The Riha Paten*, 6th century

24. *The Chalice of the Abbot Suger from St. Denis*, French, 12th century

25. *Sacrifice of Abel and Melchizedek*, San Vitale, Ravenna, 6th century

# II. *Sacraments and Liturgy in Latin Christianity*

### PIERRE-MARIE GY

RATHER THAN TREAT each of the principal sacraments separately, we will examine different moments in the spiritual history of the sacraments. Our purpose is to understand the internal articulations of sacramental spirituality during the times of Hippolytus, Ambrose and Augustine, the periods of the great Roman sacramentaries, the Carolingian and post-Carolingian periods, and finally the twelfth century.

## The First Roman Liturgy in Greek: The *Apostolic Tradition* of Hippolytus of Rome

The author of the *Apostolic Tradition* was apparently Hippolytus, a Roman priest and the founder of a small schismatic community, who died in exile with Pope Pontianus in 235. His work (lost in the original Greek) described the liturgy as he envisioned it and the tradition as reconstructed according to his personal theological ideas. The interest of this document is not only that it presents the state of Christian liturgy (still in Greek) in Rome during the early third century but also that it advances the first theological synthesis of the liturgy, which was to have a widespread influence later on, especially in the East. The two principal Christian teachers of the third century, Hippolytus in Rome and Origen in the East, were contemporary opponents of the rabbis who provided Jewish prayer with its fully developed structure.

In Christian spirituality, baptism was the most important sacrament, because in spite of persecutions—or more likely because of them—Christianity spread rapidly. According to Tertullian, "The blood of Christians is a seed," that is, it increases their numbers (*Apology* 50.13). The majority of those baptized were adults, although children of Christian parents were baptized at an early age—in spite of Tertullian's injunction to the contrary, which was summed up in his formula "Christians are made, not born" (*Apology* 18.4). The cases of children of Christian families being baptized only when they became adults, as attested to in the fourth century, seems due more to a fear of the demands of penance than to the perpetuation of an early Christian praxis.

The baptismal rites themselves already had a communitarian structure, with a time of preparation by personal conversion, instructions, and exorcisms of the devil. The time of preparation, which in the fourth century evolved into the liturgical season of Lent, led to the baptismal celebration during the Easter vigil. To be admitted to the catechumenate it was necessary to renounce all life-styles incompatible with the Gospel. The rites of baptism constituted an ensemble: the actual sacrament consisted of a triple interrogation of faith in the Father, Son, and Spirit accompanied by a triple immersion. No other baptismal formula was known in the West until the seventh and eighth centuries, at which time the interrogation of faith was combined with the formula "And I baptize you in the name of the Father, Son, and Holy Spirit"—which preserved a distinctly epicletic character in its invocation of the Trinity. The baptism was followed by a double anointing with oil (by the priest and by the bishop), an imposition of hands, and finally by communion. The prayers expressed the action of the Trinity during baptism and the rites that followed and distinguished the effect of baptism, which is the remission of sins and regeneration, from the imposition of hands "to be filled with the Holy Spirit" (Hippolytus *Apostolic Tradition* 21). Hippolytus's distinction is better than that of Tertullian, who stated that the sole effect of baptism is the remission of sins.

In Hippolytus's conception the Eucharist is situated within the second-century framework according to which the word *eucharistia* designated both the prayer of thanksgiving over the bread and wine and the bread and wine themselves once "eucharistized." The coupling of the eucharistic prayer and the eucharistic sacred elements (Justin called them "the flesh of Jesus made flesh" [*Apology* 1.66]), essential to all eucharistic spirituality, was to be lost in the East because the Eucharist came to be considered only an obligation, and in the West because of Latin usage, which provided two separate expressions to describe the two senses of *eucharistia*. The prayer was termed *gratiarum actio* and the body and blood of Christ were called *eucharistia*. (Medieval Latin completely ignored the fact that *eucharistia* signified thanksgiving, a sense that was rediscovered during the Renaissance.)

In treating these two aspects of the Eucharist, Hippolytus attempted to reveal Christian originality as opposed to Jewish prayer. In his eyes, both shared the glorifying of the Father, but giving thanks and doing Eucharist was proper to Christians since only they recognized the Son, that is, the gift of God made human (*Against the Heresies* 14). Thus it was because of the incarnation that the Eucharist is the essential act of the cult of the new covenant. We give thanks because the eucharistic bread and wine are and become "the flesh of Jesus made flesh."

In the *Apostolic Tradition*, the text of the eucharistic prayer has a twofold character: the unified nature of the prayer (as opposed to the series of Jewish benedictions); and its trinitarian structure, which could have motivated the unity of the prayer. At approximately the same time that the rabbis were giving the prayer of benediction (*berakah*) its definitive structure of blessing addressed to God for his salvific action culminating in the glorification of the divine Name, Hippolytus constructed the Eucharist as thanksgiving to the Father, through Christ the Redeemer, who gave his body and blood, followed by supplication for the Spirit, and finally a trinitarian glorification in the church. In Hippolytus this request for the Spirit was not yet developed into a eucharistic epiclesis that asked for the changing of the bread and wine into the body and blood of Christ, as would follow in the Antiochene anaphora, or eucharistic prayer. But he did have a precise theology of the church as the place where the Trinity was confessed and glorified and the Spirit flourished (*Apostolic Tradition* 35). The word *ekklēsia*, which was not applied to the church building until the end of the third century, designated both the church community and the church assembled in prayer as in the New Testament. It was necessary to go to the *ekklēsia* because the Spirit flourished within it.

## The Roman Liturgy in Latin:
## The Time of Ambrose and Augustine

Although it is now established that the use of Latin by Christians began in Rome and not in Africa by the second half of the second century, it was only sometime between the mid-third century and the second half of the fourth that the liturgy passed into Latin. It was precisely the second half of the fourth century that saw the simultaneous appearance of the major liturgical texts which form the fundamental fabric of Christian liturgies and the principal patristic catecheses whose authors remain the fathers of sacramental theology and spirituality. In general it is difficult to identify liturgical texts dating from the fourth century. In the West, however, it is possible in the case of the primitive version of the Roman eucharistic prayer and for at least four hymns of Ambrose. Furthermore, when Ambrose commented on the Roman *prex*, his personal contribution is original when compared with the liturgical text. If he did not quote the Roman canon, it would not be possible to reconstitute it from his teachings. Two witnesses to his sacramental catechesis during Easter week are extant: the *De sacramentis* (*On the Sacraments*), a transcription of his spoken words (the Roman canon is cited therein), and the *De mysteriis* (*On the Mysteries*), a literary rendering based on his preaching. The difference between the two is interesting and shows that his recourse to the notion of initiation is a literary technique rather than a spontaneous element of live preaching (the same is true for Augustine).

The season of Lent originated in the fourth century out of the time of preparation for paschal baptism. In the Latin liturgies this time was structured by the three Johannine pericopes of the Samaritan woman (John 4:5–42), the man born blind (9:1–41) and the resurrection of Lazarus (11:1–46). One can compare this with the application of Romans 6 to baptism, which had minor significance in the baptismal theology of the early church and until this time played no role in the Syrian baptismal tradition, which was completely inspired by the baptism of Christ. Concerning penance, the primary evangelical paradigm is much less Jesus' conferring the power of the keys on Peter than the latter's repentance at the cock's crow, which made the apostle the model of repentance for the *lapsi* who had denied their faith in Christ.

In the ritual texts it is probable that the Roman prayer during the post-baptismal imposition of hands already asked for the newly baptized to be endowed with the seven gifts of the Holy Spirit as enumerated in Isaiah 11:2: "Almightly God, Father of Our Lord Jesus Christ, who has regenerated your servants through water and the Holy Spirit and who has granted them the remission of all sins, pour out on them your Holy Spirit the Paraclete and give them the spirit of wisdom and knowledge . . . in the name of our Lord Jesus Christ with whom you live and reign and with the Holy Spirit" (*Gelasian Sacramentary* n. 451; *On the Sacraments* 3.8). The Roman eucharistic prayer adopted in Milan seems already to have been the one that insisted the most on the sacrificial aspect of the Christian Eucharist among all those that were to follow in East and West. In contrast to the anaphora of Hippolytus and those influenced by it, this composition is not unified and contains no special mention of the Holy Spirit. It has never emphasized the awesome character (*tremendum*) of the sacramental mysteries, as will be the case in the Antiochene anaphoras. This would explain why the recitation of the prayer in a low voice, attested to in the East from the fourth century, did not appear in the West until the eighth century, in Frankish countries rather than in Rome.

The sacramental catecheses of Ambrose and Augustine, the most important for Western spirituality, are marked by their different personalities as well as by the differences between the local churches to which they were the heirs. In this case, Augustine is much less the catechumen baptized and initiated by Ambrose than an African bishop taking a stand with regard to

Tertullian and Cyprian and against the Donatists. Along with the other major Christian authors of their time, Ambrose and Augustine shared the same conception of initiation, as well as a biblical and ecclesial catechesis of the sacraments whose principles have been part of Christian understanding since its origins. "To be initiated" (*by* the sacraments rather than *to* them) did not connote a progressive growth. Within these sacramental actions the eyes of the heart received the light of faith and discovered the divine and invisible realities that Christ gives us to participate in. This is the essential part of Platonism which the fathers recognized as Christian. Moreover, according to Christian interpretation, the major salvific acts of God recounted in the Old Testament are images and prefigurations of what happens in the sacraments of the new covenant. A modern reader of the patristic catecheses or liturgical texts that rely heavily on such a typology (for example, the Roman ordination prayer of a priest, which could date from the first half of the fifth century) may sometimes have the impression of a return to the Old Testament. The contrary is actually true: early Christianity in general was so convinced of the Old Testament's transparent role in prefiguring the New that its own human and religious value vanished into an explanation of Christian realities.

Concerning the ecclesial dimension of the sacraments, the fathers thought that baptism and Eucharist make Christians by first creating the church, or more precisely the church-mother, which is the entire community and which bears new children by baptism. She is similarly active in the other sacraments, for example, the reconciliation of penitents. The fathers' sacramental catechesis was ecclesiological before it dealt with the spiritual destiny of individual persons—the reverse of the catechetical and theological approach developed from the twelfth century on.

Ambrose and Augustine each have their respective emphases within this more general context. In the case of the Eucharist, Ambrose used Old Testament prefigurations to explain that the bread and wine are changed by the words of Christ. In the eucharistic prayer especially, he made a clear distinction between the words of the entire prayer pronounced by the priest and those of Christ himself found at the center. He explained that they are not simply Christ's words being quoted by the priest but that "the Lord Jesus Christ himself says (*clamat*) 'This is my Body'" (*On the Mysteries* 54). Before these words there are just ordinary bread and wine on the altar. After, there are the body and blood of Christ. Thus Ambrose is presenting a newly developing theology of eucharistic consecration. His spirituality of communion, however, is prior to the vision of the mysteries as awesome (or in opposition to this notion), and he relies on the Song of Songs to describe the eucharistic experience with intensity.

The eucharistic spirituality of Augustine developed in a quite different direction, much more ecclesiological, in which the role of Christ is situated in another manner. The change of the bread and wine into the body and blood of Christ occupied little of his attention, a somewhat astonishing fact for the West, which was afterward highly influenced by Ambrose. Augustine's focus shifted rather quickly toward the ecclesial body nourished and in some way created by the Eucharist: "This bread which you see on the altar, sanctified by the word of God, is the Body of Christ. The cup, or rather its contents sanctified by God's word, is the Blood of Christ. If you have received them in a worthy state, you are what you have received" (*Sermon 227*).

With this ecclesiological vision of the Eucharist, which was to have little effect on the Roman liturgy itself but a profound influence on medieval eucharistic theology, one could compare Augustine's interpretation of Psalms. Once again there is a striking difference between his reading and that of Ambrose. The personal relationship with Christ is the focus for Ambrose: "Drink Christ because he is the river whose current gladdens the city of God; drink Christ because he is peace; drink Christ because from his side flow living waters; drink Christ to drink the blood which redeemed you; drink Christ to drink his words" (*Commentary on Psalm 1* n. 33). Augustine, on the other hand, regarded Psalms as the praying voice of the total Christ, the head and ecclesial body united:

> When the body of the Son is praying, it is not separated from its head. Our Lord Jesus Christ, Son of God, alone is the 'Savior of his body,' the One who prays for us, who prays in us and who is prayed to by us. He prays for us as our priest; He prays in us as our head; and He is prayed to by us as our God. Let us acknowledge then our voice in Him and His voice in us. (*On Psalm 85*, n. 1).

And so there seems to be a correlation between Ambrose's interpretation of Psalms and his eucharistic theology. A similar coherence may also be observed in Augustine's approach to Psalms and the Eucharist even though his interpretation of Psalms exerted a greater influence on liturgical piety in the centuries that followed than did his approach to the Eucharist itself. In return, the poet Ambrose established the principal form of Latin liturgical hymnody. It complemented the psalmody (especially in the monastic Office) without ever supplanting it, which was the case to a certain degree in the East.

Penitential rites of Christian antiquity, reserved only for serious sins and received only once, had little to do with the subject of liturgical spirituality except for the fact that the entire community interceded for the sinner's forgiveness in the sight of God. Augustine, however, attempted a further integration of penance into general spirituality, especially monastic. In the first place, he proposed a reorganization of the penitential aspects of Christianity no longer in two stages (baptismal conversion and sacramental penance) but in three, by allotting an important role to penitential behavior in the whole Christian life (*Sermon* 352). To this he added the penitential prayer of his last days on earth, which is recounted by his friend Possidius:

> He had the habit of telling us during private conversation that after baptism even praiseworthy Christians and priests mustn't leave this world without doing fair and reasonable penitence. This is what he himself did during the illness from which he never recovered. He had David's penitential psalms recopied, which are not that numerous; and during the days of his sickness, lying on his bed, he looked at the quaternions placed along the wall, reading and weeping constantly and copiously. And ten days before his death, he asked us to stay out of his room so as not to divert his attention. . . . His wish was respected and he attended only to prayer during the whole time. (*Life of Augustine* 31)

## The Books of the Roman Liturgy

We know of the existence of books of the different Western liturgies from the sixth century on—in particular those of the Roman liturgy, which were to replace the others throughout most of the West. Concerning these Roman liturgical books, three general traits can be observed: (1) the distinction between what may be referred to as the varying degrees of "ecclesiality" of the liturgy; (2) the attenuation of certain sacramental characteristics proper to Christian antiquity; and (3) the stability for many centuries to come of most elements developed during the highly formative period between the fourth and the eighth century.

The first of these traits should not be understood in the light of a modern definition of liturgy, according to which things liturgical are ascribed to the body of the prayer of the church by competent ecclesiastical authority. In the ancient church this aspect was not denied, but it was less emphasized than a prayer's or a celebration's attachment to an actual ecclesial assembly. Key examples of this were the Eucharist of a bishop and his people, and Sunday Eucharist in general, the reconciliation of penitents on Holy Thursday, and Christian initiation during the paschal vigil. Sacramental marriage and funerals, on the other hand, were more often acts of familial prayer than liturgies of the assembled *ekklēsia*. Monk's Offices were organized and celebrated in complete autonomy, although a sort of fusion was taking place between the ecclesial Offices of lauds and vespers (which the Hispanic liturgy and modern historians call "cathedral Offices") and the prayer assemblies of monks during the other liturgical hours of day and night. The Office organized in this fashion was to be considered the Roman Office during the Carolingian period, and the Office according to the *Rule of St. Benedict* was the only alternative. This monastic Office was, in turn, later assumed into the official prayer of the church under the Gregorian Reform.

In the second place, in connection with the degrees of ecclesiality of the liturgy delineated above, certain changes in the liturgical praxis and spirituality appeared by the end of antiquity. The pre-Gregorian orations of the Easter vigil, contained in the Gelasian sacramentary of the eighth century and probably written by Leo the Great (d. 461), admirably expressed how the death and resurrection of Christ, the history of salvation, and the mystery of the church were tied together in Easter baptism, in much the same manner as the fourth-century catecheses. For example, the prayer that accompanied the reading of the sacrifice of Abraham: "God, veritable Father (*pater summe*) of the faithful, who in outpouring your adoption multiplies the children of your promise throughout the whole world, and who makes your son Abraham the father of all nations as you promised, allow your people to enter worthily into the grace of your call" (*Gelasian Sacramentary*, n. 434). But to the extent that entire populations were becoming Christian, infant baptism prevailed over that of adults and baptismal catecheses disappeared almost completely. In Rome during the sixth century, the pre-baptismal scrutinies, performed up until that time on the Sundays of Lent, ceased to be celebrated in the presence of the entire community and were moved to weekdays. The whole tone of Lent became more penitential than baptismal, so that the Gregorian orations during the Easter vigil, without entirely losing their baptismal theme, took on a moralizing and interiorizing connotation in harmony with the monastic dimension of Gregory the Great's spirituality. For confirmation, little is known of the proportion of baptized people who had to receive it from the bishop outside of the paschal vigil. The number would appear to have increased during the high Middle Ages, and the sacrament was often celebrated quite summarily and almost privately, even on the occasion of encountering the bishop during one of his journeys. Furthermore, the reconciliation of penitents, and with it their public status, disappeared progressively, and prayer for the forgiveness of sins assumed a greater place in the liturgy in general and more particularly in prayers for the dead.

It must be stressed, however, that the majority of the Roman liturgy created between the fourth and eighth century with its liturgical year, biblical readings, chants and prayers, remained substantially unchanged until the present century. This fact is of enormous importance when considering

Western Christian spirituality, which has been profoundly impregnated both directly and indirectly, consciously or unconsciously by this period of liturgical fecundity.

This phenomenon appears mainly in the course of the liturgical year—its meaning, its principal seasons and feasts, and even the details of specific rites and texts. Neither patristic nor medieval authors considered the liturgical year (an eighteenth-century expression) a sort of ritual specificity within human (profane) time. It was rather this human time considered within the time of salvation and intersected by its dynamism that carries the church to its eschatological accomplishment. Such a theology, developed already by Augustine in the case of Easter, was extended by Leo the Great to include the ensemble of liturgical feasts. Around the same time (fourth and fifth centuries or even earlier) there appeared the principal feasts and seasons of the year common to East and West: Lent and the fifty days of Easter, Christmas and Epiphany, Ascension and Pentecost. Within this shared festive framework there is one notable difference: the significance of Epiphany. In Rome and elsewhere in the West, this feast celebrated the adoration of the Magi, the first of the Gentiles in whom the *vocatio gentium* was inaugurated: the approach of pagan peoples to faith in Christ. To this train of common liturgical development the West added the season of Advent (in the second half of the sixth century in Rome) which both opened and closed the liturgical year. It was only around the twelfth century that the eschatological tension between the two comings of Christ present in this and other seasons of the year and essential to the Christian understanding of salvation history from the time of the New Testament began to disintegrate.

The celebration of the feasts of martyrs, other saints, and the Virgin Mary, Mother of God, placed less emphasis on their lives as models for spirituality than on their relationship to the paschal mystery, their entry (*natale*) into the afterlife, their tomb as the scene of local cult, as well as their intercession and efficacious presence in the church. A good example of this last point is the preface to the eucharistic prayer for the feast of Sts. Peter and Paul, which entreats the Lord: "Eternal Shepherd, do not abandon your flock, but safeguard it under the continual protection of Saints Peter and Paul so that they be directed by these same heads whom you have charged as their shepherds and vicars of your action" (*Gregorian Sacramentary* n. 591).

From the seventh century on, in Rome and in Constantinople and in other places to which the Roman liturgy was later diffused, the cult of the saints lost its strictly local character and developed into the cult of relics. It was not until the end of the Middle Ages, however, that a sort of competition between saints' feasts and the seasons of the liturgical year developed. In the high Middle Ages there did exist in Rome and elsewhere certain major feasts including those for saints (Peter and Paul for example) which helped to provide a framework to the liturgical year. The variations among these feasts are quite important in a consideration of the history of spirituality. Such is the case for the importance attributed to Christmas in relation to Easter, or, for example, the accentuation of the feast of the Assumption (August 15), which started in the twelfth century.

The pre-Carolingian Roman liturgy contained several distinguishing characteristics that were either uniquely its own or more pronounced than in other traditions. Among these are the predominance of biblical elements, the sacrificial and eschatological aspects of the Eucharist and the christological prayers on feast days. The biblical preoccupation is witnessed in the chants of the Mass and Office where the use of Psalms is almost exclusive, apart from the position given to hymns in the monastic Office and several responses or antiphons introduced into the Office in Rome by seventh- or eighth-century Greek monks. The respective space allotted to Mass readings from both the Old and the New Testament is significant in Rome and elsewhere. In Constantinople, and perhaps already in Antioch, only the New Testament was read (except at the Easter vigil and the other great vigils within the year), with the possible intent of clearly discriminating Christian and Jewish liturgies, even though the Old Testament enjoyed wide usage in Syria and Egypt. In Rome, the Sunday and paschal ferial readings were always from the New Testament, whereas those for ferial days at other times of the year—especially during Lent—were taken from the Old Testament. To this list must be added the biblical readings of the Office. Beginning in the seventh century, the principle seems to have been the total coverage of the Bible at the night Office within the space of a year. All things considered, those Christian liturgies that included numerous Old Testament readings held a strong typological interpretation, whereas Antioch, taking into consideration the Jewish critique of Christian typological exegesis, probably insisted on a quasi-exclusive use of the New Testament at Eucharist.

The Roman eucharistic *prex* of the fourth century was complemented during the following centuries by additional elements that reveal the Roman church's understanding of the Eucharist. Once the *Sanctus* was inserted into the eucharistic prayer (under Eastern influence in the first half of the fifth century), the preface varied from one Mass to another, but in general the other parts of the prayer did not. These were, however, to remain or become variable in Gallican and Hispanic liturgies. By the fifth century, the meaning of the Eucharist was also expressed by two variable prayers: the oration over the offerings, which immediately preceded the canon, and the prayer after communion. Several characteristics can be ascribed to the quantity of these texts and the themes they articulate. First, the fundamental notion of giving thanks appears only in the first words of the preface and is almost never developed in the rest of the prayer, which makes room for prayers of supplication and of emphasis on the sacrificial aspect of the Eucharist. It should be noted, however, that the post-communion oration occasions the request "that we remain in thanksgiving" (*Gregorian Sacramentary*, supplement 1128). It is not simply a question of giving thanks after receiving communion, but of a more general attitude of Christian living which is the fruit of eucharistic action and sacramental communion. Nevertheless, this eucharistic action, in both the Roman canon and its accompanying set of prayers, appears more sacrificial than in any other liturgy. It is a "spiritual sacrifice," and we ask that it make of us an offering and an eternal liturgy (*munus aeternum*) (*Gregorian Sacramentary* n. 553; see also the prayer of the Roman Missal of Vatican II, eucharistic prayer 3, following the anamnesis).

As has already been noted, the Roman canon never accepted the inclusion of an epiclesis (calling down) of the Holy Spirit, even though it may have had its origin in Hippolytus's *Apostolic Tradition*. Roman eucharistic tradition relegated it to the feast of Pentecost and the days that followed. Furthermore, this euchology, or ritual book, did not incorporate the individual eucharistic themes of Ambrose or Augustine. It preserved instead a more global flavor, perhaps archaic and more fundamental. In these prayers the fruit of the Eucharist is salvific medicine in the life of the church, which already begins its eschatological realization. Thus it was asked "that the holy things received (*sancta*) vivify and prepare us, while purifying us, for eternal mercy" (*Gelasian Sacramentary* n. 1217), and "that by the celestial sacraments we grow within eternal salvation" (*Gelasian Sacramentary* n. 1212), or even "that what we accomplish in this time [the Eucharist] may be obtained in eternal joy" *Gregorian Sacramentary* n. 541).

The place of Christ in the euchological structure never deviates from the schema considered by historians to be the most fundamental within Christian liturgy. The orations, like the eucharistic prayer itself, are addressed to the Father through Christ's mediation. After stating their entreaties they evoke this mediation with a trinitarian formula of glorification at the end. This mediation, however, is not only ascending (we ask you this through Christ) but also descending (you accord us these favors through Christ). This manner of praying through Christ is found partially in the use of Psalms (Passiontide for example); wherever the liturgical feast enjoys the greatest rapport with christological dogma, as in the case of Christmas and Ascension, there is a predominance of psalmody addressed to Christ as God. Christ is also addressed as God in the invocation of the *Agnus Dei*, introduced in the Mass under Greek influence in the seventh century as a chant for the fraction rite, and in the interpretation appearing in the *Rule of St. Benedict* of the initial verses of the Office, "Lord, open my lips" (Ps 50:17), "God come to my aid" (Ps 69:2), and of the opening verses of the nocturnal Office as well with Psalm 94 (*Venite exultemus*) and the accompanying invitatory antiphon.

## The Roman Liturgy in Carolingian and Post-Carolingian Piety

Roman liturgy (and chant), having been progressively transmitted throughout Frankish territories, was officially imposed by Charlemagne in his empire. It therefore became the school of prayer for most of the Western world even though linguistic evolution deprived most of the faithful of an understanding of Latin.

Among the major Carolingian contributions to the liturgy and sacramental life are the spread of private penance and the interpretation of the liturgy expounded by Amalarius. Private penance, of insular origin, seems rather far removed from spirituality if considered only on the basis of the penitentials with their catalogues of sins and the corresponding penances. And yet there was a spirituality of repentance especially among the monks which played a major role in collections of private prayers first in England and later on the continent because of the work of Alcuin. A typical example of this perspective is Alcuin's response to Benedict of Aniane's question about how he prayed for himself: "This is how I pray to Christ: 'Lord, help me to understand my sins, to make an honest confession and satisfactory penance, and grant me forgiveness of my sins'" (*Life of Alcuin* 9.17). Private prayers of this genre were said during the Mass not only by the faithful but by the priest himself, as seems to have already been the case for several centuries in Syria. Their importance diminished only around the time of the Gregorian Reform. It was probably during the Carolingian period that the general Western practice of private sacramental confession before communion became customary. The Carolingian penitential rituals also mentioned the possibility of giving absolution immediately after confession without having completed the prescribed penance, the exception becoming the rule with the passage of time.

The controversies among members of the generation that followed Alcuin —Agobard and Florus in Lyons on the one hand, and Amalarius of Metz on the other—are indicative of both a new liturgical mentality (especially Amalarius) and the reactions against it by those who rigorously adhered to the ancient understanding of the liturgy. Agobard held that the liturgy had to be purely biblical and purged the antiphonary that came from Rome of the several ecclesiastical compositions it contained. Florus defended the traditionally patristic (Latin) notion that the Mass in its entirety is the mystery of salvation, while Amalarius interpreted each portion of the Mass and Office as containing an individual mystery, much along the lines of the liturgical exegesis applied by the Antiochene Theodore of Mopsuestia in the early fifth century. At the time, Florus succeeded in having Amalarius's ideas condemned, but the paths they opened were to be those of subsequent spirituality. The liturgy was conceived of as a staging of biblical scenes, which allowed for a much greater inclusion of poetic creations. This dramatic element, which is a particular realization of the sacramental character of the liturgy, took many diverse forms. During ordination, a priest was in some sense visually constituted: he was vested, his hands were anointed, and he was presented with chalice and paten. The impression created was so strong that the faithful could no longer be given communion in their hands. And when the priest pronounced the words of consecration, they were accompanied by certain mimetic elements reminiscent of Christ himself (e.g., lifting the eyes to heaven). But, above all, during Masses on major feast days, the chant was complemented by tropes, words inserted into the middle of a liturgical text to elaborate and embellish its meaning. In the Introit for Easter, the Son says to the Father:

> Behold, I am coming, "I have arisen and am always with You" with whom I have been eternally through participation in your divinity. He who sits at the supreme right of the Father and sings: "Your hand rests upon me," And we, on earth, we honor, we marvel, we love the splendor of a man whose body is like our own. "Your wisdom has been made wonderful."

It was also at Easter, and perhaps around the Introit, that the first liturgical drama was woven, the *Quem quaeritis* ("Whom seek you?").

The two most important poetic elements of the Carolingian and post-Carolingian liturgy are the hymns of the Office and the sequences. Originally only the monastic Office included hymns, but as they grew in number they were to be generally adopted by the secular Office. These and other texts imbued the liturgy with an innovative equilibrium between the biblical chants and the creations of the church—precisely what Agobard's mono-biblism wished to exclude. These newly developing literary genres at the heart of the church's prayer brought forth several masterpieces that were to have a lasting spiritual influence. To mention only a few, there was the hymn "Veni Creator," perhaps by Rabanus Maurus, in which the confession of faith in the *Filioque* is accompanied by an originally polemical connotation which the centuries have mitigated; the sequence "Victimae paschali laudes," by the eleventh-century imperial chaplain Wipo; or the grand cry (*clamor*) to the Mother of God, "Salve Regina," composed in eleventh-century Aquitaine, possibly at the Marian sanctuary of Le Puy—though here we are not far from the spiritual evolution of the following period.

## Liturgical Spirituality and Sacramental Piety in the Twelfth Century

One of the greatest historians of medieval piety, the Benedictine André Wilmart, thought that a spiritual text from the middle of the eleventh century was much closer to a patristic work written many centuries earlier than to something written only a few decades later. In effect, the end of the eleventh century witnessed profound changes of spirituality regarding the interiorization of prayer, an approach to the humanity of Christ, and Marian piety. Similar observations can be made for the twelfth-century theology and canon law taught in the schools. Even if the liturgy itself changed very little at this time, the encounter of diverse liturgical spiritualities produced new factors that would significantly modify sacramental practices in the second half of the twelfth century.

The conflict between Bernard of Clairvaux and the abbey of Cluny is quite characteristic of the period, if one considers his personality and stature and the fact that he did not recognize the authentic spiritual value of Cluny and its liturgy. Cluny's significance in the history of liturgical spirituality is found less in the developments that its liturgical prayer underwent in the eleventh century than in the way tangible elements were integrated into the cultic practice it rendered to God. Cluniac usage indicated the degree of solemnity of feast days (albs, capes, carillons). The same was true at Saint-Denis where Abbot Suger used the most precious objects to honor the book of the Gospels or the sacred Eucharist—all of which simply continues the Carolingian liturgical spirituality. Furthermore, at the time of his introduction of Gothic art with its stained glass illumination of liturgical space, Suger provided an interpretation drawn from the theological works of Pseudo-Dionysius, who was purportedly buried in the church that he was currently reconstructing. At Clairvaux and elsewhere Bernard, nourished by Origen, fought against the contemporary continuation of this kind of traditional spirituality of the liturgy in favor of one marked by an interiority advanced (though in a totally different fashion) by the Parisian theologian Peter Abelard. In the Cistercian liturgy, which in some ways is much closer to that of Cluny than the disputes waged by Bernard would have one believe, the rank of feast days was not manifested by exterior solemnity, but in the number of lessons, the exceptional celebration of two conventual Masses, and above all in preaching. At Cîteaux and Clairvaux it was the feasts with sermons that corresponded to Cluny's pealing of bells. Bernard's spiritual itinerary seems to have led him to a systematic exclusion of all human artistry, which in Cluny contributed to God's glory, as dangerous to the quest of God.

To judge from the limited treatment of the Eucharist in his writings, it would seem that here too Bernard's spirituality was marked by this sort of Origenist interiorization. This did not prevent the Cistercians, however, from taking the lead during the last quarter of the twelfth century in the eucharistic piety movement, something which did indeed coincide with the devotion of Bernard and his contemporaries to the humanity and sufferings of Christ. Here it is important to note that the new accent in devotion to Christ—and to some extent to Mary—had little concrete effect on liturgical forms but profoundly influenced the manner in which they were lived, for example in Christmas piety, in Holy Week, and in eucharistic devotion. But the latter evolution is attributable to other causes as well, which will now be examined.

In the middle of the eleventh century, Latin eucharistic theology was considerably affected by the teachings of Berengar, canon and headmaster of Saint-Martin's in Tours. Through a dialectical interpretation of citations from Augustine which he collected, Berengar attacked the traditional understanding of the Eucharist and forced theological thinkers to make a choice between symbolism and realism. The two had been linked together by the theologians before him and by the fathers. Even though Berengar's Augustinian citations played an important role in the mid-twelfth-century reflection that led to a theological articulation of the notion of sacrament and the list of the seven sacraments, the reaction against Berengar's doctrine by the theologians and the papacy was violent and expressed itself in an ultra-realistic form. Berengar had to admit that the true body and blood of Christ are present on the altar after the consecration, that the body of Christ is broken by the priest's hands and chewed by the communicants' teeth. This same doctrine seems implied in the numerous eucharistic miracles at this time, in which a piece of flesh appeared or blood flowed. This doctrine, as well as the term transubstantiation (whose usage began in the mid-twelfth century), was in turn to be reinterpreted by scholastic theologians, who made a distinction between the substantial eucharistic presence and the accidents of bread and wine. But the devotion to Christ undoubtedly played a stronger role than the theological debate in the development of eucharistic cult. Eucharistic piety addressed itself to Jesus on the cross, whereas eucharistic theology concentrated on the consecration and presence of Christ in the Eucharist rather than on the memorial of his passion.

The intense religious perception of the sacredness of the Eucharist, all the while developing into the cult of the real presence, also led to a growing awareness of the requirements for receiving communion. It was about the twelfth century that communion from the chalice disappeared (except by the priest), mainly because of the fear of spilling the precious blood. The baptismal communion of infants was also abandoned at this time, since it was also done with the wine. Up until this period, the practice appeared to have been commanded by John's teaching that communion was necessary for salvation (John 6:53). By the twelfth century the Pauline rejoinder to self-scrutiny before communicating (1 Cor 11:28) took the forefront. Theology and pastoral practice initiated the steps toward a new configuration of sacramental practice, codified by the Fourth Lateran Council's canon 21. Infants who were baptized soon after birth (even the day of their birth) now had to attain the years of discretion, the time when they would be capable of confessing, in order to receive communion.

The twelfth century attached at least as much importance to confession as to eucharistic devotion. The mode of penance (officially prescribed by the Fourth Lateran Council) differed from the antecedent "tariff" confession only in the abandonment of the catalogues of penances, their determination being henceforth made by the priest. From now on the primacy of interior contrition was much more underlined. The Christians of this time went to confession more often than communion and this emphasis given to the sacrament of penance replaced in some sense a part of the baptismal spirituality of Christian antiquity.

*Translated by Craig McKee*

## Bibliography

### Studies

Bouyer, Louis. *Eucharistie: Théologie et spiritualité de la prière eucharistique.* Tournai: Desclée, 1966. Synthetic view of the historical development, with a number of deep insights.

Camelot, Pierre-Thomas. *Spiritualité du baptême.* Paris: Cerf, 1960. In-depth patristic synthesis.

Daniélou, Jean. *The Bible and the Liturgy.* Notre Dame, IN: University of Notre Dame Press, 1956. Fundamental to an understanding of biblical typology.

Fischer, Balthasar. *Die Psalmen als Stimme der Kirche: Gesammelte Studien zur christlichen Psalmenfrömmigkeit.* Trier: Paulinus-Verlag, 1982. Important continuation and critique of Jungmann's work on prayer.

Gy, Pierre-Marie. "Liturgies occidentales." In *Dict. Sp.* 9, cols. 899–912. A general survey with additional bibliography.

Jungmann, Josef Andreas. *The Mass of the Roman Rite: Its Origins and Development.* 2 vols. New York: Benziger, 1951–55. A true classic.

———. *The Place of Christ in Liturgical Prayer.* London: Chapman, 1965. Basic work on the place of Christ in the structure of prayer.

———. *Christian Prayer through the Centuries.* New York: Paulist Press, 1978. Deals with the history of Christian prayer in general.

Mayer, Anton. *Die Liturgie in der europäischen Geistesgeschichte.* Darmstadt: Wissenschaftliche Buchgesellschaft, 1971. Collection of articles on the place of the liturgy in cultural history, somewhat affected by the "Romantic" approach of the liturgy.

Wilmart, André. *Auteurs spirituels et texts dévots du Moyen Age latin.* Paris: Études augustiniennes, 1971. Collection of articles on the history of piety, some treating the periods covered herein.

# 15

# Icon and Art

## Leonid Ouspensky

ONE OF THE FEATURES that distinguish Eastern Orthodoxy from other Christian confessions is the attitude toward icons or sacred images. In the Orthodox tradition, icons are essential and irreplaceable. They not only adorn the church and illustrate sacred writings; they also are a necessary condition for the fullness of worship.

This means that the icon is not merely the expression of an autonomous sphere of human creative activity that the church happens to use in an accessory way. Rather, the icon belongs to the *esse* or essential being of the church; it is a vital part of that general order of human activity within the church that serves to express Christian revelation. "The Church speaks many languages; however, each of them is the language of the Church only in as much as it corresponds with the other true expressions of the Christian faith."[1] Through its content and meaning, therefore, the icon conveys the same truth that is expressed by other essential elements of the church's life and faith, including Holy Scripture.

As a necessary element of worship, the icon is essentially a *liturgical* art form. Accordingly, the church's teaching concerning icons situates them within the overall context of the divine economy and views them as ontologically related to the whole content of Orthodox teaching. This means that an aesthetic evaluation of a particular iconographic representation must be based upon its theological as well as its artistic merits. The ultimate value of an icon lies in its significance for the spiritual life of the worshiper. This fact alone distinguishes the icon from any other art form.

Contrary to prevailing opinion, sacred images have existed in the Orthodox tradition from the very beginning of Christianity, as has the theology that underlies them. The Seventh Ecumenical Council (Nicaea II, 787) proclaimed: "The tradition of making painted images . . . existed already in the time of apostolic preaching, as we learn everywhere from the very appearance of Christian churches. The holy fathers witness to it, and the historians, whose writings have been preserved until our times, confirm it." In making this affirmation, the Orthodox church was guided not so much by documents and other material evidence that served merely as external confirmation as by the very foundation of the church's faith, that is, by the content and meaning of Christian revelation. As an expression of the very essence of Christianity, the sacred image is above all an incontrovertible witness to the incarnation. When God became human, God's image appeared in the created world. Because the icon testifies that Old Testament archetypes have been fulfilled in the person of the incarnate Son of God, it is no longer subject to Old Testament prohibitions against created images either of God or of human beings. The prohibition of the second commandment has been abolished, for, in the person of the Son, God has become visible and thus representable in graphic form.

The primary iconographic representation depicts the tradition of the image "not-made-by-hands" (Greek *acheiropoiētos*): an image which, according to legend, was sent by Christ himself to King Abgar of Edessa and was celebrated in liturgical hymns to the Savior on 16 August. Of nearly equal importance in the church's living memory are traditions concerning icons of the *Theotokos*, the Mother of God, painted by the evangelist Luke (see, e.g., the liturgical celebration of the Vladimir icon of the *Theotokos*, 21 May). These two figures, the incarnate Son of God and his Holy Mother, the Ever-Virgin Mary, manifest the very essence of the divine economy and Christian revelation. According to the lapidary formulas of the church fathers, "God became man so that man could become God," that is, so that humanity could participate in the fullness of eternal, divine life. These two prototypical icons bear witness to the incarnation of the divine Son in the person of Jesus Christ and to the "deification" of humanity in the person of the Mother of God. Through them, we can come to understand the entire program of the church's art in the form of sacred images. It is for this reason that the church's traditions concerning these two icons—however much they may have been overgrown with legendary elements—were incorporated into the living fabric of Orthodox worship.

## A New World View

The radical change brought about in the world by Christianity introduced a radical transformation in world view—a veritable regeneration of consciousness and thought regarding human destiny and creative human work. This regeneration was expressed first of all in a new attitude toward matter and, specifically, toward the human body. Unlike pagan cults of the flesh on the one hand and disdain of the body on the other, Christianity refused to

"dematerialize" matter. On the contrary, it affirmed the actual transfiguration
of human nature and the salvation of the body through material resurrection. Matter becomes a vehicle of salvation and thus acquires decisive significance. In the words of John of Damascus: "I do not worship matter. I
worship the Creator of matter who became matter for my sake, who willed
to take his abode in matter, and who through matter wrought my salvation."[2]
This saving quality of matter comes to expression in the church's sacred art.

From the very beginning the church was engaged in a struggle against
idolatry, and simultaneously it strove to eliminate those elements of pagan
culture that threatened the Christian world view. In order to create its own
language in images, the church had to purify existing art forms of all that
was ambiguous, sensuous, or illusory. From the first centuries it struggled
against tendencies in art that threatened, in the words of Clement of Alexandria, to "fascinate and deceive" by presenting themselves as expressions of the
truth (*Protrepticus* 4). This required a process of selection: only those graphic
forms that would permit the manifestation and affirmation of Christian
revelation were to be maintained and incorporated into the new language of
Christian art. The dominant element in this process was not the influence
of paganism on Christianity, as is widely held, but the christianizing and
"churching" of pagan customs and art forms. Therefore it is improper to
speak of the "pagan orientation" of early Christian art.

Borrowed forms and means of expression were filled with new content,
and this new content in turn changed the forms.

> [Christian art] being to a great extent in continuity with Greek antiquity . . .
> nonetheless posed, from the very first centuries of its existence, a series of
> independent problems for itself. It can by no means be described as Christian
> antiquity. . . . The new subjects of early Christian art are not merely an exter-
> nal fact. They reflect a new worldview, a new religion, essentially a new
> understanding of reality. That is why these new subjects could not be clothed
> in the old classical forms. . . . All the creative efforts of Christian artists were
> directed toward working out this new style.[3]

This new art first acquired its basic features in the catacomb paintings. To
express the new world view, catacomb artists employed the customary
artistic language of their time. This language, however, acquired a different
meaning. The focus was no longer upon the relative beauty of the pre-
Christian world but upon the divine beauty manifested in creation and
particularly in the incarnation. Beauty itself was beheld no longer in the
ephemeral aspect of creaturely existence but rather in the future transfiguration of the creature and creation. In Christian iconography the sense of
rhythm and harmony is preserved. The aim of the artist, however, is not
that of his pagan counterpart. Whereas the art of antiquity reproduced

externals as closely as possible, in Christian iconography it is precisely these illusory aspects—in the depiction of space, the human body, and objects— that are done away with. Light and shading, optical perspective, and other marks of a transient, three-dimensional world simply disappear.

Of course, an adequate artistic language for the expression of the faith was not created immediately, anymore than an adequate theological language was found at the very beginning of the church's existence. Furthermore, the conditions of early Christian life and the existence of early iconoclastic tendencies were hardly conducive to wide dissemination of sacred images. Consequently, we find an abundant use of symbols in the early centuries of Christianity. Nevertheless, already in the catacombs there appeared scenes from the Old and New Testaments, dating from the first centuries of this era. In addition, there exist written testimonies to the existence of portrait icons and of their veneration even in apostolic times. One such testimony is a second-century apocryphal writing, the *Acts of John*, which tells of the veneration of the icon of John the Evangelist by one of his disciples during the apostle's lifetime. There is also the testimony of Eusebius of Caesarea, who describes a statue of Christ erected by the woman with the issue of blood from the Gospel episode. Eusebius added: "The features of His Apostles Paul and Peter, and indeed of Christ Himself, have been preserved in colored portraits that I have examined."[4] Yet despite the rarity of these images, by the year 330, when Constantinople was founded, Christian art already had a long history both in Rome and in the Eastern part of the empire.

In the fourth century, the church situation changed. Under the emperor Constantine, the church was given the opportunity freely to preach its faith in words and in images. As a result, Constantinople became the artistic center of the Byzantine Empire. Until that time Christians had considered martyrs to be the true pillars of the church. After Constantine, fathers and teachers as well as ascetic monks became the recognized heroes of Christianity. This was the time of the great church fathers: Basil the Great, Gregory the Theologian, John Chrysostom, Athanasius, Cyril of Alexandria, and others.

The experience of the holy ascetics and their writings became known throughout the Christian world. The teaching of the church and the living spiritual experience of the holy fathers and ascetics thus became the primary nourishing source of church art, providing direction and inspiration. On the one hand, art faced the task of conveying the truths which at that time were being formulated as dogmas. On the other, it manifested the living, concrete experience of those truths in the form of a living Christianity in which dogma and life express each other. In this period, as in the previous one, the main role of the image was to witness to the reality and living relevance of Christian revelation.

As theological thought developed, many church fathers based their arguments on sacred images. They appraised church art not from the viewpoint of its artistic or aesthetic value; rather, they saw it as a means of preaching with greater power of persuasion. Referring to the two basic means of acquiring knowledge, seeing and hearing, the holy fathers repeatedly emphasized that what the word is to hearing, the image is to seeing.

The fourth century brought liturgical change as well, with the emergence of what may be called a "canon of worship" that set a limit to improvisation. The canon of worship was formed in the period of dogmatic definitions and controversies, and a parallel definition of a canon of church art also took shape at this time.

As the number of converts grew, more spacious churches were needed, as was a change in the manner of preaching. The symbols of the first centuries filled the requirements of a small number of initiates who clearly understood their content and meaning. For the mass of neophytes of the fourth and fifth centuries, however, these symbols were not so easily understandable. A clearer and more concrete visual expression became necessary. The church not only taught by means of images; it also relied on them in the struggle against heresy. The church's answer to false teaching was the orthodox teaching on worship and images. Iconographic details and entire programs of wall paintings reflected the opposition of church teaching to doctrinal errors. In the fourth and fifth centuries, this need led to the appearance of large monumental frescoes that depicted entire historical cycles of Old and New Testament events. Many churches built in Palestine at the sites of major Gospel episodes were adorned with mosaics. Some of these date back to the time of Constantine, others to later centuries. By the fifth or sixth century, their subjects were basically defined, and we find them reproduced on the famous ampules of Monza and Bobbio.[5] The scenes depicted there represent an already established iconography, which we also find in Orthodox festal icons.

## First Doctrinal Definitions on Icons

Revealed truth was concretely and directly experienced by the first Christians, without being theoretically defined. Dogmatic definitions were produced by the church in response to the requirements of historical crises, as an answer to heresies or false teachings, or in order to correct verbal obscurities in the Scriptures. The same is true of definitions concerned with images.

The first formal theological reference to the dogma of the incarnation substantiating the use of images, is found in a decree of the Sixth Ecumenical Council (Trullanum, 692). The same council, responding to practical necessity, defined for the first time the fundamental notion and character of holy images. At that time, the dogmatic struggle of the church for the true confession of the two natures of Christ, his divinity and his humanity, had ended. The formula concerning sacred images was justified by the following conciliar explanation: "Some remains of pagan and Jewish immaturity have become mixed with the ripe wheat of the truth." In other words, along with direct portrayal, the sacred art of the seventh century used Old Testament symbols to replace the human image of Christ. As long as the wheat was not yet ripe, the existence of symbols was necessary, because they furthered the ripening, but with the appearance of the "ripe wheat of the truth," their role ceased to be constructive.

The council was chiefly concerned with the symbol of the lamb. The immaculate lamb of the Old Testament not only prefigured Christ; it was a basic symbol expressing Christ's major function as the expiatory sacrifice. The text of canon 82 of the council reads as follows:

> We decree that henceforth Christ our God, the Lamb who took away the sin of the world, be represented in His human form and not in the form of the ancient lamb, so that the humiliation of God the Word be understood, His life in the flesh be remembered, as well as His Passion, His saving death and, thus, the redemption of the world.

Thus, the truth is not only revealed by the Word but is also shown by the image ("I am the Truth . . ." John 14:6). Since the Word became flesh and dwelled among us, the image should show directly, and not symbolically, that which appeared on earth in time, thereby becoming visible, representable and describable.

But the council went further. "Having thus welcomed these ancient figures and shadows as symbols of the truth transmitted to the church, we prefer today grace and truth themselves as a fulfillment of the law." The council ordered that the symbols of the Old Testament and the first centuries of Christianity be replaced by direct representation of the truth they prefigured, and it called for an unveiling of their meaning. Iconographic symbolism is not excluded entirely, but it is placed in the background. The artistic language of the icon should itself become symbolic. Here the task of sacred art, which existed since the very first ages of Christianity, is formulated in concrete terms. Icon painting is concerned not only with the *subject* of the image—since the same subject can be expressed by other means also—but also with the *manner*, the *way* in which it is represented. The historical reality of the subject reveals spiritual and eschatological truth. By demanding that "the humiliation of God the Word" be discernible in the image, canon 82 gives theoretical foundation to what we call the iconographic canon.

If "Jewish immaturity" consisted in an adherence to biblical symbols in place of the human image, "pagan immaturity" expressed itself in vestiges of an art form which the church had fought from the very beginning, but which still influenced sacred art.

The text of canon 100 of the Quinisext Council reads as follows:

"Let your eyes look straight ahead; keep your heart with all vigilance" (Prov 4:23, 25), Wisdom demands. For bodily sensations easily enter the soul. We therefore ordain that misleading representations which corrupt the intelligence by exciting shameful pleasures, whether these be paintings on boards or any other similar objects, are not to be used in any way, and that anyone who undertakes to make such an object be excommunicated.

## Iconoclasm and the Triumph of Orthodoxy

The development of church art was slowed for more than a century by the iconoclastic movement of the eighth and ninth centuries (there were two iconoclastic periods: 730–787 and 813–843).[6] The iconoclasts were not enemies of art; on the contrary, they promoted it. They persecuted only cultic images—those of Christ, of the Mother of God, and of the saints. During the time of the iconoclastic controversy, everything was destroyed that could be destroyed. The concern of the iconoclasts was not only with icons as such but also with the orthodox confession of the divine incarnation. The controversy was essentially dogmatic, and it involved the very heart of theology. As G. Florovsky has shown, the iconoclastic heresy was rooted in a persistent Hellenistic spiritualism represented by Origen and the Neoplatonists. It was a return to pre-Christian Hellenism or, more precisely, to the Greek separation of spirit and matter.[7] In such a system, the image is understood as an obstacle to prayer and spiritual life, not only because it is made out of "crude matter," but also because it represents the human body, which itself is substantially matter. In other words, iconoclasm signified a denial of the witness of the Gospel and the reality of the incarnation.

The first iconoclastic period ended with the Seventh Ecumenical Council (787), which sealed the faith of the church in the dogma of the veneration of icons. This council concluded the period of ecumenical councils with their major teachings on the Holy Trinity and divine incarnation. But the Seventh Council also turned toward the future. The iconoclastic controversy

26. *Enthroned Pantocrator Receiving Obeisance of Leo IX*, Hagia Sophia, Istanbul, 11th century

27. *Our Lady of Vladimir*, Dormition Cathedral, Moscow, 12th century

28. *Nativity of Christ*, Monastery Church at Daphne, 11th century

moved the church to establish the christological basis of the image, and this led to a clarification and purification of the language of sacred art. In its struggle with iconoclasm, as in the overcoming of other heresies, the church found adequate forms to express the theology of the Gospel in images.

The *horos*, or definition, of the Seventh Council affirmed first of all the conformity of the icon to the Gospel teaching, "for things that presuppose each other are mutually revelatory." The same witness is expressed in two forms, verbal and pictorial. Each presents the same revelation in the light of the same holy tradition of the church. In the incarnation, both the Word and the image of the Father are revealed to the world in the one divine person of Jesus Christ. The Gospel and the icon together constitute a unity of verbal and pictorial expression of divine revelation.[8] The council also decreed that the book of the Gospels and the holy cross, which witness to the cooperation and union of divine human action, are the proper objects of an identical veneration.

The dogmatic definition of the council reads as follows: "The honor rendered to the image passes to its prototype, and the person who venerates an icon venerates the person (*hypostasis*) represented in it" (*NPNF* 14:549ff). The icon of Christ depicts the divine person according to the human nature that he assumed from his Mother. This concept of the person as bearer of divinity and humanity is the key to the Chalcedonian doctrine and, thereby, to the theology of the image. Indeed, the definition of the Seventh Council made specific reference to Chalcedon. Therefore, it is essential that any image, whether of the God-man or of a saint, be doctrinally authentic. The image of a concrete person, divine or human, cannot, if it is authentic, be replaced either by a natural phenomenon or by any human idea, however lofty it may be. Thus, there is consistency in Orthodox iconography of the saints. Only through communion with a person is it possible to partake of what that person bears.

The doctrine of the veneration of icons is not a doctrine of the veneration of art. Veneration is rendered not to images in general but to the image of a person, thereby realizing the words of Christ: "The kingdom of God is within you" (Luke 17:21). In other words, an icon is the gospel expressed in artistic form; it is the fulfillment of the gospel, manifesting the participation of human nature in divine life. Therefore it represents realization of the patristic formula: "God became man so that man might become God."

In Orthodox sacred art, the main theme is thus the human being. No art gives so much attention to the human person, nor raises it to such a height, as does the icon. Everything depicted in an icon has reference to humanity. In the hierarchy of existence, humanity occupies the supreme position. We stand at the center of creation, and the surrounding world is depicted such as it is rendered by human holiness. The icon is a visual anticipation of the eschatological kingdom of Christ, the manifestation of Christ's glory in the multitude: "The glory which thou hast given me I have given to them" (John 17:22).

All dogmatic controversies of the past, both christological and trinitarian, were concerned with the relation between divinity and humanity, that is, with Christian anthropology. Therefore the catholic consciousness of the church celebrates the victory over iconoclasm as the Triumph of Orthodoxy; it proclaims the icon itself as this Triumph, insofar as it is the church's witness to revealed truth. It is precisely in the Orthodox icon that Christian anthropology finds its most vivid and direct expression. The icon, being a revelation of the truth and the fruits of divine incarnation, expresses in the fullest and deepest way the Christian teaching about the relation of God to human life and of human life to the world. And the Triumph of Orthodoxy, which closes the second period of iconoclastic dispute and is celebrated as the feast of the victory of the icon, also marks the final triumph of the dogma of the divine incarnation.

## Immutable Tradition and Mutable Forms

Since the christological basis of the image was definitively affirmed by the Seventh Ecumenical Council, after that council a definite and clearly conscious tendency emerged to reveal the content and spiritual essence of the image, based on previous and present spiritual experience. Thus, the center of gravity shifted from the predominantly christological aspect of the icon, which was stressed during the preceding period, to its pneumatological content, which found expression in the liturgy of the Triumph of Orthodoxy.

In the tenth century a revival of spiritual life occurred in Orthodoxy and reached its pinnacle with Symeon the New Theologian (949–1022). Along with spiritual revival came a flourishing of sacred art. During that period, the original task of church art was realized in all its fullness: the classical language of the Orthodox icon was formed, visually expressing—as far as is possible by human means—the truth of Christian revelation. This artistic language attained the form that most fully conveys the spiritual experience of Orthodoxy. Beginning with that period, the image reached the highest precision, clarity, and form. Art inseparably merged with the reality of spiritual experience. Form was conceived and realized as the most convincing and lucid transmission of content. By fixing the attention of the believer on the prototype, the icon aids the believer in the inner process of becoming like the prototype. The artistic language of Orthodox art is both changeable, since its forms are those of living experience and therefore naturally vary with time, and immutable, since spiritual experience itself is essentially unchanging.

In the post-iconoclastic period, new groups of people entered the church, most of whom were of Slavic origin. Each nation accepted Christian tradition as a whole, with its past, its present, and its future. For the new converts, the heresies of Nestorius, Eutyches, or the iconoclasts were not foreign problems, but represented a distortion of their own faith and life.

Newly converted peoples inherited the already formed language of sacred art, together with its theological foundation. On this basis, each people developed its own original artistic language. This expression of originality was favored by the fact that in the Orthodox church the unity of faith not only does not exclude diversity in forms of worship and other expressions of the church's life, but—quite the opposite—requires such diversity. This is because faith must be constantly renewed through the original and creative experience of tradition. Each nation that entered the church brought its own national peculiarities and grew according to its own character, in holiness as well as in its external, artistic manifestation. Sacred art was received not passively but creatively, and therefore it merged with local artistic traditions. Both holiness and the sacred image acquired a national coloring and form as fruits of living experience. As there emerged specific forms of Russian, Serbian, and Bulgarian holiness, so correspondingly there arose specific types of icons.

The content of the icon and its significance for Orthodoxy make clear why the church felt obliged to defend the icon through intense struggle for more than a century during the iconoclastic period. For Orthodoxy, the content of the icon offers authentic spiritual guidance on the pathway of Christian life, particularly in prayer. Through the icon, a believer enters into communion with Christ or the saint portrayed. As an essential element of worship and as genuine liturgical art, the icon witnesses to the unity of the earthly and the heavenly church—a unity realized in and through Orthodox worship.

The order of the icon and its role and composition grew out of the liturgical experience of the church, as did other forms of sacred art. It confronts the universal experience of the church with the consciousness and individual experience of the artist and the artist's particular vision. Icons are not merely the fruit of an artist's conception, nor are they the artist's own invention. The artist does not create them in a burst of inspiration, however lofty. They are created in accordance with, and as an expression of, the immutable tradition of the universal church. The character of the church's artistic language is determined by the norm developed by the catholic consciousness of the church. It has become customary to refer to that norm as the iconographic "canon." In art as in other spheres of the church's life and work, the canon is a means by which the church guides humanity on the way toward salvation. It is within the canon, and only within the canon, that the iconographic tradition realizes its function as the artistic language of the church. Therefore, any "canonical" icon, regardless of its artistic merit, reflects the content of the unique witness of faith and spiritual life in Orthodoxy, its true "order." This "order of the icon" is aimed at making human beings participants in Christian revelation by revealing in visual forms the essence of the revolution brought about by Christianity. The "order" was developed through ascetic effort, prayer, self-denial, and contemplation by generations of icon painters. Only a concretely lived, personal experience of revelation can enable one to find the words, forms, and colors that truly correspond to what they seek to express in sacred images. This correspondence is expressed by the whole order of the icon. Hence the development of a definite "style" of the canonical icon; hence too the selection of materials used in creating the icon.

As the artistic language of the church, the icon thus participates in the whole complex of our offerings to God through which human destiny is realized: the destiny—indeed, the vocation—to sanctify and transfigure the world, to heal matter corrupted by sin, and to transform all things into a means of eternal communion with God.

*Translated by Larissa Pavear*

### Notes

1. John Meyendorff, "Philosophy, Theology, Palamism, and 'Secular Christianity,'" *St. Vladimir's Seminary Quarterly* 10 (1966) 207.

2. John of Damascus *On the Divine Images* 1.16 (trans. David Anderson; Crestwood, NY: St. Vladimir's Seminary Press, 1980) 23.

3. V. N. Lazarev, *Istoriya visantiiskoy zhivopisi* (Moscow: Gosudarstvennoe Izdatel'stvo "Iskusstvo," 1947) 38.

4. Eusebius *Ecclesiastical History* 7.18 (trans. G. A. Williamson; Baltimore: Penguin Books, 1967) 302.

5. André Grabar, *Les Ampoules de la Terre Sainte* (Paris: Klincksieck, 1958).

6. André Grabar, *L'Iconoclasme byzantin* (Paris: Collège de France, 1957).

7. Georges Florovsky, "Origen, Eusebius, and the Iconoclastic Controversy," *Church History* 19 (1950) 96.

8. Vladimir Lossky, *In the Image and Likeness of God* (Crestwood, NY: St. Vladimir's Seminary Press, 1974) 125-39.

## Bibliography

### Studies

Bryer, Anthony, and Judith Herrin, eds. *Iconoclasm.* Center of Byzantine Studies. University of Birmingham, 1976.

Graber, André. *Christian Iconography: A Study of Its Origins.* Princeton, NJ: Princeton University Press, 1968.

Ouspensky, Leonid. *Theology of the Icon.* Crestwood, NY: St. Vladimir's Seminary Press, 1978.

———, and Vladimir Lossky. *The Meaning of Icons.* Translated by G. E. H. Palmer and E. Kladlovbovsky. Crestwood, NY: St. Vladimir's Seminary Press, 1982.

Trubetskoy, Eugene N. *Icons: Theology in Color.* Translated by Gertrude Vakar. Crestwood, NY: St. Vladimir's Seminary Press, 1973.

Weitzmann, Kurt, et al. *The Icon.* New York: Alfred A. Knopf, 1982.

# 16

# Ways of Prayer
and Contemplation

## I. *Eastern*

### KALLISTOS WARE

### The Spiritual Journey:
### an Outline Map

"THE PRINCIPAL THING is to stand before God with the intellect in the heart, and to go on standing before him unceasingly day and night, until the end of life." The words are those of a Russian bishop in the nineteenth century, Theophan the Recluse (1815–1894),[1] but they reflect accurately the understanding of prayer to be found also in Greek and Syriac writers of the first eleven centuries. Three points of basic significance for early patristic spirituality stand out in Bishop Theophan's statement. First, to pray is to *stand before God*—not necessarily to ask for things or even to speak in words but to enter into a personal relationship with God, a meeting "face to face," which at its most profound is expressed not in speech but in silence. Second, it is to stand *in the heart,* in the deep center of the person, at the point where created humanity is directly open to uncreated love. It is significant Theophan avoids making any sharp contrast between head and heart, for he tells us to stand with the "intellect" or "mind" in the heart; the two are to be united. Third, this attitude or relationship of "standing" is to be *continual,* "unceasingly day and night, until the end of life." Prayer is to be not merely one activity among others but *the* activity of our entire existence, a dimension present in everything else that we undertake: "Pray constantly" (1 Thess 5:17). It should constitute not so much something that we *do* from time to time as something that we *are* all the time.

Since prayer is in this way a direct encounter between living persons, it

395

cannot be restricted within precise rules; it remains free, spontaneous, unpredictable. Out of respect for this freedom, therefore, many Eastern Christian writers offer no abstract theories about prayer and contemplation, no exact definitions, no map of the various stages upon the spiritual way. This unsystematic, existential approach is to be found notably in the *Apophthegmata* or *Sayings of the Desert Fathers* (Egypt, fourth–fifth centuries). These are texts that speak in the language of direct experience, not of rational speculation. The advice is simple and forthright: "Abba Macarius was asked, 'How should we pray?' The old man said, 'There is no need to use a lot of words; just stretch out your hands and say, *Lord, as you will and as you know best, have mercy.* And if the conflict grows fiercer, say *Lord, help!* He knows very well what we need and he shows us his mercy.'"[2] Verbal "icons" are given of the human person at prayer, but usually there is no attempt to explain things in argued, abstract terms:

> A brother came to the cell of Abba Arsenius at Scetis. Looking through the window, he saw the old man entirely like a flame; for the brother was worthy to see this. When he knocked, the old man came out and saw the brother bewildered, and he said to him, "Have you been knocking long? You didn't see anything here, did you?" The other answered, "No." So then he talked with him and sent him away.

> They also said this of him, that on Saturday evening, preparing for the glory of Sunday, he would turn his back on the setting sun and stretch out his hands towards the heaven in prayer; and so he continued until the rising sun shone in his face. Then he would sit down.[3]

There is a deliberate reticence here before the mystery of living prayer. What precisely was involved in Arsenius's bodily transfiguration, what he contemplated in the long hours of nightly solitude—of this nothing explicit is said.

But there are other sources that, although by no means neglecting the element of personal experience, also speak of prayer in a more systematic way. A distinction is often made between two basic stages on the spiritual journey: the active life (*praxis, praktikē*) and the contemplative life (*theōria*). This is a distinction found already in Clement of Alexandria (ca. 150– ca. 215) and in Origen (ca. 185–ca. 254), where Martha is treated as the symbol of the active and Mary of the contemplative life (cf. Luke 10:38–42).[4] The early use of these two terms is somewhat different from that commonly found today. In modern Western and especially Roman Catholic usage, the active life normally denotes members of religious orders engaged in teaching, preaching, or social work, whereas the contemplative life refers to religious such as the Carthusians, who live in enclosure. But in Greek patristic authors the terms apply to inner development, not to external situation: the active life means ascetic effort to acquire virtue and to master the passions, whereas the contemplative life signifies the vision of God. Thus, according to this second usage, most hermits and enclosed religious are still struggling at the active stage, whereas a doctor or social worker, fully committed to outward service in the world, may yet at the same time be pursuing the contemplative life, if he or she is practicing inner prayer and has attained silence of heart.

The contemplative life in its turn may be subdivided into the contemplation of God and the contemplation of nature, thus transforming the twofold pattern into a scheme of three stages: the active life (*praktikē*), the contemplation of nature or "natural contemplation" (*physikē*), and contemplation in the strict sense, the vision of God (*theōria*), also termed *theologia*, "theology," or *gnōsis*, spiritual "knowledge." Making use of this threefold scheme, Origen speaks of "ethics," "physics," and "enoptics" or mystical theology, and he associates each stage with a particular book of the Bible: "ethics" with Proverbs, "physics" with Ecclesiastes, and mystical theology with the Song of Songs.[5] The scheme is rendered more precise by Evagrius of Pontus (346–399), and employed by most subsequent authors in the Greek tradition, especially by Maximus the Confessor (ca. 580–662).

Let us look more closely at the three stages, mainly according to Evagrius:

*Praktikē.* The active life begins with repentance (*metanoia*), understood not merely as sorrow for sin but as a "change of mind" (which is the literal sense of the Greek term), as a radical conversion, the re-centering of our entire life upon God. The spiritual aspirant strives, with the help of God's grace, to overcome the deep-rooted passions that distort his or her human nature. In Evagrius and most Greek writers the term "passion" (*pathos*) signified a disordered impulse, such as jealousy, lust, or uncontrolled anger, which violently dominates the soul. So the passions are seen as unnatural, intrinsically evil, a "disease" and thus no true part of our human personhood. But occasionally a more positive view prevails: Theodoret of Cyrus (ca. 393–ca. 466) regarded the passions, including the sexual instinct, as impulses originally placed in humanity by God, essential to our survival, and capable of being turned to good purposes. It is not the passion as such but its misuse that is sinful.[6] In the later Byzantine period Gregory Palamas (ca. 1296–1359) adopted a similar view, insisting that our aim is the "redirection" of the passions, not their suppression or "mortification," and he even spoke of "divine and blessed passions."[7]

The Christian is called to struggle not only against the passions but also against "thoughts" (*logismoi*), as soon as they first emerge in consciousness and long before they have issued in outward actions or taken root as passions. Evagrius gave a list of the eight basic evil "thoughts," and, after certain modifications, it became the catalogue of the seven "deadly sins" current in the medieval West. In Evagrius the list runs: gluttony, lust, avarice, dejection (*lypē*), anger, despondency or listlessness ("accidie," *akēdia*), vainglory, and pride. Keeping watch over his heart, growing in self-awareness, the aspirant acquires *nepsis* ("sobriety" or "watchfulness") and *diakrisis* ("discernment" or "discrimination," the power to distinguish between good and evil thoughts). These qualities should be accompanied by *penthos* (inward "grief") and *kata-nyxis* ("compunction"), together with the gift of tears. But tears are not only penitential: what begin as "bitter" tears of sorrow are gradually changed into "sweet" tears of gratitude and love. In what remains the classic treatment of the gift of tears in orthodox spirituality, the seventh step of *The Ladder of Divine Ascent,* John Climacus (seventh century) spoke of "joy-creating sorrow."

For Evagrius the final aim of the active life was to achieve *apatheia* ("dis-passion," freedom from passion). This term, taken over from the Stoics and first employed regularly in a Christian context by Clement of Alexandria, was sometimes used by Evagrius in a suspect way. Yet on the whole he understood it not negatively but positively. It is not apathy in the modern sense of the word—for this Evagrius used the terms *akēdia* ("listlessness") or *anaisthēsia* ("insensitivity")—but the replacing of our sinful desires by a new and better energy from God. It is a state of reintegration and spiritual freedom, not the absence of all feeling. Transmitting Evagrius's teaching to the Latin West, John Cassian (ca. 369–435) rendered *apatheia* as *puritas cordis,* "purity of heart," and Diadochus of Photice (mid-fifth century) even spoke of the "fire of dispassion."[8] Evagrius himself linked dispassion closely with love: "*Agapē* is the offspring of *apatheia*."[9] Having ceased to lust, we are free to love.

*Physikē.* The second stage, natural contemplation, is to be understood not in an aesthetic fashion or in terms of nineteenth-century romanticism, but theologically. It is to see God in all things and all things in God—to discern, in and through each created reality, the divine presence that is within it and at the same time beyond. It is to treat each thing as a sacrament, to view the whole of nature as God's book. In Evagrius's words: "There came to the righteous Anthony one of the wise men of that time and said: 'How ever do you manage to carry on, Father, deprived as you are of the consolation of books?' He replied: 'My book, philosopher, is the nature of created things, and it is ready at hand whenever I wish to read the words of God.'"[10] Evagrius further subdivided *physikē* into "second natural contemplation," which has as its object the physical world perceived by the bodily senses, and "first natural contemplation," which is directed toward things non-material, toward the angelic realm of spiritual reality. An important aspect of *physikē* is meditation on the inner meaning of Holy Scripture.

*Theoria.* At the third stage, the contemplation of God, the Christian no longer approaches the Creator through the works of creation, but meets God directly, face to face, in an unmediated union of love. Since the deity is a mystery beyond words and understanding, it follows that in such contemplation the human mind has to rise above concepts, words, and images—above the level of discursive thinking—so as to apprehend God intuitively through simple "gazing" or "touching." As Evagrius put it, the mind is to become "naked," passing beyond multiplicity to unity. Its goal is "pure prayer," prayer that is not only morally pure and free from sinful thoughts but also intellectually pure and free from *all* thoughts. Accordingly he wrote:

> When you are praying, do not shape within yourself any image of the Deity, and do not let your mind be stamped with the impress of any form; but approach the Immaterial in an immaterial manner. . . . Prayer means the shedding of thoughts. . . . Blessed is the intellect that has acquired complete freedom from sensations during prayer.[11]

At the higher levels of contemplation, then, awareness of the subject-object differentiation recedes, and in its place there is only a sense of all-embracing unity. In the words of Anthony of Egypt, as recounted by Cassian: "A monk's prayer is not perfect if in the course of it he is aware of himself or of the fact that he is praying" (*Conferences* 9.31). To use T. S. Eliot's phrase, "You are the music while the music lasts."

In this way the apophatic attitude is to be applied not only to theology but also to prayer. In theology it means—as the Cappadocians insisted, reacting against the rationalism of Eunomius and the extreme Arians—that all positive statements about God must be qualified and counterbalanced by negative statements, for no verbal formula can contain the fullness of the transcendent mystery. In the realm of prayer it means that the mind is to be stripped of all images and concepts, so that our abstract concepts about God are replaced by the sense of God's immediate presence. Accordingly, Gregory of Nyssa (ca. 330-ca. 395) gave a symbolical interpretation to the first of the Ten Commandments, which prohibits graven images (Exod 20:4). Reliance on pictures and intellectual abstractions made by humans is a form of idolatry, for we are substituting our notion of the deity for the living reality of God. It is not only images of stone but also conceptual images that must be shattered (*Life of Moses* 1.165-66).[12] "Every concept grasped by the mind becomes an obstacle in their quest to those who search," he wrote. Our aim is to attain, beyond all words and concepts, a "certain sense of presence"; "the Bridegroom is present, but he is not seen."[13] This noniconic, nondiscursive consciousness of God's presence is often designated in Greek sources by the term *hesychia,* meaning tranquillity and inner still-ness (hence "hesychasm" and "hesychast"). *Hesychia* means silence, not negatively in the sense of an absence of speech, a pause between words, but positively in the sense of an attitude of listening. It signifies plenitude, not emptiness; presence, not a void.

It should not be thought that noniconic *hesychia* is the only form of inner prayer practiced in the Christian East. Many writers also recommended detailed, imaginative meditation upon the life of Christ and, more especially, on the passion. This was emphasized, for example, by Mark the Monk or Hermit (early fifth century?) and by Nicolas Cabasilas (fourteenth century); Peter of Damascus (eleventh–twelfth century) even discussed imageless prayer and imaginative meditation side by side in the same chapter. The two ways of praying are not mutually exclusive but complementary.

The faculty or aspect of the human person that apprehends God in con-templative prayer was described by Evagrius as the *nous,* the intellect or mind. He defined prayer as "the highest intellection of the intellect."[14] By *nous,* however, he meant in this context not the discursive reason but the direct understanding of spiritual truth through intuition or inner "sight." If, then, he is to be termed an "intellectualist," it should be recognized that the word is being used in a sense very different from that commonly assigned to it today. Other Greek fathers regard prayer as a function not so much of the *nous* as of the *kardia* or heart. It thus seems possible, on the basis of this differing usage, to make a distinction between two schools or currents of early spirituality, the one "intellectualist" and the other "affective." But the difference should not be exaggerated, and in particular the term "heart" needs to be correctly understood. Just as those patristic authors who spoke in terms of the *nous* do not mean by this exclusively or primarily the discursive reason, so those who spoke in terms of the heart do not mean by this solely the affections or emotions.

The Macarian Homilies (Syria?, late fourth century), for example, looked on the heart as the moral and spiritual center of the whole human person, the true self, the place where each is most authentically "in the image of God":

> The heart governs and reigns over the whole bodily organism; and when grace possesses the pasturages of the heart, it rules over all the members and the thoughts. For there, in the heart, is the intellect (*nous*), and all the thoughts of the soul and its expectation; and in this way grace penetrates also to all the members of the body. . . . The heart is Christ's palace. . . . There Christ the King comes to take his rest.[15]

Here there is no head–heart dichotomy, for the intellect is *within* the heart. The heart is the meeting point between body and soul, between the sub-conscious, the conscious, and the supraconscious, between the human and the divine. The word bears an all-embracing sense: in the words of John Climacus, "I cried out with all my heart, says the psalmist (Ps 118 [119]:145): that is, with my body and soul and spirit."[16] In the phrase of Gregory Palamas, it is "the instrument of instruments" (*Triads* 2.2.28)—what in Zen Buddhism is styled "the centre of the lotus."[17] When "heart" is understood in this inclusive fashion, it becomes clear that for Eastern Christian writers "prayer of the heart" means, not merely "affective prayer" in the Western sense, but prayer of the whole human person, prayer in which the one who prays is totally identified with the act of praying.

Combining these two approaches to prayer—the one emphasizing the role of the *nous,* the other that of the heart—Greek hesychast writers of the four-teenth century spoke of "descending with the *nous* into the heart" and of the "prayer of the *nous* in the heart." This, as we have seen, was also Bishop Theophan's way of speaking.

Such, then, is the basic threefold scheme proposed by Origen, Evagrius, and Maximus. Triadic patterns of a slightly different type can be found in other authors. Gregory of Nyssa, in *The Life of Moses,* spoke of three stages, each corresponding to a "theophany" or manifestation of God in Exodus: *light* (the burning bush, Exod 3:2); *cloud* (i.e., mingled light and darkness; cf. the pillar of cloud and fire, Exod 13:21); *darkness* (on the summit of Sinai, Exod 20:21). In the writings attributed to Pseudo-Dionysius the Areopagite (ca. 500), the three stages are purification, illumination, and union. This scheme was widely adopted in the medieval West, but in the Greek tradition the Evagrian scheme was more common.

Two shortcomings may be noted in Evagrius's "map." First, he often spoke as if the three stages were successive, but should they not rather be envisaged as three deepening levels, interdependent and coexisting simultaneously? This is in fact the view adopted by others, and even Evagrius recognized that the passions of the soul "persist up to death,"[18] which implies that no one in this life passes altogether beyond the first or "active" stage. Second, in the Evagrian scheme love is set on a lower level than *gnōsis* or knowledge. Love is linked with *apatheia* and so comes at the end of the first stage, that of *praktikē*, and *gnōsis* occupies the highest point of the third stage. As Evagrius put it, "The perfection of the *nous* is immaterial *gnōsis*" (*Gnostic Chapters* 3.15). The perspective is rightly reversed by Gregory of Nyssa, who assigned the highest place to love: "*Gnōsis* is transformed into love" (*On the Soul and*

*Resurrection* [*PG* 46, col. 96C]). Maximus the Confessor, although he used the Evagrian scheme, also insisted unambiguously upon the supremacy of love: "Nothing is greater than divine love. . . . Love makes man god, and reveals and manifests God as man."[19] In the words of Isaac the Syrian (Isaac of Nineveh, seventh century), another author who was influenced by Evagrius but adapted what he borrowed: "When we have reached love, we have reached God and our journey is at an end."[20]

And yet, from another point of view, the journey is *never* at an end. Since God is infinite, the blessed even in heaven will never cease to grow in the knowledge and love of God. As Origen affirmed:

> Those who devote themselves to the pursuit of wisdom and knowledge have no end to their labours. How could there be an end, a limit, where the wisdom of God is concerned? The nearer someone comes to that wisdom, the deeper he finds it to be; and the more he probes into its depths, the more he sees that he will never be able to understand it or express it in words. . . . Travellers, then, on the road to God's wisdom find that the further they go, the more the road opens out, until it stretches to infinity. (*Homilies on Numbers* 17.4)

All this is true, so Gregory of Nyssa insisted, not only in this present life but equally in the age to come. He described this unending progress into divine infinity by the term *epektasis*, "straining forward," which he took from Philippians 3:13: ". . . forgetting what lies behind and straining forward (*epekteinomenos*) to what lies ahead." Adopting a dynamic view, he maintained that the very essence of perfection lies in the fact that we never become totally perfect but unceasingly advance "from glory to glory" (2 Cor 3:18). Gregory's standpoint was well summed up by Jean Daniélou: "God becomes ever more intimate and ever more distant . . . known by the smallest child and yet unknown to the greatest mystic. For the soul possesses God and yet still seeks him."[21] Not in time only but also in eternity, the road goes ever, ever on.

## A Way of Ascent: The Jesus Prayer

But how are we to set out upon this spiritual way? How, more specifically, are we to acquire inner stillness or *hesychia*, progressing from the level of discursive thinking to that of unmediated, nondiscursive union? How are we to stop talking and to start listening?

The Christian East has always been reluctant to regard any particular "technique," taken in isolation, as a privileged way of entry into *hesychia*. Stillness of heart cannot be pursued on its own but presupposes all the different expressions of the Christian life: true Orthodox faith in the dogmas of the church, liturgical prayer, the sacraments, the reading of Scripture, the observance of the commandments, acts of service, and practical compassion toward our neighbor. All these form an organic unity. Nevertheless, within this undivided totality, there is one way of praying that has been found especially valuable as an aid to inner silence: the Jesus Prayer.

This is a short invocation, designed for frequent repetition and addressed to the Savior. Most commonly it takes the form "Lord Jesus Christ, Son of God, have mercy on me." Although this may be regarded as the "standard" formula, there is a wide variety in the actual phrasing: for example, "the sinner" may be added at the end; the plural may be used, "have mercy on *us*"; the formula may be shorter—"Lord Jesus Christ, have mercy on me," or simply, "Lord Jesus, have mercy." But, whereas the name "Jesus" was often invoked on its own in the medieval West, this is not usual in Orthodox practice. The Holy Name is felt to be so powerful, so charged with spiritual energy, that it needs to be as it were "diluted" with other words; repeated constantly on its own, it might lead to a state of inner tension.

The Jesus Prayer is used in two main situations. Either it may be recited as part of our formal "prayer time," when we are alone in church or in our own room, not engaged in any other activity; or else it may be said in a "free" way as we go about our daily work, in particular when we are engaged in some repetitive or mechanical task, as also during all the scattered moments of the day that would otherwise be wasted, when we are waiting for something to happen.

The Jesus Prayer has been called a "Christian mantra," but this is misleading. It is not simply a rhythmic incantation, but implies a specific personal relationship and a consciously held belief in the incarnation. The aim is not simply the suspension of all thought, but an encounter with Someone. The prayer is addressed directly to another person and embodies an explicit confession of faith in that person as the incarnate Son of God, at once truly divine and completely human, our Savior and our Lord. Without this personal relationship, without this explicit confession of faith, there is no Jesus Prayer.

The Western public has become familiar with the Jesus Prayer above all through *The Way of the Pilgrim*, the narrative of an anonymous Russian layman who lived in the middle of the nineteenth century. But the prayer itself is far more ancient. Orthodox authors generally hold that it dates back to the very beginnings of Christianity and was taught by the Lord himself to the apostles. Clear evidence for this is lacking, but certainly its origins extend back at least to the fourth and fifth centuries. In the practice of the Jesus Prayer, as found in the Orthodox tradition, four constituent elements may be distinguished: (1) the invocation of the Holy Name "Jesus"; (2) the appeal for God's mercy, accompanied by a sense of *penthos* or sorrow for sin; (3) the discipline of frequent or continual repetition; (4) the desire to attain nondiscursive or apophatic prayer.

The second and third of these elements are found already in the desert spirituality of fourth-century Egypt, particularly in such centers as Nitria and Scetis. As the *Sayings of the Desert Fathers* indicate, the early monks sought to maintain the "remembrance of God," the awareness of the divine presence, at every moment and in every place—not only during the times of liturgical prayer in church, but throughout the day. "Pray constantly" (1 Thess 5:17): for them, as for Bishop Theophan the Recluse, Paul's words meant that prayer is to accompany and imbue every other activity. As they put it, "The monk who prays only when he stands up to say prayers is not really praying at all."[22]

The daily work of the desert fathers was usually a simple form of manual labor, such as basket making or plaiting rush mats. As a method for retaining the "remembrance of God" while performing this work, the monk was encouraged to recite the Psalms and other texts from Scripture which he knew by heart; and instead of reciting long passages he might repeat the same phrase again and again. This practice of reiterating a short phrase or formula had come to be known, by the time of John Climacus, as "monologic prayer," prayer consisting of a single *logos* or phrase. Through such "monologic prayer" the monk was enabled, in combination with the "outer work" of his manual labor, to practice also the "inner work" of prayer. In the words of the *Apophthegmata*, "A man should always be inwardly at work."[23] The aim is summed up by Bishop Theophan: "The hands at work, the mind and heart with God."[24]

Initially a variety of formulas were used in frequent repetition. One monk repeated the first verse of Psalm 50 [51], "Have mercy upon me, O God, according to thy great mercy . . .";[25] another constantly said the words "As man, I have sinned; as God, forgive."[26] In both these instances the element of *penthos* and contrition is strongly to the fore. Cassian, drawing on his Egyptian experience, recommended the repeated use of the opening of Psalm 69 [70], "O God, come to my aid; O Lord, make haste to help me" (*Conferences* 10.10). Sometimes the phrase might be very brief indeed, as in the prayer suggested by Abba Macarius, "Lord, help" (but nothing is explicitly said here about frequent repetition).[27] Although in the *Sayings of the Desert Fathers* there are a few prayers that include the name of Jesus, no special priority is assigned to it, nor had it yet begun to act as a decisive focus for devotion.

Early Egypt, then, provides clear evidence for the second and third of the four elements that we have mentioned—for *penthos* and monologic prayer—

but not for the first, the particular invocation of the Holy Name. As for the fourth element, nondiscursive prayer and the "shedding of thoughts," this was taught in fourth-century Egypt by Evagrius, although he was drawing here not upon the Coptic monks around him in the desert but rather upon Origen and the Cappadocians. Indeed, most of the Coptic monks, simple men with no philosophical education, were "anthropomorphites," who took Genesis 1:26 literally in ascribing a human form to God. They would scarcely have understood what was meant by noniconic, apophatic prayer. But although Evagrius urged the renunciation of concepts and images, he nowhere proposed a specific method whereby this kind of "pure" prayer might in practice be achieved. Although he said on one occasion, "Use a brief but intense prayer,"[28] no connection is made between this piece of advice and the "stripping" of the intellect. So the fourth element, nondiscursive prayer, although known in early Egyptian monasticism, was not initially connected with the third element, the discipline of repetition.

In the fifth century, however, a "Jesus-centered" spirituality began to emerge, although the earliest evidence comes not from Egypt but from Asia Minor and northern Greece. At four points in his voluminous correspondence, Nilus of Ancyra (d. ca. 430) advocated the continual "remembrance" or "invocation" of the Name of Jesus, but these allusions are scattered and incidental. The Jesus Prayer occupied a central place in the teaching of Diadochus of Photice, who wrote about a generation after Nilus. He linked closely together three of our four elements, seeing the repeated invocation of Jesus as a way of attaining nondiscursive prayer—although he gave no special prominence to the second element, *penthos* or inner grief.

How, asked Diadochus, can our fragmented memory be reduced to unity? How can our ever-active intellect be brought from restlessness to stillness, from multiplicity to "nakedness"? This is his answer:

> When we have blocked all its outlets by means of the remembrance of God, the intellect (*nous*) requires of us imperatively some task which will satisfy its need for activity. For the complete fulfillment of its purpose we should give it nothing but the prayer "Lord Jesus." . . . Let the intellect continually concentrate on this phrase within its inner shrine with such intensity that it is not turned aside to any mental images.[29]

It is noteworthy that Diadochus says *"nothing* but the prayer 'Lord Jesus'"': the variety of formulas that existed in fourth-century Egypt is now being replaced by a greater uniformity. Through this constant, unvarying repetition, the invocation of Jesus grows ever more spontaneous and "self-acting": "The soul now has grace itself to share its meditation and to repeat with it the words 'Lord Jesus,' just as a mother teaches her child to repeat with her the word 'father,' until she has formed in him the habit of calling for his father even in his sleep."[30]

The Jesus Prayer is thus a way of "keeping guard" over the intellect or heart, to use a phrase common in Eastern Christian texts. Although it is a prayer in words, the invocation of the Name is of such brevity and simplicity that it enables the seeker to reach out beyond language into the living silence of God. Here, then, in commending imageless prayer, Diadochus made a decisive advance beyond Evagrius by proposing a *practical method* for the attainment of such prayer. His *Gnostic Chapters,* unifying as they do devotion to the Name, monologic repetition, and the "shedding" of thoughts, serve as an all-important catalyst in the history of the Jesus Prayer.

According to Irénée Hausherr, Diadochus had in view only the "remembrance" of Jesus in a diffused sense and not an explicit invocation through a specific formula.[31] But the language of the *Gnostic Chapters* implies more than a mere recollection of the person of Jesus. It remains uncertain, however, whether Diadochus intended the words "Lord Jesus" to be followed by something further, such as "have mercy." At any rate he did not propose the invocation of the name "Jesus" entirely by itself. Lev Gillet holds that the Jesus Prayer began with the use of the word "Jesus" on its own, but this is unlikely.[32] All the surviving evidence from the early centuries suggests, on the contrary, that the Holy Name formed part of a longer formula of prayer.

It was during the sixth and seventh centuries that what we have termed the "standard" form of the Jesus Prayer was first explicitly mentioned. In Barsanuphius and John of Gaza (early sixth century), and in their disciple Dorotheus, we find the form "Lord Jesus Christ, have mercy on me" (without "Son of God"); Barsanuphius also commended other short phrases such as "Jesus, help me."[33] The "standard" form, "Lord Jesus Christ, Son of God, have mercy on me," is found in the *Life* of Abba Philemon, an Egyptian monk, possibly of the sixth or early seventh century.[34] The Jesus Prayer is also mentioned by three writers linked with Sinai, John Climacus (seventh century), Hesychius (eighth–ninth century?), and Philotheus (ninth–tenth century?), but none of them gave an exact formula of invocation. Agreeing closely with Diadochus, they saw the Prayer as a way of unifying the inward attention, stripping the mind of images, and so attaining *hesychia*. It is, however, misleading to attribute the early development of the Jesus Prayer primarily to Sinai.[35] It is only one among a number of centers with which the Prayer is associated in the early evidence. The most ancient testimonies do not in fact come from Sinai, and its role seems to have been to transmit rather than originate the tradition of the Jesus Prayer.

Between the fifth and the eighth century, then, the Jesus Prayer emerged in Eastern Christendom as a recognized spiritual "way." It should not, however, be imagined that its use was universal. It is nowhere mentioned in the writings of Pseudo-Dionysius the Areopagite, Maximus the Confessor, or Isaac of Syria, nor in the authentic works of Symeon the New Theologian, to mention but a few examples. When Gregory of Sinai (d. 1346) came to the holy mountain of Athos early in the fourteenth century, searching for guidance in the practice of "*hesychia* or the guarding of the intellect and contemplation"—from the context it is clear that the Jesus Prayer is included in this general description—he could at first find no one to help him. Only after many inquiries did he eventually discover three monks with some understanding of these matters; all the others, so it is claimed by his disciple and biographer Kallistos, were concerned solely with the pursuit of the "active life."[36]

It was only during the fourteenth century, and more especially through the writings of Gregory of Sinai himself, that the Jesus Prayer became far more generally known. Its use was further promoted by the publication in 1782 of the *Philokalia,* a vast collection of spiritual texts edited by Macarius of Corinth and Nicodemus of the Holy Mountain. Translations of the *Philokalia* led to a much greater knowledge of the Jesus Prayer in Russia and Romania, and in the last forty years the prayer has come to be practiced also by large numbers of Western Christians. Although limited in the past mainly to monastic circles, it is today part of the spiritual life of many laypersons. The invocation of the Holy Name has probably never been so widely valued and practiced as it is at the present time.

There are in particular three aids or means of support in the use of the Jesus Prayer, the one inner, the other two external. As an inner aid, the personal guidance of a spiritual father or "elder" (Greek *gerōn* or *geronta;* Slavonic *starets*) plays a vital part. The need for obedience, in the use of the Jesus Prayer as in all aspects of the life in Christ, is frequently underlined in Orthodox teaching from the time of the desert fathers on. In the words of the *Apophthegmata,* "If you see a young man climbing up to heaven by his own will, seize him by the foot and pull him down, for this is to his profit."[37] "What is more to be desired," asked Theodore of Studios (795–826), "than a true father, a father-in-God?" (*Letter* 1.2 [*PG* 99, col. 909B]). Readers of *The Way of a Pilgrim* will recall the decisive role of the *starets* in the Pilgrim's quest. The Orthodox sources refer also to the spiritual mother as well as the spiritual father, to the "amma" as well as the "abba."

Of the two external aids, the first is the use of a prayer rope (Greek *komvoschoinion;* Russian *chotki*), similar in appearance to the Western rosary, except that in Orthodox practice it is commonly made of knotted wool rather than of beads. Evidence for its use in combination with the

Jesus Prayer can be traced back for at least 250–300 years, and it is probably much older. The primary purpose of the prayer rope is not so much to measure the number of times that the prayer is said as to ensure a regular, rhythmic invocation. It is a fact of experience that it is easier to concentrate in prayer if the hands also have their part to play.

Second, a physical technique, involving in particular the control of the breathing, has come to be recommended in connection with the Jesus Prayer. The origins of this method are obscure. Early authors give the advice, "Remember God more often than you breathe" (Gregory Nazianzen *Oration 27* 4 [*PG* 36, col. 16B]). "Just as we breathe the air continually, so we ought to praise and sing to God continually" (Nilus of Ancyra *Letter 1* 239 [*PG* 79, col. 169D]). Probably the sense here is no more than metaphorical: prayer is to be as constant, as much part of us, as is the very act of breathing. But John Climacus was slightly more definite: "Let the remembrance of Jesus be present with your every breath," or "be united with your breathing" (*Ladder* step 27). Hesychius was more specific still: "Let the Jesus Prayer cleave to your breath" (*On Watchfulness and Holiness* 2.80 [*PG* 93, col. 1537D]).[39] Here a metaphorical sense is not excluded, but it is also possible that John and Hesychius had in view some kind of coordination between the words of the Prayer and the rhythm of the respiration. More explicit still is a phrase in the Coptic Macarian cycle (seventh–eighth century?): "Is it not easy to say with every breath, 'My Lord Jesus Christ, have mercy on me; I bless you, my Lord Jesus Christ, help me'?"[40] Such language implies more than a mere analogy and surely indicates some form of breathing technique.

But it is not until considerably later, in the thirteenth and fourteenth centuries, that clear and detailed evidence about such a physical method can be found in the Greek sources. Even then the description is far from complete. For reasons of prudence many aspects of the technique were not committed to writing, but were taught orally by each spiritual father to his immediate disciples. The fullest accounts are given in two short treatises: *On Watchfulness and the Guarding of the Heart*, by Nicephorus the Hesychast, a monk of Mount Athos in the late thirteenth century; and *On the Three Methods of Prayer*, attributed to Symeon the New Theologian (949–1022), but almost certainly later in date and very possibly also by Nicephorus.[41] Supplementary details can be found in the writings of Gregory of Sinai and of Kallistos and Ignatius Xanthopoulos (late fourteenth century).

The method comprises three main features: (1) A particular bodily posture is adopted: seated, with the head and shoulders bowed, and the gaze directed toward the place of the heart or the navel. (2) The speed of the breathing is slowed down, and the words of the Jesus Prayer are coordinated with the inhalation and exhalation of the breath. In *The Way of a Pilgrim* the prayer is also synchronized with the rhythm of the heartbeats, but no such suggestion is made in the texts of the thirteenth and fourteenth centuries. (3) Through a discipline of "inner exploration," attention is concentrated upon specific psychosomatic centers, more especially the heart: along with the inhalation of the breath, the intellect is made to "descend" into the heart, thus bringing about "prayer of the intellect in the heart." There are striking similarities between this "hesychast" method and the techniques used in Yoga and Sufism, but it is difficult to find proof of direct influence.

Used in a self-willed and uncontrolled fashion, the technique suggested by Nicephorus could easily prove harmful on both the physical and psychic levels, and it is in fact little used in its full form by contemporary Orthodox. The personal guidance of an experienced teacher is essential. Gregory Palamas, however, defended the physical method as resting upon a sound doctrine of the human person: since body and soul form an integral unity, the body as well as the soul should play a positive role in prayer. But he did not in fact attach primary significance to the method, which he regarded as chiefly useful for beginners.[42] It is in any case no more than an exterior aid, and the Jesus Prayer may be offered in its integrity without the use of any psychosomatic technique at all.

Modern Orthodox writers, summarizing the teaching of earlier centuries, commonly distinguish three levels in the practice of the Jesus Prayer: (1) It begins as a *prayer of the lips*, an oral prayer recited aloud (but not chanted). In the early stages, heavy stress is placed upon the need to repeat faithfully the actual words of the prayer. Beginners should concentrate all their energies on this, not deluding themselves with the thought that they are perhaps advancing at once to wordless prayer of the heart. (2) By degrees the invocation grows more interior, becoming *prayer of the intellect* or mind (*nous*). Perhaps the words are no longer recited aloud but are expressed inwardly. The images that incessantly arise in the consciousness are gently but firmly "shed" or laid aside, while the sense of Christ's immediate presence, unaccompanied by any mental picture or concept, grows ever more powerful. (3) Finally the prayer descends from the intellect to the heart. Intellect and heart are united, and so the invocation becomes *prayer of the heart* or, more exactly, prayer of the intellect in the heart prayer, that is, of the whole human person. In a few rare cases such prayer may be continual, but for others it is an exceptional state, attained only occasionally and for brief moments. Prayer of the heart is by no means granted automatically to all who practice the invocation of the Name, but it is a special gift of God's grace. It is the result not simply of human effort but of divine energy at work within us: "not I, but Christ in me" (Gal 2:20). Like the prayer of

"Christ in me," the Jesus Prayer becomes on its deeper levels "self-acting," and leads in this way to a state corresponding to what is termed "infused contemplation" in Western mystical theology. The soul is not so much active as passive: in the words of Pseudo-Dionysius, ". . . *suffering* things divine, not just learning about them" (*On the Divine Names* 2.9 [*PG* 3, col. 648B]).

## Journey's End:
## The Dazzling Darkness

The final end of the threefold way, contemplative union with God, is described in the Christian East, as in the Christian West, through the symbolism of both darkness and light. The symbol of darkness was used especially by Clement of Alexandria —drawing on the Jewish author Philo (ca. 20 B.C.E.—ca. 50 C.E.)—and by Gregory of Nyssa and Pseudo-Dionysius the Areopagite. These authors took as their model for the mystical ascent the figure of Moses going up Mount Sinai to encounter God in the "thick darkness" (Exod 20:21). By darkness in this context is meant not a preliminary stage of purification—as with the "dark night of the senses" in the theology of John of the Cross—but the ultimate union "face to face" with the divine mystery. More frequent than the symbol of darkness, however, is that of divine light, which was employed by Irenaeus (ca. 130–ca. 200), Origen, Gregory of Nazianzus, Evagrius, the Macarian Homilies, Symeon the New Theologian, and Gregory Palamas. These writers took as their model not the darkness of Sinai but Moses' vision of the "pavement of sapphire stone" and the "firmament of heaven in its clarity" (Exod 24:10), Ezekiel's vision of the chariot (Ezekiel 1)—also important in Jewish mysticism—and Christ's transfiguration on Mount Tabor. In either instance, of course, the description is no more than symbolical, for in himself, as Pseudo-Dionysius pointed out, God is "neither darkness nor light" (*Mystical Theology* 5 [*PG* 3, col. 1048A]). Reconciling the two symbols, the Areopagite spoke of the "dazzling darkness which with utter obscurity outshines the brightest light" (*Mystical Theology* 1 [*PG* 3, col. 997B]).

More strikingly than any other author, Symeon the New Theologian set the divine light at the center of his spiritual teaching:

> We bear witness that God is light, and that those counted worthy to see him have all beheld him as light, and those who have received him have received him as light, for the light of his glory goes before him. Without light it is impossible for him to be made manifest, and those who have not seen his light have not seen him, for he is the light, and those who have not received the light have not yet received grace.[43]

Symeon's own life, from the age of about twenty when he was still a layman, was marked by a series of visions of the divine light. Although he termed this light "nonmaterial," he clearly did not mean by it simply a metaphorical light of the intelligence. It is for him an existent reality, beheld through the senses, even though itself transcending them. Three centuries later Gregory Palamas was to elucidate the character of this "nonmaterial" light by identifying it with God's uncreated energies. These energies, so he maintained, are God himself, God in action, yet they are to be distinguished from God's essence, which remains unknowable and beyond all participation, alike in this age and in the age to come. Symeon, however, is less precise, sometimes speaking in the same way as Palamas, yet at other times affirming that human beings can participate not only in the energies but in the very essence of God.

What remains clear is that for Symeon God is a mystery beyond all understanding; and so, even though he sometimes said that we participate in God's essence, this does not mean that we can ever know God exhaustively. It is also clear that for Symeon the vision of divine light is a direct, unmediated union with God himself and not merely the experience of some created gift that God confers. It is, moreover, a transforming union: Symeon was conscious of sharing in the light that he contemplated and of being himself changed into light. As he wrote in one of his *Hymns of Divine Love:*

O Light that none can name, for it is altogether nameless,
O Light with many names, for it is at work in all things . . .
How do you mingle yourself with grass?
How, while continuing unchanged, altogether inaccessible,
Do you preserve the nature of the grass unconsumed?
How, while keeping it unaltered, do you yet transform it entirely?
Remaining grass it is light, and yet the Light is not grass;
But you, the Light, are joined to the grass in a union without confusion,
And the grass becomes light; it is transfigured, yet without changing.[44]

Here Symeon points to the basic mystical paradox: God is both unknown and yet well known, beyond all being and yet everywhere present. The Wholly Other is at the same time uniquely close to us, and without ceasing to be transcendent he joins himself to created human persons in a union of love. We humans for our part are "deified" by this union, and without forfeiting our personal identity we are assumed entirely into the divine life.

The majority of the authors to whom we have referred were monks, writing in the first instance for other monks. Yet it should not therefore be assumed that they regarded the way of hesychasm and the use of the Jesus

Prayer as impossible outside a monastic setting. On the contrary, in their eyes this way possessed universal value. Symeon the New Theologian insisted that one "who has wife and children, crowds of servants, much property, and a prominent position in the world" can yet attain the "vision of God"; it is possible to live "a heavenly life here on earth . . . not just in caves or mountains or monastic cells, but in the midst of cities."[45] Gregory of Sinai told one of his disciples, Isidore (later patriarch), to return from the solitude of Mount Athos to Thessalonica so as to act in the heart of the city as a spiritual guide to laypeople. And Gregory Palamas held that the command to "pray constantly" applied not only to monks but to all Christians without exception. In the words of Nicolas Cabasilas:

> Everyone may continue to exercise their art or profession. The general may continue to command, the farmer to till the soil, the workman to pursue his craft. No one need desist from his usual employment. It is not necessary to retire into the desert, or to eat unaccustomed food, or to dress differently, or to ruin one's health, or to do anything reckless; for it is quite possible to practice continual meditation in one's own home without giving up any of one's possessions.[46]

Contemporary Christians who have learned to use the Jesus Prayer will testify from their own experience that Cabasilas is speaking the truth. Because of its shortness and simplicity, it is a prayer that can be said at all times and everywhere, particularly in situations of anxiety and stress when more complex forms of prayer are impossible. It is a prayer for all seasons, never out of place. The Jesus Prayer makes it possible for each of us to be an "urban hesychast," preserving inwardly a secret center of stillness in the midst of outward pressures, carrying the desert with us in our hearts wherever we go.

## Notes

1. Quoted in Igumen Chariton of Valamo, *The Art of Prayer: An Orthodox Anthology* (London: Faber & Faber, 1966) 63. Here and in some other quotations I have modified the translation.

2. *The Sayings of the Desert Fathers: The Alphabetic Collection,* trans. Benedicta Ward (London: Mowbray, 1975) Macarius the Great 19 (p. 131).

3. *The Sayings,* Arsenius 27, 30 (trans. Ward, pp. 13, 14).

4. Origen *Commentary on John,* fragment 80.

5. Origen *Commentary on the Song of Songs,* prologue (ACW 26, 1957) 40–41.

6. Theodoret *The Cure of Pagan Maladies* 5 (PG 83, col. 952BC).

7. Gregory of Palamas *Triads in Defence of the Holy Hesychasts* 2.2.19–22; 3.3.15. See Gregory Palamas, *The Triads,* ed. John Meyendorff; trans. Nicholas Grendle (New York: Paulist Press, 1983).

8. Diadochus of Photice *Gnostic Chapters* 17, in G. E. H. Palmer, P. Sherrard, and K. Ware, *The Philokalia* (London: Faber & Faber, 1979) 1:258.

9. Evagrius of Pontus *Praktikos* 81 in *Evagrius Ponticus: The Praktikos: Chapters on Prayer,* trans. John Eudes Bamberger (Spencer, MA: Cistercian Publications, 1970) 36.

10. *Praktikos* 92, in *Evagrius Ponticus,* 39.

11. *On Prayer* 67, 71, 120, as translated in Palmer et al., 63, 64, 68.

12. See the translation by A. J. Malherbe and E. Ferguson, *Gregory of Nyssa: The Life of Moses* (New York: Paulist Press, 1978) 95–96.

13. Gregory of Nyssa *Commentary on the Song of Songs* 6 and 11, in *Gregorii Nysseni in Canticum Canticorum,* ed. H. Langerbeck (Leiden: Brill, 1960) 183, 324.

14. *On Prayer* 35, as translated in Palmer et al., 60.

15. *Homilies,* collection H, 15.20 and 33. See A. J. Mason, *Fifty Spiritual Homilies of St. Macarius the Egyptian* (London: S.P.C.K., 1921) 116, 122.

16. John Climacus, *The Ladder of Divine Ascent,* trans. C. Luibheid and N. Russell (New York: Paulist Press, 1982) step 28, p. 281.

17. P. Reps, *Zen Flesh, Zen Bones* (Harmondsworth: Penguin Books, 1971) 155.

18. *Praktikos* 36, in Bamberger, 25.

19. *On Love* 1, 9; *Letter* 2 (*PG* 91, col. 401B); see Palmer et al., 2:54, 171.

20. *Mystic Treatises,* trans. A. J. Wensinck (Amsterdam: Akademie van Wetenschappen, Verhandelingen, XXIII, 1, 1923) 212.

21. See *From Glory to Glory: Texts from Gregory of Nyssa's Mystical Writings,* ed. Jean Daniélou and Herbert Musurillo (New York: Scribner, 1961; repr. Crestwood, NY: St. Vladimir's Seminary Press, 1979) 54.

22. F. Nau, ed., *Apophthegmata,* the Anonymous Supplement, §104, *Revue de l'Orient chrétien* 12 (1907) 402. The normal posture for prayer in early Christendom was to stand, not to kneel or sit.

23. F. Nau, ed., Anonymous Supplement, §241, *Revue de l'Orient chrétien* 14 (1909) 363.

24. Chariton, p. 92.

25. *The Sayings,* Lucius 1 (trans. Ward, p. 121).

26. *The Sayings,* Apollo 2 (trans. Ward, p. 36).

27. *The Sayings,* Macarius the Great 19 (trans. Ward, 131).

28. *On Prayer* 98, as translated in Palmer et al., 1:66.

29. *Gnostic Chapters* 59, as translated in Palmer et al., 1:270.

30. *Gnostic Chapters* 61, as translated in Palmer et al., 1:271.

31. Irénée Hausherr, *The Name of Jesus,* 220–29.

32. Lev Gillet, "A Monk of the Eastern Church," 68; against this view, see Hausherr, 104.

33. See F. Neyt, "The Prayer of Jesus," *Sobornost* series 6, no. 9 (1974) 641–54.

34. See Palmer et al., 2:348.

35. As is done, for example, by "A Monk of the Eastern Church," 24; see the criticisms of Hausherr, 279–80.

36. Patriarch Kallistos, *Life of St. Gregory of Sinai* 7; cited in K. Ware, "The Jesus Prayer in St. Gregory of Sinai," *Eastern Churches Review* 4 (1972) 5.

37. F. Nau, ed., Anonymous Supplement, §244, *Revue de l'Orient chrétien* 14 (1909) 364.

38. Trans. C. Luibheid and N. Russell, 270.

39. For a translation, see Palmer et al., 1:195.

40. See A. Guillaumont, "The Jesus Prayer among the Monks of Egypt," *Eastern Churches Review* 6 (1974) 67.

41. For an English translation of these two works, made from the Russian (which omits parts of the Greek), see E. Kadloubovsky and G. E. H. Palmer, *Writings from the Philokalia on Prayer of the Heart* (London: Faber & Faber, 1951) 22–34, 152–61. See I. Hausherr, *La méthode d'oraison hésychaste* (Orientalia Christiana 9, 2 [36]; Rome, 1927).

42. *Triads* 1.2.7 (ed. Meyendorff and trans. Gendle, 45).

43. *Discourse (Catechesis)* 28, in *Symeon the New Theologian: The Discourses,* trans. C. J. de Catanzaro (New York: Paulist, 1980) 298.

44. *Hymn* 28.114–15, 160–67, in *Hymns of Divine Love by St. Symeon the New Theologian* (Denville, NJ: Dimension Books, n.d.) 150–51.

45. *Discourse* 5 and 6 (trans. de Catanzaro, 93, 123).

46. Nicholas Cabasilas, *The Life of Christ,* trans. C. J. de Catanzaro (Crestwood, NY: St. Vladimir's Seminary Press, 1974) 173–74.

# Bibliography

## Studies

Hausherr, Irénée. *The Name of Jesus.* Kalamazoo, MI: Cistercian Publications, 1978.

Lossky, Vladimir. *The Mystical Theology of the Eastern Church.* Translated by the Fellowship of St. Alban and St. Sergius. Cambridge: James Clarke, 1957; reprint, Crestwood, NY: St. Vladimir's Seminary Press, 1976.

———. *The Vision of God.* Translated by A. Moorhouse. London: Faith Press, 1963; reprint, Crestwood, NY: St. Vladimir's Seminary Press, 1963.

Louth, Andrew. *The Origins of the Christian Mystical Tradition: From Plato to Denys.* Oxford: Oxford University Press, 1981.

Maloney, George A. *The Mystic of Fire and Light: St. Symeon the New Theologian.* Denville, NJ: Dimension Books, 1975.

Meyendorff, John. *St. Gregory Palamas and Orthodox Spirituality.* Crestwood, NY: St. Vladimir's Seminary Press, 1974.

Gillet, Lev. "A Monk of the Eastern Church," In *The Prayer of Jesus.* New York: Desclée, 1967.

Regnault, L. "La prière continuelle 'monologistos' dans la littérature apophtegmatique," *Irénikon* 47 (1974) 467–93.

# II. *Western*

## JEAN LECLERCQ

THE UNDERSTANDING AND PRACTICE of prayer that had been conveyed to the West by antiquity evolved very little before the end of the eleventh century. At that time a change occurred with regard to methods of meditation. Monasticism played a decisive role in this evolution. It is important first to establish the fundamental and enduring conception of prayer in general, then to situate the appearance and development of "meditation" among the forms of this prayer, finally to recall that monastic prayer is inseparable from a "way of life" that creates the conditions under which it can exist and yield its fruits.

### Sixth to Eleventh Century: The Unity of Prayer and the Diversity of Its Practice

The unity and diversity of prayer are manifest in the very terms by which prayer has been designated. An important witness in the ninth century was Smaragdus of St. Michael, because of the synthesis he presented and the influence he exerted.[1] The names given to prayer have been diverse, but all of them attempt to express different aspects of a common reality, different movements or different stages of a common activity. These names can be used somewhat interchangeably, and apparently with confusion, as is the case in innumerable texts. By means of some examples, we can at least discern the meaning that is proper to certain of these terms and recognize the bond that exists between the ideas they express.

The dominant concern was that of praying unceasingly, in accordance with the precept of the Lord (Luke 18:1). Augustine had clearly stated that this continuity could be achieved through desire. The periods of medieval monasticism during which uninterrupted choral prayer was instituted were only exceptions. Continuous prayer was always carried out partly in private, each person in his or her own behalf, in the silence of the heart. Nevertheless, monastic life has often been presented as promoting prayer without interruption as a goal, to the extent that and in whatever form this is possible here on earth. In what way was this goal judged to be possible,

29. *Transfiguration of Christ,* Apse, Church of the Virgin,
Monastery of Saint Catherine, Mount Sinai, 6th century

desirable for all, and achieved by the saints? By means of an alternation between various "exercises" that would enable the spirit to remain caught up in God and would sustain its attention in accordance with normal human psychology. The vocabulary itself suggests the conclusion that the life of prayer was so conceived.

*Oratio,* properly speaking, took place when the spirit, without the intermediary of words borrowed from any text, spoke with God and was united with God. Three qualifications were traditionally attributed to *oratio,* which corresponded to three qualities it was supposed to assume, each one flowing into the others: *pura, brevis, frequens.* "Pure": it had to be without distraction. Since this normally and habitually could not be done for very long, pure prayer had to be "brief." But one could compensate for the short duration by coming back to it often: it became "frequent." This, in summary, was the consistent teaching of the Western tradition. It is found, for example, in Augustine, Cassian, Benedict, Hildemar, Rabanus Maurus, and Robert of Arbrissel. Prayer, a profound activity, was designated as "private," "solitary," "personal." It could consist of rapid and spontaneous exclamations, that is, "ejaculatory" prayers—also called "furtive" because they were done as if stealthily, between other kinds of spiritual activity. It could come after the chanting of psalms, whether privately or in community; in that case, it alternated with psalmody as with another form of prayer. The two blended together. A continuity and coalescence was established between them—it was as if they became identical.

## Prayer and Reading

*Oratio* was most often associated with *lectio.* The latter was essential to the life of prayer. Numerous sources have led scholars to this conclusion and have enabled them to discern the reasons for it. Monastic hagiography gives us a glimpse of the way the monks thought that reading should be practiced and of the importance it had in their psychology. Like ascetical exercises, it was a requisite observance, one of the normal channels through which one was initiated into the spiritual tradition. It was a means by which the monks learned to know themselves, to enter into themselves, and to consider what they had to change. It became a vital necessity—we know that some of them even read while traveling, that is, on horseback. The story was told that for Wulstan reading had become indispensable to the point where it was necessary for someone to read in his presence during his afternoon nap, and, if the reader paused, he would wake from his sleep. His biographer, William of Malmesbury, added: "They read to him the lives of the saints and other edifying writings" (*Life of Wulstan* 3.3), but the basic text that was read was the Holy Scripture and the various commentaries on it. Reading was done attentively, and one of the qualities it had to assume, which was most insisted upon, was continuity. Unlike the *oratio*, which was brief, the *lectio* could be prolonged. It was also supposed to be done as often as possible, and thus it contributed to the frequency of prayer, with which it was associated. All these exercises were meant to lead to purity of heart, because they all united one to the Lord. Thus, frequency became a kind of continuity. Such, at least, was the ideal program.

*Lectio* followed *oratio*, which in turn prepared one for the resumption of reading, prompted it, and sustained it. But *oratio* remained the goal: it was to this that one had to come, and one was not to stop along the way. *Oratio* was supposed to follow from *lectio*. In the latter, God reveals himself; in the former, one offers oneself to God. The two, therefore, were inseparable; monks had to devote themselves to both. They had to establish a sponta-neous and necessary alternation between them, to the point where these exercises blended together and even became identical. For example, we read concerning Isarn of Marseille that "his reading was itself a prayer," and his biographer added: "In reading, he sought less the instruction of the intellect than the touching of the heart" (*Life of St. Isarn* 1.9). Thus, he saw in reading a means of carrying out the word of the Lord, which exhorted people to pray unceasingly.

Finally, one of the forms and manifestations of the life of prayer, one of its exercises, was *meditatio*. This word was sometimes used in the plural, but more often in the singular, to designate a practice appropriated from two traditions—the Bible and the teaching practice of antiquity. On this point, the two traditions were somewhat related, and they merged during the Middle Ages. One can at least occasionally identify what was appropriated from each. Following the Bible and the tradition of the rabbinical schools, meditation was chiefly an act of memory in which the basic exercise was the repeated pronunciation of words and phrases. In Latin pedagogy there was sometimes a further insistence on an effort at reflection, properly speaking. In either case, since in fact the practice inherited from these two traditions customarily combined their respective elements, meditation was marked by the same characteristics.

In the first place, meditation had as its object the initial reading of the text. The reading was followed by repetition in which the "mouth" and the "tongue" played a role. This was never an abstract exercise devoted to ideas alone; it was always meditation on some word of God that was conveyed through Sacred Scripture and explained by those who had commented on it in one way or another. Among the books of the Bible, the Psalter, interpreted from the traditional Christian perspective, was a privileged text for meditation. It sustained within the soul the presence of Christ. In the second place, meditation was exercised without constraint; it sufficed for it to be fostered by reading. Attention was aroused, stimulated by the text, and when it disappeared, this was the sign that it was time to resume reading in order to rekindle reflection. Meditation was therefore bound neither to a fixed span of time nor to a method; indeed, it implied the absence of method. It was a "free" exercise, unlike *lectio*, which followed certain rules, that is, those of grammar. Thus, meditation was an extension of reading and a preparation for *oratio*. It induced contemplation and elicited admiration for the deeds and words of God. Finally, by very reason of its calling attention to the divine mysteries and giving the spirit the freedom to consider them, meditation was a delightful spiritual activity. It was never presented as a test of endurance, of patience during dark times, of courageous perseverance in times of aridity. It was called "pleasing" and "fragrant" and had an essential link to scriptural texts. In this form, it was one of the exercises responsible for the Christian's resisting temptations and preserving unity with God.

## Bible and Liturgy

Prayer was practiced within the framework of the Divine Office and consequently in an atmosphere created by the liturgy. In the Christian tradition —and also in synagogue worship—every part of the Divine Office always consisted of an alternation between readings and an element of hymnody (often called psalmody in the Latin Middle Ages). This included not only psalms, but other canticles, biblical and nonbiblical, and, more or less according to the time, other formulas of prayer and moments of silence. This was particularly the case with the "vigils" or night Offices, for which extensive collections of texts were assembled: lectionaries, collections of homilies, passionaries. The act of reading during the Divine Office constituted a *lectio divina*. Certainly, *lectio divina* was not confined to readings that were done as part of the Office; nevertheless, the readings done during the Office were one of its elements, and *lectio*, when practiced fully, complemented the Office. The "raw material," so to speak, of all reading was Scripture par excellence, that is, the Bible. But this was never utilized without reference to the tradition. Likewise, the liturgical books always drew their commentaries from the writings of the fathers, who, using the seed of God's word as their starting point, gave birth to the doctrine of the church. What distinguished the kind of reading described here was the way in which it was practiced: it was identified neither with scientific study properly speaking (which it presupposed for those who had the taste) nor with exhortations to fervor. Going beyond precepts for moral action, *lectio* taught prayer itself, as well as the involvement of the whole person in the service of God's word in human society. The specific form of involvement was left to the discernment and generosity of each individual. Rather than teach a "lesson" in the strict sense of the word, *lectio* contributed to a formation that was integral and permanent. It created a mentality in which every occasion of study, or every activity supporting the spiritual quest, could become prayer. It was not at all an act of psychological concentration or scientific investigation. *Lectio* promoted calm and relaxed meditation, a loving disposition, and a fervent interest in exegesis or at least in its results. It created a spiritual atmosphere within which the problems dealt with by biblical science remained religious problems—an atmosphere of faith in which one learned, in a manner always mysterious, to enter into the experience of the inspired authors, and especially of Christ.

*Lectio* with the elements of tranquil reflection and of memorization which it included disposed a person to "remember" God easily and continuously. This "perpetual remembrance of God," as Cassian put it (*Conferences* 10.10), purified the human memory for its proper instinctive and free functions. Thus, to learn something "by heart," that is, with the heart (using the word in the sense of the fullness of the inner life) made it possible to re-present actively what one had read or heard read, to interiorize it, and to picture it to oneself. *Lectio* developed sacred imagination. It was not a question of knowing but of becoming reacquainted with, or discovering in a new way, what one believed—of consenting to it anew and translating it into experience, the experience of love.

A particularly important aspect of this formation was the way the Psalms were used in the life of prayer. The Psalms were a summary of the Bible; they were filled with allusions to biblical persons and events, yet they summarized the Bible and recalled its events in a way that was already transformed into prayer. The Bible was the best commentary on prayer, but without the Psalter it would have lacked the hymnic expression peculiar to this collection of poems composed under God's inspiration to be chanted in God's presence. The liturgy taught an appreciation and understanding of the Psalms not as historical and literary documents that were worthy of being studied, but as the expression of a kind of prayer which, throughout the ages of the history of God's people, contributed to the development of a piety and a culture. This was conditional upon their being read prayerfully, in the manner in which the tradition read and interpreted them. The Psalms gave witness to a long evolution of piety, a gradual and progressive formation. They were not meant to be taken literally. The liturgy fostered the discernment of their profound and abiding truth and the beauty of their expression. A "poetic" reading of this collection of works of art helped people to understand the creativity with which the Spirit of God composed them and gave them to God's people. The Psalms were often eminently useful in the fruitful process of illuminating the Old Testament by means of the New, and vice versa.

The liturgy offered the keys for entering the world of the Psalms. Through the readings, antiphons, introductions, summaries, titles, collects, and other prayers that traditionally preceded or followed the Psalms in the manuscripts, the liturgy unpacked their themes. This Christian interpretation of the Psalter developed into a school of prayer within the liturgical tradition. Through the liturgy's poetic style of juxtaposing texts that came from different biblical books, each text shed new light on the others. The result was a unique aesthetic genre, especially when chant and ritual were added. A text read in an atmosphere of beauty left a more profound impression than it would have otherwise. "Only the one who sings hears . . ." wrote Bernard of Clairvaux (*Sermons on the Song of Songs* 1.6.11).[2]

Because worship was not individualistic, neither was *lectio*. It was always done in union with the church, receiving from it the texts from the tradition. *Lectio* was therefore done *through* and necessarily *for* the church. It promoted participation in the church's abiding and universal character. Traditionally, one of the preferred means of arriving at this kind of communion was communicating with others within the very environment in which one lived, read, and prayed. This activity was described by the terms "colloquy," "conference," "conversation." Today we prefer to speak of "sharing," and this word corresponds exactly to the conception of the medievals. They saw in these exchanges, in this opportunity for each person to give and to receive, a natural—some would even say, necessary—complement to *lectio*. Smaragdus of St. Michael went so far as to write: "It is better to converse than to read. Conversations are likely to lead to learning. Indeed, obscurities are avoided by means of the questions posed; often the hidden truth comes to light as a result of objections. In consultation, one can discover immediately what is obscure or ambiguous" (*Diadem of Monks* 40 [*PL* 102, col. 636AB]). Previously Gregory the Great had had the simplicity to admit: "While there were many things in the sacred word that I could not come to understand by myself, I could often grasp their sense when I was in the presence of the brothers" (*Homilies on Ezekiel* 7.1.8 [*PL* 76, col. 843]). In monasticism this sharing, associated with *lectio* and often called "night reading," preceded or followed vespers or compline. As a result of these efforts, little by little, *lectio* bore its fruits: those of joy. *Lectio* was necessary, remarked Jerome, "not for the toil, but for the delight and instruction of the soul" (*Letter* 130.15). A monk of the Middle Ages would add: "without any toil." An initial discovery was normally followed by a thorough investigation that led to an experience of wonder; this wonder tended to become continuous. Monks spoke of this "enjoyment," this *frui* on which the ancients had insisted. *Lectio* brought peace in that it unified all the activities of prayer, and other activities as well: the studies to which one turned before and after it, the proclamation and the pastoral work of those who were involved in these tasks, the communal sharing. Above all, the Bible sustained all prayer. It was not a succession of books to be read one after the other, but the unfolding of something unique and even mysterious, centered totally on Christ. It is ultimately Christ whom *lectio* helps us to find in order to bring to our life and experience what was in him—to meet him, receive his Spirit, and enter into communion with his entire Mystical Body. To read God's word while praying it, to read about God in accordance with the tradition of the ages (including the present one), to study God—these were the means of encountering God in a vital way in order to be able to radiate God's presence throughout the universe. Reviving an idea and term used by Gregory the Great, Smaragdus, speaking about reading and sharing after having discussed prayer and psalmody and before coming to love of God and neighbor, wrote: "Sacred Scripture, in a manner of speaking, sprouts and grows with those who read it. Uncultivated readers are led to explore it, while those who are instructed find it ever new" (*Diadem of Monks* 3 [*PL* 102, col. 598A]).

## Contemplative Prayer

In order to convey expressively the frequent, diligent, and repetitive character that was proper to prayerful activity, people in the Middle Ages liked to compare the monks to ruminant animals. The texts that indicate this are numerous. There is one in the *Life* of St. Gerard of Brogne which defends the legitimacy of applying words that designated the various stages of rumination (mastication, the sense of taste, digestion and its effects) to spiritual activity (*Life of Gerard* 20).[3] Such images attempted to show the importance of incorporating the word of God into one's life in order to become assimilated into divinity and to nourish prayer. All these practices constituted what the Middle Ages called "spiritual exercise," and the fact that this expression was deliberately used in the singular is indicative of the unity that existed between the various "exercises." *Lectio*, meditation, and prayer were inseparable from asceticism and penance; like the latter, they presupposed repentance and were supposed to lead to "contemplation."

*Contemplatio* was a term that was often associated with *lectio, meditatio,* and *oratio.* This term must be properly understood. It did not designate solely, or primarily (as was often the case in later periods), highly elevated states of prayer that belong to the order of the contemplative life and are exceptional and rare. The words that have been used here—*oratio, lectio, meditatio,* etc.—designate the activities and spiritual attitudes that together constituted "contemplative prayer."

Descriptions of this contemplative prayer became especially frequent in the *Lives* of saints from the beginning of the thirteenth century, before they became in later centuries the object of more developed accounts or even of actual treatises. But what is said in these documents, hagiographical or otherwise, conforms to what the most ancient sources reveal. It was always a question of one unified activity and of one contemplative life, where prayer was surrounded by other spiritual activities, which prepared for it and extended it. If the act of prayer was ordinarily brief, the state of prayer could and had to be habitual and continuous. It was constituted by an enduring attitude of meditation and attentiveness to God, as a result of which everything became prayer and longing. This latter word reveals the reason for all this activity: "We must not devote ourselves to prayer once or twice, but frequently, diligently, letting God know the longings of our hearts and letting him hear, at times, the voice of our mouth. This is why it is said: 'Let your petitions be made known to God,' which happens as a result of persistence and diligence in prayer" (Bernard of Clairvaux *Sermon on Advent* 9).[4]

## After the Eleventh Century

From the end of the eleventh century, one of the activities of prayer began to be the object of a special kind of literature, which came to include two genres. The first consisted in the extension of texts in which Augustine addressed God or himself in prayer (e.g., the *Confessions* and *Soliloquies*). John of Fécamp (d. 1078) composed three successive editions of a long prayer of praise and supplication. The edition entitled *The Theological* (i.e., "contemplative") *Confession* was afterwards divided into short sections which, combined with similar selections from Augustine and other authors, was widely read under the title of *Meditations of St. Augustine.* The idea was to propose formulas that a reader could make the object of private reading. Anselm (d. 1109) composed a collection, *Meditations and Prayers,* which was of the same genre.[5] There was nothing methodical in any of this: it was simply a question of providing material for *lectio divina.* Nor was there anything laborious: the criterion that fixed the duration of the exercise was the pleasure it provided. Similarly, Arnold of Bonneval (d. after 1156) edited some texts dealing with the mysteries of Christ, which were to be read in the same way. Some of these were given the title *Meditations* by later editors. William of St. Thierry (d. 1148) also produced a volume entitled *Meditative Prayers,* which came close to the genre of the texts attributed to Augustine and John of Fécamp. Among the Cistercians, Bernard of Clairvaux inserted into the second half of his treatise *In Praise of the New Knighthood* a series of lofty reflections on each of the mysteries of Christ that were accomplished in the holy places. Aelred of Rievaulx (d. 1166), in his *Rule for Recluses,* also proposed themes for contemplation of the mysteries. All of these texts provided material for meditative reading but presented neither an elaborate reflection on the nature of meditation nor a method.

It was outside the Benedictine tradition that texts began to appear which dealt with these latter two issues. The canons regular, such as Hugh of St. Victor and others whose writings circulated under his name, tried to situate meditation among the other activities of prayer with more precision than the monastic tradition had achieved.[6] This resulted in several series of classifications, which became more and more systematic but still did not include a method for how to enter into each of these activities. The same thing holds true for the *Ladder of Monks* of the Carthusian Guigo II (d. ca. 1188). It was out of these distinctions and schemas that there later developed the beginnings of a method for the practice of meditation and for the activities associated with it. This second genre of literature began to encourage "methodical prayer."

The imagination held a strong place in this. Bernard justified this emphasis by putting forth the idea of the incarnate Word "descending into our imagination" (*Sermon on the Nativity of the Blessed Virgin* 10).[7] Since God, first in the Bible and then in the incarnation, made himself visible in order to save and sanctify our imagination, the good use to which we put it helps us to come to our primary attitude and activity in relation to God, that is, prayer. Following upon the principle set forth by Bernard, practical applications were soon presented under the form of meditations elaborated from the imagination by an anonymous twelfth-century monk, by Aelred of Rievaulx, and later by many others.

## Conditions for and Effects of Diligent Prayer

The ensemble of prayerful exercises discussed above could only be conceived and actualized within a way of life, that is, monasticism, which, for all its variations according to era, environment, and traditions, included common elements. It goes without saying that all prayer was introduced, sustained, and nourished by what was often called psalmody, a word that included the entire Divine Office, whose basic text was the Psalter. The history of actual life in most monasteries, which is gradually becoming better known, reveals that they were (except during some exceptional periods) circumscribed communities that often contained a small number of monks and nuns. Many of these innumerable "priories" (or similar houses that were called by a different name) had only a limited liturgical life for want of having at their disposal all the necessary manuscripts for a complex liturgy. It was, however, the Divine Office which, wherever possible, facilitated all other prayer and provided for its expansion. As for the *laus perennis,* which consisted in groups successively reciting the psalms without interruption, this was only achieved in certain places from the sixth to the eighth century. Prolonged psalmody, called "prolix," although not continuous, was practiced at Cluny and elsewhere.

All of this prayer involved meditation and therefore separation from the noise and tumult of secular life; it involved asceticism, therefore fasting, vigils, and the whole gamut of monastic observance. It involved silence, purification of the heart, humility, repentance, and patience. A certain ennui (*taedium*), which was engendered by the continuity and monotony of the regular life, became one of the forms of mortification that one had to accept generously. Work of various kinds was also a part of daily life.

To judge it according to all the evidence we have at our disposal, this existence was centered in prayer. It possessed an aspect of variety introduced by the succession of daily activities and the unfolding of the liturgical cycle, and it engendered a peace without exultation or sadness, as well as a tranquil joy which manifested itself in so many works of art of every kind. The quiet and leisure (*quies, otium*) which the life of monastic prayer required and promoted was indeed a source of artistic creativity. All the works it produced attest to the importance of imagination and hope in monastic spirituality: an imagination that was thoroughly biblical and a hope that spontaneously looked toward the heavenly Jerusalem.

*Translated by Dennis Tamburello*

### Notes

1. Smaragdus's primary work on prayer is the *Diadem of Monks,* which may be found in *PL* 102, cols. 593–690. He also wrote a commentary on the *Rule of St. Benedict.*

2. *Sancti Bernardi opera,* ed. J. Leclercq et al. (8 vols.; Rome: Editiones Cistercienses, 1957–77) 1:8.

3. *MGH, SS* 15, p. 671.

4. *Sancti Bernardi opera,* 5:18.

5. See the discussion of these prayers in the article by Benedicta Ward in this volume.
6. See the article by Grover Zinn in this volume.
7. *Sancti Bernardi opera,* 5:282.

## Bibliography

### Studies

Butler, Cuthbert. *Western Mysticism: The Teaching of Augustine, Gregory and Bernard on Contemplation and the Contemplative Life.* 3rd ed. London: Constable, 1967. A classic treatment.

Leclercq, Jean. *The Love of Learning and the Desire for God: A Study of Monastic Culture.* New York: Fordham University Press, 1961.

———. "*Otium Monasticum* as a Context for Artistic Creativity." In *Monasticism and the Arts,* 63–80. Edited by Timothy Gregory Verdon. Syracuse, NY: Syracuse University Press, 1984.

———. "Prayer at Cluny." *Journal of the American Academy of Religion* 51 (1983) 351–65.

Rousse, Jacques, and Hermann Joseph Sieben. "Lectio divina." In *Dict. Sp.* 9, cols. 470–96.

Severus, Emmanuel von, Aimé Solignac, and Matthias Gossens. "Méditation." In *Dict. Sp.* 10, cols. 906–19.

Szarmach, Paul, ed. *An Introduction to the Medieval Mystics of Europe.* Albany: State University of New York Press, 1984.

Vaggagini, Cipriano, ed. *La pregheria nella Bibbia e nella tradizione patristica e monastica.* Rome: Biblioteca di cultura religiosa, 1978.

Vogüé, Adalabert, de. "*Orationi frequenter incumbere:* Une invitation à la prière continuelle." *Revue d'ascétique et de la mystique* 41 (1965) 467–72.

# 17

# The Notion of Virginity in the Early Church

PETER BROWN

FROM AN EARLY PERIOD, in some sectors, and universally after around 300 C.E., the ideal of virginity, practiced equally by men and women, enjoyed a moral and cultural supremacy in the Christian church that remained unchallenged until the Reformation. The leadership of the church itself—certainly its most articulate and authoritative leadership—tended to coagulate (to varying degrees, and at varying speeds, according to the differences of the Christian regions) into the hands of those known to be sexually continent. As a result, both the structures of authority and the dominant ideals of Christianity communities came to contrast irrevocably with those of their pagan, Jewish, Zoroastrian, and, later, Muslim neighbors. "For you have received a curse," Jews would tell Aphraat, a bishop in early fourth-century Iraq, "and have multiplied barrenness" (Aphraat *Demonstration* 18.1). "This virtue," John Chrysostom would reply, in Antioch, "is above human nature; it is an alien force in human affairs" (*Religious Women* 1.5 [*PG* 47, col. 514]). And for that reason alone virginity was frequently paraded as yet one further manifestation of the suprahuman origins of the Christian faith.

By "virginity" Christians tended to mean lifelong abstinence from sexual intercourse. Thus, the precise physical state of virginity was upheld as the state to which all human beings—men quite as much as women—had every right to aspire. The virginity of a young woman conventionally held to be guarded by her family until it could be terminated (frequently at an age far closer to puberty than is the case in modern Western societies) by marriage, by penetration, and by consequent conception and childbirth. Continence, however, was the more usual option for many males. This involved the irrevocable renunciation of all future sexual relations. Such renunciation might follow youthful sexual activity, it might come with widowerhood, or it might even be practiced within marriage itself by withdrawal from the marriage bed. It was the intended perpetuity of the renunciation that mattered. Thus, temporary continence, like fasting, was widely practiced in the early church; however, since it lacked the overtones of perpetuity, such temporary abstinence from sexual relations never came to bear the same symbolic charge. It is not the purpose of this essay to explain why this ideal gained such prominence in the early church. Rather, it might be helpful to explain precisely *what* this ideal meant to Christians of the "classical" age of its expression, in the fourth and fifth centuries. In that period, writers such as Athanasius, Gregory of Nyssa, John Chrysostom, Ephrem the Syrian, Ambrose, and Jerome (to name only the better known) mobilized all the resources of a late classical culture in its Christian form to glorify the practice of virginity. In so doing they laid bare, frequently with rare candor and precision, the wider human and social implications of such an ideal. This essay will concentrate, therefore, less on what these writers said than on the seriousness of the concerns that underlay their discourse.

It is easy for the modern reader, with modern, frequently post-Puritan, notions of sexuality, to trivialize the implications of the notion of virginity for the members of an ancient Mediterranean society. For ancient persons, the center of gravity of the notion did not lie—as we might automatically expect that it must lie—solely in the repression of sexuality in the individual as an end in itself. We must learn to be more faithful to the harsh precision of the imagery current in the ancient world: virginity was a state that was expected to be terminated by a *social* act. In losing her physical intactness in the consummation of an arranged marriage—and, so it was hoped, conceiving a child that was a mixture and a new departure for both families— the young woman was conscripted as a fully productive member by her society, as, indeed, was her spouse, in a less obvious but equally definitive manner. Intercourse was the necessary act on which the solidarity and the perpetuity of the human race depended. It was also, fortunately, an act that could be habitually associated with considerable personal enjoyment: indeed, it was an act presented for both parties as one of the most delightful, and hence one of the most irresistible, of human sensations. Thus, the loss of virginity, though an act of irrevocable recruitment into and possession by society, was at the same time associated on the personal level with the sweet violence of a passion from which no human being could wish to feel himself or herself exempt. Hence personal experiences of sexuality and the desire for such experiences merged so inextricably with the social implications of marital intercourse that it is easy to read an early Christian treatise on virginity as if it were simply an attack on the joys of sex. Yet the muted logic of the argument was plain: solidarity in accepting the strength and the delight of the sexual urge implied solidarity in a willingness to be married. And this, in turn, implied a willingness to be conscripted into society as normally constituted in a late classical, Jewish, or Zoroastrian environment. Thus, when those who wished to maintain their state of virginity were told, in no uncertain terms, that they must learn "to war against human nature itself," the writers had in mind not solely the struggle against the tensions of an unfulfilled sexuality—serious though that might be and frequently expatiated upon by writers such as Jerome (whose writings have contributed heavily, and disastrously, to modern stereotypes). Behind these inner physical conflicts there lay the effort to brace the person against the force of social convention that threatened to sweep the individual, with the silent violence of a landslip, into his or her "natural" social role as a married person, sexually active in order to produce children.

To uphold virginity, therefore, was to commit oneself, by implication, to a different image of the grounds of cohesion of society. In ancient views, virginity was there to be lost—as a beautifully flowering meadow must bloom and then be scythed, or as the green earth must be tilled before it can bear fruit. It was one stage only (if a poignantly precious stage) in a cyclical movement by which all boys and girls were swept, by the process of physical maturation, into the enduring human compact of those "who marry and are given in marriage." To render that one stage permanent was to halt the benign circulation of marriage partners and to deny the solidarities that sprang from such circulation. By the fourth century, such a view had come to mean, in practice, that a number of young, well-placed persons, by deciding "to make their bodies holy," had, in fact, made plain that they considered that they had the right to dispose of their bodies as they pleased, by keeping them in their virgin state, out of circulation in society. Thus, the body itself was held to be no longer permeable to the demands that society made upon it. In that sense, a young man's body could be as "intact," as free from penetration by society, as that of any young woman's and a virgin woman could present as "hard" a boundary to the outside world as did any man. The body, indeed, had become a tangible *locus* on which the freedom of the will could be exercised, in choices that intimately affected the conventional fabric of society.

The radical social implications of this notion were spelled out in many ways. The life of the sexually continent was presented as an exact imitation on earth of the "life of the angels." By this Christians meant a life in society—for what group was more harmonious than were the angels of heaven?—but in a society no longer formed by bonds of marriage, family, and kinship. Such was the interpretation that was given to the promise of Christ to the "sons of God": "For when they rise from the dead, they neither marry nor are given in marriage, but are like angels in heaven" (Mark 12:25; cf. Matt 22:29–30 and Luke 20:34–36).

Exegesis of the story of the fall of Adam and Eve concentrated insistently on the virginal state of the first human couple. In sharp contrast to rabbinic exegesis of Genesis (which may have been elaborated to counter Christian views), Adam and Eve were presented as presexual, and, by implication, as presocial beings. They had not been created so as to be given in marriage to each other by God, duly consummating the divinely arranged match by sexual intercourse in Eden. On the contrary, the fall of Adam and Eve had either consisted in, or had necessarily led to, their joining together in the wrong manner—that is, in sexual intercourse. The more radical view saw the fall itself as due to the manner in which Adam and Eve had abandoned their "angelic" status by imitating beasts in having intercourse. The less radical interpretation (as expressed by writers such as Gregory of Nyssa and John Chrysostom) nonetheless insisted that the present human need for the consolations of marriage, for intercourse, and for the joy of children sprang directly from the chill dread of death and sense of physical transience that had followed fast upon the fall. In either case, the ideal structures of a truly "human" society—that is, a society formed of purely voluntary joinings, as harmonious as the vibrant unison of the angels around the throne of God— came to form a yardstick with which to judge, and to find sadly wanting, the present structures of a human society based upon marriage, upon the family, and hence, in the last analysis, upon those ambiguous sexual drives which men and women, in their fallen, "post-angelic" state, shared with the animal world.

At its most bleak, we have a "de-mystified" vision of society. It is no longer natural, in that it can no longer claim to base its cohesion and recruitment on the fulfillment of natural drives—toward sexual joining and, hence, toward marriage and the joys of progeny. Rather, the existing human community is seen as no more than the factitious creation of a sexual social contract. Like Adam and Eve, each individual is free to withhold or to surrender his or her body to society. And the majority of choices are "falls" in miniature, by which weakened human beings lightly surrender their inalienable right to join the harmonious society of the angels and decide instead to swell the abrasive, transient, and tarnished "communion" of the married.

It is important to realize that the most radical exponents of such views were usually those most fervently committed to the ideal of the creation, within the Christian church, of alternative forms of social grouping. The notion of virginity and the radical exegesis of the story of Adam and Eve provided conceptual tools of great emotive power with which to explore the possibilities of the Christian community as a voluntary association. For a society no longer held together by a sexual social contract was, in many ways, a *tabula rasa:* it might regroup itself in a very different manner from that current in the surrounding world. Along with marriage, it might abandon also those other great "dividing walls" associated with a normal, marriage-based, society—the institution of slavery and the exclusion of women.

Such radicalism was surprisingly widespread in the early church. It had its roots, as far as we can now see, in currents of sectarian Judaism exemplified by the Essenes and now illustrated in the Dead Sea Scrolls. By around 300 C.E., the dividing line that had come to separate radical groups—who were named, largely for the sake of scholarly convenience, Encratites, "abstainers"—from the main consensus of the Christian communities tended to be drawn between the radicals who expected that such a total restructuring of society, based on sexual abstinence, would be applied to the community of Christians as a whole, and those who thought that the potent mirage of an "angelic" solidarity should be set to work among the members of the elite alone. Ever since Paul's first letter to the Corinthians in the year 54 there had been a strong tendency within the Christian communities, and especially in the urban communities, to limit such perilous and fascinating experiments to their leaders. The radical current constantly tended to spill out so as to form little groups of total "abstainers." Many of these communities lived up to the radical conclusions that they had drawn from the myth of the fall of Adam and Eve. They shocked contemporaries by the freedom from restraint of their womenfolk, who mixed easily with their virginal "brothers" and frequently exercised roles of leadership. More usually, however, the radical current was canalized into the upper echelons of the "great church."

Thus canalized, it impinged with the force of a millrace. The creation of a cultivated elite of "virgin" teachers, equally accessible to men and women, from Origen to Jerome; the emergence of great monasteries and nunneries as alternative societies in miniature, perched on the edge of the settled world throughout the Mediterranean; the huge esprit de corps of an increasingly celibate upper clergy—these all sprang from the need to create in the church groupings that had all the solidarity, the will to survive over time, and the authority of a political community, and yet which pointedly lacked the one ingredient on which political communities had usually rested in the ancient world—the solid flesh and blood of family and kinship. The virgin state was praised as the state of "true" joining, and so as the source of "true" and abiding progeny. We should be careful not to dismiss such hyperboles as if they were merely rhetoric or as if they betrayed a somewhat pathetic sublimation of the procreative urge in so many useless male bodies, so many empty wombs. For in such a statement we can touch on the zest with which the clergy and ascetics of the fourth and fifth centuries had set about creating enduring institutions and lasting forms of cultural transmission on a foundation as seemingly etherial, and yet as tenacious, as the will of a gifted minority to construct a society that they could regard as a society based ideally on freedom of choice and not on the usual, "organic" bonds of a family-based society. This was in the light of their high theory of virginity, if not always in practice; for children were frequently "donated" to monasteries and to the clergy with as little respect for their wills as once they had been married off.

Such considerations were implied in the notion of virginity in its classical form. Important though it may be for a modern reader to recapture them, they are not the only ones that would have occurred to a Christian of late antiquity. Equally important was the appeal of the virgin state as a form of "mediation" between the divine and the human. In the words of Gregory of Nyssa:

> For in the Virgin Birth, virginity has led God to partake in the life of human beings, and in the state of virginity the human person has been given the wings with which to rise to a desire for the things of heaven. And so virginity has become the linking-force that assures the intimacy of human beings with God; and by the mediation of the virgin state there comes about the harmonious joining of two beings of such widely distant natures. (*On Virginity* 2)

When we read such a passage, we must remember the corollary, as this has been spelled out by a recent tradition of structural anthropology: that is, although "the central 'problem' of religion is . . . to reestablish some kind of bridge between Man and God . . . 'mediation' (in this sense) is always achieved by introducing a third category which is 'abnormal' in terms of ordinary 'rational' categories. . . . The middle ground is abnormal, nonnatural, holy. It is typically the focus of all taboos and ritual observances."[1]

Indeed, a heavy sense of paradox always surrounded the figure of the virgin. For here were ordinary men and women, the fruit of sexual intercourse, only too well aware in most cases of the abiding strength of their own sexual nature; still bound to their fellows by a common need to eat, to sleep, to breathe; and, like them all, doomed to death. Yet, at the same time, they "lived the life of the angels of heaven" on earth; they maintained in their unconscripted bodies the primal integrity of Adam and Eve; they enjoyed the "first fruits of the resurrection." They were frequently made ritually separate from their fellows as the privileged "betrothed of Christ": ceremonies of the veiling of nuns, based on marriage rituals, grew in dramatic explicitness and in binding power in the course of the fourth century, and the monastic "profession" of a male was an equally solemn undertaking. As a result of all this, their frail bodies were believed to have become "temples of the Holy Spirit."

Seen in this light, that is, in terms of a potent emphasis on the virgin body as the "abnormal" mediator between the human and the divine, the causes usually invoked to explain the emergence of the ideal of virginity in late antiquity may need to be reassessed. Explanation can never be limited—as it is only too easy for a modern scholar to limit it—exclusively to attitudes to sexuality. The emergence of the ideal, therefore, cannot be explained solely in terms of a mounting disquietude in pagan and Christian circles with the physical, and particularly with the sexual, components of the human person. This is a secondary cause and may well be quite a superficial one in comparison with the voiceless, geological pressures set up within the religious system of late antique Christianity itself, by its search for cogent and tangible forms of mediation between God and humanity.

For Christians shared with their contemporaries of late antiquity a haunting sense of the distance between God and humanity, between the heavenly and the earthly, between God's invisible creation—the angelic society—and God's visible creatures—the material world and the human race. Yet to this they added a quite peculiar insistence on the possibility of a joining of these antithetical spheres—and especially on the possibility that such a joining could happen through the persons of human beings. Christianity had rendered itself patently absurd to thinking pagans—and even more so to Jews, as later to Muslims—by its doctrine of the direct, unmediated joining of the highest God to human flesh in the person of Christ. A stunned sense of the mystery of the incarnation loomed over the mind of every great Christian writer who turned the pen, in more peaceful moments, to the easier topic of the praise of the virgin life. The religion included dramatic rituals of participation, of transformation, of ritual promotion, by which human beings were moved from one antithetical category into the other. Baptism raised the believer from a being of clay to the fiery essence of the angels. The faithful sang with the cherubim before the throne of God at the Eucharist and then proceeded to participate in the body and blood of that God. Prophecy, martyrdom, ascetic sanctification were believed to have raised human beings to an intimacy with God as close as that of any angel. The universe rang with the supplications of the saints in behalf of the faithful on earth, and the explosion of the cult of saints and of their physical remains rendered magnificently concrete the heady belief in the unceasing possibility of a joining of heaven and earth.

It is worthwhile to note how little other religious systems shared this distinctive ordering of experience. In Judaism, as later in Islam, the antithesis of God and humanity, Creator and created, was sensed to be too mighty to admit the insertion of "angelic" human beings as mediating figures. This may be one reason, among so many, why a notion of the peculiar excellence of the virgin state never gained a central place in either religion. Contemporary pagan thought of the Platonic school shared the obsession of the Christians with the possibility of mediating antithetical categories. Yet it arrived at significantly different conclusions. For if the primary antithesis that needed to be mediated, for the Platonist, was that between the invisible world of pure spirit, the world of the Ideas and of the intelligible gods, and the visible world of matter, then human beings appeared too deeply tainted with matter—in their earthly existence, at any rate—ever to rise to a mediating position. The etherial *daemones*, abnormal creatures in that they shared immortality with the gods and bodily emotions with the human race (along with the few great souls who, after death alone, had joined their ranks), were the towering, etherial figures who filled the gap in pagan minds between heaven and earth.

Faced with these alternative responses to the burning issue of mediation, what the historian has to explain is less why the notion of virginity rose to such prominence in late antiquity than one very peculiar feature of this notion in Christian circles—that is, the enormous symbolic weight placed on the individual human body as an obsessively significant locus of that "abnormal, not-natural, holy" mediation of human and divine. Virginity was an intensely physical state of the body. The intact body of the virgin woman remained throughout the organizing image of the whole notion. A body in this state—or, at least, a body perpetually removed from future sexual experience—was treated as a "temple of the Holy Spirit" in the most concrete manner: in the words of one treatise, a virgin was "the Holy Spirit given a body." The shift in perspective is a dramatic one. The joyful, transforming embrace between the divine and the material world, which Plotinus, the great pagan Platonist, was prepared to see above all in the "holy" body of the cosmos as a whole, made most visible in the shimmering order of the stars, has narrowed down, in Christian spirituality, to the embrace of Christ with his betrothed, the individual virgin. This embrace was sincerely expected to render the body itself holy—to penetrate with its fine perfume the frail, physical frame of the good Roman nun. Little wonder, then, that she was solemnly advised not to lean back in her tub while having a bath, lest "common" water lap over a body made sacred by the Holy Spirit!

It is here that we might fruitfully return to the overwhelming importance of the *social* implications of the virgin state in late antiquity. For what was "abnormal" about the virgin body was not necessarily that it was a human body whose sexual drives had been overcome, an uncanny enough achieve-ment though that might seem to the average observer. On the deeper level that we have explored, the virgin body was abnormal largely because it was, by normal categories, profoundly asocial—it did not belong to society as naturally defined.

The emphasis on the withdrawal of the person as a whole from the claims of society led to a significant modification of long-established views of the human person. Many writers on virginity, such as Gregory of Nyssa and Ambrose, still moved unthinkingly in a Platonic universe. Yet although they might use phrases borrowed from the works of Plato, their distinctive con-centration on the specifically social implications of the ideal of virginity came to erode one crucial facet of the thought of classical Greece—that "sharp dichotomy between the self and the body . . . the most far-reaching, and perhaps the most questionable, of her gifts to human culture."[2]

For in their works on virginity, the "withdrawal" of the soul from the body, on which Socrates had spoken so resonantly in Plato's *Phaedo*, came to be overshadowed by a different concern— the withdrawal of the body itself from society. Socrates was the well-rooted inhabitant of the Greek *polis*. He was a man who had married, who had begotten children, who had served in the armies of Athens. He might have wished, in the hours before his execution, that he had spent all his life learning gradually how to say good-bye to the body—to that garrulous, flighty, and uninformative com-panion who would soon lie silent, as the draft of hemlock took its effect, leaving the true Socrates, Socrates the soul, to feast undistracted on the eternal beauty. But Plato never doubted for a moment that the *polis* had complete control over the bodies of its young: that the fertility of its young females must be mobilized for childbirth and that the high spirits of its young males must be made available for procreation and for the organized violence of war. In contrast, the young men and women envisioned by Gregory of Nyssa, who had decided to "make their bodies holy," made them holy by setting them aside from the demands made upon them by society. They took the body itself across the mighty divide that separated the self from society.

This body, of course, frequently remained as unruly as ever before. The commonplaces of ascetic exhortation did, indeed, draw all too heavily on the old Platonic dichotomy of self and body when faced with the powers of the untamed flesh. Only a few ascetic writers of outstanding insight, reared in the harsh yet perspicacious school of the desert fathers—men such as Evagrius and John Cassian, later Dorotheus of Gaza and John Clima-cus—realized that a different image of the body implied, in fact, a subtly different approach to the moral struggle. This struggle was directed no longer to the dismissal of the body but to its intimate sanctification: hence an attention to the precise ebb and flow of sexual feelings in the body. These came to be treated at times less as the stirrings of an area alien to the true self than as merciful reminders of the deeper tensions of the soul, made manifest by God's patient kindness in the mysterious recesses of the body. For, as John Climacus wrote in around 630: "I do not think that anyone should be classed as a saint until he has made his body holy, if indeed that is possible" (*Ladder of Divine Ascent,* step 15).

*C'est le premier pas qui coûte.* To have withdrawn the body as a whole from society was to make a particularly concrete and intimate statement about the nature of one form of human solidarily—the common bonds of society, expressed at their lowest common denominator in terms of sexual needs, of sexual joining, and of the natural forms of union that sprang from such joining: family, offspring, kin. It was to assert, instead, the right of the individual to seek for himself or herself different forms of solidarity, more consonant with the high destiny of free persons, able to enter into a freely chosen harmony of wills, which, so Christians of late antiquity believed, was the particular joy of the undivided life of the "angels of heaven."

The early Byzantine cult of the Virgin Mary throws into high relief the concerns that had underlain the classical Christian discourse on virginity, by approaching these from an unfamiliar angle. For behind the mounting fervor of the cult of the Virgin as *Theotokos*—she who gave birth to God— and as intercessor for the human race, we can detect the final playing out of the half-conscious logic of the virgin state. In the art, the liturgy, the poetry, and the preaching of the fifth and sixth centuries, we see these concerns as they were viewed not only by a restricted elite of ascetics and patrons of nuns but also by the populations of the great Christian cities of the Byzantine Near East.

The debate about virginity, as we have seen, was in large part a debate about the nature of human solidarity. It was a debate about what the individual did and did not need to share with fellow humans. In the figure of the Virgin and in her peculiar relationship with Christ the paradoxes inherent in the early Christian notion of virginity came to a head. For God, as Christ, had chosen to assert his solidarity with the human race in the most intimate possible manner, by taking his flesh from Mary's womb and then by nurturing that flesh through dependence on her breasts. To a Byzantine, no natural bond of society could be as strong or as unambiguously good as was the double bond of the womb and of the nurturing breast. As a queen said, when pleading for the life of a prince in a Coptic tale: "Wilt thou not bear in thy mind, O king, that it was the womb of a woman that carried this prince, like any other person, and that it was the breasts of a

30. *Roundel of Saint Thecla in the Lions' Den,*
Egyptian, 5th century

31. *Icon of the Virgin: Tapestry Panel,*
Egyptian, 6th century

woman that suckled him, even as my beloved child was suckled at my breasts."[3]

The inhabitants of the Byzantine cities were members of a society notorious for its abrasiveness and marked by chasms between the rich and the poor, the powerful and the helpless, which bruised the soul of preachers such as John Chrysostom. These inhabitants instinctively fell back upon the potent trace memory of a warm and nurturing solidarity between mother and child as the last, vestigial right of all to a common human nature and so to a common claim to human love in a divided and inhumane world. And God had chosen precisely that bond with which to make plain his intimate union with a suffering humanity.

Yet, for mere human beings, the impetus of the notion of virginity had been precisely to evaporate all such merely natural bonds. If Christ was to be considered a member of the human race, it could not possibly be a membership gained through the conventional, deeply tarnished solidarity of the sexual social contract. Rather, he had to be the fruit of a virgin womb. With unfailing circumstantiality, writers on the virgin birth made plain that Christ had always been spoken of as the "fruit of the womb": that is, he had been conceived within the womb alone, without male penetration of the vagina. In this, he had recaptured the presocial majesty of Adam's first state. No joining of two bodies, no penetration of the one by the other, no admixture of male seed had produced Adam—molded by God from the "virgin," untilled earth of Eden—or Eve—taken from Adam's side—or Christ—formed from the flesh of the virgin entirely within the womb of Mary, without the intervention of male seed. And so Christ had entered the human race marvelously exempt from those cloying solidarities against which mere human virgins had to battle ceaselessly and with such great pain of spirit throughout their lives—solidarities seen, in contrast to the solitary forming of Christ in Mary's womb, to be as intimate and as pervasive as the unruly admixture associated with the act of conception.

Yet, so perfect a triumph of the classical paradigm of virginity left part of the mind and heart unsatisfied. The figure of Christ as the New Adam could only too easily come to be surrounded by the eerie flicker of the "earthborn," of the imperfectly human; whereas Christ as God might remain separated from humanity by the towering majesty of his divine status. For how could a human being who had not been born through human society ever come to show that *sympatheia,* that deep strain of human compassion for one's fellow beings, which enjoyed such poignant esteem among Byzantines, who knew only too well that such fellow feeling was a rare human trait? Hence the enormous emotional importance to the early Byzantine believer of that double bond of the womb and the breasts established between the human

Mary and her divine child. God might be prayed to as a God who "alone loves humanity," and as the Compassionate One. But to be reassured that such high epithets were really true and, above all, relevant to day-to-day existence, Byzantines turned to their icons and to their hymns of the Virgin. For, in enabling God, as Christ, to become human, by carrying him in her womb and by maintaining his physical life through her breasts, Mary, in fact, had made God humane.

In so doing, Mary enjoyed a closeness to the very emperor of heaven at the thought of which all Byzantines shuddered. The sense of a divine majesty made totally available to a single, frail human being brought out the best in the great Christian poets of the Byzantine East, Ephrem the Syrian in the fourth century, Romanos Melodes in the sixth. For the style of a whole Christian society was rendered visible in the figure of the Virgin holding the Ruler of All on her knees. All its deepest hopes and fears about the access of the weak to the powerful, of humanity to God clustered around the crib at Bethlehem:

> The One of Fire Mary now carries in her fingers.
> The Holy Flame is hugged to her side.
> The Burning God grasps at her breasts.
> . . . . . . . . . . . . . . . . . . . . . . .
> O, who has seen the Holy Fire
> wrapping itself in swaddling bands?
> (Ephrem the Syrian *Carmina Soghita* 1)

Contemplating that hushed moment, one could easily assume that a half millennium of obstinate and frequently shrill debate on how human beings might draw close to God, but at the cost of so great a portion of that warm fabric woven by the ancient solidarities of the flesh, had suddenly been resolved—and resolved in a moment of loving contact that hymn-writers and preachers of late antiquity (good monks or admirers of the monks) could express only in terms of haunting sensuality:

Thou didst stretch out thy right arm (O Mother of God), thou didst take Him and make Him lie on thy left arm. Thou didst bend thy neck, and let thy hair fall over Him. . . . He stretched out His hand, He took thy breast, as he drew into His mouth the milk which was sweeter than manna. . . . And He at Whom the Seraphim could not gaze, and into Whose face the angels were never able to look, did the Holy Virgin dandle in her hands . . . and she made bold without fear, and called Him "My Son," and He called her also, "My Mother." (Cyril of Jerusalem *Discourse on the Theotokos*)[4]

## Notes

1. Edmund Leach, *Genesis as Myth* (London: Cape, 1969) 10.
2. E. R. Dodds, *Pagan and Christian in an Age of Anxiety* (Cambridge: Cambridge University Press, 1965.
3. *Encomium on Theodore the Anatolian,* in *Miscellaneous Coptic Texts in the Dialect of Upper Egypt,* ed. E. A. W. Budge, 593.
4. *Discourse on the Theotokos by Cyril Archbishop of Jerusalem,* in *Miscellaneous Coptic Texts in the Dialect of Upper Egypt,* ed. E. A. W. Budge, 701, 717.

## Bibliography

### Sources

Ambrose of Milan. *Concerning Virgins.* Translated by E. de Romestin and H. T. F. Duckworth. NPNF, 2nd series, 10. 1955.

Gregory of Nyssa. *Grégoire de Nysse: Traité de la Virginité.* Edited by M. Aubineau. Sources chrétiennes 119. Paris: Cerf, 1966.

———. *Ascetical Works.* Translated by V. W. Callahan. Fathers 58. 1967. See especially *On Virginity* (pp. 3–75) and *Life of Saint Macrina* (pp. 161–91).

Jerome. *Letters.* Translated by C. C. Mierow. ACW 33. 1963. See especially *Letter 22* (pp. 134–79).

John Chrysostom. *Jean Chrysostome: La Virginité.* Edited by H. Musurillo and B. Grillet. Sources chrétiennes 125. Paris: Cerf, 1966.

Methodius of Olympus. *Méthode d'Olympe: Le Banquet.* Edited by H. Musurillo. Sources chrétiennes 95. Paris: Cerf, 1963.

———. *The Symposium: A Treatise on Chastity.* Translated by H. Musurillo. ACW 27. 1958.

### Studies

One should always bear in mind that the statements of the classic sources, on which most accounts depend, emerged from a plethora of lesser exhortations to the virgin state, mostly anonymous; see especially Amand and Moons, Aubineau. For the Latin world, the works of Ambrose have been particularly well studied by Duval, Consolino ("Dagli 'exempla'").

The views described in this article are those of a vocal and influential segment of early Christian opinion, but they were by no means dominant at every time or in every region. Forms of expression varied greatly from region to region, as can best be appreciated by comparing the Greek authors with those of the Syriac-speaking world of Syria and Mesopotamia; see Murray ("The Exhortation") and the vivid introductory survey of Vööbus. Some leading thinkers were impermeable to the idea in its classic form, most notably Augustine of Hippo; see Müller, Brown.

The growth of celibacy in the church was not a development that is linked at every stage to the deployment of a classic notion of virginity. Indeed, many other unrelated factors contributed to the emergence of a celibate male clergy in the upper echelons of the Christian church; see Gryson.

Ever since the Reformation, the study of the ideal of virginity in the early church has been bemired in a quest for its origins. Celibate militancy can be seen to have existed in later Judaism; see Black, Guillaumont ("Monachisme"). Baltensweiler and Nieder-wimmer are careful surveys. On the views of Paul and his communities, Chadwick ("All Things") remains exceptionally level-headed. On discipleship and the abandonment of marriage, see Kretschmar.

The idea that the renunciation of sexuality is explicable (and, by implication, excusable) as an overreaction to the depravity of the surrounding pagan world must be abandoned. If anything, the ideal represented a radical challenge to the emphasis increasingly placed on conventional marriage as a privileged symbol of social order among the elites of the Roman Empire; see Veyne. Rousselle is particularly revealing on the medical notions associated with virginity and on the problems of marital sexuality in the Roman world.

On Encratite radicalism, see especially Pagels. Chadwick ("Enkrateia") is a judicious survey.

On the presexual nature of Adam and Eve in radical Christian and Gnostic exegesis, see especially Klijn. On the expectation of a transcendence of sexuality and of gender differences associated with the rite of baptism, see particularly Meeks, Smith. We should not underestimate the tenacity with which such ideas recurred in ascetic circles; see Guillaumont ("Le nom"), Patlagean ("L'histoire"). Within the ascetic movement itself, however, not every exegete drew the same radical consequences from the story of the fall; see the contrasts revealed by Harl.

On virginity and the end of society, see Van Eijk. The disruption of social arrangements by young converts to the virgin state was a scenario treasured in Christian hagiography; see Gaiffier, Consolino ("Modelli"), Clark. One should remember, however, that virginity was not always an unwelcome choice for families who had to dispose of surplus children; see Patlagean ("Sur la limitation").

The problems of sexuality within an ascetic environment have been well treated by Rousselle, Foucault, Refoulé.

Theological concern with the mediation of divine and human, especially in the person of Christ, was never far from the minds of those who wrote on virginity; see especially Roldanus, Gregg and Groh. It is instructive to compare Origen's notion of the soul as the bride of Christ, one that would be crucial to the later sensibility of the virgin state (see Crouzel), with the views of his near-contemporary, Plotinus, on the "mystical body" of the universe, beautifully evoked by Armstrong.

Alvarez Campos is a remarkably complete assembly of early Christian texts on the Virgin Mary. Cameron opens up a new approach to the early Byzantine cult of the Virgin. The reader is best advised to browse widely in the sermons and liturgical compositions of the fifth and sixth centuries, most especially the works of Romanos the Melodist, now edited and commented on by Grosdidier de Matons, and the sermons collected by Budge.

Alvarez Campos, Sergio. *Corpus Marianum Patristicum.* Burgos: Ediciones Aldecoa, 1974–

Amand, D., and M. C. Moons, "Une curieuse homélie grecque sur la virginité, addressée aux pères de famille." *Revue bénédictine* 63 (1953) 18–69, 211–38.

Armstrong, A. H. *St. Augustine and Christian Platonism.* Villanova, PA: Villanova University Press, 1967.

Aubineau, M. "Les écrits de S. Athanase sur la virginité." *Revue d'Ascétique et Mystique* 31 (1955) 140–71.

Baltensweiler, H. *Die Ehe im Neuen Testament.* Zurich and Stuttgart: Zwingli, 1967.

Black, M. "The Tradition of Hasidaean-Essene Asceticism: Its Origins and Influence. In *Aspects du Judéo-christianisme,* 19–33. Edited by M. Simon. Paris: Presses universitaires de France, 1965.

Brown, P. "Sexuality and Society in the Fifth Century: Augustine and Julian of Eclanum." In *Tria Corda: Studi in onore di Arnaldo Momigliano,* 49–70. Edited by E. Gabba. Biblioteca di Athenaeum 1. Como: New Press, 1983.

Budge, E. A. W., ed. *Miscellaneous Coptic Texts in the Dialect of Upper Egypt.* London: British Museum, 1915.

Cameron, Averil. "The Theotokos in Sixth-Century Constantinople: A City Finds Its Symbol." *Journal of Theological Studies* 29 (1978) 79–108.

Chadwick, H. "'All Things to All Men:' 1 Cor. 9.22," *New Testament Studies* 1 (1955) 261–75.

———. "Enkrateia." In *Reallexikon für Antike und Christentum,* 5:343–365. Stuttgart: Hiersemann, 1960.

Clark, Elizabeth A. "Ascetic Renunciation and Feminine Advancement: A Paradox of Late Ancient Christianity." *Anglican Theological Review* 63 (1981) 240–57.

Consolino, F. E. "Dagli 'exempla' ad un esempio di comportamento cristiano: Il 'de exhortatione virginitatis' di Ambrogio." *Rivista storica italiana* 94 (1982) 455–77.

———. "Modelli di santità femminile nelle più antiche passioni romane." *Augustinianum* 24 (1984) 83–113.

Crouzel, H. *Virginité et Mariage selon Origène.* Paris: Desclée de Brouwer, 1963.

Duval, Y. M. "L'originalité du *de virginibus* dans le mouvement ascétique occidental: Ambroise, Cyprien, Athanase." In *Ambroise de Milan: xvième centénaire de son élection épiscopale,* 9–66. Edited by Y. M. Duval. Paris: Études augustiniennes, 1974.

Foucault, M. "Le combat de la chasteté." *Communications* 35 (1982) 15–24.

Gaiffier, B. de. "Intactam sponsam relinquens." *Analecta Bollandiana* 65 (1947) 157–95.

Gregg, R., and D. Groh. *Early Arianism: A View of Salvation.* Philadelphia: Fortress, 1981.

Grosdidier de Matons, J. *Romanos le Mélode.* Sources chrétiennes 99, 110, 114, 128, 283. Paris: Cerf, 1964, 1965, 1967, 1981.

Gryson. R. *Les Origines du célibat ecclésiastique du premier au septième siècle.* Gembloux: Duculot, 1970.

Guillaumont, A. "Monachisme et éthique judéo-chrétienne. In *Judéo-christianisme: Volume offert au Cardinal Jean Daniélou,* 199–218. Recherches de sciences religieuses 60. Paris: Centre nationale des lettres, 1972.

———. "Le nom des Agapètes." *Vigiliae Christianae* 23 (1969) 30–37.

Harl, M. "La prise de conscience de la 'nudité' d'Adam: Une interprétation de *Genèse* 3.7 chez les Pères grecs." *Studia Patristica* 7 (1966) 486–95.

Klijn, A. F. J. "The 'Single One' in the Gospel of Thomas." *Journal of Biblical Literature* 81 (1962) 271–78.

Kretschmar, G. "Ein Beitrag nach der Ursprung frühchristlicher Askese." *Zeitschrift für Theologie und Kirche* 61 (1964) 27–67.

Meeks, W. A. "The Image of the Androgyne: Some Uses of a Symbol in Earliest Christianity." *History of Religions* 13 (1974) 165–208.

Müller, M. *Die Lehre des heiligen Augustinus von der Paradiesehe und ihre Auswirkung in der Sexualethik des 12. u. 13. Jahrhunderts.* Regensburg: Pustet, 1954.

Murray, Robert. "The Exhortation to Candidates for Ascetical Vows at Baptism in the Ancient Syriac Church." *New Testament Studies* 21 (1974–75) 59–80.

———. *Symbols of Church and Kingdom: A Study in Early Syriac Tradition.* Cambridge: Cambridge University Press, 1975.

Niederwimmer, K. *Askese und Mysterium.* Göttingen: Vandenhoeck & Ruprecht, 1975.

Pagels, E. "Adam and Eve, Christ and the Church: A Survey of Second Century Controversies Concerning Marriage." In *The New Testament and Gnosis: Essays in Honour of Robert McL. Wilson,* 146–75. Edited by A. H. B. Logan and A. J. M. Wedderburn. Edinburgh: T. & T. Clark, 1983.

Patlagean, E. "L'histoire de la femme déguisée en moine et l'évolution de la sainteté féminine à Byzance." *Studi medievali* 3rd series 17 (1976) 597–623.

———. "Sur la limitation de la fécondité dans la haute époque byzantine." *Annales* 24 (1969) 1353–69.

Refoulé, F. "Rêves et vie spirituelle d'après Évagre le Pontique." *La vie spirituelle: Supplément* 14 (1961) 470–511.

Roldanus, J. *Le Christ et l'Homme dans la Théologie d'Athanase d'Alexandrie.* Leiden: Brill, 1977.

Rousselle, A. *Porneia: De la maîtrise du corps à la privation sensorielle.* Paris: Presses universitaires de France, 1983.

Smith, J. Z. "The Garments of Shame." In *Map is Not Territory,* 1–23. Leiden: Brill, 1978.

Van Eijk, Ton H. C. "Marriage and Virginity, Death and Immortality." In *Epektasis: Mélanges J. Daniélou,* 209–35. Edited by C. Kannengiesser. Paris: Beauchesne, 1972.

Veyne, P. "La famille et l'amour sous le haut Empire romain." *Annales* 33 (1978) 35–63.

Vööbus, A. *A History of Asceticism in the Syrian Orient.* 2 vols. Corpus scriptorum Christianorum Orientalium 184, 197. Louvain: Corpus scriptorum Christianorum Orientalium, 1958–60.

# 18

# Spiritual Guidance

### (Sr.) Donald Corcoran

S TRICTLY SPEAKING, spiritual guidance in the modern sense was not a formalized and self-conscious practice in early Christianity. However, the guidance and care of souls in its widest sense was certainly a major theme in much early Christian literature—sermons, letters, treatises of moral exhortation, etc. Numerous letters of Ambrose, Augustine, Anselm of Canterbury, for example, were directed to explicit spiritual guidance of individuals. Christian writers of the first several centuries to some extent inherited from classical antiquity the concern of the philosophers for moral guidance. Thus, Clement of Alexandria's *The Teacher*, for example, is largely directed to questions of Christian moral life. One finds in Gregory of Nyssa's *On Virginity* and John Climacus's *The Ladder of Divine Ascent* strong exhortations on the necessity of having a spiritual guide. Gregory the Great's *Pastoral Care*, which greatly influenced the spirituality of the Middle Ages, was directed to the spiritual formation of the clergy in general and was not a manual for spiritual direction.

The Christian tradition has always emphasized that Christ or the Holy Spirit is the true guide of souls. We find here a notable difference from some of the other major spiritual traditions where the role of a spiritual master, teacher, or guide is central if not indispensable. For some traditions the master–disciple relationship is something of a semi-institutionalized form of transmission.[1] The battle of the early church with the Gnostics established that transmission is in the whole of the community of the church and is, therefore, public and exoteric rather than private and esoteric. The spiritual master, in the sense of an extraordinary spiritual teacher responsible for person-to-person transmission, is very rare in Christianity though there are two subtraditions, as it were, that somewhat approximate this phenomenon: the early monastic desert fathers and the Russian startsy of the eighteenth and nineteenth centuries.[2]

Though the presence of the spiritual master is somewhat exceptional in

Christianity it can readily be admitted that certain individuals have stood out as great guides even in Western Christianity, where spiritual direction was increasingly formalized, institutionalized, and linked to sacramental confession. The seventeenth century in France is often called the great age of spiritual direction because of figures such as Bossuet, Fénelon, Francis de Sales, and Bérulle. Or one might point to the great French priest director of souls, Abbé Huvelin (d. 1910), who was the spiritual guide of Baron von Hügel, who in turn was the spiritual guide of the noted Anglican writer on mysticism, Evelyn Underhill. There are many great spiritual guides in the Christian tradition. There is, however, no semiformalized line of transmission (spiritual genealogies, as it were) as in Zen, for example.

Spiritual direction in Western Christianity, in particular, has usually connoted a more limited, less personal relationship than the phenomenon of spiritual master and disciple in other spiritual traditions. Spiritual direction in Western Christianity became increasingly the province of ordained clergy. Because of the link to sacramental confession it often tended to have a strong moral emphasis, especially in the last two centuries. In France, for example, the spiritual director was called "le directeur de conscience." The Christian East, in contrast, has always retained a greater distinction between spiritual direction and the remission of sins. The Russian startsy were almost exclusively nonordained monks. Irénée Hausherr comments, therefore, that the term "spiritual direction" as it is commonly understood is insufficient when describing the care of souls in the Christian East.[3] The care of souls in Orthodox Christianity focused on the pursuit of holiness in general rather than the more narrow concern of morality. Above all, the Christian East has always retained a strong sense of the role of the Holy Spirit—the pneumatic element in guidance of souls.

Notions of spiritual guidance in the patristic era and throughout the early Middle Ages were strongly indebted to the monastic tradition and experience. Though we can certainly assume that there has always been a concern for the guidance and care of souls in the Christian tradition, there is little literary evidence of it in the first twelve centuries. Even in the monastic tradition the gradual institutionalization of monastic life would substitute a specific rule of life and community formation for the highly personal and charismatic interaction of elder and disciple in primitive monasticism. Only in the twelfth century, with the rise of popular movements and the mendicant orders, did spiritual guidance of the laity become a concern in itself. The emergence of somewhat abstract, generalized notions of spiritual progress meant that any person could be guided through a somewhat objective process. Thus, the term spiritual direction became common only in the later Middle Ages.

The monastic tradition of spiritual fatherhood/motherhood is the phenomenon in early Christianity that most closely resembles the phenomenon of spiritual master and disciple in the other great spiritual traditions. The "abba" of early Christian monasticism played a role quite similar to that of the Hindu guru, Zen master, or Sufi sheik. The desert fathers/mothers stand out as the preeminent spiritual guides of the early Christian era. These desert fathers/mothers were the first Christian monks and nuns who from the fourth to the sixth century peopled the deserts and wilderness regions of Egypt, Palestine, and Syria. Though the origins of Christian monastic life are complex, certainly one of the strongest factors was the simple fact that people were drawn to the desert to find an "elder," an accomplished ascetic and spiritual teacher capable of leading other persons to a greater experience of God.

The desert elder was addressed by the Aramaic term father (*abba*) or mother (*amma*). There is a rather extensive literary witness to the teaching of these desert fathers/mothers contained largely in collections of sayings known as the *Apophthegmata Patrum*, the *Sayings of the Fathers*.[4] These collections of sayings resemble a genre of spiritual literature found also in other traditions—Sufi stories, Hasidic tales, Zen mondos, etc. The apophthegms or sayings were transmitted orally at first and so are very concise. The sayings reveal the rich wisdom of the desert elders but tell us little about techniques of spiritual guidance.

The first generations of desert fathers/mothers made no attempt to elaborate a spiritual doctrine for general use. There was simply the elder's response out of deep life in the Spirit to the persons, situations, and problems that were encountered. Later visitors to the desert would develop a more conceptualized summation of desert ascesis—writers such as Evagrius of Pontus and John Cassian. Thus, though John Cassian described purity of heart as the goal of ascetic practice, in the *Apophthegmata* literature it does not stand out among other aims of ascetical effort, for example, spiritual vigilance (Greek, *nēpsis*) or freedom from anxiety (Greek, *amerimnia*) or the remembrance of God, which was a prominent theme in the desert fathers of Gaza. Since there was no self-conscious concern with methods of instruction, nor formalized formation, the personal charismatic nature of the master–disciple interaction is revealed only through a great variety of concrete stories that have come down to us in the collections of sayings. The varieties of instruction are as diverse and rich as the panoply of the masters' personalities. The master was, in some sense, the teaching. John Cassian, who spent ten years in the desert, wrote in his *Conferences:* "A saintly life is more educative than a sermon."[5] Another apophthegm advises: "Abraham was hospitable and God was with him, and Elisha loved quiet, and God was with him. So whatever you find your soul wills in the following God's will, do it, and keep your heart."[6]

## Spiritual Paternity/Maternity

What distinguished the Christian guide in the early monastic context was the notion of fatherhood/motherhood in the Spirit.[7] Despite Christ's injunction to "call no man father" (Matt 23:9), early Christianity readily saw the human spiritual guide as sharing both the loving kindness of God the Father and the charismatic gift of the Spirit to engender others in the spiritual life. Thus Paul spoke of begetting disciples in the Spirit, and Origen wrote "Happy is he who without ceasing is engendered by God" (*On Jeremiah* 9.4). The qualities that characterized the desert fathers/mothers as spiritual guides reflected their own deep experience of the qualities of the divine.

One finds in each form of spiritual guidance in the major religious traditions a distinct or dominant tonality. Thus, the classic Hasidic spiritual guide was characterized by overflowing joy and his close bond with his community. The Zen master is characterized by his austere and insistent iconoclasm of thoughts. Though the notion of spiritual fatherhood/motherhood may be found incidentally in other traditions, that notion is not the dominant image of the guide as it was for the early Christian monks and nuns. Thus fatherhood/motherhood—"begetting in the Spirit"—is the distinctive character of Christian spiritual direction, particularly in the monastic context, compared with other traditions of spiritual direction.

The great desert spiritual guides displayed extraordinary patience, gentleness, and forbearance with their disciples—but also the necessary strength to confront and admonish. The desert elders had remarkable insight, delicacy, and compassion in dealing with the weaknesses of others. Charity and nonjudgment were, without question, the outstanding qualities of the desert fathers/mothers. Barsanuphius, the great desert father of Gaza, wrote to a disciple: "In effect, my concern for you is more than yours for yourself and God's is even greater."[8] The gentleness of the desert elders is also exemplified in a story told of the great Abba Poemen:

> Some old men came to see Abba Poemen and said to him, "When we see brothers who are dozing at the synaxis [liturgy], shall we rouse them so that they will be watchful?" He said to them, "For my part when I see a brother who is dozing, I put his head on my knees and let him rest."[9]

> Charity far exceeds in value even the greatest of self-imposed austerities. Thus one anonymous elder said that a brother who fasts six days, even if he hung himself up by his nostrils, could never be equal to him who ministers to the sick.[10]

## *Exagoreusis:*
## The Manifestation of Thoughts

One of the least understood practices of desert ascesis was the "manifestation of thoughts." If anything approached a technique of guidance it was this practice. It has been described as a "spirituality of opening one's heart."[11] The disciple was encouraged to make known to the spiritual elder all that was going on interiorly. It had a much broader meaning than sacramental confession. The aim was not absolution from guilt but rather an increase in discernment about the propensities of the deep will in one's personality. *Exagoreusis* brought true self-knowledge and gave the opportunity for the charismatically endowed elder to be a physician for one's soul. When John Cassian wrote of the necessity of "bringing them [the fathers] every thought that rises in our heart," the reason he gave was that "the foul serpent from the dark underground cavern must be released; otherwise it will rot."[12] There is an obvious psychological wisdom in this practice and it was never done under constraint. *Exagoreusis* also enabled the young ascetic to have greater awareness of the disperse nature of "thoughts" (Greek, *logismoi*) and helped the ascetic to quiet the mind in order to achieve inner peace of heart (Greek, *hesychia*). The aim was to become a person of one thought (Greek, *monologistos*), a person centered on the awareness of God.[13] There is a remarkable parallel here with Eastern spiritual disciplines such as Yoga and Zen. *Exagoreusis* was not an indiscriminate unburdening of one's soul to any ready ear. Abba Poemen advised "Do not open your soul to anyone whom you do not trust in your heart."[14] *Exagoreusis* was a practice that came naturally since it stemmed from confidence and deep trust.

## *Diakrisis* and Prophecy

The spiritual gift of discernment, for the desert elders, meant moderation, balance, and prudence, but especially the insight into the spiritual state and needs of others (Greek, *diakrisis*)—the ability to read hearts. This was a power given by God and went far beyond mere natural sensitivity and insight into human nature. There was widespread agreement in primitive monastic literature that no progress in the spiritual life was possible without discernment. Abba Moses in Cassian's *Conferences* warned of the example of monks who did not have discernment and called them "ancient and modern shipwrecks."[15] Abba Anthony counseled, "Some have afflicted their bodies by asceticism, but they lack discernment, and so they are far from God."[16] Discernment is like the foundation upon which all the virtues are built.

Some desert elders showed particular ability to read hearts. Abba Mios, for

32. *Relief of a Bearded Saint, Coptic, 6th–7th century*

example, was called a "true reader of hearts."[17] Yet the ability to read hearts is presumed in every case in which an elder spoke a "word" (Greek, *rhēma*), an inspired statement of spiritual counsel. The ability to give such a "word" was called prophecy. Prophecy was the direct inspiration of the Holy Spirit given for the purpose of guiding others. Certain desert elders had the title prophet added to their name because of their extraordinary gift of counsel— for example, John the Prophet, the disciple of Barsanuphius. *Diakrisis,* prophecy, and outstanding charity are the principal characteristics of the great spiritual guides of the desert.

One phrase from an apophthegm came to summarize, especially in later Eastern Christian monastic tradition, the whole process of Christian trans- formation: "Give your blood and receive the Holy Spirit."[18] All the effort of the desert elder was directed to increasing the receptivity of the disciple to the Holy Spirit. The elders frequently did not have the gift of prophecy unless a disciple was open. Cassian's *Conferences* mentions Abba Moses, who had an inflexible rule never to give instruction except to persons who sought it in faith and heartfelt contrition.[19] The earnest search and openness in the disciple in some sense created the power in the master, though the desert elders did not perhaps believe this to the extent that it was held in the Hindu and Sufi traditions. The efficacy of the Holy Spirit depended on the mutual openness of master and disciple.

The early monks looked to Elijah as one model for the desert ascetic. The transmission of Elijah's spirit to Elisha, symbolized in the giving of Elijah's mantle (2 Kings 2:13), finds its parallel in the story that the great Anthony inherited the tunic of Paul of the Desert.[20] One finds some indication, but not commonly, of an extraordinary ability of the spiritual father/mother to invoke the Spirit and to create a felt experience of transmission of spiritual power similar to the *shaktipat* experience in Hinduism and the *baraka* experience in Sufism. A particularly beautiful description of this was given in the eighteenth century by Motovilov, a lay disciple of the Russian starets, Seraphim of Sarov.[21]

In our own day there is a widespread revival of interest in spiritual direction. The model of friendship seems to be the favored model for the director–directee relationship.[22] This is certainly a more egalitarian model than the parent–child model; yet it must be remembered that the early monastic movement never took human parenting as a literal role model for the spiritual guide. Their sense of "begetting in the Spirit," which under- scored the necessity of prayer and striving for holiness, has much to teach the contemporary practice of spiritual direction. There is a danger of seeing spiritual direction merely as a specialized form of ministry, a skill that can be bolstered by counseling and psychological insights. The desert elders, along with the great Christian guides of all times, strongly emphasized that the Holy Spirit is the true guide of souls.

## Notes

1. For an excellent study of the master–disciple relationship in most of the major spiritual traditions, see *Le Maître Spirituel dans les grandes traditions d'occident et d'orient*.

2. For a general introduction to the history of the early monastic movement, see Derwas Chitty, *The Desert a City*. For the best history of the Russian startsy, see Igor Smolitsch, *Leben und Lehre der Startzen* (Cologne: Jacob Hegner, 1952), or the French version of the same work, translated by Josse Alzin and Pierre Chambard, *Moines de la Sainte Russie* (Paris: Mame, 1967).

3. Irénée Hausherr, "Direction spirituel," in *Dict. Sp.* 3, col. 1009.

4. There are two main collections. The so-called alphabetical collection lists sayings alphabetically by name of the *abba* or *amma*. This collection is now available in English; see *The Sayings of the Desert Fathers*, trans. Benedicta Ward. The so-called systematic collection lists apophthegms by topics such as discernment, obedience, and so on; see "The Sayings of the Fathers," in *Western Asceticism*, ed. Owen Chadwick, 33–181.

5. John Cassian, "First Conference of Abba Chaeremon," *The Conferences*, trans. Owen Chadwick, in *Western Asceticism*, 247.

6. "The Sayings of the Fathers," trans. Owen Chadwick, in *Western Asceticism*, 39.

7. For the question of spiritual paternity/maternity, see Basil Steidle, "Heilige Vaterschaft," *Benediktinische Monatschrift* 14 (1932) 214–26; see also Adalbert de Vogüé, "Experience of God and Spiritual Fatherhood," *Monastic Studies* 9 (1972) 83–99.

8. *Barsanuphe et Jean de Gaza: Correspondence*, 38.

9. *The Sayings*, Poemen 92 (trans. Ward, p. 151).

10. "The Sayings of the Fathers," trans. Owen Chadwick, in *Western Asceticism*, 184–85.

11. François Neyt, "A Form of Charismatic Authority," *Eastern Churches Quarterly* 6 (1974) 60.

12. John Cassian, "The Second Conference of Abbot Moses," *The Conferences*, trans. Edgar C. S. Gibson, in *NPNF* 11:312.

13. Lucien Regnault, "La prière continuelle 'monologistos' dans la littérature apophtegmatique," *Irenikon* 47 (1974) 467–93.

14. *The Sayings*, Poemen 201 (trans. Ward, p. 163).

15. John Cassian, "The Second Conference of Abbot Moses," *The Conferences*, trans. Owen Chadwick, in *Western Asceticism*, 308.

16. *The Sayings*, Anthony 8 (trans. Ward, p. 2).

17. *The Sayings*, Mios 2 (trans. Ward, p. 127).

18. *The Sayings*, Longinus 5 (trans. Ward, p. 104).

19. John Cassian, "The First Conference of Abba Moses," *The Conferences*, trans. Owen Chadwick, in *Western Asceticism*, 195.

20. Helen Waddell, *The Desert Fathers* (Ann Arbor, MI: University of Michigan Press, 1966) 38–39.

21. "The Conversation of St. Seraphim with Nicholas Motovilov," in *A Treasury of Russian Spirituality*, ed. G. P. Fedotov (New York: Sheed & Ward, 1948) 266–80.

22. See Kenneth Leech, *Soul Friend* (New York: Harper & Row, 1977); see also Tilden Edwards, *Spiritual Friend* (New York: Paulist Press, 1980).

## Bibliography

### Sources

*Barsanuphe et Jean de Gaza: Correspondence.* Translated and edited by Lucien Regnault and Phillipe Le Maire. Solesmes, France: Abbaye Saint-Pierre, 1972.

*The Sayings of the Desert Fathers: The Alphabetical Collection.* Translated by Benedicta Ward. Kalamazoo, MI: Cistercian Publications, 1975.

*Western Asceticism.* Edited by Owen Chadwick. LCC 12. 1958.

### Studies

Chitty, Derwas. *The Desert a City: An Introduction to the Study of Egyptian and Palestinian Monasticism under the Christian Empire.* Oxford: Blackwell, 1966.

Corcoran, (Sister) Donald. "The Spiritual Guide: Midwife of the Higher Spiritual Self." In *Abba: Guides to Wholeness and Holiness East and West.* Kalamazoo, MI: Cistercian Publications, 1982.

Hausherr, Irénée. *Direction spirituelle en Orient autrefois.* Rome: Pontifical Institute of Oriental Studies, 1955.

*Le Maître Spirituel dans les grandes traditions d'occident et d'orient.* Hermes 4. Paris, 1966–67.

McNeill, John T. *A History of the Cure of Souls.* New York: Harper, 1951.

Merton, Thomas. "The Spiritual Father in the Desert Tradition." *Cistercian Studies* 3 (1968) 3–24.

Vogüé, Adalbert de. "Experience of God and Spiritual Fatherhood." *Monastic Studies* 9 (1972) 83–99.

# 19

# The Practice of Christian Life: The Birth of the Laity

JACQUES FONTAINE

T O PROCLAIM AND TO WITNESS to the good news of salvation in Jesus Christ in words and deeds can only be done by each baptized person for and in each one's own proper time and in the condition where grace finds one (see 1 Cor 7:20). Thus, in order to discuss some religious practices and interior attitudes of the Christian people in the West in the course of the first millennium, it is necessary to approach the problem of the origins of a spirituality specific to the laity.

But is it legitimate to study the life of a Christian people from this perspective without playing on words? What relation is there in fact between the people of God in Scripture, the *laos theou*, and that which we call in the twentieth century the laity? Indeed, the notion of "the people of God," with which it is best to begin, has preserved throughout time a precise sense that doubly verifies the continuity of the ecclesial tradition. On the one hand, every baptized person has received and ought to "preserve" and transmit the "deposit" of the one faith (1 Tim 6:20), spoken, lived, and made progressively explicit, but unchanged in its essential content. On the other hand, at the same time as the scriptural authors and the exegetes incessantly "reread" the same foundational events of salvation, this transmission requires a constant actualization of the word of God, which "will not pass away" (Matt 24:35) in a world in which the "figure" does not cease "to pass" (1 Cor 7:31), a congenital contradiction in the life of the whole church and therefore eminently in the life of the "laity" of the church.

A traditional sociology, and one could say clerical sociology, of this people of the church has for a long time defined the laity by a sort of "method of the remainder." From the time of the most ancient Christian communities, the development of individual charisms and of the hierarchy has "set apart" those who have chosen the better part (*klēros*): not only the *clerici,* but also,

453

as the *Rule of St. Augustine* says so nicely, all the "lovers of perfect beauty." There remain then by simple subtraction the ordinary baptized persons, the laity. Would not these be, then, just a long line of followers in the immense column of those whom Augustine called the *civitas Dei peregrinans* (e.g., *City of God* 15.2.1)? This condescending and negative view of the laity is ancient. It originates in an elitism, that is to say a dualism that is not the best legacy to Christianity of an aristocratic and Platonizing antiquity, relayed thereafter through the oligarchical and monarchical structures of Germanic societies but also through an encratism just as ancient as Judeo-Christians—that of the second-century sermon on "one hundred, sixty, and thirty for one" (an allusion to the parable in Mark 4:20), which reserved the better spiritual "return" to the martyrs and to continent ascetics (one hundred for one, and sixty for one!). The simple "just ones" of the Christian people were not allocated more than thirty for one.

Two fundamental scriptural verses in Revelation and 1 Peter define the religious dignity of the laity. Augustine held both as valuable in his *City of God* (20.10): "They are priests of God and of Christ, and will reign with him during a thousand years (Rev 1:6). That was certainly not said only of bishops and priests." One can add without hesitation: it is said of all the baptized people and therefore of those whom we call laity. Augustine continued: "But at the same time that we say that all are christs, by reason of the same mystical chrism, or same mystical anointing, at the same time they are all priests insofar as they are the ministers of the unique priest—those of whom the apostle Peter has said: 'a holy people, a priestly community of the king'" (1 Pet 2:9). In this community of the baptized the laity are in all times those Christians "of whom the domain of service is primordially the world"; or again those who "are at the same time of the world and of the church; those who are truly neither clerics nor monks."[1] It follows then that these are above all the laity who "*take profit* from this world as though they did not *profit* by it truly" (1 Cor 7:31).

From the first millennium, there appear in the life of the Christian people some specific traits of such a spirituality. The practice of faith and of charity during these ten centuries manifests the difficult vicissitudes of such a spiritual understanding. It becomes clear only slowly and in the measure that clerics are more clearly distinguished from laity in Christian society. The faithful of the first three centuries insufficiently discerned the spiritual value of temporal existence, but the Constantinian turning point in the first third of the fourth century, followed by the official suppression of ancient paganism in the age of Theodosius (from 379 to 395), started a new course open to the penetration of Christianity in all of Roman society. The laity began to bring to bear all their weight, both for better and for worse. By the beginning of the sixth century, the fall of Rome, which had politically disappeared in 476, handed over medieval society in the West to the spiritual authority and often, involuntarily, to the temporal authority of the clergy, at first of the bishops, but also of the abbots. But the Carolingian "reform" of the eighth and ninth centuries gave new attention to the laity and to reflection on their way of life. These three great phases are the starting points for this sketch of the difficult birth of a "spirituality of the laity" in the life of the Christian people.

## Early Christianity
## (First to Third Century)

It is natural that the oldest Latin text on the life of a Christian community took scarcely any notice of its structure or of the activities of its members. The Christians who in in the year 112 were brought before the tribunal of Pliny the Younger, then governor of the eastern province of Bithynia, made allusion to their morning religious office, to their baptismal vows, and to their common meal. Two of them who were slaves called themselves deaconesses (*ministrae*, Pliny wrote). The governor did not understand them nor did he detain them longer. In his perplexity before the anti-Christian agitation and the rapid progress of Christianity in his province he wrote a justly celebrated letter to submit the case to the emperor Trajan (*Epistle* 10.96.7ff.).

It is even more interesting to see Clement of Rome, who wrote in Greek from the city of Rome, employing for the first time the word layman (*laikos*) in a sense that does not differ very much from our own (see his *Epistle to the Corinthians*, written at the end of the first century). It was in noticing the continuity between the Jewish sacerdotal hierarchy and that of the Christian communities that Clement was drawn to use the word and to define it. If the function of "a particular service has fallen upon the high priest," as well as upon priests and Levites (the context suggests that he sees in them the "figures of bishops, priests, and Christian deacons"), "those of the laity are bound by precepts proper to laity" (*Epistle to the Corinthians* 40.5). Clement's phrase proposes in the church of Christ a positive *specificity* for the lay tradition. It postulates the existence of rules of life distinct from those of the future *ordo sacerdotalis* and particular to the lay tradition.

At the beginning of the third century, Tertullian reflected the lack of precision at Carthage regarding the distribution of "ministerial" tasks between laity and clergy. Well before the Augustinian text of the *City of God* cited above, Tertullian based on Rev 1:6 the question he posed in chapter 7 of his *Exhortation to Chastity:* "Is it not true that we also, the laity, are priests? . . . that which constitutes the difference between the order of priests and the people is the authority in the church, and the honor which God consecrates in making the members of this order sit down together." The function of exercising *authority*—with all the social, judiciary, and, in the large sense, political nuances of the Old Latin word *auctoritas*—is translated visibly by the privileged place that the members of the clergy of the church occupy materially in what will be called the *presbyterium*, that is, the semicircular bench that surrounds, along the wall of the apse, the "cathedra" of the bishop, in opposition to the *quadratum populi*. Tertullian insisted on the fact that in case of necessity a layperson may just as well baptize as preside over the Eucharist: "There where the members of the ecclesiastical order do not sit together, you are alone to make the offering, to baptize, to be priest on your own account, because there where the three are reunited the church is found—even though these are the laity" (*Exhortation to Chastity* 7.3)[2]

This debate grew into a conflict in the churches tried by the persecution in the middle of the third century under Decius and under Valerian. The problem of the reconciliation of apostate Christians—the "fallen" (*lapsi*) or cynical buyers of "bills of confession" delivered by pagan authorities (*libellatici*)—opposed in effect the rights of an episcopate become "monarchial" to the pretensions of certain "confessors." Escaped from torture without having apostasized, these confessors tried to use their charismatic privilege to grant to the *lapsi* immediate reconciliation, that is, to return to the Christian community without performing a penance imposed by the bishop. Cyprian of Carthage rose up against such pretensions with a vigor equal to that with which he opposed the "rigorous" who wished to refuse all reconciliation to the *lapsi* during their lifetime. This effort to find a reasonable via media shows that one would err greatly in seeing in Cyprian only the champion of a sort of will to episcopal power over against a Christian people subjected to the absolute power of the clergy, that is, first of all of the bishop. Thus, from the beginnings of the organization of the African church, the bishop had to be assisted by a council of *seniores laici* elected by the Christian people, a council whose origin may go back to the Jewish community. This council assured, with the bishop, an administrative and governmental function and also jurisdiction and teaching.

The correspondence of Cyprian contains the same message. If the bishop of Carthage was convinced that his authority was delegated to him by God, he knew that concretely he held it just as much from the Christian people as from his clergy. He saw himself, like Cornelius of Rome, "ordained bishop in the church by the judgment of God and the suffrage of the clergy and of the people" (*Epistles* 68.2.1). If he felt himself gifted by personal charisms, if he received, under diverse forms, "admonitions" of the Spirit, the lay confessors of the faith could not but be also gratified by it.

This prophetic pneumatism is better understood by looking at the lived experience of conversion. Cyprian has left us a detailed narrative of his own life at the beginning of his apologetic treatise *To Donatus*. There are four points that one should retain from this picture of the interior upheaval lived by a layperson who became a believer. Irreducible to an intellectual adhesion, to an "assent" of pure reason to the content of the Christian faith, this experience is inseparable from the anxious search for personal salvation and from a communication with the divine that had, at the end of the preceding century, guided the spiritual journey of the pagan Apuleius of Madaura. The one, like the other, reveals that which we today call the ancient "second religiosity." Darkness, anxiety, discouragement, and interior bitterness: this first Cyprian resembles Lucius at the beginning of the *Metamorphoses* of Apuleius. A certain analogy is even found between the psychological manifestations of salvation brought to Lucius in book 11 of this novel by the revelation of a universal mother, Isis, and the effects of Christian baptism on Cyprian: it is for him an interior illumination (this is one of its ancient Greek names: *phōtismos*) from which came a firm certitude, an unbreakable confidence. But the most original element is without doubt the consciousness of the presence and of the animating power of the Spirit: "It is to God that one's whole person belongs"; it is God who comes into us. Cyprian had, therefore, the double interior experience of liberty and of the divine gift of spiritual grace, of *gratia spiritualis,* which allows the proper exercise of liberty. He experienced finally, in these events, the dual power to pacify hearts and to restrain demons, ". . . to dominate by imperial rights over all armed attack of an adversary"—or of *the* adversary, that is to say, of Satan.

This militant vision of the new existence of the baptized who become "new persons" goes back to Paul and also reflects a metaphorical understanding long dear to Roman Stoicism (e.g., Seneca). But in the third century it knew an exceptional revival, to the extent that the Christian ideal of martyrdom was exalted by the cruelty of the persecutions. Tertullian gave it a first literary expression in one of his oldest works: the pamphlet of exhortation *To the Martyrs*. The battle against Satan began in prison, where "you have come to trample the wicked one under foot even in his own house." This captivity was also for the future martyr a "retreat," where the warrior of God withdrew before going forth to battle: it is "for the Christian what the desert was for the prophets" but also the supreme accomplishment of the imitation of Christ even to his passion, because "we have been called to the service of the living God from the moment when we responded to the demands of our enlistment" (1.4; 2.8; 3.1).[3]

This "army of Christ" became one of the major themes of Cyprian's preaching. In his *Letter 58*, to the people of Thibaris—who wanted some preparation for, if not an inflamed exhortation, to martyrdom. This martyrdom had the value of "a baptism of blood" (*Epistles* 73.22.2), of the eucharistic sacrifice (*Epistles* 76.3.2). The martyr taught in the Roman manner, in acts and not in words, *rebus non verbis:* all these sentiments of an exalted faith, Cyprian continued, "have allowed you to penetrate into the souls of your brothers by putting into act that which you taught before in words" (*Epistles* 76.6.1). But Cyprian insisted more often on a daily rather than a bloody martyrdom as the ideal of a Christian ethic; he invited the reader to see in the biblical model of martyrdom those who lived a style of Christian life founded on patience, sweetness, and peace in the "following Christ," more than on intrepidity and endurance. The narrative of the tortures of the martyrs of Lyons in 177 (Eusebius *Church History* 5.1) as well as that of the *Passion of Perpetua and Felicitas* at Carthage in 202–203 or the letter of Cyprian to some confessors of the faith condemned to the mines in 256 (*Epistles* 76) show the eminent part taken by the laity of both sexes. One sees manifest there, with simplicity and dignity, a dramatic heroism— "reasonable, grave, without tragic fracas"—of the kind that Marcus Aurelius wished to see in the soul of a philosopher ready for death, even though he reproached Christian martyrs with a fanaticism inspired "by a simple spirit of opposition" (*Meditations* 11.3). The greatest joy for Cyprian was to be able to call to the *ordo sacerdotalis* lay confessors of the faith who had justly escaped martyrdom, such as the young Aurelius, in whom the grace of martyrdom was a sort of family tradition, because his grandmother had been martyred as well as two of his soldier uncles (*Epistles* 39.3).[4]

This conjuncture of the great persecutions of the middle of the century coincided with the acme of a crisis without precedent in the Roman Empire. Epidemics, famines, invasions, civil wars: the horsemen of the sixth chapter of Revelation all were united—and that includes the white horseman in which Christian tradition saw Christ. He receives the crown once again, through the paradoxical victory of his suffering members triumphing as he had over death through the offering of their own deaths. It is understandable that in this disastrous occurrence one could believe that the "end of time" was imminent: "The voice of the Lord and the witness of the Apostles has taught us in advance about the decline of the ages and the approach of Antichrist; all that is good will fall away and all that is evil and hostile will profit." That is what an African council presided over by Cyprian wrote in a message addressed in 254 to the Spanish priest Felix and to the faithful people of Leon and Astorga (*Epistles* 67.7). This new eschatological expectation, which bordered on an anguished "adventism," gave fresh actuality to dramatic visions of the final catastrophe, already carried for centuries by the apocalyptic literary genre, first Jewish and then Christian. One can see this in the powerful half-barbaric verses of the poet Commodian, who reflected well the common mentality of the Christian people. This Christian, who did not hesitate to shock, preached nonetheless a meticulous and demanding Christian morality; he was sarcastically critical toward all the weakness of his brothers, whom he incited as did Cyprian to the "daily martyrdom" of the true "soldiers of Christ."

In these satirical portraits, traced in the short poems of the *Instructions* of Commodian, one can recognize a social and psychological reality much less heroic than that of the narratives of the martyrs but no less veracious. The majority of these Christians did not live in the paralyzing expectation of the catastrophe of the end of time. They did not reserve the totality of their activity for liturgical services and prayer; they lived engaged in temporal activities, even if they saw such activities as first an obstacle or even a risk. In reminding his clergy (*Epistles* 1.1) of Paul's verse (2 Tim 2:4), according to which "no one who serves God engages in the distractions of the things of the world, in order to be able to please him who has called him," Cyprian seems at first to have been the founder of this negative conception of the laity, against which we protested at the beginning; but in fact it marked a difference of degree more than an opposition, and he thus allowed to the laity all the more liberty to be, throughout the world, the avant-garde of the apostolic mission.

From the end of the second century, Christians, especially in Africa, had penetrated into all the areas and all the ranks of Roman society. "We arrived only yesterday, and already we fill the earth as well as all that is yours: cities, islands, towns, municipalities, fields of harvest, and even camps, tribes, the councils, the palace, and the senate. We have left you only your temples" (Tertullian *Apology* 37.4). In a Roman world which began to fall apart in the great crisis that began at the end of the reign of Marcus Aurelius, it was more than easy for Tertullian to underline the political loyalty of Christians. They engaged in neither secession nor rebellion; their *positive* attitude was that of a *presence to the world*, which made them "witness their good intentions toward the Emperor as sincerely as towards all people" and "to do good without paying attention to anyone's rank" (*Apology* 36.2–3). That is why, in accord with his contemporary, the Greek author of the *Letter to Diognetus*, Tertullian was able to say to his audience, "We have the same kind of life as you . . . without taking ourselves out of the forum and the market-place, without renouncing the baths and the shops and the boutiques and the inns and all the other places of commerce, we *live* in this world *with* you" (*Apology* 42.3).[5]

This solidarity is, for the laity, like the natural form and the prefiguration of a true, lived charity. It is affirmed in the Christian family, between the spouses (see the end of the treatise of Tertullian *To His Wife*) and also by the "education in Christ" of which Clement of Rome had already spoken (*Epistle to the Corinthians* 21.8). It is manifested in all walks of life: "With you we sail the seas, with you we serve as soldiers, with you we work the earth, we engage in commerce. It is thus that we mix our activities and that we put the product of our labor at the disposition of the public, for your service" (*Apology* 42.3).

Day after day the evangelical ardor of the Christian laity was regularly nourished by Christian assemblies. These were not limited to the great liturgies of prayer or eucharistic celebrations; they included also the *agapē* meals and the funeral meals on or in the *tricliae* that were very early set near the family tombs or even on top of them. "Works of charity" recommended by Christ according to the Jewish tradition (Matt 25:35ff.) required a stricter organization in communities that were becoming more and more numerous. This active charity no longer was organized on the model of the primitive church (the "service of tables," probably at the origins of the deaconate: Acts 6:2). It tended to be modeled on the usages of professional *collegia* in the shelter of which Christians could come together in associations that became less and less secret. Tertullian presented the Christian community as a *corpus* (*Apology* 39.1), and this word had a connotation no less juridical than *collegium*, because the *Digest* speaks of the *corpus fabrorum et naviculariorum*. But it is "a body" that is constituted by "the common understanding of one same belief, the unity of one discipline, and the bond of one hope." The reading in common of the Scriptures allowed for the community to "bind our discipline more closely and to inculcate its precepts" (*Apology* 39.3); and a common treasury fed by voluntary gifts was shared among the less well-off. It was the spectacle of this efficacious charity toward the dead, the poor, orphans, old servants, the shipwrecked, deportees, the imprisoned, that appeared, with martyrdom, like the ferment par excellence of the daily evangelization. This *dilectionis operatio* made the pagans say: "See how they love one another" (*Apology* 39.7).

There remained, then, great permeability between the Christian people and a clergy that was far from constituting a clerical class. In large part, it was still recruited directly from among the best of the laity. The adjustment between the "ecclesiastical discipline" promulgated by Cyprian and concrete cases of conscience posed by a formal but still omnipresent paganism was not eased, however. Many of the treatises of Tertullian and Cyprian show us the points of major friction. From Roman spectacles to women's make-up, from the wearing of crowns to the wearing of the veil by young women, from remarriage to all the forms of the cult of idols, from the school to the forum and to the army, Tertullian preached a hardly livable rigorism that constituted a sort of apartheid between Christians and pagans. But these startling *theses* of the rhetorician were often accompanied by the *hypotheses* of the casuist: one could attend pagan engagement parties, on the condition that one remain a little apart at the moment of the sacrificial rite; one could remain in the army, on the condition that one would no longer shed blood and that one would refuse to adore the imperial effigy. Could one ask for a transfer into the police or into the administration? Tertullian does not say, but there are modern scholars who justly suppose so.

The *Apostolic Tradition*, which reflects the casuistry of the communities of the city of Rome in the middle of the third century, expressed with a certain involuntary humor the tolerance of Christians in the capital with regard to the career of the professor—that is to say, of a master of mythology and therefore of polytheism, as Tertullian made clear with great indignation: "If anyone (that is, a recently converted Christian) teaches children the learning of this world," says the *Tradition*, "it would be better if that person renounced doing so; nevertheless if one has no other way to make a living, then it is excusable" (*Apostolic Tradition* 16). The embarrassment of Tertullian some fifty years earlier before these "school masters" and "professors of literature," these "preachers of idolatry," suggests strongly that even he had to resign himself to the fact that one must learn the alphabet in order to read and to comprehend the Scripture and its meaning (*On Idolatry* 10). These interdictions are evidently clearer with regard to the careers that profited by violence and debauchery, that is to say, pornography and the sadism of the spectacles, if not of the pagan cults: gladiators, actors of mimes, pimps, and makers of statuettes of gods. But the situation was much less clear for the soldiers. It was the same for the magistrates to whom the *ius gladii* delegated the responsibility of inflicting the death penalty, should the occasion arise. Seneca had already condemned in very strong terms all legal use of violence and even "the glorious crimes of genocide." Is it then surprising that the love of neighbor had given, for Christians, a new depth to the maxim of Seneca in this same letter to Lucilius: *homo res sacra homini* (*Epistles* 95.33)?

If the principles were clear, their application was much less so. The debate between rigor and generosity of spirit had already begun among the Christian people. Martyrs and Christians, already too ingenuously tolerant, were already working in a complementary manner for the coming of the kingdom. Thus, the margin of liberty left to the initiative of lay Christians remained greater than the convinced authority of Cyprian would allow one to suppose. The double constraint of an often offensive paganism and of a sometimes coercive hierarchical authority had not suppressed this margin. Tertullian himself had already opened the door a crack to a certain prudent tolerance. He had recognized the existence of a profane domain, in which there was nothing either specifically Christian or pagan (*On the Crown* 8.4ff.). He had thus encouraged among the laity an understanding of their own responsibilities in the moral order, and especially in the spiritual order, in their actions as well as in what one would one day call "the direction of intention." Not without risk, a layperson could thus find a way in daily contact with a civilization into which Christianity had inserted itself and to which Christianity had acculturated itself more and more deeply during the third century.

The laity's respect for personal conscience can be illustrated by an example. When the proconsul Dion proposed to the conscientious objector Maximilian of Tebessa the example of Christian soldiers who remained in the service of the emperors, the young conscript answered: "They know what is best for them. But I am a Christian and I cannot do wrong." What he meant by "wrong" (*mala facere*) was to shed blood and to assist at the ceremonies of the "camp religion." Without concessions for himself, this conscript did not interfere and tell his brothers their duty when they served in the army: each one is responsible for his or her own actions before God and before the people, but first of all before one's own conscience.

Forty years earlier (Maximilian was executed in 295, and Cyprian's *Letter 59* was written in 255), Cyprian was also slow to impose on the laity his personal point of view with regard to the reconciliation of the *lapsi*. He intended not to constrain freedom of decision for his apostate interlocuters. "The laity themselves must see what they have to do on this point—*Viderint laici* . . . !—It is on the bishops," continued Cyprian, "that the heavier task falls to defend the glory of God and to watch over God's interests" (*Epistles* 59.13.5). One finds there again the notion of "precepts proper to the laity," which Clement's *Epistle* had explained a century and a half earlier. Cyprian also had to recognize that he had taken a false route by paradoxically imposing his own indulgence on a Christian people who had found him too rigorous toward one of the *lapsi*. He understood then that he would have to respect the opinion of his community: "The resentment of the community was found to be justified by the fact that the individual, in spite of contrary advice and the opposition of the people, nevertheless had been reintegrated through my own weakness, and he was found to be worse than before since he could not remain faithful to the penance imposed" (*Epistles* 59.15.4). That points to Cyprian's respect for those whom he called alternately (the hesitation is significant) his "people" (*populus* or *plebs*) or his "brothers" (*fratres* or *fraternitas*).

In moments of crisis the Christians knew that they had nothing more to do than to die courageously in the face of a hating and sadistic crowd drugged by the taste of blood, ready to lynch the *tertium genus,* the Christians. So it was at Lyons in 177. But not all pagans were animated by the hatred of Christians that impregnated the *True Discourse* of the philosopher Celsus. Galen thought that the Christian martyrs behaved like true philosophers, "because we have before our eyes their contempt for death."[7] In the intellectual companionship of the cultivated milieus of the liberal professions, even apologetic combat was no longer thought necessary, and a true dialogue could begin between pagans and Christians. This is shown in the first third of the third century in the work of a lawyer pleading at Rome, the *Octavius* of Minucius Felix. In its form the work significantly belonged to the literary genre of the dialogue. In two contrasting discourses, the pagan Cecilius Natalis and the Christian Octavius Januarius discussed, turn by turn, the ancient objections to Christianity. Octavius's responses, not less courteous than firm, gave a seductive vision of certain articles of the faith of Christians and of their style of life. Minucius reduced invective to a smile; he explained and proposed. He tried to bring his interlocutor to "move ahead" toward this true philosophy; the *Octavius* is in this sense a Christian protreptic, a philosophical genre that Aristotle illustrated as did Cicero in his *Hortensius.* Minucius did not risk submitting himself to a premature catechesis: he never says the name of Christ. This reserve did not proceed from a tepid and quasi-aseptic Christianity. Minucius intended only "to prepare the way" in the manner of John the Baptist—to disarm the prejudices and calumnies of the pagans, to open minds and souls, to show that these women and these infant martyrs demonstrated that "no one without the help of God can endure these tortures" (*Octavius* 37.6).

In this sense the layman Minucius is a good witness to this sort of "evangelical preparation," without which the first communication of the Christian message would have remained as impossible as it had been for Paul in the midst of the jeering Athenians at the Areopagus of Athens (Acts 17:16–34). It was thus that the apostolate of intellectual Christians, laity, lawyers, or rhetoricians, could be exercised with the greatest delicacy and often efficacy in the service of the evangelization of the governing classes. Soon Lactantius, in his *Divine Institutions,* would present the theory and the practice of this adaptation of ancient culture to the service of the conversion of cultivated Romans.

# The Laity in the Christian Roman Empire
## (Fourth and Fifth Centuries)

"The dialectical relation of opposition and participation in the surrounding world" (Y. Congar), which, in the church, defines the stimulating discomfort of the lay condition, begins with the ambiguity of the scriptural term "world," whether one adopts, in the manner of the Latin translations of the Bible, the spatial metaphor of *mundus* or the temporal image included in the word *saeculum*. The world is "vanity of vanities and pursuit of the wind"; but it is also, thanks to the verse in John 3:17, the world into which God sent the Son, "not to condemn the world, but that the world might be saved through him." This "frontier" vocation of the laity at the intersection of the church and the world became, in the fourth century, more paradoxical than it had been in the course of the three preceding centuries. There are many historical reasons for that. We will distinguish five principal ones here.

Chronologically first was the devaluation of world in the general sense of temporal existence, because of the crisis of the third century and its repercussions on pagan and Christian spiritualities. Devaluation of the body, of time, of ancient civilization in all its forms of expression is the important current that E. R. Dodds perhaps too strongly systematized in his lectures of 1963 under the title *Pagan and Christian in an Age of Anxiety*. Even if it were true that "the figure of this world," that is, the Roman world, seemed to be about to "pass away"—in the sense of an ultimate agony—"What does it matter in the light of eternity?" Beyond the great persecution of 303, would it be again, but in truth this time, *Apocalypse Now*? Some believers had continued to feel this anguish during the whole of the fourth century: the political and military history of the century shows that they did not lack objective reasons.

The second fact, however, was exactly the reverse: the Constantinian turning point, the conversion of the emperor to Christianity, without doubt in the year 312. In the following year, it led to not only the official proclamation of freedom of religion but also the beginning of privileges given to the Christian clergy, which had become an *ordo sacerdotalis*, a social body defined by the law. The distinction (the official distinction, to speak sociologically) was thereby established between clergy and laity.

The third fact—which was perhaps more the cause than the consequence of the preceding—was the growing avalanche of conversions. The Christian people, for such a long time a minority healthily marginalized and suspect, now increasingly ran the risk of coinciding, in their human reality, with the civil society. The bishops, for their part, began to consider themselves also as functionaries of a particular type within a Christian empire. Let us content ourselves to refer on this point to the sarcastic anticlericalism of the pagan Ammianus Marcellinus or to that of the virulent Christian Sulpicius Severus at the end of the century.

An event that was both contemporaneous with and correlative to the preceding points is the fourth fact, what one could call the "turning point of Anthony." Monasticism appeared from its beginning in continuity with the ideal of a martyrdom, which had become "daily" and "unbloody." It did not truly emerge in the West until the middle of the fourth century, but it was in the preceding century that Anthony appeared as a "layman who began a (spiritual) movement in the church" (as Dom Lanne said). The Western monks, however, at the end of the fourth century no longer cut off an ear to escape from priesthood, as had been done by a certain desert father in Egypt. It is true that a good part of the Western hierarchy had for its own good "contained" the monastic movement very early by cutting back the autonomy of certain ascetic communities and their attraction for the clergy who joined them. One can see this well in Spain in the last quarter of the century.

The fifth and last fact was the Theodosian turning point, which involved a spate of repressive imperial edicts against pagan rites, a failed pagan coup d'etat and the triumph of the Christian armies of Theodosius over these pagan insurgents. The theology of the imperial victory then turned against paganism itself. Imperial legislation dealt paganism the most fatal blow by suppressing the official subventions for the pagan priests of the city of Rome.

Through the influence of these five changes a certain life-style of baptized laypeople became better defined, that of the *fideles,* of the *plebs,* kept outside the chancel in the *quadratum populi* of the naves of the basilicas. It was still too early for Ambrose or Augustine to be able to pose the question as we would pose it, but both of them had been laymen for a long time—more than thirty years not baptized. Ambrose even became a bishop before receiving baptism. Their sermons are, then, to be considered as a continuing catechesis of one-time laity who spoke to a laity whose life problems they had known by personal experience. That is why the pastors of the fourth century always took care to be mediators between faith and life: their teaching began often enough from the daily life of the faithful in order to return to it. It is thus that Augustinian preaching on the Psalms contained a veritable pedagogy of the Christian daily rhythms of life; it was destined to nourish and to deepen daily the lived faith of the Christian laity.

But there is more. We possess a number of quite diverse pieces of literature that were written by and for the laity: accounts of conversions, correspondence, funerary inscriptions, and the last great apologetic works—from the writings of Firmicus Maternus to the two books *Against Symmachus* of

Prudentius. These documents have only rarely been exploited from this precise angle. We also must not forget the Latin hymnody, which had first been conceived and realized to be sung and meditated on by the assemblies of the Christian people and not by a specialized choir.

In this large documentation we shall draw out here only three themes in order to continue to respond to the question posed. The life of the laity in the fourth century was still a hard interior conflict between the old pagan and the new Christian; but liberated by the Constantinian turning point the laity— and, in particular, the educated laity—invented new spiritual itineraries. Finally, the debate between the earliest monastic asceticism and the more worldly faction of the clergy centering on the value of the temporal ought not to hide the silent but considerable search for a via media by and for convinced Christians who were also engaged in the world. More than the clergy and monks in their little priestly and ascetic communities, a large part of the laity of the fourth century continued to live what one could call the paradox of Tertullian. In the sacral civilization, which remained that of the Roman empire, it is true that the gods were still everywhere, and therefore (if one accepts the demonological exegesis of the pagan rites and cults) the baptized believed themselves to come up against a satanic presence everywhere they went.

In spite of, or perhaps because of, the religious liberalism proclaimed in 313, the virulence of the pagan reaction that still challenged the baptized in the fourth century was not due solely to the tenacity of the Roman *mos maiorum*. This pagan religiosity continued to express itself in daily life and in public monuments, in collective ritual ceremonies, in games and spectacles. It had gained new vigor under the tetrarchy which ended in the great persecution at the beginning of the fourth century, even if this was much less virulent and prolonged in the West.

The difficulty that the recently converted lay Christians experienced in detaching themselves from these ancestral rites was picturesquely illustrated in the interdicts of the Spanish Council of Elvira at the beginning of the fourth century. One can see here the quasi-syncretist liberties that many of the baptized took at that time in Baetica with their baptismal vows. Converted *flamini* continued to sacrifice. Other Christians married their daughters to pagan priests, went to cemeteries where they lit candles "capable of troubling the souls of the dead," and even had their harvests blessed by Jews. This is to say nothing of innumerable sins of a sexual order. It has been alleged that the fathers of Elvira were rigorist Novatian heretics. They condemned the practice of playing at all the tables, so to speak, and of multiplying supernatural assurances with regard to both temporal and eternal life evoked pagan spirituality and the cumulative devotions of Apuleius at the end of the second century and of Pretextatus at the end of the fourth. These liberties were in accord with the dispositions taken by Licinius and Constantine at Milan in 313: the two emperors said that they were concerned with seeing that "every sort of celestial divinity might be appeased and propitiated with regard to us and toward all of those who are under our power" (Lactantius *On the Death of Persecutors* 48.2).

Such religious incertitude had to disappear in time. A sermon of Augustine teaches us that certain of his parishioners had accepted analogous compromises. They prayed to Christ to have eternal life, but they preferred to pray to their ancient gods, who were nearer and more familiar, for the success of their little temporal affairs! In the middle of the fourth century in the heart of Cisalpine Italy Zeno of Verona found out about Christians who still kept pagan chapels on their rural estates (*Sermon* 1.25). He publicly denounced those who continued to consult their daily horoscope or who had recourse to haruspices and to augury. He also denounced the dissipated husbands who are "exasperated by the bond of marriage": in brief, these "equivocal and wavering Christians" who were neither faithful nor unfaithful (*Sermon* 1.35).

These Veronese Christians in the middle of the century appeared very weak in the face of Jewish and Manichaean proselytism. A wandering preacher could thus regain a whole community. That is what happened in Aquitaine, in the little town of Eauzé with the heresiarch Priscillian, if one is to believe Sulpicius Severus (*Chronicle* 2.48). At the extreme opposed to such compromises one finds pathological scrupulosity—as in the case of Publicola, whom Augustine gently mocked, showing him that a clear-minded and well-balanced Christian ought not to fall into the malady of abusive scruples but ought to exercise a mature judgment regarding relations with others and things that he believed to be contaminated by the remains of a dying paganism (*Epistle* 47). This response is remarkable because of the appeal that it makes to the autonomy of the personal judgment of laypersons in matters of conscience. Such a respect for their personal responsibility is completely opposed to clerical domination—which Publicola's letter could not but have helped encourage.

The conversion of the laity, even the catechized and baptized, seemed to be constantly continuing, if not renewed, throughout the fourth century. Was quantity compatible with quality? One thing is sure, Christianity such as it was lived by the laity of the fourth century was extremely ambiguous, and it was the same for their morality. Chaff and good grain were found in an inextricable *permixtio*. Watch out for the harvest and the threshing and the crushing of grapes at the end of time!—Augustine never ceased repeating this to his flock, and he surely had good reason to do so.

Insofar as this Christianity, having become official, acculturated itself more profoundly to the Latin world of the *pars Occidentis,* some of the laity found new forms of personal and collective relation to the mystery of Christ, which they lived simultaneously in the church and in the world. They did no more, actually, than bring an original note to that religious revival which put its mark upon the centuries of late antiquity—those which the historians of art have come to designate precisely as an "age of spirituality."

Even if the ministerial functions assumed by the laity in the course of the first centuries were taken over more and more by the clergy, it still remains true that in its *quadratum populi* the people of God remained, after God, the essential subject and object of the liturgy in its great public development in the fourth century. The participation of the laity was expressed in many ways: responses and acclamations of praise, listening to the readings and the homilies (often mixed with interruptions of the preacher by the crowd), bringing up the offerings, both eucharistic and other kinds. It was to associate the faithful more closely with the liturgy that Hilary in Gaul and Ambrose in Cisalpine Italy created hymnody. According to the admirable definition of Hilary of Poitiers, this hymnody is "the response of a pious profession of faith." Its effect is "to cast fear over any adversary, to knock out the devil, to conquer death by faith in the resurrection through this jubilation of our exulting voices" (*On Psalms* 65.4). Multiplied day by day, on Sundays and annual feasts especially, the liturgies wove the seasons together for the laity in a stream of celebrations that culminated in the great sacraments of their terrestrial journey: the Word of God and the Eucharist. Christ in glory, who dominated the iconography of the church apses of this time, is indeed the one "who is, who was, and who is to come" (Rev 1:4). Through and in him the *actuality* of humble daily life was constantly represented, that is, rendered present in this *actualization* of the presence of God to human beings and of human beings to God, which is the essence of the Christian liturgy. The laity were the active auditors of a preaching that often took its images, its parables, its pedagogy of the faith and the theological and moral virtues from their daily life in all the modalities and difficulties of Christian presence in the Roman world of their time and of their city.[8]

The other strong moment of this collective spirituality is to be found in the extraordinary rise of the cult of martyrs and the development of pilgrimages, which took place for the most part in relation to this rise of the liturgy. The cult of the dead, the ancient veneration for the *mediae potestates,* which literally "intercede" between the human being and the divinity, were beliefs and ritual forms too profoundly anchored in Roman spirituality for the laity to be able to content themselves with basilical liturgies. These were the human roots (specifically Jewish and some also Christian) of this cult of Christian martyrs, concretized in the cult of their tombs and then of their relics. The forms of its architectural, liturgical, literary, and epigraphical expressions were prodigiously diversified, above all in the second half of the century.[9]

The rise of the cult coincided with the entrance into the Christian church of the popular masses and of the aristocratic elite. The phenomenon should not be considered purely popular nor mounted by impresarios of the aristocracy. Without doubt it could have been a pretext for orgies and funerary drunkenness, but also and more largely it was a transfer and a survival from ancient cults of heroes, if not sometimes of gods—for example, when the cult of a saint succeeded *in situ* to the cult of a Gallo-Roman god. Nevertheless, from this original period Damasus of Rome, Ambrose of Milan, and Augustine of Hippo tried to "canalize" and to purify the cult of these privileged spiritual intercessors by subordinating it to the cult of their model, Christ, the unique mediator celebrated by the Epistle to the Hebrews in the New Testament.[10] It is still true that the cult of relics continued to grow, above all during the course of the following centuries, in proportion to the "virtues" of healing both body and soul attributed to them by believing people.

It was as much for devotion as to ask a saint for healing, exorcism, or pardon that the pilgrims went to visit sanctuaries raised over the tombs of the martyrs or sanctified by the presence of their relics. This new expression of Christian piety is well attested in literature from the end of the fourth century by two great women of the Western aristocracy who gave themselves over to asceticism: Egeria, probably a Spanish Roman of Galicia, a pilgrim in the East in 383–384 and author of *A Journal of a Voyage*, and Paula, a rich Roman matron whose *iter* of 385–386 is told in the epitaph which Jerome, her director of conscience, wrote when she died in 404 (Jerome *Letter 108*). Both women went "to see Jerusalem and the saints' places," but also "the tombs of the martyrs" and of the people of God of the two Testaments, and "the innumerable crowds of monks" in the desert of Egypt (*Letter 108*).

This pious tourism was directed also toward three types of privileged places, and such visits corresponded to three types of intentions, which were not mutually exclusive: to relive intensely the great events of salvation in the very same places from Sinai to Palestine where they occurred; to visit the living "holy men" and especially the monks of the desert; to venerate the remains of the martyrs in the basilicas in which they rested with the sentiments of devotion that Damasus expressed in his verse *Epigrams*, destined to be carved on the tombs of the martyrs of Rome and read there by pilgrims. At the end of the fourth century or the beginning of the fifth the Hispano-Roman poet Prudentius took advantage of a voyage to Rome to visit devoutly along his route the tomb-sanctuaries of the martyrs of Italy and of the city. Many poems from his *Book of Crowns,* consecrated to these martyrs, are like leaves along the road of this journey, which was both material and spiritual. Pilgrimages, whether in the city or in the region, gathered crowds of Christians from the surrounding area for the annual celebration of the *dies natalis* of a martyr or a confessor, such as the feasts of Peter and Paul at Rome on 29 June, or of the confessor Felix at Nola on 14 February. But already Jerusalem and Rome were the poles most frequented by a *peregrinatio* that one could call international. Also popular was Tours in Gaul, which became very lively after the death of Martin, whose cult thus promised an exceptional medieval development.[11]

The spiritual invention of these generations is not limited to this domain of collective liturgies or personal devotions. These are only the more visible aspects of an acculturation at once more vast and more profound because it concerned also literary forms and through them the ultimate forms of ancient thought and aesthetic. In this varied bouquet of individual formulas we shall turn only to the figures of four well-educated laymen whose works appeared throughout the century.[12] They were also poets who through the interior transparency of poetry allow us to hear more immediately the existential dialogue between a human being and God through which one can define "spirituality" at the personal level.

Lactantius, official rhetorician and teacher of the son of Constantine, offered, in his *Divine Institutions,* a reconciling apologetic: the best of the cultural and religious pagan tradition is presented there as a sort of Old Testament of the Gentiles. Lactantius legitimized and guaranteed the use of rhetoric and even poetry in the service of a refined expression of the Christian message. This work of mediation between the church and the cultural world in which it was incarnated was typical of a specific function of the lay writer. Like Minucius Felix in the preceding century, but with fewer "crypto-Christian" detours, the prose work of Lactantius is in some way at the leading edge of evangelization during the century of Constantine.[13] Very probably destined for an official ceremony in a court still largely pagan, the poem of Lactantius *On the Phoenix,* probably written in 327, was no longer "crypto-Christian." The poet here inherited the Christian interpretation of this myth of resurrection, which already appeared at the end of the first century in Clement of Rome, but the message, both political and religious, was enveloped in the energy of a descriptive imagination that was still very Alexandrine. The shadow of the resurrection of Christ appeared in it only furtively behind the political symbolism of the continuity of imperial power.[14] This polyvalence, in which the mystery of the risen Christ appears only through elaborate figures whose legitimate political use had been defended by the *Institutions,* characterized the quasi-syncretic spirituality of Constantinian Christianity. The protreptic concessions of the myth form an only too appropriate prelude to the "grand siècle" of acculturation of Latin Christianity.

Ausonius of Bordeaux was of an ancient Christian Gallo-Roman family. He well represents a Christianity established in the empire, or else a spirituality tempered by the imperial establishment. Although he was a rhetorician and not much of a philosopher, his faith was still both sincere and interior. One finds in his work spiritual attitudes that are curiously situated at quite different levels. In the *Ephemeris,* the poet opens his day with a long prayer in hexameters beginning with a litany of the divine attributes, the tone of which makes one think of the Neoplatonic poem of Tiberianus. Then follows a painting from the beyond under the sign of a heaven that is closer to the *Dream of Scipio* than to the Bible.[15] Ausonius was not the man who "prays without ceasing" of Paul; at the end of his long prayer he declared, "that's enough of my prayer to God" (*satis precum datum Deo . . .*). This formalist practitioner, attentive to the daily rite of morning prayer, seems scarcely to have been inhibited in addressing to the emperors a poem for the new year in which the refrain was a pagan prayer: *Iane veni; novus anne, veni; renovate veni sol!* (*Carmina* 3.5).[16] Ausonius reacted strongly to the surprising conversion of his student and friend Paulinus to asceticism, but was he so very wrong to be scandalized by the disorderly selling off of the immense domain of Paulinus? Where were the true spiritual responsibilities of this great lay landed proprietor?[17]

In the wake of this composite and, so to speak, plural spirituality, the profession of faith and the autobiographical confidences of the Roman senator Antonius appeared around 384. They illustrate, in elegant verses, the limpid confession of a spiritual journey, which brings to mind the witness of Justin two centuries earlier: "I traveled through all the sects, but I could find nothing better to believe in than Christ" (*Dialogue with Trypho* 2). It is notable that this Christ was essentially celebrated by Antonius in connection with the creation of the universe in ways that were not dissonant with the ancient Hellenistic and Roman theology of the "cosmic god." But also, on the other side, this Christ was the God of mercy and of pardon, he in whom goodness surpasses justice: *plus pius quam iustus erit.* This much more evangelical aspect is the one Antonius held the dearest and he says as much with moving fervor.

Let us conclude this "quartet" with the greatest of these Latin Christian

poets, Prudentius of Calagurris, one-time governor of a province and private
counselor of the emperor Theodosius.[18] One should emphasize at once his
conception of poetry as a spiritual exercise integrated into the devotional
exercises of the perfect life. Given the enduring influence of the poetic work
of Prudentius on the Middle Ages, this conception seals for centuries a
definitive alliance between the love of letters, even poetic literature, and the
desire for God. The poetry of Prudentius was foundational for the spiritual
poetry of the West in the same way as the hymns of Hilary of Poitiers and
Ambrose of Milan were fundamental for liturgical poetry. The second center
of particular interest in his work is found, for our purposes, in the two songs
of the *Against Symmachus,* where one discovers the most perfect expression
of the "official spirituality" of the Theodosian Christian empire. In a dangerous way it associates the religious triumph of Christianity with the political
triumph of the Theodosian dynasty. Without embarrassment Prudentius
opposed the civilized world of the Roman and Christian cities to the bar-
baric world of the countryside that was still pagan, as well as that of the
heretical Germanic invaders. He continued to believe in the divine mission
of a Christian empire that would inaugurate the kingdom of God in a world
submissive to Rome, and he probably died in this illusion some years before
Rome was taken by the Goths. It was time indeed that Augustine should
come to correct these perspectives to some degree in his *City of God.*

This collective and individual creativity of the Christian people turned to
good use the internal contradictions of the Constantinian Church and its
more and more ambiguous establishment in the empire. That is why one
must read *cum grano salis* the disastrous and grandiloquent balance sheets
with which Sulpicius Severus finished his *Chronicle:* that of a Christian
people abandoned by their pastors in discord.[19] This vengeful *sententia* of
a morose ascetic is far from doing justice to the slow deepening of the Christianization of the laity. In the first place, the vogue of monastic asceticism
and the exaltation of consecrated virginity had not yet overshadowed, except
among certain extremists (like Jerome), the eminent and recognized sanctifying values that marriage and the family retained. Two citations will suffice
to make this understood. First, the admirable and gracious prayer of Zeno
of Verona to Christ present in the community of the married couple: "Like
a skilled coachman you harmonize by these tender loins those who submit
their yet inexperienced necks to the very holy yoke of marriage so that their
effort may be equal in labor and affection" (*Sermons* 1.4). By itself this phrase
is worth all the laborious and deceiving explanations of Augustine's *On the
Good of Marriage.*[20] Elsewhere, in a rather astonishing page of his commentaries on John, the same Augustine knew how to exalt the family as a little
cell of the church. In the exercise of his functions, the father of the family,

33. *Reliquary Box of the True Cross,* 7th–8th century

Augustine says, "will fulfill even in his own house an ecclesial office and, in a certain manner, an episcopal office by serving Christ in his family."[21]

A second essential point in this positive evaluation of the activities of the laity in the world is the rehabilitation of manual labor. The *artes libero dignae*, the "liberal arts," are not the only occupations worthy of the children of a God who became "the son of a carpenter." In this sense the gist of the treatise of Augustine *On the Work of Monks* surpassed the problem posed by the "angelist" ascetics, who pretended to occupy all their time in praying and meditating on the Scripture without doing any manual labor. In point of fact, the first monks of the East, since Pachomius, had accorded a place of honor to manual labor in a program of life entirely ordered to the search for God. They were thus in line with a very ancient Roman tradition (that of the magistrate-laborer, like Cincinnatus). Such an esteem of manual laborers was revolutionary in a slave-holding and aristocratic society that more and more had a tendency to depreciate as servile this sort of work. It is also necessary to situate this reconsideration of work in a much larger context, that is, in the amazing celebration of the creations of human genius that crowned book 22 of the *City of God:* "It is," said Augustine, "its high natural value which permits human talent to invent all that, to learn it and to practice it." From material techniques to the fine arts, from poetry to the sciences, the litany of human creations that followed this passage loudly affirmed the value and the sense of all these temporal activities, which were in fact the lot of the laity engaged in its diverse professions (*City of God* 22.24).[22]

The whole tissue of social life was therefore given value by the diversified activity of the Christian laity in all the ranks of the society of the late empire. This society was thus open to an incessant exercise of fraternal charity, which transfigured the old Roman virtue of *humanitas*. It is this charity, said Zeno of Verona, which "keeps towns and peoples in an assured peace; it is she who keeps weapons at rest in the guard of the prince who suppresses trials, muzzles ferocity and stifles anger . . ." (*Sermons* 1.36). This litany is without doubt not so idealized as one would be tempted to think. Only a few years later Ammianus Marcellinus painted a sinister picture of contemporary society in the court and in certain great families of Rome. To some it was certain that the interior peace of the Christians and the peace that the empire retained as a Virgilian mission to defend and to impose were strictly bound together: this is the main lesson of book 19 of the *City of God.* Like Martin of Tours (*Life of Martin* 3), many converted soldiers did not, for all that, quit at once the service of Caesar, in spite of the fact that this was said in a letter of Jerome. Thus many holy laypeople of the fourth century still practiced the *vobiscum militamus* of Tertullian. When the barbarians menaced the frontiers, one must not flee the world and take refuge in a cloister. Augustine said this firmly to one person, Boniface, Count of Africa. As a responsible leader and as a Christian, he must continue to defend courageously a peace that was so necessary to the church and to the empire.

The *City of God*—even the *City of God*—had in other contexts brought a notable corrective to the risks of confusion between the service of God and that of Caesar. Profoundly attached to *romanitas,* convinced of the real benefits of a Christian empire for the advancement of the kingdom of God, Augustine nevertheless kept his distance with regard to the prestige of the terrestrial city founded on the will of collective power, the famous *amor laudis* of the old Romans. But he was not less on guard against possible illusions about the nature of a *City of God* which in fact is built mysteriously but which will not be achieved in a stable and visible manner in this world. Insisting on the citizenships more than on the cities (it is the double sense of the Latin word *civitas*), Augustine interiorizes the problems posed for lay Christians by their political engagements in the two *militiae* of the Christian empire (the army and the public function). With faith and with fear, they had to live the mystery of a *permixtio,* where the future elect and the future reprobates walk together here below, without as well as within the church.[23]

Thus, the fourth century clearly promised the free expression of spiritual values among a laity deeply engaged in the life of this world, at the same time sinning and saved. That is because even when they had become monks or bishops, if not both, the great spiritual leaders of this time were long-time laity with their rich political, military, and cultural experience. It is thus easier to explain why so many of the forms and themes of their most personal spirituality are found in implicit or direct rapport with the problems posed to both the conscience and the faith of the Christian laity. Confronted by the double defiance of the monastic profession and the hierarchical priesthood, the laity were constrained, then, to define better the specificity of their singular vocation—as uncomfortable in the church as in the world.

## Lay Practice and Piety in the Early Western Middle Ages (Sixth to Tenth Century)

The time of incubation of European civilization from the fifth to the tenth century saw the modification, in its forms and even in its content, of the religious life of the Christian people without denying the rich heritage of the preceding centuries. Four principal factors in these changes should be underlined.

After the interregnum of Roman power, made more serious in the West by the definitive migrations of Germanic peoples into Roman territory from 406 until the deposition of the last emperor in the *pars Occidentis* in 476, the power of the bishops—who often remained the only officials left to bear all the responsibility in the cities—and that of the German kings came to challenge each other in the temporal order as well as in the spiritual. This tension, at the same time destructive and fruitful, worked itself out in a difficult face-to-face situation, especially from the time of the crowning of Charlemagne at Rome by Leo III on Christmas Day in the year 800 (a French poet has spoken of "these two halves of God, the pope and the emperor").[24] The new sacralization of sovereign power had already found liturgical expression in the Davidic anointing of the Visigothic kings (certainly of Wamba in 672), and of Pepin, the father of Charles, by Boniface in 751. The chief of the laity became, thus, a sacred personage at the top of a social pyramid that became more and more sacred. A comparable alliance had been established between the Roman senatorial aristocracy and the Germanic nobility, on the one hand, and, on the other, the monastic and clerical hierarchy over which they increased their power until the Merovingian scandals. The result was that ignorant laity without morality became abbots and bishops through the action of the princes. Compared with these privileged persons whose nobility rested on birth, culture, and riches, the *populus Christianus* declined, destined to poverty, obscurity, and a veritable "deculturation." This last was accelerated by the destructions of the invasions, the disappearance of the public school as it had existed in antiquity, and the deterioration of a language given over to a purely oral culture. The opposition between *litterati* and *illitterati* requires some nuances, but it would often accentuate the radical distinction between clergy and laity in the medieval sense of the two words.

This cleavage of the Christian people was clearer still in the countryside, where the Christian poet and imperial functionary Prudentius of Calagurris from the beginning of the fifth century saw a rural and pagan barbarism in opposition to the civilization of Roman villages already Christianized. In spite of the increase of the evangelization of rural dwellers and then the creation of rural parishes, Christ was still above all and for a long time "the God whom one adores in the cities," according to the verse written by the Gallo-Roman poet Endelechius in the second part of the fourth century.[25]

In those regions of northern Europe that had not been conquered by Rome (Ireland, Scotland, Germany), and to a lesser degree in the ancient Roman provinces of the *Romania*, above all in the territories that had either been only slightly or not at all Romanized, the close connivance remained between Christianity and ancient ethnic forms of expression, social structures, moral values, languages, religions. One could demonstrate this in the Christian rites relating to death, to burial, to the cult of tombs.[26] In Rome itself, in the midst of the fifth century, Leo the Great was scandalized by the celebration of the *Lupercalia,* or by the kisses that his flock turned around to throw to the sun before entering the basilica of St. Peter. What must it have been like far from Rome—a fortiori at a distance from towns! The Christianization of the feasts and cultic places of rural paganism was a good risk taken by the church in the early Middle Ages in reaction to the expeditionary vandalism of the monastic "commandoes" carried out in the fourth century by Martin and his emulators against the pagan sanctuaries. The monks would continue this tradition, as is proved by the violent installation of Benedict at Monte Cassino in the place of a sanctuary of Apollo and of a sacred wood. (Benedict began by destroying both; see Gregory the Great, *Dialogues* 2.8.11).

Medieval society structured itself little by little according to a new division of the *ordines,* which left the laity consisting of nonnoble Christians and married Christians on a lower level. Following upon the tripartition found in Gregory the Great (see his *Pastoral Care* and *Moralities on Job*) among monks, preachers of the word (clergy), and married people (*conjugati*), there succeeded by a sort of progressive return to the ancient Indo-European tripartition, the distinction between *oratores* (those men of prayer who are clergy and monks), *laboratores* (the laity devoted to manual work, essentially in the fields), and finally the *equites* (the nobility who went to war on horseback and became knights). Thus, the laity were doubly "cornered" within a framework common to civil society and the Christian church. From this resulted a regression in the quality of the religion of the laity and a relation that one could call "dialectic" between monks and laity, even if the pastors tried constantly to preserve the dignity and fervor of the spirituality of their congregations of baptized laypeople, and even if the Carolingian Reform (*reformatio in melius*—according to an ancient Roman formula) tried, not without some success, to improve the level of religion lived by the Christian people.

The lowering of the cultural level provoked by the often dramatic events of the fifth and sixth centuries, the progressive extinction of the Roman Christian elite and the installation of Germanic barbarian peoples (who were pagans or heretic Arians), brought about a general collapse not only of evangelization but also of the spiritual tone of populations evangelized much earlier in a West that had been Roman. In the face of the definitive invasion by the barbarians of a Roman Christian empire, trouble and skepticism disturbed consciences. One reads this interior crisis in the mirror of the Latin literature of the fifth century. This questioning is found in the *Histories against the Pagans,* which Paul Orosius wrote against Roman imperialism, or in the invectives of Salvian against the hardened vices of the Romans—in his eyes justly chastised—in his *The Government of God.*

This deep and lasting trauma shook the faith without many seeing in it, as did Paulinus of Pella (grandson of Ausonius), a providential invitation to change one's customs. Paulinus addressed to God, who had converted him in this way, a *Poem of Thanksgiving* (in 459). In spite of the passage of the ancient nobility from "red" to "black," as Stendhal would say—in fact, from public charges to "episcopal responsibility" (*sarcina episcopalis,* as Augustine had already said)!—the number of people who could not read increased in proportion to the disappearance of schools and did not cease to spread even among the clerics until the sixth century, when episcopal and monastic schools were created. The children of the laity were especially welcomed in these schools so that they could become clergy or monks. Those who returned to the lay condition were drawn into a world of violence, where there reigned among the nobility surrounding the Germanic kings what Tertullian had called the irremissible sins (*peccata irremissibilia*): murder, adultery, idolatry. One has only to open at any place the truculent *History of the Franks* of Gregory of Tours (d. 594) to conjure up an image that was not at all flattering to the Merovingian "elites" during the sixth century. The people were subjected to malnutrition if not famine, to insecurity and epidemics, as well as to the brutalities of the nobility. How could the values of temporal existence not be objectively much more devalued than in the time of the *Pax Romana*—even as unstable as this was in the last centuries of the empire? In such a situation Christianity became for the majority of the laity a religion of supernatural power at the disposition of those who belonged to Christ. Rather than a God distant and feared for his justice more than loved for his mercy, the Christian people confided themselves with passion to the intercession of the saints, made present by their tombs and their relics—if not by the material that one had touched to the tombs (*brandea*). "Relics were the main channel through which supernatural power was available for the needs of ordinary life."[27] Thus, rites of contact of a suspect magical-religious character were generalized and institutionalized. The anxious believers waiting for material and spiritual salvation looked to these rites and objects for healing of illness and infirmity, deliverance from diabolical possession, and security in this life and in the next.

The abundant literature on the *Miracles of St. Martin*—above all at his tomb in the basilica of Tours placed under his patronage—says much on these elementary expressions of the faith. The sanctuaries and the feasts that surrounded the tombs and the relics of the saints crisscrossed time and space. Crowds of pilgrims started out on the roads, often traveling great distances. They flowed across the West in a spiritual *peregrinatio* that, since the fourth century, had chiefly moved toward the goal of the Holy Land, Egypt, and the whole of the Roman East. When the Islamicized Arabs took Jerusalem, an act that in 637 crowned their conquest of the greater part of the ancient Middle East, pilgrims then found their way to the Holy Land difficult and perilous. The centuries of the crusades approached, in which crusaders considered themselves to be pilgrims in arms. That is why, from the Carolingian epoch on, centers of pilgrimages multiplied in the West. They did not cease to draw crowds for more than a millennium. Believers came from all the regions of the empire and of the future duchies and kingdoms. They came to venerate sanctuaries of Christian antiquity, such as those of Rome and of Tours, but also to new places reputed to be holy, such as Mont Saint-Michel "in peril of the sea" in Normandy; Monte Gargano in southern Italy; and lastly, near to the Spanish "Land's End," the Galician tomb said to be of the apostle James, at the *Campus stellae* of Campostella.

These pilgrimages continued to attract a devotion with intentions as diverse as those of the ancient pilgrims, even if a faith (often very elementary) in supernatural power affected and enhanced the prestige of these holy places, which were as fearful as they were beneficent. But the pilgrimages took on new significance, in particular under the influence of the idea of spiritual detachment, in a wandering that was a material and spiritual quest for God. This ideal was lived and spread by the Irish monks—the *Scotti peregrini*, especially on the continent in the seventh and eighth centuries. These are the ones who, at the same time as they laid tariffs on their penitents, encouraged the ambiguous development of penitential pilgrimages. As brutal as he was devoted, the count of Anjou, Fulk Nerra, died at a very old age during his fourth pilgrimage to Jerusalem, where he flagellated himself ostentatiously before the Holy Sepulchre.

If true Christianity did not take refuge in monasticism alone, it is true that the cultural and spiritual role of monasticism was irreplaceable in the centuries of the early Middle Ages. It was a source for the spirituality of the best laity, even if these did not end their lives in a monastery, as did the Merovingian dignitary Wandrille at Fontenelle or again Queen Radegonde at Sainte-Croix of Poitiers.[28]

From the fifth century on, conversion to the perfect life was not expressed only in the practices of the hermitage or the cenobium. Laypersons continued to live in the world—if not to assume their diverse temporal responsibilities—and at the same time lead the lives of converts (*conversi*). They might well be represented as the ancestors of the members of the third orders and of the secular institutes of the modern age. One of the most startling examples was Count Gerald of Aurillac (d. 909), whose biography was written by Odo, the abbot of Cluny, as a model for the noble layman. Detached from his earthly goods, Gerald nevertheless continued to administer them in the service of the poor. Without leaving the world, he shared the trials of those in the world, even in armed conflicts, and made at least seven pilgrimages to Rome. A man of justice, humble and charitable toward all, faithful to his word, chaste without being a monk, Gerald created a monastery, which was placed under the patronage of Saint Severus of Rome at the end of the ninth century. He seemed to be the very type of the pious layman.[29]

The richness of the experience of the perfect life in the course of the first centuries of the early Middle Ages contrasted with the uniformity imposed (at least in intention and prescription) on Western monasticism by the Carolingians when they tried to generalize the use of the *Rule of St. Benedict*.[30] Even in this—which appears to us today more as the fruit of a reform than as an absolute beginning—it is appropriate to remember the capital importance of chapter 53 of the *Rule*, "On the Welcome of Guests," reserved "above all to brothers in the faith and to pilgrims," who are not only clergy and monks. One owes them every civility possible (*omnis exhibeatur humanitas*). This style of balanced life transmitted to the laity the values of *romanitas* and of the older form of Christianity, the example of spiritual liberty founded on the observance of a common law, the actualization of the model of the first evangelical and apostolic community, the sense of the *conversio morum* and of the *stabilitas* in a world often derailed and constantly destabilized by the diverse forms of collective and individual violence.

More simply, but on a point in every sense fundamental, the Western monks saved and maintained the heritage of ancient and patristic culture while ordering their love of letters to the monastic desire for God. But very early they played an equally important role in the education of the laity. This softened the disappearance of the ancient school, as can be seen through the little-known example of a small school that the picturesque hermit Valerius Bergidensis kept in his Galician solitude of Bierzo in the seventh century. The monastic communities rapidly developed their schools and gave to the young students who came from the world (many of whom returned to it) the respect and the taste for books, reading, and writing, without which the Scriptures would not have been able to retain the fundamental place that they ought to hold always in Christian spirituality, including that of the laity.

Often formed by the exercise of the perfect life in the great cenobia of the West—in Gaul, at Marmoutier from the fourth century and Lérins from the fifth century—many bishops took to heart the doctrinal, moral, and spiritual formation of the flocks confided to them, exercising toward them by both pastoral word and activity their *cura animarum*. To animate and reanimate the urban communities, to encourage evangelization in the countryside—indeed, even of the barbarian nations, where Christianity more often than not had not penetrated further than a kind of Romanization— these were the tasks to which a majority of bishops continued to give themselves with patience and ingenuity. The majority, even when their names are known to us from their signatures at regional synods, have remained "foot soldiers of history" in H.-I. Marrou's phrase. For their flocks the missionary bishops multiplied attempts at new acculturations of Roman Christianity in Celtic, Saxon, and Germanic milieus. An outstanding example of such efforts occurs in the correspondence of Gregory the Great in the last ten years of the sixth century. The pope had seen to the intellectual and religious formation of English slaves, so that these *Angli* could aid their brothers in race and language to become *angeli* (one must pardon this great missionary pope an expressive play on words). He even recommended that during the evangelization of the Saxons of England the missionaries at first make use of the local pagan sanctuaries by transforming them into churches (*Epistles* 11.56).

Not less was the concerted effort to forge a new Christian society in a Europe formerly Roman and already become mission lands. It is possible to stake out, by precise literary works, catechisms for the laity, which differ among themselves by their dates and by the situations to which their authors dedicated these plainly pastoral works. At the beginning of the sixth century, we have the *Sermons to the People* addressed by Caesarius of Arles to the Arlesians and to the country people from round about who came to assist at the liturgies of their central church and to hear the word of their bishop. A *sermo humilis* developed, in form and content, "little with little ones." At the end of this century, the Galician bishop Martin of Braga wrote for the Suevian king Miro some "precepts which can easily be followed by the laity of good conduct according to the laws of natural human intelligence, without the precepts of the divine scriptures" (*Formula of the Moral Life*, prologue [*PL* 72, col. 23]). In these same years, Pope Gregory dedicated his *Moralities on Job* to the monks, and his *Pastoral Rule* to the clergy charged with the *regimen animarum*; but it was directly to the lay audience of his Roman diocese that he commented on Scripture, in particular on the Gospels.

In the beginning of the seventh century, the lay catechumens, the baptized, the confirmed, the married, and the penitent, did not all get equal attention in Isidore of Seville's treatment of the "Duties of Members of the Church"

in his *Synonyms or Lamentations of a Sinful Soul.* This is a manual of
teaching at the same time linguistic, rhetorical, and spiritual, in which
young laypeople of Seville—and thereafter of the whole of Europe—as well
as young clergy and young monks, could find instruction. The "spiritual
testament" of Isidore, which constitutes his *Sentences,* sketched as in a miniature model the Christian society that he dreamed of inaugurating in the
Visigothic kingdom. Care for the humble and the poor held a place in his
*Sentences,* as well as the duties of state of all those who exercised functions
of authority: the bishops in the church, and the king and all his representatives (*iudices*) across the kingdom. The call to the perfect life and to its
religious and moral exigencies was addressed to all the orders of the church
of Spain. It was finally at the demand of the first layman of the kingdom—
the Visigoth king Sisebut—that Isidore wrote his vast encyclopedia, the
*Etymologies,* a compendium of knowledge, largely profane, destined first of
all for the laity.[31]

From an entirely different horizon, at the beginning of the eighth century
in Ireland, came the schematic and piquant satire the *Twelve Abuses of the
Age* (*PL* 4, cols. 869–82): twelve significant portraits, in which the laity have
the best part. In this satire there are back to back the rich man without alms
and the poor proud man, the master without virtue and the unjust king,
the citizen without discipline and the people without law, the old man
without religion and the young man without docility, the querulous Christian and the unchaste woman.[32] The Irish author foreshadowed the fabliaux,
at least insofar as his Celtic humor is not to be compared to the portraits
of Latin satire and to the more somber depiction of evils of Roman society
that were transmitted to him through the treatise of Cyprian *To Donatus.*
But that did not prevent him from observing, in its natural state, lay society
in an Ireland slow to become Christian. The little work, under the name
of Cyprian, enjoyed an exceptional success throughout the early Middle
Ages, no less than the Isidorian works and the sermons of Caesarius.

To these tumultuous contradictions of lay religion in the early Middle
Ages what new was brought by the Carolingian *reformatio*? There were
several new factors: an even more precise effort to ensure the formation of
the laity and their religious practice; an attention to the conjugal and
familial formation of laity by laity; a clerical reflection on lay moral and
spiritual education; and some attempts to invent or develop new *media* for
the Christian message.

As the first layman of a new empire, Charlemagne preached by example.
"He never failed to go to this church [the famous Palatine Chapel of
Aachen] morning and evening; he returned there for the night office. . . . He

also used to correct the manner of reading the liturgical lessons and to sing the Psalms, being himself very expert in both matters" (Eginhard *Life of Charles* 26). In his *General Monition* of 789, the sovereign prescribed "the establishment of schools where children could learn to read. May each monastery and each diocese learn the Psalms, writing, singing, computation [the calculation of dates and movable feasts on the basis of astronomical data], grammar; and let the students have well-corrected books [Psalters and missals]." In raising thus the intellectual level of the formation of the clergy, the prince intended to restore among the laity a better understanding of the Christian faith and of its diverse requirements, participation in liturgical ceremonies that was less passive, and thereby a successful moral and spiritual rearmament of the Christian people. As a result, under the influence of the Irish, there developed a practice of auricular confession (from the mouth of the faithful to the ear of the confessor). The *Chapters* of Charlemagne's counselor, the Spaniard Theodulf, prescribed for all the laity a minimum of religious practice: to learn and be able to recite the *Pater* and the *Credo;* to pray morning and evening and, if they did not know these two prayers, to say, "Lord, you have formed and created me, have pity on me; God have pity on me, a sinner"; to observe scrupulously the day of rest on Sunday; to assist at vespers on Saturday and at matins on Sunday before the principal Mass. But in what measure was this excellent program applied?

The formation of the nobility by a Christian family education is witnessed to by a text unique in its genre, the *Manual for My Son*,[33] composed at Uzès (province of Gard) by a laywoman with the Germanic name of Dhuoda, who wrote in Latin, without doubt at the beginning of the year 843. She was the wife of Bernard, who was himself the son of a close cousin of Charlemagne, and she dedicated her treatise to her son William, then age sixteen. This "rule, model and manual" was to serve as a vade mecum for the young man, who was going to make his debut in high Carolingian society. Dhuoda wanted to transmit to her son the best of religious culture, nourished by the Bible, by the Latin fathers, and by Carolingian religious writers. William was to read there constantly "that which he ought to do for the love of his mother," as the text says at the outset. The picture of religion is curious: the grandeur of a transcendent God is practically eclipsed by the Christ; only hope can save a man from his despairing fragility, thanks to the gifts of the Spirit, which will aid him in rooting out vices under the blows of virtues ("psychomachy" in the tradition of Prudentius, but taken also from the page of Ephesians on spiritual arms). William was to "accommodate himself to the great and the small" and remain always faithful to his Lord. But six years later, in the revolt against King Pepin of Aquitaine under the count of Bordeaux, William was taken prisoner and decapitated. The *Manual* is, in its way, one of the mirrors of princes, a literary genre that was beginning to develop.

It was also for a high personage, Count Matfrid, that Jonas of Orleans wrote (before 828) his treatise *Instruction of the Laity,* in response to the question: How ought those who are bound by marriage to lead a life agreeable to God? Jonas, in this patristic anthology, refers too often to Augustine and Jerome for us to be able to see in him any progress toward a less strictly puritan conception of conjugal life. He becomes more interesting when he gives general advice on the Christian life of the laity: to communicate frequently; not to hold back the tithes due to the church (!); to respect priests (an order in vogue under Louis the Pious) and the poor—without allowing oneself to be turned from these duties by too great a passion for the hunt and for dogs; to practice hospitality by observing "the rule proper to Christians." This *Regula Christiana* is certainly not without relation to chapter 53 of the Benedictine *Rule.* But from such mirrors are we able to see the image of Carolingian laypeople such as they are or such as they ought to be? Only meticulous comparison of these texts and their patristic lessons would permit a response, which would require very delicate discrimination. On their side, the councils protected the marriage of slaves and the liberty of the mutual consent of spouses, prescribed monogamy, and fulminated against endogamy, adultery, and divorce. But such texts, theoretical or canonical, allow us to see only very indirectly the real Christian life common to mortals. There was obviously a great deal of work to do to restore faith and morals and above all to achieve a total renunciation of pagan practices. The *General Monition* of 789 effectively proscribed astrologers, those who cast lots, and magicians; it also forbade lighting candles before trees, stones, and springs. Are we then so far from the sermon of Martin of Braga two centuries earlier against the pagan practices of the Galician countrypeople—the celebrated *On the Correction of the Peasants?* Or from the effort of Isidore, at the beginning of the seventh century, to instruct the Spaniards given to rites of sympathetic magic that were intended to help the stars in eclipse?

To accelerate this difficult Christianization of ancestral customs, it was important that pastoral oratory be understood and comprehended. But Latin was still the exclusive liturgical language, although even the laity of the Roman countries understood it less and less. That is why the Council of Tours in 813 prescribed repeating the sermon in a "rustic Roman language"—we would say today in proto-Romance. We have from the ninth century an embryo of a sermon of Jonas in the Romance of the north of France, and from the tenth century, sermons in Anglo-Saxon. But it was difficult to bring down the barrier between the Latin-speaking and educated clergy and a Christian people who understood Latin less and less and did not truly participate except in the processional parts of the liturgies, such as the offertory of the Mass, or those of the periodic and seasonal feasts like Rogation Days (which were a Christianized form of the ancient *Robigalia* of 25 April). Song in the vernacular language appeared along with dance in the churches of Verona in the tenth century, but outside the church proper.

There remains the medium of frescoes. The Carolingian West, which had rightly escaped the complications of Byzantine iconoclasm, knew how to use the artistic cycles illustrating the two Testaments on the walls of its churches in this pre-Romanesque epoch. It even made a place for hagiography, as one can see from the inscriptions preserved from the vanished frescoes of Saint-Martin de Tours. But the reliquary statues dear to the Aquitainians (such as Sainte-Foy de Conques in Aveyron, where the statue is taken in procession to the sound of cymbals—as earlier was done in the processions to Cybele) did not please the clergy at all!

Thus, the development of a spirituality of the laity made its way with difficulty in the Christian West of the first millennium. It was a victim of a triple confiscation: political and social, monastic, and above all cultural. But the clergy and monks themselves were very often drawn from among those who had long been laymen, and it was difficult for them to break with the experiences of years of secular life. Pastors had been at first among the flock; Pope Gregory I himself had been a prefect of Rome. This layman who became monk, priest, and finally pope, the most holy of clergy and of monks, retained this wise maxim, so merciful to human weakness and so well aware of the difficulty of being a good layperson: "The holy church corrects certain things with fervor, she tolerates others with meekness, she closes her eyes on still others and bears them with reflective attention. . . ."

*Translated by Jill Raitt*

## Notes

1. See *The Layman in Christian History*, ed. S. C. Neill and H. R. Weber; and Y. Congar, *Lay People in the Church*.

2. Is this a hypothetical argument that is being pushed (as is often the case in Tertullian) to the extreme paradox? Is it a trace of Montanist heresy (the treatise dates from the years 211–212), or is it simply the expression of a practice that still existed in the African communities? In any case, the text brings into sharp focus the dispute that took place in the great church, and a fortiori in the sects, which were still very

"charismatic," but especially between these latter and the catholic communities, which were in the process of becoming more rigorously structured. This dispute involved the affirmation of the clerical hierarchy over against the protestations of a Christian people who from the beginning were accustomed to more flexibility in the division of functions, even liturgical functions.

3. In this metaphor, drawn from the *militia Dei* or *Christi*, Tertullian plays on the two senses of the word *sacramentum:* a military oath, and baptismal promises to "renounce the devil, and all his pomp (*pompa diaboli*) and all his angels" (see *On the Crown* 3.3).

4. For him, the institution crowns the charism—an elegant solution to the dispute referred to above. Cyprian will resolve it in the same way, but inversely. He will personify the great exemplary figure of the martyred bishop on 14 September 258, after Cornelius of Rome's martyrdom on 14 September 253, and before that of Fructuosus of Tarragona on 21 January 259. These solemn executions were like liturgies in which the whole community took part, before reclaiming and solemnly burying the mortal remains and distributing as relics the linens stained with the blood of the victim. Thus was already born the cult of the martyrs, which was still closely associated with the cult of the dead.

5. The word *cohabitamus* implies duties and rights, intentions and acts of a free "cohabitation," which places Christians at the heart of this human world, like the leaven hidden in the dough of the gospel to make it rise.

6. "Acta Maximiliani," in H. Musurillo, *The Acts of Christian Martyrs* (Oxford: Oxford University Press, 1979) 247.

7. Fragment from *Liber de Sententiis politiae Platonicae* of Galen.

8. This aspect of the spirituality of laypersons is better known to us through studies that are both theological and literary, such as Pascuale Borgomeo, *L'Église de ce temps dans la prédication d'Augustin;* and Suzanne Poque, *La langage symbolique dans la prédication de saint Augustin.*

9. The anthropological and social conditioning of this cult, its evolution, and the development of its concrete forms has recently been clarified in three substantial books by Victor Saxer (*Morts, martyrs, reliques en Afrique chrétienne aux premiers siècles*), Peter Brown (*The Cult of the Saints*), and Yvette Duval (*Loca Sanctorum Africae*).

10. If it could be reduced to the superstitious veneration of the smallest relic, it was also purified into a new form of "spiritual sacrifice" for Christ, venerated in the memorial in one of his suffering members who had "fulfilled in himself what was lacking in the sufferings of Christ," according to the mysterious verse of Colossians (1:24).

11. The words *peregrinatio* and *peregrinus* had first designated in classical Latin the voyage and the voyager abroad (from *per agros-externos*, "across territories, foreign"). In particular, the "cultural" voyage into the Greek Orient had become, since the final centuries of the empire, a usage accepted in literary circles. The "pilgrimage" to places where great people had lived or had been buried was a forerunner of the future Christian pilgrimages, as were trips to the sanctuaries and to the centers of initiation rites in the Greek Orient. For the first, note the rediscovery of the tomb of Archimedes by Cicero on the outskirts of Syracuse (*Tusculanae disputationes* 5.23) or his "pilgrimage" to the Academy of Plato and to the remains of the house of Epicurus in Athens (*De finibus* 5.1, 3); for the second, note the voyages of Hadrian.

12. The rhetorician Lactantius in 327, the Bordelaise professor Ausonius in the second half of the century, the Roman senator Antonius around 384, and finally the high official Prudentius during the Theodosian period. An African, a Gaul, a Roman, a Spaniard: the sampling could hardly have been better.

13. I am inclined to believe that he was both the spokesman for and the inspiration of this.

14. It was a question of celebrating this continuity first in Rome in 327 and in these *uicennalia* of Constantine, which were also the *decennalia* of his son Crispus.

15. But did not Petronius Probus do as much in juxtaposing in his two funeral inscriptions a vertical imagery of ascension to heaven and a voyage to the land of the dead worthy of the ancient "*katabasis,*" or journey to the lower world?

16. Ornamental paganism? An image warranted by the contemporary recovery of solar iconography applied to Christ? It is difficult to understand, let alone to judge.

17. The cause of asceticism of Paulinus appears, upon serious reflection today, to be less easy to defend than had generally been thought. And in the ninth century, Gerard of Aurillac showed himself to be more circumspect (see above, p. 461–62).

18. With only his diverse poems as a starting point, it would have been possible to describe the major characteristics of the spirituality of cultured laypersons during the century of Theodosius and of his son. It appeared more advisable to confine our discussion of this rich work to two particular characteristics.

19. Having painted with a Sallustian darkness the divisions successively provoked within the clergy by the Arian controversy and by the "Priscillian affair," he opposed to the bishops torn by theological passions "the people of God and all the best Christians held in shame and in derision" (*plebs dei et optimus quisque probo ac ludibrio habebatur* [*Chronicle* 2.51.8]).

20. Even if it is true that Emile Schmitt has shown that Augustine developed, through all his works, a baptismal theology of conjugal *life*, thus making baptism the source of the sanctification of spouses (see *Le mariage chrétien dans l'oeuvre de saint Augustin*).

21. *Episcopale implebit officium, ministrans Christo.* Augustine forthwith invited all laypersons to do the same "in their own way," by their good conduct, their almsgiving, and even "in preaching the name of Christ to whomever they can" (*On John* 51.13).

22. As of all things created, Augustine could say of these things what he wrote to be engraved on the paschal candle: "All this is yours, and it is good, since it is you who have created it in your goodness" (*City of God* 15.22).

23. The state of lay Christians, in this domain also, is "to live together with all people, joined together by this great thread of the gospel, and in this world as in an ocean . . . until the moment when, arriving at the shore, the evil will be separated from the good" (*City of God* 18.49).

24. Victor Hugo, *Hernani,* v. 1480.

25. It is thus that the term *paganus* (source of the words which designate the "pagan" in the European languages) is definitely linked with its ancient meaning of "peasant" and of *pagi* (our "countries," from the original Latin sense of "villagers" and their territory), that of a fidelity to the beliefs and rites of the pre-Roman rural religions.

26. See the article by P. Riché in this volume.

27. R. W. Southern, *Western Society and the Church in the Middle Ages* (Baltimore, MD: Penguin Books, 1970) 31. People often returned to the "bargaining" of the Roman with his gods: "I give to you so that you will give to me" (*do ut des*). To this God, the just judge, it was necessary to be rigorously accountable for one's sins, through penances that the Irish would teach the West.

28. See the article of J. Leclercq, "Monasticism and Asceticism, II: Western Christianity," in this volume. But if the osmosis between clergy and monasticism was accentuated during the course of this century, it must not be thought that monasticism, for all this, had deviated from its fundamental objectives: to strive for the sanctity of perfect life through the triple renunciation of the flesh, material goods, and personal will, and

through searching for God in the liturgy, the private and public reading of Scripture, personal and communal prayer, and all the fraternal activities of the common life. Between this spirituality of the monks and that of laypeople, there had neven been a complete division. God is one, and the interior roads that led to him could be distinct, yet not incompatible.

29. See "Life of Gerald of Aurillac," by Odo of Cluny, in *St. Odo of Cluny*, trans. and ed. G. Sitwell (New York: Sheed & Ward, 1958) 89–180.

30. See the article by J. Leclercq, "Monasticism and Asceticism, II: Western Christianity," in this volume.

31. The next-to-last paragraph of book 7, *De Deo, angelis et sanctis*, in chapter 14, "Of the Rest of the Faithful," was content with the gloss *Laicus popularis. Laos enim Graece populus dicitur.*

32. No monk is represented here, which could signify in a negative way the original milieu of this work.

33. If we leave out of consideration the treatise on education entitled *Methods of Instruction (Institutionum disciplinae)*, taken to be Visigothic from the seventh century by some, and by others as later, perhaps of the Carolingian era.

# Bibliography

## Studies

*General Bibliography*

For present conceptions of the spiritual theology of the laity and the way in which the Christian churches portray the history of the laity, from the Catholic point of view, see the important work of Congar (*Lay People*). The same author has a more properly historical and spiritual sketch in the article "Laïc et Laïcat." For the non-Catholic view, see Neill and Weber, an excellent history whose first three chapters treat of our period. See also the recent studies in Schroer and Mueller. On the text of 1 Pet 2:9, see Sandevoir. See also the first part of *Histoire vécue*, Vol. 1, *De la clandestinité à la chrétienté*, in which five chapters concern our period. Consult also the substantial syntheses of the two first volumes of Bouyer et al. and the remarkable prologue of Karl Rahner to the anthology *Kirchenväter und Laien*. Notable summaries with important bibliographies on liturgies during the course of the first millennium can be found in E. Lanne and P.-M. Gy. Artistic expressions of the spiritual life during these centuries are presented in the exceptional catalogue of the Metropolitan Museum of Art's exposition *Age of Spirituality*, ed. Weitzmann. See also the accompanying volume of papers, *A Symposium*.

*The first three centuries*

A small though weighty and personal book is that of the biblical scholar Jaubert. See also the collection of Hamman (*La vie quotidienne des premiers chrétiens*). On the status and function of laity during these centuries, begin with Meslin. See also E. Lanne ("Le laïcat") and A. Faivre. Of a more general nature, Grant is useful. On the tendency to devalue temporal existence, Dodds should be compared with the rather different view of Brown (*Making of Late Antiquity*). On Tertullian's openness to ancient civilization, the distinguished book of Fredouille should be completed by a look at the paradoxical work of Rambaux. Cyprian's relation to our inquiry is treated by Saxer (*Vie liturgique*). A fine study of a central theme of Cyprian's pastoral spirituality is Deléani. On the origins of the cult of the martyrs, see Saxer (*Morts, martyrs*).

*The age of Constantine and Theodosius*

The work of Augustine remains the essential and richest witness. For his pastoral attitude toward the laity, begin with the classic book of Van der Meer. See also Brown (*Augustine*). The practical ecclesiology of Augustine and the spirituality of the laity found in his preaching have been renewed through the brilliant thesis of Borgomeo, which should be completed by the suggestive book of Poque. A good synthesis can be found in Hamman (*La vie quotidienne en Afrique*). On daily sanctification, see Fontaine ("Le pédagogie"). On the rehabilitation of the temporal in Augustine's thought, see the capital work of Marrou. For the poetic evidence about the diverse spiritualities of lettered laypeople and the Christian people in general, see Fontaine (*Naissance*). On the cult of the martyrs, besides the detailed and accurate study of Saxer (*Morts, martyrs*), see the very personal essay of Brown (*Cult of the Saints*), with the corrections suggested in Fontaine ("Le culte des saints"). Archaeology allows a concrete view of the origin and forms of expression of the cult in the work of Duval. On the spirituality of marriage, see the new study of Pietri. Augustine's conception of marriage has been given a positive evaluation in the work of Schmitt.

*The early Middle Ages*

The fundamental works on lay culture and that of the clerics who instructed them are those of Riché. On beliefs and culture, see the particular but rich work (especially on Gerard of Aurillac) by Poulin. On the forms of popular religion, consult Boglioni. On pilgrimage, the fundamental work is Koetting. See also Sumption and, now in press, Maraval. On the role of miracles, see Ward. For Spain, there is the detailed paper of Hillgarth, and Meslin ("Persistances"). For Gaul, see *Césaire d'Arles*, ed. Delage, with an important introduction. On lay converts and religious practices in fifth-century Gaul, see Griffe. The spirituality of the aristocracy during the Carolingian period is illustrated by *Dhuda*, ed. Riché. For the spirituality of the princes, see the recent thesis of Rey-dellet, which should be complemented by the study of the "mirrors of the princes" beginning with Hadot.

Boglioni, P., ed. *La culture populaire au Moyen Age*. Montreal: University of Montreal Press, 1977.

Borgomeo, Pascuale. *L'Église de ce temps dans la prédication d'Augustin*. Paris: Études augustiniennes, 1972.

Bouyer, Louis, Jean Leclercq, and François Vandenbroucke. *A History of Christian Spirituality*. New York: Seabury, 1982. Vol. 1, *The Spirituality of the New Testament and the Fathers*. Vol. 2, *The Spirituality of the Middle Ages*.

Brown, Peter. *Augustine of Hippo: A Biography*. Berkeley: University of California Press, 1967.

———. *The Cult of the Saints: Its Rise and Function in Latin Christianity*. Chicago: University of Chicago Press, 1981.

———. *The Making of Late Antiquity*. Cambridge, MA: Harvard University Press, 1978.

*Césare d'Arles: Sermons au peuple*, I. Edited by M. J. Delage. Sources chrétiennes 175. Paris: Cerf, 1971.

Congar, Yves. *Lay People in the Church: A Study for a Theology of the Laity*. Westminster, MD: Newman Press, 1965. The third French edition of 1964 has a fascicle of addenda and corrigenda.

———. "Laïc et Laïcat." In *Dict. Sp.* 9, cols. 79–108.

Deléani, Simone. *Christum sequi: Étude d'un thème dans l'oeuvre de saint Cyprian*. Paris: Études augustiniennes, 1979.

*Dhuda: Manuel pour mon fils.* Edited by P. Riché. Sources chrétiennes 225. Paris: Cerf, 1975.

Dodds, E. R. *Pagan and Christian in an Age of Anxiety.* Cambridge: Cambridge University Press, 1965.

Duval, Yvette. *Loca Sanctorum Africae: Le culte des martyrs en Afrique du IV<sup>e</sup> au VII<sup>e</sup> siècle.* 2 vols. Rome: École française de Rom, 1982.

Faivre, A. "Clerc/Laïc, histoire d'une frontière." *Recherches de sciences religieuses* 57 (1983) 195-220. Treats the period down to the sixth century.

Fontaine, J. "Le culte des saints et ses implications sociologiques." *Analecta Bollandiana* 100 (1982) 17-41.

———. "La pédagogie augustinienne des rythmes du temps dans les *Enarrationes in psalmos.*" In *Le temps chrétien.* Paris: CNRS, 1984. Forthcoming.

———. *Naissance de la poésie dans l'Occident chrétien du III<sup>e</sup> au VI<sup>e</sup> siècle.* Paris: Études augustiniennes, 1981.

Fredouille, J. C. *Tertullien et la conversion de la culture antique.* Paris: Études augustiniennes, 1972.

Grant, Robert M. *Early Christianity and Society.* San Francisco: Harper, 1977.

Griffe, E. *La Gaule chrétienne à l'époque romaine.* Paris: Letouzey et Ané, 1965.

Hadot, P. "Fürstenspiegel." In *Reallexikon für Antike und Christentum,* vol. 8, cols. 555-632. Stuttgart: Hiersemann, 1972.

Hamman, A. G. *La vie quotidienne des premiers chrétiens (95-197).* Paris: Hachette, 1960.

———. *La vie quotidienne en Afrique du Nord au temps de saint Augustin.* Paris: Hachette, 1979.

Hilgarth, J. N. "Popular Religion in Visigothic Spain." In *Visigothic Spain: New Approaches,* 3-60. Edited by Edward James. Oxford: Clarendon Press, 1980.

*Histoire vécue du peuple chrétien.* Vol. 1, *De la clandestinité à la chretienté.* Edited by Jean Delumeau. Toulouse: Privat, 1979.

Jaubert, Annie. *Les premiers chrétiens.* Paris: Seuil, 1967.

Koetting, B. *Peregrinatio religiosa: Wallfahrten in der Antike und das Pilgerwesen in der alten Kirche.* Regensburg: Münster, 1950.

Lanne, E. "Le laïcat dans l'église ancienne." *Verbum Caro* 18 (1971-72) 105-26.

Lanne, E., and P.-M. Gy. "Liturgie et vie spirituelle." In *Dict. Sp.* 9, cols 884-911.

Maraval, P. *Lieux saints et pèlerinages dans l'Orient byzantin jusqu'aux invasions arabes (IV<sup>e</sup>-VII<sup>e</sup> siècle).* In press.

Marrou, H.-I. "Le dogme de la resurrection des corps et la théologie des valeurs humaines selon l'enseignement de saint Augustin." *Revue des études augustiniennes* 12 (1966) 112-36.

Meslin, M. "Ecclesiastical Institutions and Clericalization in the Early Church." In *Sacralization and Secularization,* 41-52. Concilium 47. New York: Paulist Press, 1969.

———. "Persistances païennes en Galice vers la fin du VI<sup>e</sup> siècle." In *Hommages à Marcel Renard,* 2:72-124. Brussels: Latomus, 1969.

Neill, S. C., and H. R. Weber, eds. *The Layman in Christian History.* Philadelphia: Westminster, 1963.

Pietri, C. "IV<sup>e</sup>-V<sup>e</sup> siècles, le mariage chrétien à Rom." In *Histoire vécue du peuple chrétien,* 105-31.

Poque, Suzanne. *Le langage symbolique dans la prédication de saint Augustin.* Paris: Études augustiniennes, 1984.

Poulin, J. C. *L'ideal de sainteté dans l'Aquitaine carolingienne d'après les sources hagiographiques (750-900).* Quebec: University of Laval Press, 1975.

Rahner, Karl. Prologue to *Kirchenväter und Laien: Briefe der Seelenführung*. Translated by L. W. Weussenheimb. Freiburg: Herder, 1954.

Rambaux, C. *Tertullien face aux morales des trois premiers siècles*. Paris: Les Belles Lettres, 1979.

Reydellet, M. *La royauté dans la littérature latine de Sidoine Apollinaire à Isidore de Séville*. Rome: École française de Rome, 1981.

Riché, Pierre. *Daily Life in the World of Charlemagne*. Philadelphia: University of Pennsylvania Press, 1978.

———. *Les écoles et l'enseignement dans l'Occident chrétien de la fin du Ve siècle au mileau du XIe siècle*. Paris: Aubier, 1979. Contains an important bibliography.

———. *Education and Culture in the Barbarian West, Sixth through Eighth Centuries*. Columbia, SC: University of South Carolina Press, 1976.

Sandevoir, P. "Un royaume de prêtres." In *Études sur la première Epître de Pierre*, 219–29. Paris: Cerf, 1980.

Saxer, V. *Morts, martyrs, reliques en Afrique chrétienne aux premiers siècles: Les témoignages de Tertullien, Cyprien et Augustin à la lumière de l'archéologie africaine*. Paris: Beauchesne, 1980.

———. *Vie liturgique et quotidienne à Carthage vers le milieu du IIIe siècle: Le témoignage de saint Cyprien et de ses contemporains d'Afrique*. Rome: Città del Vaticano, 1969.

Schmitt, Emile. *Le mariage chrétien dans l'oeuvre de saint Augustin*. Paris: Études augustiniennes, 1983.

Schroer, H., and G. Mueller, eds. *Von Amt des Laien in Kirche und Theologie: Festschrift für Gerhard Krause*. Berlin: de Gruyter, 1982.

Sumption, Jonathan. *Pilgrimage: An Image of Medieval Religion*. London: Rowman & Littlefield, 1975.

*A Symposium: Age of Spirituality*. New York: Metropolitan Museum of Art, 1980.

Van der Meer, Frederic. *Augustine the Bishop: Church and Society at the Dawn of the Middle Ages*. New York: Sheed and Ward, 1961.

Ward, Benedicta. *Miracles and the Medieval Mind*. Philadelphia: University of Pennsylvania Press, 1982.

Weitzmann, Kurt, ed. *Age of Spirituality: Late Antique and Early Christian Art, Third to Seventh Centuries*. New York: Metropolitan Museum of Art, 1979.

# Contributors

BERNARD McGINN, coeditor of this volume, is Professor of Historical Theology and the History of Christianity at the Divinity School of the University of Chicago. His books include *Visions of the End* (1979), *Apocalyptic Spirituality* (1979), and *The Calabrian Abbot: Joachim of Fiore in the History of Christian Thought* (1985).

JOHN MEYENDORFF, coeditor of this volume, is Professor of History at Fordham University and Professor and Dean at St. Vladimir's Orthodox Theological Seminary in Crestwood, New York. His books include *St. Gregory Palamas and Orthodox Spirituality* (1959), *Christ in Eastern Christian Thought* (1969), and *Byzantium and the Rise of Russia* (1981).

JEAN LECLERCQ, O.S.B., consulting editor of this volume, is a monk of the Benedictine Abbey of Clervaux in Luxemburg and Professor in the Institute of Religious Psychology at the Gregorian University in Rome. Author of over fifty books, he was the principal editor of the modern edition of Bernard of Clairvaux's works (1957ff.)

ROBERTA C. BONDI is Professor of Church History at the Candler School of Theology of Emory University and author of *Three Monophysite Christologies: Severus of Antioch, Philoxenus of Mabbug, and Jacob of Sarug* (1976).

PETER BROWN is Professor of History at Princeton University. His recent books include *The Making of Late Antiquity* (1978), *The Cult of the Saints* (1981), and *Society and the Holy in Late Antiquity* (1982).

J. PATOUT BURNS, S.J., is Professor of Theology at Loyola University in Chicago and author of *The Development of Augustine's Doctrine of Operative Grace* (1982).

MARY T. CLARK, R.S.C.J., is Professor of Theology at Manhattanville College in Purchase, New York. Her books include *Marius Victorinus: Theological Treatises on the Trinity* (1981).

DONALD T. CORCORAN, O.S.B., is a member of the Benedictine community of Transfiguration Monastery in Windsor, New York. Sister Donald is presently completing a dissertation at Fordham University on the history of spiritual guidance.

JACQUES FONTAINE is Professor of Latin at the Sorbonne. His books include *Isidore de Séville et la culture classique dans l'Espagne wisigothique* (1959), *Aspects et problèmes de la prose d'art latine au IIIᵉ siècle: La genèse des styles latins chrétiens* (1968), and *Études sur la poésie latine tardive d'Ausone à Prudence* (1980).

ROBERT M. GRANT is Buck Professor in the Divinity School and the Division of the Humanities of the University of Chicago. His books include *Gnosticism and Early Christianity* (1959), *Gnosticism* (1961), and *Early Christianity and Society* (1977).

JEAN GRIBOMONT, O.S.B., is a monk of the Benedictine Abbey of Clervaux in Luxembourg and the foremost contemporary authority on the monastic traditions connected with St. Basil of Caesarea. His books include *L'Histoire du texte des Ascétiques de S. Basile* (1953) and *Saint Basile, Évangile et Église* (1984).

PIERRE-MARIE GY, O.P., is Director of the Institut Supérieur de Liturgie of the Institut Catholique in Paris. He is author of numerous works on the history of Western liturgies.

THOMAS HOPKO is Associate Professor of Theology at St. Vladimir's Orthodox Theological Seminary in Crestwood, New York. His books include *The Spirit of God: Christian Spirituality East and West* (1976) and *All the Fulness of God* (1982).

CHARLES KANNENGIESSER, formerly of the Institut Catholique in Paris, is presently Huisking Professor of Theology at the University of Notre Dame. His books include *Athanase d'Alexandrie évêque et écrivain* (1983).

PAUL MEYENDORFF is presently completing a doctoral dissertation at the University of Notre Dame on the problems of liturgical reform in Russia in post-Byzantine times.

KARL F. MORRISON is Ahmanson-Murphy Professor of History at the University of Kansas. His books include *Tradition and Authority in the Western Church, 300–1140* (1969) and *The Mimetic Tradition of Reform in the West* (1982).

LEONID OUSPENSKY is a well-known interpreter of traditional Eastern Christian iconography. His books include *Theology of the Icon* (1978) and, with Vladimir Lossky, *The Meaning of Icons* (1982).

BASIL PENNINGTON, O.C.S.O., is a Trappist monk of St. Joseph's Abbey in Spencer, Massachusetts. His books include *Centering Prayer* (1980), *Monastic Journey to India* (1982), and *The Eucharist Yesterday and Today* (1984).

PIERRE RICHÉ is Professor of Medieval History at the University of Paris (Nanterre). His books include *Education and Culture in the Barbarian West, Sixth through Eighth Centuries* (1976), *Daily Life in the World of Charlemagne* (1978), and *Les écoles et l'enseignement dans l' Occident chrétien de la fin du V^e siècle au milieu du X^e siècle* (1979).

PAUL ROREM is pastor of Our Savior's Lutheran Church in Edison, New Jersey, and author of *Biblical and Liturgical Symbols in the Pseudo-Dionysian Synthesis* (1985).

SANDRA M. SCHNEIDERS, I.H.M., is Professor of New Testament at the Jesuit School of Theology at Berkeley, California, and author of numerous articles on the Gospel of John and on the relation between Scripture and spirituality.

LARS THUNBERG of Aarhus, Denmark, is author of *Microcosm and Mediator* (1965) and *Man and the Cosmos: The Vision of St. Maximos the Confessor* (1985).

KALLISTOS WARE is a Fellow of Pembroke College and Spalding Lecturer in Eastern Orthodox Studies at Oxford University. In 1982 he was consecrated titular bishop of Diokleia, auxiliary of the Orthodox Archdiocese of Great Britain. His books include *The Orthodox Church* (1963) and *The Orthodox Way* (1979).

BENEDICTA WARD, S.L.G., is a member of the Sisters of the Love of God at Fairacres in Oxford, and author of *Miracles and the Medieval Mind* (1982).

GROVER A. ZINN is Professor of Religious Studies at Oberlin College. He has written extensively on the Victorines and has translated the works of Richard of St. Victor for the Classics of Western Spirituality.

JOHN ZIZIOULAS is Professor of Theology at the University of Thessaloniki in Greece. His books include *Being as Communion: Studies in Personhood and the Church* (1984).

# Photographic Credits

The editors and publisher wish to thank the custodians of the works of art for supplying photographs and granting permission to use them. In particular, the art editor wishes to acknowledge the research assistance of Charlotte Burke and her staff at Dumbarton Oaks.

1. Courtesy of the Michigan-Princeton-Alexandria Expedition to Mount Sinai
2. Courtesy of The Metropolitan Museum of Art, The Cloisters Collection, Purchase, 1950
3. Sovfoto/Eastfoto
4. Courtesy of A La Vieille Russie, New York
5. Courtesy of Dumbarton Oaks, Trustees for Harvard University © 1985
6. Courtesy of The Institute for Antiquity and Christianity, Claremont, California
7. Courtesy of Dumbarton Oaks, Trustees for Harvard University © 1985
   Photo by Cyril Mango
8. Scala/Art Resource, New York
9. Courtesy of the Michigan-Princeton-Alexandria Expedition to Mount Sinai
10. Bildarchiv Foto Marburg/Art Resource, New York
11. Courtesy of the Department of Rare Books and Special Collections, The Princeton University Library
12. Courtesy of the Michigan-Princeton-Alexandria Expedition to Mount Sinai
13. Courtesy of The Cleveland Museum of Art, The John Huntington Art and Polytechnic Trust
14. Alinari/Art Resource, New York
15. Bildarchiv Foto Marburg/Art Resource, New York
16. Courtesy of The Pierpont Morgan Library, New York
17. Courtesy of Dumbarton Oaks, Trustees for Harvard University © 1985
18. Alinari/Art Resource, New York
19. Alinari/Art Resource, New York
20. Courtesy of Dumbarton Oaks, Trustees for Harvard University © 1985
21. Bildarchiv Foto/Marburg/Art Resource, New York
22. Courtesy of The Pierpont Morgan Library, New York
23. Courtesy of Dumbarton Oaks, Trustees for Harvard University © 1985
24. Courtesy of The National Gallery of Art, Washington, D.C., The Widener Collection
25. Scala/Art Resource, New York
26. Courtesy of Dumbarton Oaks, Trustees for Harvard University © 1985
27. Sovfoto/Eastfoto
28. Courtesy of Dumbarton Oaks, Trustees for Harvard University © 1985
29. Courtesy of the Michigan-Princeton-Alexandria Expedition to Mount Sinai
30. Courtesy of The Nelson-Atkins Museum of Art, Kansas City, Missouri, The Nelson Fund
31. Courtesy of The Cleveland Museum of Art, Leonard C. Hanna, Jr., Bequest
32. Courtesy of Dumbarton Oaks, Trustees for Harvard University © 1985
33. Courtesy of The Metropolitan Museum of Art, Gift of J. Pierpont Morgan, 1917

# Indexes

## Subjects

anchoritism, 90, 92–95, 96, 101, 102, 106; medieval forms of, 189; rules of, 124; spiritual discernment and, 448, 450; Syriac Christianity and, 153–54, 156

angels, 44, 47–48, 56, 57, 60; Christ's identification with, 231, 232; Dionysian exegesis and, 135–38, 144; sexual continence and, 429–30, 432–34

anti-semitism, 76, 186

Arianism, 59, 61, 65, 68, 78; Ambrose, Augustine and, 80, 81, 85; among Germans, 171; Hilary's refutation of, 78–79, 280; refutation by Marius Victorinus of, 281–82

asceticism, 35, 38–40, 42, 45, 48, 59; *See also* anchoritism; monasteries, European; monasticism; Anthony and, 92–95, 107–9; cenobitic form of, 96–98, 101, 109; church art and, 385–86; of Cistercians, 207–8; extremism and, 102–4; gnostic forms of, 54–55; of Gregory of Nazianzus, 70, 99; hospices and, 91, 99; Irish forms of, 166–67, 169; in Italy, 116–19; Norbert of Xanten and, 189, 190, 220; patristic forms of, 62, 63, 77, 92–93, 113; serenity and, 110–11; in Spain, 115–16; Syriac forms of, 155–57; virginity and, 435–36, 472; visions of Zacharias and, 109–10

Augustinian concepts, 14, 61, 78, 82, 85–86; of divinization, 254, 277, 279; of free will, 307, 320–21, 324–25, 336–38; of humanity, 307, 317–21; of knowledge and love, 202–3, 289, 333–34; of the laity, 454, 465, 467, 474–75; of monasticism, 85–86, 107, 115, 120, 218; Roman liturgy and, 368–71; of salvation, 342–48; of spirit and matter, 333–36; of the Trinity, 277, 282–86, 319–20; of two cities, 338–40, 342

baptism, 5, 28–30, 48, 51, 52; controversies over, 103, 353, 465; Cyprian and, 457; as

death and resurrection symbols, 352, 353; exegesis of, 354–55; as an initiative rite, 350, 351, 355; of Jesus, 284, 352, 353; liturgy and, 353, 354, 366; love and, 287; as rebirth, 352; as remission of sin, 355–56, 366; salvation and, 339, 340, 345; of the soul, 282; Tertullian and, 365, 369, 456; theology and, 352, 353, 355; *theōsis* and, 350–51, 356

bishops, concepts of, 31–32, 34–35, 40, 62, 70; Ambrose of Milan, 79–82, 331, 465; Athanasius, 62–66, 92–93, 97; Augustine, 62, 82, 85–86, 115 (*see also* Augustinian concepts); Basil of Caesarea, 62, 67–69, 99–101; Cyprian of Carthage, 340, 456–59; Gregory of Nazianzus, 62, 68, 69–71; Gregory of Nyssa, 62, 67–68, 71–72, 74–75, 99; Hilary of Poitiers, 62, 77–79; Jerome, 62, 82–84; John Chrysostom, 62, 75–77; Martin of Tours, 119, 122

Celtic concepts; of asceticism, 166–67; of martyrdom, 167; missionary spread of, 170, 479; of monasticism, 119–22, 165–71; paganism and, 163–64; of penances, 167–69

charism, 17, 27, 40, 100, 103

Christology, 8, 9, 17, 18, 108. *See also* messianic concepts; of Anselm, 256–57; of Appolinaris, 234; of Athanasius, 64–65, 232, 236, 238; of Bernard of Clairvaux, 253–54, 257; Christ's dual nature and, 308; Council of Chalcedon and, 234–39, 308; of Cyril, 232–39, 241, 295; of Dionysius the Areopagite, 144–46; earthly sovereignty of humanity and, 302; Eucharist and, 242, 244–46, 249; of Eutyches, 236; Holy Spirit and, 241, 242, 244–47; of Jacob of Sarug, 158; Mary and, 239–40, 436, 438–39; of Maximus the Confessor, 240–42, 249, 253; of Monophysites, 144–45; of Nestorius, 233, 234; patristic forms of, 76, 79, 248, 254; of Symeon, 247–48; theology and, 235–39; *theōsis* and, 292; transubstantiation and, 245, 257, 360

# Names

## Colophon

*Christian Spirituality: Origins to the Twelfth Century,*
Volume 16 of World Spirituality: An Encyclopedic History of the
Religious Quest, was designed by Maurya P. Horgan and Paul J. Kobelski.
The type is 11-point Garamond Antiqua and was set by
The Scriptorium, Denver, Colorado.